Complete Applications of Law and Ethics for California Licensed Marriage and Family Therapists ©

Fourteenth Edition 2015

Federico C. Grosso, D.D.S., Ph.D., M.F.T., B.C.F.E., B.C.P.D.
Licensed Marriage and Family Therapist
Diplomate of the American Board of Forensic Examiners

First Edition — January 2001
Fourteenth Edition – July 2015

Published by
FGrosso.com
Federico C. Grosso, D.D.S., Ph.D., M.F.T., B.C.F.E.
138 Palm Coast Parkway, NE
Suite 114
Palm Coast, FL 32137-8241
tel 805-962-3628
fcgt@fgrosso.com
http://www.FGrosso.com

This book in only available from the publisher.

Table of Contents

Table of Contents

Table of Contents

About the Author

Federico Grosso, DDS, PhD, MFT, BCFE, is a licensed marriage and family therapist in private practice; his practice is limited to forensic psychotherapy. He is a board-certified pediatric dentist who retired from Dentistry due to a career-ending accident. In addition to his forensic practice as a malpractice expert witness, he is an author, academician, consultant, lecturer, and publisher in the area of the clinical application of legal and ethical guidelines for marriage and family therapists, clinical social workers, alcohol and drug abuse counselors and certified addictions treatment specialists, and licensed professional counselors.

He serves as an expert witness in malpractice and administrative actions in this field and provides consultation to attorneys and universities. His publications are widely used in psychotherapy and academic programs and by attorneys involved in malpractice actions against clinicians. He has help define the standard of care for mental health records. His success, effectiveness, and ability as an expert witness have been recognized and appreciated by attorneys. Having served in many difficult cases, he translates his experience into practical and effective course content, which allows clinicians to create a protective clinical practice.

Dr. Grosso is currently an official lecturer for the California Chapter of the National Association of Social Workers and teaches at the annual conferences of the California Association of Alcohol and Drug Abuse Counselors and the California Association of Alcohol and Drug Educators. He regularly teaches on the legal and ethical standard of care for MFT, LCSW, LPCC, and D&A Counseling clinical practices.

From the Author

I have come to realize that in the realm of human services, religious, physical, social etc., psychotherapy is sui generis. This point is underscored when we say that the scope of practice varies according to the license, we see this not as a constriction but as the charge to enter a special world, the world of the Self and of its connection to others. Indeed, one can make the case that it is through connectedness that the human psyche is most effectively challenged to evolve to its fullness. Because of this, in the powerful interpersonal encounter that constitutes therapy, the clinician is called upon to exercise unusual sensitivity, extraordinary listening skills, and liberating creativity. It is therefore of the essence that the therapist develop the kind of relationship that provides the client with a grounded feeling of safety, which in turn will strengthen the client's resolve to accept the challenge and make significant personal and interpersonal changes.

It is precisely because of this orientation that we must, perhaps with some reluctance, turn to the practical steps providing the safety and respect that can enhance our chances of a successful outcome, and that will help us avoid any threats of harm to the client as well as to the therapist.

This book is based on my years of work both as a therapist and as a forensic expert. Initially, I had interacted with the legal system as an expert witness in pediatric dentistry, and later, as an expert witness in malpractice and administrative actions involving MFTs, LCSWs, D & A Counselors and now LPCCs.

My focus here will be on the art of protecting the clinician. The material I present may seem distant from connectedness, even mundane and arduous, triggered only by the litigiousness of modern society. But since in large part it is meant to enhance our chances of helping our clients, it is far more than that. Among other things it provides us a focus on discerning the real problem, not just what the client presents. It helps us truly listen, that is, hear what the client is and is not saying. It helps us come to the realization that we ourselves have perhaps not really heard something that the client has only implicitly said. It makes us aware of the range of possibilities of help and enables us to choose an alternative best suited to the client's immediate and long-term needs. This is the important process that we should hear beneath the requirement that our therapy manifest "reasonable and prudent behavior". The latter makes at least two contributions to our clinical work.

The first is to enhance our work with the client by helping us to focus on what we have heard and seen in our sessions. What is the real problem brought in by the client? Can we situate it? The second is to provide safety for both the client and the therapist. It does this by assuring that we assess and diagnose the client. It pushes us to envision a goal and means by which to achieve it. It charts progress toward this goal and moves us consciously toward a conclusion.

Introduction to the Clinical Application of California Law and CAMFT Ethical Standards for Marriage and Family Therapists

Law and ethics in the practice of marriage and family therapy in California provides the perimeter or boundary for the therapeutic "playing field." The state legislature, the courts and case law, the professional organization of marriage and family therapists (MFTs), and the California Association of Marriage and Family Therapists (CAMFT), created these rules or boundaries guiding MFTs to provide a safe therapeutic environment for everyone involved in this profession (see figure 1). Those protected include MFTs, trainees, interns, instructors, students, supervisors, supervisees, employers, employees, and, most importantly, clients. The Board of Behavioral Sciences (BBS), under the auspices of the Department of Consumer Affairs, has the legal responsibility to protect the consumer or the client in California.

The political, economic, and professional climate continues to change in this profession and clients obtain a greater protection under state law. Additionally, MFTs continue to experience greater professional demands for clinical accountability. As the competition among psychiatrists, psychologists, licensed clinical social workers (LCSWs), and MFTs increases, MFTs must familiarize themselves with legally defined concepts such as scope of practice, scope of competence, standard of care, therapeutic duty, and informed consent. Although these terms cause confusion for some, and possibly fear in other therapists, these concepts actually represent the structural foundation of a safe and responsible clinical practice.

Figure 1

Note that the combination of California Laws, Case Law, CAMFT ethical standards, and the therapist's personal values define the perimeter of safe therapy: also known as the therapeutic duty. As long as therapists stay within these boundaries, the therapy they provide will be safe for all involved and they will protect themselves. There are some instances where therapists must act beyond the usual and customary boundaries of clinical practice due to requirements in the law. For example, breaching confidentiality to protect the life of a suicidal client or reporting child abuse are examples of these challenging situations. The danger lies in the breaching of confidentiality. This action will undoubtedly affect the therapeutic relationship, treatment, and possibly end in a malpractice action against the therapist. (See figure 2).

California law and ethical standards provide therapists who face these crisis issues with a mechanism that extends the boundary of safety when these difficult situations arise. (See circle below). This mechanism includes recognized reasonable and prudent steps defined by experts in the field of psychotherapy, which serve to protect the client's welfare. Additionally, therapists rely on their scope of competence (training, experience and education) to assess the nature and level of danger of the crisis at hand. Should therapists face a malpractice action in court, they are best protected with appropriate documentation of their rationale for making the clinical decisions attempting to manage the present crisis.

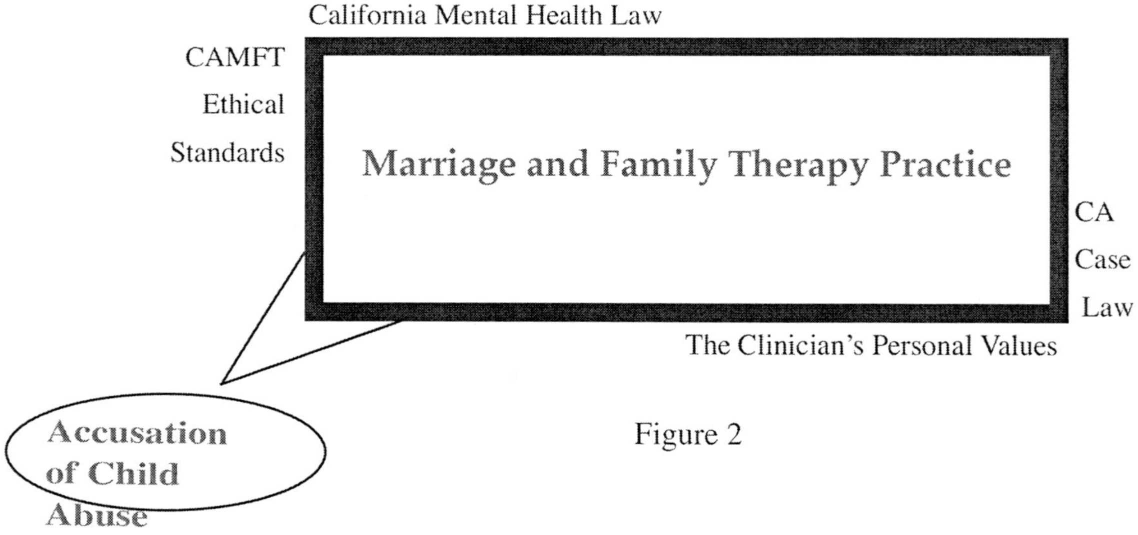

Figure 2

Some therapists may question the need to attend to legal and ethical mandates. After all, they have not experienced a legal challenge. Utilizing my forensic experience as an expert witness, I remind clinicians that crisis issues are unpredictable and they can occur at any time to any one of us. Those clinicians I have testified for and against them in court would agreed with me. I recommend to therapists that they practice in a manner that protects their clients and themselves from harm. For clients, this harm is physical and/or emotional. For MFTs, they protect themselves from a malpractice action and/or action against their license. Reading, learning, and applying the clinical applications of law and ethics can serve clinicians to provide their clients safety and peace of mind for themselves.

Dr. Grosso provides clinical examples obtained from his experience as a forensic expert witness involving MFTs, LPCCs, LCSWs, and drug and alcohol counselors in malpractice actions and consultations for attorneys. The questions following each clinical example intend to challenge the reader's ability to develop a personal reasoning process that leads to clinical objectivity when addressing legal decisions. Some questions may be difficult to answer because the possible answer may be uncomfortable or because there may not be a pleasant solution to the clinical challenge. Rather than attempting to find an immediate answer, I recommend that the reader take time to consider possibilities as he or she establishes the pattern of being a "reasonable and prudent" clinician. Doing so allows the clinician to obtain all available information, integrate his or her scope of competence into the presenting issue, consider his or her internal reality, maintain clinical objectivity, and determine the best approach that meets the needs of the client

Figure 3

Chapter 1

The Therapist's Personal Belief System

Personal Frame of Reference

Practicing psychotherapy can be a challenging endeavor. Each person entering therapy is unique and presents his or her own therapeutic issues. The therapist may also present his or her own challenges and must assure that his or her personal issues do not interfere with those of the client. Our ethical codes, California Law as well as Case Law place the responsibility, or therapeutic duty, on the MFT to "do no harm" as he or she addresses the well-being of clients. Adhering to this responsibility of "no harm," either physical or emotional, creates safety in therapeutic practice and helps build a strong therapeutic alliance. The foundation of doing no harm is based on the clinician's ability to know his or her personal frame of reference.

Internal Reality, Clinical Safety, and Protecting the Clinician

The first step MFTs take in creating safety in clinical practice requires that they have an understanding of their internal and external schema. I use the term internal reality to describe the therapist's unique perspective of the world. Internal reality is a cluster of factors that include, but are not limited to, individual life experiences, beliefs, biases, fears, myths, personal history, past emotional injuries, religious values, financial values, morality, socioeconomic values, relational power differentials, cultural values, and life expectations. Internal reality is the reference point from which MFTs process clinical, legal and ethical issues. Self-awareness contributes to the creation of safety in therapy by helping MFTs avoid personal emotional reactivity and maintain an objective perspective throughout the duration of the therapeutic relationship.

The second step in creating clinical safety requires that MFTs acquire appropriate knowledge, training, clinical skills, and take appropriate steps to obtain these. Specialized education allows MFTs to assess, diagnose, and treat the client's presenting issues appropriately throughout the duration of therapy. Integration of these two steps is necessary to create a strong and safe therapeutic structure that can withstand a legal challenge.

Clinical safety is frequently challenged when MFTs face high-risk issues involving the possibility of child abuse, elder/dependent abuse, spousal abuse, suicide, and dangerous clients. A sound knowledge base can help MFTs weather a storm. However, it may not be enough to protect the clinician. Any of these high-issues can trigger MFTs' personal blind spots. These unmanaged blind spots will likely lead to the loss of clinical objectivity, which can trigger reactive and inappropriate decisions. Ultimately, the client, the client's family, and/or clinicians can face injury. MFTs base the best protective mechanism on sound clinical knowledge, continuous self-awareness, and the maintenance of clinical objectivity.

The Complexity of Making Safe Legal and Ethical Decisions

Legal and ethical issues can push the boundaries of clinical practice as well as the personal boundaries of MFTs. These pressures can also create difficult challenges for MFTs. Some clinical issues may increasingly challenge MFTs depending on their personal internal reality. Addressing child abuse, elder/dependent abuse, suicide, spousal abuse, violence or substance abuse can be laden with personal emotional reactivity and can alter their ability to maintain clinical objectivity.

Additionally, the boundaries of legal/ethical issues are not always well defined. For example: In court, expert witnesses and attorneys continuously attempt to define what constitutes a "reasonable suspicion" of child abuse. Courts also attempt to define the appropriate steps MFTs must take to document and manage a client in imminent danger of hurting self or others. MFTs can make these and similar clinical decisions from their personal Internal Reality Structure. Accordingly, clinicians will experience their unique set of feelings, which can range from self-assurance to relief, anxiety, frustration, concern, fear, and in some cases even terror. MFTs' internal realities can be harmful or beneficial to the client and to the clinician. At best, MFTs use their knowledge and internal reality to distinguish challenging clinical issues and make appropriate clinical decisions. At the other extreme, other MFTs choose not to address their legal/ethical duties out of ignorance or fear. This choice of inaction has been costly to many clinicians. Their personal, emotional, and financial well-being has been disturbed when facing a difficult and protracted malpractice lawsuit. In court, judges have ruled that 1) ignorance of the law is not an excuse for injuring clients and 2) maintaining clinical objectivity is a legal and ethical therapeutic duty for MFTs.

MFTs may also be unclear about the implications of their legal and ethical decisions on the therapeutic relationship and treatment. For example, a therapist might face questions such as 1) How will the client react if I breach confidentiality when I believe that suicide is imminent? 2) Will the client experience abandonment or betrayal? 3) Will the client leave therapy? 4) Will he or she kill him/herself? 5) Will my decision lead to a lawsuit? 5) Must I make this decision? When MFTs have not fully resolved their own similar personal issues, they will likely experience greater emotional difficulty in the decision making process. Notably, MFTs who have faced and resolved personal issues tend to develop a sound foundation of clinical objectivity and be able to make clear decisions with little or no emotional discomfort.

Potential Loss of Objectivity

MFTs can lose objectivity when a clinical or legal/ethical issue intersects with an unresolved personal issue. This intersection can trigger a "blind spot." A blind spot is a form of personal defense that prevent MFTs from fully exploring the necessary implications required to address a challenging clinical issue. Consider the following examples, 1) a therapist fails to notice that his or her 20-year-old female client is grossly underweight. His or her family severely judged his or her own appearance as an adolescent. 2) A therapist fails to consult with an anorexic client's physician because of his or her own mistrust of physicians. While personal defenses helps therapists avoid experiencing uncomfortable emotions, they may also lead to making unsafe decisions for themselves and their clients.

Loss of objectivity can harm the client and leave the MFT vulnerable. If a client becomes injured from the MFTs' acts of omission or commission arising from loss of objectivity, they will likely face an accusation of malpractice. Additionally, a BBS investigation could also result in the loss of license. Rather than assessing for malpractice, the BBS evaluates MFTs for unprofessional conduct, which is defined in Business and Professions Code 4982.

Ultimately, safe MFTs clearly know their own internal reality perspective. The BBS advocates that students undergo their own therapy before graduating. It serves MFTs to continue personal therapy as needed to maintain clinical objectivity. MFTs familiar with their own internal reality are aware of their blind spots and the issues that trigger these. In being aware, MFTs can relate from their internal reality perspective with greater freedom and clarity. This freedom and clarity allows MFTs to obtain all necessary clinical information, seek consultation when necessary and, most importantly, avoid loss of objectivity.

Clinical Example # 1

> Imagine the following clinical scenario: An MFT has been treating a young man for anorexia. He tells his therapist that he doesn't want the therapist to contact his physician. He says: "If you trust me, you won't ask me to give you written consent to speak to him. If you ever call him, I'll stop coming to see you." She agrees to treat him under these conditions because she mistrusts physicians. She once experienced a personal problem with an M.D. and since then, has avoided contact with the medical profession. She continues to treat the young man for several months and one day she receives a phone call from the client's brother telling her that the young man

has died of a heart attack. The question an expert witness would ask in this case is: "Did she allow her "blind spot" regarding physicians to interfere with her treatment?"

Questions for Clinical Example # 1

1. If this MFT was consulting with you, what would you tell him about your impression of his internal reality?
2. How could this MFT have maintained clinical objectivity?
3. On the one hand, the clinician wanted to support the client and, on the other he had a therapeutic duty to obtain the client's medical information. How can she carry out both duties and still maintained a healthy relationship with the client? If not, what other options are available to the MFT?
4. What recommendations can you make to this MFT upon your initial consultation? How do you think she will react upon hearing these recommendations?
5. What would you do differently?
6. If you refer the client to someone else, how would you manage him feeling abandoned and betrayed by you? If you fail to manage his feelings, do you believe these feelings could be strong enough to lead him to initiate legal action against you for abandonment? Imagine yourself in his place.

Chapter Questions

1. What does internal reality mean to you? What is your personal internal reality?
2. What are the individual life experiences, beliefs, biases, fears, myths, personal history, past emotional injuries, religious values, morality, socioeconomic values cultural values, and expectations that were important in your path to becoming a therapist?
3. If you identified you "blind spots" regarding therapeutic issues, what are they? How can these "blind spots" affect your decision-making process regarding legal/ethical issues?
4. What does "therapeutic safety" mean to you?
5. How can you create therapeutic safety for yourself and your clients when facing personal feelings arising from issues such as child abuse, spousal abuse, suicide, client dangerousness and other similar crisis issues?

Chapter 2

Informed Consent

Informed Consent and the Therapeutic Contract

The concept of informed consent originates generally from the battery and negligence areas of tort law. Battery is the unlawful and intentional touching of a person that can result in injury. A negligent act is an action that a reasonable person would not have taken. In American law, a client is entitled to adequate information from the therapist before the client provides consent to treat. For mental health clinicians, using the informed consent document is the first step toward creating clinical safety for all involved and for protecting themselves. By informing the client in advance of the requirements and expectation of services to be provided, the clinician clarifies the therapeutic boundaries and establishes accountability within the therapeutic relationship.

Clinicians can use informed consent as the first step toward protecting all those involved in providing treatment because it documents specific conditions for continuing as well as for terminating treatment. By informing the client in advance of these requirements and expectation of services to be provided, MFTs define the therapeutic boundaries and establish accountability within the therapeutic relationship.

Informed Consent and Case Law

Listed below are several of the case laws that addresses the therapeutic duty to obtain informed consent.

Cobbs v. Grant (1972) — Informed consent was required of physicians.

Truman v. Thomas (1980) — The mental health professional must disclose the material risks of not undergoing the recommended procedure.

Legally-Defined Elements of Informed Consent

Therapists must comply with these four conditions when obtaining informed consent:

1. The competency of the client: The client must have sufficient mental ability to reasonably understand the condition, nature and effect of the proposed treatment. Additionally, the client must have sufficient mental ability to reasonably understand the risks of pursuing and not pursuing the offered treatment. This issue becomes increasingly important when a client presents any measure of diminished capacity. For example, a developmental disorder or a mood disorder may interfere with a client's capacity to understand the possible consequences of treatment. In such a case, the client would be unable to give *Informed Consent*. To address this, a thorough initial assessment would include utilizing tools such as a mental status exam to determine the client's competency.

2. The disclosure of material information: A therapist needs to provide the client with all information that a "reasonable" person would want to know before deciding to accept or reject the proposed treatment. The more complicated or aggressive the treatment, the greater care the therapist must exercise in providing in-depth information and making sure that the client understands the proposed treatment. For example, a couple who is in extreme conflict needs to be informed that the results of therapy are unpredictable so that reconciliation and divorce are both possible outcomes of therapy.

3. The client's understanding of the presented material: The therapeutic contract needs to be worded in language that a "reasonable" person would understand.

4. Voluntary consent: The client must be free of coercion, duress, or fraud when giving consent for treatment.

Though not legally required, the best tool clinicians can use to protect themselves and their clients is using a therapeutic contract. This addresses a range of issues including : a) a description of the therapy process and the risks and benefits of treatment; b) the therapist's education and clinical orientation; c) an outline of the client's rights in treatment including the management of confidentiality; d) how the clinician will manage emergencies; e) the fee charged per session and how other fee related issues will be managed; f) the reasonable expected length of treatment; g) a description of office policies including termination; h) and other pertinent information.

The lack of informed consent in psychotherapy resembles a situation where client walks down a darkened path. At any moment an unpredictable event may unbalance the client and both untoward and uncomfortable events may injure him. With informed consent, the client walks with a light in his hand and has the choice how to manage an unpredictable or uncomfortable because he knows what to expect and can respond accordingly. The clinician can also do likewise and thus, can protect him/herself from the unpredictable vagaries of the therapeutic process.

Ethical Therapeutic Duty to Obtain Informed Consent

CAMFT has established an ethical therapeutic duty to obtain informed consent via several standards. These include the following:

CAMFT Ethical Standard 1.5 — Marriage and family therapists provide adequate information to patients in clear and understandable language so that patients can make meaningful decisions about their therapy.

CAMFT Ethical Standard 1.5.2 — Marriage and family therapists inform patients on the extent of their availability for emergencies and for other contacts between sessions. When a marriage and family therapist is not located in the same geographic area as the patient, he/she shall provide the patient with appropriate resources in the patient's locale for contact in case of emergency.

CAMFT Ethical Standard 1.4 — Marriage and family therapists respect the right of patients to make decisions that help them to understand the consequences of their decisions. When clinically appropriate, marriage and family therapists advise their patients that decisions on the status of their personal relationships, including dissolutions, are the responsibilities of the patients.

CAMFT Ethical Standard 1.5.4 — Marriage and family therapists are encouraged to inform patients as to certain exceptions to confidentiality such as child abuse reporting, elder and dependent adult abuse reporting, and patients dangerous to themselves or others.

CAMFT Ethical Standard 1.5.5 — Marriage and family therapists are encouraged to inform patients at an appropriate time and within the context of the psychotherapeutic relationship of their experience, education, specialties, and theoretical and professional orientation, and any other information deemed appropriate by the therapist.

CAMFT Ethical Standard 1.4.1 — When patients are not physically present (e.g., therapy by telephone or Internet) during the provision of therapy, marriage and family therapists take extra precautions to meet their responsibilities to patients. Prior to utilizing electronic therapy, marriage and family therapists consider the appropriateness and suitability of this therapeutic modality to the patient's needs. When therapy occurs by electronic means, marriage and family therapists inform patients of the potential risks, consequences, and benefits, including but not limited to, issues of confidentiality, clinical limitations, transmission difficulties, and ability to respond to emergencies. Marriage and family therapists ensure that such therapy complies with the informed consent requirements of the California Telemedicine Act.

CAMFT Ethical Standard 9.3 — Marriage and family therapists disclose, in advance, their fees and the basis upon which they are computed, including but not limited to, charges for canceled or missed appointments and ay interest to be charged on unpaid balances, at the beginning of treatment and give reasonable notice of any changes in fees or other charges.

These standards create direction and guidance for MFTs to define the standard of care regarding the content of an appropriate informed consent document. For a complete discussion of these ethical guidelines on treatment and the therapeutic relationship, see Chapter 28.

Sample Therapeutic Contract, Part I: The Therapy Process

The following is an example of Part I for a therapeutic contract.

Part I: The Therapy Process • Participating in therapy can result in a number of benefits to you, including a better understanding of your personal goals and values, improved interpersonal relationships, and resolution of the specific concerns that led you to seek therapy. Working toward these benefits, however, requires effort on your part and may result in your experiencing considerable discomfort. Change will sometimes be easy and swift, but more often it will be slow and frustrating. Remembering unpleasant events and resolving them through therapy can bring on strong feelings of anger, depression, fear, etc.. Attempting to resolve issues between marital partners, family members, and other individuals can also lead to discomfort and may result in changes that were not originally intended. As part of my therapeutic process, I use several techniques, including hypnosis and Eye Movement Desensitization and Reprocessing. My theoretical perspective is a combination of Family Systems, "Cognitive-behavioral" and "Self-psychology."

Sample Therapeutic Contract, Part II: The Client's Rights

Part II of this sample therapeutic contract establishes what the client can expect from the therapist. It addresses in part Health and Safety Code 123100 regarding the release of mental health records to clients when requested and the consequences of releasing those records. Additionally, limits of confidentiality are discussed. Questioning the therapeutic process and terminating therapy are also important elements of informed consent. Specific statements describe how the client and the therapist can end the therapeutic relationship. Lastly, should the therapist experience incapacitation, disability, or death, the contract establishes the means to continue the client's therapeutic process, which prevents the possibility that clients could suffer therapeutic abandonment.

Part II: Client's Rights • You have the right to a confidential relationship with me. Within certain legal limits (see #3 below), information revealed by you during the course of therapy will be kept completely confidential and will not be revealed to any person without your written permission.
1. You have the right to know the content of your records at any time, and I have the right to provide you with either the complete records or a summary of their content.
2. If you ask me, I can release any part of your records on file with me to any person you specify. I will tell you when you make your request whether or not I think releasing that information to that agency or person might be harmful to you at any time.
3. Under certain legally defined situations, I have the duty to reveal information you tell me during the course of therapy to other persons without your written consent. I am not required to inform you of my actions if this occurs. These legally defined situations include:
a. If you reveal information to me about active child abuse or neglect, elder abuse, or dependent physical abuse, I must make a report to protective services. When a perpetrator of child abuse is in contact with minors and there is a reasonable suspicion that

he or she may still be abusing minors, I must also report that information.
b. If you seriously threaten harm or death to another person, I am required to warn the intended victim and notify the appropriate law enforcement agencies.
c. If you are in therapy or being tested due to an order of a court or lawyer, the results of the treatment or tests ordered must be revealed to that court or lawyer.
d. If a court of law issues a legitimate subpoena, I am required by law to provide the infor mation specifically described in that subpoena.
e. If you are in a lawsuit where emotional harm is being claimed, the opposing side may subpoena your therapy records.
4. You have the right to ask questions about any of the procedures used in the course of your therapy. If you ask, I will explain my customary approach and methods to you.
5. You have the right to choose NOT to receive therapy from me. If you choose this, I will provide you with names of other qualified professionals whose services you might prefer.
6. You have the right to terminate therapy with me at any time without any financial, legal, or moral obligations other than those you've already incurred. I have the right to terminate therapy with you under the following conditions:
a. When I believe that therapy is no longer beneficial to you.
b. When I believe that you will be better served by another professional, whom I will recommend. If I determine during the first three sessions that I cannot help you, I will assist you in finding someone qualified. If I have written consent from you, I will provide that professional with the essential information she or he requires.
c. When you have not paid for the last two sessions, unless special arrangements have been made with me.
d. When you have failed to show up for your last two therapy sessions without a 24-hour notice of cancellation.
e. When you've failed to cooperate with treatment.
If any of these situations apply, I will send you a certified letter to your address of record to inform you of my decision, and I will give you the names of several therapists for your future counseling needs.

As life can bring unexpected circumstances, should I be unable to continue your therapy, my trusted colleague, Ross Smith, Ph.D., will contact you to discuss what would be best for you at that time.

Sample Therapeutic Contract, Part III: Fees and Length of Therapy

Together, Parts III and IV of this sample therapeutic contract fulfill three important facets of legal and ethical therapeutic duty: the agreement concerning fees at the beginning of therapy, informed consent regarding the length of therapy and documentation that the client has provided consent for treatment. CAMFT ethical standards "encourage" MFTs to explain to clients the potential benefits and risks of services, as was done in Part I of the sample contract. MFTs discuss with clients the possible length of treatment and notify clients regarding this issue. The importance of this document is paramount. Should MFTs face legal action, they can refer to this document as proof that they discuss these and similar issues with the client or clients.

Obtaining a client's signature after she or she has reviewed and approved the conditions of therapy places the onus of responsibility on the client for having made an appropriate decision without coercion from the therapist or a third party. Since clinicians cannot predict when a therapeutic relationship may sour, a client may hurt him/herself and or others, and a malpractice action or legislative complaint may arise from therapy, it is in the best interest of MFTs to obtain adequate documentation (via the client's signature) on the informed consent document.

> **Part III: Fees and Length of Therapy • I agree to enter into therapy with John Q. Sample, MFT, for _________ 50-minute sessions during the next ______weeks. I agree to pay the standard fee of $_____ for each completed 50-minute session (prorated for longer sessions). I will make payment in cash or by check at the time of the therapy appointment, unless we have made other arrangements. I understand that I can leave therapy at any time and that I have no financial, legal, or moral obligation to complete the maximum number of sessions listed in this contract. I am contracting only to pay for completed therapy sessions, sessions I miss without providing 24-hour notice, and telephone time as outlined in Part V of this contract.**
>
> **Date____________ Client's Signature________________________________**
>
> **Therapist's Signature____________________________**

Sample Therapeutic Contract, Part IV: Client's Consent for Treatment

> **Part IV: Consent for Treatment • I, ______________, authorize and request John Q. Sample, MFT, to carry out psychological examinations, diagnostic procedures, and/or treatments that are advisable now or during the course of my care as a patient.**
> **I understand that the purpose of any procedure will be explained to me and be subject to my agreement. I have read and fully understand this Consent for Treatment form.**
>
> **Date________________ Client's Signature________________________________**
>
> **Therapist's Signature____________________________**

Sample Therapeutic Contract, Part V: Office Policies

> **Part V: Office Policies**
> **<u>Payment for Service:</u> You are expected to pay for services at the time they are rendered unless other arrangements have been made. Please notify me if any problem arises regarding your ability to make timely payment.**
> **<u>Insurance Reimbursement:</u> Patients who carry insurance will bill their own insurance. I will provide you with the appropriate billing information, which you will send for reimbursement. I do not bill insurance companies nor do I accept payment from them.**
> **<u>Cancellations:</u> Since an appointment reserves time specifically for you, a minimum of 24-hour notice is required for rescheduling or cancellation of an appointment. The full fee will be charged for sessions missed without such notification. Most insurance companies do not reimburse for missed sessions.**

<u>Office Hours:</u> My office hours are from 8:00 A.M. to 6:00 P.M., Monday to Friday. If you need to contact me between sessions, please leave a message and I will return your call.
Telephone Time: After 5 minutes of telephone time, you will be charged at your regular fee.
<u>Sessions Greater Than 50 Minutes:</u> Sessions that go beyond 50 minutes will be prorated to the nearest quarter hour, unless you have made prior arrangements with me.
<u>Emergency Procedure:</u> An emergency is an unexpected event that requires immediate attention and can be a threat to your health. If an emergency arises, please state this when you leave your message and I will return your call as soon as possible. After 5 minutes of telephone time, you will be charged on a prorated basis. If I have not called you back within 60 minutes, the emergency persists, and the emergency requires it, please call your physician or admit yourself to a hospital for observation.

The entire informed consent document creates safety for the client and protects the therapist. With this document, MFTs address their therapeutic duty, establish clear therapeutic boundaries, outline the potential advantages and disadvantages of therapy, document the client's consent, identify emergency issues and procedures, and set the fee and probable length of therapy. These are important components of any therapeutic contract. As our society continues to utilize the courts as a means of conflict resolution, it serves MFTs to protect themselves by using the therapeutic contract effectively. The example presented in this section is only for illustration purposes. It is not a legal document. I recommend that the reader consider which components are appropriate for his or her practice and then consult with an attorney to develop a legal instrument that will best serve the reader and his or her clients.

Informing Clients of the Potential Risks and Benefits of Treatment

Experienced MFTs know that unpredictable outcomes are a reality of treatment. CAMFT Ethical Standard 1.5 addresses creating safety for all involved as follows:

> **CAMFT Ethical Standard 1.5 — Marriage and family therapists provide adequate information to patients in clear and understandable language so that patients can make meaningful decisions about their therapy.**

When an unintended or unpredictable outcome results from therapy, a client may experience strong and at times difficult feelings. If MFTs lead their clients to believe that their desired outcome is a reasonable result, then they can blame MFTs for any unpredictable result or injury. It is quite reasonable to consider that clients will hold their MFTs responsible for the perceived breach of contract. A breach of contract occurs when MFTs promise their clients an outcome and they cannot deliver on their promise. Since MFTs cannot guarantee a specific outcome, they can best protect themselves by applying their ethical therapeutic duty to inform clients of possible outcomes, which includes both risks and benefits of treatment. When MFTs inform their clients of possible outcomes, then the therapist has taken "reasonable and prudent" steps to inform their clients in an ethical manner. Thus, MFTs act within the standard of care while providing clients with a reasonable range of possible therapy outcomes. This approach respects the client and protects MFTs should they face a malpractice action.

Clinical Example

> **A marriage and family therapist is asked to treat a client for unresolved childhood trauma because this trauma affects her marital relationship. At the beginning of this treatment, the therapist considers possible outcomes of the proposed treatment. The MFT considers outcome possibilities and he advises his client as follows: "I cannot predict or guarantee that your treatment will give you exactly what you are asking for now. I can, however offer you a range of possibilities. One possibility is that your childhood trauma does resolve and your marriage improves. Another possibility might be that you childhood trauma does resolve, however, your marriage does not improve or may even deteriorate. It may be even be that neither your childhood trauma resolves nor your marriage improves. Additionally, during the course of your therapy, you could recall very traumatic and unwanted memories. These memories could retraumatize you. You may actually get worse before getting better." The therapist then goes on to explore with his client how they can both monitor the therapy to ensure the best possible outcome.**
>
> **What impression do you have about this MFT's approach to discussing risks and benefits of treatment?**

Informed Consent When Using "Challenging" Therapies

Challenging therapies can be those therapies that are new, untested, exotic, experimental, difficult, potentially dangerous, scientifically unproven, and/or controversial. When using these modalities, reasonable and prudent MFTs consider that they have a therapeutic duty to obtain a distinct and separate informed consent from their clients prior to engaging in any of these therapies. One would ask: "Why go that far?"

The answer lies in the concept of being "reasonable and prudent" MFTs and these clinicians obtain additional informed consent when they provide challenging therapies.

> **CAMFT Ethical Standard 1.0 states: Marriage and family therapists advance the welfare of families and individuals, respect the rights of those persons seeking their assistance, and make reasonable efforts to ensure that their services are used appropriately."**
>
> **CAMFT Ethical Standards 1.5.1 states: Marriage and family therapists inform patients of the potential risks and benefits of therapy when utilizing novel or experimental techniques or when there is a risk or physical harm that could result from the utilization of any technique.**

The separate informed consent address legally required elements. These are: a) Discuss the risks and benefits of the modality, b) Present all information allowing the client to make an informed decision, c) present the material in language the client can understand, and d) avoid any form of coercion to obtain consent. Reasonable and prudent clinician consider additional necessary elements, which include but are not limited to the following:

- Discuss the nature of the proposed modality. Accuracy is paramount regarding the standing of the modality in the scientific and professional community. Provide information regarding the research (or lack of) done on the modality and the results from such research.
- Inform the client regarding the clinician's depth of knowledge in using this specific modality, duration of usage, training received, and other pertinent information about the modality (i.e., scope of competence).
- Provide the client with accurate risks and benefits of using this modality. If the modality is untested and experimental, obviously no one has defined the benefits of the theory and the client must assess this important information before proceeding with treatment. If the modality is exotic or potentially harmful (consider the re-birthing technique used by the clinician in Colorado several years past), then inform the client that in using this modality, one of the potential risks could be the specific potential harm to the client.
- Inform the client how she or he can stop the modality should it prove to be extremely threatening or frightening to him or her.
- The client signs the original document and the clinician keeps the original. Provide the client with a copy.

Reasonable and prudent MFTs consider how they would be viewed by the Court should they face legal action. The opposing attorney will surely attempt to discredit MFTs by establishing that these clinicians failed to provide a separate and appropriate informed consent. The use of this type of informed consent will not stop a lawsuit, however it establishes that MFTs acted reasonably and prudently, which may ameliorate any negative impact or injury suffered by the client. An appropriate informed consent may even have the lawsuit dismissed on behalf of the clinician because the Court may reason that the client received appropriate information to continue with therapy.

Hugging and Psychotherapy

Hugs, as any other clinical intervention in psychotherapy, can benefit or destroy the therapeutic relationship. A misinterpreted hug may confuse the client and he or she may act on this confusion. The client may act on a misperception of the therapeutic relationship, may consider that the clinician holds special and possibly romantic feelings or that the therapeutic relationship is now balanced and equal.

If the client acts on this confusion and the clinician reactively rejects the client's advances, the rejection will likely harm the client emotionally and most likely will destroy the therapeutic relationship. On the other hand, there are MFTs who "hug" their clients indiscriminately and are likely seeking to satisfy their personal emotional needs. Reasonably stated, they most likely aren't taking into consideration the client's emotional needs. Both conditions discussed in this paragraph can lead to various accusations against the clinician, including client abandonment or sexual harassment.

There are times when client request a hug. Managing this situation appropriately requires a delicate approach. MFTs consider that the client is requesting a clinical intervention and MFTs must consider if the client is therapeutically developed to manage it appropriately without misinterpreting the intent of the hug and becoming confused. MFTs consider their therapeutic duty and consider the hug as a clinical intervention. MFTs assess if the therapeutic relationship is at a stage where this form of clinical intervention is appropriate. Therapists also assess if they are therapeutically and personally comfortable with this form of expression with this client and at this time. MFTs avoid injuring the client. Reasonable and prudent MFTs take the time to explore their internal reality about hugging clients and refer to their established policy about using hugs as a clinical intervention. To go a step further, MFTs can clarify this policy in advance either verbally or in writing, depending on the preference of the clinician.

Informed Consent And Touching Therapies

The scientific literature is replete with articles supporting "touch" as a healing modality in the medical and psychotherapy arenas. Some forensic experts will testify that touching a client without the client's consent is considered as battery. As a result, psychotherapists and counselors must carefully consider the issue of crossing a client's personal boundary when using touch in the clinical setting. Consider any modality that utilizes touch as a form of clinical intervention as part of the psychotherapeutic process. Examples of touch therapies include Somatic Psychology, Perinatal Psychology, Energy Psychology where touching is used, or any other kinesthetic based modality.

One of the foundations of creating clinical safety rests in providing appropriate informed consent. When MFTs provide documentation of the theoretical perspectives, clients receive adequate information needed to make a decision whether or not to participate in a particular touch therapy. When using touch therapies, MFTs are well advised to include in their discussion and documentation those risks and benefits that are specific to touch. Importantly, informing the client about the MFTs' rationale and intention for the use of touch, as well as the scientific validity of the particular touch therapy helps document that informed consent was obtained appropriately.

Touch Therapies and Boundary Violations

The next step in protecting the client and clinician requires that MFTs explore their own internal reality regarding the use of touch. This includes assessing their conscious and unconscious motivation for using touch as a theoretical model. We ask the following question and seek an honest answer: "Am I providing this touch therapy solely for the welfare of the client?" The quick answer is, "Yes, the clinical intervention is for the welfare of the client." Unfortunately, a number of mental health professionals have taken advantage of the power differential between client and clinician and abused touch in the clinical setting.

Having addressed numerous legal cases as an expert witness, I have consulted with attorneys who were attempting to discern whether a clinician's motives were an innocent mistake or predatory behavior. Regardless of the outcome, involvement in a legal or administrative action of this kind will injure both client and MFT. Using touch as a clinical tool raises the responsibility of MFTs to a higher level. This responsibility requires MFTs to maintain healthy boundaries and respect them.

Steps to Help Prevent an Accusation of a Boundary Violation When Using Touch Therapies

Although some accusations of boundary violations are unavoidable, the following recommendations can help protect MFTs when facing a legal action.

- Learn and apply the scope of competence to use touch as a therapeutic modality.
- Thoroughly explore your internal reality regarding the use of touch. Separate your emotional needs from the client's needs and respect this clinical boundary.
- Stay abreast of the scientific literature regarding the particular clinical modalities that you use. Document your education on your curriculum vitae.
- Create a separate and clearly written informed consent document outlining the scientific validity, clinical use, benefits, risks, and other necessary information regarding the touch modalities used.
- Retain a qualified attorney to review your informed consent form.
- Confirm that your treatment plan is in line with your treatment.
- Apply consistent standard of care to all clients.
- Create a procedure by which the client can communicate his or her physical or emotional discomfort during the touch therapy. Listen and respect the client's feedback.
- Carefully document unanticipated or strong reactions that arise during the process of touch therapy.
- Know your state's laws concerning sexual harassment.

Remember that the use of touch therapy can increase the risk of malpractice or administrative action. It is easier to prevent difficulties than to manage them after they have taken place. Practice safely and make sure you know your legal and ethical duties in this sensitive and challenging area of treatment.

Termination and Standard of Care

Ending therapy can bring up a myriad of feelings, reactions and responses for a client. This important phase of treatment may continue the client's healing process and allow for utilization of learned skills or it may be traumatic for the client. A positive therapeutic outcome during the termination phase of therapy usually requires that a strong therapeutic relationship exists. Additionally, a positive outcome most likely occurs when the client has developed a healthy meaning of self, and has created (and learned to use) appropriate internal and external resources. With continuing therapeutic work to process feelings and gain self awareness throughout the termination phase, the client can take another step in his or her growth.

Initiating the ending phase can be traumatic or frightening for a client. Trauma or regression can occur with the end of therapy if a client re-experiences emotional trauma and is unable to process this thoroughly. Abandonment by a parent in childhood might trigger a client's emotional reactivity. If the client had not developed sound internal and external resources to manage this emotional turmoil, and/or the therapist fails to help the client work through challenge, a new trauma can occur. A client terminated prematurely may seek resolution a perceived injury through a formal Board of Behavioral Sciences complaint, or a malpractice action against the MFT.

Managing Termination Safely

Prudent and reasonable MFTs consider the following:

- They address necessary factors contained in their informed consent when terminating the therapeutic relationship. These include, but are not limited to the following: a determination that therapy is no longer serving the client, failure to pay for services, non-compliance of treatment, failure to show up for sessions, or that the client has met the goals of therapy.
- They assess the client's mental status and determine if termination will enhance the client's process or harm the client.
- They assess the client's internal and external resources. They ask if the client can utilize these resources without the help of the therapist.
- They assess if the therapist terminates treatment due to lack of client cooperation with therapy.

- They know risk factors and high-risk populations for suicide. They recognize that the scientific knowledge base has addressed age differences, gender differences, ethnic differences, substance abuse/dependence, mental disorders, and any recent loss experiences related to harm issues.
- They know the legal and ethical standards and apply them.
- They discuss the process of termination with the client, its possible impact on the client's emotional process, and the feelings that the client may experience as a result of termination.
- They create a written systematic plan for terminating clients.

Reasonable and Prudent Steps to Take When Terminating Difficult and Uncooperative Clients

Margarite has been in treatment for several years with the same psychotherapist. She has had a troubled personal history with failed relationships complicated with moderate borderline features that she has experienced throughout the life. She also has had difficult relationships with previous therapists and does not want to lose her present one. She has been "fired" by some, she has "fired" others and afterwards she has felt betrayed and abandoned by these clinicians. She can sense that her current therapist, Arnette, is having difficulty managing her borderline features but she does not want to experience another episode of feeling betrayed and abandoned should their relationship end suddenly. She vows to hang on to Arnette "come hell or high water."

Arnette is indeed facing difficulties managing Margarite's borderline features. She finds herself caught between being appreciated and being hated and this is emotionally very difficult for her. Though she has had experience treating difficult clients, she never thought that treating Margarite would be this difficult, chaotic, and at times even scary. Just last week, the anniversary of her last non-lethal suicide attempt, Margarite was feeling despondent and told Arnette she felt compelled to hurt herself. Arnette determined that she could manage Margarite's emotional reactivity in an in-patient treatment program and referred her to a local treatment program. Margarite agreed yet failed to keep her appointment. She told Arnette that she was the best therapist she ever had and did not want anyone else treating her. She also said that she knew her rights, that Margarite could not abandon her, and that she would sue her if Arnette ended her treatment and therapeutic relationship.

Arnette feels stuck in a bind; she's scared that Margarite could hurt herself, scared of being sued, and scared of continuing to treat her. She asks herself "How did I get into this mess?" She would like to know how she can extricate herself from continuing to treat Margarite without the client accusing of client abandonment. If Arnette were to consult with an expert witness regarding this issue, the expert witness would address the following points:

- First, what questions would you, the reader, ask or would you feel overwhelmed and stuck just like Arnette?
- The expert assesses the initial use informed consent to establish the protection of the client and the clinician and determines if the content is sufficient to allow the MFT to terminate the

relationship with this client in a reasonable and prudent manner.

- Next, the expert witness reviews existing records establishing that the client signed the appropriate forms.
- The expert witness examines the mental health records searching for existing psychometric testing assessing the client's mental state throughout the duration of the treatment. His purpose is to establish that the client's mental state was perturbed.
- He continues reviewing the mental health records for notations of the client's lack of cooperation with treatment and the clinician's management of this issue.
- The expert witness assesses for consultations with clinically objective colleagues regarding the treatment.
- The expert witness reviews the treatment plan as proposed treatment and assessment tool.
- The expert witness now evaluates the format used by the clinician to initiate termination, including appropriate referrals to assure continuity of care.
- The expert witness knows that if these elements are missing in the records, he or any other expert witness will have a difficult time testifying on behalf of the client.

Though it appears that termination is a natural and easy progression in the treatment process, if it isn't managed appropriately the clinician can face a challenging and difficult malpractice action for client abandonment. The latter means that the clinician failed to transition the client into continuity of care using standard of care practices.

Sudden Termination of Therapeutic Services

There are times when MFTs must close their practices. Regardless of the reason, clinicians can use the informed consent document to protect themselves in case a bereft or reactive client initiates a malpractice action for client abandonment. The important clause is known as the "life will in psychotherapy." It informs clients that in case the MFT is unable to continue providing therapeutic services, The MFT or a trusted colleague informs the client and either one activates an appropriate referral process. Regardless of the reason for the interruption of psychotherapy, of importance is the fact that the client signed the informed consent document agreeing to this treatment condition. If a client began legal action for client abandonment, an opposing attorney and expert witness would have a hard time supporting the claim that the MFT acted inappropriately.

Sample Sudden Termination Clause: As life can bring unexpected circumstances, should I be unable to continue your therapy, my trusted colleague, Ross Smith, Ph.D., will contact you to discuss what would be best for you at that time.

Termination and CAMFT Ethical Standards

The following ethical standards apply to managing an appropriate termination of treatment:

CAMFT Ethical Standard 1.0 — Marriage and family therapists advance the welfare of families and individuals, respect the rights of those persons seeking their assistance, and make reasonable efforts to ensure that their services are used appropriately.

CAMFT Ethical Standard 1.3.1 — Marriage and family therapists use sound clinical judgement when terminating therapeutic relationships and do so in an appropriate manner. Reasons for termination may include, but are not limited to, the patient is not benefiting from treatment, continuing treatment is not clinically appropriate, the therapist is unable to provide treatment due to the therapist's incapacity or extended absence, in order to avoid an ethical conflict or problem.

CAMFT Ethical Standard 1.3.2 — Marriage and family therapists do not abandon or neglect patients in treatment. If a therapist is unable or unwilling to continue to provide professional services, the therapist will assist the patient in making clinically appropriate arrangements for continuation of treatment.

CAMFT Ethical Standard 1.4 — Marriage and family therapists respect the right of patients to make decisions and help them to understand the consequences of their decisions. When clinically appropriate, marriage and family therapists advise their patients that decisions on the status of their personal relationships, including dissolution, are the responsibilities of the patient(s).

Clinical Example # 1

Andrea is a recently arrived immigrant from Italy. He works as a fashion designer for a local company. His insurance company refers him to a therapist because he was rear-ended on the freeway a few weeks ago and he is having difficulty driving. Though he speaks enough English to get by, he has difficulty with reading. The therapist gives him several forms to read and tells him he must sign before he will provide treatment. Andrea is confused but he wants to be treated and he signs the forms.

Questions for Clinical Example # 1

1. Is the document signed by Andrea legal? Why or why not?
2. Which component of informed consent did Andrea's therapist fail to comply with?
3. Should a legal dispute arise from the therapy, would the jury support Andrea or the therapist?
4. Does Andrea need to understand the informed consent document? Why or why not?

Clinical Example # 2

Charlene, an attractive 45-year old begins treatment for emotional issues arising from sexual harassment at work. Her therapist is compassionate and assures her that they will work together but she is adamant that she won't testify in court and requires that Charlene sign a statement to this issue. Charlene assures her that she only wants to heal her injury and won't sue. One year later, Charlene's therapist receives a phone call from Charlene requesting her to testify regarding her previous treatment because she was in an auto accident and needs to show that the present symptoms were not present one year ago. Her therapist refuses.

Questions for Clinical Example # 2

1. Is the informed consent statement signed by Charlene legal? Why or why not?
2. Even though Charlene signed this statement, can the therapist legally refuse to testify?
3. If you were another therapist working with Charlene, what recommendations would you make to her?
4. Would you ask Charlene to have you talk to her previous therapist? Why or why not?
5. Charlene requests that her previous mental health records be sent to you to help document the genesis of her present injuries. You find that these records don't comply with standard of care. What would you tell Charlene about what you can or can't support with these records? What are your legal duties?

Clinical Example # 3

Doreen and Richard receive a recommendation to see a friend's therapist for couples counseling. They try twelve sessions and Richard decides to stop. Doreen continues individual treatment and the therapist tells her that it's time to focus on her repressed sexuality. He tells her he will use dream work with elements of Somatic Psychology involving touch. Though unsure, she eventually complies. During the course of treatment, she notices that at times he touches her in a way that can only be described as "sexual." She is confused yet afraid of challenging his expertise.

Questions for Clinical Example # 3

1. Did Doreen provide appropriate informed consent for the "touch" therapy? Why or why not?
2. As you relate from your internal reality, do you consider the therapist to be unaware of his actions or is he "predatory" in his approach to women? What leads you to make this conclusion?
3. You are a therapist and Doreen's friend. She confides her confusion and fear with you. What do you advise her to do? How would you make sure that you are prudent and reasonable in your recommendations?
4. Doreen follows your recommendation and shares her confusion with her therapist. He tells her: "It's all in your mind. That's part of your problem and we're working towards helping you release your inhibitions." She shares this with you. What do you recommend to her?
5. She tells you that her insurance pays for his services and that he is the only therapist on her insurance's panel. She is afraid of not obtaining treatment if she challenges him any further. What do you recommend to her?

Chapter Questions

1. What is informed consent?
2. What purpose does obtaining an informed consent to treat serve?

3. How does it create therapeutic safety?
4. What are the components of informed consent?
5. What are the advantages and disadvantages of using this document in practice?
6. If you were providing your clients with a document of informed consent regarding your treatment and office policies, what would you include in the document?
7. Begin creating a document of informed consent as it would apply to your current situation. Even if you are not seeing clients at this time, make it as applicable as possible. As your clinical experience continues to grow, how do you think this document will change?

Chapter 3

Confidentiality

Confidentiality

Confidentiality is the foundation of safe therapy. (Confidentiality differs from privilege in that privilege relates to released information in a legal setting. Confidentiality relates to holding information in private practice.) Under California law, MFTs must hold all information concerning clients. There are no exceptions to maintaining confidentiality unless a client gives a written consent to release confidential information or there is a legal mandate or legal permission to release information. For MFTs, the legal foundation of confidentiality lies in the Business and Professions Code 4982(m) which states:

> **It is unprofessional conduct for failure to maintain confidentiality, except as otherwise required or permitted by law, of all information that has been received from a client in confidence during the course of treatment and all information about the client, which is obtained from tests or other means.**

Additionally, CAMFT Ethical Standard 2.1 complements the issue of confidentiality by stating:

> **Marriage and family therapists do not disclose patient confidences, including the names or identities of their patients, to anyone except a) as mandated by law, b) as permitted by law, c) when the marriage and family therapist is a defendant in a civil, criminal or disciplinary action arising from the therapy (in which case patient confidences may only be disclosed in the course of that action), or d) if there is an authorization previously obtained in writing, and then such information may only be revealed in accordance with the terms of the authorization.**

Based on these legal and ethical requirements, MFTs have a dual responsibility to maintain confidentiality when treating clients. The Board of Behavioral Sciences (BBS) has made it clear that it considers violating confidentiality as unprofessional conduct. Many therapists have lost their licenses because they have breached a client's confidentiality. The law and ethical standards dictate that, in some instances, MFTs must breach confidentiality and in others, they can breach it depending on the clinical circumstances. MFTs must remember that when they decide to breach confidentiality, they must have a strong legal foundation to do so based on their assessment, diagnosis, and treatment of the challenging issue. Examples of a strong legal foundation are: 1) an MFT appropriately determines that a "reasonable" suspicion of child abuse exists, 2) another MFT determines that his or her client will commit suicide unless he or she notifies a family member or 3) a third MFT hears her or his client make a credible and serious threat to harm his sister-in-law and the sister-in-law has no way of knowing about this threat (The Tarasoff Case Law). In cases where MFTs decide to breach confidentiality, they can best protect themselves by documenting their decision-making process carefully and extensively. This type of documentation serves MFTs should they face a malpractice or administrative action.

The legal and ethical standards recognize that in specific circumstances confidentiality must be breached to protect client welfare. Some circumstances mandate and other circumstances permit therapists to breach confidentiality. The mandated breaches are the following: 1) a serious threat to harm an identifiable victim who can't protect him/herself (Tarasoff), 2) child abuse (Penal Code 11166-11174)), 3) elder abuse (Welfare and Institutions Code 15600-15755), and 4) dependent abuse (Welfare and Institutions Code 15600-15755). The permitted circumstances are the following: 1) a client's mental or emotional condition is such that he or she is a danger to self or others or the property of others, such as suicide (Evidence Code 1024), 2) permitted written releases of information (Civil Code 56-56.37), and 3) when a therapist is a defendant to a malpractice action, criminal action, or disciplinary action involving the treatment provided per Evidence Code 1020.

Mandated Breaches of Confidentiality

In California, MFTs must breach their client's confidentiality in four situations. The first situation is when a client makes a serious threat, in front of the MFT, to harm an identifiable victim who is unable to protect him/herself because they do not know about the threat. In this case, California Law requires that MFTs take reasonable steps to protect the identifiable victim by warning the identifiable victim and notifying the police. This is known as a Tarasoff situation. The Tarasoff Case Law mandates protecting the identifiable victim and Civil Code 43.92 mandates the breach of confidentiality. The second situation is when treating MFTs determine that a "reasonable" suspicion exists that child abuse took place. In this event, the law requires that MFTs protect the abused child. Treating MFTs provide the required information to Child Welfare Services (CWS) immediately and within 36 hours submit a written report. Penal Code 11166 or the "Child Abuse Law" mandates these steps. The third mandated situation occurs when MFTs have a reasonable suspicion that their client, 65 years of age or over, has been the victim of: 1) physical abuse, 2) sexual abuse, 3) neglect, 4) abandonment, 5) financial abuse, or 6) abduction. In this situation, treating MFTs must call Adult Protective Services immediately and then submit a written report within two working days. The fourth and last mandated situation is when MFTs have a reasonable suspicion that her or his client who is a person between the ages of 18-64, is dependent on another person for his or her well-being (developmentally disabled, for example), and has been the victim of 1) physical abuse, 2) sexual abuse, 3) neglect, 4) abandonment, 5) financial abuse, or 6) abduction. In this situation, treating MFTs must call Adult Protective Services immediately and submit a written report within two working days. The Elder and Dependent Abuse Laws (Welfare and Institutions Code 15600-15755) mandate the last two situations.

Permitted Breaches of Confidentiality

In California, MFTs can breach confidentiality in three situations. First, MFTs have the choice to breach confidentiality and create safety for a client when a client's mental or emotional state is such that he or she presents a danger to self or others, or the property of others. Evidence Code 1024 addresses this. The second permitted breach is when MFTs obtain a written release of information from the client to speak to a third party about the client or to obtain information from a third party about the client. Civil Code 56.11 defines this release. The third permitted breach occurs when MFTs face a legal action against them initiated by the client, the BBS, or a district attorney. Evidence Code 1020 defines this.

Written Releases of Information

MFTs have a legal and ethical therapeutic duty to assess, diagnose and treat appropriately. To accomplish this task, exchanging information with other sources is often necessary. Civil Code 56.11 establishes the guidelines to accomplish this task safely. The written release of information provides the parameters for obtaining or releasing information. This law requires the following specific content to make the exchange of confidential information legal. The complete requirements from Section 56.11 are below:

56.11. Any person or entity that wishes to obtain medical information pursuant to subdivision (a) of Section 56.10, other than a person or entity authorized to receive medical information pursuant to subdivision (b) or (c) of Section 56.10, shall obtain a valid authorization for the release of this information.

An authorization for the release of medical information by a provider of health care, health care service plan, pharmaceutical company, or contractor shall be valid if it:

(a) Is handwritten by the person who signs it or is in a typeface no smaller than 14-point type.

(b) Is clearly separate from any other language present on the same page and is executed by a signature which serves no other purpose than to execute the authorization.

(c) Is signed and dated by one of the following:

(1) The patient. A patient who is a minor may only sign an authorization for the release of medical information obtained by a provider of health care, health care service plan, pharmaceutical company, or contractor in the course of furnishing services to which the minor could lawfully have consented under Part 1 (commencing with Section 25) or Part 2.7 (commencing with Section 60).

(2) The legal representative of the patient, if the patient is a minor or an incompetent. However, authorization may not be given under this subdivision for the disclosure of medical information obtained by the provider of health care, health care service plan, pharmaceutical company, or contractor in the course of furnishing services to which a minor patient could lawfully have consented under Part 1 (commencing with Section 25) or Part 2.7 (commencing with Section 60).

(3) The spouse of the patient or the person financially responsible for the patient, where the medical information is being sought for the sole purpose of processing an application for health insurance or for enrollment in a nonprofit hospital plan, a health care service plan, or an employee benefit plan, and where the patient is to be an enrolled spouse or dependent under the policy or plan.
(4) The beneficiary or personal representative of a deceased patient.
(d) States the specific uses and limitations on the types of medical information to be disclosed.
(e) States the name or functions of the provider of health care, health care service plan, pharmaceutical company, or contractor that may disclose the medical information.
(f) States the name or functions of the persons or entities authorized to receive the medical information.
(g) States the specific uses and limitations on the use of the medical information by the persons or entities authorized to receive the medical information.
(h) States a specific date after which the provider of health care, health care service plan, pharmaceutical company, or contractor is no longer authorized to disclose the medical information.
(i) Advises the person signing the authorization of the right to receive a copy of the authorization.

Omitting any part or parts of the requirements above is a breach of client confidentiality. Before MFTs communicate with another party regarding a client's confidential information, they must always obtain a written release of information. There are times when other clinicians will call the MFT and indicate that they hold a written release of information and thus would like to confer about the client. From a forensic perspective, it is best to request the other clinician to fax a copy of the release. This gives the recipient an opportunity to review the written release and determine if it meets legal requirements. If it does not, obviously the communication will not take place until the sender provides the legaly correct one. Imagine a therapist who receives such a phone call, proceeds to provide information, and never receives a copy for his or her records. Later, this MFT becomes involved in a legal action. The opposing attorney requests a copy of the records and finds that the conversation with the other clinician was logged in the progress notes, yet he cannot find a copy of the release of information for this conversation. At this moment, the attorney considers adding an accusation of breaching confidentiality. MFTs can protect themselves by obtaining a legally correct written release of information before every conversation and keeping a copy in their records. This helps avoid an accusation of breaching confidentiality without legal authority.

HIPAA mandated clinicians face more restrictive requirements than the California ones regarding a written release of information. When HIPAA mandated clinicians receive a California mandated one, they are unable to honor it because the legally mandated requirements differ. Thus, to avoid any harm to a client, it serves non-HIPAA mandated MFTs to use a HIPAA form at all times. A sample HIPAA written release of information follows on the next page. For additional information on HIPAA, see "HIPAA Made Easy: A Workbook for Mental Health Clinicians." (Grosso, 2003).

Sample of a Release of Information Document

Name of the Therapist
Address
City, State, Zip Code

Lic. No. MFC XXXXX
Tel 555-555-5555
Fax 555-555-5556

AUTHORIZATION TO USE AND DISCLOSE HEALTH INFORMATION

Name of Patient: ______________________________, hereby authorizes
(Name or Function of Clinician Releasing Information): ______________________________ and

Name or Function of Clinician Receiving Information): ______________________________
to exchange my health records and information obtained during the course of treatment.

The disclosure of such records authorized herein is required for the purpose of carrying out treatment, payment activities, and / or healthcare operations.

Such disclosure shall be limited to the following specific information:
____
____

Such disclosure shall be limited for the following use of information:
____
____

Such disclosure shall be limited for the following type of information:
____
____

This consent shall expire on:______________________________

The patient can request a copy of this authorization. The patient has a right to refuse to sign this form. The patient understands that information that is used or disclosed according to this authorization may be subject to re-disclosure by the recipient. The Provider will not make providing treatment a condition of signing this Authorization. The Patient is entitled to receive a copy of this form. For revocation of this form, the Patient must provide a written request to the clinician named above.
(For California Use Only): California law may provide additional protection regarding the possible re-disclosure stated above.

Dated____________________ Signature of Patient____________________

This form is for illustration purposes only! It meets federal HIPAA requirements.
Always check with your attorney prior to using a published form
to determine if it is appropriate for your practice.
This form must be in size 14 to meet California legal requirements.

Releasing Outpatient Psychotherapy Records for Diagnosis and Treatment Only

Section 56.10 of the California Civil Code permits health care providers, health care service plans or contractors to release medical information relating to a patient's participation in outpatient treatment with a psychotherapist to other health care providers, plans or professionals without obtaining a previously mandated and specified written release of information if the release is made for the purpose of diagnosis or treatment of the patient (BBS News, # 13). A reasonable and prudent clinician remembers that the application of this law be made conservatively. The diagnosis and treatment information is equal in scope to that information found on a HICFA insurance form. Diagnosis is that information used by the clinician on the insurance form. Treatment information would involve the name of the patient, dates of treatment, the treatment provided, duration of treatment, and progress of treatment. All other "confidential" information would require a written release of information form before releasing it.

Though it is true that MFTs can release the above information, they can still face a lawsuit if the client learns that the MFT released or obtained information without their consent. Likely, the opposing attorney will happily present this MFT to the court as being incompetent and unprofessional. Even if the MFT is correct, the opposing attorney will attempt to show that the MFT acted without the client's authorization. It is important for MFTs to avoid releasing any medical information without the client's written consent. Should MFTs face this situation, it would be best to consult with a practicing attorney familiar with mental health law and its application in court.

Group Therapy

At this time, there are no California laws specifically addressing confidentiality in group therapy. However, CAMFT Ethical Standard 2.7 clearly establishes the ethical therapeutic duty for MFTs working with groups. This standard reads as follows:

> **Marriage and family therapists, when working with a group, educate the group regarding the importance of maintaining confidentiality, and are encouraged to obtain written agreement from group participants to respect the confidentiality of other members of the group.**

In a legal action against an MFT, the courts will look to CAMFT Ethical Standard 2.7 for guidance when determining the MFTs' ethical therapeutic duty to protect group confidentiality. This ethical standard directs MFTs to apply reasonable and prudent steps to manage group confidentiality. They consider the following steps:

- MFTs inform group clients regarding the importance of respecting each other's confidentiality and they protect their clients' personal and clinical needs.
- MFTs inform group members that a condition to participating in group therapy is to sign a confidentiality contract. The contract directs the responsibility of maintaining confidentiality to each member.
- Should he or she breach someone else's, the injured party can seek legal action against the person who breached it and thus the contract protects all involved.
- This action helps protect the clinician and the group members. Should the clinician face a malpractice action for failing to protect a group member's confidentiality, the contract serves to document that he or she took appropriate steps to protect the members of the group.
- Having a contract establishes that MFTs acted reasonably and prudently to protect their clients.

Group contracts serve to not only inform and clarify client responsibility regarding managing confidentiality but also serve to enhance group safety and stimulate group process. It is important for MFTs to consult with an attorney before applying a group contract.

"Holding Information" Policy (Secrets) and Its Clinical Implications

Marriage and family therapy practice focuses specifically on the enhancement of relationships. In many cases, MFTs provide treatment to more that one person as part of the treatment unit. For example, a treatment unit could involve a mother, father, and child. CAMFT recognizes that providing treatment under these conditions poses a unique confidentiality challenge. For example, the unit is covered under "group" confidentiality. This means that when the unit participates in therapy, all share the information provided within the group session. However, when an individual separates from the unit for individual treatment, the individual is entitled to his or her own confidentiality. This situation becomes problematic should any member of the unit receives individual therapy from the same MFT. Here's the difficulty for the MFT: If this clinicians fails to establish an appropriate "Holding Information" policy and the member of the unit shares injurious information to the group, legally the MFT is not allowed to release this information to the unit when the client integrates him/herself into group treatment. Failure to address "held information" results in a clinical bind for the therapist. For example:

> **An MFT treats a family unit. He treats one of the members separately to obtain additional family information. Before the clinician has the chance to speak, the client blurts out: "I am glad I had the chance to talk to you apart from my family. I owe lots of money due to uncontrollable gambling and I do not want you to tell my family about it. This stays between you and me."**

To avoid such a clinical bind, CAMFT has established the following ethical standard. CAMFT Ethical Standard 2.0 addresses a "holding information" policy, as follows:

> **Marriage and family therapists have unique confidentiality problems because the "patient" in a therapeutic relationship may be more than one person. The overriding principle is that marriage and family therapists respect the confidences of their patient(s).**

Ethically, MFTs must respect the confidentiality needs of the unit and simultaneously respect the confidentiality needs of an individual member of the unit as previously presented. Thus, the solution is the "Holding Information" policy, which addresses how the clinician will manage the confidentiality needs of the unit and the individual and assure that all agree on this policy. The policy may be; hold all individual's clinical information, do not hold any of the individual's information, or hold some of this information and the clinician will share it at his or her discretion. MFTs who release this information to the group without consent from the individual member breach this individual's confidentiality illegally.

How the "Holding Information" Policy Affects Treatment and the Therapeutic Relationship

MFTs must be aware of how holding sensitive information can affect both treatment and the therapeutic relationship. The reason being that awareness can prevent a malpractice action. In some cases, holding information can have beneficial effects. For example, a husband may need time to process his feelings and find a safe manner to tell his wife that he has had an affair. If the clinician were to help him expose this betrayal to his wife, it could be that the relationship, with the help of the therapist, could develop renewed commitment to the marriage, to therapy, and develop greater trust in the therapist. On the other hand, holding information can also be detrimental to those involved in treatment. For example, the wife in the above example might feel betrayed by the therapist because he or she failed to tell her about the betrayal and therapy may slow down or end. At the other extreme, holding no information in a family system full of secrets might threaten the family members to the point that they consider therapy as unproductive and they terminate immediately. On the other hand, it might increase the courage of family members to break the pact of silence and ultimately strengthen the therapeutic relationship.

A "reasonable and prudent" MFT considers in advance how holding information will affect those involved and attempts to manage it before their clients experience an injury. If clinicians injure their clients, it is reasonable to expect that they will initiate legal action against the clinician. It is good clinical judgment to address how the MFT's "holding information" policy affects clients. We have known this policy as the "secrets" policy. I have found that many clients attach negative connotations to this word. The name implies deceit and separation. For this reason, I have chosen to label this policy as "holding information". Clients feel comfortable with the idea that therapist "hold" information they consider to be personally sensitive and share it when they are ready.

Minors and Confidentiality

When MFTs treat minors (persons under the age of 18), they must remember that the patient or client, in this case the child, holds confidentiality. The exception occurs when the client has a guardian or conservator or if the client is dead, the trustee. However, because the minor is unable to enter into a legal contract or authorize for treatment, the parent or guardian provides the legal consent for the minor's treatment. Therefore, it is reasonable and required to obtain written consent from the parent or guardian to release confidential information about a minor in treatment. (A later chapter discussed treatment of emancipated minors and providing treatment without parental consent.)

When the treatment involves children with parental consent, there are occasions in which the parent becomes part of the treatment unit and will want the MFT to keep him/her informed about their child's progress and process. Therefore, to protect the minor's and the parent's confidentiality needs, it is prudent to discuss the nature and application of the "holding information" policy with both child and parent. This step establishes how the minor's confidentiality is protected, allows the minor to trust the therapist, and reduces conflict that may develop when a parent later demand access to his or her child's therapy information.

Since the parent makes legal decisions for the minor, situations may come up in treatment that require consulting with the parent. For example, the child's behavior poses a danger to self or others. Another example involves a minor who shares sensitive information with the MFT and asks the therapist not to share it with the parent. The problem arises when withholding this information from the parent could create a dangerous situation for the child. The MFT may be in a bind. Sharing the information will likely destroy the trust between the minor and therapist. On the other hand, not providing the information could cause the minor to injure him/herself. Both of these situations require that MFTs inform the parent. Having established a clear "holding information" policy, the clinician avoids the bind, includes the parent in the management of the danger, and protects the clinician.

Minors and Privilege

In all instances, minors in California hold the patient-psychotherapist privilege. However, because minors are unable to make legal decisions or enter into legal contracts for themselves, parents usually make these decisions for the minor. There are some situations where the minor will make his or her own decision concerning holding or waiving the privilege. For example: there is alleged child abuse in a family, and the parents want access to this child's mental health records to disprove the alleged child abuse. In this case, some courts have awarded children the right to hold their own separate privilege. That is, in this situation, only the child can release the mental health records. In a complicated case such as this, the child would likely have his or her own legal representation. The court will have appointed a legal representation to serve the interests of the child. The issue of minors holding their own privilege was tested in court and the Courts have ruled in favor of the minors (Daniel v. Daniel, 1990). Legally emancipated minors treated without parental consent, (See Chapter 26) also have the right to make this decision.

Safeguarding Sensitive Clinical Information Involving Minors From Insurance Companies

At times, parents of minors receiving treatment ask the MFT to avoid releasing sensitive information to the insurance company paying for the minor's treatment. This request can place the clinician in a bind. If the MFT receives payment for treatment and does not provide this information to the insurance company, an investigator will likely consider this as fraud. Conversely, providing it can be considered a breach of confidentiality. Consider the bind in the following example:

> **A parent initiates treatment for her daughter, an anxious 12 year-old. During the evaluation process, the minor tells the clinician that at times, her anxiety is so severe that she wishes she were dead. The clinician asks: "Do you ever think of harming yourself?" The 12 year-old answers "kind of." The clinician remembers the "holding information" policy she established at the beginning of treatment and shares this information with the parent.**
>
> **The parent is concerned that if her insurance company should learn this information, her daughter could face the possibility of having future medical insurance limited or denied to her as an adult. She knows that insurance companies share this information with each other and once this information is placed in her daughter's records, she could be affected negatively. The parent requests that treatment be limited to the daughter's anxiety and that the MFT avoids discussing suicidal ideation. The clinician, afraid for the daughter's safety, contacts the insurance company and requests additional services to address the suicidal ideation.**

Reasonable and prudent MFTs know that appropriate documentation of the "holding information" policy serves to protect them in case they face a malpractice action. If these clinicians were to consult with another colleague, the latter would ask: how did you assess the child's statement regarding at times wanting to die and rule possible harm to self? Therapeutic duty expects MFTs to know that the suicide scientific literature clearly indicates that the clinician must assess multiple risk factors to determine if imminent danger exists. If these risk factors are not present within the clinical context, it is reasonable to consider that the child may only be expressing frustration instead of a serious intent to harm herself.

The clinician addresses the parent's request and she withholds the minor's statement from the insurance company. Next, the clinician provides the parent with reasonable alternatives to treatment, which conform to benefits under the medical insurance program. For example, the MFT informs the mother that she can pay for her daughter's treatment "out-of-pocket" to avoid sharing sensitive information with the insurance company. Informed consent addresses this specific issue. If MFTs release this sensitive information with the insurance company with or without informed consent, an opposing attorney will consider this act as an illegal breach of confidentiality. When the parent makes the request to hold this sensitive information from the insurance company, MFTs avoid a bind by discussing with the parent the risks and consequences of holding this information. If MFTs withholds this information from the insurance company and continue to receive payment, an insurance investigator would consider this action as insurance fraud.

If MFTs bill the insurance company under false pretenses, their investigators will likely consider this as insurance fraud. The latter takes place when MFTs obtain insurance payment under false pretenses. In this case, providing false information to the insurance company for the purpose of obtaining treatment is considered insurance fraud. At this point, it seems that MFTs are in a bind; either commit insurance fraud or breach confidentiality illegally. Avoiding this bind requires consulting with an objective and experienced colleague. MFTs assure that an appropriate informed consent document discusses the issues previously discussed and exists in the mental health records. They confer with the parent regarding the consequences of these actions. If the parent wishes to continue treatment under these circumstances, MFTs consider how their licensing status will be affected if they pursue this course of action. It may be that MFTs must terminate the therapeutic relationship appropriately, assure the client's continuity of treatment, and document the rationale for this decision thoroughly and carefully.

Electronic Devices

At this time, no specific legal mandates exist regarding breaching confidentiality through electronic devices. However, CAMFT Ethical Standard 2.3 places the responsibility on MFTs to recognize and prevent the possible adverse effects of technology with respect to the dissemination of confidential patient information. Additionally, MFTs take reasonable care to maintain confidentiality when using such devices to transmit confidential client information. This means that MFTs recognize that a breach of confidentiality can occur when electronic devices are used. Such devices include cellular telephones, smart phones, cordless telephones, fax machines, Internet e-mail, computers, hard drives, web site servers, hand-held palm devices, and other electronic media. Such instruments, by their nature, do not maintain confidentiality.

What steps can a therapist take to maintain safety when using these devices? First, avoid using them and use a regular telephone line whenever possible to communicate confidential information. Courts have recognized that information transmitted on a "hard-wired" telephone line is confidential and a government agency cannot monitor these without a court order. Therefore, these lines maintain confidentiality. If using a hard line is not possible, then the alternative is to remember that electronic communications are not secure and MFTs must use precautions. With this in mind, the third step available to MFTs is to avoid using any identifiers when discussing a client's confidential information. In an emergency, a cellular telephone is a wonderful adjunct; however, the rest of the time, it can be a detriment to maintaining confidentiality. For storage devices (hard drives), these must have a password to protect access and stored confidential information. When discarding these, a special "sweeper" program assures that the confidential information is completely erased and unrecoverable from the hard drive. Should a third party access any confidential information after the storage device has been discarded, the failure to protect confidential information would be a considered a serious breach of client confidentiality by the responsible MFT.

The Internet

The Internet is a powerful tool and clinicians can use it to communicate with patients and other clinicians. MFTs must know that before transmitting sensitive information, they must know its confidentiality vulnerabilities. For example, anyone can access servers (the hard drives storing this information) storing transmitted confidential information without encryption. Confidential information transmitted to insurance companies is best sent via the insurance company's web site. Evaluate the computer used for transmitting information via the Internet. Some computers used a software based firewall versus others use a hardware based firewall. The latter, which is not prone to SPAM and Internet attacks, is far more secure than the former.

Reasonable MFTs weigh the benefits of speed versus the potential of breaching confidentiality before deciding on how to transmit electronic information. Though insurance companies may require the use of the Internet, MFTs remember that the Internet is not a confidential medium. Witness the many warnings that arise while using Internet browsers telling users that their communication can be intercepted by a third party. Any third person wishing to intercept information on the Internet can do so. Hackers are notorious for accessing "secure" servers holding credit card numbers of businesses. The United States government has been attempting to prevent the sale of encryption software to countries that could pose a threat to this country and continues to struggle with this issue.

Fax Machines

Fax machines communicate with each other across "hard" lines and are "secure" unless the phone connection occurs via a cell phone. Fax machines are a wonderful invention and can speed up communication between two parties. Unfortunately, a breach of confidentiality can take place if the therapist dials an incorrect FAX number. To decrease the chances of this happening, the first step reasonable MFTs take is to double-check the outgoing number. The second step includes creating test FAX containing a cover page with a warning like the one printed below. This message informs the receiver that if they are the unintended recipients of this document, they must destroy it immediately and call the sender. This warning places the responsibility on the receiver, rather than on the sender to respect confidentiality. The third step involves sending a test fax asking the recipient to notify the sender when he or she receives the fax. Each step is reasonable and prudent to ensure that maintaining confidentiality is as reasonable as possible.

Fax Warnings

When sending a fax, a fax warning like the sample below is important to include as part of the cover page. (Always consult with your attorney to create a message that meets your needs) Doing so establishes that the clinician acted reasonably and prudently to protect the client's confidentiality. Though the message by itself does not prevent a breach of confidentiality, it shows that the psychotherapist acted to protect the client in the event the FAX was sent to the wrong FAX number.

Sample Fax Warning

> **The information contained in this fax message is intended only for the personal & confidential use of the recipients named above. This message may be a communication that, as such, is privileged & confidential. If the reader of this message is not the intended recipient, you are hereby notified that you have received this document in error & that any review, dissemination, distribution, or copying of this message is strictly prohibited. If you have received this communication in error, please notify us immediately by phone & return the original to us by mail. Thank you.**

HIV Status

Federal law mandates how to manage confidentiality regarding a client's HIV status. The American With Disabilities Act specifically states that health professionals must protect a client's HIV status as confidential information when the client does not want this information released because no other party knows his or her status. Its intent is to prevent insurance companies or employers intently or inadvertently finding out and discriminating against a client because he or she is HIV positive.

Therefore, it is important to protect this information in a reasonable manner and simultaneously respect the clinician's duty to document assessment, diagnosis, and treatment protocols. MFTs keep all references to HIV status separate from the treatment notes in a separate manila folder attached to the inside of the front cover of the chart. The word "private" appears on the front of the chart and MFTs store a duplicate of all forms in the treatment record that indicates the client's HIV status. For example, therapists take the intake form and copy it. On the original, the clinician blacks out the information about HIV. He or she places the copy in the manila envelope. The MFT repeats this process with other forms identifying the HIV status information, such as treatment plan, 5-Axis diagnosis, etc. In other forms, such as progress notes, the clinician substitutes the term "HIV" with "general medical condition." Taking these steps protect the confidentiality of the client's HIV status and simultaneously protect the MFT's duty to document his or her therapeutic duty.

Should a subpoena demand these records, MFTs discuss the subpoena with their clients and their attorneys and proceed according to their instructions regarding the release of this information. MFTs also protect themselves by discussing to need to protect HIV confidentiality, the implications of releasing this information. This discussion addresses the potential harmful outcome if clients use their insurance for payment and want to prevent the insurance company or an employer from obtaining this information. If the employer and/or the insurance company are aware of the client's HIV status, then protecting HIV confidentiality is a moot point.

Confidentiality and Mandated Reporting

As mandated reporters of Tarasoff situations, child and elder/dependent abuse, psychotherapists have a window of opportunity to make the mandated report within a certain time. For child abuse, MFTs make the report immediately by telephone or fax and follow up with a written report within 36 hours. For elder dependent abuse, MFTs make the report immediately by telephone or fax and follow up with a written report within two working days. The reporting laws do not permit MFTs to communicate with Child Protective Services, Adult Protective Services, or law enforcement agencies after MFTs made the mandated report if these agencies call the clinician to request additional information. These agencies must have a valid court order or an appropriate signed released of information for the parent to obtain additional information unless they seek clarification of unclear or missing data. Opposing attorneys consider any unauthorized communication an illegal breach of the client's confidentiality.

Should a legal action against the clinician arise, the opposing attorney will view the reporting dates carefully. Any deviation invalidates the "immunity" clause and thus strengthens the lawsuit against this clinician. Breaching a client's confidentiality assures that this opposing attorney will succeed in the outcome of the lawsuit. This breach of confidentiality is also ground for a BBS disciplinary action.

Making a Decision to Report or Not Report a Legally-Mandated Breach of Confidentiality

Clinicians can get into trouble when managing mandated reporting for child/elder/dependent abuse. Clinicians tend to forget that the reporting requirement balances between the legal requirements of determining if a "reasonable" suspicion of the abuse exists versus it does not. Expert witnesses emphasize that MFTs have the duty to report only that abuse that the clinician has personal knowledge of or when the clinician has a reasonable suspicion, that abuse had taken place. Opposing attorneys will consider reporting of any abuse else that does not fit the "reasonable" suspicion parameters as a breach of the client's confidentiality. Likely, they will use it as grounds for a malpractice action against MFTs who caused emotional harm to the client.

Expert witnesses also remind us that the legislature provides an accused person of child/elder/dependent abuse the right to sue reporting therapists in spite of the immunity clause for reporting parties. Opposing attorneys initiate legal actions for the following reasons: clinicians knew that the report was done maliciously, was inappropriate, failed to meet the legal requirements such as the time reporting requirements, or did not meet the condition of being "reasonable." Consider the following vignette:

> **Jose recently obtained his license as an MFT. He helps mostly Hispanic clients manage immigration related issues as these affect families. He finds himself working beyond the time required by his employer due to the large number of clients seeking help. His clients speak mostly Spanish or Portuguese, both of which Jose is fluent in. He finds that many of his clients do not know the legal nuances of surviving in the United States and act as if they were in their country of origin. He reminds these clients that they must conform to the laws of the state they live in. Recently, a client informed Jose that he had an argument with his 14 year-old daughter who wanted to go out with her boyfriend to an all-night party. The father reported that in attempting to stop his daughter from going out, he grabbed her by her blouse and it ripped. During the scuffle her breast was exposed and the father looked at his daughter's breast. Believing that he must report this circumstance, Jose begins the reporting process by calling Child Welfare Services immediately and later sends a written report within 36 hours. He is still confused and apprehensive about this reporting situation. Up to now, he has never made a mandated report. He knows it will be for the best of all involved. When Child Welfare Services contacts the father for an interview, he is stupefied. He cannot believe his friends and neighbors ridicule him. He tells himself: "It must be that stupid counselor. It is his fault." He is going to pay for this. Soon thereafter, the father contacts an attorney and consult about suing Jose. The attorney agrees to take the case and soon contacts an expert witness regarding the standard of care when making mandated reports.**

Consider the following questions:

- What specific information led Jose to believe that he faced a possible issue of child abuse?
- Did Jose have any information from a previous communication that supported or denied his impression that child abuse had taken place?
- Did Jose communicate with any person to determine if child abuse had or had not taken place?
- Did Jose have any mental health records that supported or denied that child abuse had taken place?
- How did Jose maintain personal clinical objectivity when making the determination that child abuse had taken place?
- What consultations did Jose carry out to support or deny that child abuse had taken place? Did one of the consultations involve an expert in the alleged perpetrator's cultural values?
- Did Jose specifically document his sequential process of how he determined that child abuse had taken place?
- Did Jose clearly identify and document the foundation of his "reasonable" suspicion of child abuse?
- Did Jose make the reports according to the legally defined limits? That is, immediately by phone and within 36 hours in writing?

These are the questions that an expert witness would ask when attempting to establish clinical liability. For clinicians, the best protection is to assure that they have answered these questions for themselves and documented them thoroughly when facing a possible mandated reporting situation to avoid being sued for making as well as not making the mandated report.

Failure to Maintain Confidentiality Nulls Immunity in a Child Abuse Reporting Situation

Clinicians are reminded to be aware of the conditions the Child Abuse Law imposes regarding immunity. Immunity is only provided when the clinician follows the legally established steps during the reporting process. In Cuff v Grossmont (2013), the Appeals Court ruled that a clinician would not be protected by immunity for violating the confidentiality of the reported party. In this case, the clinician provided the spouse a copy of the child abuse report, which is confidential. Thus, the violation of the reported party's confidentiality, will results in the lack of immunity protection for the clinician.

Documenting the Decision to Report or Not Report a Legally Mandated or Permitted Breach of Confidentiality

There are times when MFTs must breach confidentiality due to a legal mandate, i.e., child abuse reporting. In this, as well as other mandated conditions, the act of reporting is a serious issue with potentially damaging consequences. Opposing attorneys have sued clinicians for breaching as well as for not breaching confidentiality, according to the clinician's decision. Where MFTs reviewed the clinical information and determined that they did not have a "reasonable" suspicion of abuse and thus did not have the duty to report, these attorneys sued the clinician for failing to protect the client due to failure to report. Where MFTs reviewed the clinical information and determined that they did have a "reasonable" suspicion of abuse and thus reported the abuse, these attorneys sued the clinician for harming the client due to making an illegal report and harming the client.

To protect MFTs from this bind, they must document their decision to report or not report. Making this protection even stronger, MFTs would do the following:

- MFTs conduct this process using clinical objectivity.
- MFTs consider their duty to assess, diagnose, and treat this issue.
- MFTs assure that they conduct appropriate assessments and obtain the necessary information to transition into the diagnosis phase.
- MFTs arrive at a diagnosis, which does not mean that an Axis 1 diagnosis. The diagnosis comprises of a simple "yes or no." Have I determined with the available information that a "reasonable" suspicion of child abuse exists? They observe their rationale used to arrive at this "diagnosis."
- If the answer is yes, then I report and if the answer is no, then I do not report.
- Appropriate documentation of the above protects clinicians. Should MFTs face a legal challenge years later, the documentation of the components above indicates the specific information obtained, how (rationale) MFTs used this information to make a decision, and the steps taken to carry out this mandate.

Consider the following vignette:

An elderly and severely ill client tells his therapist that he wants to die with dignity. He says: "I am afraid that if I wait any longer, I will be ravaged by my illness and will have to suffer severe pain. I also will be angry with myself for allowing my illness progress this far. I'm ready to die and will die tonight." The clinician, assessing that the client presents a danger to self, calls the client's daughter under Evidence Code 1024 (breaching the client's confidentiality due to the client wanting to harm himself). The client's daughter forces the client to enter voluntary hospitalization for 72 hours. After leaving the hospital, the client makes another appointment with the client and shares his sense of betrayal. He tells the clinician: "If you breach my confidentiality again, I will sue you!" Fearing a lawsuit, the clinician assures the client he will not do it again. The client again shares with the clinician that he is now ready to kill himself that evening. They say goodbye and the client goes home. The next day, his daughter finds him dead in his bed: he drank half a bottle of vodka and took a bottle of

sleeping pills. She believes the clinician betrayed her father when the therapist failed to call her. She is sure her father shared his intent to die with the clinician. She decides to sue for wrongful death and for failure to take reasonable steps to protect her father's life.

In this vignette, the clinician found himself in a bind. If he breaches his client's confidentiality, the client will sue him. If he does not and the client dies, the daughter will sue him. The only way this clinician can exit this bind is to determine if the presenting situation presents a legal mandate or permission to breach confidentiality. Next, he obtains all necessary information to determine if all of the legal requirements to breach confidentiality exist. Identify the rationale he used to make this determination. If he is legally required or permitted to report, he follows the mandated reporting conditions carefully. Finally, he documents this information thoroughly.

Confidentiality Challenges: Employees and Volunteers

Business and Professions Code requires licensed clinicians to maintain confidentiality, except as mandated or permitted by law. However, this requirement does not apply to unlicensed clinicians, non-licensed employees, volunteers, and trainees/interns who decide later stop to their licensing MFTs (trainees and inters in the licensing tract must comply with this law). MFTs who work with unlicensed clinicians, employees, and volunteers must recognize their vulnerability. These unlicensed individuals most likely are unaware of the confidentiality duty placed upon MFTs. These individuals may inadvertently breach the confidentiality of the MFT's client in the work setting. The outcome may be a lawsuit against this MFT for failing to protect the client's confidentiality, failing to educate the employees on how to protect client confidentiality, and for causing harm to the client. Some MFTs might say: "This will never happen to me." I remind these clinicians that opposing attorneys will sue for malpractice when their assessment of a situation indicates a high potential of winning the lawsuit.

Consider this vignette:

A prominent member of the community seeks services from a mental health clinic. One of the volunteers provides clerical services and observes this individual come regularly for treatment. A few weeks later, the volunteer ends her service to the agency and tells a friend about the prominent person seeking treatment. The friend tells someone else and soon the information is disseminated throughout the community. Later, the client sues the agency and the therapist for malpractice due to the breach of his confidentiality.

An expert witness asked to review the facts first determines if the agency routinely requires volunteers and/or employees to sign a confidentiality agreement contracts with appropriate restrictive clauses. Next, they ask if the contract defines an appropriate amount of time for the management of confidentiality after termination of the volunteer or employee position. Third, did an attorney knowledgeable in contract and mental health law draft the contract? The employer and licensed clinician have the responsibility to implement and enforce such a contract. Should such a contract not exist and the volunteer/employee violates confidentiality, then the responsibility of the breach of confidentiality falls on the clinician. A reasonable and prudent clinician is aware of her or his ethical mandates regarding this issue and manages confidentiality risks involving non-licensed volunteers and employees in a way that protects against reasonable possibilities. Therefore, to create safety for his or her clients and him/herself, a clinician would consider the following:

- Assure that employees and volunteers receive appropriate training regarding the legal requirements of maintaining confidentiality at all times. Update the training on a regular basis.
- Document the training in the employee/volunteer file.
- Have a knowledgeable attorney versed in mental health and contract law prepare an applicable contract that meets California contract law and applicable ethical standards.
- Have all employees sign and date the contract after they have received training. Keep the original in the employee/volunteer file.
- Develop an appropriate confidentiality management protocol for the office and post it in an accessible location for staff to review as needed.

If the clinician is required to comply with HIPAA, he or she has an additional requirement to assure his or her employees comply with the secure management of protected patient information, which includes providing the necessary education to employees to learn how to comply effectively with the HIPAA requirements. Should a legal action involving this issue ensue, a confidentiality management contract between employer and employee would be of paramount importance to document that the clinician took reasonable and prudent action. Clinicians are not expected to be "perfect" in managing confidentiality issues with employees. They are expected to be reasonable and prudent in their actions.

Confidentiality Challenges With Ex-Associates, Ex-Interns, and Ex-Trainees

Clinical supervisors can face a problematic area in the management of confidentiality involving clinical associates, interns, and trainees when they decide not to continue the licensing track. This is significant because once an ex-associate, intern, or trainee stops the licensing track, the Business and Professions Code regarding confidentiality no longer applies to him or her. Therefore, clinical supervisors may find themselves in a legal quandary should one of the ex-clinicians above breach a client's confidentiality.

Consider the following clinical scenario:

> **Dorothy faces a personal challenge. She is undecided about becoming a licensed MFT. She has completed a fair number of her pre-licensed hours, however she is not satisfied by her clinical work in her private practice internship. Finally, she informs her supervisor that she will terminate her clinical duty to her clients and will transfer her clients to other clinicians. Satisfied that she has managed termination appropriately, her supervisor wishes her well in her future endeavor. A year later, Dorothy begins teaching self-development seminars. She integrates her previous clinical experience in her work and discusses her previous cases freely in her seminars. She is not careful to disguise the identities of neither her previous clients nor their presenting issues. She is unaware that one of her previous clients is in the audience and Dorothy just happens to use this client's history in the seminar. The client is shocked in disbelief. Her painful story and her identity are shared freely with the audience.**
>
> **She consults with an attorney who obtains all records pertaining to the supervisory relationship. After providing these to a forensic expert, his feedback indicates that he has a strong case. He initiates legal action against Dorothy and soon realizes that Dorothy has few assets, has no malpractice insurance, and has no legal requirement to uphold this client's confidentiality since she is no longer involved in the mental health licensing track. Neither her state's mental health laws nor her professional ethical standards apply to her. Additionally, a malpractice action against her would be wasteful since he could never collect any financial damages from her. Therefore, the opposing attorney turns to the clinical supervisor seeking financial redress.**

Consider the following steps:

- When working with interns, associates, and trainees, consider that they could stop their licensing track at any time.
- Create a life-long legal contract holding them accountable to maintain confidentiality of all clinical information considered confidential at all times. This contract become active should the intern/associate/trainee fail to complete the licensure track.
- Specify this clearly in the contract and state that this is contract is applicable even if the associate, trainee, or intern stops the licensing tract and is no longer bound by his or her state's mental health laws.
- Consult with an attorney knowledgeable in mental health law and contract law to develop such a contract.

Potential Breaches of Confidentiality in Settings With Multiple Clinicians

Managing client confidentiality in settings with multiple clinicians can be challenging and problematic because not all clinicians involved with client care may be aware of their duty to protect client confidential information. Additionally, some of the clinicians involved in client care may not be licensed and state law regarding client confidentiality may not apply to them. Consider the following scenario:

> **A young man lives in a residential setting for the mentally disturbed. He has a history of being aggressive though he has never been violent with anyone. The owner of the facility is concerned that this client may hurt himself or someone else and wants him assessed by an expert in violent behavior who is not a licensed mental health clinician. The retained expert is under contract with the owner and begins to interview the client, the licensed mental health clinical staff, and other residents. Eventually, the expert submits his report to the owner of the facility and the report clearly states that this client is a serious threat to the safety of other residents. Based on this information, the owner terminates this client's contract and refers him to several other residential facilities.**
>
> **The client becomes confused and bewildered and begins to decompensate because he is out of his comfort zone and familiar environment. He attempts suicide and an attentive residential monitor at his new facility finds him barely alive. After consulting with a malpractice attorney, the young man's family decided to initiate legal action against the owner of the facility and the consultant. The family's attorney extends the malpractice legal action against the licensed mental health clinicians for not preventing their client's breach of confidentiality. The attorney's contention is that this caused severe physical and emotional harm to the client. Regardless of the outcome, the licensed clinicians will have a challenging experience during the lawsuit.**

This problematic scenario tends to arise in situations where multiple clinicians interact as part of the same treatment facility. It becomes even more complicated when licensed and non-licensed mental health clinicians interact. State law requires licensed clinicians to maintain confidentiality, except as mandated or permitted by law (Mandated-Child Abuse, Elder/Dependent Abuse, Tarasoff, Permitted-Evidence Code 1024). Non-licensed clinicians are only ethically required to maintain confidentiality and the laws do not protect them or their clients since California laws do not protect them. MFTs working under similar parameters can take the following actions to assure compliance with legal aspects of confidentiality:

- Distinguish who in the treatment facility is and is not a licensed mental health clinician.
- Determine which clinicians have access to confidential clinical information.
- Establish that an appropriate written release of information permits the exchange of confidential clinical information.
- When consultants are integrated into the treatment team, determine if they are licensed as an independent contractor or an employee of the organization. Licensed clinicians must uphold confidentiality. Independent contractors operate as separate entities whereas employees are part of the treatment team.
- Document any consultation with an outside person. State the name of the client, date of

consultation, reason for consultation, and outcome of consultation.

Ultimately, each clinician has the therapeutic duty to know the legal and ethical implications of confidentiality. The opposing attorney will make sure that he or she uses errors of omission and commission to undermine the professionalism and credibility of the clinician.

Other CAMFT Ethical Standards Related to Confidentiality

These ethical standards help to further define the ethical therapeutic duty of applying standard of care in relation to confidentiality and client privacy issues.

CAMFT Ethical Standard 2.2
When there is a request for information related to any aspect of psychotherapy or treatment, each member of the unit receiving such therapeutic treatment must sign an authorization before a marriage and family therapist will disclose information received from an member of the treatment unit.

CAMFT Ethical Standard 2.4
Marriage and family therapists store, transfer, transmit, and/or dispose of clinical records in ways that protect confidentiality.

CAMFT Ethical Standard 2.5
Marriage and family therapists take appropriate steps to ensure, insofar as possible, that the confidentiality of patients is maintained by their employees, supervisees, assistants, and volunteers.

CAMFT Ethical Standard 2.6 Marriage and family therapists use clinical materials in teaching, writing, and public presentations only if a written authorization has been previously obtained in accordance with 2.1 d, or when appropriate steps have been taken to protect patient identity.

Clinical Example # 1

A licensed MFT knows he has a therapeutic duty to obtain informed consent from clients yet he finds it burdensome to "deal with all this paperwork." His clinical supervisor never obtained informed consent and she was comfortable with a verbal agreement regarding fees. As part of his licensing requirement, he attended a course on law and ethics and learned that he was in violation of CA law (Rains v. Superior Court, 1984) and CAMFT ethical standards. He returns to his office and creates the necessary forms, yet he finds it very difficult presenting them to his clients. He is afraid they might be offended and will stop treatment. Instead, he leaves the forms in his client's mental health records completed and unsigned.

Questions for Clinical Example # 1

1. From your perspective, what prevents this clinician from "dealing with this paperwork"?
2. What is this clinician failing to understand regarding his therapeutic duty to obtain informed consent? What are the potential legal and ethical ramifications of not presenting the forms and leaving them in the client's records?
3. Is he afforded the same level of protection by having the forms in the records and not presenting them to the client for signature? What could be a potential ramification of this action should a legal action ensue?
4. What would be of help to him and enable him to present these documents to his clients and have them sign them? Is his fear that his clients will stop treatment valid? How would you address this issue if you were in his place?
5. If a client refused to sign this form after many months of treatment, what would a reasonable and prudent clinician do in this situation?

Clinical Example # 2

A young couple begins treatment to attempt to stop their fighting, which has been gradually escalating and at times has become physical. In a recent session, the fighting was so severe that the therapist decided to separate them and begin individual sessions to help them calm down and reduce their emotional reactivity. During the individual session with the wife, she begins to cry inconsolably and tells the therapist she can't hold this secret any longer: "I'm having an affair with my boss and I can't stop. If I tell my husband, he'll divorce me and I don't want that to happen. I don't want you to tell him!"

Questions for Clinical Example # 2

1. If this clinician were consulting with you about her dilemma, what would you want to know first?
2. She tells you she did not discuss a "holding information" policy with her clients in advance. What steps can a reasonable and prudent clinician take at this point to avoid the present clinical impasse?
3. The therapist tells the wife that she cannot continue treating her individually if she does not provide the therapist with the consent to bring the "sensitive" information to couples therapy. This client refuses and she threatens the therapist with client abandonment. Is this a valid threat? Why or why not? Is this an ethical issue, a legal issue, or both?
4. The therapist recognizes she made a mistake in not having the clients agree in advance to a "Holding Information" policy. She tells you that in the future, she will not hold any "sensitive" information for clients. Do you consider this to be an appropriate policy for all clients? What are the clinical implications of her choice?
5. Fearful of similar situations happening again, she decides to have all future clients sign her "Holding Information" policy. Does this approach follow standard of care? What would you advise her instead?

Clinical Example # 3

A young woman begins treatment with a faith-based therapist. The therapist's fee is paid by a church fund assisting members of the congregation. Three months after treatment was initiated, the accountant for the church conducts an audit. The therapist sends him the treatment dates for this client including the fees charged and payments for each date.

Questions for Clinical Example # 3

1. Is this an appropriate action? Is it legal, ethical, or both?
2. What steps should this clinician have taken before releasing this information to the accountant?
3. The therapists presents a written release of information document to the client and she refuses to sign. The therapist tells the accountant that she cannot comply with the audit and the accountant refuses to pay for further treatment. What would you advise this therapist? Can the therapist tell the accountant that the client refused to sign the above document? Why or why not?
4. What is the therapeutic duty owed to the person paying for psychotherapy services? What is the extent of this duty?

Clinical Example # 4

> A young adult man, John, tells his therapist that a priest sexually abused him several years ago and that the priest is still in contact with children. After consulting with an attorney, the clinician makes the appropriate reports to Child Welfare Services. Three weeks later, the therapist receives a call from the assistant to the district attorney. This person seeks additional information about the client and the alleged child abuse. The district attorney assistant's contacts the therapist and informs her of her legal duties under California law to report all instances of child abuse. As a last measure, he threatens the therapist with jail if she refuses to comply. Fearful of jail, she provides all informtion in her records about this client6.

Questions for Clinical Example # 4

1. What does the Child Abuse law state about such disclosures? Are they permitted under this or other law?
2. Is this a breach of confidentiality? Why or why not?
3. In your opinion, what prompted this clinician to react to the threat, rather than respond appropriately?
4. Eventually the case goes to trial and the priest's attorney initiates a complaint to the Board of Behavioral Sciences against this therapist for unprofessional conduct regarding the manner in which the report was made. Is there any validity to this complaint? Why or why not?

Chapter Questions

1. What are the unique confidentiality problems encountered by MFTs when treating more than one person as part of the treatment unit?
2. What are the required elements of a legal written release of information document? Can you release more information than that defined by the document?
3. How would you manage confidentiality when doing group therapy? What is your legal and ethical therapeutic duty? What would you do if a client breached group confidentiality?
4. How does a "holding information" (secrets) policy create therapeutic safety?
5. What are the clinical implications of the different forms of "holding information" policies?
6. You are seeing a couple with differing ego strengths. He cannot handle conflict and she can. How would you manage a "holding information" (secrets) policy with such a couple? Would you work with such a couple, why or why not?
7. Would you breach confidentiality if a minor was seeing you with parental consent and the minor

asked you not to tell his or her parents even though he or she was in a situation that could harm him or her? What would be the impact of your decision on the progress of treatment?

8. What are the dangers of using electronic devices in a psychotherapy practice? How can a therapist diminish the danger of breaching confidentiality?

9. If you were developing your own release of information form, what would it look like? Create one for your own practice.

10. What potential clinical challenges can be faced by an MFT trainee or registered intern when managing confidentiality as he or she begins clinical training?

11. How would you manage the clinical scenario that follows? You have a written release of information from your client to speak to his or her previous therapist. The document permits the other therapist to release information to you. During the course of the conversation, the therapist asks you "Has Mary told you about the child abuse accusation yet?"

Chapter 4

Privilege

Privilege

Privilege is similar to confidentiality. Privilege relates to the confidential information that will be released the legal system. When any legal system attempts to have the client's confidential information released, the client's confidentiality is protected by "privilege". Some of the reasons that an MFT might come into contact with the federal, state, or local courts include the receipt of subpoenas, treatment of court-mandated clients, divorce court actions, expert witness testimony, malpractice legal actions and criminal legal actions. Evidence Code ranging from 1010-1027 are the laws that outline privilege for psychotherapists. Like confidentiality, privilege has exemptions too. These are clearly defined by California law.

Evidence Code 1010–1027

Evidence Code 1010 and 1013 describe the licensed clinicians that are considered as psychotherapists and the person who holds the privilege for a client.

> **Evidence Code 1010:** The term "psychotherapist" includes licensed psychologists, licensed clinical social workers, school psychologists, licensed MFTs, MFT registered interns and trainees.
>
> **Evidence Code 1013:** The "holder of the privilege" is:
>
> a. The patient when the patient has no guardian or conservator.
> b. The guardian or conservator of the patient when the patient has a guardian or conservator.
> c. The personal representative of the patient if the patient is dead.

Evidence Code 1014 and 1015 address privilege and the requirement that psychotherapist "claim privilege" (they will not release this information until the client authorizes the release).

> **Evidence Code 1014: The holder of the privilege has the right to refuse to disclose, and to prevent another from disclosing, a confidential communication between the patient and psychotherapist if the privilege is claimed by: a) the holder of the privilege, b) the person who is authorized to claim the privilege by the holder of the privilege, or c) the person who was the psychotherapist at the time of the confidential communication, but such person may not claim the privilege if there is no holder of the privilege in existence or if**

he or she is otherwise instructed by a person authorized to permit disclosure.
Evidence Code 1015: The psychotherapist "shall claim privilege whenever he or she is present when the communication is sought to be disclosed and is authorized to claim privilege."

Exemptions to Privilege

Evidence Code 1016: There is no privilege in any proceeding when the patient's emotional condition has been raised as an issue by the patient or the patient's representative.

Evidence Codes 1016 - 1027 and Penal Code 11171 address the exceptions to "privilege". Evidence Codes 1016 specifically addresses the situation in which a client initiates a lawsuit in which he or she claims he or she has been emotionally injured. In this case, the attorneys for the opposing side are entitled to the records of the client claiming injury.

Evidence Code 1017: There is no privilege if the psychotherapist has been appointed by the court to examine the patient. This does not apply when the court has appointed the psychotherapist at the request of the defendant's lawyer in a criminal proceeding for the purpose of determining whether the defendant should enter a plea based on insanity or base the defense on the defendant's mental or emotional condition.

Evidence Codes 1017 applies to the MFT who is appointed by the court such as an expert witness or child custody evaluator.

Evidence Code 1018: There is no privilege if the services of the psychotherapist were sought to help anyone "commit or plan to commit a crime" or escape punishment for a crime.

Evidence Code 1018 addresses the uncomfortable situation of a client enlisting the help of an MFT in his or her criminal activities. For example, if a client tells his or her therapist that he or she had robbed a bank and asks the therapist to tell the police that he or she was in therapy at the time of the robbery, there is no privilege. In the unlucky event of this happening, it would be important for the MFT to consult with an attorney who is knowledgeable in this arena before taking action.

Evidence Code 1020: There is no privilege when either the psychotherapist or patient alleges a breach of duty arising out of the therapeutic relationship.

Evidence Code 1020 addresses the situation of a client suing a therapist and vice versa. Importantly, if a therapist sues a client for non-payment of fees, only essential information should be disclosed to the court. Such information may include the therapeutic contract, attendance, and moneys owed.

Evidence Code 1023: There is no privilege "in a proceeding initiated at the request of the

defendant in a criminal action to determine insanity."

Evidence Code 1023 applies to psychologists and psychiatrists since it involves a non-relational intrapersonal issue (determining a client's sanity). This type of intrapersonal issue is outside of the scope of practice of MFTs.

Evidence Code 1024: There is no privilege "if the psychotherapist has a reasonable cause to believe that the patient is in such a mental or emotional condition as to be dangerous to himself or the person or property of another" and if the disclosure of confidential information "is necessary to prevent the threatened danger."

Evidence Code 1024 addresses violent and/or suicidal clients and allows MFTs to break confidentiality if necessary to prevent the violence.

Evidence Code 1025: There is no privilege in a "proceeding brought on behalf of the patient to establish his competence."

Evidence Code 1025 addresses issues such as assessing a person with Alzheimer's disease. These are non relational intrapersonal issues that are outside of the scope of practice for MFTs.

Evidence Code 1027: There is no privilege when the patient is under the age of 16 and the psychotherapist has reason "to believe that the patient has been the victim of a crime" and that disclosure of confidential information is in the best interest of the patient.

Evidence Code 1027 extends protection to minors who have been victim of a crime. A reasonable and prudent therapist usually seeks consultation from an attorney in this situation.

Penal Code 11171: The Child Abuse and Neglect Reporting Law takes precedence over laws governing the psychotherapist-patient privilege. Therefore, no privilege exists in situations involving reports of a known or reasonable suspicion of child abuse.

Penal Code 11171 addresses knowledge of child abuse and that the psychotherapist cannot withhold information involving a "reasonable" suspicion of child abuse.

Clinical Example # 1

Jane, a seasoned MFT, tells her clients in advance that she won't testify in court and includes that statement in her informed consent form. She receives a subpoena from an attorney defending a claim of sexual harassment and emotional pain by her client against an employer. Jane calls the opposing attorney and her client's attorney and tells them both she will not appear in Court on the specified date because her conversations with the client are confidential and she does not have a written release of information form signed by the client. They try to reason with her to no avail. She is adamant about not testifying or producing the records.

Questions for Clinical Example # 1

1. Jane is apparently unaware of an important law stating an exemption to privilege. Which one is it?
2. Can Jane refuse to testify if required to do so by a subpoena? Is she required to obtain a written release of information from her client to testify in court? Why or why not?
3. Who holds the privilege in this case? How does Evidence Code 1016 affects this case?
4. If Jane were sharing her frustration about this situation with you, what would you tell her?
5. What steps can Jane take to remedy this situation?
6. What do you believe will happen if Jane continues to refuse to testify?

Chapter Questions

1. What are the differences between privilege and confidentiality?
2. What are the similarities between privilege and confidentiality?
3. When can privilege be violated?
4. Who is the holder of the privilege?
5. How does a licensed therapist assert privilege for the client?
6. If a marshall came to your office and demanded to see a client's mental health records, and threatened to take you to jail if you didn't cooperate, how would you claim privilege for your client and still stay centered emotionally? What would be the first step you would take?
7. A therapist is afraid that a client's records will be subpoenaed. The client is facing a possible contentious divorce and does not want the client's therapeutic information to be available to the spouse's attorney. She chooses to not keep any mental health records to protect her client's privilege. What advice would you have for this therapist?
8. What makes an auto accident a challenging situation for clinicians regarding keeping mental health records?

Chapter 5

Important Legal Concepts in MFT Practice

Scope of Practice

Business and Professions Code 4980.02 states:

The Scope of Practice for MFTs shall include individuals, couples, or groups wherein interpersonal relationships are examined for the purpose of achieving more adequate, satisfying, and productive marriage and family adjustments.

California law permits MFTs to practice psychotherapy when the focus of treatment is the enhancement of relationships. Regardless of the number of clients who are in the treatment room, the focus must be to improve or address relationships. Determining who is treatable within the scope of practice for MFTs can be confusing. For example, an individual presents for therapy a mood disorder or a personality disorder. The MFT must determine whether to treat this client and/or refer to a psychologist or psychiatrist. This requires a thorough assessment and a determination concerning whether the focus of attention will be within the MFT's scope of practice. The litmus test here is this: Will this therapy focus on improving any aspect of the client's relationships? If the answer is yes, then the therapy is within the MFT's scope of practice. Practicing outside of the scope of practice can be considered to be unprofessional (illegal) conduct and can lead to disciplinary action by the Board of Behavioral Sciences.

Scope of Competence

Business and Professions Code 4982 (s) states:

(It is unprofessional conduct for an MFT to be) performing, holding oneself out as being able to perform, or offering to perform any professional services beyond the scope of one's competence as established by one's education, training, or experience.

CAMFT Ethical Standard 3.9 states:

Marriage and family therapists do not assess, test, diagnose, treat, or advise on problems beyond their scope of competence as determined by their education, training and experience. While developing new areas of practice, marriage and family therapists take steps to ensure the competence of their work through education, training, consultation, and/or supervision.

California law and CAMFT Ethical Standard 3.10 clearly state that before an MFT is eligible to treat a client for a specific issue, the MFT must have the knowledge, training, and experience to treat that issue. Additionally, MFTs must know how to assess, diagnose, treat, and/or advise appropriately throughout the duration of therapy without causing harm to the client; also known as the legal and ethical therapeutic duty. A reasonable and prudent MFT will determine if the treatment necessary for his or her client is within her or his scope of competence.

There will be times in treating clients when issues come up that are beyond the scope of competence for the clinician. This opens the question, how can an MFT treat new issues that will arise in therapy when he or she does not currently have the competence to do so? The MFT can gain competence by obtaining additional education, training, and experience in the new clinical arena. This course of action will enable the MFT to treat new issues. Examples of how clinicians might increase their scope of competence are: 1) participating in a weekly case discussion meeting with a mentor who is experienced in a new area of treatment (while maintaining confidentiality); 2) taking courses dealing with the new issue; 3) reading literature on the topic or; 4) utilizing training courses to increase treatment skills.

CAMFT Ethical Standards Related to Scope of Competence and Integrity

> **CAMFT Ethical Standard 3.1** Marriage and family therapists are in violation of this Code and subject to termination of membership, or other appropriate action if they: a) are convicted of a crime substantially related to their professional qualifications or functions; b) are expelled from or disciplined by other professional organizations; c) have licenses or certificates that are lapsed, suspended or revoked or are otherwise disciplined by regulatory bodies; d) continue to practice when they are no longer competent to practice due to physical or mental causes or the abuse of alcohol or other substances; or e) fail to cooperate with the Association or the Ethics Committee at any point from the inception of an ethical complaint through the completion of all proceedings regarding the complaint.
>
> **CAMFT Ethical Standard 3.5** Marriage and family therapists remain abreast of developments in their field through educational activities and clinical experiences. Marriage and family therapists, when acting as teachers, supervisors, and researchers, stay abreast of changes in the field, maintain relevant standards of scholarship and present accurate information.
>
> **CAMFT Ethical Standard 3.6** Marriage and family therapists actively strive to identify and understand the diverse cultural backgrounds of their clients by gaining knowledge, personal awareness, and developing sensitivity and skills pertinent to working with a diverse client population.
>
> **CAMFT Ethical Standard 3.7** Marriage and family therapists make continuous efforts to be aware of how their cultural/racial/ethnic identity, values and beliefs affect the process of therapy.

> **CAMFT Ethical Standard 3.9** Marriage and family therapists do not assess, test, diagnose, treat, or advise on problems beyond their level of their competence as determined by their education, training, and experience. While developing new areas of practice, marriage and family therapists take steps to ensure the competence of their work through education, training, consultation, and/or supervision.

For a complete review of CAMFT Ethical Standards relating to competence, see Chapter 30.

Therapeutic Duty

Therapeutic duty is a legal concept rather than an actual law. It encompasses all the legal and ethical responsibilities imposed upon MFTs by California Case Law, California Law, and CAMFT Ethical Standards. Therapeutic duty places upon MFTs, the responsibility of assessing, diagnosing and treating appropriately. Additionally, MFTs must incorporate all legal and ethical standards during the assessment, diagnosis and treatment of each client. Throughout the duration of treatment, MFTs must consider their first duty to the client, which is to "do no harm". This is found in CAMFT Ethical Standard 1.0, which addresses advancing the welfare of clients. Additionally, Business and Professions Code as well as Contract Law delineate specific clinical actions for MFTs to assure they "do no harm" to their clients.

Therapeutic duty begins as soon as the client enters into a therapeutic contract and the agreement happens implicitly or explicitly. MFTs create an implicit therapeutic contract when they provide any type of a therapeutic service to a person, thus creating the expectation of a continuing therapeutic relationship. MFTs create an explicit therapeutic contract when they produce a written contract to their clients. When clients sign the contract, they agree to the explicit contract conditions. Therapeutic duty ends when the client completes treatment successfully or terminates prematurely.

Some Clinical Examples of Therapeutic Duty

Legal and ethical standards address therapeutic duties. For example, confidentiality falls into this category. The overlap between laws and ethics is found in Business and Professions Code 4982 (a-v), case law, and CAMFT ethical standards. The following is a sample of therapeutic duties gleaned from the literature. Some address scope of competence, advertising, referrals, and releases of information. This is only a partial list.

- Duty to avoid making unauthorized disclosures
- Duty to avoid breaches of confidentiality when keeping, storing, and transferring mental health records

- Duty to recognize symptoms
- Duty to assess client appropriately, per standard of care (addressed in later section)
- Duty to diagnose properly
- Duty to use appropriate diagnostic procedures (must stand up to *Dauber v Dow Chemical*, 1993 which was a landmark case establishing the scientific basis of testimony)
- Duty to analyze diagnostic procedures properly
- Duty to make proper decisions in light of results of the diagnostic procedures
- Duty to know whether a specialist or consultant should be utilized
- Duty to know when hospitalization is required
- Duty to provide proper treatment
- Duty to give proper advice, instructions, and warning
- Duty to keep proper and accurate records and reports
- Duty to avoid abandoning the client

To protect themselves and their clients, MFTs must have a thorough knowledge of California law and CAMFT ethical standards and apply them appropriately in practice. Failure to adhere to the laws and ethical guidelines constitute practicing unethically and unprofessionally, which is the fastest path to lose one's license and/or experience a malpractice action for harming a client. When challenged in a legal action, an opposing attorney will question MFTs about their knowledge of the laws and ethical standards and how they apply to MFT practice.

Therapeutic Duty Regarding Assessing Appropriately

A thorough assessment protocol requires obtaining the client's personal, medical, and family history and the presenting issues. MFTs obtain additional information consultations with previous therapists, current mental health clinicians, physician and psychiatrist. Furthermore, it is important to assess a client's mental state and if necessary, assess for depression.

In 1984, the Attorney General of California wrote an opinion concerning MFTs and psychometric testing. This opinion stated that MFTs had the right to use any psychometric test in the course of practice when: 1) the scope of practice (the enhancement of relationships) was applied and 2) when the MFT had the knowledge, training, and experience to use these tests (scope of competence). One can reasonably interpret this opinion as also permitting MFTs to utilize any psychometric test in the course of practice when these conditions apply: 1) the scope of practice (the enhancement of psychosocial adjustments) is applied and 2) when the MFT has the knowledge, training, and experience to use these tests (scope of competence).

An important part of assessment includes the observing client's general appearance, behavior, affect, perception, intellectual functioning, memory, attention, concentration, insight and judgment. Any of these areas can prove of significance during the course of treatment. Fortunately, the Mental Status Exam addresses the former components, which define an appropriate assessment of a person's mental and emotional state. The Mental Status Exam organizes all of these elements in a concise format. When MFTs use the formal version of the Mental Status Exam or an unstructured version, doing so establishes that MFTs took a "reasonable and prudent" step to assess the client. Documenting the Mental Status Exam protects MFTs because they carried out their duty to assess their clients and assessed within the standard of care.

Other tests, which may be important as assessment tools include, but are not limited to the following: a) Beck's Depression Inventory, b) Beck's Hopelessness Scale, and c) the MMPI.

Therapeutic Duty Regarding Diagnosing Appropriately

The Diagnostic and Statistics Manual of Mental Health Disorders of the American Psychiatric Association (DSM) identifies a 5-Axis diagnosis as standard of care. Including each component of the 5-Axis system constitutes a complete diagnosis. Axis 1 notes diagnoses of mental disorders and/or developmental disorders. Axis 2 addresses all personality disorders. Axis 3 allows for notation of any medical disorder. Note that this indicates the need to obtain a complete medical history from the client. Axis 4 identifies and acknowledges all psychosocial and environmental problems the client faces. The final category, Axis 5, asks the therapist to rate the current global assessment of functioning in comparison to last year. When diagnosing, MFTs would be wise to document observable clinical behaviors and their behaviors symptomatic of the diagnoses mental disorder(s). These noted clinical observations are useful in supporting MFTs should they face a legal challenge for their diagnoses.

Therapeutic Duty Regarding Treating Appropriately

Treating appropriately requires that MFTs practice within the standard of care, which means that MFTs provide "reasonable and prudent" treatment and apply a treatment modality that best addresses the client's presenting issue. Treatment modalities that meet the standard of care are found in the psychology literature including refereed journals evaluated by objective experts in the field, lectures and presentations given by recognized experts, and textbooks written by recognized experts. The latter provide excellent sources of treatment information considered appropriate and acceptable to manage clinical issues.

Some MFTs use modalities not yet recognized by experts in the field. However, should they injure the client using this modality, the client can claim that these MFTs provided substandard care. To protect themselves against a legal challenge resulting from the claimed injury, the best approach for MFTs is to provide a separate informed consent. This consent informs the client of the nature of the modality, discusses the benefits and risks of treatment of this modality, and obtains a written consent signed by the client. Even when using these protective steps, in case of a legal challenge MFTs must explain their rationale for using this treatment modality.

Collaborating With Others

CAMFT Ethical Standard 1.11 addresses collaboration to benefit the client as follows:

> **When appropriate, marriage and family therapists consult, collaborate with, and refer to physicians, other health care professionals, and community resources in order to improve and protect the health and welfare of the patient.**

Experienced MFTs acknowledge that they are unable to provide a broad range of treatment to their clients. When the need arises for a treatment modality that MFTs cannot provide due to inexperience or unfamiliarity, reasonable and prudent MFTs consult with more experienced peers. Should that approach prove insufficient, MFTs refer the client to a professional who can provide adjunctive, concurrent, or sequential treatment. This approach supports the MFTs ethical therapeutic duty to collaborate or refer to improve and protect the health and welfare of the client. Collaborating with another professional serves to expand the treatment structure and provide the client the necessary treatment to address presenting issues. This cooperative effort creates a stronger treatment team, balances out therapeutic responsibility among the treating professionals, and creates greater clinical objectivity.

This ethical standard implicitly requires MFTs to be knowledgeable about other clinicians and services available in their community. When a presenting condition may have a medical etiology, MFTs refer to a physician to rule out this possibility. In legal cases where MFTs failed to obtain information about a client's medical condition, juries found them negligent of their legal an ethical therapeutic duty. Ethical Standard 1.12 requires MFTs to know their clinical limitations, avoid practicing beyond this clinical boundary, and refer to appropriate professionals when appropriate.

Standard of Care

The definition of standard for MFTs describes them as "reasonable and prudent" therapists in the community who provide appropriate and scientifically accepted modalities to treat their clients.

Experts consider standard of care as a dynamic standard that is continually defined by California Law, Case Law (such as the Tarasoff case), CAMFT Ethical Standards, research and publications, and the testimony of expert witnesses in court after a client experiences an emotional injury arising from treatment. Standard of care is also defined by the client's history, presenting issues, cultural background, treatment history, socio-economic status, and other similar factors. Prudent MFTs consider their psychotherapy within the format of the latter clinical factors presented by the client.

An example of standard of care in couples therapy follows: The clinician addressees all confidentiality needs, including addressing a "holding information" policy at the beginning of treatment. The MFT completes a thorough assessment of the presenting conflict, including the severity and intensity of the conflict. The MFT attempts to determine if the couple requires individual treatment until they are able to handle conjoint treatment or are they able to manage conjoint treatment cooperatively. The MFT completes an appropriate treatment plan addressing the individual and/or conjoint treatment. Thus, the clinician approached this challenge progressively while assessing the needs of the client. The MFT avoided rushing the couple into treatment they were not yet ready to begin. The MFT prepared the clients for treatment and applied the necessary modalities.

Attending to Standard of Care in Clinical Practice

Below is a list of some of the duties in clinical practice. It is important for MFT to consider how each one relates to the standard of care.

- Utilizing psychometric assessment instruments.
- Evaluating clinical needs based on culture, cognitive capabilities, as well as socioeconomic, age, gender and other demographic factors.
- Choosing a theoretical approach or methodology that best serves the client.
- Being knowledgeable concerning research about clinical interventions.
- Applying scope of competence to determine personal clinical limitations.
- Obtaining consultation and utilizing referrals.
- Applying current legal and ethical standard.
- Documentation.

The Clinician's Therapeutic Duty to Assess for Clinically Important Issues Thoroughly and Completely

Juan's priest refers him for treatment. Juan tells the clinician that his wife complains that he is abusive to her and harsh with the children. Juan says that he wants to make sure his kids do not end up in a gang and that is why he is so harsh with them. Juan's clinician begins his assessment process to determine the nature of the abusiveness, conflict with his children, and the nature of his parenting style. Eventually, the therapist asks Juan: "Did

your father drink?" Juan answers: "Just like everyone else." He asks Juan: "And you, do you drink?" Juan answers: "Yes, just like everyone else." The clinician moves on to obtain more information about the cultural and structural aspects of the family.

Several months later, Juan's clinician is stymied because he cannot understand the lack of progress with Juan's treatment. The therapist has addressed structural and cultural issues, as well as attempting to improve Juan's communication with his wife and children. From Juan's report, it appears that the conflict with his family is only getting worse. Juan tells the therapist he wants to stop spending all this money on treatment that is not working.

A few days later, Juan's parish priest called the clinician and left him a message on his voice mail saying that Juan was involved in an auto collision and was in intensive care in the hospital. Since the clinician had asked Juan to sign a written release of information to speak with the priest, he called and spoke to the priest. The priest told the clinician that Juan had been drunk when he was driving and hit a telephone pole. The therapist asked: "Did he just begin drinking?" The priest answered: "No, he's been drinking heavily for several years now. That's why I sent him to you." The therapist felt a tightening feeling in the pit of his stomach. He realized he failed to thoroughly assess Juan's drinking and it is impact on his life.

Juan's wife spoke with her husband's physician and he told her that Juan would most likely end up with a severe brain injury. After she realized the extent of his injuries, she decided to engage the services of an attorney to help her and her family. The attorney informed her that both her and her husband had a strong case against the clinician for negligence. She decided to begin a lawsuit against him.

The clinician in the previous vignette is facing a malpractice action. "What did I do wrong?" he asks? His first error was in failing to assess Juan appropriately. For example, in his mental health records, Juan's clinician made the notation that Juan drinks a "docecito" every day. The clinician thought it was a 12 oz. can of beer. Had he asked further, he would have found that Juan was drinking a 12-pack of beer every day. An expert witness involved in this case testified that Juan's clinician failed to assess him thoroughly and did not address Juan's minimization of his drinking. Additionally, Juan's clinician failed to address how the drinking affected his life, his relationships, his work, and his marriage. This vignette deals with substance abuse and it is applicable to other instances where clients present with similar challenges involving equally challenging issues. It is up to each clinician to assess appropriately for potentially harmful behaviors that could place the client at risk.

Mental Health Case Law

Case law in California consists of rulings made either by the Court of Appeals or the California Supreme Court. After a court ruling has been made in a county Superior Court, that ruling may be appealed. The first appeal would take place at the Appeals Court level. If their decision is appealed, the case would continue to the California Supreme Court. When a ruling is made by either of these two judicial bodies, it becomes "Case Law." Case law is as binding as legislative law.

1. ***Bellah v. Greenson* (1978)** No legally mandated duty to warn exists when a client threatens suicide; however, a therapist has a legal duty to take reasonable steps to protect the life of the client. *(Tarasoff does not apply to suicide, i.e., there is no duty to warn. However, the therapist must protect the life of his or her client when he or she is suicidal).*

2. ***Landeros v. Flood* (1976)** A physician and the hospital where he practiced were found guilty of medical malpractice for the physician's failure to diagnose and report a suspected case of child abuse. In this case, due to the failure of the physician to report child abuse, the child was returned home, where he received permanent physical injury. *(If a therapist does not report reasonably suspected child abuse, in addition to breaking the law and facing criminal charges, the therapist can also be sued for malpractice if the report is not made and the child is consequentially injured).*

3. ***Planned Parenthood Affiliates v. Van de Kamp* (1986)** Consensual, non abusive, non coercive sex involving minors between ages 14 and 18 is not reportable. *(A therapist is not mandated to report consensual sex between minors when they are between the ages of 14-18)*

4. ***Tarasoff v. Regents of University of California* (1976)** The California Supreme Court ruled that the psychotherapist's obligation to protect a patient's confidences must be suspended when a psychotherapist determines, or should determine, that a patient presents a serious danger of violence to another person and that person does not know of the threat. *(A therapist has a duty to warn when he or she hears a client make a serious threat to harm against an identifiable victim who cannot protect himself or herself because he or she does not know of the threat).*

5. ***Hedlund v. Superior Court of Orange County* {1982}** The court extended the protective warning to include not only the direct victim of such violent threats but anyone who is foreseeable and identifiable as a person who might be injured if the threatening person carried out her or his threat. *(In a Tarasoff situation, therapists must protect those living at the same address as the intended victim. This includes children, spouses, or parents).*

6. ***Cooper v. Board of Medical Examiners* (1975)** The Court of Appeals stated that the negligent diagnosis of a child's mental condition caused emotional distress to the child's parents. Parents have the right to sue a psychotherapist for malpractice when psychotherapists are negligent in diagnosing children. *(If a therapist does not diagnose a child correctly, he or she can be sued for malpractice).*

7. ***Thompson v. County of Alameda* {1983}** There is no duty to warn when threats are made against unspecified persons. *A Tarasoff condition applies only when an identifiable victim exists. It does not apply to persons who are not identifiable).*

8. ***Jablonski ex rel. Pahls v. United States* (1983** —Psychotherapists have a duty to maintain mental health records and to obtain records from previous mental health providers early in treatment. In this case, the Veterans' Administration had an obligation to obtain, review, and, if necessary, communicate information from prior psychiatric records to avoid a possible risk of violence by a patient. *(Mental health records must be maintained by therapists).*

9. *Inabnit v. Berkson* (1988) Privilege applies to protect the client from unauthorized disclosures by the mental health professional. It does not protect the client from a subpoena for records that complies with specific statutory provisions or from a court order requiring a mental health professional to testify. If a subpoena is served with a "notice to consumer" and the patient does not object in a timely fashion or act as specified in the statute to protect his or her legal rights to confidentiality, the records can be produced and the mental health professional can testify because the patient's failure to act is deemed to be a consent to disclosure. *(If a subpoena is carried out correctly, it must be respected by the therapist).*

10. *Cutter v. Brownbridge* (1983) Mental health professionals must be aware of the requirements and limitations of the law not only so they can advise their clients of its limitations but also so they will not be misled into inadvertent and improper disclosure due to ignorance of the precise parameters of the law. Where information is disclosed in contravention of the constitutional and statutory provisions, a plaintiff can recover compensatory damages. *(If a therapist breaches confidentiality because of ignorance of the law, he or she can still be sued for malpractice).*

11. *Mavroudis v. Superior Court* (1984) Confidential communication includes information learned in an examination of the patient, any diagnosis made, and any advice given by the psychotherapist in the course of that relationship. If a vague threat to harm is made, it is not the responsibility of the psychotherapist to interrogate or investigate to determine the identity of the intended victim. *(A Tarasoff condition only exists if a serious threat to harm an identifiable victim is made. A vague or unclear threat does not require that the therapist investigate the identity of the victim).*

13. *Farell L. v. Superior Court* (1988) The Court of Appeals held that a crime victim's communication with other patients in group therapy were privileged and that she could not be cross-examined on the communications. The court concluded that the other group therapy participants were persons who were present to further the patient's interest within the meaning of Evidence Code 1012. *(Group therapy communications are privileged and cannot be disclosed by the therapist).*

14. *Menendez v. Superior Court* (1992) The California Supreme Court stated that privilege can cover information that was never confidential but was communicated to the therapist in confidence, as well as information that had lost its confidential status. The court stated that privilege may survive even the broadest disclosure of the most secret information, particularly if the patient is unaware of the disclosure. *(In this case, the Menendez brothers told their psychologist they had killed their parents. This was privileged information and could not be disclosed to the court. However, it was disclosed to the Court because the therapist made a Tarasoff report to the police after they had threatened to kill him, his girlfriend and coworkers were the identifiable victims).*

15. *People v. Wharton* (1991) Where the threatening statements are disclosed to the prospective victim, the statements are no longer confidential and the therapist can therefore testify about the substance of the warning and the statement in therapy that led to the warning being made. *(In a Tarasoff situation, the information given to the identifiable victim by the therapist is not confidential).*

16. *Howard v. Drapkin* (1990) As a general rule, information received by a mental health practitioner in a consultation or examination is confidential; however, this is not true when the evaluation is for the purposes of a custody evaluation. *(In custody evaluations, information given to the therapist is not confidential).*

17. *James W. v. Superior Court* (1993) The Court held that when therapists go from reporting to investigating abuse, they are beyond their area of competence and are not immune from being sued. *(In child abuse situations, therapists have the duty to report a reasonable suspicion of child abuse. Their duty is not to investigate the child abuse. That duty belongs to the police or C.W. S. workers).*

18. *Searcy v. Auerbach* (1993) Immunity did not protect a California psychologist from a civil suit for defamation over a report of child abuse made to authorities in Texas when no report was made in California. *(Making a child abuse report to a state other than California is considered as a breach of confidentiality since the therapist is not mandated to obey the laws of other states).*

19. *People v. Stritzinger* (1983) The California Supreme Court has interpreted the waiver of confidentiality imposed by the child abuse reporting law to be limited in scope. When a mental health practitioner made an initial report of child abuse, the confidentiality was waived; however, when a deputy sheriff subsequently called the mental health practitioner and sought additional details, confidentiality was not waived, and a subsequent criminal conviction was reversed. (In child abuse reporting, the mandate to report only applies to the initial statement made to CWS. Any additional statements made by the therapist to the police or CWS are considered a breach of confidentiality).

20. *People v. Battaglia* (1984) Even though reporting may lead to criminal prosecution, a mental health practitioner is not required to give a patient warning against self-incrimination. *(If a therapist is mandated to report, the therapist is not mandated to warn the client about the impact of telling the therapist about the abuse).*

21. Daniel C. H. (Court of Appeals) Ruled that noncustodial parents had no entitlement to breach a child's psychotherapist-patient privilege. *(Parents who are not legal custodians of a child in a divorce case cannot breach the client-psychotherapist privilege of the child which is protected by law).*

22. *Molien v. Kaiser Foundation Hospital* (1980) A person who is not physically present when an injury ocurrs may be a direct victim by virtue of his or her relationship with either the allegedly negligent party or another victim of negligence. In this case, a hospital was held liable to a man for negligently advising his wife that she had a venereal disease when in fact she did not. When the woman communicated the erroneous diagnosis to her husband, their marital relationship was destroyed. Subsequently, when it was determined that the diagnosis was incorrect, the husband brought an action against the hospital for negligent infliction of emotional distress. The court held that it was reasonably foreseeable that a negligent diagnosis of a venereal disease would cause emotional distress to a married couple. *(Psychotherapists can be sued by third parties, i.e. spouses, when they experience direct harm from indirect clinical interventions).*

23. *Cooper v. Board of Medical Examiners* (1975) An appellate court upheld an administrative law judge's decision that an MFT could not testify to the standard of care for a psychologist. *(MFTs cannot testify against a psychologist or psychiatrist regarding issues of Standard of Care).*

24. *People v. Kelly* (1976) The California Supreme Court held that the rationale of *Frye v. United States* (1923) applied to California cases. The U.S. Supreme Court in *Daubert v Merrell Dow Pharmaceutical, Inc.* (1993) held that the federal rules of evidence provided the standard for federal courts to use in determining the admissibility of scientific and expert evidence. The court concluded that the federal rules of evidence superseded the Frye case. Thus federal courts in California are now required to apply the federal rules of evidence, not the Frye decision. However, the principles of the Frye case have been accepted by the California Supreme Court in *People v. Kelly* and made a part of state law. Thus, state courts can probably continue to use the Kelly-Frye criteria until the California Supreme Court indicates to the contrary. The Kelly-Frye criteria can be met by establishing the general acceptance of the technique or device through expert testimony, by citation of authoritative scientific or legal journals that reflect the acceptance of the technique (assuming that the hearsay objection can be overcome), and by reference to any judicial opinions that have applied to the Kelly-Frye test and accepted the technique or device as accurate. Some of the areas that have met the Kelly-Frye test in recent years include Child Sexual Abuse Accommodation Syndrome (this syndrome is used to explain inconsistent behaviors of a child witness) and the use of the MMPI. Some areas where the Kelly-Frye test has been held to bar testimony include the use of hypnotically refreshed memory, Rape Trauma Syndrome to show that a rape has occurred, and the use of anatomically correct dolls. *(The Kelly-Frye rule is a rule to measure scientifically acceptable testimony).*

25. *People v. Harlan* (1990) Two criteria must be met for admission of testimony of Child Sexual Abuse Accommodation Syndrome: (a) the testimony must be directed to specific misconceptions jurors might have, and (b) the court must instruct the jury not to take the evidence as proof that the child was abused. *(For the Child Abuse Accommodation Syndrome to be accepted as evidence in a trial, the two conditions set above must be met).*

26. *Miller v. Los Angeles County Flood Control District* (1973) An expert witness cannot testify as to whether a defendant is guilty of a crime. *(Expert witnesses cannot testify as to the guilt or innocence of a defendant. Only the jury or judge can determine that).*

27. *Cobbs v. Grant* (1972) Physicians are required to obtain informed consent. *(Obtaining informed consent to clients is required of health practitioners and mental health practitioners are affected).*

28. *Truman v. Thomas* (1980) The mental health professional must disclose the material risks of not undergoing the recommended procedure. *(See above).*

29. *Moore v. Regents of the University of California* (1990) The patient's interest and information does not extend to a lengthy polysyllabic discourse on all possible complications. A mini-course in medical science is not required. A mental health professional who is seeking a patient's consent for a therapeutic procedure must, in order to satisfy the fiduciary duty to disclose and obtain informed consent, disclose all personal interests unrelated to the patient's health that may affect his or her professional judgment. This includes economic and research interests. However, mental health professionals are not required to disclose every contingency that might affect the patient's nonmedical rights and interests. *(Mental health practitioners are required to discuss any personal interests in the client's treatment, for example a research project that benefits the therapist. However, the disclosure need not cover every possible complication).*

30. *Davis v. Superior Court,* 7 Cal. App. 4th 1008 (1992) California courts held that the constitutional right to privacy applies to a relationship between a patient and a health care professional and supersedes nearly all other statutory provisions. (Confidentiality applies to a client and the therapist).

31. People v. Randy Lee Cain, 82 Cal. App. 4th 81(1997) California courts held that the psychotherapist-patient privilege outweighs a criminal defendant's constitutional right to question his or her accusers. (Confidentiality is held by the psychotherapist in spousal abuse cases when the psychotherapist is subpoenaed to testify by the abuser).

32. *Engstrom v. Engstrom,* Superior Court, Los Angeles County, California, No. VC016157, Oct. 11, 1995. The judge excluded the testimony of the plaintiff and his witnesses, including expert witnesses, regarding "repressed memories," "repression," or "dissociation," finding that the "phenomenon of 'memory repression' is not generally accepted as valid and reliable by a respectable majority of the pertinent scientific community and that the techniques and procedures utilized in the retrieval process have not gained general acceptance in the field of psychology or psychiatry."

33. Engstrom v. Engstrom, California Appellate Court, Division 2, No. B098146, June 18, 1997. In an unpublished opinion, a California Court of Appeals affirmed the previous ruling (see above) by the Superior Court judge. The court did not allow the suit to continue because the appellant had no memories of childhood abuse other than those generated during the period he was in therapy, and "compelling" evidence showed that those memories did not meet the Kelly-Frye standard of admissibility. Therefore, the appellant could not testify regarding recovered repressed memories.

34. Thomason v. Vice, Superior Court, San Joaquin County, California, No. 236209, June 25, 1996. A Superior Court judge excluded expert testimony as to repressed memories because "there is no general acceptance by the scientific community of this scientific technique."

35. Ramona v. Ramona, California Appellate Court, District 2, Aug. 19, 1997. The Second District Court of Appeals ordered a lower court to dismiss a claim of "repressed memory" because, the court concluded that the testimony was tainted by the use of the drug sodium amytal, which was administered during therapy. The court concluded that the repressed memory testimony of the plaintiff was "inadmissible under Kelly-Frye due to the lack of general acceptance in the scientific community of the reliability of memories recalled after a sodium amytal interview."

36. Ewing v. Goldstein (2004)—This case law expands the duty to warn under Tarasoff. It now includes statements made by a client's intimate family members regarding the client's serious danger to harm as meaningful "communications" under Civil Code 43.92 and must be considered when a clinician determines if a client presents a serious threat to harm under Tarasoff.

37. Calderon v. Glick (2005)—The Applellate Court ruled that a clinician doesn't have duty to warn unless the specific legal conditions exist, such as a communication of a serious threat to harm between client and psychotherapist. Without these legal conditions, the clinician doesn't have a duty to warn.

Business and Professions Code 865 - Definition of Sexual Orientation Change Efforts

This law requires licensed clinicians to avoid seeking the change of sexual orientation of their clients or to eliminate or reduce sexual or romantic attractions or feelings toward individuals of the same sex. Additionally, these clinicians musty provide acceptance, support, and understanding to clients or the facilitation of their client's coping, social support, and identity exploration and development, including sexual orientation.

As of February 2014 this law is on hold. A legal challenge by those opposed to this law has been successful in having the California Appellate Court review this law. It is likely that the constitutionality of this law may be decided by the U.S. Supreme Court. Until then, MFTs are nor bound by this law.

Chapter 5

Clinical Example # 1

Judy, an intern in a private practice internship, is supervised by an MFT. Judy has a small number of clients and her supervisor wants to refer as many clients as she can manage. One referral turns out to be a difficult case and Judy is afraid of telling her supervisor she is over her head because he might stop referring to her. Meanwhile, the clinical supervisor keeps referring her new clients.

Questions for Clinical Example # 1

1. Judy recognizes that she doesn't have the scope of competence to treat this client. What reasonable and prudent steps is she now required to take?
2. Did her supervisor fail in his therapeutic duty? How did she do so?
3. If Judy does not take any steps to correct her present situation, what do you foresee happening to her?
4. If she were to injure a client, what could the BBS accuse her and her clinical supervisor of?
5. What is Judy's overall therapeutic duty to clients?
6. How can Judy keep her referral base and treat within her scope of competence?

Clinical Example # 2

John refuses to use treatment plans in his mental health records. He states: "I know how to treat clients and I don't need a piece of paper telling me how to do my work." One of his clients asks John: "All we seem to do is sit and talk. Am I ever going to get any better?" John replies: "This is a long process and you must be patient." A few weeks later, the client calls to cancel an appointment and soon thereafter, John receives a letter from an attorney requesting this client's records.

Questions for Clinical Example # 2

1. John appears to be ignoring an important therapeutic duty. Which one is he ignoring?
2. How is he failing in this duty?
3. Since John does not have a treatment plan, how can John assess the progress of treatment?
4. What would a reasonable and prudent clinician tell John about his belief about using treatment plans?
5. What options does John have to comply with the request for records since he does not have a treatment plan for this client?

Chapter Questions

1. How does the scope of practice define what kind of issues and clients you will treat? Define an intrapersonal issue in psychotherapy. Define an interpersonal issue in psychotherapy.
2. How does a therapist develop scope of competence in new areas? What areas of psychotherapy would currently challenge your scope of competence?
3. What aspects about your professional experience would you examine to determine your scope of competence with each presenting clinical issue?
4. What do you believe is the most important aspect in assessing your own scope of competence?
5. How would you maintain objectivity in assessing your scope of competence?
6. What language would you use to define your understanding of what is your therapeutic duty?
7. How does therapeutic duty differ from informed consent?
8. Therapeutic duty is based on which concept?
9. How can a therapist use the concept of therapeutic duty to create therapeutic safety and protect him or herself?
10. You begin therapy with a client and you have the competence to manage the presenting issue. After a few sessions it becomes clear to you that you don't like the client as a person. What is your

therapeutic duty to this client?
11. What is your understanding of standard of care?
12. What is scientific standard of care?
13. What is clinical standard of care? How do you currently expand you clinical standard of care?
14. What is legal/ethical standard of care?
15. How does standard of care affect therapy?
16. How does case law affect the practice of psychotherapy?
17. How can you stay abreast of case laws as they develop?
18. What could prevent you from referring to others to expand the treatment team for this case?

Chapter 6

BUSINESS AND PROFESSIONS CODE
As It Applies To Marriage and Family Therapists
SECTIONS 4980–4989

Business and Professions Code

These codes dictate legally the clinical behavior expected from an MFT practicing in California. This includes students, trainees, interns, licensed therapists, and those therapists acting as clinical supervisors. All the legal and relevant information to practice as an MFT in California is contained in the following legal codes. The BBS requires that MFTs, interns, trainees, and their supervisors know their content prior to practicing. Per the BBS or the courts, ignorance is no excuse.

4980. (a) Many California families and many individual Californians are experiencing difficulty and distress, and are in need of wise, competent, caring, compassionate, and effective counseling in order to enable them to improve and maintain healthy family relationships.
Healthy individuals and healthy families and healthy relationships are inherently beneficial and crucial to a healthy society, and are our most precious and valuable natural resource. Marriage, family, and child counselors provide a crucial support for the well-being of the people and the State of California.
(b) No person may for remuneration engage in the practice of marriage, family, and child counseling as defined by Section 4980.02, unless he or she holds a valid license as a marriage, family, and child counselor, or unless he or she is specifically exempted from that requirement, nor may any person advertise himself or herself as performing the services of a marriage, family, child, domestic, or marital consultant, or in any way use these or any similar titles to imply that he or she performs these services without a license as provided by this chapter. Persons licensed under Article 4 (commencing with Section 4996) of Chapter 14 of Division 2, or under Chapter 6.6 (commencing with Section 2900) may engage in such practice or advertise that they practice marriage, family, and child counseling but may not advertise that they hold the marriage, family, and child counselor's license.

4980.01. (a) Nothing in this chapter shall be construed to constrict, limit, or withdraw the Medical Practice Act, the Social Work Licensing Law, the Nursing Practice Act, or the Psychology Licensing Act.
(b) This chapter shall not apply to any priest, rabbi, or minister of the gospel of any religious denomination when performing counseling services as part of his or her pastoral or professional duties, or to any person who is admitted to practice law in the state, or who is licensed to practice medicine, when providing counseling services as part of his or her professional practice.
(c) This chapter shall not apply to an employee of a governmental entity or of a school, college, or university, or of an institution both nonprofit and charitable if his or her practice is performed solely under the supervision of the entity, school, or organization by which he or she is employed, and if he or she performs those functions as part of the position for which he or she is employed.

(d) Notwithstanding subdivisions (b) and (c) all persons registered as interns or licensed under this chapter shall not be exempt from this chapter or the jurisdiction of the board.

4980.02. For the purposes of this chapter, the practice of marriage, family, and child counseling shall mean that service performed with individuals, couples, or groups wherein interpersonal relationships are examined for the purpose of achieving more adequate, satisfying, and productive marriage and family adjustments.

This practice includes relationship and premarriage counseling. The applications of marriage, family, and child counseling principles and methods includes, but is not limited to, the use of applied pyschotherapeutic techniques, to enable individuals to mature and grow within marriage and the family, and the provision of explanations and interpretations of the psychosexual and psychosocial aspects of relationships.

4980.03. (a) "Board," as used in this chapter, means the Board of Behavioral Sciences.

(b) "Intern," as used in this chapter, means an unlicensed person who has earned his or her master's or doctor's degree qualifying him or her for licensure and is registered with the board.

(c) "Trainee," as used in this chapter, means an unlicensed person who is currently enrolled in a master's or doctor's degree program, as specified in Section 4980.40, that is designed to qualify him or her for licensure under this chapter, and who has completed no less than 12 semester units or 18 quarter units of coursework in any qualifying degree program.

(d) "Advertise," as used in this chapter, includes, but is not limited to, the issuance of any card, sign, or device to any person, or the causing, permitting, or allowing of any sign or marking on, or in, any building or structure, or in any newspaper or magazine or in any directory, or any printed matter whatsoever, with or without any limiting qualification. It also includes business solicitations communicated by radio or television broadcasting. Signs within church buildings or notices in church bulletins mailed to a congregation shall not be construed as advertising within the meaning of this chapter.

4980.07. The board shall administer the provisions of this chapter.

4980.08. (a) The title "licensed marriage, family and child counselor" or "marriage, family and child counselor" is hereby renamed "licensed marriage and family therapist" or "marriage and family therapist," respectively. Any reference in any statute or regulation to a "licensed marriage, family and child counselor" or "marriage, family and child counselor" shall be deemed a reference to a "licensed marriage and family therapist" or "marriage and family therapist."

(b) Nothing in this section shall be construed to expand or constrict the scope of practice of a person licensed pursuant to this chapter.

(c) This section shall become operative July 1, 1999.

4980.10. A person engages in the practice of marriage, family, and child counseling who performs or offers to perform or holds himself or herself out as able to perform such a service for remuneration in any form, including donations.

4980.30. Except as otherwise provided herein, a person desiring to practice and to advertise the performance of marriage, family, and child counseling services shall apply to the board for a license and shall pay the license fee required by this chapter.

4980.31. A licensee shall display his or her license in a conspicuous place in the licensee's primary place of practice.

4980.34. It is the intent of the Legislature that the board employ its resources for each and all of the following functions:

(a) The licensing of marriage, family, and child counselors, clinical social workers, and educational psychologists.

(b) The development and administration of written and oral licensing examinations and examination procedures, as specified, consistent with prevailing standards for the validation and use of licensing and certification tests. Examinations shall measure knowledge and abilities demonstrably important to the safe, effective practice of the profession.

(c) Enforcement of laws designed to protect the public from incompetent, unethical, or unprofessional practitioners.

(d) Consumer education.

4980.35. (a) The Legislature acknowledges that the basic obligation to provide a complete and accurate application for a marriage, family, and child counseling license lies with the applicant. At the same time, the Legislature recognizes that an effort should be made by the board to ensure that persons who enter degree programs and supervisorial training settings that meet the requirements of this chapter are enabled to discern the requirements for licensing and to take the examination when they have completed their educational and experience requirements.

(b) In order that the board, the educational institutions, and the supervisors who monitor the education and experience of applicants for licensure may develop greater cooperation, the board shall do all of the following:

(1) Apply a portion of its limited resources specifically to the task of communicating information about its activities, the requirements and qualifications for licensure, and the practice of marriage, family, and child counseling to the relevant educational institutions, supervisors, professional associations, applicants, trainees, interns, and the consuming public.

(2) Develop policies and procedures to assist educational institutions in meeting the curricula requirements of Section 4980.40 and any regulations adopted pursuant to that section, so that those educational institutions may better provide assurance to their students that the curriculum offered to fulfill the educational requirements for licensure will meet those requirements at the time of the student's application for licensure.

(3) Notify applicants in the application procedure when applications are incomplete, inaccurate, or deficient, and inform applicants of any remediation, reconsideration, or appeal procedures that may be applicable.

(4) Undertake, or cause to be undertaken, further comprehensive review, in consultation with educational institutions, professional associations, supervisors, interns, and trainees, of the supervision of interns and trainees, which shall include, but not be limited to,
the following, and shall propose regulations regarding the supervision of interns and trainees which may include, but not be limited to, the following:

(A) Supervisor qualifications.

(B) Continuing education requirements of supervisors.

(C) Registration or licensing of supervisors, or both.

(D) Responsibilities of supervisors in general.

(E) The board's authority in cases of noncompliance or negligence by supervisors.

(F) The intern's and trainee's need for guidance in selecting well-balanced and high quality pofessional training opportunities within his or her community.

(G) The role of the supervisor in advising and encouraging his or her intern or trainee regarding the necessity or value and appropriateness of the intern or trainee engaging in personal psychotherapy, so as to enable the intern or trainee to become a more competent marriage, family, and child counselor.

4980.37. (a) In order to provide an integrated course of study and appropriate professional training, while allowing for innovation and individuality in the education of marriage, family, and child counselors, a degree program which meets the educational qualifications for licensure shall include all of the following:

(1) Provide an integrated course of study that trains students generally in the diagnosis, assessment, prognosis, and treatment of mental disorders.

(2) Prepare students to be familiar with the broad range of matters that may arise within marriage and family relationships.

(3) Train students specifically in the application of marriage and family relationship counseling principles and methods.

(4) Encourage students to develop those personal qualities that are intimately related to the counseling situation such as integrity, sensitivity, flexibility, insight, compassion, and personal presence.

(5) Teach students a variety of effective psychotherapeutic techniques and modalities that may be utilized to improve, restore, or maintain healthy individual, couple, and family relationships.

(6) Permit an emphasis or specialization that may address any one or more of the unique and complex array of human problems, symptoms, and needs of Californians served by marriage, family, and child counselors.

(7) Prepare students to be familiar with cross-cultural mores and values, including a familiarity with the wide range of racial and ethnic backgrounds common among California's population, including, but not limited to, Blacks, Hispanics, Asians, and Native Americans.

(b) Educational institutions are encouraged to design the practica required by subdivision (b) of Section 4980.40 to include marriage, family, and child counseling experience in low-income and multicultural mental health settings.

4980.38. (a) Each educational institution preparing applicants to qualify for licensure shall notify each of its students by means of its public documents or otherwise in writing that its degree program is designed to meet the requirement of Section 4980.37 and shall certify to the board that it has so notified its students.

(b) In addition to all the other requirements for licensure, each applicant shall submit to the board a certification by the chief academic officer, or his or her designee, of the applicant's educational institution that the applicant has fulfilled the requirements enumerated in Sections 4980.37 and 4980.40, and subdivisions (a) and (d) of Section 4980.41.

(c) An applicant for an intern registration who has completed a program to update his or her degree in accordance with subdivision (k) of Section 4980.40 shall furnish to the board certification by the chief academic officer of a school, college, or university accredited by the Western Association of Schools and Colleges, or from a school, college, or university meeting accreditation standards comparable to those of the Western Association of Schools and Colleges, that the applicant has successfully completed all academic work necessary to comply with the current educational requirements for licensure as a marriage, family, and child counselor.

4980.40. To qualify for a license an applicant shall have all the following qualifications:

(a) Applicants applying for licensure on or after January 1, 1988, shall possess a doctor's or master's degree in marriage, family, and child counseling, marital and family therapy, psychology, clinical psychology, counseling psychology, counseling with an emphasis in marriage, family, and child counseling, or social work with an emphasis in clinical social work, obtained from a school, college, or university accredited by the Western Association of Schools and Colleges, or approved by the Bureau for Private Postsecondary and Vocational Education, pursuant to Section 94774.5 of the Education Code. For purposes of this chapter, the term "approved by the Bureau for Private Postsecondary and Vocational Education" shall not include temporary, conditional, or any other type of interim approval. In order to qualify for licensure pursuant to this subdivision, any doctor's or master's degree program shall contain no less than 48 semester or 72 quarter units of instruction. The instruction shall include no less than 12 semester units or 18 quarter units of coursework in the areas of marriage, family, and child counseling, and marital and family systems approaches to treatment.

The coursework shall include all of the following areas:

(1) The salient theories of a variety of psychotherapeutic orientations directly related to marriage, family, and child counseling, and marital and family systems approaches to treatment.

(2) Theories of marriage and family therapy and how they can be utilized in order to intervene therapeutically with couples, families, adults, children, and groups.

(3) Developmental issues and life events from infancy to old age and their effect upon individuals, couples, and family relationships.

This may include coursework that focuses on specific family life events and the psychological, psychotherapeutic, and health implications that arise within couples and families, including, but not limited to, childbirth, child rearing, childhood, adolescence, adulthood, marriage, divorce, blended families, stepparenting, and geropsychology.

(4) A variety of approaches to the treatment of children.

The board may, by regulation, further define the content requirements of required courses specified in this subdivision.

(b) (1) In addition to the 12 semester or 18 quarter units of coursework specified above, the doctor's or master's degree program shall contain not less than six semester or nine quarter units of supervised practicum in applied psychotherapeutic techniques, assessment, diagnosis, prognosis, and treatment of premarital, couple, family, and child relationships, including dysfunctions, healthy functioning, health promotion, and illness prevention, in a supervised clinical placement that provides supervised fieldwork experience within the scope of practice of a marriage, family, and child counselor.

(2) For applicants who enrolled in a degree program on or after January 1, 1995, the practicum shall include a minimum of 150 hours of face-to-face experience counseling individuals, couples, families, or groups.

(3) (A) Supervised practicum hours, as specified in this subdivision, shall be evaluated, accepted, and credited as hours for trainee experience by the board.

(B) The practicum hours shall be considered as part of the 48 semester or 72 quarter unit requirement.

(c) As an alternative to meeting the qualifications specified in subdivision (a), the board shall accept as equivalent degrees, those master's or doctor's degrees granted by educational institutions whose degree program is approved by the Commission on Accreditation for Marriage and Family Therapy Education.

(d) All applicants shall, in addition, complete the coursework or training specified in Section 4980.41.

(e) All applicants shall be at least 18 years of age.

(f) All applicants shall have at least two years' experience that meets the requirements of this chapter in interpersonal relationships, marriage, family, and child counseling and psychotherapy under the supervision of a licensed marriage, family, and child counselor, licensed clinical social worker, licensed psychologist, or a licensed physician certified in psychiatry by the American Board of Psychiatry and Neurology. Experience shall not be gained under the supervision of an individual who has provided therapeutic services to that applicant. For those supervisorial relationships in effect on or before December 31, 1988, and which remain in continuous effect thereafter, experience may be gained under the supervision of a licensed physician who has completed a residency in psychiatry. Any person supervising another person pursuant to this subdivision shall have been licensed or certified for at least two years prior to acting as a supervisor, shall have a current and valid license that is not under suspension or probation, and shall meet the requirements established by regulations.

(g) The applicant shall pass a written examination and an oral examination conducted by the board or its designees.

(h) The applicant shall not have committed acts or crimes constituting grounds for denial of licensure under Section 480. The board shall not issue a registration or license to any person who has been convicted of any crime in the United States that involves sexual abuse of children or who has been ordered to register as a mentally disordered sex offender or the equivalent in another state or territory.

(i) Applicants applying for licensure on or before December 31, 1987, shall possess all of the qualifications specified in subdivisions (e) to (h), inclusive, and shall possess a doctor's or master's degree in marriage, family, and child counseling, social work, clinical psychology, counseling, counseling psychology, child development and family studies, or a degree determined by the board to be equivalent, obtained from a school, college, or university accredited by the Western Association of Schools and Colleges, the Northwest Association of Secondary and Higher Schools, or an essentially equivalent accrediting agency as determined by the board.

(j) For applicants applying for a license pursuant to subdivision (i), the board may make a determination that an applicant's master's or doctor's degree is an equivalent degree if it finds that the degree was issued upon completion of a course of academic study primarily designed to train persons as a marriage, family, and child counselor. The course of study completed by the applicant shall contain not less than 30 semester or 45 quarter units of coursework as follows: (1) human biological, psychological, and social development, (2) human sexuality, (3) psychopathology, (4) cross-cultural mores and values, (5) theories of marriage, family, and child counseling, (6) professional ethics and law, (7) human communication, (8) research methodology, (9) theories and applications of psychological testing, and (10) not less than six semester or nine quarter units of supervised practicum in applied psychotherapeutic techniques, assessment, diagnosis, prognosis, and treatment of premarital, family, and child relationship dysfunctions. The applicant shall submit to the board satisfactory written verification by the chief academic officer of the accredited or approved school, or by an authorized designee, that the applicant has successfully completed courses, including the practicum required by the board. The verification shall include, but need not be limited to, descriptions of the completed courses. The board may request further written verification of course content and academic experience to determine that the applicant's training and experience is equivalent to the course of instruction required by this section.

(k) (1) An applicant applying for intern registration who, prior to December 31, 1987, met the qualifications for registration, but who failed to apply or qualify for intern registration may be granted an intern registration if the applicant meets all of the following criteria:

(A) The applicant possesses a doctor's or master's degree in marriage, family, and child counseling, marital and family therapy, psychology, clinical psychology, counseling psychology, counseling with an emphasis in marriage, family, and child counseling, or social work with an emphasis in clinical social work obtained from a school, college, or university currently conferring that degree that, at the time the degree was conferred, was accredited by the Western Association of Schools and Colleges, and where the degree conferred was, at the time it was conferred, specifically intended to satisfy the educational requirements for licensure by the Board of Behavioral Sciences.

(B) The applicant's degree and the course content of the instruction underlying that degree have been evaluated by the chief academic officer of a school, college, or university accredited by the Western Association of Schools and Colleges to determine the extent to which the applicant's degree program satisfies the current educational requirements for licensure, and the chief academic officer certifies to the board the amount and type of instruction needed to meet the current requirements.

(C) The applicant completes a plan of instruction that has been approved by the board at a school, college, or university accredited by the Western Association of Schools and Colleges that the chief academic officer of the educational institution has, pursuant to subparagraph (B), certified will meet the current educational requirements when considered in conjunction with the original degree.

(2) A person applying under this subdivision shall be considered a trainee, as that term is defined in Section 4980.03, once he or she is enrolled to complete the additional coursework necessary to meet the current educational requirements for licensure.

(l) This section shall become operative on January 1, 1997.

4980.41. All applicants for licensure shall complete the following coursework or training in order to be eligible to sit for the licensing examinations:

(a) A two semester or three quarter unit course in California law and professional ethics for marriage, family, and child counselors, which shall include, but not be limited to, the following areas of study:

(1) Contemporary professional ethics and statutory, regulatory, and decisional laws that delineate the profession's scope of practice.

(2) The therapeutic, clinical, and practical considerations involved in the legal and ethical practice of marriage, family, and child counseling, including family law.

(3) The current legal patterns and trends in the mental health profession.

(4) The psychotherapist/patient privilege, confidentiality, the patient dangerous to self or others, and the treatment of minors with and without parental consent.

(5) A recognition and exploration of the relationship between a practitioner's sense of self and human values and his or her professional behavior and ethics.

This course may be considered as part of the 48 semester or 72 quarter unit requirements contained in Section 4980.40.

(b) A minimum of seven contact hours of training or coursework in child abuse assessment and reporting as specified in Section 28 or any regulations promulgated thereunder.

(c) A minimum of 10 contact hours of training or coursework in human sexuality as specified in Section 25, and any regulations promulgated thereunder. When coursework in a master's or doctor's degree program is acquired to satisfy this requirement, it shall be considered as part of the 48 semester or 72 quarter unit requirement contained in Section 4980.40.

(d) Except for persons who began graduate study prior to January 1, 1986, a master's or doctor's degree qualifying for licensure shall include specific instruction in alcoholism and other chemical substance dependency as specified by regulation. When coursework in a master's or doctor's degree program is acquired to satisfy this requirement, it shall be considered as part of the 48 semester or 72 quarter unit requirement contained in Section 4980.40.

(e) Except for persons who began graduate study prior to January 1, 1995, a master's or doctor's degree qualifying for licensure shall include coursework in spousal or partner abuse assessment, detection, and intervention. Coursework required under this subdivision may be satisfactory if taken either in fulfillment of other educational requirements for licensure or in a separate course. The requirement for coursework in spousal or partner abuse detection and treatment shall be satisfied by, and the board shall accept in satisfaction of the requirement, a certification from the chief academic officer of the educational institution from which the applicant graduated that the required coursework is included within the institution's required curriculum for graduation.

(f) Except for persons who began graduate study prior to January 1, 2001, an applicant shall complete a minimum of a two semester or three quarter unit survey course in psychological testing. When coursework in a master's or doctor's degree program is acquired to satisfy this requirement, it may be considered as part of the 48 semester or 72 quarter unit requirement of Section 4980.40.

(g) Except for persons who began graduate study prior to January 1, 2001, an applicant shall complete a minimum of a two semester or three quarter unit survey course in psychopharmacology. When coursework in a master's or doctor's degree program is acquired to satisfy this requirement, it may be considered as part of the 48 semester or 72 quarter unit requirement of Section 4980.40.

(h) The requirements added by subdivisions (f) and (g) are intended to improve the educational qualifications for licensure in order to better prepare future licentiates for practice, and are not intended in any way to expand or restrict the scope of licensure for marriage and family therapists.

4980.42. (a) Trainees performing services in any work setting specified in subdivision (e) of Section 4980.43 may perform those activities and services as a trainee, provided that the activities and services constitute part of the trainee's supervised course of study and that the person is designated by the title "trainee." Trainees may gain hours of experience outside the required practicum. Those hours shall be subject to the requirements of subdivision (b) and to the other requirements of this chapter.

(b) On and after January 1, 1995, all hours of experience gained as a trainee shall be coordinated between the school and the site where the hours are being accrued. The school shall approve each site and shall have a written agreement with each site that details each party's responsibilities, including the methods by which supervision shall be provided. The agreement shall provide for regular progress reports and evaluations of the student's performance at the site. If an applicant has gained hours of experience while enrolled in an institution other than the one that confers the qualifying degree, it shall be the applicant's responsibility to provide to the board satisfactory evidence that those hours of trainee experience were gained in compliance with this section.

4980.43. (a) For all applicants, a minimum of two calendar years of supervised experience is required, which experience shall consist of 3,000 hours obtained over a period of not less than 104 weeks. Not less than 1,500 hours of experience shall be gained subsequent to the granting of the qualifying master's or doctor's degree. For those applicants who enroll in a qualifying degree program on or after January 1, 1995, not more than 750 hours of counseling and direct supervisor contact may be obtained prior to the granting of the qualifying master's or doctor's degree. However, this limitation shall not be interpreted to include professional enrichment activities. Except for personal psychotherapy hours gained after enrollment and commencement of classes in a qualifying degree program, no hours of experience may be gained prior to becoming a trainee. All experience shall be gained within the six years immediately preceding the date the application for licensure was filed, except that up to 500 hours of clinical experience gained in the supervised practicum required by subdivision (b) of Section 4980.40 shall be exempt from this six-year requirement.

(b) All experience shall be at all times under the supervision of a supervisor who shall be responsible for ensuring that the extent, kind, and quality of counseling performed is consistent with the training and experience of the person being supervised, and who shall be responsible to the board for compliance with all laws, rules, and regulations governing the practice of marriage, family, and child counseling. Experience shall be gained by interns and trainees either as an employee or as a volunteer in any allowable work setting specified in this chapter. The requirements of this chapter regarding gaining hours of experience and supervision are applicable equally to employees and volunteers. Experience shall not be gained by interns or trainees as an independent contractor.

(c) Supervision shall include at least one hour of direct supervisor contact for each week of experience claimed. A trainee shall receive an average of at least one hour of direct supervisor contact for every five hours of client contact in each setting in which experience is gained. An intern shall receive an average of at least one hour of direct supervisor contact for every 10 hours of client contact in each setting in which experience is gained. For purposes of this section, "one hour of direct supervisor contact" means one hour of face-to-face contact on an individual basis or two hours of face-to-face contact in a group of not more than eight persons. The contact may be counted toward the experience requirement for licensure, up to the maximum permitted by subdivision (d). All experience gained by a trainee shall be monitored by the supervisor as specified in regulation. The 5-to-1 and 10-to-1 ratios specified in this subdivision shall be applicable to all hours gained on or after January 1, 1995.

(d) (1) The experience required by Section 4980.40 shall include supervised marriage, family, and child counseling, and up to one-third of the hours may include direct supervisor contact and other professional enrichment activities.

(2) "Professional enrichment activities," for the purposes of this section, may include group, marital or conjoint, family, or individual psychotherapy received by an applicant. This psychotherapy may include up to 100 hours taken subsequent to enrolling and commencing classes in a qualifying degree program, or as an intern, and each of those hours shall be triple counted toward the professional experience requirement. This psychotherapy shall be performed by a licensed marriage, family, and child counselor, licensed clinical social worker, licensed psychologist, licensed physician certified in psychiatry by the American Board of Psychiatry and Neurology, or a licensed physician who has completed a residency in psychiatry.

(e) The experience required by Section 4980.40 may be gained as a trainee in the following settings: a governmental entity, a school, college or university, a nonprofit and charitable corporation, a licensed health facility, as defined in Sections 1250, 1250.2, and 1250.3 of the Health and Safety Code, a social rehabilitation facility or a community treatment facility, as defined in subdivision (a) of Section 1502 of the Health and Safety Code, a pediatric day health and respite care facility, as defined in Section 1760.2 of the Health and Safety Code, or a licensed alcoholism or drug abuse recovery or treatment facility, as defined in Section 11834.02 of the Health and Safety Code, if the experience is gained by the trainee solely as part of the position for which he or she is employed.

(f) The experience required by Section 4980.40 may be gained as an intern as specified in subdivision (e), or when employed in a private practice owned by a licensed marriage, family, and child counselor, a licensed psychologist, a licensed clinical social worker, a licensed physician and surgeon, or a professional corporation of any of those licensed professions. Employment in a private practice setting shall not commence until the applicant has been registered as an intern. When an intern is employed in a private practice setting by any licensee enumerated in this section, or by a professional corporation of any of those licensees, the intern shall be under the direct supervision of a licensee enumerated in subdivision (f) of Section 4980.40 who shall be employed by and practice at the same site as the intern's employer. An intern employed in a private practice setting shall not pay his or her employer for supervision. While an intern may be either a paid employee or a volunteer, employers are encouraged to provide fair remuneration.

(g) All interns shall register with the board in order to be credited for postdegree hours of experience gained toward licensure, regardless of the setting where those hours are to be gained. Except as provided in subdivision (h), all postdegree hours shall be gained as a registered intern.

(h) Except when employed in a private practice setting, all postdegree hours of experience shall be credited toward licensure so long as the applicant applies for the intern registration within 90 days of the granting of the qualifying master's or doctor's degree and is thereafter granted the intern registration by the board.

(i) Trainees and interns shall not receive any remuneration from patients or clients, and shall only be paid by their employer.

(j) Trainees and interns shall only perform services at the place where their employer regularly conducts business, which may include performing services at other locations, so long as the services are performed under the direction and control of their employer and supervisor, and in compliance with the laws and regulations pertaining to supervision. Trainees and interns shall have no proprietary interest in the employer's business.

(k) An intern or trainee who provides volunteered services or other services, and who receives no more than a total, from all work settings, of five hundred dollars ($500) per month as reimbursement for expenses actually incurred by that intern or trainee for services rendered in any lawful work setting other than a private practice shall be considered an employee and not an independent contractor. The board may audit applicants who receive reimbursement for expenses, and the applicant shall have the burden of demonstrating that the payments received were for reimbursement of expenses actually incurred.

(l) Each educational institution preparing applicants for licensure pursuant to this chapter shall consider requiring, and shall encourage, its students to undergo individual, marital or conjoint, family, or group counseling or psychotherapy, as appropriate. Each supervisor shall consider, advise, and encourage his or her interns and trainees regarding the advisability of undertaking individual, marital or conjoint, family, or group counseling or psychotherapy, as appropriate. Insofar as it is deemed appropriate and is desired by the applicant, the educational institution and supervisors are encouraged to assist the applicant in locating that counseling or psychotherapy at a reasonable cost.

4980.44. (a) An unlicensed marriage, family, and child counselor intern employed under this chapter shall:

(1) Have earned at least a master's degree as specified in Section 4980.40.

(2) Be registered with the board prior to the intern performing any duties, except as otherwise provided in subdivision (e) of Section 4980.43.

(3) File for renewal of registration annually for a maximum of five years after initial registration with the board.

(4) Inform each client or patient prior to performing any professional services that he or she is unlicensed and under the supervision of a licensed marriage, family, and child counselor, licensed clinical social worker, licensed psychologist, licensed physician certified in psychiatry by the American Board of Psychiatry and Neurology, or a licensed physician who has completed a residency in psychiatry and who is described in subdivision (f) of Section 4980.40, whichever is applicable. Continued employment as an unlicensed marriage, family, and child counselor intern shall cease after six years unless the requirements of subdivision (b) are met.

(b) When no further renewals or extensions are possible, either because the applicant has exhausted the number of renewals and extensions available or because of the repeal of Section 4980.44, as amended by Chapter 1114 of the Statutes of 1991, an applicant may apply for and obtain new intern registration status if the applicant meets the educational requirements for registration in effect at the time of the application for a new intern registration. An applicant who is issued a subsequent intern registration pursuant to this subdivision may fulfill the required hours of experience in all allowable work settings except in private practice, and shall fulfill all of the required hours of experience for licensure within that intern registration period. Hours of experience fulfilled under a prior intern registration shall not be used to satisfy licensure requirements.

(c) This section shall become operative on January 1, 1999.

4980.45. (a) A licensed professional in private practice who is a marriage, family, and child counselor, a psychologist, a clinical social worker, a licensed physician certified in psychiatry by the American Board of Psychiatry and Neurology, or a licensed physician who has completed a residency in psychiatry and who is described in subdivision (f) of Section 4980.40 may supervise or employ, at any one time, no more than two unlicensed marriage, family, and child counselor registered interns in that private practice.

(b) A marriage, family, and child counseling corporation may employ, at any one time, no more than two registered interns for each employee or shareholder who is qualified to provide supervision pursuant to subdivision (f) of Section 4980.40. In no event shall any corporation employ, at any one time, more than 10 registered interns. In no event shall any supervisor supervise, at any one time, more than two registered interns. Persons who supervise interns shall be employed full time by the professional corporation and shall be actively engaged in performing professional services at and for the professional corporation. Employment and supervision within a marriage, family, and child counseling corporation shall be subject to all laws and regulations governing experience and supervision gained in a private practice setting.

(c) Within 30 days of employment and within 30 days of termination of employment, in any allowable work setting, a registered intern shall notify the board in writing of the employment or termination of employment. The notice shall include the name of the registered intern, the full name and business address of the employer, the type of work setting where the intern is gaining hours of experience, and the date employment commenced or terminated. If an intern fails to notify the board within 30 days after the date of his or her employment or termination of employment, the board shall not accept any hours of experience gained during that period of employment prior to notification for the purposes of meeting the experience requirements for licensure. The board may, at its discretion, waive this requirement when it believes good cause exists. "Employment," as used in this section, means the gaining of hours of experience in an allowable setting as an employee or as a volunteer. This subdivision does not apply to hours gained on or after January 1, 1994.

4980.46. Any licensed marriage, family, and child counselor who conducts a private practice under a fictitious business name shall not use any name which is false, misleading, or deceptive, and shall inform the patient, prior to the commencement of treatment, of the name and license designation of the owner or owners of the practice.

4980.48. A trainee shall inform each client or patient, prior to performing any professional services, that he or she is unlicensed and under the supervision of a licensed marriage, family, and child counselor, a licensed clinical social worker, a licensed psychologist, or a licensed physician certified in psychiatry by the American Board of Psychiatry and Neurology.

4980.50. Every applicant who meets the educational and experience requirements and applies for a license as a marriage, family, and child counselor shall be examined by the board. The examinations shall be as set forth in subdivision (g) of Section 4980.40. The examinations shall be given at least twice a year at a time and place and under supervision as the board may determine. The board shall examine the candidate with regard to his or her knowledge and professional skills and his or her judgment in the utilization of appropriate techniques and methods.

The board shall not deny any applicant, who has submitted a complete application for examination, admission to the licensure examinations required by this section if the applicant meets the educational and experience requirements of this chapter, and has not committed any acts or engaged in any conduct which would constitute grounds to deny licensure.

The board shall not deny any applicant, whose application for licensure is complete, admission to the written examination, nor shall the board postpone or delay any applicant's written examination or delay informing the candidate of the results of any written examination, solely upon the receipt by the board of a complaint alleging acts or conduct which would constitute grounds to deny licensure.

When an applicant for examination who has passed the written examination is the subject of a complaint or is under board investigation for acts or conduct which, if proven to be true, would constitute grounds for the board to deny licensure, the board shall permit the applicant to take the oral examination for licensure, but may withhold the results of the examination or notify the applicant that licensure will not be granted pending completion of the investigation.

Notwithstanding Section 135, the board may deny any applicant who has previously failed either the written or oral examination permission to retake either examination pending completion of the investigation of any complaints against the applicant. Nothing in this section shall prohibit the board from denying an applicant admission to any examination, withholding the results, or refusing to issue a license to any applicant when an accusation or statement of issues has been filed against the applicant pursuant to Sections 11503 and 11504 of the Government Code, respectively, or the applicant has been denied in accordance with subdivision (b) of Section 485 of the Business and Professions Code.

The board shall retain all written examinations for at least one year following the date of the examinations. The board shall keep an accurate record of all oral examinations for at least one year following the date of the examinations.

An applicant who has qualified pursuant to this chapter shall be issued a license as a marriage, family, and child counselor in the form that the board may deem appropriate.

4980.54. (a) The Legislature recognizes that the education and experience requirements in this chapter constitute only minimal requirements to assure that an applicant is prepared and qualified to take the licensure examinations and, if he or she passes those examinations, to begin practice.

(b) In order to continuously improve the competence of licensed marriage, family, and child counselors and as a model for all psychotherapeutic professions, the Legislature encourages all licensees to regularly engage in continuing education related to the profession or scope of practice as defined in this chapter.

(c) (1) Except as provided in subdivision (e), on and after January 1, 2000, the board shall not renew any license pursuant to this chapter unless the applicant certifies to the board, on a form prescribed by the board, that he or she has completed not less than 36 hours of approved continuing education in or relevant to the field of marriage, family, and child counseling in the preceding two years, as determined by the board.

(2) For those persons renewing during 1999, the board shall not renew any license pursuant to this chapter unless the applicant certifies to the board, on a form prescribed by the board, that he or she

has completed not less than 18 hours of approved continuing education in or relevant to the field of marriage, family, and child counseling, as determined by the board. The coursework of continuing education described in this paragraph may be taken on or after the effective date of the continuing education regulations adopted by the board pursuant to the other provisions of this section.

(d) The board shall have the right to audit the records of any applicant to verify the completion of the continuing education requirement. Applicants shall maintain records of completion of required continuing education coursework for a minimum of two years and shall make these records available to the board for auditing purposes upon request.

(e) The board may establish exceptions from the continuing education requirements of this section for good cause as defined by the board.

(f) The continuing education shall be obtained from one of the following sources:

(1) An accredited school or state-approved school that meets the requirements set forth in Section 4980.40. Nothing in this paragraph shall be construed as requiring coursework to be offered as part of a regular degree program.

(2) Other continuing education providers, including, but not limited to, a professional marriage, family, and child counseling association, a licensed health facility, a governmental entity, a continuing education unit of an accredited four-year institution of higher learning, or a mental health professional association, approved by the board.

(3) The board shall establish, by regulation, a procedure for approving providers of continuing education courses, and all providers of continuing education, as described in paragraphs (1) and (2), shall adhere to procedures established by the board. The board may revoke or deny the right of a provider to offer continuing education coursework pursuant to this section for failure to comply with the requirements of this section or any regulation adopted pursuant to this section.

(g) Training, education, and coursework by approved providers shall incorporate one or more of the following:

(1) Aspects of the discipline that are fundamental to the understanding, or the practice, of marriage, family, and child counseling.

(2) Aspects of the discipline of marriage, family, and child counseling in which significant recent developments have occurred.

(3) Aspects of other disciplines that enhance the understanding, or the practice, of marriage, family, and child counseling.

(h) A system of continuing education for licensed marriage, family, and child counselors shall include courses directly related to the diagnosis, assessment, and treatment of the client population being served.

(i) The board shall submit a report to the Legislature no later than January 1, 2001, evaluating the progress of continuing education required by this section, and making recommendations therefor.

(j) On and after January 1, 1997, the board shall, by regulation, fund the administration of this section through continuing education provider fees to be deposited in the Behavioral Science Examiners Fund. The fees related to the administration of this section shall be sufficient to meet but shall not exceed the costs of administering the corresponding provisions of this section. For purposes of this subdivision, a provider of continuing education as described in paragraph (1) of subdivision (f) shall be deemed to be an approved provider.

(k) The continuing education requirements of this section shall comply fully with the guidelines for mandatory continuing education established by the Department of Consumer Affairs pursuant to Section 166.

4980.55. As a model for all therapeutic professions, and to acknowledge respect and regard for the consuming public, all marriage, family, and child counselors are encouraged to provide to each client, at an appropriate time and within the context of the psychotherapeutic relationship, an accurate and informative statement of the therapist's experience, education, specialties, professional orientation, and any other information deemed appropriate by the licensee.

4980.57. (a) The board shall encourage marriage, family, and child counselors to take continuing education classes in spousal or partner abuse assessment, detection, and intervention.
(b) In the event the board establishes a requirement for continuing education coursework in spousal or partner abuse detection or treatment, that requirement shall be met by each licensee within no more than four years from the date the requirement is imposed.
(c) This section shall only become operative if Senate Bill 404, adding Sections 4980.56 and 4996.22, is enacted and takes effect on or before January 1, 1995.

4980.60. The board may adopt those rules and regulations as may be necessary to enable it to carry into effect the provisions of this chapter. The adoption, amendment, or repeal of those rules and regulations shall be made in accordance with Chapter 3.5 (commencing with Section 11340) of Part 1 of Division 3 of Title 2 of the Government Code.
The board may, by rules or regulations, adopt, amend, or repeal rules of advertising and professional conduct appropriate to the establishment and maintenance of a high standard of integrity in the profession, provided such rules or regulations are not inconsistent with Section 4982. Every person who holds a license to practice marriage, family, and child counseling shall be governed by such rules of professional conduct.

4980.70. Except as provided by Section 159.5, the board may employ whatever additional personnel is necessary to carry out the provisions of this chapter.

4980.80. The board may issue a license to any person who, at the time of application, has held for at least two years a valid license issued by a board of marriage counselor examiners, marriage therapist examiners, or corresponding authority of any state, if the education and supervised experience requirements are substantially the equivalent of this chapter and the person successfully completes the written and oral licensing examinations administered in this state and pays the fees specified. Issuance of the license is further conditioned upon the person's completion of the following coursework or training:
(a) A two semester or three quarter unit course in California law and professional ethics for marriage, family, and child counselors which shall include areas of study as specified in Section 4980.41.
(b) A minimum of seven contact hours of training or coursework in child abuse assessment and reporting as specified in Section 28, and any regulations promulgated thereunder.
(c) A minimum of 10 contact hours of training or coursework in human sexuality, as specified in Section 25, and any regulations promulgated thereunder.
(d) A minimum of 15 contact hours of training or coursework in alcoholism and other chemical substance dependency as specified by regulation.
(e) Instruction in spousal or partner abuse assessment, detection, and intervention. This instruction may be taken either in fulfillment of other requirements for licensure or in a separate course.
(f) With respect to human sexuality and alcoholism and other chemical substance dependency, the board may accept training or coursework acquired out of state.

4980.90. (a) Experience gained outside of California shall be accepted toward the licensure requirements if it is substantially equivalent to that required by this chapter provided that the applicant has gained a minimum of 250 hours of supervised experience in direct counseling within California while registered as an intern with the board.

(b) Education gained outside of California shall be accepted toward the licensure requirements if it is substantially equivalent to the education requirements of this chapter, provided that the applicant has completed all of the following:

(1) A two semester or three quarter unit course in California law and professional ethics for marriage, family, and child counselors which shall include areas of study as specified in Section 4980.41.

(2) A minimum of seven contact hours of training or coursework in child abuse assessment and reporting as specified in Section 28, and any regulations promulgated thereunder.

(3) A minimum of 10 contact hours of training or coursework in sexuality as specified in Section 25, and any regulations promulgated thereunder.

(4) A minimum of 15 contact hours of training or coursework in alcoholism and other chemical substance dependency as specified by regulation.

(5) Instruction in spousal or partner abuse assessment, detection, and intervention. This instruction may be taken either in fulfillment of other educational requirements for licensure or in a separate course.

(6) With respect to human sexuality and alcoholism and other chemical substance dependency, the board may accept training or coursework acquired out of state.

(c) For purposes of this section, the board may, in its discretion, accept education as substantially equivalent if the applicant has been granted a degree in a single integrated program primarily designed to train marriage, family, and child counselors and if the applicant's education meets the requirements of Sections 4980.37 and 4980.40 provided, however, that the degree title and number of units in the degree program need not be identical to those required by subdivision (a) of Section 4980.40. Where the applicant's degree does not contain the number of units required by subdivision (a) of Section 4980.40, the board may, in its discretion, accept the applicant's education as substantially equivalent if the applicant's degree otherwise complies with this section and the applicant completes the units required by subdivision (a) of Section 4980.40.

4981. This article applies to licenses to engage in the business of marriage, family, and child counseling, and does not apply to the licenses provided for in Article 5 (commencing with Section 4986) except that the board shall have all powers provided in this article not inconsistent with this chapter.

4982. The board may refuse to issue any registration or license, or may suspend or revoke the license or registration of any registrant or licensee if the applicant, licensee, or registrant has been guilty of unprofessional conduct. Unprofessional conduct shall include, but not be limited to:

(a) The conviction of a crime substantially related to the qualifications, functions, or duties of a licensee or registrant under this chapter. The record of conviction shall be conclusive evidence only of the fact that the conviction occurred. The board may inquire into the circumstances surrounding the commission of the crime in order to fix the degree of discipline or to determine if the conviction is substantially related to the qualifications, functions, or duties of a licensee or registrant under this chapter. A plea or verdict of guilty or a conviction following a plea of nolo contendere made to a charge substantially related to the qualifications, functions, or duties of a licensee or registrant under this chapter shall be deemed to be a conviction within the meaning of this section. The board may order any license or registration suspended or revoked, or may decline to issue a license or registration when the time for appeal has elapsed, or the judgment of conviction has been affirmed on appeal, or, when an order granting probation is made suspending the imposition of sentence, irrespective of a subsequent order under Section 1203.4 of the Penal Code allowing any such person to withdraw a plea of guilty and enter a plea of not guilty, or setting aside the verdict of guilty, or dismissing the accusation, information, or indictment.

(b) Securing a license or registration by fraud, deceit, or misrepresentation on any application for licensure or registration submitted to the board, whether engaged in by an applicant for a license or registration, or by a licensee in support of any application for licensure or registration.

(c) Administering to himself or herself any controlled substance or using of any of the dangerous drugs specified in Section 4211, or of any alcoholic beverage to the extent, or in a manner, as to be dangerous or injurious to the person applying for a registration or license or holding a registration or license under this chapter, or to any other person, or to the public, or, to the extent that the use impairs the ability of the person applying for or holding a registration or license to conduct with safety to the public the practice authorized by the registration or license, or the conviction of more than one misdemeanor or any felony involving the use, consumption, or self-administration of any of the substances referred to in this subdivision, or any combination thereof. The board shall deny an application for a registration or license or revoke the license or registration of any person, other than one who is licensed as a physician and surgeon, who uses or offers to use drugs in the course of performing marriage, family, and child counseling services.

(d) Gross negligence or incompetence in the performance of marriage, family, and child counseling.

(e) Violating, attempting to violate, or conspiring to violate any of the provisions of this chapter or any regulation adopted by the board.

(f) Misrepresentation as to the type or status of a license or registration held by the person, or otherwise misrepresenting or permitting misrepresentation of his or her education, professional qualifications, or professional affiliations to any person or entity.

(g) Impersonation of another by any licensee, registrant, or applicant for a license or registration, or, in the case of a licensee, allowing any other person to use his or her license or registration.

(h) Aiding or abetting, or employing, directly or indirectly, any unlicensed or unregistered person to engage in conduct for which a license or registration is required under this chapter.

(i) Intentionally or recklessly causing physical or emotional harm to any client.

(j) The commission of any dishonest, corrupt, or fraudulent act substantially related to the qualifications, functions, or duties of a licensee or registrant.

(k) Engaging in sexual relations with a client, or a former client within two years following termination of therapy, soliciting sexual relations with a client, or committing an act of sexual abuse, or sexual misconduct with a client, or committing an act punishable as a sexually related crime, if that act or solicitation is substantially related to the qualifications, functions, or duties of a marriage, family, and child counselor.

(l) Performing, or holding one's self out as being able to perform, or offering to perform, or permitting any registered trainee or registered intern under supervision to perform, any professional services beyond the scope of the license authorized by this chapter.

(m) Failure to maintain confidentiality, except as otherwise required or permitted by law, of all information that has been received from a client in confidence during the course of treatment and all information about the client which is obtained from tests or other means.

(n) Prior to the commencement of treatment, failing to disclose to the client or prospective client the fee to be charged for the professional services, or the basis upon which that fee will be computed.

(o) Paying, accepting, or soliciting any consideration, compensation, or remuneration, whether monetary or otherwise, for the referral of professional clients. All consideration, compensation, or remuneration shall be in relation to professional counseling services actually provided by the licensee. Nothing in this subdivision shall prevent collaboration among two or more licensees in a case or cases. However, no fee shall be charged for that collaboration, except when disclosure of the fee has been made in compliance with subdivision (n).

(p) Advertising in a manner which is false, misleading, or deceptive.

(q) Reproduction or description in public, or in any publication subject to general public distribution, of any psychological test or other assessment device, the value of which depends in whole or in part on the naiveté of the subject, in ways that might invalidate the test or device.

(r) Any conduct in the supervision of any registered intern or registered trainee by any licensee that violates this chapter or any rules or regulations adopted by the board.

(s) Performing or holding one's self out as being able to perform, professional services beyond the scope of one's competence, as established by one's education, training, or experience. This subdivision shall not be construed to expand the scope of the license authorized by this chapter.

(t) Permitting a registered trainee or registered intern under one' s supervision or control to perform, or permitting the registered trainee or registered intern to hold one's self out as competent to perform, professional services beyond the registered trainee's or registered intern's level of education, training, or experience.

(u) The violation of any statute or regulation governing the gaining and supervision of experience required by this chapter.

(v) Failure to keep records consistent with sound clinical judgment, the standards of the profession, and the nature of the services being rendered.

4982.05. (a) Except as provided in subdivisions (b) and (c), any accusation filed against a licensee pursuant to Section 11503 of the Government Code shall be filed within three years from the date the board discovers the alleged act or omission that is the basis for disciplinary action, or within seven years from the date the alleged act or omission that is the basis for disciplinary action occurred, whichever occurs first.

(b) An accusation filed against a licensee pursuant to Section 11503 of the Government Code alleging the procurement of a license by fraud or misrepresentation is not subject to the limitations set forth in subdivision (a).

(c) The limitation provided for by subdivision (a) shall be tolled for the length of time required to obtain compliance when a report required to be filed by the licensee or registrant with the board pursuant to Article 11 (commencing with Section 800) of Chapter 1 is not filed in a timely fashion.

(d) If an alleged act or omission involves a minor, the seven-year limitations period provided for by subdivision (a) shall be tolled until the minor reaches the age of majority.

4982.1. The board may refuse to issue any registration or license whenever it appears that an applicant may be unable to practice his or her profession safely due to mental illness or chemical dependency. The procedures set forth in Article 12.5 (commencing with Section 820) of Chapter 1 shall apply to any denial of a license or registration pursuant to this section.

4982.15. (a) The board may place a license or registration on probation under the following circumstances:
(1) In lieu of, or in addition to, any order of the board suspending or revoking the license or registration of any licensee or intern.
(2) Upon the issuance of a license to an individual who has been guilty of unprofessional conduct, but who had otherwise completed all education and training and experience required for licensure.
(3) As a condition upon the reissuance or reinstatement of any license that has been suspended or revoked by the board.
(b) The board may adopt regulations establishing a monitoring program to ensure compliance with any terms or conditions of probation imposed by the board pursuant to subdivision (a). The cost of probation or monitoring may be ordered to be paid by the licensee, registrant, or applicant.
(c) The board, in its discretion, may require any licensee or registrant who has been placed on probation, or whose license or registration has been suspended, to obtain additional professional training, and to pass an examination upon completion of that training, and to pay any necessary examination fee. The examination may be written, oral, or a practical or clinical examination.

4982.2. (a) A licensed marriage, family, and child counselor, licensed clinical social worker, or educational psychologist whose license has been revoked or suspended or who has been placed on probation may petition the board for reinstatement or modification of penalty, including modification or termination of probation, after a period not less than the following minimum periods has elapsed from the effective date of the decision ordering the disciplinary action, or if the order of the board, or any portion of it, is stayed by the board itself, or by the superior court, from the date the disciplinary action is actually implemented in its entirety:
(1) At least three years for reinstatement of a license which was revoked for unprofessional conduct, except that the board may, in its sole discretion at the time of adoption, specify in its order that a petition for reinstatement may be filed after two years.
(2) At least two years for early termination of any probation period of three years, or more.
(3) At least one year for modification of a condition, or reinstatement of a license revoked for mental or physical illness, or termination of probation of less than three years.
(b) The petition may be heard by the board itself, or the board may assign the petition to an administrative law judge pursuant to Section 11512 of the Government Code. The board shall give notice to the Attorney General of the filing of the petition. The petitioner and the Attorney General shall be given timely notice by letter of the time and place of the hearing on the petition, and an opportunity to present both oral and documentary evidence and argument to the board. The petitioner shall at all times have the burden of production and proof to establish by clear and convincing evidence that he or she is entitled to the relief sought in the petition. The board, when it is hearing the petition itself, or an administrative law judge sitting for the board, may consider all activities of the petitioner since the disciplinary action was taken, the offense for which the petitioner was disciplined, the petitioner's activities during the time his or her license was in good standing, and the petitioner's rehabilitative efforts, general reputation for truth, and professional ability.
(c) The hearing may be continued from time to time as the board or the administrative law judge deems appropriate.
(d) The board itself, or the administrative law judge if one is designated by the board, shall hear the petition and shall prepare a written decision setting forth the reasons supporting the decision. In a decision granting a petition reinstating a license or modifying a penalty, the board itself, or the administrative law judge may impose any terms and conditions that the agency deems reasonably

appropriate, including those set forth in Sections 823 and 4982.15.
Where a petition is heard by an administrative law judge sitting alone, the administrative law judge shall prepare a proposed decision and submit it to the board.

(e) The board may take such action with respect to the proposed decision and petition as it deems appropriate.

(f) The petition shall be on a form provided by the board, and shall state any facts and information as may be required by the board including, but not limited to, proof of compliance with the terms and conditions of the underlying disciplinary order.

(g) The petitioner shall pay a fingerprinting fee and provide a current set of his or her fingerprints to the board. The petitioner shall execute a form authorizing release to the board or its designee, of all information concerning the petitioner's current physical and mental condition. Information provided to the board pursuant to such a release shall be confidential and shall not be subject to discovery or subpoena in any other proceeding, and shall not be admissible in any action, other than before the board, to determine the petitioner's fitness to practice as required by Section 822.

(h) The petition shall be verified by the petitioner, who shall file an original and sufficient copies of the petition, together with any supporting documents, for the members of the board, the administrative law judge, and the Attorney General.

(i) The board may delegate to its executive officer authority to order investigation of the contents of the petition, but in no case, may the hearing on the petition be delayed more than 180 days from its filing without the consent of the petitioner.

(j) The petitioner may request that the board schedule the hearing on the petition for a board meeting at a specific city where the board regularly meets.

(k) No petition shall be considered while the petitioner is under sentence for any criminal offense, including any period during which the petitioner is on court-imposed probation or parole, or subject to an order of registration as a mentally disordered sex offender pursuant to Section 290 of the Penal Code. No petition shall be considered while there is an accusation or petition to revoke probation pending against the petitioner.

(l) Except in those cases where the petitioner has been disciplined for violation of Section 822, the board may in its discretion deny without hearing or argument any petition that is filed pursuant to this section within a period of two years from the effective date of a prior decision following a hearing under this section.

4982.25. The board may deny any application, or may suspend or revoke any license or registration issued under this chapter, for any of the following:

(a) Denial of licensure, revocation, suspension, restriction, or any other disciplinary action imposed by another state or territory or possession of the United States, or by any other governmental agency, on a license, certificate, or registration to practice marriage, family, and child counseling, or any other healing art, shall constitute unprofessional conduct. A certified copy of the disciplinary action decision or judgment shall be conclusive evidence of that action.

(b) Revocation, suspension, or restriction by the board of a license, certificate, or registration to practice as a clinical social worker or educational psychologist shall also constitute grounds for disciplinary action for unprofessional conduct against the licensee or registrant under this chapter.

4982.26. Notwithstanding Section 4982, any proposed decision or decision issued under this chapter in accordance with the procedures set forth in Chapter 5 (commencing with Section 11500) of Part 1 of Division 3 of Title 2 of the Government Code, that contains any finding of fact that the licensee or registrant engaged in any act of sexual contact, as defined in Section 729, when that act is with a patient, or with a former patient when the relationship was terminated primarily for the purpose of engaging in that act, shall contain an order of revocation. The revocation shall not be stayed by the administrative law judge.

4982.3. The proceedings conducted under this article shall be held in accordance with Chapter 5 (commencing with Section 11500) of Part 1 of Division 3 of Title 2 of the Government Code.

4983. Any person who violates any of the provisions of this chapter is guilty of a misdemeanor punishable by imprisonment in the county jail not exceeding six months, or by a fine not exceeding two thousand five hundred dollars ($2,500), or by both.

4983.1. In addition to other proceedings provided for in this chapter, whenever any person has engaged, or is about to engage, in any acts or practices which constitute, or will constitute, an offense against this chapter, the superior court in and for the county wherein the acts or practices take place, or are about to take place, may issue an injunction, or other appropriate order, restraining such conduct on application of the board, the Attorney General, or the district attorney of the county.

The proceedings under this section shall be governed by Chapter 3 (commencing with Section 525) of Title 7 of Part 2 of the Code of Civil Procedure.

4984. Licenses issued under this chapter shall expire no more than 24 months after the issue date. The expiration date of the original license shall be set by the board in a manner as to best distribute the renewal work throughout each year.

To renew an unexpired license, the holder thereof, on or before the expiration date of the license, shall apply for a renewal on a form prescribed by the board, and pay a two-year renewal fee prescribed by the board.

4984.1. A license that has expired may be renewed at any time within five years after its expiration on filing an application for renewal on a form prescribed by the board and payment of the renewal fee in effect on the last regular renewal date. If the license is renewed after its expiration, the licensee, as a condition precedent to renewal, shall also pay the delinquency fee prescribed by this chapter.

4984.2. A suspended license is subject to expiration and shall be renewed as provided in this article, but such renewal does not entitle the licensee, while it remains suspended and until it is reinstated, to engage in the activity to which the license relates, or in any other activity or conduct in violation of the order or judgment by which it was suspended.

4984.3. A revoked license is subject to expiration as provided in this article, but it may not be renewed. If it is reinstated after its expiration, the licensee shall, as a condition precedent to its reinstatement, pay a reinstatement fee in an amount equal to the renewal fee in effect on the last regular renewal date before the date on which it is reinstated, plus the delinquency fee, if any, accrued at the time of its revocation.

4984.4. A license that is not renewed within five years after its expiration may not be renewed, restored, reinstated, or reissued thereafter, but the licensee may apply for and obtain a new license if:

(a) No fact, circumstance, or condition exists that, if the license were issued, would justify its revocation or suspension.

(b) He or she pays the fees that would be required if he or she were applying for a license for the first time.

(c) He or she takes and passes the current licensing examinations.

4984.5. The board shall report each month to the Controller the amount and source of all revenue received pursuant to this chapter and at the same time pay the entire amount thereof into the State Treasury for credit to the Behavioral Sciences Fund.

4984.6. (a) The Behavioral Sciences Fund is continuously appropriated, without regard to fiscal years, to the Board of Behavioral Sciences for carrying out and enforcing the provisions of this chapter.

(b) The board shall keep any records as will reasonably ensure that funds expended in the administration of each licensing or registration category shall bear a reasonable relation to the revenue derived from each category, and shall so notify the department no later than May 31 of each year.

(c) Surpluses, if any, may be used in such a way so as to bear a reasonable relation to the revenue derived from each category, and may include, but not be limited to, expenditures for education and research related to each of the licensing or registration categories.

4984.7. The amount of the fees prescribed by this chapter that relate to licensing of persons to engage in the business of marriage, family and child counseling is that established by the following schedule:

(a) The fee for applications for examination received on or after January 1, 1987, shall be one hundred dollars ($100).

(b) The fee for issuance of the initial license shall be a maximum of one hundred eighty dollars ($180).

(c) For those persons whose license expires on or after January 1, 1996, the renewal fee shall be a maximum of one hundred eighty dollars ($180).

(d) The delinquency fee shall be ninety dollars ($90). Any person who permits his or her license to become delinquent may have it restored only upon the payment of all fees that he or she would have paid if the license had not become delinquent, plus the payment of any and all outstanding delinquency fees.

(e) For those persons registering as interns on or after January 1, 1996, the registration fee shall be ninety dollars ($90).

(f) For those persons whose registration as an intern expires on or after January 1, 1996, the renewal fee shall be seventy-five dollars ($75).

(g) The written examination fee shall be one hundred dollars ($100). After successfully passing the written examination, each applicant for oral examination shall submit two hundred dollars ($200). Applicants failing to appear for any examination, once having been scheduled, shall forfeit any examination fees paid.

(h) An applicant who fails any written or oral examination may within one year from the notification date of that failure, retake the examination as regularly scheduled without further application upon payment of one hundred dollars ($100) for the written reexamination and two hundred dollars ($200) for the oral reexamination. Thereafter, the applicant shall not be eligible for further examination until he or she files a new application, meets all current requirements, and pays all fees required. Persons failing to appear for the reexamination, once having been scheduled, shall forfeit any reexamination fees paid.

(i) The fee for rescoring a written examination shall be twenty dollars ($20). The fee for appeal of an oral examination shall be one hundred dollars ($100).

(j) The fee for issuance of any replacement registration, license, or certificate shall be twenty dollars ($20).

(k) The fee for issuance of a certificate or letter of good standing shall be twenty-five dollars ($25).

With regard to all license, examination, and other fees, the board shall establish fee amounts at or below the maximum amounts specified in this chapter.

4984.8. A licensed marriage, family and child counselor may apply to the board to request that his or her license be placed on inactive status. Licensees who hold an inactive license shall pay a biennial fee of half of the active renewal fee. Licensees holding an inactive license shall be exempt from continuing education requirements specified in Section 4980.54, but shall otherwise be subject to this chapter and shall not engage in the practice of marriage, family and child counseling in this state. Licensees on inactive status who have not committed any acts or crimes constituting grounds for denial of licensure and have completed any required continuing education equivalent to that required for a single renewal period may, upon their request, have their license to practice marriage, family and child counseling placed on active status. Licensees requesting their license be placed on active status at any time between a renewal cycle shall pay the remaining half of their renewal fee.

4984.9. A licensee or registrant shall give written notice to the board of a name change within 30 days after each change, giving both the old and new names. A copy of the legal document authorizing the name change, such as a court order or marriage certificate, shall be submitted with the notice.

4986. Persons licensed under this article by the board may practice pursuant to this article.

4986.10. A licensed educational psychologist shall be authorized to perform any of the following professional functions pertaining to academic learning processes or the educational system or both:

(a) Educational evaluation, diagnosis, and test interpretation limited to assessment of academic ability, learning patterns, achievement, motivation, and personality factors directly related to academic learning problems.

(b) Counseling services for children or adults for amelioration of academic learning problems.

(c) Educational consultation, research, and direct educational services.

4986.20. A person who desires a license under this article shall meet all of the following qualifications:

(a) He or she shall possess at least a master's degree in psychology, educational psychology, school psychology, or counseling and guidance, or a degree deemed equivalent by the board under regulations duly adopted under this article. Such degree or training shall be obtained from educational institutions approved by the board according to the regulations duly adopted under this article.

(b) He or she shall be at least 18 years of age.

(c) He or she shall not have committed acts or crimes constituting grounds for denial of licensure under Section 480. The board shall not issue a registration or license to any person who has been convicted of any crime in the United States that involves sexual abuse of children or who has been ordered to register as a mentally disordered sex offender or the equivalent in another state or territory.

(d) He or she shall have successfully completed 60 semester hours of postgraduate work devoted to pupil personnel services or have experience deemed equivalent by the board in regulations duly adopted under this chapter.

(e) He or she shall furnish proof of three years of full-time experience as a credentialed school psychologist in the public schools or experience which the board deems equivalent. If the applicant provides proof of having completed one year's internship working full time as a school psychologist intern in the public schools in an accredited internship program, one year's experience shall be credited toward this requirement.

(f) He or she shall furnish written statements from two sponsors having personal knowledge of his or her professional competence. These statements shall include a description of the applicant's functioning and evaluation of his or her professional competencies. The sponsor of this applicant shall be qualified to be a licensed educational psychologist under this article.

(g) He or she shall be examined by the board with respect to the professional functions authorized by this article.

(h) He or she shall have at least one year of supervised professional experience in an accredited school psychology program, or under the direction of a licensed psychologist, or such suitable alternative experience as determined by the board in regulations duly adopted under this chapter.

4986.30. The board may, in its discretion, provide for a continuing education program in connection with the professional functions and courses described in this article.

4986.40. The board shall issue an educational psychologist license to all applicants who meet the requirements of this article and who pay the board the fees required by this chapter.

4986.41. A licensee shall display his or her license in a conspicuous place in the licensee's primary place of practice.

4986.50. It is unlawful for any person to use any title or letters which imply that he or she is a licensed educational psychologist unless at the time of so doing he or she holds a valid, unexpired and unrevoked license issued under this article.

4986.60. The provisions of Sections 4984 to 4984.40, inclusive, shall apply to this article.

4986.70. The board may refuse to issue a license, or may suspend or revoke the license of any licensee if he or she has been guilty of unprofessional conduct which has endangered or is likely to endanger the health, welfare, or safety of the public. Unprofessional conduct includes, but is not limited to, the following:

(a) Conviction of a crime substantially related to the qualifications, functions and duties of an educational psychologist, the record of conviction being conclusive evidence thereof.

(b) Securing a license by fraud or deceit.

(c) Using any narcotic as defined in Division 10 (commencing with Section 11000) of the Health and Safety Code or any hypnotic drug or alcoholic beverage to an extent or in a manner dangerous to himself or herself, or to any other person, or to the public and to an extent that such action impairs his or her ability to perform his or her work as a licensed educational psychologist with safety to the public.

(d) Improper advertising.

(e) Violating or conspiring to violate the terms of this article.

(f) Committing a dishonest or fraudulent act as a licensed educational psychologist resulting in substantial injury to another.

(g) Denial of licensure, revocation, suspension, restriction, or any other disciplinary action imposed by another state or territory or possession of the United States, or by any other governmental agency, on a license, certificate, or registration to practice educational psychology or any other healing art, shall constitute unprofessional conduct. A certified copy of the disciplinary action, decision, or judgment shall be conclusive evidence of that action.

(h) Revocation, suspension, or restriction by the board of a license, certificate, or registration to practice as a clinical social worker or marriage, family and child counselor shall constitute grounds for disciplinary action for unprofessional conduct against the licensee or registrant under this chapter.

(i) Failure to keep records consistent with sound clinical judgment, the standards of the profession, and the nature of the services being rendered.

4986.71. The board shall revoke any license issued under this chapter upon a decision made in accordance with the procedures set forth in Chapter 5 (commencing with Section 11500) of Part 1 of Division 3 of Title 2 of the Government Code, that contains any finding of fact that the licensee engaged in any act of sexual contact, as defined in Section 729, when that act is with a patient, or with a former patient when the relationship was terminated primarily for the purpose of engaging in that act, shall contain an order of revocation. The revocation shall not be stayed by the administrative law judge.

4986.75. The board may refuse to issue any license whenever it appears that an applicant may be unable to practice his or her profession safely due to mental illness or chemical dependency. The procedures set forth in Article 12.5 (commencing with Section 820) of Chapter 1 shall apply to any denial of a license pursuant to this section.

4986.80. The amount of the fees prescribed by this chapter that relate to the licensing of educational psychologists is that established by the following schedule:

(a) Persons applying for an original license after July 1, 1986, shall pay an application fee of one hundred dollars ($100).

(b) The fee for issuance of the initial license shall be a maximum of one hundred fifty dollars ($150).

(c) Persons whose license expires after January 1, 1991, shall pay a renewal fee of a maximum of one hundred fifty dollars ($150).

(d) The delinquency fee shall be seventy-five dollars ($75). Any person who permits his or her license to become delinquent may have it restored only upon the payment of all fees that he or she would have paid if the license had not become delinquent, plus the payment of any and all delinquency fees.

(e) The written examination fee shall be one hundred dollars ($100). After successfully passing the written examination, each applicant for oral examination shall submit two hundred dollars ($200). Applicants failing to appear for any examination, once having been scheduled, shall forfeit any examination fees paid.

(f) The fee for each reexamination shall be the fee for each examination specified in subdivision (e). An applicant who has failed the written or oral examination may within one year from the notification date of failure, retake that examination as regularly scheduled without further application. Thereafter, the applicant shall not be eligible for further examination until he or she files a new application, meets all current requirements, and pays all fees required. Persons failing to appear for reexamination, once having been scheduled, shall forfeit any reexamination fees paid.

(g) The fee for rescoring a written examination shall be twenty dollars ($20). The fee for appeal of an oral examination shall be one hundred dollars ($100).

(h) The fee for issuance of any replacement registration, license, or certificate shall be twenty dollars ($20).

(i) The fee for issuance of a certificate or letter of good standing shall be twenty-five dollars ($25).

With regard to all license, examination, and other fees, the board shall establish fee amounts at or below the maximum amounts specified in this chapter.

4986.81. Any person who violates any of the provisions of this article is guilty of a misdemeanor.

4986.82. A licensed educational psychologist may apply to the board to request that his or her license be placed on inactive status. Licensees who hold an inactive license shall pay a biennial fee of half of the active renewal fee. Licensees shall be subject to this chapter and shall not engage in the practice of educational psychology in this state. Licensees on inactive status who have not committed any acts or crimes constituting grounds for denial of licensure may, upon their request, have their license to practice educational psychology placed on active status. Licensees requesting their license be placed on active status between renewal cycles shall pay the remaining half of their renewal fee.

4986.90. In addition to other proceedings provided for in this article, whenever any person has engaged, or is about to engage in any acts or practices which constitute, or will constitute, an offense against this article, the superior court in and for the county wherein the acts or practices take place, or are about to take place, may issue an injunction, or other appropriate order, restraining that conduct on application of the board, the Attorney General, or the district attorney of the county.

The proceedings under this section shall be governed by Chapter 3 (commencing with Section 525) of Title 7 of Part 2 of the Code of Civil Procedure.

4987. The board may, by rules or regulations, adopt, amend or repeal rules of professional conduct appropriate to the establishment and maintenance of a high standard of integrity and dignity in the profession, provided those rules or regulations are not inconsistent with Section 4986.70. Every person licensed under this article shall be governed by those rules of professional conduct.

4987.5. A marriage, family, and child counseling corporation is a corporation that is authorized to render professional services, as defined in Section 13401 of the Corporations Code, so long as that corporation and its shareholders, officers, directors, and employees rendering professional services who are marriage, family, and child counselors, physicians and surgeons, psychologists, licensed clinical social workers, registered nurses, chiropractors, or acupuncturists are in compliance with the Moscone-Knox Professional Corporation Act
(Part 4 (commencing with Section 13400) of Division 3 of Title 1 of the Corporations Code), this article, and any other statute or regulation pertaining to that corporation and the conduct of its affairs. With respect to a marriage, family, and child counseling corporation, the governmental agency referred to in the Moscone-Knox Professional Corporation Act is the Board of Behavioral Sciences.
4987.6. It shall constitute unprofessional conduct and a violation of this chapter for any person licensed under this chapter to violate, attempt to violate, directly or indirectly, or assist in or abet the violation of, or conspire to violate, any provision or term of this article, the Moscone-Knox Professional Corporation Act (Part 4 (commencing with Section 13400) of Division 3 of Title 1 of the Corporations Code), or any regulations duly adopted under those laws.

4987.7. The name of a marriage, family, and child counseling corporation shall contain one or more of the words "marriage," "family," and "child" together with one or more of the words "counseling," "counselor," or "therapist," and wording or abbreviations denoting corporate existence. A marriage, family, and child counseling corporation that conducts business under a fictitious business name shall not use any name which is false, misleading or deceptive, and shall inform the patient, prior to the commencement of treatment, that the business is conducted by a marriage, family, and child counseling corporation.

4987.8. Except as provided in Section 13403 of the Corporations Code, each director, shareholder, and officer of a marriage, family, and child counseling corporation shall be a licensed person as defined in the Moscone-Knox Professional Corporation Act.

4988. The income of a marriage, family, and child counseling corporation attributable to professional services rendered while a shareholder is a disqualified person (as defined in the Moscone-Knox Professional Corporation Act) shall not in any manner accrue to the benefit of such shareholder or his or her shares in the marriage, family, and child counseling corporation.

4988.1. A marriage, family, and child counseling corporation shall not do or fail to do any act the doing of which or the failure to do which would constitute unprofessional conduct under any statute, rule or regulation now or hereafter in effect. In the conduct of its practice, it shall observe and be bound by such statutes, rules and regulations to the same extent as a person holding a license as a marriage, family, and child counselor.

4988.2. The board may formulate and enforce rules and regulations to carry out the purposes and objectives of this article, including rules and regulations requiring (a) that the articles of incorporation or bylaws of a marriage, family, and child counseling corporation shall include a provision whereby the capital stock of such corporation owned by a disqualified person (as defined in the Moscone-Knox Professional Corporation Act), or a deceased person, shall be sold to the corporation or to the remaining shareholders of such corporation within such time as such rules and regulations may provide, and (b) that a marriage, family, and child counseling corporation shall provide adequate security by insurance or otherwise for claims against it by its patients arising out of the rendering of professional services.

4989. The powers and duties of the board, as set forth in this chapter, shall be subject to the review required by Division 1.2 (commencing with Section 473). The review shall be performed as if this chapter were scheduled to become inoperative on July 1, 2005, and would be repealed as of January 1, 2006, as described in Section 473.1.

Clinical Example # 1

> Mary Anne has practiced for many years and in the last year and has faced many personal problems ranging from illness to death in the family. She tells herself that she must keep working to keep busy. Her colleagues note that she has difficulty staying focused and at times slurs her words. After a particularly difficult day at work, she stopped at a friend's house and had several glasses of wine. On her way home, she was stopped by a policeman for running a stop sign and after receiving a sobriety test, was arrested for driving under the influence.

Questions for Clinical Example # 1

1. Mary Anne appears to have violated a Business and Profession Code law. Which one?
2. Based on what you have read in this chapter, what do you think will happen to her license?
3. What is Mary Anne's legal obligation regarding her professional conduct?
4. If she had been visiting you before being arrested, what would be your legal obligation as a fellow therapist? What would be your moral obligation to her as a fellow therapist? What would be your

options if she refused your help?
5. As you check your internal reality, would you be willing to call the police to stop her and possibly expose her to lose her license?

Clinical Example # 2

> James is a seasoned therapist who considers himself to be from "the old school." He has not attended legal and ethical seminars because he believes they are "a bunch of bull." He is your friend and asks you to see his patients for a period of time to recuperate from an illness. You agree because you could benefit from the extra money and soon find out that he doesn't keep any sort of mental health records on any of his patients.

Questions for Clinical Example # 2

1. You've begun to see his clients at his office. How do you manage this situation?
2. As you refer to Business and Professions Code 4982 (v), which of the two therapists, you or him, must comply with this legal therapeutic duty?
3. Can you be held accountable for not complying with this law?
4. What steps could you have taken to avoid this situation?
5. What would you recommend James do after he returns to his practice?

Clinical Example # 3

> Mary, a single mother on a fixed budget, calls a therapist for an appointment. Mary asks about the fee and the therapist tells her that they can work it out later. Several weeks pass and Mary still does not have an idea about the fee. Finally, after three months of treatment, she receives a bill at home for $175 for each session.

Questions for Clinical Example # 3

1. Is Mary obligated to pay this fee? Why or why not?
2. What is the legal therapeutic duty that Mary's therapist must comply with regarding fees?
3. Mary's therapist decides to take her to Small Claims Court after she refuses to pay this fee. What do you believe will happen in Court?
4. Mary decides to call a malpractice attorney. What do you believe she will be told by the attorney?
5. Mary submits a complaint to the BBS. What will be the first item the investigator will ask Mary's therapist?

Chapter Questions

1. Look at Business and Professions Code (BPC) 4980.02, which is the defined scope of practice. What is the scope of practice for California MFTs? How can a marriage and family therapist abuse this law? Do you agree with it?
2. What does BPC 4980.10 state about how the state of California differentiates MFTs from other counselors?
3. What does BPC 4980.55 expect MFTs to provide their clients?

4. What does BPC 4982 define as "unprofessional conduct" that would require administrative action against the MFT? Notice that violating ethical standards can also be considered unprofessional conduct by the BBS. Which specific subsection of the Code applies to the latter?
5. What does BPC 4982 (m) state about maintaining confidentiality?
6. What does BPC 4982 (n) state about disclosing fees?
7. What does BPC 4982.26 state regarding having sexual contact with a client and the impact on the MFT's license?
8. There are two legally mandated situations where an MFT (including interns and trainees) must disclose information to her or his client. What are they?

Chapter 7

Malpractice and Unprofessional Conduct

Malpractice

Malpractice is a legal action against an MFT for breaching therapeutic duty and/or providing treatment below the standard of care. The result is always an injury to the client. When these take place, the client, with the help of an opposing attorney, will likely initiate a malpractice action against the therapist. The attorney will ask the jury and the judge to determine if the MFT was negligent. If so, the client has a strong basis to pursue the malpractice action. If the jury finds in favor of the client, that means that the jury will consider the degree of the injury, the nature of the substandard treatment, and will determine how much the therapist and/or his or her insurance will pay in damages.

The plaintiff (the party suing the MFT) must prove that the MFT injured him or her due to a violation of the therapeutic duty owed to the client. To prove negligence, the client's attorney must prove that four elements are present. These are a) the MFT owes a therapeutic duty to the client; b) the therapist must have breached the duty through an act of omission or commission; c) the therapist's act of omission or commission caused the resulting injury, and d) the therapist's breach of duty directly harmed the client. Only then can the opposing attorney substantiate a malpractice action. Even if there was no intention to harm the client, the mere fact that an injury took place is enough for the jury to find against the therapist.

When consulted to render an opinion of the client's injury, the expert witness will rely on treatment records including intake and assessment protocols, consultations and referrals, treatment plan and diagnosis, progress notes and discharge summaries. Interrogatories of collateral parties serve as additional informational resources. Sometimes, interviews with the client or MFT, depending on who retained the expert, are necessary. Finally, the expert witness presents his or her information to attorney. A deposition and court testimony follows. After hearing all necessary and appropriate information, the jury will base their decisions on the extent of the injury and the degree of therapist negligence. Some of the types of malpractice actions against therapists include the following:

- Breach of contract—Promising results to clients and not delivering.
- Physical assault—Restraining or touching the client without consent.
- Sexual assault—Having sex with the client.

- Abandonment—Not providing continued care when the client is in need.
- Wrongful death—A patient kills him/herself and the family sues for lack of protection.
- Failure of the duty to protect and warn—Failing to comply with the Tarasoff/Civil Code 43.92 or similar mandated reporting requirement.
- Breach of confidentiality—breaching confidentiality without authorization from the client.
- Practicing medicine without a license—Telling clients that they require psychotropic medication or treating a physical problem via psychotherapy. For example, treating depression using psychotherapy methodologies when it is caused by a hormonal imbalance or pituitary dysfunction.

Any of these actions can create a situation in which the client believes he or she has been injured by the therapist and that this warrants a malpractice action against the therapist. It is in the best interest of therapists to carry the maximum malpractice insurance they can afford.

Unprofessional Conduct

Unprofessional conduct is the legal term the BBS uses to describe illegal behavior by MFTs. The specific behaviors that define "unprofessional conduct" are found in Business and Professions Code 4982. Violating CAMFT ethical standards is also considered unprofessional conduct because the following subsection applies:

> **4982(d) Gross negligence or incompetence in the performance of marriage, family, and child counseling (is considered unprofessional conduct).**

Clients can initiate a complaint against a therapist with the BBS. The BBS reviews the complaint, then decides to either drop the case or initiate an investigation. If enough evidence is found against the MFT, then legal action through the Administrative Law Judge begins. This is not a regular court of law; instead, it is an administrative court where the therapist can lose his or her license. Should MFTs find themselves in this situation, they must obtain legal advice. A synopsis of the list of unprofessional conduct as defined by Business and Professions Code 4982 follows:

a) Conviction of a crime related to the practice of marriage and family therapy.
b) Obtaining a license or registration fraudulently.
c) Using drug and/or alcohol to the degree of impairment.
d) Practicing below the standard of care.
e) Violating any of the laws of B. and P.C. 4980-4989.
f) Practicing below the scope of competence (education, training, and experience).
g) Impersonating another licensee or registrant for the use of their status.
h) Helping another person practice fraudulently.

i) Harming a client physically or emotionally.
j) Lying to the BBS.
k) Having a sexual relationship with a client.
l) Practicing outside of the scope of practice.
m) Breaching confidentiality.
n) Failing to disclose the fee at the first session.
o) Receiving payment or paying for referrals.
p) Advertising falsely.
q) Providing answers to a psychometric test to the public.
r) Supervising interns/trainees below the standard of care.
s) Practicing outside of the scope of competence.
t) Permitting a supervisee to practice outside of her or his scope of competence.
u) Violating the law regarding obtaining supervision hours.
v) Not keeping mental health records that meet the standard of care.
w) Failure to comply with the Child Abuse reporting law.
x) Failure to comply with the Elder/Dependent Abuse law.
y) Failure to comply with the "patient access to records" law, Health Code 123130.
z) Violating the Telemedicine Act.
aa) Committing any sexual misconduct with a minor.
ab) Subverting any license examination in any manner.

The BBS upholds these laws when examining complaints. Should an accusation be deemed valid, the BBS has the authority to discipline the MFT and/or revoke an MFT's license.

Creating Therapeutic Safety: Learning the Hard Way

John, a licensed marriage and family therapist for many years, is facing his first malpractice action. He does not know how this misunderstanding got out of hand. Yes, he had not kept up with all the new legal and ethical changes, but he thought of himself as a good therapist. Surely, that must count for something in court.

It all started after John came back from a weekend course and was thrilled to initiate an experimental technique he learned there with a difficult client. John knew that this would help create the much-needed catharsis for his client. Although he was reminded at the course to discuss the implications of the technique with his clients and obtain informed consent, John believed this "legal stuff" only got in the way of the real therapeutic relationship. He had never bothered to review CAMFT ethical standards or applicable mental health law before and his clients had never complained. "Besides," he thought, "this legal and ethical stuff really scares me." Now, the client was claiming that John had hurt her horribly. Her emotional injury began after he used this new technique on her. John believed the technique had been a success. His client, however, had not experienced it as a positive intervention; rather, she was severely injured by this experience and felt traumatized again. Since John refused to believe he had hurt this client, he rationalized that his client had underlying borderline features that were beginning to surface.

> **After looking at the clinical records, which were minimal, John's attorney wisely pointed out how the opposing attorney would use all available material to discredit John as a therapist. His attorney also recommended that they settle the case; however, John wanted his day in court since he had done nothing wrong. His attorney told him, "You are in for a rough ride." After the opposing attorney took his deposition, which took two full days, John felt confused, angry, betrayed, and beaten. The opposing attorney asked him questions that triggered feelings of being insensitive, ignorant, reckless, and arrogant.**
>
> **During the deposition, The opposing attorney asked John about Health and Safety Codes 121100, 123105, and 123130 and the legally required content of his mental health records. This attorney also asked him and why he had failed to provide these to him. The attorney wanted to know if John knew that he had a duty to provide these to attorneys when subpoenaed. John had no idea what the opposing attorney was asking him. When asked if John had consulted with a more experienced peer regarding the newly learned technique, John had answered, "No." When asked if he ever consulted with other therapists, John also answered, "No." When asked to explain his treatment plan, John did not have one. He also answered that he never used treatment plans because he followed his clinical sense. When asked about the scope of practice regarding the treatment for the issue the client presented, John stated he was not familiar with this concept. When asked about the scientific literature discussing this new intervention, John could not cite any articles he had read. When asked when was the last time he had taken a legal and ethical issues review course, John admitted that the last time was in graduate school. As the depositions ended, John sensed that this case was not going well for him.**

A prudent and reasonable therapist in the community would agree that John is not a "bad" therapist. John is able to affect his clients in a positive manner. However, John appears to be forgetting that the purpose of psychotherapy is to help clients create safety out of crisis, create healing out of injury, and create health out of dysfunction. To accomplish this goal, the therapeutic environment must be safe for all involved, especially the client. If John had applied the appropriate CAMFT ethical standards, California law, and case law and had thus created therapeutic safety, most likely this malpractice action would not be taking place.

John's attorney warned him that though John may not have intended to hurt his client, due to his cumulative legal and ethical violations the jury would not view him favorably. The opposing attorney would accentuate John's lack of knowledge of applicable CAMFT Ethical Standards regarding competence, empowerment of the client, and consultation to describe a "reckless" and "incompetent" therapist. Additionally, the opposing attorney would use John's lack of informed consent regarding his treatment to discredit him. The attorney focused on John's use of experimental techniques and did not discuss this action fully with his client. The opposing attorney would use John's lack of appropriate mental health records and treatment plan and his disregard of current MFT legal and ethical developments to personify John as a "harmful and dangerous" therapist. Individually, one ethical or legal breach would not be significant; however, as a composite, the opposing attorney would use them to create an image of a therapist who is unconcerned or disdainful about the safety of his clients. In retrospect, John acknowledged that settling this case would be the best solution to a difficult problem. Though he hated to admit it, he recognized how he had allowed himself to become complacent regarding legal and ethical issues.

Mental Health Records and Lawsuits: A Direct Correlation

MFTs often ask expert witnesses how they failed to keep appropriate mental health records. This clinical scenario describes how a lawsuit can happen as a result of this failure.

A client has been seeing a psychotherapist for treatment of a specific issue. The client, injured in an auto accident, is claiming that the collision caused him emotional injury. At this point, the mental health records are no longer privileged (Evidence Code 1016). As the focus of therapy changes to support and document the emotional suffering, inadequate mental health records can be detrimental to the client's case. When subpoenaed, excessive records provide a wealth of information for the opposing attorney to discredit the client's emotional suffering. On the other hand, insufficient records do not support the client's emotional suffering. The therapist's poor record keeping becomes the cause for the client losing the emotional injury case. By keeping inappropriate records, the psychotherapist has opened the door to a lawsuit for the damages entailed by the client's financial loss.

This is how MFTs invite a malpractice lawsuit. In California, it is unethical and illegal (unprofessional conduct per the BBS) for LCSWs and MFTs not to keep mental health records. At this time, no specific law dictates the mandated content of mental health records. However, standard of care considers Health and Safety Code 123130 as a guideline to establish minimally acceptable content of mental health records. This law requires the following content when a client requests her or his records in writing from her or his psychotherapist:

a. Chief complaints, including pertinent history
b. Findings from consultations and referrals to other health care workers
c. Diagnosis, when determined
d. Treatment plan
e. Progress of treatment
f. Prognosis, including significant continuing problems or conditions
g. Pertinent reports of diagnostic procedures and tests and all discharge summaries
h. Objective findings from the most recent physical examination

Another aspect to consider is therapeutic duty. A psychotherapist has the legal and ethical duty to assess, diagnose, and treat appropriately throughout the duration of therapy. Appropriately does not mean accurately. It means following an established and accepted procedure known as standard of care. Incorporating the eight elements described above may not be sufficient. Additionally, the psychotherapist must consider how each of the eight components appropriately support and document the therapist's duty to assess, diagnose, and treat according to the standard of care. To review the standard of care for mental health records, see Chapters 15-18 in this book.

How Small Clinical Issues Become Malpractice or BBS Administrative Actions

Expert witnesses who review clinical documents arising from a BBS administrative or malpractice action against therapists or counselors often wonder, "How did this case get this far?" In some situations, emotional reactivity that can exist between client and therapist can injure the therapeutic relationship. Many times, the severity of this reactivity will prevent these two from healing a rift in the therapeutic relationship. When perceiving an injury arising from a clinician's behavior, the client enters into his or her own reactivity and attempts to seek redress through a BBS complaint or malpractice action against the therapist.

The "Transference-Countertransference" theory is too limited to explain how a minor clinical infraction can turn into a maelstrom for the therapist or counselor. From my experience as a forensic expert, I have witnessed how each potentially harmful clinical situation has a "critical mass" of its own. Critical mass is reached once the litigant's attorney or the BBS investigator believes with a degree of reasonable certainty that a violation has taken place. At this point, the accusation reaches "critical mass." After this critical mass is reached, the "energy" of the action turns against the clinician. The following forensic case will help outline this process.

After obtaining parental consent, an experienced clinician begins treating a minor for suicidal ideation. The clinician conducts her assessment, including a family history. She obtains a "no-suicide" contract from the minor and initiates treatment considered to fall under the standard of care. After months of treatment, she believes she has developed a strong therapeutic relationship with the minor and the parents. Her observation is supported after several family sessions where both parents thank her for helping their child. The clinician attempts to help the minor develop a strong sense of self that at times challenges the family's belief system. Here, she is called on to make an intervention that addresses the minor's need to individuate in a healthy fashion and still maintain the parents in their role as leaders of the family. Though the clinician attempted to prepare the parents to view this intervention as a necessary part of treatment, she was not prepared for the negative emotional reactivity both parents showed after they interpreted her clinical intervention as attempting to undermine their parental authority. The minor, who experienced his parent's anger, withdrew into his depression and became actively suicidal. Now, the parents blamed the therapist for the minor's suicide attempt. Though the attempt was "low lethality," from a system's perspective, the minor again succeeded in getting all members of the family to focus their attention on him. The parents experienced fear and anger, which they then displaced onto the therapist.

In anger, the parents initiated a BBS administrative complaint for unprofessional conduct and began a malpractice action against the therapist for practicing below the standard of care. Upon consultation with the expert witness, the therapist and her defense attorney decided to settle the malpractice case rather than have exposure to a large financial judgment against her. Rather than losing her license, she agreed to the BBS's charge of unprofessional conduct as defined by Business and Professions Code 4982 (d) & (v). As part of the BBS's action, she was also required to inform future clients of the disciplinary status. What went wrong?

Upon reviewing the mental health records, the expert witness reported the strengths and weaknesses of the case to the defense attorney. One of the strengths of the case was the therapist's intention to help the family. Another strength was that the therapist's treatment of the minor fell within the standard of care. Unfortunately, the weaknesses of the case overwhelmed the strengths. The first major weakness of the case was the inadequate content of the mental health records. Secondly, the treatment plan did not substantiate the treatment. Third and most important, the therapist failed to substantiate her assessment of the impact of her last intervention upon the parental subsystem. In combination, these omissions prevented the defense attorney from presenting an appropriate defense.

The therapist's failure to follow the standard of care by keeping appropriate mental health records, lack of treatment plan, and failure to document her reasoning and clinical objectivity in using a challenging intervention, strengthened the perception that she acted unprofessionally, was negligent and breached her therapeutic duty to her clients. Rather than facing a potentially devastating outcome, all agreed to settle the case. The "critical mass" in this case erupted when the therapist could not support her side of the case with appropriate documentation.

To avoid reaching a similar "critical mass" in similar situations, a reasonable and prudent psychotherapist or counselor would consider following these steps:

- Always keep appropriate mental health records that meet the standard of care.

- Treatment plans, a required component of mental health records, must accompany all mental health records.
- Document the process of making challenging clinical interventions that could affect the therapeutic relationship negatively.
- Remember the maxim, "It never happens, until it happens, and when it happens, it happens." It is impossible to predict the future in psychotherapy, therefore apply the standard of care for mental health records to all clients.
- Stay informed of the current standard of care regarding treatment planning and keeping appropriate mental health records.

Some therapists and counselors are not aware of how difficult it is to defend a case with inadequate or inappropriate mental health records. These types of records do not support the therapist's contention that he or she acted in a reasonable and prudent manner.

How Attorneys Develop Malpractice Cases Against Clinicians In Conjunction With an Expert Witness

Once an attorney decides to initiate a malpractice action against a mental health clinician, he or she begin a process to show how the clinician's clinical treatment fell below the standard of care and violated her or his therapeutic duty to assess, diagnose, and treat the client in a "reasonable and prudent" manner. This attorney will attempt to find "actual" or at least real and arguable deficiencies in the clinician's work, which may be hidden from view. Through the discovery process the goal is to find these, as well as any legal and/or ethical violations that the clinician carried out by omission and commission during the course of treatment. Non-existent, poor, or excessive mental health records can serve to make the defense attorney's task much harder and help strengthen the opposing attorney's premise that malpractice took place.

The opposing attorney will start by issuing a subpoena of the existing mental health records to determine the strengths and weaknesses of the clinician's care and approach. Upon receiving these, he or she will turn them over to an expert witness to determine the following: a) Are these the actual records? b) Did the clinician alter these records in any way? c) If computerized, were they created and printed after the lawsuit began? If these are the actual records, then the expert witness will be asked to review them and identify the strengths and weaknesses of the case. If there is any doubt that the records have been recreated by hand (ink is dated and an expert can determine if the ink and paper correspond to the time of records creation) or recreated by computer (word processing software does not "fix" data and opens the possibility that the clinician's hard drive will be subpoenaed to determine the creation date of the document, which is readily obtainable from the internal data structure of the hard drive) the attorney has now won the case. A clinician tampering with records after the fact is altering legal evidence and this action now opens the door for the clinician to be accused of perjury (lying in court) and an accusation of unprofessional conduct to the state's licensing agency (the BBS and the Board of Psychology in California).

If the records are legitimate, the expert witness begins his or her examination to determine the following: a) Does the quality of the existing treatment records conform to the standard of care? B) Did the clinician follow standard of care to assess the client appropriately throughout the treatment process? c) Did the clinician diagnose the client appropriately throughout the treatment process? d) Did the clinician treat the client appropriately throughout the treatment process? The expert witness develops a time line beginning with the initial visit and ending with the final visit meanwhile attempting to answer the following question:

1. Is the presenting issue identified in the treatment records?
2. Does the clinician have the scope of competence (training, knowledge, and experience) to treat the presenting issues?
3. Does a treatment plan exist addressing the four phases of treatment?
4. If so, is the proposed treatment plan reasonable in attempting to resolve the presenting issues with appropriate goals and objectives in each phase?
5. Do the assessments conform to the standard of care?
6. Does the diagnosis conform to the presenting symptoms?
7. Is the diagnosis supported by documented symptoms and their duration?
8. Is a written informed consent document part of the treatment records?
9. Does the informed consent document conform to the legal and ethical standard of care and is there any additional consent required for unconventional or experimental treatment provided?

With these initial questions, the expert witness compiles a list of strengths and weakness specific to this case. For example, the clinician's competence may come into question if he or she treated a suicidal client and has not taken a course on managing suicidal clients within the last two years. The clinician may have not obtained previous treatment information pertinent to the assessment process: a history of suicide attempts known to the previous treatment providers. A Mental Status Exam and a Beck Depression Inventory may be lacking. The treatment plan does not address the suicidal behavior. The client was not referred to a psychiatrist. The informed consent form may be inadequate or non-existent. A separate informed consent form may not have addressed challenging or unorthodox therapeutic modalities used. The diagnosis was not supported by specific behavioral symptoms and their duration.

Each one of these violations may be minor, however together they serve to demonstrate in their totality a significant deviation from the reasonable and prudent practice lawfully expected of the practitioner. I can imagine this conversation between the opposing attorney and the clinician during a deposition:

- **Attorney: In your training as a ________ you learned certain skills and practices that allowed you to have an understanding of the prevailing standard of care in matters of ________________________"You are a reasonable and prudent clinician, are you not?"**
- **Clinician: "Yes."**
- **Attorney: "As such the reasonable and prudent clinician, would make his best efforts to conform with these legal and ethical standards correct?"**
- **Clinician: "Yes."**
- **Part of that would be to understand the importance of obtaining your patient's informed consent before treating the patient, correct?**
- **That would be the reasonable and prudent course of action for a clinician, would it not?**
- **Attorney: "Can you tell me what specific things you did in obtaining your patient's informed consent form in your records?"**

From this moment on, the clinician's credibility as a reasonable and prudent clinician has been damaged. Imagine each ethical and legal violation as a black mark on a white paper. The opposing attorney will present that image to a jury.

After completing the initial aspect of the document review, the expert witness is ready to complete the next part of the assessment process: the assessment of the initial complaints as they appear on the legal document titled "Complaint of Damages." This legal form registered with the Court will have a myriad of complaints ranging from practicing below the standard of care to willfully inflicting harm on the client and causing severe emotional injuries.

The expert witness will review the deposition of the clinician. The opposing attorney attempts to ask questions during the deposition that attempt to point out the clinician's weakness (See above). Upon reviewing this deposition and the deposition of others involved in the malpractice action, specific items will be identified that will help support the accusation that the clinician acted below the standard of care and if applicable of willfully injuring the client by acts of omission or commission.

The opposing attorney will use the compilation of all material that supports his or her premise and bases it on the evidence that the clinician is at fault for injuring the client. His intent is to obtain an acceptable financial settlement from the insurance carrier. Should a settlement not be forthcoming, he or she will obtain a settlement conference date where the judge attempts to have both parties resolve this action. Should a settlement not be reached then the case will go to trial. This process can take anywhere between two to three years from the time the malpractice action is filed with the court to the time a trial is finished and a verdict reached by a jury.

A Malpractice Lawsuit Arising For Reporting As Well As Not Reporting Child Abuse

When clinicians face the issue of child abuse, at times the issue of abuse may not be clearly defined. Should the clinician report the abuse, it is possible that the reported party could initiate legal action against the clinician for causing emotional injury. On the other hand, if the clinician fails to make a report and the child experiences physical harm in the future, one of the parents could sue the clinician for malpractice due to failure to protect. Though MFTs cannot prevent a malpractice action, they can protect themselves by documenting their rationale for reporting or not reporting the abuse. Consider the following vignette:

> **A parent drinks two glasses of wine, drives a car with his child in the back seat and the child is in his restraining seat. The parent tells the clinician that he drove "under the influence" of alcohol. The clinician makes a child abuse report for child endangerment.**

It is feasible that the parent will initiate a malpractice action against the clinician for breach of confidentiality. Though the MFT may have determined appropriately that the father endangered the child, the father can still sue the therapist for a myriad of reasons. Now consider the following vignette:

> **A parent consistently drives a car with his child in the back seat. The child sits outside of his restraining seat. The parent has had two narrow escapes where he almost hit someone else. Proudly, he tells his clinician: "That's how real men drive." The clinician reminds him that he has his son in the back seat without a restraint and that he could get hurt. The father replies: "That's how I learned to drive." A few weeks later, the father is involved in a severe auto collision and his son dies.**

It is quite likely that the clinician's failure to make a mandated report to Child Welfare Services will be considered as negligence and failure to protect the child and the other parent will likely sue the therapist using the latter accusation as ground for the lawsuit.

Clinical Example # 1

> After receiving his MFT license, Mark begins sharing an office with an established clinician. Mark notices laxity in this clinician's approach to practice: unclear boundaries with clients, using extra time even though clients are waiting, charts left on the desk, talking with clients in the reception room, and hugging every client for extended periods of time. Mark questions this clinician about his cavalier attitude and his response is: "Mark, you are too uptight. You'll never get sued if you are friendly with your clients."

Questions for Clinical Example # 1

1. Do you agree with the established clinician's attitude toward clinical practice? Why or why not?
2. What is the probability that Mark could get sued? What is the one aspect of lawsuits that Mark can't predict nor control?
3. Sometimes well-meaning clinicians make mistakes of omission and commission. What possible mistakes could the established clinician make based on Mark's observations of his clinical practices?
4. The housekeeping staff comes in every night for cleaning and one of them notices a familiar name on a chart. He picks up the chart and reads damaging information about this person. He goes home and shares this information with his wife, who shares it with her friend, etc. What could the injured party accuse the therapist of?
5. Mark decides to inform this therapist of how to become reasonable and prudent in his clinical practices. What would Mark tell him?

Clinical Example # 2

> Mark, the therapist in the previous vignette,receives a referral from the therapist above above because the second therapist has a full schedule and cannot schedule this client within a reasonable period of time. Mark conducts an interview and this client reveals that she had a sexual relationship with the previous therapist. Mark is shocked and confused.

Questions for Clinical Example # 2

1. Mark calls you after this appointment and shares his confusion and shock with you. What do you advise him to do?
2. Mark does not want to betray his friend, the therapist, yet he recognizes he has a therapeutic duty to this client. What must Mark do legally?
3. Mark is extremely angry with this therapist and he recommends to the client that she sue him. Do you agree with this recommendation? Why or why not?
4. The therapist approaches Mark in the office and asks him to help him avoid a lawsuit and tells him that this client is "crazy." Is this interaction appropriate? Why or why not? What must Mark do immediately?
5. The therapist sues Mark for slander. Can Mark be sued? What do you think the outcome of the lawsuit will be?

Chapter Questions

1. What does "a greater professional responsibility" mean to you?
2. How can a therapist practice "unidimensionally?"
3. How do clinicians rely solely on the therapeutic relationship for the healing process?
4. What other elements of psychotherapy did John fail to incorporate in this therapy?
5. What is the difference between creating therapeutic safety versus protecting oneself? Visualize a therapist taking both stances and ask, "What is the therapist communicating to his or her clients with each posture?

Chapter 8

The Therapeutic Relationship

The Therapeutic Relationship

In general terms, therapy is the process of helping a client become aware of her or his emotional reactivity, exploring the underlying dynamics that have created and promoted these reactions, working with the client to establish healthy emotional boundaries, and become congruent with him/herself and with others. The importance of the therapeutic relationship is integral to the work of psychotherapy. Without it, psychotherapy will be difficult and challenging.

Most schools of psychotherapy view the therapeutic relationship as the foundation from which client growth takes place. The healthy therapeutic relationship becomes a safe platform from which a client can work with difficult emotions. Part of the therapist's job is to help her or his client work through their emotions without causing the client personal harm. At times, the client and therapist may challenge each other and yet, the healthy therapeutic relationship remains intact. As each challenge is successfully resolved, trust, respect and empathy increase. This strengthened therapeutic relationship provides additional safety, allowing the client to explore deeper issues and continue his or her growth. Because the therapeutic relationship is an integral part of the therapeutic work, the therapist has a unique responsibility to respect this relationship.

Additionally, clients usually initiate therapy when they are in emotional discomfort or turmoil. They choose therapy because they believe that the therapist has some expertise in this arena or field. This belief creates an immediate power differential between the therapist and the clients. Therefore, another important task of the therapist is to balance this power differential during the course of therapy.

CAMFT Ethical Standards Related to the Therapeutic Relationship

CAMFT Ethical Standard 1.2 — Marriage and family therapists are aware of their influential position with respect to patients, and they avoid exploiting the trust and dependency of such persons. Marriage and family therapists, therefore, avoid dual relationships with patients that are reasonably likely to impair professional judgment or lead to exploitation. A dual relationship occurs when a therapist and his or her patient engage in a separate and distinct relationship either simultaneously with the therapeutic relationship, or during a reasonable period of time following the termination of the therapeutic relationship. Not all dual relationships are unethical, and some dual relationships cannot be avoided. When a concurrent or subsequent dual relationship occurs, marriage and family therapists take appropriate professional precautions to insure that judgment is not impaired and that no exploitation occurs.

CAMFT Ethical Standard 1.2.1 — Other acts which would result in unethical dual relationships include, but are not limited to, borrowing money from a patient, hiring a patient, engaging in a business venture with a patient, or engaging in a close personal relationship with a patient. Such acts with a patient's spouse, partner or family member may also be considered unethical dual relationships.

CAMFT Ethical Standard 1.2.2 — Sexual intercourse, sexual contact or sexual intimacy with a patient, or a patient's spouse or partner, or a patient's immediate family member, during the therapeutic relationship or during the two years following the termination of the therapeutic relationship, is unethical.

CAMFT Ethical Standard 1.2.3 — Marriage and family therapists do not enter into a therapeutic relationship with persons with whom he/she has had a sexual relationship or enter into a therapeutic relationship with a partner or the immediate family member of a person with whom he/she has had a sexual relationship.

CAMFT Ethical Standard 1.6 — Marriage and family therapists do not use their professional relationships with patients to further their own interests.

CAMFT Ethical Standard 1.3.2 — Marriage and family therapists do not abandon or neglect patients in treatment. If a therapist is unable or unwilling to continue to provide professional services, the therapist will assist the patient in making clinically reasonable arrangements for continuation of treatment.

CAMFT Ethical Standard 1.7 — Marriage and family therapists continually monitor their effectiveness and take steps to improve when necessary. Marriage and family therapists continue therapeutic relationships only as long as it is reasonably clear that patients are benefiting from the relationship.

CAMFT Ethical Standard 1.8 — When terminating employment or contractual relationships, marriage and family therapists primarily consider the best interest of the patient when resolving issues of continued responsibility for patient care.

For a more complete discussion on the ramifications of these ethical standards, see Chapter 28.

Protecting the Therapeutic Relationship

The above list of ethical standards cover a number of issues relating to the therapeutic relationship. Although these ethical standards cover different areas, and some are general while others are specific, they share an underlying theme. This theme concerns the clinical safety of the client and the MFT. The clinicians apply these ethical standards in a manner to their clients and ultimately themselves as well.

Perhaps the first measure MFTs can take is to provide the client with informed consent (see the chapter on informed consent). This consent includes a legal document that outlines specific information concerning therapy, such as the therapist's theoretical orientation, confidentiality management in therapy, a list of mandated reporting situations and office policies, and how the MFT will manage difficult and challenging clinical issues. A client having this knowledge of the parameters of therapy is free to decide for him/herself what the limits of safety are within the therapeutic relationship. Conversely, if the client attempts to test these limits and place him/herself or the MFT in danger, the clinician can refer to the informed consent document and use it to set appropriate boundaries for the client. Should the client fail to cooperate, the clinician can use the informed consent document to terminate the therapeutic relationship in a safe and protective manner for the client and for him/herself.

Ultimately, MFTs can empower the client through the development of a "partnership," the interactive strengthening of the therapeutic relationship. For example, when a client and therapist decide together to report an incident of child abuse, they are acting in partnership. Utilizing partnership in therapy addresses the ethical standard to incorporate the client in the decision-making process when legal/ethical issues occur.

Using the Therapeutic Relationship Appropriately

Above all ethical duties, MFTs have a primary one, the one requiring them to enhance the welfare of the client. Every time MFTs apply this standard to the therapeutic relationship, they use it as a "lens" or "filter" to determine the appropriateness of every clinical intervention used or clinical action taken in therapy. This ethical duty is also a powerful tool when deciding how and when to use the therapeutic relationship as a model to enhance the client's growth. MFTs can also use the therapeutic relationship in a powerful manner to enhance every aspect of therapy. For example, it may be appropriate to use the influence of such in order to provide the client with difficult information; for example that an MFT must make a child abuse report immediately. The MFT can use it to invite the client to consider a reframe and he or she accedes. Just a few weeks before, client would not have listened to the MFT and consider the possibility of accepting a reframe.

In addition, using the therapeutic relationship appropriately extends into the area of boundaries. When working with a client who has problems setting and maintaining boundaries, the therapist can be a healthy role model. Each time the therapist respects a boundary that he or she has previously set, whether it is a time boundary or a touch boundary, the client's respect for boundaries can be solidified. The client then has the opportunity to experience how a relationship with healthy boundaries feels. This then, affords the client the opportunity to make a knowledgeable decision about what he or she wants for his or her own life regarding maintaining and respecting boundaries. All of this arises from the appropriate use of the therapeutic relationship.

Injuring the Therapeutic Relationship

It is possible to injure the therapeutic relationship through the MFT's inadvertent or direct actions. For example, the therapist does or says something that triggers a client's memory of emotional abuse by an intimate family member. When the therapist does not recognize the retraumatization or handles it clumsily, the therapeutic relationship suffers. At times, countertransference issues result in a therapist avoiding an issue while becoming defensive and even blaming a client. This could shake the client's confidence and trust in the therapist and diminishing the effectiveness of the therapeutic relationship.

Another injury to the therapeutic relationship occurs when MFTs take an action that the client opposes. For example, an MFT makes a mandated report of child abuse involving a client. This client may experience the clinician's legal duty as a betrayal of trust. Gently referring to the informed consent document a the basis of therapeutic safety for all including the client in making the report, and working with the client's resulting feelings can go a long way to healing an injury to the therapeutic relationship. Sometimes, however, the injury is so severe that it destroys the relationship. Perhaps the most dramatic illustration of injury during therapy is when a therapist violates a sexual boundary. MFTs can avoid some injuries by using their good common sense and clinical objectivity. There are times when other injuries others are unavoidable. When injuries do occur to the therapeutic relation, the therapist can take reasonable steps to heal the wound. Consider the following:

- Listen to what your client has to say.
- Acknowledge your client's feelings and his or her courage in confronting you.
- Allow your client to express his or her full range of feelings and "hold" these feelings respectfully.
- As a therapist, accept responsibility for the part you played in the misunderstanding or wrongdoing and apologize when appropriate.
- Always obtain appropriate and objective consultation regarding legal and ethical matters.

Giving special attention to such injuries may not only promote the welfare of the client, but may also helps protect the clinician and avoid legal and/or disciplinary action.

The Power Differential of the Therapeutic Relationship

Marriage and family therapists continuously face the task to provide therapeutic safety for clients while simultaneously protecting themselves. An important way in which they accomplish this is to acknowledge the inherent power differential that exists in the therapeutic relationship. CAMFT recognizes the potential for violating the power differential of the therapeutic relationship and addresses this in CAMFT Ethical Standard 1.6:

> **Marriage and family therapists do not use their professional relationships with patients to further their own interests.**

Some examples of violating the power differential during the course of therapy are: a) a therapist asks a client to introduce him or her to an influential friend the client has mentioned in therapy, b) an MFT asks a client, who is a physician, for a consultation on a personal illness and/or requests a prescription for medication or c) a successful business person, who is a client, offers to give a summer job to the therapist's daughter and the therapist accepts. In these situations, the therapist's needs supersede the needs of the client. One important question MFTs must ask before making a clinical decision in a case such as these would be "Does this action benefit me at the expense of the client?" Violating the power differential leave MFTs open to disciplinary action.

It is up to MFTs to be aware of their own issues that may tempt them to abuse the power differential within the therapeutic relationship. When MFTs are fully aware of their personal" blind spots" that lead to loss of clinical objectivity, they develop the best chance of safely handling those legal and ethical decisions that impact personal objectivity and the therapeutic relationship. At times, consultation with objective colleagues or pursuing additional therapy serves to sort out unresolved issues regarding the therapeutic power differential.

Clinical Example # 1

Your colleague, a prominent psychologist who is your main referral source, tells you that he regularly plays tennis with his clients. He states: "This is the best way to get to know them, stay connected, and have them refer to me." You don't know what to say!

Questions for Clinical Example # 1

1. What is this psychologist not understanding about the use of therapeutic relationship?
2. Are MFTs permitted legally or ethically to use the therapeutic relationship for these purposes? Would you? Why or why not?
3. What are the potential problems that could arise should you follow the psychologist's example?
4. Your psychologist friend invites you to play tennis with him. At the courts, he introduces you to other players who are his clients. They invite you to play a foursome. During the game, a disagreement takes place about a specific play and soon one of the players leaves the court fuming. Months later, you are being subpoenaed as a witness of fact in a malpractice case against the psychologist by this client. If you testify against him, you'll lose your main referral source and if you don't, you'll be in contempt of court. What are your options?
5. In hindsight, how would you have managed the situation with the psychologist differently?

Clinical Example # 2

A young attractive model in psychotherapy with an MFT is having a difficult time staying focused in session. She notices that the therapist gives her furtive looks, especially when she wears short skirts. Though he is much older than her, she's still is uncomfortable with his gazing. She brought this up in session and he denied it. He told her it was her imagination. She's confused.

Questions for Clinical Example # 2

1. From your Internal Reality Perspective, is this an appropriate response? Why or why not?
2. Imagine her confusion and now ask the question: "What is the impact of his continued denial on the therapeutic relationship?"
3. As a reasonable and prudent MFT, what would you have done instead?
4. She consults with you for a second opinion. What do you tell her?
5. How do you avoid "criticizing" the other clinician, yet maintain your objectivity in describing his behavior?

Chapter Questions

1. What is the importance of the therapeutic relationship in therapy?
2. How can the therapeutic relationship be damaged? How is treatment affected?
3. A therapist is treating a difficult client. He is resisting treatment and the therapist is becoming frustrated. How is the therapeutic relationship possibly being affected?
4. How is malpractice action against a therapist linked to the therapeutic relationship?
5. A therapist receives a letter from the BBS stating that he or she is being investigated for unprofessional conduct. A month later, the same therapist receives a letter in the mail stating that a

malpractice action is being filed against him or her. What are the differences between the two? What would you advise this therapist to do?

Chapter 9

Dual Relationships

Dual Relationships

Dual relationships are those relationships between a therapist and client that involve more than one "identity." For example, an MFT who also serves as his client's massage therapist is engaging in a dual relationship. Several CAMFT ethical standards address dual relationships.

> **CAMFT Ethical Standard 1.2** — Marriage and family therapists are aware of their influential position with respect to patients, and they avoid exploiting the trust and dependency of such persons. Marriage and family therapists, therefore, avoid dual relationships with patients that are reasonably likely to impair professional judgment or lead to exploitation. A dual relationship occurs when a therapist and his or her patient engage in a separate and distinct relationship either simultaneously with the therapeutic relationship, or during a reasonable period of time following the termination of the therapeutic relationship. Not all dual relationships are unethical, and some dual relationships cannot be avoided. When a concurrent or subsequent dual relationship occurs, marriage and family therapists take appropriate professional precautions to insure that judgment is not impaired and that no exploitation occurs.
>
> **CAMFT Ethical Standard 1.2.2** — Sexual intercourse, sexual contact or sexual intimacy with a patient, or a patient's spouse or partner, or a patient's immediate family member, during the therapeutic relationship, or during the two years following the termination of the therapeutic relationship, is unethical. Should a marriage and family therapist engage in sexual intimacy with a former patient or a patient's spouse or partner, or a patient's immediate family member, following the two years after termination or last professional contact, the therapist shall consider the potential harm to or exploitation of the former patient or to the patient's family.
>
> **CAMFT Ethical Standard 1.2.1** — Other acts which would result in unethical dual relationships include, but are not limited to, borrowing money from a patient, hiring a patient, engaging in a business venture with a patient, or engaging in a close personal relationship with a patient. Such acts with a patient's spouse, partner or family member may also be considered unethical dual relationships.
>
> **CAMFT Ethical Standard 1.2.3** — A marriage and family therapists does not enter into therapeutic relationships with a person with whom he/she has had a sexual relationship or enter into a therapeutic relationship with a partner or the immediate family member of a person with whom he/she has had a sexual relationship.

California law does not specifically address dual relationships. However, CAMFT Ethical Standard 1.2, which addresses harmful dual relationships, views MFTs who violate this standard and cause harm to a client as acting unethically and unprofessionally. Business and Professions Code 4982 defines unprofessional conduct for MFTs in subsection "d." This legal statute defines gross negligence or incompetence as grounds for disciplinary action constitutes unprofessional conduct, i.e., entering into a harmful dual relationship. Additionally, subsection "k" prohibits a sexual relationship with a client and subsection "i" establishes that disciplinary action will be taken when the therapist intentionally or recklessly causes physical or emotional harm to a client. Using these legal and ethical standards, MFTs can expect legal action by the BBS when the Board becomes aware of an accusation of a harmful dual relationship. Regardless of whether the dual relationship was or was not harmful, the burden of proof lies with the therapist.

Dual relationships are not inherently harmful. At times, dual relationships are unavoidable. For example, in a small town, a therapist's client is the only high school physics teacher. Her son enrolls in his class and his performance is less than average. This MFT must take serious and reasonable steps to avoid entering into a dual relationship with her son's teacher who is also her client. Consider another therapist and client may be in a church choir together. They practice regularly and meet afterwards to discuss the choir's progress and improvement. This MFT must ask: "What must I do to avoid harming my client? Have I lost objectivity or coerced my client?" It is prudent for this MFT to obtain a clear and objective consultation with a respected and unrelated professional. If faced with a dual relationship, the therapist increases the ability to protect him/herself by documenting the steps taken to maintain objectivity and avoid coercion.

Harmful Dual Relationships

Dual relationships are harmful when one of the following two conditions exist: a) loss of objectivity by the therapist, or b) coercion of the client by the clinician. When therapy begins, a power differential exists by default between therapist and client. This power differential sets up a condition where a therapist can take advantage of a client due to his or her greater knowledge and expertise. The literature is replete with examples of therapists engaging in dual relationships and harming their clients.

First, any sexual relationship with a client during therapy or during the two years following the termination of the therapy constitutes a harmful dual relationship and prohibited (CAMFT ethical standard 1.2.1, Business and Professions Code 4982 (k), and Civil Code 43.93). These legal and ethical standards are very clear and well defined. Examples of harmful dual relationships follow. Bear in mind that this is an illustrative list, not a comprehensive list. Before engaging in a dual relationship with a patient, it is best to consult with an expert in this field.

1. An MFT runs out of his personal medication. When he does, he asks his severely depressed client, who is a physician, to write a prescription for him. The physician does not want to write the prescription because he believes that the therapist's physician needs to evaluate him. However, he writes the prescription because he is depressed and afraid that if he refuses, his therapist will stop treating him. This is a dual relationship. The therapist has become the client's patient. It is a harmful dual relationship because of its coercive nature.

2. A client lives in a guest room belonging to her treating therapist. The MFT felt sorry for her abused client and invited her to move in after the client's husband threatened to beat her up for the third time. This is a harmful dual relationship. The therapist is now the client's roommate. This therapist has lost objectivity.

3. An MFT has a long-standing professional relationship with a wealthy client. In therapy, the client has showered the MFT with expensive gifts. Afraid of losing this client, she has accepted the gifts. The client invites the MFT to a gala event at her house and says to the therapist: "You will come, dear." The MFT complies with this command because she is afraid that if she says no she will lose the client. The therapist now has a social relationship with her client. This is a harmful dual relationship because the therapist has lost objectivity.

Friendships With Clients

Therapists do not have any legal or ethical restrictions preventing them from entering into a friendship with an ex-client. However, if they do, the relationship must not include any type of sexual behavior even after the client terminates therapy. Legal and ethical standards address friendships with former clients, stating that MFTs can face difficulties arising from this relationship. They can also cause injury to the ex-client and clinicians can face a malpractice action or a BBS investigation. The injury arises from a misunderstanding, from unmanageable conflict, from an abrupt ending, or from abandonment. MFTs who find themselves in this type of relationship are always in a bind. If they do not meet the ex-client's expectations and the latter feels taken advantage of or slighted, he or she can always complain to the BBS. Even if the ex-client is not injured, their complaint to the BBS will be enough to cause severe anguish to the therapist. Therefore, it is important that MFTs question their motive for entering into this relationship.

Sexuality and Clients

California law specifically addresses sexuality and psychotherapy. Business and Professions Code 4982, clearly states that the following behaviors are considered unprofessional conduct: a) engaging in sexual relations with a client within two years following termination of therapy, b) soliciting sexual relations with a client, c) committing an act punishable as a sexually related crime, if that act or solicitation is substantially related to the qualifications, functions, or duties of a marriage and family therapist.

Ethical standards also recognize that a therapeutic boundary must exist regarding sexuality. CAMFT Ethical Standard 1.2.2 states: "Sexual intercourse, sexual contact or sexual intimacy with a patient, or a patient's spouse or partner, or a patient's immediate family member during the therapeutic relationship, or during the two years following the termination of the therapeutic relationship, is unethical." CAMFT Ethical Standard 1.2 addresses the power differential in the therapeutic relationship: "Marriage and family therapists are aware of their influential position with respect to patients, and they avoid exploiting the trust and dependency of such persons." Therapists must accept that involving him/herself with a client will take advantage of the power differential inherent in the therapeutic relationship. Additionally, CAMFT Ethical Standard 1.3.1 establishes that MFTs terminate therapeutic relationships for clinically sound reasons and in an appropriate manner. Adhering to this ethical standard, then, precludes MFTs from ending a client's therapy to being a sexual relationship.

If MFTs violate a sexual boundary with a client, an injury will follow. Inappropriate sexual intimacy includes an array of behaviors. Boundary violations may be a look, a touch, or sexual activity including intercourse. The BBS considers any physical or emotional gratification connected to sexual activity as sexual involvement. When this occurs in a dual relationship, it violates Business and Professions Code 4892 and the corresponding CAMFT Ethical Standards.

Civil and Criminal Actions Specific to Sexual Boundary Violations

California created specific laws intended to protect clients injured by licensed psychotherapist due to a sexual violation. These laws help them obtain monetary remedy. Civil Code 43.93 allows for civil action, which is a malpractice action attempting to recover moneys from the therapist, against a licensed psychotherapist who has had sex with a client during the course of therapy, within two years following termination of therapy, and/or by means of deception. If MFTs misrepresent sexual contact to the client by claiming it is a part of treatment, this act is deceptive. This law also requires that subsequent MFTs, who have knowledge of the sexual boundary violation, must provide a brochure to the client. This brochure, "Therapy Never Includes Sex," informs the client about civil and criminal legal actions against the violating psychotherapist.

In addition to civil action, Business and Professions Code 729 allows a criminal prosecution against a therapist who has had sex with a client during the course of therapy, or after terminating with the client for having sex. Due to this law, district attorneys are empowered to pursue criminal action against the therapist and the resulting punishment could be prison.

Mandated Brochure "Therapy Never Includes Sex"

When a client informs subsequent MFTs that he or she had sex with a previous therapist, they must maintain the client's confidentiality and, therefore cannot contact authorities. However, Civil Code 43.93 mandates MFTs to provide the patient a brochure: "Therapy Never Includes Sex". This brochure is available from the Department of Consumers Affairs, Sacramento, CA: Telephone # 1-800-952-5210. MFTs must discuss the contents of the brochure with the client including all possible legal and clinical actions available to the client. An important point to discuss is CAMFT Ethical Standard 1.7, which states that the client must come to her or his own decisions. The client has the responsibility to decide that action he or she will take. The focus of the ensuing therapy addresses helping the client heal from the previous injury. Should the case go to trial, the client's attorney will subpoena the latter therapist to testify on behalf of the client. This necessitates that MFTs keep complete and appropriate mental health records.

Administrative Actions by the BBS

Senate Bill 1394 became law, effective January 1, 1993. This law states that engaging in sexual relations with a patient either during a therapist-patient relationship or for two years following termination of a relationship is unprofessional conduct. This unprofessional conduct can constitute the basis for disciplinary action by the BBS. As part of it's investigation, the BBS would fully explore whether the therapeutic relationship was terminated to begin engaging in a sexual relationship with the client. Should the BBS find that the therapist engaged in sexual relations during the time frame, or terminated therapy for this purpose, it would then pursue action against the therapist. This may result in revocation of license.

Sexual Harassment: A Workplace Hazard for MFTs

MFTs and their supervisees are not immune from an accusation of sexual harassment. California law considers a sexual advance that is unsolicited, unwelcome, hostile, pervasive or severe in nature from one person towards another as sexual harassment. MFTs and their supervisees are in a vulnerable position about sexual harassment because of the emotional exchange and physical contact that occurs in therapy. Under present California law, the person who perceives the sexual advance, even if the intention was innocent, can accuse the alleged perpetrator of sexual harassment. Sexual harassment can be a look, a touch, or a statement considered as sexual and coercive in nature.

Civil Code 59.1 states that any verbal, visual or physical conduct of a sexual or hostile nature, which is based on gender and can be considered to be engulfing (it may be continuous or only happen once) and, if the receiver experiences some form of loss, then the act will be considered to be sexual harassment. Further, a person who believes he or she has been harassed need not inform the person, nor ask that person to stop. Additionally, with the present law, a malpractice or other legal action can begin at any time without time limit.

MFTs can attend to their conduct and the conduct of their supervisees to ensure that they do not engage in sexual harassment. However, it is impossible to predict every action that may be perceived as sexual harassment. Therefore, reasonable and prudent clinicians attends carefully to each client's general capacity to understand concepts, their belief system, and perceptions of the world as part of assessment at the beginning of and throughout therapy. Additionally, before using any intervention or technique that might possibly be construed as sexual harassment, MFTs should first thoroughly discuss their expected outcome with the client. After that, MFTs obtain a written informed consent for the intervention or technique.

Testifying On Behalf of Clients Can Create a Harmful Dual Relationship

Clients often ask MFTs to testify on their behalf in a variety of cases. In some cases, the client sued the driver who caused a collision, which resulted in a major physical injury affecting the client. The client needs the MFT's testimony to prove that the resulting injuries were due to the collision. In another situation, a client facing a divorce needs the MFT's testimony to strengthen her position as a custodial parent. Some clients face a situation where the client is requesting disability funds and only the treating MFT can testify regarding the emotional disability. When MFTs enter into such relationships, they may find themselves burdened by extra work, greater amount of preparation, and long hours. To obtain fair compensation, some MFTs have told clients who require their testimony that they will charge a higher fee for testimony than the regular fee for therapy. This is where the problem for MFTs begins.

The moment the client feels coerced: if he or she does not pay the increased fee to the MFT, he or she will not testify and the client will definitely lose the case. Thus, he is in a bind and he must pay the fee: this is client coercion. MFTs may not know that their actions are coercive, yet the consequences are potentially severe for MFTs. What can MFTs do? View the following recommendations:

- MFTs learn the different roles of an expert witness versus a witness of fact, their responsibilities, their duties, and their billing practices.
- MFTs review the meaning of a dual relationship, a harmful dual relationship, and how to avoid the latter when agreeing to testify for clients.

- MFTs benefit from exploring healthy versus coercive therapeutic relationships.
- MFTs review the appropriate use of informed consent, it is content, and address of risks and benefits of providing testimony.
- MFTs educate themselves about a fee structure that is not coercive, illegal, or unethical.
- MFTs benefit from having an appropriate referral structure to manage clients who cannot afford her fee, thus avoiding the possibility of abandoning clients when they need continuity of care.

Subtle Dual Relationships

Dual relationships can be overt or subtle. The latter are harder to discern. MFTs, regardless of their training and experience, can become absorbed into the latter type of dual relationship. Imagine a couple presenting a high degree of conflict. The treating MFT established an appropriate "holding information" policy with both individuals. The therapist knew she would see them individually to obtain additional information separate from each other. In the wife's individual session, she indicated that her husband was an abusive bully. In his session, he indicated that his wife was cold, calculating, and sexually unavailable to him. Before his session terminated, he turned around and gave the MFT a check for $5000 to pay for his individual therapy. As therapy progressed, the MFT found herself siding with the husband and labeling his wife as cold and unavailable. Eventually the couple divorced.

It appears that this MFT allowed the husband to disarm her clinical objectivity and he used money as the key to do so. It is impossible to determine if his action was overt or covert. The outcome is the important matter. The therapist lost her objectivity, she inappropriately labeled the wife as cold and unavailable, and her actions harmed the wife. Had the wife become aware of this harmful dual relationship, she had the option to begin a BBS complaint and a malpractice action against this therapist.

Clinical Example # 1

John runs a successful electronics distribution company. He begins treatment with an MFT because his wife tells him he is "boring" due to the excessive time he spends at work. He tells the therapist that soon he will be expanding his company and must hire an extensive sales force to meet the demand for new products introduced by his company. The MFT realizes that this would be an excellent opportunity for her unemployed brother. After the session, she calls her brother and tells him that he can call and ask to speak to the owner because before the last session ended he said: "If you know of anyone who is in sales, send them to me." She says to her brother: "Tell him I sent you. He'll definitely talk to you." The therapist's brother calls John.

Questions for Clinical Example # 1

1. Imagine how John felt when he received the phone call from the therapist's brother. How would you feel in the same situation?
2. Is this an appropriate use of the therapeutic relationship? Why or why not?
3. Is this a dual relationship? How did you determine this? If we consider that the therapist is acting both as therapist and employment broker, then the answer is yes. Is this a harmful dual relationship? Why or why not?
4. A reasonable and prudent clinician considers the possibility that loss of objectivity or coercion could take place. Describe the possibility of how any of these two issues could happen in this relationship.
5. If you were the therapist above and your brother needed a job desperately to avoid bankruptcy would you help him in the same manner? What would allow you to do it? What would prevent your from doing it?

Clinical Example # 2

Virginia considers herself a spiritual therapist. She believes that clients are sent to her for a special purpose. She has been a successful "matchmaker" in several relationships between of her clients who were looking for a spouse. The last couple invited her to speak at their wedding and she accepted.

Questions for Clinical Example # 2

1. Do you believe Virginia is aware of the dual relationships she is engaging with her clients? Why or why not?
2. If she is serving as a matchmaker, a therapist, and a friend at the wedding, does the possibility exist that she could lose objectivity or coerce her clients? Describe how.
3. What could happen if one of the relationships ended in acrimonious divorce and they blamed her for their problems? How would you feel if she were responsible for the divorce?
4. If she was being sued for malpractice by a divorcing couple, what would the lawsuit attempt to establish?
5. What specific charges would the BBS investigate is she were accused of unprofessional conduct?

Clinical Example # 3

An MFT began working as a drug and alcohol counselor at a rehabilitation center. She specifically wanted to avoid MFT related activities. During her employment, she fell in love with a client and soon began dating. Though they never engaged in sex, they kissed often. The director of the program threatened to fire her if she did not stop the relationship with her client. She did and he felt confused and betrayed. Eventually he submitted a complaint to the BBS.

Questions for Clinical Example # 3

1. Even if her job description is as an alcohol and drug abuse counselor, will the BBS still hold her accountable for the scope of practice as an MFT?
2. Imagine that the answer is "yes." What therapeutic duty did she violate and how did she violate it?
3. What action did she take to aggravate his feelings and trigger feelings of abandonment and betrayal?
4. How could she have ended the relationship in a way to avoid triggering these feelings in him?
5. Would that have prevented him from initiating an accusation with the BBS?
6. What is the foundational error she made besides entering into a sexual relationship with the client? Could she have possibly believed that she was not acting as an MFT and thus the laws did not apply to her?

Chapter Questions

1. What is your internal reality about harmful dual relationships? What countertransference issues are raised for you?
2. What is the current legal position regarding a therapist having sex with a client during the therapeutic process? What are your beliefs about this issue?
3. A therapist who has had sex with a client during the therapeutic process can be prosecuted through civil and criminal courts. What does this mean?
4. Therapists in California have been educated about the dangers of having sex with their clients, yet, some still do. What is the reason behind this?

Chapter 10

Managing Crisis Issues And Creating Therapeutic Safety

The Danger for Clinicians When Facing Crisis Issues

One of the major clinical challenges mental health clinicians will most likely face in their practice involves attempting to manage an unpredictable crisis issue. These clinical challenges can occur at any time during treatment. They may begin subtly with a mildly depressive symptom, mild anxiety, or a slight mood elevation. Because these issues are unpredictable, MFTs can miss important information required to manage the issue appropriately and end up caught off guard. In some cases, clinicians may lack the appropriate training, knowledge, and/or experience necessary to manage the issue appropriately. In this case, "appropriately" does not mean "accurately"; it means according to the standard of care that a reasonable and prudent clinician is expected to provide the client facing a high-risk issue.

The scientific literature is replete with studies showing that mismanagement of the presenting issue can lead to the client experiencing severe emotional and/or physical injury including death. In these outcomes, the repercussions for the clinician can be emotionally, professionally, and/or financially disastrous. In some cases, clinicians have faced multi-million dollar verdicts in court, while others faced the possible loss of their license to practice due to a board investigation. As a result of these clinical outcomes, mental health case law (for example; Bellah v. Greenson, 1978; Tarasoff, 1976) continues to define the legal and clinical standard of care when MFTs address crisis issues. Generally, Case Law continues to impose increased professional duties on clinicians to prevent harm to the client and/or other identifiable victims. Though the clinician may not be able to stop someone from causing injury to him/herself or others, the clinician is required to take reasonable steps to protect the life of the client and/or others. Should the client or others experience physical or emotional injury arising from the client's actions, they will most likely initiate legal action against treating MFT and other collateral clinicians, via a malpractice and/or Board administrative action.

If MFTs are unprepared to manage a presenting crisis issue according to the standard of care, he or she will most likely make errors of omission or commission, which can be damaging to the well-being of the client and/or the clinician. To avoid these potentially disastrous possibilities, MFTs must be aware of the how courts view the therapeutic duty expected of them when they address crisis issues.

Additionally, clinicians must be prepared to manage these presenting crisis issues by having the scope of competence (training, knowledge, and experience) to recognize the obvious and subtle clinical risk factors associated with an increased potential of harm to self/others that a reasonable and prudent clinician must know. Next, it is imperative that the clinician puts into effect a previously created crisis management plan when he or she finds him/herself facing one of these circumstances. Attempting to create an action plan during the crisis issue is asking for trouble; the emotional charge and the lack of predictability of the situation will most likely prevent the clinician from being emotionally centered, focused, and clinically objective regarding the clinical path required to create safety. Such a plan is presented later in this chapter.

The Clinician's Scope of Competence Regarding Crisis Issues

The mental health scientific literature has addressed the necessary scope of competence required of MFTs when addressing crisis issues. Dr. Bruce Bongar, an eminent author in the field of suicidology, establishes the required elements in the area of professional competence when treating suicidal clients. His guidelines are applicable to all MFTs who assess, diagnose, and treat any clinical crisis issue. He reminds clinicians that ordinary clinical issues can fulminate into a full-blown high-risk issue.

- Clinicians must have a broad-spectrum training, including the benefits and limitations of psychosocial and organic therapies.
- Clinicians must have ready access to appropriate inpatient hospitalization facilities, in case a voluntary or involuntary hospitalization is required for the client and/or others' safety.
- Clinicians must know the specific clinical and research literature on all recommended psychosocial interventions for high-risk mental disorders.
- Clinicians must know when to request a consultation for psychotropic medication for the treatment of patients with high-risk mental disorders.
- Clinicians must be able to distinguish acute suicidal states related to DSM Axis I clinical syndromes and chronic suicidal states related to an Axis II personality disorder.
- Clinicians are required to differentiate between acute and chronic risk predictor variables in clinical issues involving harm to self or others.
- Clinicians must understand the impact of cultural values regarding harm to self/others.
- Ultimately, clinicians must have the necessary clinical objectivity to know their personal limitations when treating clients presenting crisis issues.

When facing a malpractice case arising from a crisis issue, the clinician can expect to questions about his or her training, knowledge, and experience as stated in the above guidelines. It is important to remember that the opposing attorney will likely retain an expert witness, a board certified psychiatrist or psychologist, who is familiar with the standard of care required to treat crisis issues and this expert will testify that any clinician providing treatment in these circumstances without the required competence is practicing below the standard of care. Imagine the impact on the jury when they hear this statement!

Reasonable and Prudent Steps Required to Manage Crisis Issues

At this point, it is important to define what are "reasonable and prudent" MFTs. These clinicians obtain all necessary information available to them and determine, based on their training, knowledge, experience, and the presenting issues, which treatment approach best meets the need of the client. Reasonable and prudent MFTs make sure that they comply with their therapeutic duty to assess, diagnose, and treat according to the standard of care throughout the duration of treatment. Reasonable and prudent clinical steps begin as conservative measures and become increasingly more aggressive as necessary to manage the presenting crisis issue as it worsens. The clinician must remember that courts do not expect clinicians to be "perfect" or "accurate" in their actions. Instead, the courts expect clinicians to be reasonable and prudent. This means that the courts recognize that clinicians cannot predict the exact moment when a client will hurt him/herself or others. However, the courts do expect clinicians to assess, diagnose, and treat the client in a manner that protects the client and/or other identifiable victims.

Assessing The Client's Competence

First, MFTs determine the client's competence to enter into or continue with treatment. Performing a Mental Status Exam can help determine if the client presents any form of physical, emotional, or cognitive impairment that prevents him or her from entering into treatment. It is inappropriate for MFTs to allow a client who cannot provide informed consent due to incompetence to enter into treatment or continue in treatment. If a client presents this degree of impairment, it is best for MFTs to refer him or her to a psychiatrist or physician for immediate hospitalization depending on the presenting clinical issue.

Initial Assessment of the Client

The next step requires a complete assessment of the client. MFTs obtain a personal, medical, family, psychiatric and other previous treatment histories. They perform any necessary psychometric testing. A required and fundamental test is the Mental Status Exam, which establishes that when used, establishes that MFTs assessed the client's emotional and mental state. This test also establishes a baseline for future reference to establish improvement or lack of improvement as treatment progresses. MFTs repeat the Mental Status Exam as often as the clinical conditions require it. Should clients present any form of mood disorder, a required psychometric test would be a Beck Depression Inventory. This is a standardized test with reliability and validity, which documents the degree of the client's clinical depression. It also serves as baseline for future comparisons as needed. If the client presents any personality disorder traits, then MFTs consider the use of an MMPI or similar personality test. MFTs and LCSWs can perform any psychometric test as long as they have the training, knowledge, and experience to use it and as long as it is used as part of the treatment, which involves the enhancement of relationships for the former or helping the client address psychosocial adjustments for the latter. As unlicensed clinicians, drug and alcohol counselors do not have authorization to use psychometric testing except for a Mental Status Exam.

Consultation With Past and Current Treatment Providers

It is imperative that treating MFTs obtain a written release of information and consult with previous treatment providers. Previous providers may have information that can affect current treatment. If MFTs fail to integrate this information into the current treatment plan and should the client harm him/herself or others, these MFTs can find themselves accountable for practicing below the standard of care in their assessment protocol.

MFTs must obtain the client's current medical information. If the client has not had a complete medical evaluation within two years, it is reasonable and prudent to refer the client for a complete medical check-up. The client's medical status is essential because without it, the client's physical condition may be at risk. This is especially true for clients presenting with mood disorders or eating disorders, and substance related disorders. Mood disorders can have a physical origin, such as a thyroid problem, an adrenal problem, a hormonal imbalance, or a tumor. If MFTs treat these issues using psychotherapy, they opens the door for an accusation of treating below the standard of care. Eating disorders place the client at risk because of the possibility of an unpredictable heart attack in anorexia or a possible burst aneurism in bulimia. Only a physician can rule out the possibility of immediate risk of death in both conditions and hospitalize as necessary.

Consulting with psychiatrists when the client presents a mental disorder that can benefit from medication is of primary importance. Only psychiatrists can assess and provide psychotropic medication. MFTs providing any treatment without a psychiatric consultation, when warranted, are considered as practicing below the standard of care. Consulting with previous mental health care providers is considered part of the standard of care protocol. This is significant because these clinicians can hold important information regarding the client's previous clinical history. In one case, a treating psychotherapist providing treatment to a severely distraught client failed to consult with the previous psychotherapist. Had he done so, he would have found that this client had attempted five non-lethal suicide actions and was hospitalized after each attempt. Had he known these facts about his client, he would have been more aggressive in attempting to manage her risk of suicide. Instead, his laxity allowed the client to try a sixth attempt, which ended in her death. He faced malpractice action for wrongful death and had difficulty explaining how he practiced below the standard of care. Other significant consultations include providers of substance related treatment, if present. This information is extremely important; it helps rule out complicating factors, which could impede current treatment. Other consultations may be required and these depend on the presenting clinical history and psychosocial factors.

There are times when clients refuse to comply with a request for consultation or with a referral to a physician or a psychiatrist. When this happens, it serves MFTs to document the refusal and consider this refusal as a clinical issue that must be addressed as part of the immediate treatment. It could be that the client is challenging the MFT's boundaries. If so, it serves the clinician to maintain appropriate boundaries regarding these referrals and requests for consultation. If the client continues to refuse to cooperate, MFTs must ask themselves if they are willing to jeopardize their careers by providing treatment that falls below the standard of care. An appropriate informed consent document serves to inform the client that lack of cooperation serves as grounds for the termination of treatment and appropriate referrals provided for continuity of treatment. Of course, ending treatment and providing referrals can only take place if the client does not present a risk to self/others. It serves MFTs to document the client's mental and emotional state should treatment terminate because the client refused to comply.

Observable Clinical Behavior

When clients face crisis issues, it is likely that they are expressing a degree of emotional reactivity. Each client expresses affect and emotions in a unique manner depending on a variety of factors. It is important that MFTs begin identifying the cluster of presenting clinical behaviors and their duration associated with the crisis issue at hand. Clinicians must do so because this documentation serves to establish a baseline for future comparison, to determine the progress of treatment. In addition, the clinician uses these clinical behaviors as part of the overall assessment, as a means to determine if immediate action is required to stabilize the client to prevent him or her from harming him/herself or others, such as immediate hospitalization. Failing to document presenting clinical behaviors and their duration supports an accusation of failing to assess the client properly and of practicing below the standard of care. Of specific concern to clinicians are the following clinical behaviors: a) hopelessness, b) loss of pleasure or interest, c) mood cycling, d) impulsivity, e) suicidal ideation and f) homicidal ideation. The scientific literature has associated these behaviors with a high degree of risk to self/ others.

Psychosocial Stressors and Environmental Problems

The DSM 5 defines psychosocial stressors and environmental problems as being negative life events, environmental difficulties or deficiencies, a personal or interpersonal stress, limited social support system or personal resources, or any other problem relating to the context in which a person's difficulties have developed (DSM 5, 2013).

These factors can potentiate a presenting clinical issue into becoming a crisis issue. For example, the loss of a job, the loss of a marriage, an impending divorce, the loss of a loved one, financial difficulties, etc., can lead a client to experience destabilization in their current life. Should the stressor be severe enough to diminish the client's ability to manage the immediate challenge, then he or she can react emotionally and transition into destructive behavior directed at self and/or others.

In documenting the current psychosocial stressor, the clinician attempts to distinguish and identify those factors that serve to diminish the client's ability to cope with stress. The clinician can use these to assess the strength of the client's external and internal structure of safety and available resources. For example, a client presenting with a limited social structure with a lack of available relatives, siblings, spouse, or children, with illness, with use of alcohol or drugs, or who lacks other available resources may present a greater degree of emotional reactivity that can lead to a crisis issue. Clinicians must be aware of how psychosocial stressors affect potential crisis issues and address these as necessary during the management of the crisis issue.

Culturally Sensitive Assessments

When managing crisis issues, MFTs must take into consideration cultural factors as these relate to the presenting crisis issue. Cultural manifestation of emotional pain takes place in different forms. This pain can appear as acute stress, anxiety, worry, somatization, denial, stoicism, obsessions, projection, sublimation, or in other forms. Regardless of how it is manifested, the clinician has the legal and ethical therapeutic duty to be cognizant of how each culture manifests emotional pain when he or she provides treatment to a client who relates from a specific cultural framework or belief system.

When treating culturally sensitive clients, it is important to remember that the predominant zeitgeist may not be appropriate when assessing, diagnosing, and treating crisis issues presented by these clients. For example, when managing suicidality the model of "sharing" feelings utilized by non hispanic psychotherapists is deficient in understanding the emotional manifestations expressed by a bilingual and bicultural Mexican-American client. This is generally true from the anthropological perspective that men from this culture do not "open" themselves up nor share their true feelings to anyone, especially those feeling arising from a perceived weakness such as depression. Some view this expression as a sign of loss of manhood and as a great shame when a woman witnesses this. Thus, should this client deny suicidal ideation or wanting to harm another party, a reasonable and prudent clinician takes time to explore this denial within the client's cultural perspective.

Specific ethical standards further clarify the duty placed upon clinicians who treat culturally sensitive clients. For example, MFTs are ethically mandated, per CAMFT Ethical Standards 3.6 and 3.7 to understand the interaction of culture, be educated about the client's cultural values, and continue developing their scope of competence when treating culturally sensitive clients. MFTs who avoid this therapeutic duty can be considered as exhibiting unprofessional conduct, which is a legal violation of the Business and Professions Code related to gross negligence in the duties of MFTs.

An expert witness will likely state that a psychotherapist or counselor will meet the standard of care by following these steps:

- Understand the cultural undercurrents of the client's culture passed on as part of the transgenerational transmission process and can manifest themselves in the clients cultural psyche.
- Assess and diagnose the interplay of cultural values and the presenting crisis issues.
- The process of assessment, diagnosis, and treatment must address ethical guidelines and reflect standard of care.
- The process of assessment, diagnosis, and treatment considers and incorporates the client's foundational cultural issues.
- The treating therapist or counselor obtains appropriate consultation when treating such clients.

If MFTs are unable or unwilling to provide standard of care, they refer in an appropriate manner.

Assessing For Risk Factors

The scientific literature is clear on this issue: clinicians cannot predict that client will harm him/herself and/or others. However, the same literature established that MFTs have a requirement to recognize risk factors that can lead to actions resulting in harm to self and/or others. Upon recognizing these risk factors, MFTs must take appropriate action to protect the life of the client and/or others who are at risk of harm (Bellah v. Greenson, 1978; Tarasoff, 1976).

MFTs must rely on observable clinical factors when attempting to assess the potential of harm to self and/or others. The value of these clinical factors is much greater for short-term assessment than for long-term determination of harm. Legal experts agree that a reasonable and prudent clinician considers these clinical factors as they relate to acts that may result in the harm to self and/or others. First, MFTs assess the therapeutic relationship potential (strong v. weak or non-existent). Next, meaningful social relationships (present v. non-present) are considered. MFTs integrate the history of previous acts to harm self or others (number of attempts into the assessment protocol. The degree of harm, intent to harm, plan to harm are viewed carefully. In addition, the client's physical distress or illness present is determined. Any present Axis I or Axis II mental disorders are assessed. Finally, attention is paid to short-term and long-term psychosocial stressors present (short-term include loss of job, divorce, death of family member, grave illness, etc. Long-term include ongoing illness, long-term unemployment, loss of socioeconomic status, etc.), demographic data associated with high risk of harm to self/others.

Assessing for these risk factors requires conducting a personal interview with the client, obtaining collateral interviews of relatives or significant others, obtaining previous medical, mental health, and substance-related treatment information, completing a Mental Status Exam, Beck Depression Inventory and any other necessary psychometric testing, and reviewing the complete clinical history of the client.

Documenting risk factors involves identifying elements of the client's clinical history that points to an increase risk of harm to self and/or others. For example, the clinician determines if the client fits into a high-risk or low-risk group based on the client's race, marital status, and living situation. Also, the clinician would establish any previous actions taken by the client that identify him or her with a high-risk group, such as having committed previous acts of harm to self and/or others. Additionally, it's important to identify and document statements made by the client that imply having an immediate plan of action, a weapon, or serious intent to harm him/herself and/or others.

A treatment plan identifying the proposed goals and objectives to resolve the crisis issue serves both as a documentation of appropriate treatment, as an assessment tool to determine if the proposed treatment is effective, and to assess the progress of the client. Not having such a treatment plan presents the MFT as practicing below the standard of care (See Dinnerstein v. State, 1973). It is also reasonable and prudent for the clinician to document continuing changes in mental and affective states as often as required. The best tools to accomplish this task are the Mental Status Exam and the Beck Depression Inventory. Not having this degree of documentation indicates that the clinician is practicing below the standard of care.

Establishing An Appropriate DSM 5 Diagnosis

One of the legal foundations for malpractice actions against clinician is the lack of appropriate diagnosis. Attorneys strongly take the position that MFTs must take reasonable and prudent steps in making a diagnosis. For example, what steps did MFTs take to determine that the client was suicidal (Dillman v. Hellman, 1973)? An appropriate diagnosis involves obtaining all necessary clinical information, clinical symptoms and their duration. The first diagnostic component identifies mental disorders. The second identifies personality disorders. The third identifies concurrent medical conditions. The fourth identifies current psychosocial stressors. The fifth identifies current Global Assessment of Functioning and compares it to last year's level. In addition to establishing the mental disorder, adding the other four component strengthens the clinician's diagnostic protocol.

It is prudent for MFTs to accurately identify those observable clinical behaviors and their duration supporting a given diagnosis. For example, if MFTs identify the client as presenting a major depressive episode it is reasonable that the identified clinical behaviors would be: a) social isolation, b) flat affect, c) overeating or under eating, d) oversleeping or insomnia, and e) suicidal ideation. These clinical symptoms would have lasted for a period of at least two weeks. When diagnosing any mental disorder that is associated with a possibility that the client will exhibit harm to self and/or others, MFTs must be aware that their therapeutic duty increases and they must take any necessary steps to prevent potential harm. When questioning MFTs during a deposition, opposing attorneys will ask them how they developed a diagnosis and their documentation.

The Presenting Crisis Issue

A crisis issue is a presenting clinical issue that involves an actual or potential physical or emotional threat to the well being of the client and/or to others who are or are not directly involved in the actual treatment. For example, a client may be contemplating suicide or may be taking actual steps towards committing suicide. Another example involves a client who presents with an undefined eating disorder. A third example involves a client who tells the clinician he is extremely angry with his girlfriend and will make sure "she learns her lesson for cheating on me." The dynamics involved in a crisis issue reflect the following: a) a threat or perceived threat, b) the clinical context of the crisis issue, and c) the potential outcome of the crisis issue. The threat could be a direct or perceived threat of direct or potential injury to the client or to others involved in some manner with the client. The overt or covert threat is also expressed through acts of omission or commission.

Examples of overt threats of injury follow: a) A parent sexually abusing his or her child, b) A young woman showing signs of an eating disorder in a family gathering, c) An adolescent telling his friends he is considering suicide, d) A man telling his neighbor "You're going to pay for this," after a dispute. Examples of indirect threats are: a) A thin young woman in therapy asks her MFT if she has ever considered hospitalization for a client, b) a depressed client asks a therapist: "Is it wrong for clients to kill themselves?" and c) an adolescent "innocently" asks his therapist: "What would you do if you ever found out one of your clients was sexually abused by a relative?" Should clients ask indirect questions such as these, MFTs must clarify the intent of the question and rule out any possible threat of harm to self and/or others. Not doing so means that MFTs failed in their duty to assess the client appropriately.

These issues require special attention in order to address the safety of the client and other people. If these issues are present at the beginning of therapy, MFTs address them immediately before they provide any other treatment. Should a crisis issue arise during the course of therapy, it takes precedence over other issues and MFTs deal with it immediately. Crisis issues, by their nature, place a higher degree of responsibility on MFTs. They must have the scope of competence to recognize and address these issues in a safe manner. Their duty is to create safety, structure, and stability when crisis issues are present. Legal therapeutic duty requires that the treatment plan reflect the specific treatment that is required to manage the crisis issue. Additionally, it is extremely important to document the decision-making process that MFTs follow to manage crisis issues. The latter serves as a means to establish that MFTs acted in a reasonable and prudent manner when managing the presenting crisis.

When managing crisis issues, MFTs determine which legal and ethical guidelines apply specifically to the immediate crisis. Next, they assess the full potential impact his or her legal or ethical decision will have on treatment and the therapeutic relationship. Finally, MFTs gather all necessary information and utilize it to make an appropriate treatment plan to manage the crisis issue. MFTs understand and apply California laws and professional ethical standards as they apply to crisis issues. These include the Child Abuse Law (Penal Code 11164–11174.3), Elder and Dependent Abuse Law (Welfare and Institutions Code 15600-15755), Tarasoff Case Law, Civil Code 49.82, Evidence Code 1024, and other Case laws that apply to crisis issues. Each crisis issue will be discussed more fully in subsequent sections. A more complete list of California laws, CAMFT Ethical Standards follows later in this chapter.

The Emergency "Plan of Action" To Manage Crisis Issues

Should a crisis issue arise, having a clinical "plan of action" is one of the best preventive measures for MFTs. The components of such a plan involve the following:

- Assessment protocols to determine the seriousness of the crisis issue.
- Diagnostic protocols to label the seriousness of the crisis issue.
- Treatment protocols to manage the crisis issue.
- Available collateral resources to extend and strengthen the treatment team.
- Post-care management protocols to extend the safety net after the immediate crisis issue is managed.

Malpractice attorneys only accept a case against a mental health clinician when the case has merit due to the alleged injury suffered by the client. Opposing attorneys seek cases where MFTs fail to document their scope of competence or their assessment, diagnosis, and treatment required to meet the standard of care. Imagine an attorney who is considering initiating a malpractice against a mental health clinician. This attorney reviews the subpoenaed mental health records. As the attorney reads the records, he or she finds that the clinician had an emergency "plan of action" in place that preceded the crisis issue and had planned his or her management of crisis issue according to this plan. This attorney would not want to become involved in this case; his or her determination would be that the chances of winning this case are minimal. The applicable lesson for clinicians is to create an emergency "plan of action" prior to the onset of any clinical crisis issues and practice it on a regularly basis.

Applicable California Laws in Managing Crisis and High Risk Issues

The following laws relate to crisis issues. These provide the legal standard of care for mental health clinicians. These apply directly to licensed clinicians.

Business and Professions Code 4982 (m) (Confidentiality and MFTs) Unprofessional conduct includes the failure to maintain confidentiality, except as otherwise required or permitted by law, of all information that has been received from a client in confidence during the course of treatment and all information about the client that is obtained from tests or other means.

Business and Professions Code 4982 (d) (For MFTs - Unprofessional Conduct and Practicing Below the Standard of Care): A clinician that provided treatment or services that fall below the standard of considered as acting illegally action and with unprofessional conduct.

Business and Professions Code 4982 (i) (For MFTs - Unprofessional Conduct and Harming a Client Physically or Emotionally): A clinical action by an MFT that causes physical or emotional harm is considered an illegal action and unprofessional conduct.

Business and Professions Code 4982(v) (Unprofessional Conduct and Mental Health Records): Not keeping mental health records that meet the standard of care is considered illegal and unprofessional conduct.

Evidence Code 1024 (Confidentiality and Danger to Self/Others): A psychotherapist is permitted to break confidentiality when a client's mental or emotional state is such that this person presents a danger to self or others, or the property of others.

Penal Code 11600-11163.2 (Reporting Spousal Abuse in Medical Settings): Anyone who is employed by a physician, a licensed health clinic, or a licensed health facility and provides direct medical care to clients must report stated spousal abuse. This law applies to physicians and emergency rooms. They must report observed bruises to the police.

Civil Code 43.92 (Defines the Mandated Reporting for Tarasoff): A psychotherapist must take reasonable steps to warn the identifiable victim and the police of the intended crime. Be sure to document in your case notes the dialogue with the police officer and the identifiable victim.

Welfare and Institutions Code 5150 (Permits an Involuntary Hospitalization): Involuntary hospitalization is permissible when a client's mental or physical state causes him or her to be in imminent danger of harming self or others. The MFT cannot hospitalize a client. Only a physician is permitted to do so.

Bellah v. Greenson (Case Law-Standard of Care for Suicide Management): There is no duty to protect and warn (Tarasoff) in a suicide situation; however, a psychotherapist must take reasonable steps to protect the life of his or her client.

Tarasoff v. Regents of UC (Case Law-Duty to Protect in a Serious Threat to Harm): A psychotherapist must use reasonable care to protect and warn third parties who have been identified as possible victims of a serious threat to harm versus a threat of serious harm. A serious threat is real and imminent. Also, the third party must be unaware of the threat.

Thompson v. Alameda (Case Law-Duty to Warn Extends Only to Identifiable Victims): The object of the duty to warn applies only to identifiable victims.

Hedlund v. Superior Court of Orange County (Case Law-Extends the Duty to Report Under Tarasoff to Specific Persons): The object of the duty to warn applies only to the identifiable victim. However, if several people live in the same house, they may all be identifiable victims if the perpetrator conducts a random shooting and all may be hurt.

Ewing v. Goldstein (Case Law-Expands The Meaning of "Communications" under Tarasoff and Civil Code 43.92): Communications from a client's intimate family member regarding the client's serious threat to harm (Tarasoff) can be sufficient to activate the duty to warn under Tarasoff and Civil Code 43.92

Calderon v. Glick (Case Law-Defines Limits of Duty to Warn): Psychotherapists must make a mandated breach of confidentiality only when the legally-defined conditions exists.

Dinnerstein vs. State, 1973 (Requires treatment plans for clinical services): Not having such a treatment plan would be considered that the clinician practicing is below the standard of care.

Penal Code 11165–11174 (Defines Mandated Reporting for Child Abuse): This law states that physical and sexual abuse must be reported immediately by phone to Child Protective Services and in writing within 36 hours to the same agency when "one acquires knowledge of or observes facts which give rise to a reasonable suspicion." Neglect that causes harm to the child's welfare or health must also be reported. "Reasonable suspicion" occurs when "it is objectively reasonable for a person to entertain such a suspicion, based upon facts that could cause a reasonable person in a like position, drawing when appropriate on his or her training and experience, to suspect child abuse." As of January 1, 1998, the law was amended to include two reportable categories: (a) it is unlawful to have sexual intercourse (even if it consensual) with a child under the age of 16 (determined by birth date) when the perpetrator is over the age of 21 years (determined by birth date), and (b) lewd and lascivious acts with a child of 14 or 15 years of age is a crime when the perpetrator is more than 10 years (determined by birth date) older than the victim.

Welfare and Institutions Code 15600-15755 (Defines Mandated Reporting for Elder/Dependent Abuse): Elder abuse refers to one or more of the following acts inflicted by other than accidental means on an elder by another person: physical abuse, fiduciary abuse, neglect, or abandonment. WIC 15630: Defines "dependent adult" as any person between the ages of 18 and 64 who has physical or mental limitations that restrict his or her ability to carry out the normal activities of daily living or to protect his or her own rights. Physical abuse, neglect, abandonment, isolation, abduction, and financial abuse are required to be reported. Additionally, other forms of non-mandated abuse may be reported when the mandated reporter reasonably suspects that this abuse is taking place.

CAMFT Ethical Standards and Crisis Issues

CAMFT Ethical Standard 1: Marriage and family therapists do not condone or engage in discrimination, or refuse professional service to anyone on the basis of race, gender, religion, national origin, age, sexual orientation, disability, socioeconomic, or marital status. Marriage and family therapists make reasonable efforts to accommodate patients who have physical disabilities.

This standard requires MFTs to assure that their clinical decisions about their clients are made for the best interest of the client and will not cause harm to the client.

CAMFT Ethical Standard 1.4: Marriage and family therapists respect the right of patients to make decisions and help them to understand the consequences of their decisions. When clinically appropriate, marriage and family therapists advise their patients that decisions on the status of their personal relationships, including dissolution, are the responsibilities of the patient(s).

This standard requires that MFTs avoid making decisions for clients and help clients understand the implications and consequences of their personal decisions on their lives and relationships. When clients exhibit actions that can lead to harm of self or others, MFTs discuss with clients the ramifications of their actions on all aspects of their lives and relationships. This standard also requires MFTs to provide informed consent that meets the standard of care.

CAMFT Ethical Standard 2.1: Marriage and family therapists do not disclose patient confidences, including the names or identities of their patients, to anyone except a) as mandated by law b) as permitted by law c) when the marriage and family therapist is a defendant in a civil, criminal, or disciplinary action arising from the therapy (in which case patient confidences may only be disclosed in the course of that action), or d) if there is an authorization previously obtained in writing, and then such information may only be revealed in accordance with the terms of the authorization

This standard complements Business and Professions Code 4982 and other California laws requiring MFTs to maintain confidentiality except when they determine that the client presents with the legally defined clinical conditions that mandate or permit the breaching of confidentiality to protect the client and/or others or when the client presents a danger to self and others. Of importance is the responsibility placed upon MFTs to determine that such a condition exists. Reasonable and prudent MFTs assure that they can document the presenting clinical behaviors or symptoms that create the above condition and how they determine that they must breach confidentiality to protect those involved.

Breaching Confidentiality in a Safe Manner

This standard complements Business and Professions Code 4982 and other California laws requiring MFTs to maintain confidentiality except when they determine that the client presents with the legally defined clinical conditions that mandate or permit the breaching of confidentiality to protect the client and/or others or when the client presents a danger to self and others. Of importance is the responsibility placed upon MFTs to determine that such a condition exists. Reasonable and prudent MFTs assure that they can document the presenting clinical behaviors or symptoms that create the above condition and how they determine that they must breach confidentiality to protect those involved.

- Tarasoff
- Child Abuse,
- Dependent Abuse
- Elder Abuse

The following provide a permitted breach of confidentiality when the legally defined clinical conditions are met (the clinician has the choice to breach confidentiality):

- Danger to self or others (Evidence Code 1024) and include: suicide, dangerous substance abuse, anorexia, and any other condition that meets the Evidence Code 1024 legal definition.

Remember that breaching confidentiality as required or permitted by the above regulations must not be taken lightly. This is a serious step with potentially damaging consequences. Clinicians can be sued for not breaching as well as for breaching confidentiality in the above situations depending on the clinical circumstances. The act of breaching confidentiality as required or permitted by law, must be considered like any other clinical intervention that can be both enhancing and destructive in its potential outcome.

To create safety when considering breaching client confidentiality while managing a crisis issue, reasonable and prudent MFTs remember that they must comply with the therapeutic duty to assess, diagnose, and treat appropriately. The appropriate assessment requires that MFTs obtain all necessary information regarding the crisis issue allowing him or her to be clinically objective. The appropriate diagnosis requires that the clinician review the obtained information and determine if the act of breaching confidentiality serves to satisfy the legal mandate or permission to breach confidentiality. Additionally, MFTs document how they reasoned through the decision of breaching or not breaching confidentiality and how the conditions met the legal requirement in the present case. In a malpractice action, it is important for MFTs to show how they acted as reasonable and prudent clinicians by documenting the reasoning process of how they made the decision to breach or not breach confidentiality.

Hospitalization as a Clinical Intervention

There are times when MFTs have utilized all possible clinical interventions available and they have not been successful in stabilizing the client. At this point, their last option is to consider either voluntary or involuntary hospitalization. Like any other intervention, MFTs must assess, diagnose, and use this intervention according to the standard of care. Doing so means that the clinicians assessed the client's mental or emotional state, the presenting clinical behaviors, all risk factors, the psychosocial stressors, and other important clinical information that lead them to determine that this intervention is reasonable and prudent.

Voluntary hospitalization requires that MFTs invite or direct the client to hospitalize him/herself. Clients carry this out by going to the emergency room or by having his or her physician or psychiatrist initiate the hospitalization protocols. Involuntary hospitalization is initiated through a different procedure. Marriage and family therapists, licensed clinical social workers, alcohol and drug abuse counselors, and certified addictions treatment specialists are not permitted to hospitalize clients. They must rely on Welfare and Institutions Code 5150 for the psychiatric assessment team to hospitalize the client for a 72 hour hold and when MFTs breaching the client's confidentiality under Evidence Code

1024. To create safety in relation to breaching confidentiality under Evidence Code 1024, MFTs must document their assessment protocols, the assessment results, and any other significant information that led them to determine that the client's mental or emotional state presented a danger to self or others and how they carried out this permitted breach.

Post-hospitalization Risk Factors

Once the hospital releases the client, MFTs must be aware of and assess for the possible increased risk of suicide or other harmful behavior that can occur after the client is stabilized. The scientific literature indicates that when clients develop cognitive clarity immediately after being released from the hospital, there is an increase in the risk of harm to self (Bongar, 2002). Prominent researchers, among them Simon (1988), have indicated that clinicians must take the following steps: a) determine the client's ability to participate in their post-discharge follow-up and aggressively integrate the client into a strong interpersonal support system, b) all clinicians, in outpatient and inpatient treatment facilities, must cooperate to assure that the client complies with post-discharge treatment recommendations, and c) inform the client, significant others, and family members that the responsibility for cooperating with follow-up treatment rests on the client. (Adapted from Bongar, 2002). Clinicians who do not document their post-discharge assessment and instructions to clients run the risk of being found liable in a malpractice case for failing to assess, diagnose, and treat according to the standard of care.

Suicide — Specific Laws and Codes: Managing This Issue

Applicable California Laws
Business and Professions Code 4982 (m) (Confidentiality and MFTs)
Business and Professions Code 4982 (d) (Practicing Below the Standard of Care and MFTs)
Business and Professions Code 4982 (i) (Harming a client and MFTs)
Business and Professions Code 4982 (v) (Failure to keep appropriate records and MFTs)
Evidence Code 1024
Bellah v. Greenson (Case Law)
Welfare and Institutions Code 5150
Dinnerstein vs. State, 1973

Applicable Ethical Standards
CAMFT Ethical Standard 2.1

The Malpractice Challenge: MFTs face a unique dilemma when they encounter a high-risk issue involving the possibility of suicide. Should the client present marginal symptoms of depression, MFTs must consider that these can explode into full blown depression with accompanying suicidal ideation or suicidal intent. If the client commits suicide, the client's family will likely challenge MFTs in court for failure to protect their loved one. Conversely, an MFTs thwarts a client's attempt to commit suicide even though the client shared this information with expected confidentiality. The client truly wanted to die and now feels betrayed by the MFT. His sense of betrayal turns into anger, which is directed against the MFT in a malpractice action for inappropriate breach of confidentiality.

Managing this issue: Suicide can become a crisis issue at any time during therapy, even though the client present minor and insignificant depressive symptoms. It may become a potentially severe clinical challenge due to the client's severe depression, bipolar disorder, or other complicating factor causing an emotional collapse. MFTs have the therapeutic duty to a) assess, b) diagnose, and c) treat appropriately throughout the duration of treatment and especially during the crisis phase. MFTs attend to the consideration that suicide is a possibility. This sets the stage to prevent the client from killing him/herself. For example, an MFT obtains the necessary information during assessment phase and identifies minor depressive symptoms, severe depression, suicidal ideation, or suicidal intent. Doing so prepares MFTs to determine if the minor depressive symptoms will become suicidal intent. These MFTs begin with the first step of referring the client to a physician to rule out physical problems that can present as depression. Second, MFTs refer to a psychiatrist for evaluation and possible medication. Should the client present with suicidal behavior during any other phase of treatment, clinicians redirect the focus of treatment to manage and prevent the possible suicide. Other steps MFTs can take to decrease the suicide potential include, though are not limited to, increasing the number of therapy sessions, establishing telephone contact between sessions, considering obtaining a "suicide action plan" with the client (this intervention doesn't conform to the standard of care), help the client stabilize eating and sleeping patterns, working with the client to increase social or family contacts, and consider voluntary hospitalization.

Despite the best preventive steps, at times, these interventions are insufficient and the therapist faces a client who is in imminent danger of suicide. Now, the stakes are much higher and the therapist has a greater responsibility. When the therapist believes that breaching confidentiality is necessary to prevent the suicide of a client, Evidence Code 1024 permits this breach confidentiality, this case law allows MFTs to breach confidentiality. The therapist may decide that it is necessary to contact one or more family members, a significant other or the Psychiatric Evaluation Team. Since this is an important decision, MFTs may decide to consult with other professionals to confirm and plan for another intervention. Complete documentation of each step regarding suicidality helps to maintain clarity and to protect them.

MFTs must remember that when opposing attorneys initiate a lawsuit on behalf of a client, they consider breaching confidentiality under Evidence Code 1024 as the foundation of their lawsuit of inappropriate breach of confidentiality. To avoid supporting the opposing attorney's legal case, this high-risk clinical intervention must be put into perspective according to Bellah v. Greenson. The latter requires that the clinician take reasonable steps to protect the life of the client. Thus, it is imperative that MFTs document how they determined that the client met the legal conditions to breach his or her confidentiality. Additionally, MFTs only breach confidentiality to manage the imminent suicidality. If these attorneys sue MFTs for either breaching or not breaching confidentiality depending on the circumstances, this level of documentation serves to show that they acted in a reasonable and prudent manner in managing this difficult clinical situation.

Serious Threat of Harm to An Identifiable Victim (Tarasoff Situation) — Specific Laws and Codes: Managing This Issue

Applicable California Laws
Business and Professions Code 4982 (m) (Confidentiality and MFTs)
Business and Professions Code 4982 (d) (Practicing Below the Standard of Care and MFTs)
Business and Professions Code 4982 (i) (Harming a client and MFTs)
Business and Professions Code 4982 (v) (Failure to keep appropriate records and MFTs)
Tarasoff Ruling
Civil Code 43.92
Thompson v. Alameda (Case Law)
Ewing v. Goldstein (Case Law)
Hedlund v. Superior Court of Orange County (Case Law)
Welfare and Institutions Code 5150
Dinnerstein vs. State, 1973

Applicable Ethical Standards
CAMFT Ethical Standard 2.1

The Malpractice Challenge: MFTs face a unique dilemma when they encounter a high-risk issue of a serious threat to harm an identifiable victim. Should the client communicate to an MFT a serious threat to harm, spoken or unspoken, against an identifiable victim or an intimate relative communicates the same information to this therapist, the MFT is mandated to report this serious threat. MFTs face the challenge in having to protect the identifiable victim and at the same time, assuring that the breach of confidentiality does not harm to the person making the threat because it was an unfounded breach of confidentiality or it did not meet the legal requirements for reporting. The answer lies in having appropriate documentation of assessment, diagnosis, and interventions to manage this issue.

Managing this issue: A serious threat to harm is considered as a threat against a person's physical well-being. It includes a plan and a weapon, it is imminent, and physical harm will arise if the psychotherapist fails to intervene. When a client notifies MFTs of a serious threat to harm another person or persons, or an intimate family member (Ewing v. Goldstein) communicates the same threat the relative/client, MFTs are mandated to call a law enforcement agency and take reasonable steps to warn the intended victim or victims. The law requires that the identifiable victim must not know about the threat and, therefore, cannot take steps to protect him/herself and threat to harm is serious. The threat can be "communicated" in one of two ways: spoken or unspoken. Unspoken communications include previous acts of violence directed against identifiable individuals and the "client" continues to returns to the same location where the same victims reside and these do not know that he continues to pose a serious threat to harm (Jablonki v. United States, 1983). MFTs have the responsibility of determining that the threat of physical harm is serious (as defined above) and imminent.

When a serious threat of harm is communicated to MFTs, reasonable and prudent clinicians ask: "In this situation, do I have a duty to protect the identifiable victim under Tarasoff?" MFTs act prudently when they document how they determined whether they have a duty to protect. MFTs document how they reasoned their decision to report or not report. The process includes assessing several variables including: personality traits of the client, history of violent behavior, the threat being credible and reasonable, the client having a plan and a weapon, establishing the client's relationship to the identifiable victim, and obtaining previous mental health records and reviewing prior treatment. This documentation serves to protect MFTs should they face a lawsuit for breach of confidentiality and/or a client's reputation in the community because of making the report.

If MFTs determine that they have a duty to protect, the next step is to comply with Evidence Code 43.92, which requires that they contact a law enforcement agency and provide sufficient information regarding the serious threat, it's context, the clinician's rationale for determining that this is a serious threat, identifying information regarding the client and the identifiable victim including names, addresses, phone numbers, identifying features if available, relationship between client and identifiable victim, plan and weapon, and previous history of violence only as it relates to the present threat and no more. Next, MFTs take "reasonable" steps to contact the identifiable victim. Reasonable steps include making a phone call to the identifiable victim if the clinician has the identifiable victim's telephone number available, leaving a message on the identifiable victim's answering machine asking him or her to call the clinician immediately, or sending a "next-day" certified letter if only a mailing address is available. If a telephone number or address is not available to the clinician, this information is provided to the police and this likely satisfies the "reasonable" requirement.

It serves MFTs to consult experienced colleagues or attorneys who have the scope of competence in this arena before making a mandated report. These clinical situations are unpredictable, thus it serves MFTs to "practice" these clinical possibilities with colleagues, develop the scope of competence to recognize risk factors that can predict violence, and maintain mental health records that meet the standard of care. These would document the MFTs' therapeutic duty of assessing, diagnosing, and treating appropriately throughout the duration of therapy. MFTs lacking this scope of competence will become easy prey for opposing attorneys.

Spousal Abuse — Specific Laws and Codes: Managing This Issue

Applicable California Laws
Business and Professions Code 4982 (m) (Confidentiality and MFTs)
Business and Professions Code 4982 (d) (Practicing Below the Standard of Care and MFTs)
Business and Professions Code 4982 (i) (Harming a client and MFTs)
Business and Professions Code 4982 (v) (Failure to keep appropriate records and MFTs)
Penal Code 11160-11163.2
Dinnerstein vs. State, 1973

Applicable Ethical Standards
CAMFT Ethical Standard 1
CAMFT Ethical Standard 1.4

The Malpractice Challenge: MFTs face a unique dilemma when they encounter spousal abuse as a high-risk issue. Though MFTs are not legally mandated to report spousal abuse, the challenge occurs when the abuser hurts the abusee severely or kills him or her. At this point, MFTs face several possibilities than can lead to a malpractice action. In the first situation, the immediate family members of the dead person can sue the clinician for failure to protect. In the second situation, the injured client recovers and sues the MFT for failure to protect. In the third situation, the MFT reports the abuser and he or she sues the clinician for breaching confidentiality illegally and causing harm.

Managing this issue: Spousal or domestic abuse is the physical attack of a spouse or domestic partner upon the other. Penal Code 11160-11162.2, the mandated reporting law for domestic abuse, does not apply to MFTs, since they do not provide direct medical care. However, when MFTs encounter a client abused by his or her spouse, they use specific ethical standards to protect the client. First, they ascertain that the condition is indeed spousal abuse and establish that they do not have a mandate to report. Next, they consider referring the client to the client's physician or the emergency room. The medical personnel in these facilities have a mandate to report the abuse under Evidence Code 1194 when they observe it or know that the abuser caused these injuries. MFTs who are aware that spousal abuse is taking place must discuss the pros and cons of staying in the abusive relationship. When clients request information about how to leave the abusive relationship, MFTs provide the client with the phone number of the nearest shelter, help the client prepare a plan of escape, which includes setting aside money, keys and clothes in case physical abuse reoccurs and the client must flee.

There are times when clinicians may witness spousal violence in the treatment room. In these situations, MFTs must keep themselves safe. If injured, they are useless to anyone, especially the victim and to themselves. Should the clinician face an abusive situation in the treatment room, they determine if they are in immediate danger. If so, then exiting the room and calling the police or 911 immediately are prudent actions. The police receive training to manage this type of situation, whereas MFTs do not. Calling the police or 911 breaches the client's confidentiality. At this moment, MFTs rely on Evidence Code 1024 to provide them the appropriate venue. This breach of confidentiality intends to manage the very real and immediate danger of harm to others by the actively abusive client. The appropriate documentation of the rationale used to breach or not breach confidentiality is paramount to protect MFTs should they face a malpractice action.

Child Abuse — Specific Laws and Codes: Managing This Issue

<u>Applicable California Laws</u>

Business and Professions Code 4982 (m) (Confidentiality and MFTs)
Business and Professions Code 4982 (d) (Practicing Below the Standard of Care and MFTs)
Business and Professions Code 4982 (i) (Harming a client and MFTs)
Business and Professions Code 4982 (v) (Failure to keep appropriate records and MFTs)
Penal Code 11164–11174.3
Dinnerstein vs. State, 1973

<u>Applicable Ethical Standards</u>

CAMFT Ethical Standard 1
CAMFT Ethical Standard 1.4

The Malpractice Challenge: MFTs face a unique dilemma when they encounter child abuse as a high-risk issue. MFTs, as mandated reporters of child abuse, can face a malpractice action from an opposing attorney because his or her client, the reported party, claims injury resulting from the mandated report. The attorney's claim centers on the MFT making an erroneous or inaccurate report that fails to meet the legal requirements. Conversely, an MFT refuses to make a mandated report because he or she determines that a "reasonable" suspicion does not exist and he or she can support his or her rationale for making this decision. A few yeas later, the then "minor" who is now an adult initiates a malpractice action against the MFT for failing to make a mandated report and failing to protect her from abuse that took place several years after terminating treatment with the MFT.

Managing this issue: MFTs, when acting in their capacity as licensed psychotherapists, are mandated to report a "reasonable" suspicion of child abuse or observed abuse to Child welfare Services. MFTs make the report immediately by phone or fax and within 36 hours in writing. Mandated reporters do not investigate the validity of the suspicion. That task is the responsibility of Child Welfare

Services. If the then "minor" is now over the age of 18, then he or she is no longer a minor and this law is not applicable. However, if he or she tells the mandated reporter that the alleged abuser is still in contact with children, this law attempts to protect the children exposed to the potential abuse and the MFT reports the reasonable suspicion of abuse.

Mandated reporters receive "immunity" when making a child abuse report. However, to receive this benefit, clinicians must follow the legal reporting requirements carefully. Additionally, clinicians must succeed in the lawsuit against them and then will MFTs receive $50,000 to pay for legal expenses. MFTs can face legal action when they make mandated child abuse reports. These include the breach of the therapeutic contract when clinicians promise confidentiality and do not discuss the limits of confidentiality in their informed consent document. In addition, the alleged abuser believes that the MFT harmed his or her reputation in the community when he or she made an "unfounded" report. Next, the client's parents claim that the MFT breached their confidentiality when the report did not meet a level establishing a "reasonable" suspicion of abuse. In addition, an MFT accused of practicing below the standard of care can also face an accusation of loss of clinical objectivity, which can appear as gross negligence. This accusation expands the opposing attorneys premise that the MFT failed to rely on a rational basis for his or her decision and ultimately caused harm to the plaintiff. Even if MFTs win the legal challenge, they will face a daunting and extremely uncomfortable experience for the duration of the legal action.

To protect themselves, MFTs assure themselves that they document their rationale for making a report based on a supportable premise regardless of whether they make the report. Ultimately, only the appropriate documentation of the components discussed can serve to protect MFTs.

Elder and Dependent Abuse — Specific Laws and Codes: Managing This Issue

Applicable California Laws
Business and Professions Code 4982 (m) (Confidentiality and MFTs)
Business and Professions Code 4982 (d) (Practicing Below the Standard of Care and MFTs)
Business and Professions Code 4982 (i) (Harming a client and MFTs)
Business and Professions Code 4982 (v) (Failure to keep appropriate records and MFTs)
Welfare and Institutions Code 15600-15755:
Dinnerstein vs. State, 1973

Applicable Ethical Standards
CAMFT Ethical Standard 1
CAMFT Ethical Standard 1.4

The Malpractice Challenge: MFTs face a unique dilemma when they encounter elder/dependent abuse as a high-risk issue. MFTs, as mandated reporters of elder/dependent abuse, can face a malpractice action from an opposing attorney because his or her client, the reported party, claims injury resulting from the mandated report. The attorney's claim centers on MFTs making an erroneous or inaccurate report that fails to meet the legal requirements. Conversely, an MFT refuses to make a mandated report because he or she determines that a "reasonable" suspicion does not exist and he or she can support his or her rationale for making this decision. A few yeas later, the client's guardian initiates a malpractice action against the MFT for failing to make a mandated report and failing to protect her loved one from abuse that took place several years after the session with the MFT.

Managing this issue: Licensed MFTs are mandated to report adult (age 65 and over) and dependent (between 18-64 years of age) abuse to Adult Protective Services. MFTs are required to report immediately by phone or fax and within 2 working days in writing. Thus, clinician is required to determine that a "reasonable" suspicion exists that abuse (physical, sexual, physical neglect, abandonment, financial abuse, or abduction) has taken place or is taking place. In addition, if MFTs have direct knowledge of abuse, they have a duty to report. For example, an MFT witnessed an abusive act while functioning as a licensed psychotherapist. Mandated reporters do not investigate the validity of the suspicion. That task is the responsibility of Adult Protective Services.

Mandated reporters receive "immunity" when making an elder/dependent abuse report. However, to receive this benefit, clinicians must follow the legal reporting requirements carefully. Additionally, clinicians must succeed in the lawsuit against them and then MFTs will receive $50,000 to pay for legal expenses. MFTs can face legal action when they make mandated child abuse reports. These include the breach of the therapeutic contract when clinicians promise confidentiality and do not discuss the limits of confidentiality in their informed consent document. In addition, the alleged abuser believes that the MFT harmed his or her reputation in the community when the clinician made an "unfounded" report. Next, the client's parents claim that the MFT breached their confidentiality when the report did not meet a level establishing a "reasonable" suspicion of abuse. In addition, MFTs accused of practicing below the standard of care can also face an accusation of loss of clinical objectivity, which can appear as gross negligence. This accusation expands the opposing attorneys premise that MFTs failed to rely on a rational basis for their decision and ultimately caused harm to the plaintiff. Even if MFTs win the legal challenge, they will face a daunting and extremely uncomfortable experience for the duration of the legal action.

HIV-Positive Clients — Managing This Issue

Applicable California Laws
Business and Professions Code 4982 (m) (Confidentiality and MFTs)
Business and Professions Code 4982 (d) (Practicing Below the Standard of Care and MFTs)
Business and Professions Code 4982 (i) (Harming a client and MFTs)
Business and Professions Code 4982 (v) (Failure to keep appropriate records and MFTs)
American With Disabilities Act (Federal Law)
Dinnerstein vs. State, 1973

Applicable Ethical Standards
CAMFT Ethical Standard 2.1

The Malpractice Challenge: Providing treatment to HIV infected clients can present a malpractice challenge to MFTs. The basic issue relates to unintended breach of confidentiality and this possibility increases exponentially as the number of individuals managing this information increases. Should MFTs release the client's HIV status to a third party without intention and injures the client, they can expect an opposing attorney to initiate legal action to pay for the resulting employment, medical insurance, and medical discrimination.

Managing this issue: The Americans With Disabilities Act requires mental health clinicians to protect the confidentiality of a client's seropositive or seropositive HIV status. Aside from the California confidentiality requirements, MFTs must assure that this information will be protected anytime a third party requests mental health records. MFTs must remember that thirds parties have a right to access client records when they have a valid subpoena, an appropriate release of information document, or their medical insurance company holds an appropriate release. The bind for MFTs involves having the duty to maintain appropriate records with important client information and simultaneously must protect this information. MFTs can solve this dilemma by maintaining appropriate records with the HIV information left out from the general records. They can also keept the sensitive information in a separate folder within the chart. Should a third party subpoena the records, this party only receives the general information. If MFTs are challenged in court for failing to provide complete information, they can request that their attorney speak to the judge and explain the dilemma. Of concern involves the same situation in a practice with a large number of employees who may release this information without meaning to. The repercussions can affect MFTs quite negatively. Educating these employess benefits all those involved.

At this time, clinicians are not permitted or mandated to breach confidentiality when an infected client threatens to infect others as a form of attack or retaliation. The courts have not yet determined the impact of Evidence Code 1024 nor the Tarasoff ruling regarding this issue. In this situation, MFTs may choose to refer the client to a physician who is permitted by law to warn those in danger of exposure to HIV of the danger. The clinician can take reasonable and prudent steps to address this issue.

Eating Disorders — Specific Laws and Codes: Managing this Issue

Applicable California Laws
Business and Professions Code 4982 (Confidentiality and MFTs)
Evidence Code 1024
Bellah v. Greenson (Case Law)
Welfare and Institutions Code 5150
Dinnerstein vs. State, 1973

Applicable Ethical Standards
CAMFT Ethical Standard 2.1

The Malpractice Challenge: MFTs face a unique dilemma when they encounter a high-risk issue involving the possibility of harm to self. Should the client present anorexia or bulimia with accompanying symptoms, MFTs must consider that these can explode into a heart attack or ruptured aneurism. If the client dies from one of these physical conditions, the client's family will likely challenge the treating MFTs in court for failure to protect their loved one. Conversely, MFTs breach confidentiality to protect their client; the client may initiate a legal action in retaliation for the hospitalization against their will.

Managing this issue: Eating disorders can become a crisis issue at any time during therapy. The potential death occurs from a fatal heart attack in anorexia and a ruptured aneurism in bulimia. The former contributes to a depletion of minerals required for healthy functioning of the heart leads to a heart attack. The latter leads to an erosion of the esophagus due to the continuous exposure of stomach acid upon regurgitation and cause death due to a burst large blood vessel. MFTs have the therapeutic duty to a) assess, b) diagnose, and c) treat appropriately throughout the duration of treatment and especially during the crisis phase. Thus, the initial assessment attends to evaluating for the possibility that the eating disorder client may cause passive physical harm to him/herself. Should the assessment protocol indicate the presence of an eating disorder, MFTs must obtain an immediate medical assessment to assess the possible progress of the identified medical conditions. Some clients may refuse and ultimately, MFTs have the responsibility of obtaining this information.

Clinicians at times have chosen to treat anorexic or bulimic clients without obtaining a medical assessment due to the client's refusal to cooperate. Expert witnesses have testified that treating an anorexic or bulimic client without obtaining a current medical assessment is considered to be practicing below the standard of care and failing to protect him or her. Opposing attorneys relish knowing that clinicians failed to obtain medical information. This simplifies their task of presenting the clinician as failing in their duty to protect the client.

Should clients adamantly refuse to cooperate with obtaining a medical evaluation, MFTs can rely on the informed consent document, which establishes that failure to obtain a medical consult is a condition to terminate treatment due to lack of cooperation. To provide continuity of treatment and avoid an accusation of abandonment, MFTs provide appropriate referrals to the client. To protect themselves, MFTs document the reasons for terminating treatment as stated in the informed consent document. Some MFTs manage the refusal to cooperate as a therapeutic issue and continue treatment as long as their immediate and short-term goals of treatment focus on obtaining a current medical evaluation. MFTs must be aware that should the client die of a heart attack or an aneurism during the course of this short-term treatment, they will likely face a malpractice action for contributing to the wrongful death of the client and failing to manage the client's welfare.

Even if the clinician has obtained a complete medical evaluation and is in communication with the physician, the client's clinical behavior may indicate to the clinician that he or she is a danger to self because either the anorexia or bulimia are worsening. Prudently, the clinician to considers Bellah v. Greenson as a reference and applies it here. Though the client is not presenting active suicidality, he or she is presenting harm to self with the possibility of death. Thus, the clinician is required to take reasonable steps to protect the life of the client. When all reasonable clinical steps have been exhausted and the client continues to present a danger to self, the last recourse is to consider breaching confidentiality as permitted by Evidence Code 1024. However, therapists must also remember that breaching confidentiality under Evidence Code 1024 can be a high-risk clinical intervention as previously discussed. It is imperative that the clinician document the presenting clinical issues that led the clinician to determine the following: a) that the client presents a danger to self or others, b) how the clinician determined that confidentiality required breaching to manage the imminent danger, c) did not require breaching because the assessments indicated that the client did not present a danger to self. Should the clinician face a lawsuit for either breaching or not breaching confidentiality, this documentation serves to show that the clinician acted in a reasonable and prudent manner in this difficult clinical situation.

Substance Abuse/Dependence to the Degree Where the Client Presents a Danger to Self or Others — Managing This Issue

Applicable California Laws
Business and Professions Code 4982 (m) (Confidentiality and MFTs)
Business and Professions Code 4982 (d) (Practicing Below the Standard of Care and MFTs)
Business and Professions Code 4982 (i) (Harming a client and MFTs)
Business and Professions Code 4982 (v) (Failure to keep appropriate records and MFTs)
Evidence Code 1024
Bellah v. Greenson (Case Law)
Welfare and Institutions Code 5150
Dinnerstein vs. State, 1973

Applicable Ethical Standards
CAMFT Ethical Standard 2.1

The Malpractice Challenge: MFTs face a unique dilemma when they encounter a high-risk issue involving the possibility of harm to self and/or others involving the use of substances. Should the client present intoxication to the degree of loss of control while driving, MFTs must consider that these situations can result in the severe harm or death of the client and/or others. If the client or another party die from an auto collision and the clinician had the means to prevent the client from driving, the client's family and the family of the deceased will likely challenge the treating MFTs in court for failure to protect their loved ones. Conversely, if MFTs breach confidentiality to protect the client and or others from harm, the client may initiate a legal action for causing breaching their confidentiality without any reason.

Managing this issue: The use or abuse of substance can become a crisis issue at any time during therapy. Intoxication may be a potential problem due to the client's impaired judgment during and after the session. Should the client drive under the influence, he or she can endanger his or her life and the lives of others. Each clinician has the therapeutic duty to a) assess, b) diagnose, and c) treat appropriately throughout the duration of treatment and especially during the crisis phase. Therefore, part of the assessment in the initial visit must attend to the possibility of harm address it immediately.

Should a client come impaired to the session because of the use of substances, the clinician has the therapeutic duty to determine if the client is a danger to self/others. A Mental Status Exam serves to determine the client's degree of impairment. Regardless of the results, it is in the best interest of the clinician to carefully document his or her findings. If the clinician determines that the client is not impaired, allows the client to leave the office and drive, and the client ends up in an auto collision causing harm to self or others, the clinician can face a malpractice action for failing to manage the risk of danger to self or others. If the client determines that the client is impaired and breaches confidentiality to prevent the client from causing harm to self or others in an auto collision, the client can still sue the clinician for inappropriate breach of confidentiality. The appropriate documentation of the clinician's findings and actions serves to establish that the clinician acted in a reasonable and prudent manner according to the standard of care.

When facing this difficult issue, it would be prudent for the clinician to consider Bellah v. Greenson and apply it. Though the client is not presenting active suicidality, he or she is presenting a very real threat of harm to self with the possibility of causing his or her death or the death of others in an auto collision. Thus, the clinician is required to take reasonable steps to protect the life of the client and of others. When all reasonable clinical steps have been exhausted and the client continues to present a danger to self or others, the last recourse is to consider breaching confidentiality as permitted by Evidence Code 1024. This law states that when a client's mental or emotional state is such that he or she presents a danger to self or others, the clinician can choose to breach confidentiality. However, therapists must also remember that breaching confidentiality under Evidence Code 1024 can be a high-risk clinical intervention. It is imperative that the clinician documents the presenting clinical issues that indicate to the clinician that the client presents a danger to self or others. MFTs also document the steps taken to breach or not breach confidentiality depending on whether an imminent danger to self or others exists. Should the clinician face a lawsuit for either breaching or not breaching confidentiality, this documentation serves to show that the clinician acted in a reasonable and prudent manner in this difficult clinical situation.

Documenting Intake Information

The intake form provides MFTs with initial valuable and necessary information as part of the assessment protocol to use should a crisis issue develop. This information includes residence and business, telephone numbers, social security number, insurance information, significant family contact information, personal history, treatment history, medical information, history of hospitalization, names and phone numbers of previous mental health providers, types and dosages of current medications, and any other information deemed necessary by the clinician. This information identifies those significant individuals in the client's immediate social and family network that are the best contacts in case of emergency. This information is especially useful when MFTs must breach the client's confidentiality to a family member who is the best resource of benefit to the client.

Documenting A Mental Status Exam

The Mental Status Exam (MSE) assesses the client's cognitive and emotional functioning. MFTs use it to determine if the client is an appropriate candidate for psychotherapy. This cognitive and emotional assessment establishes a baseline of the client's current mental and emotional state, which is useful for future comparisons to determine the improvement or worsening of the client's mental or emotional state. MFTs perform this assessment as often as necessary. For example, the MSE is used every time that the client presents a significant change in his or her mental or emotional status. Additionally, when MFTs document their use of the MSE as often as necessary to assess the client's progress or deterioration, supports the clinician as a reasonable and prudent clinician. Using the MSE to assess positive or negative change in the client serves to strengthen a decision to breach or not breach confidentiality and protect the client should MFTs face a legal action.

Sample Mental Status Form

Mental Status Exam Assessment

Name: ______________________________ Date: __________

APPEARANCE: (How does patient present? Appropriately dressed, disheveled, excessively neat and organized, immaculate and meticulous?)

BEHAVIOR: (How does patient behave? Congruent or incongruent, contained or expansive, appropriate or inappropriate?)

SPEECH: (Describe patient's quality of talking. Rapid, slow and deliberate, disjointed, etc?)

EMOTION/AFFECT: (Describe patient's emotional state and affect. Is emotion depressed, euthymic, dysthymic, manic, hypomanic? Is affect expansive, labile, or flat, or other?
THOUGHT PROCESSES: (Is patient delusional, hallucinating, obsessive, or compulsive, or other? Is patient's thought process continuous and connected or disconnected and choppy?)

ORIENTATION: (Is patient oriented to person/place/time?)

MEMORY: (Is patient's memory intact for recent/intermediate/remote?)

GENERAL INTELLECTUAL ABILITIES: (Is patient's intellect within normal limits?)

JUDGEMENT: (Is patient's judgment appropriate or inappropriate?)

INSIGHT: (Is patient's insight reasonable or unreasonable?)

CLINICAL RECOMMENDATIONS:

Documenting A Beck Depression Inventory

Aaron T. Beck, Robert A. Steer and Gregory K. Brown developed the Beck Depression Inventory-II (BDI-II). It assesses depression in line with the depression criteria of the Diagnostic and Statistical Manual of Mental Health Disorders—Fourth Edition (DSM–IV). It consists of 21 items to assess the intensity of depression in clinical and normal patients. Each item is a list of four statements arranged in increasing severity about a particular symptom of depression which is related to DSM–IV criteria. After testing original and new items on a large clinical sample (N = 500), test developers compared item-option characteristic curves. The new editions showed improved clinical sensitivity, with the reliability of the BDI–II (Coefficient Alpha = .92) higher than the BDI (Coefficient Alpha = .86).

A reasonable and prudent clinician treating clients with a presenting mood or affective disorder uses the BDI as necessary with this population (B. Bongar, 2002). Like the MSE, the BDI is initially to establish a baseline of depression, regardless of how minimal it presents. This baseline makes future comparisons to determine if the client's depressive symptoms continue to improve or worsen. Should these worsen and the client presents danger to self/others, the BDI and MSE serve to document the clinician's assessment and any necessary clinical intervention. The latter includes breaching or not breaching confidentiality depending on the client presenting danger to self and/or others. California MFTs can use any psychometric test as long as they use it within the scope of practice, the clinician has the scope of competence to use this test, and they use this test as part of providing treatment to the client. The BDI can be obtained from the following website: http://marketplace.psychcorp.com/psychcorp/ProductListing.aspx?Category=BehavioralHealthcare

Documenting Consultations

Consultations with other mental health clinicians serve to obtain greater clinical objectivity when facing a crisis issue, to strengthen the therapeutic team, and to obtain additional services for the client when the clinician lacks the necessary scope of competence or scope of practice in specific arenas of psychotherapy. The clinicians tend to consult physicians, a psychiatrists, suicidologists, and current and previous mental health providers including substance abuse counselors. Documenting these consultations shows that the clinician acted according to the prevailing standard of care. The following ethical standard is very clear about this issue.

> **CAMFT Ethical Standard 1.11: When appropriate, marriage and family therapists consult, collaborate with, and refer to physicians, other health care professionals, and community resources in order to improve and protect the health and welfare of the patient.**

Should the clinician face a malpractice action, consulting with other professionals strengthens the MFTs legal standing due to enhanced clinical objectivity and appropriate use of external resources.

Documenting Treatment Plans for Crisis Issues

Treatment plans perform several tasks. Primordially, they serve to document that the proposed treatment meets the standard of care and addresses the presenting issues. It also serves as an assessment tool to determine if the proposed treatment is effective in resolving the presenting issues. Upon completing the goals of treatment, the treatment plan serves to document that the client completed the goals of treatment and termination is the next appropriate phase. Treatment plans also serve to avoid an accusation of abandonment or inappropriate termination, which can have damaging legal consequences. See Dinnerstein vs. State, 1973.

Generic Crisis Issue Treatment Plan

Crisis Issues:

- Goals:
  - Create safety
  - Rule out harm to self/others
  - Rule out substance abuse/dependence
- Objectives:
  - Refer to physician for medical exam
  - Refer to psychiatrist for medication evaluation
  - Initiate voluntary or involuntary hospitalization as necessary

Beginning Phase:

- Goals:
  - Establish therapeutic relationship
  - Provide bibliotherapy
  - Complete assessments
- Objectives:
  - Normalize the therapeutic process

Inform and educate about therapy
Provide reading list of self-help resources
Complete MSE and Beck's Depression Inventory as needed
Obtain previous treatment records

Middle Phase:

Goals:

Stabilize crisis
Identify and utilize personal and interpersonal resources
Enhance personal and interpersonal well being

Objectives:

Identify and process negative symptomatology
Identify and process emotional reactivity
Separate negative thoughts and feelings
Identify and process negative self-criticism
Explore and process core issue: "damaged goods" / unlovability.
Address and explore sense of interdependent self
Address and enhance interpersonal relationships
Create crisis prevention program
Explore and create possibilities of life enjoyment

Ending Phase:

Goals:

Prepare for termination.
Model a healthy good-bye

Objectives:

Explore and address feelings arising from termination
Practice crisis prevention program
Extend visits as necessary
Leave option open for future treatment

Documenting a DSM 5 Diagnosis

Clinicians have a therapeutic duty to diagnose appropriately during the course of treatment and, in this case, "appropriately" means according to the standard of care. This level of care dictates that a clinician complete a diagnosis per the Diagnostic and Statistical Manual of Mental Disorders © published by the American Psychiatric Association. An opposing attorney considers the lack of this diagnostic protocol as a failure in providing adequate client care. The question asked by the opposing attorney is: "Without an appropriate diagnosis, how can the client receive appropriate care?"

A DSM 5 diagnosis includes the following: The first component corresponds to mental disorders and V codes, the second corresponds to developmental disorders and personality disorders, the third corresponds to medical conditions, the fourth describes factors impacting the presenting issues, and the fifth compares the present Global Assessment of Functioning to last year's. The corresponding first and second diagnostic components are documented behaviorally and by the duration of their symptoms in the progress notes. Otherwise, MFTs can have a difficult time supporting their diagnosis should an opposing attorney question their diagnosis. If the client or his or her family claim emotional injury due to the clinician's actions, a documented DSM 5 diagnosis supports that the clinician provided the appropriate diagnostic protocol. An unsupported diagnosis can lead the opposing attorney to question the validity of the assessment and diagnostic process used by the MFT.

Documenting the Legal Challenge

When documenting legal and ethical actions that arise during crisis issues, MFTs know that they must establish their reasoning process from start to finish. Crisis issues, by definition, present inordinate clinical challenges and these create an enhanced therapeutic duty to manage them safely. There are times when MFTs must determine if the alleged child abuse or elder/dependent abuse meet the "reasonable" standard and therefore requires reporting. On the other hand, in other situations MFTs must determine if breaching of a client's confidentiality is an appropriate intervention to manage a client's imminent suicide, These are challenging questions and perfect answers do not exist, only reasonable and prudent ones. Regardless of the decision made by MFTs, the most significant error of omission is the lack of appropriate documentation.

One specific example of a legal/ethical issue that arises in psychotherapy is the management of a suicidal patient. Standard of care dictates that the clinician must take reasonable steps to protect the life of the client. The suicidology literature is replete with clinical examples of what constitutes "reasonable steps." Bruce Bongar has written an excellent book on this subject (Bongar, 2002). For documentation purposes, MFTs begin writing their assessment of the presenting crisis issue. This approach includes the clinician's observation of the client's behavior related to suicidality, high risk factors, the client's high-risk statements, results of psychometric testing (including use of Beck's Depression Inventory and Mental Status Exam), complete client history related to past attempts and present suicide risk, family history involving depressive symptoms and suicides and/or attempts in the family, and history of previous mental health treatment. This information is clearly written in the progress notes, followed by the diagnosis, which is supported by observable clinical behaviors. Third, MFTs document their clinical interventions used to manage the impending suicide. These include referrals to a psychiatrist and physician, increased telephone contact, "no-suicide" contract, voluntary hospitalization, etc. If none of these interventions is successful, the clinician faces a legal challenge: does the client meet the legally defined requirements permitting a breach of confidentiality? Regardless of the answer, MFTs must document their rationale for their answer to protect themselves should they face a malpractice action. Only then can they strengthen their position to keep opposing attorneys at bay.

Writing these notes systematically and repeatedly, helps establish a beneficial pattern. The pattern begins by documenting the clinical challenge that may require a breach of confidentiality. Next, MFTs document detailed assessments and other pertinent information leading to the consideration of a breach of confidentiality to safeguard the client's well-being. A detailed description of the rationale used by the MFT to determine if the client presented a risk to self and/or others. Third, MFTs document the specific action that followed his or her decision to breach or not breach confidentiality. If the MFT decides to breach client confidentiality, he or she documents the names and roles of those individuals involved, the dates and times of involvement, and the reason for their involvement. If MFTs breach confidentiality as mandated or permitted by law, they only release that clinical information about the client, and no more, that permits the restoration of safety and satisfies the legal requirements. It is important to remember that breaching confidentiality is a serious matter; therefore, the breach releases the minimum information necessary to create clinical safety. Lastly, MFTs document the outcome clinical action necessary to create safety.

Legal/Ethical Documentation Examples

> Example # 1 — 11-29-95: Mr. Doe reports that his feelings of despair are becoming more intense and that he is afraid that he can't handle them. He states: "I don't have a way out of his problem except to end it. I am ready to die to stop these horrible feelings. Life doesn't matter anymore." He states he has a gun and will kill himself when he goes home. I reminded him of his "no-suicide" contract, his connection with his family and friends, and if he kills himself there is no return. I asked him to have himself admitted to the hospital under his own volition and he refused. Under the present circumstances, my clinical impression is that his current mental and emotional state is such that he presents a danger to self and without intervention, he could commit suicide immediately. California Evidence Code 1024 permits me to breach Mr. Doe's confidentiality after having assessed his mental state (see Beck Depression Inventory and Mental Status Exam dated: 11/29/95). Therefore, I have called his wife and disclosed to her Mr. Doe's present mental state. I have called the Psychiatric Assessment Team for an evaluation in my office for possible involuntary hospitalization as permitted by California Welfare and Institutions Code 5150. After the evaluation, the PAT Team decided that he was a danger to self and has taken him to the hospital for admission and observation for the next 72 hours. I have

privileges at the hospital and will consult with his psychiatrist to coordinate treatment after he is released. (Therapist's signature).

Example # 2 — 12-02-2003: Ms. Smith reported that when she was a child, her uncle sexually molested her. She told me that the abuse took place in Arizona and that he now lives in California. She believes he is working as a custodian in a private primary school. She does not want me to tell anyone because she does not want to relive the past. She said: "It was too traumatic then and I don't want to face it again." I reminded her of my legal obligation to report a reasonable suspicion of child abuse and since he is in contact with children, they could be in danger of sexual abuse. She said: "If you report him, I won't ever come back to therapy." I informed her that only she could make that decision and that I strongly recommended against it. However, if she refused to return, I would provide her with the names of several clinicians she could use to continue treatment. I informed her that I would be consulting with an expert and would inform her of the outcome of my consultation. After Ms. Smith left, I consulted with Mr. Johnson, an attorney who is an expert in mental health law. He recommended that I make a report to Child Welfare Services immediately because he agreed that I have a "reasonable" suspicion of child abuse and the uncle is in contact with children. He also recommended that I call Ms. Smith and inform her of my decision. At that time, I will provide her with the names and telephone numbers of 3 qualified therapists who can continue treatment should she decide to terminate with me. I left Ms. Smith a telephone message to call me. I called Child Welfare Services and spoke with Jean Adams. I provided her with the name of the uncle, the name of my client, the approximate dates of the sexual abuse, his current place of employment, his contact with children, her specific statement, and other required information. See written Child Welfare Report dated 12/02/2003, which was mailed today. (Therapist's signature).

12/03/2003: I spoke with Ms. Smith and informed her of the results of the consultation. She said she would not be returning and hung up the phone before I had an opportunity to give her the names of the referrals. I sent her a certified letter with the names and telephone numbers of the referrals and informed her that I would gladly provide the clinician of her choice a copy of her treatment records after a written request was submitted. Discharge Summary: Case closed and therapeutic duty has ended due to client's choice to terminate treatment prematurely. (Therapist's signature).

Clinical Example # 1

Meredith has had a long history of fighting bulimia and has sought therapy from different sources. Recently, her parents told her that if she did not seek help, they would hospitalize her. She sets up an appointment with Jane, a licensed MFT, and begins by stating that she will refuse to see a physician for a medical check-up because she knows what they will do to her. If the therapist is not willing to see her under these conditions, then she will stop treatment. The therapist accepts hoping to convince her to be evaluated medically eventually. After several weeks in treatment, the therapist receives a call from her parents telling her that Meredith died suddenly of a heart attack.

Questions for Clinical Example # 1

1. Did her therapist fail to perform her therapeutic duty and practice according to the standard of care? Why or why not?
2. What is the crisis issue that Meredith failed to consider when accepting to treat Jane without first having a current medical exam?
3. What would be a reasonable length of time before Meredith should have insisted that her client obtain a medical exam to continue treatment?
4. What options were available to Meredith if Jane continued to refuse obtaining a medical evaluation?
5. Several months go by and Meredith receives a certified letter from an attorney informing her that her client's parents had initiated a malpractice action against her due to failure to protect their daughter's life and for being responsible in the "wrongful death" of the client. Do the parents have a reasonable cause of action against Jane? Why or why not?
6. After reading the letter, Meredith is perplexed. She doesn't understand how they could accuse her of such wrongdoing. What is Jane not addressing? If you were counseling her, what would you help her become aware of?
7. If you were in Jane's situation, what would be your greatest concern?

Chapter Questions

1. What makes these clinical issues "crisis" issues?
2. What aspect of the law do these crisis issues have in common?
3. How do the law and CAMFT ethics interplay with crisis issues?
4. Of these crisis issues, which would be more difficult for you to manage and why?
5. What is your internal reality regarding these issues?
6. If you decided to consult with an expert, what would be your greatest personal challenge?

Chapter 11

The Suicidal Client and the Standard of Care

The Suicidal Client

The most frequently encountered mental health emergency in a psychotherapy practice is suicide. This emergency can have broad-reaching effects for MFTs. In addition to the emotional experience attached to a suicide, MFTs may also be exposed to the possibility of a malpractice lawsuit for failure to prevent the suicide. When a client attempts or commits suicide, the family can initiate a malpractice lawsuit. Multi-million dollar settlements are common because courts award damages in direct proportion to injuries suffered. MFTs can also be held personally responsible for any award that is in excess of the face value of their malpractice insurance policy. Unfortunately, even a low-lethality "cry for help" attempt may result in the tragic death of the client. Treating MFTs can be accused of causing the "wrongful death" of the client. This array of factors that produce serious consequences for client and MFTs require providing standard of care a necessity.

Legal, Ethical and Clinical Standard of Care for Treating Suicidal Clients

The courts and legislation have established some guidelines addressing the legal standard of care when treating suicidal clients, including those clients presenting with suicidal ideation. In Bellah v. Greenson (1978), the court held that MFTs have a duty to protect the life of his or her client. In Meier v. Ross General Hospital (1968), the court demanded that therapists exercise adequate care and skill in diagnosis when suicidality is well established. In Dinnerstein v. State (1973), the court stated that a therapist was negligent when her or his treatment plan neglected or overlooked a client's suicidal tendencies. In Abille v. United States (1989), the courts imposed an additional duty on therapists to take prudent and reasonable precautions when suicidal tendencies are identified. In California, Evidence Code 1024 permits a therapist to break confidentiality if a client's mental or emotional state is such that he or she is a danger to self or others. CAMFT Ethical Standard 2.1 supports the law in this regard, allowing MFTs to break client confidence as permitted by law. The laws go on to address specific actions that's available to clinicians when a client is in imminent danger. Welfare and Institutions Code 5150 states that involuntary hospitalization for 72 hours is permissible when a client's mental or emotional state causes them to be an imminent danger to self or others. Additionally, the court adds clarification concerning the parameters of hospitalization. The U.S. Court of Appeals ruled that it is unconstitutional to commit someone simply because he or she is dangerous to self or others, unless the danger is imminent. Finally, in Pisel v. Stamford Hospital, the courts ruled that when a psychotherapist fails to meet her or his clinical responsibilities, she or he faces a liability for resulting injuries.

The court, legislation, case law, and CAMFT ethical standards, provide parameters for reasonable and prudent actions a therapist might take when dealing with a suicidal client. Attorneys use these guidelines to prepare their cases and hold MFTs accountable in a lawsuit. The court attempts to determine if the therapist obtained sufficient information to assess the risk of harm, could have predicted possible suicide, and did enough to protect the life of the client. The courts have placed the additional burden on the therapist to correctly assess the risk of suicide and balance this risk with the benefits of increased control through hospitalization.

Experts in the field of psychotherapy have generated parameters for clinical standard of care. These experts attempt to generate assessment parameters as well as define reasonable and prudent actions, in this case, when a client is suicidal. To define parameters and actions, various studies have examined demographics, sociocultural perspectives, biological considerations, psychological components, theoretical approaches, and appropriate interventions. Understanding this knowledge base, being facile with the literature and using it to manage suicidal clients is part of scope of competence. Opposing attorneys readily use MFTs' failings in their application of these important factors when questioning them in court.

Reasonable and Prudent Steps to Manage Suicidality

Working with suicidal clients, a daunting and stressful task requires care, foresight, and the application of a comprehensive structure to protect the life of the client. Even with the best of care, a client may choose suicide. Should MFTs face a malpractice lawsuit because of the client's suicide or attempt, the courts will determine whether the MFTs' behavior was reasonable and prudent as defined by legal, ethical, and clinical standards of care. MFTs can minimize the risk by incorporating the guidelines presented in this section into their practice.

When a client expresses any kind of suicidal thought or behavior, the MFT must determine if this is an immediate crisis issue or if this information places the client in a high-risk client and non-lethal category. This distinction is critical because managing the former differs from the latter. The following list of steps may be necessary for both. Since each case is unique, there may be additional reasonable steps MFTs can take that are not included on this list.

- Obtain a complete patient history, including a thorough family history, a history of all previous therapy, psychological evaluations and diagnoses, previous individual and family suicidal history, and a complete medical evaluation to rule out organicity.
- Obtain an appropriate informed consent.
- Obtain written releases to speak with any former therapists, physicians, family members or other persons you believe may be helpful for assessment, diagnosis or treatment.
- As part of assessment, evaluate the client's perturbation (the degree of mental agitation), sense of hopelessness, communication of intent to a significant other or therapist, finalization of personal affairs, ability to carry out suicide plan and lethality. The following are some tools available for this task: a) Mental Status Exam, b) Beck's Depression Inventory, c) Beck's Hopelessness Scale and d) the MMPI, as necessary.
- Use a team approach to increase safety by referring the client for a psychiatric evaluation and consulting with other professionals
- Utilize your knowledge appropriately of risk factors for high-risk populations (for suicide).
- Apply the legal and ethical standards of care. Remember that confidentiality is central to therapy, however, Evidence Code 1024 (whereby a therapist may breach confidentiality when a client's mental or emotional state is such that he or she is a danger to self) supports a necessary step of last recourse to prevent suicide.
- Document in the case notes all decisions regarding suicide prevention including appropriate diagnosis and prognosis, consultations with experts or colleagues, rationale for any clinical and legal decisions, specific interventions, outreach to family members with or without the client's authorization, and updated treatment plan.
- Using sound clinical judgment to manage a suicidal client requires viewing interventions on a continuum. The choice of intervention will depend on the lethality of the suicidal client who is a <u>high-risk client and non-lethal</u> versus one who is in a suicidal state.

The following list is an example of increasingly protective interventions that a therapist can take to safeguard the life of a suicidal client according to the intent of Bellah v. Greenson.

a) Refer to a psychiatrist and physician for evaluations.
b) Maintain communication with psychiatrist and other concurrent treatment providers.
c) Obtain a signed "no suicide" contract.
d) Provide for 24-hour coverage for suicidal clients.
e) Allow for telephone contact between sessions, as needed.
f) Increase the number of therapy sessions, as needed.
g) Incorporate the family or significant others into therapy sessions.
h) Involve family and/or significant others should a 24-hour watch become necessary.
h) Encourage voluntary hospitalization, if necessary.
i) Breach confidentiality to initiate involuntary hospitalization, if necessary.

Despite the best preventive steps, there are times when these are not enough to contain the client and the therapist faces a client who does commit suicide. Complete documentation of each step regarding suicidality will help to document that the clinician took reasonable and prudent steps to protect the life of the client and increase his or her level of protection in case a malpractice action develops.

Permitted Breaches of Confidentiality Under Evidence Code 1024

> **1024: There is no privilege "if the psychotherapist has a reasonable cause to believe that the patient is in such a mental or emotional condition as to be dangerous to himself or the person or property of another" and if the disclosure of confidential information "is necessary to prevent the threatened danger."**

Despite the best proactive interventions, there are times when these do not suffice and MFTs face a client presenting imminent suicide. MFTs can use Evidence Code 1024, which permits them to breach confidentiality in this specific situation where the client presents danger of harm to self. MFTs remember that breaching confidentiality, while at times necessary, is a serious action, which can bring damaging consequences. Even though MFTs breaches confidentiality to protect a client's life, the client can feel betrayed and injured by his or her MFT and may initiate a legal action. Conversely, even if the therapist does not breach confidentiality because the client's symptoms are not severe enough to meet the legal standards, the client's family will likely sue the MFT if their loved one ends up killing him/herself. Reasonable and prudent MFTs comply with assessing the client's mental or emotional state to determine imminent danger. Next, they consult with experts in the arena of suicidology to determine the extraordinary steps necessary to treat. They make sure that they document each step thoroughly. When treating suicidality, thorough written records help the MFTs maintain clarity and clinical objectivity and protect themselves when facing a lawsuit.

Clinical Example # 1

> Roger, a therapist using a religious approach in his clinical work begins treating a woman referred by the minister of her church. Though the church is not keen on psychotherapists, Roger's religious approach is somewhat acceptable to some of the church members and they are desperate to help her manage her severe depression. Roger was never trained in using psychometric testing nor does he trust other therapists to do so. He prefers to work alone and never consults with anyone. The client has tried different anti-depressants and they make her sick to her stomach. After trying different approaches, Roger refers her to an "exorcist" to purify her of the demons possessing her. She tries this approach and it fails to heal her. A few weeks later, she takes an overdose of sleeping pills with large amounts of alcohol. She is found dead the next morning by her neighbor.

Questions for Clinical Example # 1

1. What did Roger fail to assess? What steps could he have taken to assess her properly?
2. Did Roger fail to diagnose her high risk of self-harm? Why or why not?
3. You are asked to review her whole treatment history and find out that she had attempted 5 non-lethal suicide attempts in the last two years. What does this tell you about her imminent risk of suicide? How would a reasonable and prudent clinician obtain this information after the first meeting with this client?
4. Is the referral to the "exorcist" a clinical intervention meeting the standard of care? Why or why not?
5. Did Roger meet his therapeutic duty under Bellah v. Greenson? Why or why not?

6. If you were to examine Roger's treatment plan, what would you be looking for? What is required to be documented?

Chapter Questions

1. What are your legal duties when managing a suicidal client?
2. From the perspective of clinical standard of care, how would a reasonable and prudent therapist manage suicidal clients?
3. What steps would you take to protect the life of your client per Evidence Code 1024 should he or she be in imminent danger of committing suicide?
4. How would you make the determination to break confidentiality to protect the life of your client? What are the potential dangers of breaching confidentiality?
5. You have been seeing a client for several weeks. During that time your client's spouse suddenly dies. Your client feels despondent and depressed and talks about suicide. What would be your greatest personal challenge when facing his possible death? What steps can you create to take care of yourself?
6. A fellow therapist believes that suicide is an acceptable means to end human suffering. He now faces the possible suicide of a client and decides to seek consultation with you. What guidance will you give this therapist knowing that a conflict existed between his personal beliefs and "*Bellah v. Greenson*?"

Chapter 12

The Dangerous Client In a Tarasoff Situation

The Dangerous Client

Facing a dangerous and threatening client can be the most frightening experience that MFTs can encounter. Suddenly, the degree of therapeutic responsibility magnifies as the MFT hears the client state a serious threat to harm an identifiable person. The clinician realizes that an identified person outside of the treatment unit requires protection due to the present and serious danger and he or she must act immediately to protect that person. The MFT remembers that in some cases, the duty to protect may include family members or roommates residing with the identifiable victim. MFTs can expect a daunting experience.

When a client in a therapy session states a serious threat to harm an identifiable person who is outside of the treatment unit, a number of questions may cross the MFT's mind. Many questions may cross the MFT's mind. For example: "Is this really happening? Is the threat serious? Will my client hurt this person or is this just an idle threat? What do I need to do next? How can I keep my client in my office while I call the police? Do I need to call the psychiatric assessment team? What happens if he or she is hurt? Will he hurt me?" In this tense situation, the therapist must immediately consider how to best provide safety for everyone involved including him/herself. MFTs can learn to protect all involved by continuous practice and role-playing of this difficult clinical scenario.

Dangerous Clients and Laws Affecting Psychotherapists

In 1969, a graduate student at U. C. Berkeley began treatment with a psychologist at the student health center seeking help with an obsession involving an undergraduate student who had spurned him. He felt his obsession interfered with his studies and he could not get her out of his mind. The obsession was so severe that he told the psychologist he wanted to kill her. This concerned the psychologist and he wrote a letter to the Berkeley police department warning them about the threat to the young woman's life. The police found the graduate student, questioned him, obtained from him a promise to leave her alone and released him. Shortly thereafter, he killed her. Eventually, her parents initiated a lawsuit, Tarasoff v. Regents of the University of California (1976), against the psychologist and other individuals involved in the case. Their lawsuit rested on the allegation that the psychologist was remiss in his duty to warn the young woman that she was the potential victim of harm. They contended that his warning would have prevented her death. Eventually, the California Supreme Court decided that confidentiality must yield to public safety. Therefore, the court ruled that therapists have a duty to exercise reasonable care to protect foreseeable victims of harm identified after a moment's reflection. The court also recognized that, while at times it may be possible to identify a potential victim during the course of working with a threatening client, it is unreasonable to interrogate or investigate in other instances.

Tarasoff v. Regents of the University of California (1976) addressed and changed he legal standard of care when the California Supreme Court decided that public safety takes priority over confidentiality. However, specific issues concerning the protection of the public safety were unanswered. The California legislature later revisited the unanswered question of whom to call to meet this requirement. In California Civil Code 43.92, the legislature established that when a client communicates to a psychotherapist a serious threat of physical violence directed against a reasonably identifiable victim or victims, the psychotherapists release their duty by communicating with a law enforcement agency and making reasonable efforts to communicate the threat to the victim or victims. MFTs remember that the identifiable victim has no means of knowing that a serious threat exists against him or her and thus cannot take steps to protect him/herself.

The established legislation defines the necessary steps to take to protect the identifiable victim are threefold. First, the client communicates the threat to the psychotherapist. Second, there must be "a serious threat to harm". "Serious" in this context means that a credible intent exists and that the client can carry out the threat with a plan and a weapon. It does not require that the potential injury must be severe. Third, there must be an identifiable victim. MFTs agree that "reasonable" efforts means taking different actions depending on the circumstances involved in each case. For example, telephoning the identifiable victim seems the most reasonable action. However, what does the clinician do if the identifiable victim has no telephone? Does the MFT go to their home? If the clinician has neither phone number nor address, what happens then? A reasonable step is calling the police, informing them of the situation, and asking them to warn the identified victim. Ultimately, MFTs must remember that their safety is paramount.

In 1983, the court found that an expanded level of protection was necessary. The decision of Hedlund v. Superior Court of Orange County recognized that therapists had a duty to warn individuals exposed to direct harm (in harms way) if a threat were to be carried out. This includes those individuals living in the close proximity to the identifiable victim, for example the victim's children or spouse. This law included the enactment of an immunity clause. This immunity clause allows for the dismissal of lawsuits against any therapist who follows their duty under the law as stated by Tarasoff and California Civil Code 43.92. However, for immunity to apply, MFTs must comply with all requirements established by the Tarasoff case, the Hedlund case, Civil Code 43.92, and the Ewing law. Any deviation or omission voids the immunity and allows opposing attorneys the grounds to gain an advantage in a malpractice action against an MFT.

Civil Code 43.92

> **(a) There shall be no monetary liability on the part of, and no cause of action shall arise against, any person who is a psychotherapist as defined in Section 1010 of the Evidence Code in failing to warn of and protect from a patient's threatened violent behavior or failing to predict and warn of and protect from a patient's violent behavior except where the patient has communicated to the psychotherapist a serious threat of physical violence against a reasonably identifiable victim or victims. (b) If there is a duty to warn and protect under the limited circumstances specified above, the duty shall be discharged by the psychotherapist making reasonable efforts to communicate the threat to the victim or victims and to a law enforcement agency.**

Experts explain this law to mean that MFTs are liable if they fail to warn an identifiable victim or victims of a serious threat of physical violence made against him/her/them. MFTs have the duty to take reasonable steps to warn the identifiable victim and must warn law enforcement regarding the threat.

Ewing v. Goldstein

In 2004, the California Appellate Court released a ruling in a recent case involving "duty to warn" (Ewing v. Goldstein, 2004). The court ruled that the term "communication" as used in Civil Code 43.92 was not limited to specific communications made by a client to a therapist. Rather, it expanded the use of this term to mean a communication made by a significant family member of the client to a therapist that "leads the therapist to believe or predict that the patient poses a serious risk of grave bodily injury to another." What does this mean to mental health clinicians? Forensic experts explain the application of this case law as follows: as of July, 16, 2004, licensed psychotherapists must consider this ruling to be a therapeutic duty, which applies to all MFTs who receive a communication from a significant family member of the client and relating a serious threat to harm made by the client.

In the Ewing case, a psychologist recommended that a client hospitalize himself for observation due to suicidal ideation emanating from a break up with his girlfriend who later began a relationship with a new boyfriend. During the client's hospitalization, the psychologist received a communication from the client's father indicating that his son intended to do serious harm to the boyfriend after his release from the hospital. The father requested that his son stay hospitalized for further observation. Since the psychologist determined that he did not have cause to have his client stay in the hospital any longer, the hospital released him. After his release, the client murdered the boyfriend and killed himself.

The parents of the murdered boyfriend sued the psychologist for wrongful death due to professional negligence. They contented that the psychologist failed to apply Civil Code 43.92 appropriately and did not warn their son of the serious intention to harm him by the psychologist's client. The Superior Court "threw the case" out of court in a summary judgment because the communication to do serious harm did not come from the client. However, the Appellate Court reversed the summary judgment and agreed that Civil Code 43.92 was interpreted too narrowly. It expanded the meaning of patient communication to include pertinent communications from immediate relatives of the client. It also based its ruling on the inclusion of "communications to psychotherapists by intimate family members" established by a previous Case law (Grosslight v. Superior Court, 1977), which ruled that relevant communications about a client made to a psychotherapist by intimate family members are considered privileged.

Clinical Applications Under Ewing v. Goldstein

Mental Health clinicians consider the following clinical approach regarding appropriate utilization of this ruling:

- Know Ewing v. Goldstein relates to Tarasoff v. UC.
- When a client's significant family member communicates a serious threat to harm to a therapist made by the client, clinicians must consider this communication as an indication of the client's "mental or emotional disorder, life history, current circumstances and personal or familial relationships as perceived by the family member."
- A clinician asks the following questions: a) is this statement valid? b) Does this statement make sense in light of the client's mental disorder or emotional perturbation? c) How did the intimate relative become aware of this information? d) How serious is the threat to harm?
- Once these questions have been answered, clinicians determine if the communication meets the Tarasoff standards: a) is this a serious threat to harm? and b) is there an identifiable victim who is unaware of the threat? If so, clinicians apply Civil Code 43.92 to make sure they comply with their legally mandated reporting appropriately.

- In all situations, precise documentation of clinicians' reasoning process regarding how they determined that a Tarasoff mandate exists or does not exist is required. Opposing attorneys sue clinicians for "breaching confidentiality" as well as for "failure in their duty to report a serious threat to harm" under Tarasoff. Protective documentation is necessary in such these actions.

Calderon v. Glick (2005), Ca. App. 4th

In the Calderon v. Glick case, a client killed three people and later killed himself. The family of those killed sued the therapists involved for failure to warn according to Tarasoff. The court ruled that if the therapist has not received a communication regarding a serious threat to harm and the therapist has made this determination, then a Tarasoff duty does not apply to him/her. What this means for clinicians:

- According to their legal mandate, MFTs only breach confidentiality when a client or an intimate family member communicates a serious threat to harm to the clinician. In cases where a client or third party experience harm, clinicians can expect to a malpractice lawsuit as shown in this case.
- Since it is impossible to predict when a client will become a danger to self or others, it is in the clinician's best interest to assess, diagnose, and treat appropriately throughout the duration of the professional relationship.

As an expert witness involving one of the clinicians in this case, it was evident quite early that the opposing attorney would review the mental health records of all the clinicians involved with the client's treatment. This attorney found a common theme with many other mental health records he reviewed in his practice, which were poor or non-existent. Fortunately, the records reviewed in this case did document, though minimally, the necessary assessment protocols to determine whether the client presented a danger to self and/or others. Imagine the following; had the clinician failed to document as he did, he would likely be facing a multi-million dollar judgment. Appropriate documentation includes the following elements:

- Always use a Mental Status Exam with every client to establish a baseline of mental functioning throughout the duration of treatment. Use it as often as necessary to document the client's improvement or deterioration of his or her mental state.
- If your assessment indicates that your client does or does not present a danger to self or others document this finding clearly in the progress notes by writing: "Client does or does not present a danger to self or others" and document your reasoning to support your findings.

- If the client presents a danger to self and/or others, document how this was determined.
- Should an opposing attorney sue you for malpractice, this attorney will want to know if you developed the components of your mental health records from elements that are based in standard of care. This attorney will want to know where did you document these compoents in your records.

These questions are important to ask because they help the clinician initiate a documentation process to defend against a possible malpractice action. How did the clinician determine that the client presented a danger to self or others? Did the client make a statement to the clinician directly? Did the clinician receive this information from a collateral resource? Did the client's behavior lead the clinician to determine that the he or she presented a danger to self or others? What information did the Mental Status Exam and the Beck Depression Inventory provide? MFTs remember that in a deposition, the opposing attorney will ask about their knowledge of the validity and reliability of the specific psychometric tool used. Additionally, this attorney will when MFTs use these psychometric tests. The standard of care dictates that MFTs use them initially and as often as needed to document improvement or worsening of depressive symptoms. Should MFTs fail to use these psychometric tools when warranted, they allow opposing attorney to accuse them of failing to assess the client appropriately and thus failing in their duty to protect those injured by the client.

The mental health clinicians sued in this case could not predict that the client would kill three people and later himself. This is by far the greatest risk for mental health clinicians and their greatest vulnerability is the inability to predict when a client will harm him/herself and or others. Should the client harm him/herself and/or others, the clinicians involved can expect to face a major lawsuit for failure to protect and/or wrongful death. In such cases, the best protection is appropriate documentation of how the clinician's assessment, diagnosis, and treatment throughout the duration of services. A reasonable clinician remembers to ask: "If I face a similar situation, will my records protect me? The answer is: "Only if you use your mental health records effectively."

Managing a "Serious Threat to Harm"

When working with a client who is expressing violent intent, MFTs rely on their professional judgment to determine whether the threat is serious. Arriving at this conclusion requires the integration of important factors. These include assessment of the client's perturbation (mental agitation), determination of the client's degree of dangerousness, the victim's degree of risk to harm, and the determination of who is the intended victim. In deciding how far to explore the specifics of the threat, the therapist needs to assess the possibility of danger toward him/herself. If unsure, the therapist needs to consult immediately, if available, with an experienced professional associate, preferably a suicidologist. When convinced that the threat is serious, MFTs call a law enforcement agency and take reasonable steps to contact the identifiable victim. After they identify themselves to the police, MFTs exchange and document the following: a) the name and badge number of the officer taking the report, b) the nature of the call, c) the client's exact statement, d) the reporting laws, e) the client's and victims' identities, addresses, and telephone numbers if available. Ultimately, MFTs remember that they are not investigators, only evaluators of the seriousness of the risk and act accordingly. Their best protection in these difficult cases is appropriate documentation.

Clinical Example # 1

Samantha is new to clinical practice since she was recently licensed as an MFT. She supplements her income by working with physically abusive husbands mandated by the court to obtain treatment. One of the men in the group asks her for an appointment at her private office because he would like additional individual treatment and the agency says it's fine with them. After several individual sessions, she notices that he did not show up for group the week before. She questions him and with controlled anger he tells her he drank and his wife poured his liquor down the drain. His face is red and he is livid with anger as he relates this incident. He turns to her and tells her: "When I go home tonight, she'll learn never to touch my liquor. I work hard for it and it's mine. I am going to teach her a lesson she'll never forget." Upon hearing this, Samantha is fearful and her fear stops her dead in her tracks. He quickly changes the subject and tells her he will be at the group session next week.

Questions for Clinical Example # 1

1. What do you believe happened to Samantha as she heard his statement?
2. If you were in her place, would you consider his statement to be valid? Why or why not?
3. If it were valid, what would be your next consideration? What information do you need to assess to determine if this a Tarasoff condition?
4. If it is a Tarasoff condition, what are your legal duties?
5. How would you carry these out in a reasonable and prudent manner?
6. You search in your records and you realize you don't have his wife's name or telephone number. How do you carry out your duty under Civil Code 43.92 under this circumstance?
7. Would you challenge your client about the possibility of hurting his wife after he tells you this statement? Why or why not? What is the possible danger to you if you do?

Clinical Example # 2

Anthony was recently fired by his firm due to outsourcing of jobs to another country and has recently become depressed. He has been seeing a therapist for several months due to spousal conflict and to him, this is "the last straw." He confides in his sister and tells her the company "is going to pay," however he is not specific about his plans. He refuses to share any more information with her. Worried, his sister calls the therapist and leaves a message on her answering machine telling the therapist what Anthony told her.

Questions for Clinical Example # 2

1. How would you determine whether Anthony is serious about this threat, especially since he did not communicate it directly to you?
2. If you the therapist, what would be your concerns about the risk involved for you and for the potential victim?
3. Do you have enough information to be a mandated reporter under *Tarasoff* and *Ewing v. Goldstein*? If not, what information do you need to assess to determine if this a Tarasoff condition?
4. If you breach confidentiality how will you manage your client's reaction?
5. What would be your best protection should your client decide to sue you for a breach of confidentiality?
6. If you don't breach your client's confidentiality and the identifiable victim is harmed, what is your best protection?
7. How would you document your therapeutic duty as mandated or permitted by law?

Chapter Questions

1. What makes a "serious threat to harm" such a dangerous situation in psychotherapy? What makes it difficult to manage?
2. When facing such a situation in your practice, what steps would you take to create safety for yourself and your client?
3. What would be your greatest personal challenge when facing this issue?
4. What is the difference between Tarasoff and Civil Code 43.92?
5. What does "taking reasonable steps to contact the intended victim," mean?
6. What would you do if a threat was made against you and you had a spouse and children living with you or you practiced with colleagues who could be affected by this serious threat to harm you?
7. A couple is sitting in your treatment room and suddenly the conflict escalate. He tells her "I'm going to teach you not to disrespect me when we get home and you're never going to forget it."
You believe he is serious and intends to harm her. Is this a Tarasoff situation? Why or why not?
8. The same couple sits in the therapist's reception room. He comes into your treatment room first while she waits. During the session you observe his tension and anger increasing. He tells you: "I'm sick and tired of that woman. She will learn not to disrespect me. When we get home, I'll teach her a lesson she'll never forget." You assess his mental state and determine that his threat is serious (he intends to carry it out and has the means to do it). Does Tarasoff apply? What reasonable and prudent steps would you take? How would you document your reasoning and steps taken?

Chapter 13

Child Abuse Reporting

Child Abuse and Reasonable Suspicion

MFTs have a legal mandate to report child abuse. They are also responsible to determine when a "reasonable" suspicion of child abuse exists or has occurred before they make a report. This may seem vague, however, the law goes on to specify the meaning of "reasonable suspicion."

> **"Reasonable suspicion" means that it is objectively reasonable for a person to entertain a suspicion, based upon facts, that could cause a reasonable person in a like position, drawing, when appropriate, on his or her training and experience, to suspect child abuse or neglect. "Reasonable suspicion" does not require certainty that child abuse or neglect has occurred nor does it require a specific medical indication of child abuse or neglect; any "reasonable suspicion" is sufficient. For the purpose of this article, the pregnancy of a minor does not, in and of itself,constitute a basis for a reasonable suspicion of sexual abuse. PC 11166.1**

This law appears to say that MFTs must rely on their scope of competence, which is their training, knowledge, and experience when making the determination if a "reasonable" suspicion of abuse exists. Additionally, MFTs rely on the prevalent standard of care, which relates to a reasonable person in a like position with reasonably the same knowledge, to help them determine the existence of a "reasonable suspicion" of child abuse. When practicing, MFTs determine if the presenting factors support the accusation of abuse as being reasonable. They utilize their clinical objectivity appropriately to view all available clinical information before making the decision of whether to report. If the therapist hasn't yet developed the scope of competence to manage this issue, consultation with a supervisor or objective colleague would be necessary before making a final determination. Making a child abuse report based on unreliable, false, or malicious information may lead MFTs to face legal action from separate sources. And even if the clinician's report is "reasonable," some vindictive alleged perpetrators have initiated legal actions against these therapists. These include the person reported to Child Welfare Services, the Board of Behavioral Sciences if MFTs make an inappropriate or erroneous report.

Sometimes, divorcing parents use accusation of child abuse against each other as a manipulative tool to divert custody. Though MFTs are not required to investigate the accusation, they must assure that a "reasonable suspicion" of child abuse exists before a making a report in these difficult circumstances. Some parents have initiated legal action against individual therapists for reporting alleged child abuse in custody situations and even though MFTs receive "immunity," they still must resolve a pending lawsuit initiated by the parents. MFTs can protect themselves through documentation of the information used to base their decision to report. It is paramount to document those factors that led to the determination that a "reasonable suspicion" of child abuse exists or occurred. Likewise, when a therapist determines that a "reasonable suspicion" of child abuse does not exist, documenting the factors leading to this assessment is equally important. MFTs remember that they can be sued for reporting as well as not reporting child abuse regardless of the merit of the report. Importantly, "reasonable suspicion" does not require that the therapist be "right," rather that he or she follows the standard of care.

Mandated Reporters

California law identifies the individuals and their roles who are required to make mandated reports of a "reasonable" suspicion of child abuse to the appropriate authorities. MFTs, interns, and trainees are specifically named as mandated reporters when they perform their duties as such. These clinicians may hold other positions when practicing as a marriage and family therapist. These include; an employee of a child care institution, including, but not limited to, foster parents, group home personnel, and personnel of residential care facilities, a person who is an administrator or presenter of, or a counselor in, a child abuse prevention program in a public or private school, A child visitation monitor. As used in this article, "child visitation monitor" means a person who, for financial compensation, acts as a monitor of a visit between a child and another person when the monitoring of that visit has been ordered by a court of law, an employee or administrator of a public or private postsecondary educational institution, whose duties bring the administrator or employee into contact with children on a regular basis, or who supervises those whose duties bring the administrator or employee into contact with children on a regular basis, as to child abuse or neglect occurring on that institution's premises or at an official activity of, or program conducted by, the institution.

Managing Child Abuse Reporting

Penal Code 11164–11174.3 outlines the required steps to report child abuse. This law states that MFTs report physical and sexual abuse immediately by phone to Child Welfare Services, a police department, a sheriff's department, any local department designated by the county to receive such reports, or the welfare department. and in writing within 36 hours to the same agency when "one acquires knowledge of or observes facts which give rise to a reasonable suspicion" as discussed in the previous section. Any extraneous information included in the report must be non privileged and germane to the incident.

As of January 1, 1998, the law was amended to include two other reportable categories: a) it is unlawful to have sexual intercourse, even if it consensual, with a child under the age of 16 (as determined by birth date), when the perpetrator is over the age of 21 years (as determined by birth date), and (b) lewd and lascivious acts with a child of 14 or 15 years of age are a crime when the perpetrator is more than 10 years (as determined by birth date) older than the victim.

Multiple Parties Required to Report

In situations where two or more clinicians must report a "reasonable" suspicion of child abuse, Penal Code 11166 (E) (h) states that when agreed upon, one of the clinicians must make the telephone report. The written report is signed by the selected designated reporter. Should a clinician learn that the report wasn't made, she must make the report immediately. Due to the multiple clinician involvement in these circumstances, its possible for a clinician to lose paperwork or fail to document the necessary data in the mental health records. It serves each clinician to keep copies of all appropriate records related to this case in their possession. Should the be challenged by an opposing attorney, those holding appropriate documentation can help defuse a potential legal action.

Reporting Child Abuse Involving Adults Abused as Children

The requirement for reporting child abuse after a client has become an adult can cause confusion for many MFTs. The following sentence helps clarify the confusion. When a client is over 18 years of age and discloses abuse they experienced as a child, there is no mandate to report (the client is no longer a minor child). However, if the alleged perpetrator of that child abuse is still in contact with children, then the MFT reports to the appropriate to protect children exposed to the alleged perpetrator. Confusion also occurs when an abused child does not reside in California. The child abuse laws only serve to protect children residing in California and thus, MFTs must abide only to California law. Therefore, when a client tells an MFT about child abuse that is happening in another state, the MFT does not have a mandate to report. The MFT can opt to call the local reporting agency and make the report. Calling another state places the clinician in peril. Since the clinician isn't likely licensed in that state, the action can be interpreted as practicing psychotherapy without a license. Additionally, if the reported party is also a client, this person my initiate a BBS and malpractice actions against the reporting clinician for breach of confidentiality and severe emotional harm. As a sequitur, I recommend that MFTs be careful when using the term "perpetrator" to identify an accused child abuser. This term is used only with individuals who have been found guilty in a criminal court. To avoid a possible legal action for slander, it serves MFTs to add the term "alleged" in their written and verbal descriptions when the report only involves an accusation.

Employees and the Child Abuse Law

When any person falling under the mandate of the Child Abuse Law (Penal Code 11166) becomes a salaried employee, he or she is required to sign a statement regarding the Child Abuse Law. This statement must clearly state that the employee is aware of this law and will abide by its requirements. See the code below:

> **11166.5 (a) On and after January 1, 1985, any mandated reporter as specified in Section 11165.7, with the exception of child visitation monitors, prior to commencing his or her employment, and as a prerequisite to that employment, shall sign a statement on a form provided to him or her by his or her employer to the effect that he or she has knowledge of the provisions of Section 11166 and will comply with those provisions. The statement shall inform the employee that he or she is a mandated reporter and inform the employee of his or her reporting obligations under Section 11166. The employer shall provide a copy of Sections 11165.7 and 11166 to the employee.**

This law applies to all licensed MFTs, interns and trainees in public or private employment when they function within the role of their profession. The employer keeps the signed statement in the employee's file.

Child Abuse Reporting and Immunity

Section 11172 of the Penal Code clearly established that a clinician making a mandated report of child abuse is provided immunity from civil or criminal prosecution. However, the same section states that immunity applies as long as the report wasn't false, or made with disregard to the truth or falsity of the report. Additionally, the same section states that "any person who makes a case report or with disregard of the truth of falsity of the report is liable for damages caused."

Section 11172 (d) (1) appears to indicate that clinician can be sued by those who believed they've been harmed by false or inappropriate reports. To compensate individuals who face a malpractice or criminal action, the State of California provides a clinician who's been sued with the sum of $50,000 applicable to attorney's fees. The caveat is that the clinician must win the lawsuit, otherwise the financial aid won't apply. The significance of these sections upon the wellbeing of clinicians is that to protect themselves in these challenging circumstances, they must provide the necessary documentation to an opposing attorney indicating that they determined that their child abuse report was based on an objective determination of a "reasonable" suspicion of child abuse. Additionally, its in the best interest of the clinician to document in the clinical records how he made that determination. That information can serve to indicate to the opposing attorney that the malpractice or criminal action against the clinician lacks merit.

The Use of Anatomically Correct Dolls to Prove Child Abuse

The courts have decided that anatomically correct dolls are unacceptable as a tool to determine child abuse. The reason for this is that the use of these dolls has not passed the Kelly-Frye test, a legal test that is meant to ascertain whether the testimony presented is based on proven scientific methodology. The therapeutic community of experts would most likely accuse a therapist who uses these dolls to determine child abuse of contaminating the child's testimony because she or he used material that was not scientifically acceptable

Reporting Consensual Sex Between Minors

In the late 1980's, the California Appellate Court rendered an opinion that sexual intercourse between minors under 14 years of age is not considered a reportable act under the Child Abuse Law. However, it would be prudent for the clinician to determine if one of the parties involved is mature enough to participate in consensual sex and to document his or her determination thoroughly. It may be that one of the two children could be coerced

physically or emotionally from the sexual interaction. Should this happen, it is likely that the clinician could be sued for failure to report mandated child abuse. Appropriate documentation of this determination can help to avoid potentially difficult legal challenges in the future.

Reporting Consensual Sex Between Minors and Adults

In 1998, the law was amended regarding sex and minors to include the following:

a) It is unlawful to have sexual intercourse (even if it is consensual) with a child under the age of 16 (as determined by birth date) when the alleged perpetrator is over the age of 21 years of age (as determined by birth date).

b) Lewd and lascivious acts with a child of 14 or 15 years of age is a crime when the perpetrator is more than 10 years older (as determined by birthday) than the victim.

Note that when an adult (18 and over) has sex with a minor under the age of 18, it is considered statutory rape, even though it is not reportable except in specific age brackets. See figure 5:

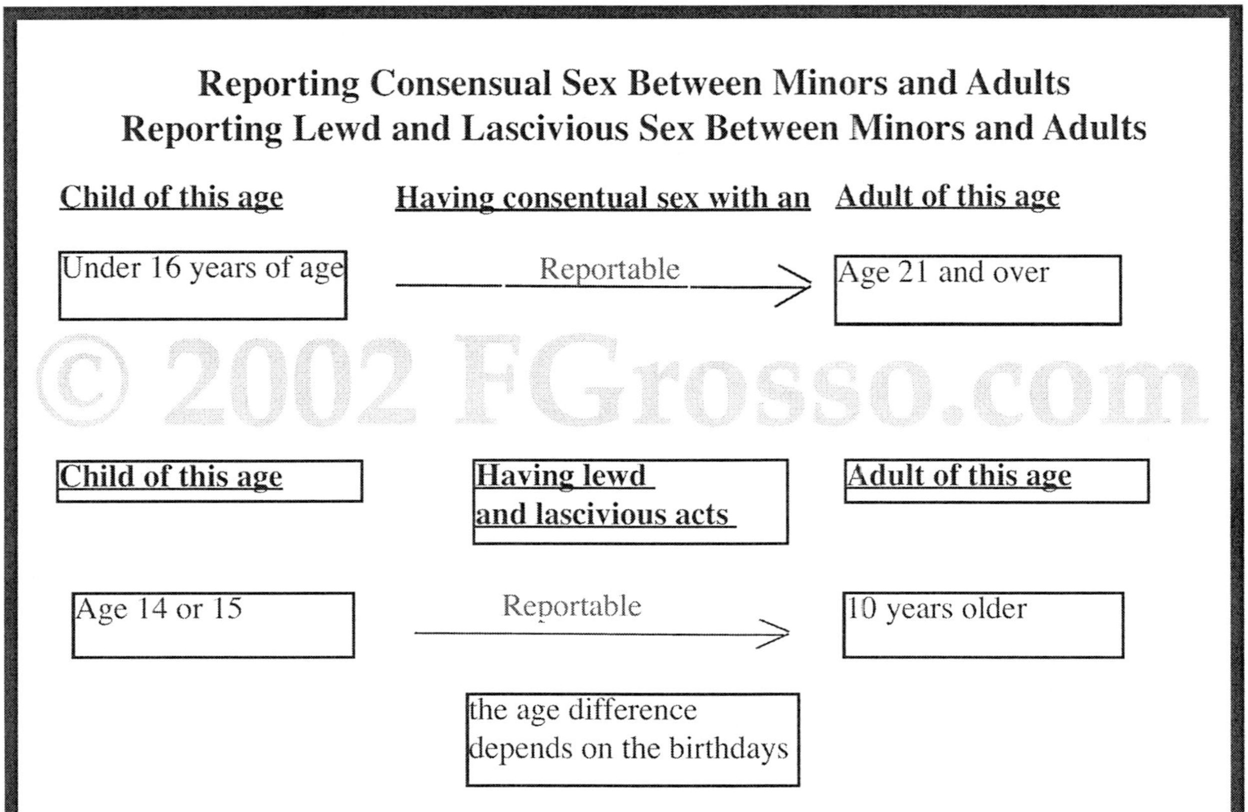

Figure 5

Copyright 2000 Federico C Grosso, DDS, PhD, MFT

Serious Emotional Damage

Another change made to the law relates to the child's emotional suffering. On January 1, 2011, the Child Abuse Laws was amended. The following changes apply to licensed MFTs: Section Penal Code 11166.05 states "Any mandated reporter who has knowledge of or who reasonably suspects that emotional suffering has been inflicted upon a child or that his or her emotional well-being is endangered in any other way may report the known or suspected instance of child abuse or neglect to an agency specified in Section 11165.9." The MFT has the option of reporting emotional suffering after determining that a reasonable suspicion of abuse exists. The law was amended to expand the inclusion of reporting agencies. These include police department, sheriff's department, county probation department (if designated by the county to receive mandated reports), or the county welfare department. MFTs are protected under the "immunity" clause should they choose to report.

Special Reporting Categories

- Neglect (negligence or maltreatment by a responsible party indicating harm to the child or his/her welfare). This act requires a mandated report.

- Emotional Suffering (suffering serious emotional damage characterized by states of severe anxiety, depression, withdrawal, or untoward aggressive behavior towards self or others, etc,). This is a permitted reportable situation.
- Mental Suffering (the willful harm or injury causing suffering, unjustifiable physical pain or mental suffering). This is a reportable condition.
- Unlawful Corporal Punishment (infliction of cruel or inhuman corporal punishment or injury resulting in a traumatic condition). This act requires a mandated report.
- Treatment by Spiritual Means (failure to receive medical treatment for religious reasons). This act is not a reportable issue.

Homelessness

Homelessness is by itself not a reportable condition. However, if the clinician reasonably suspects the child is being abused or neglected, then a report must be made. See Section 11166 for more information.

The Confidentiality Bind in Child Abuse Reporting

Though California law provides immunity to those who report child abuse, it also provides those who have been reported the opportunity to seek redress. Before they make a mandated report, MFTs must determine if a reasonable suspicion of child abuse exists before making a report. Consider a situation where a teenager accuses her uncle of touching her inappropriately. The family meets with a therapist and all agree that it was an innocent touch and the uncle accepted that his touch was inappropriate and unintended. The clinician documents her findings carefully. Several years later, the teenager, who is now an adult, initiates a malpractice action against the therapist for failure to protect her. It seems that the uncle continued his sexual advances which terminated in intercourse. Even though the therapist documented her findings carefully, she now faces legal action. Now consider the same therapist who determines that she has a reasonable suspicion of child abuse. She reports the uncle to Child Welfare Services as required by law. A few weeks later, an opposing attorney serves her with court papers indicating that the uncle is suing her for making an inappropriate and malicious report, for failing to address the legal reporting process, injuring his standing in the community, and an breaching his confidentiality without legal basis.

Regardless of the action taken, MFTs can face malpractice actions. Based on experience as an expert witness, the author recommends developing a strong foundation by writing appropriate and supportive records. This is addressed in later chapters.

Communications With Law Enforcement Investigators After Making the Report

As of January 1, 2011, mandated reporters are required to respond to post facto inquiries presented by child abuse investigators. All investigators must provide the patient and the mandated reporter a detailed written request outlining the specific requested. It is in the best interest of the mandated reporter to verify the legal standing of the person requesting information and review the written request and determine if the request addresses specificity versus generality.

The Child Abuse Laws –PENAL CODE SECTION 11164-11174.3

ARTICLE 2.5. Child Abuse and Neglect Reporting Act [11164 - 11174.3] (Heading of Article 2.5 amended by Stats. 1987, Ch. 1444, Sec. 1.)

11164.
(a) This article shall be known and may be cited as the Child Abuse and Neglect Reporting Act.

(b) The intent and purpose of this article is to protect children from abuse and neglect. In any investigation of suspected child abuse or neglect, all persons participating in the investigation of the case shall consider the needs of the child victim and shall do whatever is necessary to prevent psychological harm to the child victim.
(Amended by Stats. 2000, Ch. 916, Sec. 1. Effective January 1, 2001.)

11165.
As used in this article "child" means a person under the age of 18 years. (Repealed and added by Stats. 1987, Ch. 1459, Sec. 2.)

11165.1.
As used in this article, "sexual abuse" means sexual assault or sexual exploitation as defined by the following:
(a) "Sexual assault" means conduct in violation of one or more of the following sections: Section 261 (rape), subdivision (d) of Section 261.5 (statutory rape), 264.1 (rape in concert), 285 (incest), 286 (sodomy), subdivision (a) or (b), or paragraph (1) of subdivision (c) of Section 288 (lewd or lascivious acts upon a child), 288a (oral copulation), 289 (sexual penetration), or 647.6 (child molestation).
(b) Conduct described as "sexual assault" includes, but is not limited to, all of the following:
(1) Penetration, however slight, of the vagina or anal opening of one person by the penis of another person, whether or not there is the emission of semen.
(2) Sexual contact between the genitals or anal opening of one person and the mouth or tongue of another person.
(3) Intrusion by one person into the genitals or anal opening of another person, including the use of an object for this purpose, except that, it does not include acts performed for a valid medical purpose.
(4) The intentional touching of the genitals or intimate parts, including the breasts, genital area, groin, inner thighs, and buttocks, or the clothing covering them, of a child, or of the perpetrator by a child, for purposes of sexual arousal or gratification, except that it does not include acts which may reasonably be construed to be normal caretaker responsibilities; interactions with, or demonstrations of affection for, the child; or acts performed for a valid medical purpose.
(5) The intentional masturbation of the perpetrator's genitals in the presence of a child.
(c) "Sexual exploitation" refers to any of the following:
(1) Conduct involving matter depicting a minor engaged in obscene acts in violation of Section 311.2 (preparing, selling, or distributing obscene matter) or subdivision (a) of Section 311.4 (employment of minor to perform obscene acts).
(2) A person who knowingly promotes, aids, or assists, employs, uses, persuades, induces, or coerces a ild, or a person responsible for a child's welfare, who knowingly permits or encourages a child to engage in, or assist others to engage in, prostitution or a live performance involving obscene sexual conduct, or to either pose or model alone or with others for purposes of preparing a film, photograph, negative, slide, drawing, painting, or other pictorial depiction, involving obscene sexual conduct. For the purpose of this section, "person responsible for a child's welfare" means a parent, guardian, foster parent, or a licensed administrator or employee of a public or private residential home, residential school, or other residential institution.
(3) A person who depicts a child in, or who knowingly develops, duplicates, prints, downloads, streams, accesses through any electronic or digital media, or exchanges, a film, photograph, videotape, video recording, negative, or slide in which a child is engaged in an act of obscene sexual conduct, except for those activities by law enforcement and prosecution agencies and

other persons described in subdivisions (c) and (e) of Section 311.3. (Amended by Stats. 2014, Ch. 264, Sec. 1. Effective January 1, 2015.)

11165.2.
As used in this article, "neglect" means the negligent treatment or the maltreatment of a child by a person responsible for the child's welfare under circumstances indicating harm or threatened harm to the child's health or welfare. The term includes both acts and omissions on the part of the responsible person.
(a) "Severe neglect" means the negligent failure of a person having the care or custody of a child to protect the child from severe malnutrition or medically diagnosed nonorganic failure to thrive. "Severe neglect" also means those situations of neglect where any person having the care or custody of a child willfully causes or permits the person or health of the child to be placed in a situation such that his or her person or health is endangered, as proscribed by Section 11165.3, including the intentional failure to provide adequate food, clothing, shelter, or medical care.
(b) "General neglect" means the negligent failure of a person having the care or custody of a child to provide adequate food, clothing, shelter, medical care, or supervision where no physical injury to the child has occurred.
For the purposes of this chapter, a child receiving treatment by spiritual means as provided in Section 16509.1 of the Welfare and Institutions Code or not receiving specified medical treatment for religious reasons, shall not for that reason alone be considered a neglected child. An informed and appropriate medical decision made by parent or guardian after consultation with a physician or physicians who have examined the minor does not constitute neglect. (Repealed and added by Stats. 1987, Ch. 1459, Sec. 7.)

11165.3.
As used in this article, "the willful harming or injuring of a child or the endangering of the person or health of a child," means a situation in which any person willfully causes or permits any child to suffer, or inflicts thereon, unjustifiable physical pain or mental suffering, or having the care or custody of any child, willfully causes or permits the person or health of the child to be placed in a situation in which his or her person or health is endangered. (Amended by Stats. 2004, Ch. 842, Sec. 1. Effective January 1, 2005.)

1165.4.
As used in this article, "unlawful corporal punishment or injury" means a situation where any person willfully inflicts upon any child any cruel or inhuman corporal punishment or injury resulting in a traumatic condition. It does not include an amount of force that is reasonable and necessary for a person employed by or engaged in a public school to quell a disturbance threatening physical injury to person or damage to property, for purposes of self-defense, or to obtain possession of weapons or other dangerous objects within the control of the pupil, as authorized by Section 49001 of the Education Code. It also does not include the exercise of the degree of physical control authorized by Section 44807 of the Education Code. It also does not include an injury caused by reasonable and necessary force used by a peace officer acting within the course and scope of his or her employment as a peace officer. (Amended by Stats. 1993, Ch. 346, Sec. 1. Effective January 1, 1994.)

11165.5.
As used in this article, the term "abuse or neglect in out-of-home care" includes physical injury or death inflicted upon a child by another person by other than accidental means, sexual abuse as defined in Section 11165.1, neglect as defined in Section 11165.2, unlawful corporal punishment or injury as defined in Section 11165.4, or the willful harming or injuring of a child or the endangering of the person or health of a child, as defined in Section 11165.3, where the person responsible for the child's welfare is a licensee, administrator, or employee of any facility licensed to care for children, or an administrator or employee of a public or private school or other institution or agency. "Abuse or neglect in out-of-home care" does not include an injury caused by reasonable and necessary force used by a peace officer acting within the course and scope of his or her employment as a peace officer.
(Amended by Stats. 2007, Ch. 393, Sec. 1. Effective January 1, 2008.)

11165.6.
As used in this article, the term "child abuse or neglect" includes physical injury or death inflicted by other than accidental means upon a child by another person, sexual abuse as defined in Section 11165.1, neglect as defined in Section 11165.2, the willful harming or injuring of a child or the endangering of the person or health of a child, as defined in Section 11165.3, and unlawful corporal punishment or injury as defined in Section 11165.4. "Child abuse or neglect" does not include a mutual affray between minors. "Child abuse or neglect" does not include an injury caused by reasonable and necessary force used by a peace officer acting within the course and scope of his or her employment as a peace officer. (Amended by Stats. 2007, Ch. 393, Sec. 2. Effective January 1, 2008.)

11165.7.
(a) As used in this article, "mandated reporter" is defined as any of the following:
(1) A teacher.

(2) An instructional aide.
(3) A teacher's aide or teacher's assistant employed by a public or private school.
(4) A classified employee of a public school.
(5) An administrative officer or supervisor of child welfare and attendance, or a certificated pupil personnel employee of a public or private school.
(6) An administrator of a public or private day camp.
(7) An administrator or employee of a public or private youth center, youth recreation program, or youth organization.
(8) An administrator or employee of a public or private organization whose duties require direct contact and supervision of children.
(9) An employee of a county office of education or the State Department of Education whose duties bring the employee into contact with children on a regular basis.
(10) A licensee, an administrator, or an employee of a licensed community care or child day care facility.
(11) A Head Start program teacher.
(12) A licensing worker or licensing evaluator employed by a licensing agency, as defined in Section 11165.11.
(13) A public assistance worker.
(14) An employee of a child care institution, including, but not limited to, foster parents, group home personnel, and personnel of residential care facilities.
(15) A social worker, probation officer, or parole officer.
(16) An employee of a school district police or security department.
(17) A person who is an administrator or presenter of, or a counselor in, a child abuse prevention program in a public or private school.
(18) A district attorney investigator, inspector, or local child support agency caseworker, unless the investigator, inspector, or caseworker is working with an attorney appointed pursuant to Section 317 of the Welfare and Institutions Code to represent a minor.
(19) A peace officer, as defined in Chapter 4.5 (commencing with Section 830) of Title 3 of Part 2, who is not otherwise described in this section.
(20) A firefighter, except for volunteer firefighters.
(21) A physician and surgeon, psychiatrist, psychologist, dentist, resident, intern, podiatrist, chiropractor, licensed nurse, dental hygienist, optometrist, marriage and family therapist, clinical social worker, professional clinical counselor, or any other person who is currently licensed under Division 2 (commencing with Section 500) of the Business and Professions Code.
(22) An emergency medical technician I or II, paramedic, or other person certified pursuant to Division 2.5 (commencing with Section 1797) of the Health and Safety Code.
(23) A psychological assistant registered pursuant to Section 2913 of the Business and Professions Code.
(24) A marriage and family therapist trainee, as defined in subivision (c) of Section 4980.03 of the Business and Professions Code.
(25) An unlicensed marriage and family therapist intern registered under Section 4980.44 of the Business and Professions Code.
(26) A state or county public health employee who treats a minor for venereal disease or any other condition.
(27) A coroner.
(28) A medical examiner or other person who performs autopsies.
(29) A commercial film and photographic print or image processor as specified in subdivision (e) of Section 11166. As used in this article, "commercial film and photographic print or image processor" means a person who develops exposed photographic film into negatives, slides, or prints, or who makes prints from negatives or slides, or who prepares, publishes, produces, develops, duplicates, or prints any representation of information, data, or an image, including, but not limited to, any film, filmstrip, photograph, negative, slide, photocopy, videotape, video laser disc, computer hardware, computer software, computer floppy disk, data storage medium, CD-ROM, computer-generated equipment, or computer-generated image, for compensation. The term includes any employee of that person; it does not include a person who develops film or makes prints or images for a public agency.
(30) A child visitation monitor. As used in this article, "child visitation monitor" means a person who, for financial compensation, acts as a monitor of a visit between a child and another person when the monitoring of that visit has been ordered by a court of law.
(31) An animal control officer or humane society officer. For the purposes of this article, the following terms have the following meanings:
(A) "Animal control officer" means a person employed by a city, county, or city and county for the purpose of enforcing animal control laws or regulations.
(B) "Humane society officer" means a person appointed or employed by a public or private entity as a humane officer who is qualified pursuant to Section 14502 or 14503 of the Corporations Code.
(32) A clergy member, as specified in subdivision (d) of Section 11166. As used in this article, "clergy member" means a priest, minister, rabbi, religious practitioner, or similar functionary of a church, temple, or recognized denomination or organization.
(33) Any custodian of records of a clergy member, as specified in this section and subdivision (d) of Section 11166.

(34) An employee of any police department, county sheriff's department, county probation department, or county welfare department.
(35) An employee or volunteer of a Court Appointed Special Advocate program, as defined in Rule 5.655 of the California Rules of Court.
(36) A custodial officer, as defined in Section 831.5.
(37) A person providing services to a minor child under Section 12300 or 12300.1 of the Welfare and Institutions Code.
(38) An alcohol and drug counselor. As used in this article, an "alcohol and drug counselor" is a person providing counseling, therapy, or other clinical services for a state licensed or certified drug, alcohol, or drug and alcohol treatment program. However, alcohol or drug abuse, or both alcohol and drug abuse, is not, in and of itself, a sufficient basis for reporting child abuse or neglect.
(39) A clinical counselor trainee, as defined in subdivision (g) of Section 4999.12 of the Business and Professions Code.
(40) A clinical counselor intern registered under Section 4999.42 of the Business and Professions Code.
(41) An employee or administrator of a public or private postsecondary educational institution, whose duties bring the administrator or employee into contact with children on a regular basis, or who supervises those whose duties bring the administrator or employee into contact with children on a regular basis, as to child abuse or neglect occurring on that institution's premises or at an official activity of, or program conducted by, the institution. Nothing in this paragraph shall be construed as altering the lawyer-client privilege as set forth in Article 3 (commencing with Section 950) of Chapter 4 of Division 8 of the Evidence Code.
(42) An athletic coach, athletic administrator, or athletic director employed by any public or private school that provides any combination of instruction for kindergarten, or grades 1 to 12, inclusive.
(43) (A) A commercial computer technician as specified in subdivision (e) of Section 11166. As used in this article, "commercial computer technician" means a person who works for a company that is in the business of repairing, installing, or otherwise servicing a computer or computer component, including, but not limited to, a computer part, device, memory storage or recording mechanism, auxiliary storage recording or memory capacity, or any other material relating to the operation and maintenance of a computer or computer network system, for a fee. An employer who provides an electronic communications service or a remote computing service to the public shall be deemed to comply with this article if that employer complies with Section 2258A of Title 18 of the United States Code.
(B) An employer of a commercial computer technician may implement internal procedures for facilitating reporting consistent with this article. These procedures may direct employees who are mandated reporters under this paragraph to report materials described in subdivision (e) of Section 11166 to an employee who is designated by the employer to receive the reports. An employee who is designated to receive reports under this subparagraph shall be a commercial computer technician for purposes of this article. A commercial computer technician who makes a report to the designated employee pursuant to this subparagraph shall be deemed to have complied with the requirements of this article and shall be subject to the protections afforded to mandated reporters, including, but not limited to, those protections afforded by Section 11172.
(44) Any athletic coach, including, but not limited to, an assistant coach or a graduate assistant involved in coaching, at public or private postsecondary educational institutions.
(b) Except as provided in paragraph (35) of subdivision (a), volunteers of public or private organizations whose duties require direct contact with and supervision of children are not mandated reporters but are encouraged to obtain training in the identification and reporting of child abuse and neglect and are further encouraged to report known or suspected instances of child abuse or neglect to an agency specified in Section 11165.9.
(c) Except as provided in subdivision (d), employers are strongly encouraged to provide their employees who are mandated reporters with training in the duties imposed by this article. This training shall include training in child abuse and neglect identification and training in child abuse and neglect reporting. Whether or not employers provide their employees with training in child abuse and neglect identification and reporting, the employers shall provide their employees who are mandated reporters with the statement required pursuant to subdivision (a) of Section 11166.5.
(d) Pursuant to Section 44691 of the Education Code, school districts, county offices of education, state special schools and diagnostic centers operated by the State Department of Education, and charter schools shall annually train their employees and persons working on their behalf specified in subdivision (a) in the duties of mandated reporters under the child abuse reporting laws. The training shall include, but not necessarily be limited to, training in child abuse and neglect identification and child abuse and neglect reporting.
(e) Unless otherwise specifically provided, the absence of training shall not excuse a mandated reporter from the duties imposed by this article.
(f) Public and private organizations are encouraged to provide their volunteers whose duties require direct contact with and supervision of children with training in the identification and reporting of child abuse and neglect. (Amended by Stats. 2014, Ch. 797, Sec. 4. Effective January 1, 2015.)

11165.9.

Reports of suspected child abuse or neglect shall be made by mandated reporters, or in the case of reports pursuant to Section 11166.05, may be made, to any police department or sheriff's department, not including a school district police or security department, county probation department, if designated by the county to receive mandated reports, or the county welfare

department. Any of those agencies shall accept a report of suspected child abuse or neglect whether offered by a mandated reporter or another person, or referred by another agency, even if the agency to whom the report is being made lacks subject matter or geographical jurisdiction to investigate the reported case, unless the agency can immediately electronically transfer the call to an agency with proper jurisdiction. When an agency takes a report about a case of suspected child abuse or neglect in which that agency lacks jurisdiction, the agency shall immediately refer the case by telephone, fax, or electronic transmission to an agency with proper jurisdiction. Agencies that are required to receive reports of suspected child abuse or neglect may not refuse to accept a report of suspected child abuse or neglect from a mandated reporter or another person unless otherwise authorized pursuant to this section, and shall maintain a record of all reports received.
(Amended by Stats. 2006, Ch. 701, Sec. 2. Effective January 1, 2007.)

11165.11.
As used in this article, "licensing agency" means the State Department of Social Services office responsible for the licensing and enforcement of the California Community Care Facilities Act (Chapter 3 (commencing with Section 1500) of Division 2 of the Health and Safety Code), the California Child Day Care Act (Chapter 3.4 (commencing with Section 1596.70) of Division 2 of the Health and Safety Code), and Chapter 3.5 (commencing with Section 1596.90) of Division 2 of the Health and Safety Code), or the county licensing agency which has contracted with the state for performance of those duties.
(Added by Stats. 1987, Ch. 1459, Sec. 18.)

11165.12.
As used in this article, the following definitions shall control:
(a) "Unfounded report" means a report that is determined by the investigator who conducted the investigation to be false, to be inherently improbable, to involve an accidental injury, or not to constitute child abuse or neglect, as defined in Section 11165.6.

(b) "Substantiated report" means a report that is determined by the investigator who conducted the investigation to constitute child abuse or neglect, as defined in Section 11165.6, based upon evidence that makes it more likely than not that child abuse or neglect, as defined, occurred. A substantiated report shall not include a report where the investigator who conducted the investigation found the report to be false, inherently improbable, to involve an accidental injury, or to not constitute child abuse or neglect as defined in Section 11165.6.
(c) "Inconclusive report" means a report that is determined y the investigator who conducted the investigation not to be unfounded, but the findings are inconclusive and there is insufficient evidence to determine whether child abuse or neglect, as defined in Section 11165.6, has occurred. (Amended by Stats. 2011, Ch. 468, Sec. 1. Effective January 1, 2012.)

11165.13.
For purposes of this article, a positive toxicology screen at the time of the delivery of an infant is not in and of itself a sufficient basis for reporting child abuse or neglect. However, any indication of maternal substance abuse shall lead to an assessment of the needs of the mother and child pursuant to Section 123605 of the Health and Safety Code. If other factors are present that indicate risk to a child, then a report shall be made. However, a report based on risk to a child which relates solely to the inability of the parent to provide the child with regular care due to the parent's substance abuse shall be made only to a county welfare or probation department, and not to a law enforcement agency. Amended by Stats. 2000, Ch. 916, Sec. 11. Effective January 1, 2001.)

11165.14.
The appropriate local law enforcement agency shall investigate a child abuse complaint filed by a parent or guardian of a pupil with a school or an agency specified in Section 11165.9 against a school employee or other person that commits an act of child abuse, as defined in this article, against a pupil at a school site and shall transmit a substantiated report, as defined in Section 11165.12, of that investigation to the governing board of the appropriate school district or county office of education. A substantiated report received by a governing board of a school district or county office of education shall be subject to the provisions of Section 44031 of the Education Code. (Amended by Stats. 2000, Ch. 916, Sec. 12. Effective January 1, 2001.)

11165.15.
For the purposes of this article, the fact that a child is homeless or is classified as an unaccompanied youth, as defined in Section 11434a of the federal McKinney-Vento Homeless Assistance Act (42 U.S.C. Sec. 11301 et seq.), is not, in and of itself, a sufficient basis for reporting child abuse or neglect. This section shall not limit a mandated reporter, as defined in Section 11165.7, from making a report pursuant to Section 11166 whenever the mandated reporter has knowledge of or observes an unaccompanied minor whom the mandated reporter knows or reasonably suspects to be the victim of abuse or neglect.
(Amended by Stats. 2014, Ch. 71, Sec. 132. Effective January 1, 2015.)

11166.
(a) Except as provided in subdivision (d), and in Section 11166.05, a mandated reporter shall make a report to an agency

specified in Section 11165.9 whenever the mandated reporter, in his or her professional capacity or within the scope of his or her employment, has knowledge of or observes a child whom the mandated reporter knows or reasonably suspects has been the victim of child abuse or neglect. The mandated reporter shall make an initial report by telephone to the agency immediately or as soon as is practicably possible, and shall prepare and send, fax, or electronically transmit a written followup report within 36 hours of receiving the information concerning the incident. The mandated reporter may include with the report any nonprivileged documentary evidence the mandated reporter possesses relating to the incident.
(1) For purposes of this article, "reasonable suspicion" means that it is objectively reasonable for a person to entertain a suspicion, based upon facts that could cause a reasonable person in a like position, drawing, when appropriate, on his or her training and experience, to suspect child abuse or neglect. "Reasonable suspicion" does not require certainty that child abuse or neglect has occurred nor does it require a specific medical indication of child abuse or neglect; any "reasonable suspicion" is sufficient. For purposes of this article, the pregnancy of a minor does not, in and of itself, constitute a basis for a reasonable suspicion of sexual abuse.
(2) The agency shall be notified and a report shall be prepared and sent, faxed, or electronically transmitted even if the child has expired, regardless of whether or not the possible abuse was a factor contributing to the death, and even if suspected child abuse was discovered during an autopsy.
(3) A report made by a mandated reporter pursuant to this section shall be known as a mandated report.
(b) If, after reasonable efforts, a mandated reporter is unable to submit an initial report by telephone, he or she shall immediately or as soon as is practicably possible, by fax or electronic transmission, make a one-time automated written report on the form prescribed by the Department of Justice, and shall also be available to respond to a telephone followup call by the agency with which he or she filed the report. A mandated reporter who files a one-time automated written report because he or she was unable to submit an initial report by telephone is not required to submit a written followup report.
(1) The one-time automated written report form prescribed by the Department of Justice shall be clearly identifiable so that it is not mistaken for a standard written followup report. In addition, the automated one-time report shall contain a section that allows the mandated reporter to state the reason the initial telephone call was not able to be completed. The reason for the submission of the one-time automated written report in lieu of the procedure prescribed in subdivision (a) shall be captured in the Child Welfare Services/Case Management System (CWS/CMS). The department shall work with stakeholders to modify reporting forms and the CWS/CMS as is necessary to accommodate the changes enacted by these provisions.
(2) This subdivision shall not become operative until the CWS/CMS is updated to capture the information prescribed in this subdivision.
(3) This subdivision shall become inoperative three years after this subdivision becomes operative or on January 1, 2009, whichever occurs first.
(4) On the inoperative date of these provisions, a report shall be submitted to the counties and the Legislature by the State Department of Social Services that reflects the data collected from automated one-time reports indicating the reasons stated as to why the automated one-time report was filed in lieu of the initial telephone report.
(5) Nothing in this section shall supersede the requirement that a mandated reporter first attempt to make a report via telephone, or that agencies specified in Section 11165.9 accept reports from mandated reporters and other persons as required.
(c) A mandated reporter who fails to report an incident of known or reasonably suspected child abuse or neglect as required by this section is guilty of a misdemeanor punishable by up to six months confinement in a county jail or by a fine of one thousand dollars ($1,000) or by both that imprisonment and fine. If a mandated reporter intentionally conceals his or her failure to report an incident known by the mandated reporter to be abuse or severe neglect under this section, the failure to report is a continuing offense until an agency specified in Section 11165.9 discovers the offense.
(d) (1) A clergy member who acquires knowledge or a reasonable suspicion of child abuse or neglect during a penitential communication is not subject to subdivision (a). For the purposes of this subdivision, "penitential communication" means a communication, intended to be in confidence, including, but not limited to, a sacramental confession, made to a clergy member who, in the course of the discipline or practice of his or her church, denomination, or organization, is authorized or accustomed to hear those communications, and under the discipline, tenets, customs, or practices of his or her church, denomination, or organization, has a duty to keep those communications secret.
2) Nothing in this subdivision shall be construed to modify or limit a clergy member's duty to report known or suspected child abuse or neglect when the clergy member is acting in some other capacity that would otherwise make the clergy member a mandated reporter.
(3) (A) On or before January 1, 2004, a clergy member or any custodian of records for the clergy member may report to an agency specified in Section 11165.9 that the clergy member or any custodian of records for the clergy member, prior to January 1, 1997, in his or her professional capacity or within the scope of his or her employment, other than during a penitential communication, acquired knowledge or had a reasonable suspicion that a child had been the victim of sexual abuse and that the clergy member or any custodian of records for the clergy member did not previously report the abuse to an agency specified in Section 11165.9. The provisions of Section 11172 shall apply to all reports made pursuant to this paragraph.
(B) This paragraph shall apply even if the victim of the known or suspected abuse has reached the age of majority by the time the required report is made.
(C) The local law enforcement agency shall have jurisdiction to investigate any report of child abuse made pursuant to this paragraph even if the report is made after the victim has reached the age of majority.

(e) (1) A commercial film, photographic print, or image processor who has knowledge of or observes, within the scope of his or her professional capacity or employment, any film, photograph, videotape, negative, slide, or any representation of information, data, or an image, including, but not limited to, any film, filmstrip, photograph, negative, slide, photocopy, videotape, video laser disc, computer hardware, computer software, computer floppy disk, data storage medium, CD-ROM, computer-generated equipment, or computer-generated image depicting a child under 16 years of age engaged in an act of sexual conduct, shall, immediately or as soon as practicably possible, telephonically report the instance of suspected abuse to the law enforcement agency located in the county in which the images are seen. Within 36 hours of receiving the information concerning the incident, the reporter shall prepare and send, fax, or electronically transmit a written followup report of the incident with a copy of the image or material attached.
(2) A commercial computer technician who has knowledge of or observes, within the scope of his or her professional capacity or employment, any representation of information, data, or an image, including, but not limited to, any computer hardware, computer software, computer file, computer floppy disk, data storage medium, CD-ROM, computer-generated equipment, or computer-generated image that is retrievable in perceivable form and that is intentionally saved, transmitted, or organized on an electronic medium, depicting a child under 16 years of age engaged in an act of sexual conduct, shall immediately, or as soon as practicably possible, telephonically report the instance of suspected abuse to the law enforcement agency located in the county in which the images or material are seen. As soon as practicably possible after receiving the information concerning the incident, the reporter shall prepare and send, fax, or electronically transmit a written followup report of the incident with a brief description of the images or materials.
(3) For purposes of this article, "commercial computer technician" includes an employee designated by an employer to receive reports pursuant to an established reporting process authorized by subparagraph (B) of paragraph (43) of subdivision (a) of Section 11165.7.
(4) As used in this subdivision, "electronic medium" includes, but is not limited to, a recording, CD-ROM, magnetic disk memory, magnetic tape memory, CD, DVD, thumbdrive, or any other computer hardware or media.
(5) As used in this subdivision, "sexual conduct" means any of the following:
(A) Sexual intercourse, including genital-genital, oral-genital, anal-genital, or oral-anal, whether between persons of the same or opposite sex or between humans and animals.
(B) Penetration of the vagina or rectum by any object.
(C) Masturbation for the purpose of sexual stimulation of the viewer.
(D) Sadomasochistic abuse for the purpose of sexual stimulation of the viewer.
(E) Exhibition of the genitals, pubic, or rectal areas of a person for the purpose of sexual stimulation of the viewer.
(f) Any mandated reporter who knows or reasonably suspects that the home or institution in which a child resides is unsuitable for the child because of abuse or neglect of the child shall bring the condition to the attention of the agency to which, and at the same time as, he or she makes a report of the abuse or neglect pursuant to subdivision (a).
(g) Any other person who has knowledge of or observes a child whom he or she knows or reasonably suspects has been a victim of child abuse or neglect may report the known or suspected instance of child abuse or neglect to an agency specified in Section 11165.9. For purposes of this section, "any other person" includes a mandated reporter who acts in his or her private capacity and not in his or her professional capacity or within the scope of his or her employment.
(h) When two or more persons, who are required to report, jointly have knowledge of a known or suspected instance of child abuse or neglect, and when there is agreement among them, the telephone report may be made by a member of the team selected by mutual agreement and a single report may be made and signed by the selected member of the reporting team. Any member who has knowledge that the member designated to report has failed to do so shall thereafter make the report.
(i) (1) The reporting duties under this section are individual, and no supervisor or administrator may impede or inhibit the reporting duties, and no person making a report shall be subject to any sanction for making the report. However, internal procedures to facilitate reporting and apprise supervisors and administrators of reports may be established provided that they are not inconsistent with this article.
(2) The internal procedures shall not require any employee required to make reports pursuant to this article to disclose his or her identity to the employer.
(3) Reporting the information regarding a case of possible child abuse or neglect to an employer, supervisor, school principal, school counselor, coworker, or other person shall not be a substitute for making a mandated report to an agency specified in Section 11165.9.
(j) A county probation or welfare department shall immediately, or as soon as practicably possible, report by telephone, fax, or electronic transmission to the law enforcement agency having jurisdiction over the case, to the agency given the responsibility for investigation of cases under Section 300 of the Welfare and Institutions Code, and to the district attorney's office every known or suspected instance of child abuse or neglect, as defined in Section 11165.6, except acts or omissions coming within subdivision (b) of Section 11165.2, or reports made pursuant to Section 11165.13 based on risk to a child which relates solely to the inability of the parent to provide the child with regular care due to the parent's substance abuse, which shall be reported only to the county welfare or probation department. A county probation or welfare department also shall send, fax, or electronically transmit a written report thereof within 36 hours of receiving the information concerning the incident to any agency to which it makes a telephone report under this subdivision.
(k) A law enforcement agency shall immediately, or as soon as practicably possible, report by telephone, fax, or electronic

transmission to the agency given responsibility for investigation of cases under Section 300 of the Welfare and Institutions Code and to the district attorney's office every known or suspected instance of child abuse or neglect reported to it, except acts or omissions coming within subdivision (b) of Section 11165.2, which shall be reported only to the county welfare or probation department. A law enforcement agency shall report to the county welfare or probation department every known or suspected instance of child abuse or neglect reported to it which is alleged to have occurred as a result of the action of a person responsible for the child's welfare, or as the result of the failure of a person responsible for the child's welfare to adequately protect the minor from abuse when the person responsible for the child's welfare knew or reasonably should have known that the minor was in danger of abuse. A law enforcement agency also shall send, fax, or electronically transmit a written report thereof within 36 hours of receiving the information concerning the incident to any agency to which it makes a telephone report under this subdivision. (Amended by Stats. 2013, Ch. 76, Sec. 165. Effective January 1, 2014.)
11166.01.

(a) Except as provided in subdivision (b), any supervisor or administrator who violates paragraph (1) of subdivision (i) of Section 11166 shall be punished by not more than six months in a county jail, by a fine of not more than one thousand dollars ($1,000), or by both that fine and imprisonment.
(b) Notwithstanding Section 11162 or subdivision (c) of Section 11166, any mandated reporter who willfully fails to report abuse or neglect, or any person who impedes or inhibits a report of abuse or neglect, in violation of this article, where that abuse or neglect results in death or great bodily injury, shall be punished by not more than one year in a county jail, by a fine of not more than five thousand dollars ($5,000), or by both that fine and imprisonment. (Amended by Stats. 2006, Ch. 901, Sec. 10. Effective January 1, 2007.)

11166.05.
Any mandated reporter who has knowledge of or who reasonably suspects that a child is suffering serious emotional damage or is at a substantial risk of suffering serious emotional damage, evidenced by states of being or behavior, including, but not limited to, severe anxiety, depression, withdrawal, or untoward aggressive behavior toward self or others, may make a report to an agency specified in Section 11165.9.(Amended by Stats. 2004, Ch. 842, Sec. 9. Effective January 1, 2005.)

11166.1.
(a) When an agency receives a report pursuant to Section 11166 that contains either of the following, it shall, within 24 hours, notify the licensing office with jurisdiction over the facility:
(1) A report of abuse alleged to have occurred in facilities licensed to care for children by the State Department of Social Services.
(2) A report of the death of a child who was, at the time of death, living at, enrolled in, or regularly attending a facility licensed to care for children by the State Department of Social Services, unless the circumstances of the child's death are clearly unrelated to the child's care at the facility.
The agency shall send the licensing agency a copy of its investigation and any other pertinent materials.
(b) Any employee of an agency specified in Section 11165.9 who has knowledge of, or observes in his or her professional capacity or within the scope of his or her employment, a child in protective custody whom he or she knows or reasonably suspects has been the victim of child abuse or neglect shall, within 36 hours, send or have sent to the attorney who represents the child in dependency court, a copy of the report prepared in accordance with Section 11166. The agency shall maintain a copy of the written report. All information requested by the attorney for the child or the child's guardian ad litem shall be provided by the agency within 30 days of the request. (Amended by Stats. 2000, Ch. 916, Sec. 17. Effective January 1, 2001.)

11166.2.
In addition to the reports required under Section 11166, any agency specified in Section 11165.9 shall immediately or as soon as practically possible report by telephone, fax, or electronic transmission to the appropriate licensing agency every known or suspected instance of child abuse or neglect when the instance of abuse or neglect occurs while the child is being cared for in a child day care facility, involves a child day care licensed staff person, or occurs while the child is under the supervision of a community care facility or involves a community care facility licensee or staff person. The agency shall also send, fax, or electronically transmit a written report thereof within 36 hours of receiving the information concerning the incident to any agency to which it makes a telephone report under this subdivision. The agency shall send the licensing agency a copy of its investigation report and any other pertinent materials. (Amended by Stats. 2001, Ch. 133, Sec. 7. Effective July 31, 2001.)

11166.3.
(a) The Legislature intends that in each county the law enforcement agencies and the county welfare or probation department shall develop and implement cooperative arrangements in order to coordinate existing duties in connection with the investigation of suspected child abuse or neglect cases. The local law enforcement agency having jurisdiction over a case reported under Section 11166 shall report to the county welfare or probation department that it is investigating the case within 36 hours after starting its investigation. The county welfare department or probation department shall, in cases where a minor is a victim of actions specified in Section 288 of this code and a petition has been filed pursuant to Section 300 of the Welfare

and Institutions Code with regard to the minor, evaluate what action or actions would be in the best interest of the child victim. Notwithstanding any other provision of law, the county welfare department or probation department shall submit in writing its findings and the reasons therefor to the district attorney on or before the completion of the investigation. The written findings and the reasons therefor shall be delivered or made accessible to the defendant or his or her counsel in the manner specified in Section 859.
(b) The local law enforcement agency having jurisdiction over a case reported under Section 11166 shall report to the district office of the State Department of Social Services any case reported under this section if the case involves a facility specified in paragraph (5) or (6) of subdivision (a) of Section 1502, Section 1596.750 or 1596.76 of the Health and Safety Code, and the licensing of the facility has not been delegated to a county agency. The law enforcement agency shall send a copy of its investigation report and any other pertinent materials to the licensing agency upon the request of the licensing agency.
(Amended by Stats. 2001, Ch. 133, Sec. 8. Effective July 31, 2001.)

11166.5.
(a) (1) On and after January 1, 1985, any mandated reporter as specified in Section 11165.7, with the exception of child visitation monitors, prior to commencing his or her employment, and as a prerequisite to that employment, shall sign a statement on a form provided to him or her by his or her employer to the effect that he or she has knowledge of the provisions of Section 11166 and will comply with those provisions. The statement shall inform the employee that he or she is a mandated reporter and inform the employee of his or her reporting obligations under Section 11166 and of his or her confidentiality rights under subdivision (d) of Section 11167. The employer shall provide a copy of Sections 11165.7, 11166, and 11167 to the employee.
On and after January 1, 1993, any person who acts as a child visitation monitor, as defined in paragraph (31) of subdivision (a) of Section 11165.7, prior to engaging in monitoring the first visit in a case, shall sign a statement on a form provided to him or her by the court which ordered the presence of that third person during the visit, to the effect that he or she has knowledge of the provisions of Section 11166 and will comply with those provisions.
(2) The signed statements shall be retained by the employer or the court, as the case may be. The cost of printing, distribution, and filing of these statements shall be borne by the employer or the court.
(3) This subdivision is not applicable to persons employed by public or private youth centers, youth recreation programs, and youth organizations as members of the support staff or maintenance staff and who do not work with, observe, or have knowledge of children as part of their official duties.
(b) On and after January 1, 1986, when a person is issued a state license or certificate to engage in a profession or occupation, the members of which are required to make a report pursuant to Section 11166, the state agency issuing the license or certificate shall send a statement substantially similar to the one contained in subdivision (a) to the person at the same time as it transmits the document indicating licensure or certification to the person. In addition to the requirements contained in subdivision (a), the statement also shall indicate that failure to comply with the requirements of Section 11166 is a misdemeanor, punishable by up to six months in a county jail, by a fine of one thousand dollars ($1,000), or by both that imprisonment and fine.
(c) As an alternative to the procedure required by subdivision (b), a state agency may cause the required statement to be printed on all application forms for a license or certificate printed on or after January 1, 1986.
(d) On and after January 1, 1993, any child visitation monitor, as defined in paragraph (31) of subdivision (a) of Section 11165.7, who desires to act in that capacity shall have received training in the duties imposed by this article, including training in child abuse identification and child abuse reporting. The person, prior to engaging in monitoring the first visit in a case, shall sign a statement on a form provided to him or her by the court which ordered the presence of that third person during the visit, to the effect that he or she has received this training. This statement may be included in the statement required by subdivision (a) or it may be a separate statement. This statement shall be filed, along with the statement required by subdivision (a), in the court file of the case for which the visitation monitoring is being provided.
(e) Any person providing services to a minor child, as described in paragraph (38) of subdivision (a) of Section 11165.7, shall not be required to make a report pursuant to Section 11166 unless that person has received training, or instructional materials in the appropriate language, on the duties imposed by this article, including identifying and reporting child abuse and neglect.
(Amended by Stats. 2012, Ch. 518, Sec. 2. Effective January 1, 2013.)

11167.
(a) Reports of suspected child abuse or neglect pursuant to Section 11166 or Section 11166.05 shall include the name, business address, and telephone number of the mandated reporter; the capacity that makes the person a mandated reporter; and the information that gave rise to the reasonable suspicion of child abuse or neglect and the source or sources of that information. If a report is made, the following information, if known, shall also be included in the report: the child's name, the child's address, present location, and, if applicable, school, grade, and class; the names, addresses, and telephone numbers of the child's parents or guardians; and the name, address, telephone number, and other relevant personal information about the person or persons who might have abused or neglected the child. The mandated reporter shall make a report even if some of this information is not known or is uncertain to him or her.
(b) Information relevant to the incident of child abuse or neglect and information relevant to a report made pursuant to Section

11166.05 may be given to an investigator from an agency that is investigating the known or suspected case of child abuse or neglect.
(c) Information relevant to the incident of child abuse or neglect, including the investigation report and other pertinent materials, and information relevant to a report made pursuant to Section 11166.05 may be given to the licensing agency when it is investigating a known or suspected case of child abuse or neglect.
(d) (1) The identity of all persons who report under this article shall be confidential and disclosed only among agencies receiving or investigating mandated reports, to the prosecutor in a criminal prosecution or in an action initiated under Section 602 of the Welfare and Institutions Code arising from alleged child abuse, or to counsel appointed pursuant to subdivision (c) of Section 317 of the Welfare and Institutions Code, or to the county counsel or prosecutor in a proceeding under Part 4 (commencing with Section 7800) of Division 12 of the Family Code or Section 300 of the Welfare and Institutions Code, or to a licensing agency when abuse or neglect in out-of-home care is reasonably suspected, or when those persons waive confidentiality, or by court order.
(2) No agency or person listed in this subdivision shall disclose the identity of any person who reports under this article to that person's employer, except with the employee's consent or by court order.
(e) Notwithstanding the confidentiality requirements of this section, a representative of a child protective services agency performing an investigation that results from a report of suspected child abuse or neglect made pursuant to Section 11166 or Section 11166.05, at the time of the initial contact with the individual who is subject to the investigation, shall advise the individual of the complaints or allegations against him or her, in a manner that is consistent with laws protecting the identity of the reporter under this article.
(f) Persons who may report pursuant to subdivision (g) of Section 11166 are not required to include their names.
(Amended by Stats. 2010, Ch. 95, Sec. 1. Effective January 1, 2011.)

11167.5.
(a) The reports required by Sections 11166 and 11166.2, or authorized by Section 11166.05, and child abuse or neglect investigative reports that result in a summary report being filed with the Department of Justice pursuant to subdivision (a) of Section 11169 shall be confidential and may be disclosed only as provided in subdivision (b). Any violation of the confidentiality provided by this article is a misdemeanor punishable by imprisonment in a county jail not to exceed six months, by a fine of five hundred dollars ($500), or by both that imprisonment and fine.
(b) Reports of suspected child abuse or neglect and information contained therein may be disclosed only to the following:
(1) Persons or agencies to whom disclosure of the identity of the reporting party is permitted under Section 11167.
(2) Persons or agencies to whom disclosure of information is permitted under subdivision (b) of Section 11170 or subdivision (a) of Section 11170.5.
(3) Persons or agencies with whom investigations of child abuse or neglect are coordinated under the regulations promulgated under Section 11174.
(4) Multidisciplinary personnel teams as defined in subdivision (d) of Section 18951 of the Welfare and Institutions Code.
(5) Persons or agencies responsible for the licensing of facilities which care for children, as specified in Section 11165.7.
(6) The State Department of Social Services or any county licensing agency which has contracted with the state, as specified in paragraph (4) of subdivision (b) of Section 11170, when an individual has applied for a community care license or child day care license, or for employment in an out-of-home care facility, or when a complaint alleges child abuse or neglect by an operator or employee of an out-of-home care facility.
(7) Hospital scan teams. As used in this paragraph, "hospital scan team" means a team of three or more persons established by a hospital, or two or more hospitals in the same county, consisting of health care professionals and representatives of law enforcement and child protective services, the members of which are engaged in the identification of child abuse or neglect. The disclosure authorized by this section includes disclosure among all hospital scan teams.
(8) Coroners and medical examiners when conducting a post mortem examination of a child.
(9) The Board of Parole Hearings, which may subpoena an employee of a county welfare department who can provide relevant evidence and reports that both (A) are not unfounded, pursuant to Section 11165.12, and (B) concern only the current incidents upon which parole revocation proceedings are pending against a parolee charged with child abuse or neglect. The reports and information shall be confidential pursuant to subdivision (d) of Section 11167.
(10) Personnel from an agency responsible for making a placement of a child pursuant to Section 361.3 of, and Article 7 (commencing with Section 305) of Chapter 2 of Part 1 of Division 2 of, the Welfare and Institutions Code.
(11) Persons who have been identified by the Department of Justice as listed in the Child Abuse Central Index pursuant to paragraph (7) of subdivision (b) of Section 11170 or subdivision (c) of Section 11170, or persons who have verified with the Department of Justice that they are listed in the Child Abuse Central Index as provided in subdivision (f) of Section 11170. Disclosure under this paragraph is required notwithstanding the California Public Records Act, Chapter 3.5 (commencing with Section 6250) of Division 7 of Title 1 of the Government Code. Nothing in this paragraph shall preclude a submitting agency prior to disclosure from redacting any information necessary to maintain confidentiality as required by law.
(12) Out-of-state law enforcement agencies conducting an investigation of child abuse or neglect only when an agency makes the request for reports of suspected child abuse or neglect in writing and on official letterhead, or as designated by the Department of Justice, identifying the suspected abuser or victim by name and date of birth or approximate age. The request

shall be signed by the department supervisor of the requesting law enforcement agency. The written request shall cite the out-of-state statute or interstate compact provision that requires that the information contained within these reports is to be disclosed only to law enforcement, prosecutorial entities, or multidisciplinary investigative teams, and shall cite the safeguards in place to prevent unlawful disclosure provided by the requesting state or the applicable interstate compact provision.
(13) Out-of-state agencies responsible for approving prospective foster or adoptive parents for placement of a child only when the agency makes the request in compliance with the Adam Walsh Child Protection and Safety Act of 2006 (Public Law 109-248). The request shall also cite the safeguards in place to prevent unlawful disclosure provided by the requesting state or the applicable interstate compact provision and indicate that the requesting state shall maintain continual compliance with the requirement in paragraph (20) of subdivision (a) of Section 671 of Title 42 of the United States Code that requires the state have in place safeguards to prevent the unauthorized disclosure of information in any child abuse and neglect registry maintained by the state and prevent the information from being used for a purpose other than the conducting of background checks in foster or adoptive placement cases.
(14) Each chairperson of a county child death review team, or his or her designee, to whom disclosure of information is permitted under this article, relating to the death of one or more children and any prior child abuse or neglect investigation reports maintained involving the same victim, siblings, or suspects. Local child death review teams may share any relevant information regarding case reviews involving child death with other child death review teams.
(c) Authorized persons within county health departments shall be permitted to receive copies of any reports made by health practitioners, as defined in paragraphs (21) to (28), inclusive, of subdivision (a) of Section 11165.7, and pursuant to Section 11165.13, and copies of assessments completed pursuant to Sections 123600 and 123605 of the Health and Safety Code, to the extent permitted by federal law. Any information received pursuant to this subdivision is protected by subdivision (e).
(d) Nothing in this section requires the Department of Justice to disclose information contained in records maintained under Section 11170 or under the regulations promulgated pursuant to Section 11174, except as otherwise provided in this article.
(e) This section shall not be interpreted to allow disclosure of any reports or records relevant to the reports of child abuse or neglect if the disclosure would be prohibited by any other provisions of state or federal law applicable to the reports or records relevant to the reports of child abuse or neglect.
(Amended by Stats. 2008, Ch. 701, Sec. 9. Effective September 30, 2008.)

11168.
The written reports required by Section 11166 shall be submitted on forms adopted by the Department of Justice after consultation with representatives of the various professional medical associations and hospital associations and county probation or welfare departments. Those forms shall be distributed by the agencies specified in Section 11165.9. (Amended by Stats. 2000, Ch. 916, Sec. 26. Effective January 1, 2001.)

11169.
(a) An agency specified in Section 11165.9 shall forward to the Department of Justice a report in writing of every case it investigates of known or suspected child abuse or severe neglect that is determined to be substantiated, other than cases coming within subdivision (b) of Section 11165.2. An agency shall not forward a report to the Department of Justice unless it has conducted an active investigation and determined that the report is substantiated, as defined in Section 11165.12. If a report has previously been filed which subsequently proves to be not substantiated, the Department of Justice shall be notified in writing of that fact and shall not retain the report. The reports required by this section shall be in a form approved by the Department of Justice and may be sent by fax or electronic transmission. An agency specified in Section 11165.9 receiving a written report from another agency specified in Section 11165.9 shall not send that report to the Department of Justice.
(b) On and after January 1, 2012, a police department or sheriff's department specified in Section 11165.9 shall no longer forward to the Department of Justice a report in writing of any case it investigates of known or suspected child abuse or severe neglect.
(c) At the time an agency specified in Section 11165.9 forwards a report in writing to the Department of Justice pursuant to subdivision (a), the agency shall also notify in writing the known or suspected child abuser that he or she has been reported to the Child Abuse Central Index (CACI).The notice required by this section shall be in a form approved by the Department of Justice. The requirements of this subdivision shall apply with respect to reports forwarded to the department on or after the date on which this subdivision becomes operative.
(d) Subject to subdivision (e), any person who is listed on the CACI has the right to a hearing before the agency that requested his or her inclusion in the CACI to challenge his or her listing on the CACI. The hearing shall satisfy due process requirements. It is the intent of the Legislature that the hearing provided for by this subdivision shall not be construed to be inconsistent with hearing proceedings available to persons who have been listed on the CACI prior to the enactment of the act that added this subdivision.
(e) A hearing requested pursuant to subdivision (d) shall be denied when a court of competent jurisdiction has determined that suspected child abuse or neglect has occurred, or when the allegation of child abuse or neglect resulting in the referral to the CACI is pending before the court. A person who is listed on the CACI and has been denied a hearing pursuant to this subdivision has a right to a hearing pursuant to subdivision (d) only if the court's jurisdiction has terminated, the court has not made a finding concerning whether the suspected child abuse or neglect was substantiated, and a hearing has not previously

been provided to the listed person pursuant to subdivision (d).
(f) Any person listed in the CACI who has reached 100 years of age shall have his or her listing removed from the CACI.
(g) Any person listed in the CACI as of January 1, 2013, who was listed prior to reaching 18 years of age, and who is listed once in CACI with no subsequent listings, shall be removed from the CACI 10 years from the date of the incident resulting in the CACI listing.
(h) If, after a hearing pursuant to subdivision (d) or a court proceeding described in subdivision (e), it is determined the person's CACI listing was based on a report that was not substantiated, the agency shall notify the Department of Justice of that result and the department shall remove that person's name from the CACI.
(i) Agencies, including police departments and sheriff's departments, shall retain child abuse or neglect investigative reports that result or resulted in a report filed with the Department of Justice pursuant to subdivision (a) for the same period of time that the information is required to be maintained on the CACI pursuant to this section and subdivision (a) of Section 11170. Nothing in this section precludes an agency from retaining the reports for a longer period of time if required by law.
(j) The immunity provisions of Section 11172 shall not apply to the submission of a report by an agency pursuant to this section. However, nothing in this section shall be construed to alter or diminish any other immunity provisions of state or federal law. (Amended by Stats. 2012, Ch. 848, Sec. 1. Effective January 1, 2013.)

11170.
(a) (1) The Department of Justice shall maintain an index of all reports of child abuse and severe neglect submitted pursuant to Section 11169. The index shall be continually updated by the department and shall not contain any reports that are determined to be not substantiated. The department may adopt rules governing record keeping and reporting pursuant to this article.
(2) The department shall act only as a repository of reports of suspected child abuse and severe neglect to be maintained in the Child Abuse Central Index (CACI) pursuant to paragraph (1). The submitting agencies are responsible for the accuracy, completeness, and retention of the reports described in this section. The department shall be responsible for ensuring that the CACI accurately reflects the report it receives from the submitting agency.
(3) Only information from reports that are reported as substantiated shall be filed pursuant to paragraph (1), and all other determinations shall be removed from the central list. If a person listed in the CACI was under 18 years of age at the time of the report, the information shall be deleted from the CACI 10 years from the date of the incident resulting in the CACI listing, if no subsequent report concerning the same person is received during that time period.
(b) The provisions of subdivision (c) of Section 11169 apply to any information provided pursuant to this subdivision.
(1) The Department of Justice shall immediately notify an agency that submits a report pursuant to Section 11169, or a prosecutor who requests notification, of any information maintained pursuant to subdivision (a) that is relevant to the known or suspected instance of child abuse or severe neglect reported by the agency. The agency shall make that information available to the reporting health care practitioner who is treating a person reported as a possible victim of known or suspected child abuse. The agency shall make that information available to the reporting child custodian, Child Abuse Prevention and Treatment Act guardian ad litem appointed under Rule 5.662 of the California Rules of Court, or counsel appointed under Section 317 or 318 of the Welfare and Institutions Code, or the appropriate licensing agency, if he or she or the licensing agency is handling or investigating a case of known or suspected child abuse or severe neglect.
(2) When a report is made pursuant to subdivision (a) of Section 11166, or Section 11166.05, the investigating agency, upon completion of the investigation or after there has been a final disposition in the matter, shall inform the person required or authorized to report of the results of the investigation and of any action the agency is taking with regard to the child or family.
(3) The Department of Justice shall make relevant information from the CACI available to a law enforcement agency, county welfare department, or county probation department that is conducting a child abuse investigation.
(4) The department shall make available to the State Department of Social Services, or to any county licensing agency that has contracted with the state for the performance of licensing duties, or to a tribal court or tribal child welfare agency of a tribe, consortium of tribes, or tribal organization that has entered into an agreement with the state pursuant to Section 10553.1 of the Welfare and Institutions Code, information regarding a known or suspected child abuser maintained pursuant to this section and subdivision (a) of Section 11169 concerning any person who is an applicant for licensure or approval, or any adult who resides or is employed in the home of an applicant for licensure or approval, or who is an applicant for employment in a position having supervisorial or disciplinary power over a child or children, or who will provide 24-hour care for a child or children in a residential home or facility, pursuant to Section 1522.1 or 1596.877 of the Health and Safety Code, or Section 8714, 8802, 8912, or 9000 of the Family Code, or Section 11403.2 of the Welfare and Institutions Code.
(5) The Department of Justice shall make available to a Court Appointed Special Advocate program that is conducting a background investigation of an applicant seeking employment with the program or a volunteer position as a Court Appointed Special Advocate, as defined in Section 101 of the Welfare and Institutions Code, information contained in the index regarding known or suspected child abuse by the applicant.
(6) For purposes of child death review, the Department of Justice shall make available to the chairperson, or the chairperson's designee, for each county child death review team, or the State Child Death Review Council, information for investigative purposes only that is maintained in the CACI pursuant to subdivision (a) relating to the death of one or more children and any prior child abuse or neglect investigation reports maintained involving the same victims, siblings, or suspects. Local child

death review teams may share any relevant information regarding case reviews involving child death with other child death review teams.
(7) The department shall make available to investigative agencies or probation officers, or court investigators acting pursuant to Section 1513 of the Probate Code, responsible for placing children or assessing the possible placement of children pursuant to Article 6 (commencing with Section 300), Article 7 (commencing with Section 305), Article 10 (commencing with Section 360), or Article 14 (commencing with Section 601) of Chapter 2 of Part 1 of Division 2 of the Welfare and Institutions Code, or Article 2 (commencing with Section 1510) or Article 3 (commencing with Section 1540) of Chapter 1 of Part 2 of Division 4 of the Probate Code, information regarding a known or suspected child abuser contained in the index concerning any adult residing in the home where the child may be placed, when this information is requested for purposes of ensuring that the placement is in the best interest of the child. Upon receipt of relevant information concerning child abuse or neglect investigation reports contained in the CACI from the Department of Justice pursuant to this subdivision, the agency or court investigator shall notify, in writing, the person listed in the CACI that he or she is in the index. The notification shall include the name of the reporting agency and the date of the report.
(8) Pursuant to Section 10553.12 of the Welfare and Institutions Code, the department shall make available to a tribal child welfare agency information regarding a known or suspected child abuser maintained pursuant to this section or subdivision (a) of Section 11169 who is being considered as a prospective foster parent or adoptive parent, an adult who resides or is employed in the home of an applicant for approval, or an employee of the tribal child welfare agency who may have contact with children.
(9) The Department of Justice shall make available to a government agency conducting a background investigation pursuant to Section 1031 of the Government Code of an applicant seeking employment as a peace officer, as defined in Section 830, information regarding a known or suspected child abuser maintained pursuant to this section concerning the applicant.
(10) The Department of Justice shall make available to a county child welfare agency or delegated county adoption agency, as defined in Section 8515 of the Family Code, conducting a background investigation, or a government agency conducting a background investigation on behalf of one of those agencies, information regarding a known or suspected child abuser maintained pursuant to this section and subdivision (a) of Section 11169 concerning any applicant seeking employment or volunteer status with the agency who, in the course of his or her employment or volunteer work, will have direct contact with children who are alleged to have been, are at risk of, or have suffered, abuse or neglect.
(11) (A) Persons or agencies, as specified in subdivision (b), if investigating a case of known or suspected child abuse or neglect, or the State Department of Social Services or any county licensing agency pursuant to paragraph (4), or a Court Appointed Special Advocate (CASA) program conducting a background investigation for employment or volunteer candidates pursuant to paragraph (5), or an investigative agency, probation officer, or court investigator responsible for placing children or assessing the possible placement of children pursuant to paragraph (7), or a government agency conducting a background investigation of an applicant seeking employment as a peace officer pursuant to paragraph (9), or a county child welfare agency or delegated county adoption agency conducting a background investigation of an applicant seeking employment or volunteer status who, in the course of his or her employment or volunteer work, will have direct contact with children who are alleged to have been, are at risk of, or have suffered, abuse or neglect, pursuant to paragraph (10), to whom disclosure of any information maintained pursuant to subdivision (a) is authorized, are responsible for obtaining the original investigative report from the reporting agency, and for drawing independent conclusions regarding the quality of the evidence disclosed, and its sufficiency for making decisions regarding investigation, prosecution, licensing, placement of a child, employment or volunteer positions with a CASA program, or employment as a peace officer.
(B) If CACI information is requested by an agency for the temporary placement of a child in an emergency situation pursuant to Article 7 (commencing with Section 305) of Chapter 2 of Part 1 of Division 2 of the Welfare and Institutions Code, the department is exempt from the requirements of Section 1798.18 of the Civil Code if compliance would cause a delay in providing an expedited response to the agency's inquiry and if further delay in placement may be detrimental to the child.
(12) (A) Whenever information contained in the Department of Justice files is furnished as the result of an application for employment or licensing or volunteer status pursuant to paragraph (4), (5), (8), (9), or (10), the Department of Justice may charge the person or entity making the request a fee. The fee shall not exceed the reasonable costs to the department of providing the information. The only increase shall be at a rate not to exceed the legislatively approved cost-of-living adjustment for the department. In no case shall the fee exceed fifteen dollars ($15).
(B) All moneys received by the department pursuant to this section to process trustline applications for purposes of Chapter 3.35 (commencing with Section 1596.60) of Division 2 of the Health and Safety Code shall be deposited in a special account in the General Fund that is hereby established and named the Department of Justice Child Abuse Fund. Moneys in the fund shall be available, upon appropriation by the Legislature, for expenditure by the department to offset the costs incurred to process trustline automated child abuse or neglect system checks pursuant to this section.
(C) All moneys, other than those described in subparagraph (B), received by the department pursuant to this paragraph shall be deposited in a special account in the General Fund which is hereby created and named the Department of Justice Sexual Habitual Offender Fund. The funds shall be available, upon appropriation by the Legislature, for expenditure by the department to offset the costs incurred pursuant to Chapter 9.5 (commencing with Section 13885) and Chapter 10 (commencing with Section 13890) of Title 6 of Part 4, and the DNA and Forensic Identification Data Base and Data Bank Act of 1998 (Chapter 6 (commencing with Section 295) of Title 9 of Part 1), and for maintenance and improvements to the statewide

Sexual Habitual Offender Program and the California DNA offender identification file (CAL-DNA) authorized by Chapter 9.5 (commencing with Section 13885) of Title 6 of Part 4 and the DNA and Forensic Identification Data Base and Data Bank Act of 1998 (Chapter 6 (commencing with Section 295) of Title 9 of Part 1).
(c) (1) The Department of Justice shall make available to any agency responsible for placing children pursuant to Article 7 (commencing with Section 305) of Chapter 2 of Part 1 of Division 2 of the Welfare and Institutions Code, upon request, relevant information concerning child abuse or neglect reports contained in the index, when making a placement with a responsible relative pursuant to Sections 281.5, 305, and 361.3 of the Welfare and Institutions Code. Upon receipt of relevant information concerning child abuse or neglect reports contained in the index from the Department of Justice pursuant to this subdivision, the agency shall also notify in writing the person listed in the CACI that he or she is in the index. The notification shall include the location of the original investigative report and the submitting agency. The notification shall be submitted to the person listed at the same time that all other parties are notified of the information, and no later than the actual judicial proceeding that determines placement.(2) If information is requested by an agency for the placement of a child with a responsible relative in an emergency situation pursuant to Article 7 (commencing with Section 305) of Chapter 2 of Part 1 of Division 2 of the Welfare and Institutions Code, the department is exempt from the requirements of Section 1798.18 of the Civil Code if compliance would cause a delay in providing an expedited response to the child protective agency's inquiry and if further delay in placement may be detrimental to the child.
(d) The department shall make available any information maintained pursuant to subdivision (a) to out-of-state law enforcement agencies conducting investigations of known or suspected child abuse or neglect only when an agency makes the request for information in writing and on official letterhead, or as designated by the department, identifying the suspected abuser or victim by name and date of birth or approximate age. The request shall be signed by the department supervisor of the requesting law enforcement agency. The written requests shall cite the out-of-state statute or interstate compact provision that requires that the information contained within these reports shall be disclosed only to law enforcement, prosecutorial entities, or multidisciplinary investigative teams, and shall cite the safeguards in place to prevent unlawful disclosure of any confidential information provided by the requesting state or the applicable interstate compact provision.
(e) (1) The department shall make available to an out-of-state agency, for purposes of approving a prospective foster or adoptive parent in compliance with the Adam Walsh Child Protection and Safety Act of 2006 (Public Law 109-248), information regarding a known or suspected child abuser maintained pursuant to subdivision (a) concerning the prospective foster or adoptive parent, and any other adult living in the home of the prospective foster or adoptive parent. The department shall make that information available only when the out-of-state agency makes the request indicating that continual compliance will be maintained with the requirement in paragraph (20) of subsection (a) of Section 671 of Title 42 of the United States Code that requires the state to have in place safeguards to prevent the unauthorized disclosure of information in any child abuse and neglect registry maintained by the state and prevent the information from being used for a purpose other than the conducting of background checks in foster or adoption placement cases.
(2) With respect to any information provided by the department in response to the out-of-state agency's request, the out-of-state agency is responsible for obtaining the original investigative report from the reporting agency, and for drawing independent conclusions regarding the quality of the evidence disclosed and its sufficiency for making decisions regarding the approval of prospective foster or adoptive parents.
(3) (A) Whenever information contained in the index is furnished pursuant to this subdivision, the department shall charge the out-of-state agency making the request a fee. The fee shall not exceed the reasonable costs to the department of providing the information. The only increase shall be at a rate not to exceed the legislatively approved cost-of-living adjustment for the department. In no case shall the fee exceed fifteen dollars ($15).
(B) All moneys received by the department pursuant to this subdivision shall be deposited in the Department of Justice Child Abuse Fund, established under subparagraph (B) of paragraph (12) of subdivision (b). Moneys in the fund shall be available, upon appropriation by the Legislature, for expenditure by the department to offset the costs incurred to process requests for information pursuant to this subdivision.
(f) (1) Any person may determine if he or she is listed in the CACI by making a request in writing to the Department of Justice. The request shall be notarized and include the person's name, address, date of birth, and either a social security number or a California identification number. Upon receipt of a notarized request, the Department of Justice shall make available to the requesting person information identifying the date of the report and the submitting agency. The requesting person is responsible for obtaining the investigative report from the submitting agency pursuant to paragraph (11) of subdivision (b) of Section 11167.5.
(2) No person or agency shall require or request another person to furnish a copy of a record concerning himself or herself, or notification that a record concerning himself or herself exists or does not exist, pursuant to paragraph (1).
(g) If a person is listed in the CACI only as a victim of child abuse or neglect, and that person is 18 years of age or older, that person may have his or her name removed from the index by making a written request to the Department of Justice. The request shall be notarized and include the person's name, address, social security number, and date of birth. (Amended by Stats. 2014, Ch. 772, Sec. 7. Effective January 1, 2015.)

11170.5.
(a) Notwithstanding paragraph (4) of subdivision (b) of Section 11170, the Department of Justice shall make available to a

licensed adoption agency, as defined in Section 8530 of the Family Code, information regarding a known or suspected child abuser maintained in the Child Abuse Central Index, pursuant to subdivision (a) of Section 11170, concerning any person who has submitted to the agency an application for adoption.
(b) A licensed adoption agency, to which disclosure of any information pursuant to subdivision (a) is authorized, is responsible for obtaining the original investigative report from the reporting agency, and for drawing independent conclusions regarding the quality of the evidence disclosed and the sufficiency of the evidence for making decisions when evaluating an application for adoption.
(c) Whenever information contained in the Department of Justice files is furnished as the result of an application for adoption pursuant to subdivision (a), the Department of Justice may charge the agency making the request a fee. The fee shall not exceed the reasonable costs to the department of providing the information. The only increase shall be at a rate not to exceed the legislatively approved cost-of-living adjustment for the department. In no case shall the fee exceed fifteen dollars ($15). All moneys received by the department pursuant to this subdivision shall be deposited in the Department of Justice Sexual Habitual Offender Fund pursuant to subparagraph (C) of paragraph (9) of subdivision (b) of Section 11170. (Amended by Stats. 2004, Ch. 842, Sec. 19. Effective January 1, 2005.)

11171.
(a) (1) The Legislature hereby finds and declares that adequate protection of victims of child physical abuse or neglect has been hampered by the lack of consistent and comprehensive medical examinations.
(2) Enhancing examination procedures, documentation, and evidence collection relating to child abuse or neglect will improve the investigation and prosecution of child abuse or neglect as well as other child protection efforts.
(b) The Office of Emergency Services shall, in cooperation with the State Department of Social Services, the Department of Justice, the California Association of Crime Lab Directors, the California District Attorneys Association, the California State Sheriffs' Association, the California Peace Officers Association, the California Medical Association, the California Police Chiefs' Association, child advocates, the California Medical Training Center, child protective services, and other appropriate experts, establish medical forensic forms, instructions, and examination protocols for victims of child physical abuse or neglect using as a model the form and guidelines developed pursuant to Section 13823.5.
(c) The forms shall include, but not be limited to, a place for notation concerning each of the following:
(1) Any notification of injuries or any report of suspected child physical abuse or neglect to law enforcement authorities or children's protective services, in accordance with existing reporting procedures.
(2) Addressing relevant consent issues, if indicated.
(3) The taking of a patient history of child physical abuse or neglect that includes other relevant medical history.
(4) The performance of a physical examination for evidence of child physical abuse or neglect.
(5) The collection or documentation of any physical evidence of child physical abuse or neglect, including any recommended photographic procedures.
(6) The collection of other medical or forensic specimens, including drug ingestion or toxication, as indicated.
(7) Procedures for the preservation and disposition of evidence.
(8) Complete documentation of medical forensic exam findings with recommendations for diagnostic studies, including blood tests and X-rays.
(9) An assessment as to whether there are findings that indicate physical abuse or neglect.
(d) The forms shall become part of the patient's medical record pursuant to guidelines established by the advisory committee of the Office of Emergency Services and subject to the confidentiality laws pertaining to the release of medical forensic examination records.
(e) The forms shall be made accessible for use on the Internet. (Amended by Stats. 2013, Ch. 352, Sec. 421. Effective September 26, 2013. Operative July 1, 2013, by Sec. 543 of Ch. 352.)

11171.2.
(a) A physician and surgeon or dentist or their agents and by their direction may take skeletal X-rays of the child without the consent of the child's parent or guardian, but only for purposes of diagnosing the case as one of possible child abuse or neglect and determining the extent of the child abuse or neglect.
(b) Neither the physician-patient privilege nor the psychotherapist-patient privilege applies to information reported pursuant to this article in any court proceeding or administrative hearing. (Added by renumbering Section 11171 by Stats. 2002, Ch. 249, second Sec. 3. Effective January 1, 2003.)

11171.5.
(a) If a peace officer, in the course of an investigation of child abuse or neglect, has reasonable cause to believe that the child has been the victim of physical abuse, the officer may apply to a magistrate for an order directing that the victim be X-rayed without parental consent. Any X-ray taken pursuant to this subdivision shall be administered by a physician and surgeon or dentist or their agents.
(b) With respect to the cost of an X-ray taken by the county coroner or at the request of the county coroner in suspected child abuse or neglect cases, the county may charge the parent or legal guardian of the child-victim the costs incurred by the county

for the X-ray.
(c) No person who administers an X-ray pursuant to this section shall be entitled to reimbursement from the county for any administrative cost that exceeds 5 percent of the cost of the X-ray. (Amended by Stats. 2000, Ch. 916, Sec. 30. Effective January 1, 2001.)

11172.
(a) No mandated reporter shall be civilly or criminally liable for any report required or authorized by this article, and this immunity shall apply even if the mandated reporter acquired the knowledge or reasonable suspicion of child abuse or neglect outside of his or her professional capacity or outside the scope of his or her employment. Any other person reporting a known or suspected instance of child abuse or neglect shall not incur civil or criminal liability as a result of any report authorized by this article unless it can be proven that a false report was made and the person knew that the report was false or was made with reckless disregard of the truth or falsity of the report, and any person who makes a report of child abuse or neglect known to be false or with reckless disregard of the truth or falsity of the report is liable for any damages caused. No person required to make a report pursuant to this article, nor any person taking photographs at his or her direction, shall incur any civil or criminal liability for taking photographs of a suspected victim of child abuse or neglect, or causing photographs to be taken of a suspected victim of child abuse or neglect, without parental consent, or for disseminating the photographs, images, or material with the reports required by this article. However, this section shall not be construed to grant immunity from this liability with respect to any other use of the photographs.
(b) Any person, who, pursuant to a request from a government agency investigating a report of suspected child abuse or neglect, provides the requesting agency with access to the victim of a known or suspected instance of child abuse or neglect shall not incur civil or criminal liability as a result of providing that access.
(c) Any commercial computer technician, and any employer of any commercial computer technician, who, pursuant to a warrant from a law enforcement agency investigating a report of suspected child abuse or neglect, provides the law enforcement agency with a computer or computer component which contains possible evidence of a known or suspected instance of child abuse or neglect, shall not incur civil or criminal liability as a result of providing that computer or computer component to the law enforcement agency.
(d) (1) The Legislature finds that even though it has provided immunity from liability to persons required or authorized to make reports pursuant to this article, that immunity does not eliminate the possibility that actions may be brought against those persons based upon required or authorized reports. In order to further limit the financial hardship that those persons may incur as a result of fulfilling their legal responsibilities, it is necessary that they not be unfairly burdened by legal fees incurred in defending those actions. Therefore, a mandated reporter may present a claim to the California Victim Compensation and Government Claims Board for reasonable attorney's fees and costs incurred in any action against that person on the basis of making a report required or authorized by this article if the court has dismissed the action upon a demurrer or motion for summary judgment made by that person, or if he or she prevails in the action. The California Victim Compensation and Government Claims Board shall allow that claim if the requirements of this subdivision are met, and the claim shall be paid from an appropriation to be made for that purpose. Attorney's fees awarded pursuant to this section shall not exceed an hourly rate greater than the rate charged by the Attorney General of the State of California at the time the award is made and shall not exceed an aggregate amount of fifty thousand dollars ($50,000).
(2) This subdivision shall not apply if a public entity has provided for the defense of the action pursuant to Section 995 of the Government Code.
(e) A court may award attorney's fees and costs to a commercial film and photographic print processor when a suit is brought against the processor because of a disclosure mandated by this article and the court finds this suit to be frivolous. (Amended by Stats. 2012, Ch. 521, Sec. 3. Effective January 1, 2013.)

11174.
The Department of Justice, in cooperation with the State Department of Social Services, shall prescribe by regulation guidelines for the investigation of abuse in out-of-home care, as defined in Section 11165.5, and shall ensure that the investigation is conducted in accordance with the regulations and guidelines. (Amended by Stats. 1988, Ch. 269, Sec. 5.)

11174.1.
(a) The Department of Justice, in cooperation with the State Department of Social Services, shall prescribe by regulation guidelines for the investigation of child abuse or neglect, as defined in Section 11165.6, in facilities licensed to care for children, and shall ensure that the investigation is conducted in accordance with the regulations and guidelines.
(b) For community treatment facilities, day treatment facilities, group homes, and foster family agencies, the State Department of Social Services shall prescribe the following regulations:
(1) Regulations designed to assure that all licensees and employees of community treatment facilities, day treatment facilities, group homes, and foster family agencies licensed to care for children have had appropriate training, as determined by the State Department of Social Services, in consultation with representatives of licensees, on the provisions of this article.
(2) Regulations designed to assure the community treatment facilities, day treatment facilities, group homes, and foster family agencies licensed to care for children maintain a written protocol for the investigation and reporting of child abuse or neglect,

as defined in Section 11165.6, alleged to have occurred involving a child placed in the facility.
(c) The State Department of Social Services shall provide such orientation and training as it deems necessary to assure that its officers, employees, or agents who conduct inspections of facilities licensed to care for children are knowledgeable about the reporting requirements of this article and have adequate training to identify conditions leading to, and the signs of, child abuse or neglect, as defined in Section 11165.6. (Amended by Stats. 2000, Ch. 916, Sec. 32. Effective January 1, 2001.)

11174.3.
(a) Whenever a representative of a government agency investigating suspected child abuse or neglect or the State Department of Social Services deems it necessary, a suspected victim of child abuse or neglect may be interviewed during school hours, on school premises, concerning a report of suspected child abuse or neglect that occurred within the child's home or out-of-home care facility. The child shall be afforded the option of being interviewed in private or selecting any adult who is a member of the staff of the school, including any certificated or classified employee or volunteer aide, to be present at the interview. A representative of the agency investigating suspected child abuse or neglect or the State Department of Social Services shall inform the child of that right prior to the interview.
The purpose of the staff person's presence at the interview is to lend support to the child and enable him or her to be as comfortable as possible. However, the member of the staff so elected shall not participate in the interview. The member of the staff so present shall not discuss the facts or circumstances of the case with the child. The member of the staff so present, including, but not limited to, a volunteer aide, is subject to the confidentiality requirements of this article, a violation of which is punishable as specified in Section 11167.5. A representative of the school shall inform a member of the staff so selected by a child of the requirements of this section prior to the interview. A staff member selected by a child may decline the request to be present at the interview. If the staff person selected agrees to be present, the interview shall be held at a time during school hours when it does not involve an expense to the school. Failure to comply with the requirements of this section does not affect the admissibility of evidence in a criminal or civil proceeding.
(b) The Superintendent of Public Instruction shall notify each school district and each agency specified in Section 11165.9 to receive mandated reports, and the State Department of Social Services shall notify each of its employees who participate in the investigation of reports of child abuse or neglect, of the requirements of this section.
(c) "Inconclusive report" means a report that is determined by the investigator who conducted the investigation not to be unfounded, but the findings are inconclusive and there is insufficient evidence to determine whether child abuse or neglect, as defined in Section 11165.6, has occurred. (Amended by Stats. 2011, Ch. 468, Sec. 1. Effective January 1, 2012.)

11171.2.
(a) A physician and surgeon or dentist or their agents and by their direction may take skeletal X-rays of the child without the consent of the child's parent or guardian, but only for purposes of diagnosing the case as one of possible child abuse or neglect and determining the extent of the child abuse or neglect.
(b) Neither the physician-patient privilege nor the psychotherapist-patient privilege applies to information reported pursuant to this article in any court proceeding or administrative hearing. (Added by renumbering Section 11171 by Stats. 2002, Ch. 249, second Sec. 3. Effective January 1, 2003.)

11171.5.
(a) If a peace officer, in the course of an investigation of child abuse or neglect, has reasonable cause to believe that the child has been the victim of physical abuse, the officer may apply to a magistrate for an order directing that the victim be X-rayed without parental consent.
Any X-ray taken pursuant to this subdivision shall be administered by a physician and surgeon or dentist or their agents.
(b) With respect to the cost of an X-ray taken by the county coroner or at the request of the county coroner in suspected child abuse or neglect cases, the county may charge the parent or legal guardian of the child-victim the costs incurred by the county for the X-ray.
(c) No person who administers an X-ray pursuant to this section shall be entitled to reimbursement from the county for any administrative cost that exceeds 5 percent of the cost of the X-ray. (Amended by Stats. 2000, Ch. 916, Sec. 30. Effective January 1, 2001.)

11172.
(a) No mandated reporter shall be civilly or criminally liable for any report required or authorized by this article, and this immunity shall apply even if the mandated reporter acquired the knowledge or reasonable suspicion of child abuse or neglect outside of his or her professional capacity or outside the scope of his or her employment. Any other person reporting a known or suspected instance of child abuse or neglect shall not incur civil or criminal liability as a result of any report authorized by this article unless it can be proven that a false report was made and the person knew that the report was false or was made with reckless disregard of the truth or falsity of the report, and any person who makes a report of child abuse or neglect known to be false or with reckless disregard of the truth or falsity of the report is liable for any damages caused. No person required to make a report pursuant to this article, nor any person taking photographs at his or her direction, shall incur any civil or criminal liability for taking photographs of a suspected victim of child abuse or neglect, or causing photographs to be

taken of a suspected victim of child abuse or neglect, without parental consent, or for disseminating the photographs, images, or material with the reports required by this article. However, this section shall not be construed to grant immunity from this liability with respect to any other use of the photographs.
(b) Any person, who, pursuant to a request from a government agency investigating a report of suspected child abuse or neglect, provides the requesting agency with access to the victim of a known or suspected instance of child abuse or neglect shall not incur civil or criminal liability as a result of providing that access.
(c) Any commercial computer technician, and any employer of any commercial computer technician, who, pursuant to a warrant from a law enforcement agency investigating a report of suspected child abuse or neglect, provides the law enforcement agency with a computer or computer component which contains possible evidence of a known or suspected instance of child abuse or neglect, shall not incur civil or criminal liability as a result of providing that computer or computer component to the law enforcement agency.
(d) (1) The Legislature finds that even though it has provided immunity from liability to persons required or authorized to make reports pursuant to this article, that immunity does not eliminate the possibility that actions may be brought against those persons based upon required or authorized reports. In order to further limit the financial hardship that those persons may incur as a result of fulfilling their legal responsibilities, it is necessary that they not be unfairly burdened by legal fees incurred in defending those actions. Therefore, a mandated reporter may present a claim to the California Victim Compensation and Government Claims Board for reasonable attorney's fees and costs incurred in any action against that person on the basis of making a report required or authorized by this article if the court has dismissed the action upon a demurrer or motion for summary judgment made by that person, or if he or she prevails in the action. The California Victim Compensation and Government Claims Board shall allow that claim if the requirements of this subdivision are met, and the claim shall be paid from an appropriation to be made for that purpose. Attorney's fees awarded pursuant to this section shall not exceed an hourly rate greater than the rate charged by the Attorney General of the State of California at the time the award is made and shall not exceed an aggregate amount of fifty thousand dollars ($50,000).
(2) This subdivision shall not apply if a public entity has provided for the defense of the action pursuant to Section 995 of the Government Code.
(e) A court may award attorney's fees and costs to a commercial film and photographic print processor when a suit is brought against the processor because of a disclosure mandated by this article and the court finds this suit to be frivolous.
(Amended by Stats. 2012, Ch. 521, Sec. 3. Effective January 1, 2013.)

11174.
The Department of Justice, in cooperation with the State Department of Social Services, shall prescribe by regulation guidelines for the investigation of abuse in out-of-home care, as defined in Section 11165.5, and shall ensure that the investigation is conducted in accordance with the regulations and guidelines.
(Amended by Stats. 1988, Ch. 269, Sec. 5.)

11174.1.
(a) The Department of Justice, in cooperation with the State Department of Social Services, shall prescribe by regulation guidelines for the investigation of child abuse or neglect, as defined in Section 11165.6, in facilities licensed to care for children, and shall ensure that the investigation is conducted in accordance with the regulations and guidelines.
(b) For community treatment facilities, day treatment facilities, group homes, and foster family agencies, the Stat Department of Social Services shall prescribe the following regulations:
(1) Regulations designed to assure that all licensees and employees of community treatment facilities, day treatment facilities, group homes, and foster family agencies licensed to care for children have had appropriate training, as determined by the State Department of Social Services, in consultation with representatives of licensees, on the provisions of this article.
(2) Regulations designed to assure the community treatment facilities, day treatment facilities, group homes, and foster family agencies licensed to care for children maintain a written protocol for the investigation and reporting of child abuse or neglect, as defined in Section 11165.6, alleged to have occurred involving a child placed in the facility.
(c) The State Department of Social Services shall provide such orientation and training as it deems necessary to assure that its officers, employees, or agents who conduct inspections of facilities licensed to care for children are knowledgeable about the reporting requirements of this article and have adequate training to identify conditions leading to, and the signs of, child abuse or neglect, as defined in Section 11165.6. (Amended by Stats. 2000, Ch. 916, Sec. 32. Effective January 1, 2001.)

11174.3.
(a) Whenever a representative of a government agency investigating suspected child abuse or neglect or the State Department of Social Services deems it necessary, a suspected victim of child abuse or neglect may be interviewed during school hours, on school premises, concerning a report of suspected child abuse or neglect that occurred within the child's home or out-of-home care facility. The child shall be afforded the option of being interviewed in private or selecting any adult who is a member of the staff of the school, including any certificated or classified employee or volunteer aide, to be present at the interview. A representative of the agency investigating suspected child abuse or neglect or the State Department of Social Services shall

inform the child of that right prior to the interview.
The purpose of the staff person's presence at the interview is to lend support to the child and enable him or her to be as comfortable as possible. However, the member of the staff so elected shall not participate in the interview. The member of the staff so present shall not discuss the facts or circumstances of the case with the child. The member of the staff so present, including, but not limited to, a volunteer aide, is subject to the confidentiality requirements of this article, a violation of which is punishable as specified in Section 11167.5. A representative of the school shall inform a member of the staff so selected by a child of the requirements of this section prior to the interview. A staff member selected by a child may decline the request to be present at the interview. If the staff person selected agrees to be present, the interview shall be held at a time during school hours when it does not involve an expense to the school. Failure to comply with the requirements of this section does not affect the admissibility of evidence in a criminal or civil proceeding.
(b) The Superintendent of Public Instruction shall notify each school district and each agency specified in Section 11165.9 to receive mandated reports, and the State Department of Social Services shall notify each of its employees who participate in the investigation of reports of child abuse or neglect, of the requirements of this section.
(Amended by Stats. 2000, Ch. 916, Sec. 33. Effective January 1, 2001.)
(11) A Head Start program teacher.

Child Abuse Report

Here is an opportunity for you to complete a CWS report. Go to Page 218 and use the CWS Report as your format. This exercise is intended to familiarize you with this process. If you haven't completed a report before, pay close attention to the possible feelings and issues that you would experience should this child be your client and explain how you would manage those feelings regarding countertransference issues arising from your *Internal Reality*.

> *You are seeing a six-year-old child in therapy with parental consent. In the sixth session, she tells you that her 14 year-old cousin plays "doctor" with her and "he puts his thing into my pee-pee."*

Complete the report below to practice if needed:

1. Name/Title: Write your name and title (e.g., John Jones, MA.).

2. Address: Write your business address.
3. Phone: Write your business phone number.

4. Date of Report: Write the date of your report.

5. Signature of Reporting Party: Sign your name.

6. _______ Police Department _______Sheriff's Department ____County Welfare_____County Probation____
Check the box for the department to which you are sending the report. Usually County Welfare.

7. Agency: Write "Child Welfare Services" or "CWS."

8. Address: The address of the CWS office where you are sending the report.

9. Official Contacted: Write the name of the CWS representative to whom you gave the report by

phone.

10. Phone: Write the phone number of the CWS representative to whom you spoke.

11. Date/Time: Write the date and time when the report was made.

12. Name: Write the name of the abused child.

13. Address: Write the address of the abused child.

14. Birth date: Write the birth date of the abused child.

15. Sex: Write the gender of the abused child.

16. Race: Write the race of the abused child.

17. Present Location of Child: Write the address where the child currently lives.

18. Phone: Write the phone number at the address where the child currently lives.

19. Siblings: Write the names, birth date, sex, and race of any siblings of the abused child.

20. If Necessary, ... Check this box only when you need to include an extra sheet of paper with additional information.

21. Date/Time of the Incident: Write the time and date of the abuse incident.

22. Place of Incident: Write the address or location where the incident took place.

23. _ Occurred _ Observed: Did you witness it, or was it told to you? Check the appropriate box.

24. Type of Abuse: Check the box of the type of abuse described to you/seen by you.

25. Narrative Description: In your own words, describe what you believe is the abuse that took place.

26. Summarize What the Abused Child or Person Accompanying the Child Said Happened: Write down exactly what the child said to you. Use quotation marks if necessary.

27. Explain Known History of Similar Incident(s) for This Child: If you know of other child abuse incidents this child has experienced, write them down.

After completing the form, keep a copy for your records and mail the original to the Child Welfare Services Agency in your community. Remember, a verbal report must be made immediately by phone and the written report must be filed within 36 hours. If this procedure is not followed, the reporting party is not covered under the immunity clause.

SUSPECTED CHILD ABUSE REPORT

To Be Completed by Reporting Party
Pursuant to Penal Code Section 11166

A. CASE IDENTIFICATION
TO BE COMPLETED BY INVESTIGATING CPA
VICTIM NAME: ______
REPORT NO./CASE NAME: ______
DATE OF REPORT: ______

B. REPORTING PARTY
NAME/TITLE
ADDRESS
PHONE ( ) | DATE OF REPORT | SIGNATURE

C. REPORT SENT TO
☐ POLICE DEPARTMENT ☐ SHERIFF'S OFFICE ☐ COUNTY WELFARE ☐ COUNTY PROBATION
AGENCY | ADDRESS
OFFICIAL CONTACTED | PHONE ( ) | DATE/TIME

D. INVOLVED PARTIES

VICTIM
NAME (LAST, FIRST, MIDDLE) | ADDRESS | BIRTHDATE | SEX | RACE
PRESENT LOCATION OF CHILD | PHONE ( )

SIBLINGS

NAME	BIRTHDATE	SEX	RACE	NAME	BIRTHDATE	SEX	RACE
1.				4.			
2.				5.			
3.				6.			

PARENTS
NAME (LAST, FIRST, MIDDLE) | BIRTHDATE | SEX | RACE | NAME (LAST, FIRST, MIDDLE) | BIRTHDATE | SEX | RACE
ADDRESS | ADDRESS
HOME PHONE ( ) | BUSINESS PHONE ( ) | HOME PHONE ( ) | BUSINESS PHONE ( )

E. INCIDENT INFORMATION
IF NECESSARY, ATTACH EXTRA SHEET OR OTHER FORM AND CHECK THIS BOX. ☐
1. DATE/TIME OF INCIDENT | PLACE OF INCIDENT | *(CHECK ONE)* ☐ OCCURRED ☐ OBSERVED

IF CHILD WAS IN OUT-OF-HOME CARE AT TIME OF INCIDENT, CHECK TYPE OF CARE:
☐ FAMILY DAY CARE ☐ CHILD CARE CENTER ☐ FOSTER FAMILY HOME ☐ SMALL FAMILY HOME ☐ GROUP HOME OR INSTITUTION

2. TYPE OF ABUSE: *(CHECK ONE OR MORE)* ☐ PHYSICAL ☐ MENTAL ☐ SEXUAL ASSAULT ☐ NEGLECT ☐ OTHER

3. NARRATIVE DESCRIPTION:

4. SUMMARIZE WHAT THE ABUSED CHILD OR PERSON ACCOMPANYING THE CHILD SAID HAPPENED:

5. EXPLAIN KNOWN HISTORY OF SIMILAR INCIDENT(S) FOR THIS CHILD:

SS 8572 (Rev. 1/93)

INSTRUCTIONS AND DISTRIBUTION ON REVERSE

DO NOT submit a copy of this form to the Department of Justice (DOJ). A CPA is required under Penal Code Section 11169 to submit to DOJ a Child Abuse Investigation Report Form SS-8583 if (1) an active investigation has been conducted and (2) the incident is **not** unfounded.

[illegible]

Clinical Example # 1

Eric, an MFT intern, works at the county jail as a substance abuse counselor. He hears many stories of abuse and one in particular caused him a great deal of distress. An inmate told him that six months ago, his methamphetamine-addicted brother beat his seven-year-old daughter with a belt and left bruises on her so severe that she could not sit down. Since they live in rural Arizona and she is home schooled, the authorities did not investigate. The inmate appears worried about his niece. Upon hearing this story, Eric picked up the phone and called information for the Arizona Department of Child Welfare and made a child abuse report.

Questions for Clinical Example # 1

1. Did Eric's report conform to California law? Why or why not?
2. Since his registration as an intern applies only to California, is he mandated to make reports to Arizona? Why or why not?
3. In his attempt to protect this child, what other Business and Professions Code and ACA ethical standard did he violate?
4. How could Eric have managed this situation in a reasonable and prudent manner?
5. How did he manage to lose clinical objectivity?

Clinical Example # 2

The local family court service agency refers Elena and Arturo, a contentious couple, to Jaime for co-parenting counseling. They are undergoing a divorce and the Court requires that they complete 10 sessions prior to moving on to the next step. They begin to argue in front of Jaime and Elena screams at her husband: "You abused our daughter, you (invective). You hit her so hard she passed out. You want to hit me just like you hit her. I'm not holding your secret any longer." Arturo gets up, says: "She's a lying (invective)," and stomps out of the room. She tells Jaime: "You see, he is an abuser." Jaime stops the session and is extremely confused. He does not know whom to believe.

Questions for Clinical Example # 2

1. How would you interpret Jaime's confusion? What would you advise Jaime to do next?
2. A reasonable and prudent clinician would consider that Elena may be accusing her husband so she can get control of the children or that she is telling the truth since this is a highly antagonistic and charged situation. How would you determine that you have a "reasonable" suspicion of abuse in this case?
3. If Jaime makes the report, Arturo could sue him for slander. If he doesn't, the BBS could accuse him of failing to make a mandated report. Even though he has immunity, he still must show that he made the report as mandated by law and that he had a "reasonable" suspicion. What recommendations would you give him to make the best choice possible under these circumstances?
4. Jaime decides to interview the children without the parents present and determine if they have experienced any form of abuse. He invites a second therapist trained to interview children and both determine that father did not abuse the children. A week later, Elena's attorney initiates a BBS complaint against Jaime for failing to make a mandated child abuse report. What would be Jaime's strongest defense and how would he document it?

Clinical Example # 3

Ginny provides substance related treatment to adolescents of famous and wealthy adults. While working with the son of a powerful movie producer, he tells her that his father provides marijuana to him on a regular basis and that the father sneaks it into the treatment center when he visits. Ginny consults with her clinical supervisor about making a mandated child abuse report and is told to "drop" the case. The father is a regular contributor to the center and he has pledged $1,000,000 for the building fund of a new treatment wing.

Questions for Clinical Example # 3

1. Could the adolescent's father ruin her career if she reports him? Could the BBS attempt to take her license away if they find out she did not make the report? What would you advise her to do?
2. Ginny obtains consultation with a personal attorney who tells her that she should bring another clinician into the case and make a joint determination of a reasonable suspicion of child abuse exists. The other clinician refuses to make the report for fear of losing her job. What options does Ginny have?
3. What would you advise her to do as a reasonable and prudent clinician?
4. Realistically, how can Ginny make the best of this extremely sensitive and difficult situation?

Chapter Questions

1. Per Section 11166, what does "reasonable suspicion" of child abuse mean to you?
2. What are the legal requirements for reporting a reasonable suspicion of child abuse?
3. When two or more mandated reporters are involved in a case, who is primarily responsible for reporting?
4. What is your internal reality about child abuse? Would you be able to do therapy with an alleged perpetrator? Why or why not?
5. Regarding the child abuse report, what steps would you take to maintain objectivity and clarity in this case?
6. What are your potential blind spots in this case (Child Abuse Report) arising from your Internal Reality when dealing with all these issues? How might you lose objectivity in this case?
7. You've been working with a family for a while and you find out that the father has been sexually abusing one of the children. The mother of the child asks you not to report the husband because if you do, "he would go to jail and we would lose everything we have." Then she adds, "If you report him, it will be your fault this has happened to us!" How would you create therapeutic, legal/ethical, and clinical safety?
8. What would be the possible impact of reporting child abuse on the therapeutic relationship and on treatment? What factors could change the impact on these two issues?
9. Consider the following scenario: A divorced couple is fighting in Court for the custody of their young child. The father alleges to his or her therapist that the boyfriend of other spouse touched the child inappropriately. If this therapist were to consult with you, what other steps would you recommend in addition to seeking consultation with CAMFT attorneys?

Chapter 14

Elder and Dependent Abuse

Management of Elder and Dependent Adult Abuse

Welfare and Institutions Code 15600-15755 mandates MFTs to report a "reasonable" suspicion of physical and sexual abuse, abandonment, isolation, financial abuse, neglect or abduction, and other treatment resulting in physical or mental suffering acted upon elders (adults 65 and over), and dependent adults. A "dependent adult" is a person residing in California, between the ages of 18 and 64 years, who has physical or mental limitations that restrict his or her ability to carry out normal activities or to protect his or her rights. These persons include, but are not limited to persons who have physical or developmental disabilities or whose physical or mental abilities have diminished because of age. See important legal definitions: Sections 15610-1560.70

When MFTs develop a reasonable suspicion that an elder or dependent person is the victim of abuse, they report of the abuse to Adult Protective Services Agencies (APS) immediately by telephone and in writing within two working days. If the abuse takes place in a residential environment, MFTs report to the police. The law defines "reasonable suspicion" as meaning an objectively reasonable suspicion that a person would entertain, based upon facts that could cause a reasonable person in a like position, drawing upon his or her training and experience to suspect abuse. MFTs are exempt from reporting the described conditions of abuse when three conditions exist simultaneously. See 15630 (3) (A). The elder/dependent adult tells the MFT that he experienced any of the type of abuse described in the first paragraph, the MFT isn't aware of independent evidence supporting the statement of abuse, and the elder/dependent adult has been diagnosed with a mental illness or dementia.

Elder/Dependent Adult Abuse Reporting and Immunity for MFTs

Under Welfare and Institutions Code 15634, immunity is granted to mental health practitioners who report Elder or Dependent Abuse. Though immunity exists, it does not prevent a disgruntled individual from suing the reporting therapist for making an false report resulting in a breach of confidentiality. The law provides a refund of up to $50,000 for legal fees after the MFT is successful in the malpractice action. Immunity does not apply if the report is made outside of the required time elements, it is erroneous or incomplete, misrepresents the facts, or the MFT made the report to harm the individual.

If an MFT should face a legal action for making a mandated adult abuse report, the best defense is appropriate documentation indicating the following: the type of information the MFT obtained to make a report, consultation with a more experienced peer if necessary, determining the nature of the abuse within the professional and social history, and how the clinician made the determination that the information obtained indicated that a "reasonable" suspicion of abuse existed. The author's experience with opposing attorneys indicates that they aren't fond of MFTs who document appropriately when making mandated reports.

Employees and Elder/Dependent Adult Abuse Laws

When any person falls under the mandate of the Elder and Dependent Adult Abuse Law (Welfare and Institutions Code 15600-15755) becomes an employee, he or she is required to sign a statement, which must clearly define that the employee is aware of Welfare and Institutions Code 15600-15755 and will abide by its requirements.

> **Welfare and Institutions Code 15659: (a) Any person who enters into employment on or after January 1, 1995, as a care custodian, health practitioner, or with an adult protective services agency or a local law enforcement agency, prior to commencing his or her employment and as a prerequisite to that employment shall sign a statement on a form, that shall be provided by the prospective employer, to the effect that he or she has knowledge of Section 15630 and will comply with its provisions. The signed statement shall be retained by the employer.**

This law applies to all licensed MFTs, interns and trainees in public or private employment when they are functioning within the role of their profession. The signed statement is kept in their employee file. Should this statement be missing, both employer and employee are in violation of California law.

Multiple Parties Required to Report

In situations where two or more clinicians must report a "reasonable" suspicion of adult/ dependent abuse, WIC 15630 (5) (d) states that when agreed upon, one of the clinicians must make the telephone report. The written report is signed by the selected designated reporter. Should a clinician learn that the report wasn't made, she must make the report immediately. Due to the multiple clinician involvement in these circumstances, its possible for a clinician to lose paperwork or fail to document the necessary data in the mental health records. It serves each clinician to keep copies of all appropriate records related to this case in their possession. Should the be challenged by an opposing attorney, those holding appropriate documentation can help defuse a potential legal action.

Financial Abuse

California law describes financial abuse as taking or intending to take the real or personal property of an elder/dependent adult through any means, including fraud. In this situation, a power differential exists. Those who are willing to take advantage of the elder/dependent abuse know that due to the differential, they can take advantage of the emotional, physical, or mental status of their victim. When the MFT lears of this form of abuse, they are mandated to report it.

Isolation

California law describes this category as any act intended to prevent the elder/dependent adult from receiving any form of communication, false imprisonment, physical restraint to prevent any form of communication with others, false imprisonment,

Abandonment

California law describes abandonment as the desertion or willful forsaking of an elder or dependent adult by anyone having care or custody of that person under circumstances in which a reasonable person would continue to provide care and custody. This is a mandated reporting issue.

Neglect

According to California law, neglect is described as the negligent failure of any person having the care or custody of an elder or a dependent adult to exercise that degree of care that a reasonable person in a like position would exercise, or the negligent failure of an elder or dependent adult to exercise that degree of self care that a reasonable person in a like position would exercise. We can consider lack of assistance in personal hygiene, failure to provide clothing, food, shelter, medical, physical, or mental health needs. Additionally, we can consider the prevention of malnutrition or dehydration as examples of this type of abuse. These conditions are considered reasons to make a mandated report.

Abduction

Any elder or dependent who is restrained from returning to this state, or the restrained from returning to this state, of any elder or dependent adult who does not have the capacity to consent to the removal from this state and the restraint from returning to this state, or the restraint from returning to this state, as well as the removal from this state or the restraint from returning to this state, of any conservatee without the consent of the conservator or the court is considered as being abducted. This is a mandated reportable situation. This is also a mandated report condition.

Mental Suffering

California law describes mental suffering as being fear, agitation, confusion, severe depression, or other forms of serious emotional distress that is brought about by forms of intimidating behavior, threats, harassment, or by deceptive acts performed or false or misleading statements made with malicious intent to agitate, confuse, frighten, or cause severe depression or serious emotional distress of the elder or dependent adult. Mental suffering can include the lack of providing of physical oar mental health needs, the lack of provision of health needs, providing inadequate clothing, failure to provide heated or ventilated shelter, lack of protection from health and safety hazards, protection from malnutrition, failure to provide transportation to obtain any of the above. Though this isn't a madated category, clinician are permitted to report it.

The Elder and Dependent Abuse Laws–WELFARE AND INSTITUTIONS CODE SECTION 15600-15755

15600.

(a) The Legislature recognizes that elders and dependent adults may be subjected to abuse, neglect, or abandonment and that this state has a responsibility to protect these persons.
(b) The Legislature further recognizes that a significant number of these persons are elderly. The Legislature desires to direct special attention to the needs and problems of elderly persons, recognizing that these persons constitute a significant and identifiable segment of the population and that they are more subject to risks of abuse, neglect, and abandonment.
(c) The Legislature further recognizes that a significant number of these persons have developmental disabilities and that mental and verbal limitations often leave them vulnerable to abuse and incapable of asking for help and protection.
(d) The Legislature recognizes that most elders and dependent adults who are at the greatest risk of abuse, neglect, or abandonment by their families or caretakers suffer physical impairments and other poor health that place them in a dependent and vulnerable position.
(e) The Legislature further recognizes that factors which contribute to abuse, neglect, or abandonment of elders and dependent adults are economic instability of the family, resentment of caretaker responsibilities, stress on the caretaker, and abuse by the caretaker of drugs or alcohol.
(f) The Legislature declares that this state shall foster and promote community services for the economic, social, and personal well-being of its citizens in order to protect those persons described in this section.
(g) The Legislature further declares that uniform state guidelines, which specify when county adult protective service agencies are to investigate allegations of abuse of elders and dependent adults and the appropriate role of local law enforcement is necessary in order to ensure that a minimum level of protection is provided to elders and dependent adults in each county.
(h) The Legislature further finds and declares that infirm elderly persons and dependent adults are a disadvantaged class, that cases of abuse of these persons are seldom prosecuted as criminal matters, and few civil cases are brought in connection with this abuse due to problems of proof, court delays, and the lack of incentives to prosecute these suits.
(i) Therefore, it is the intent of the Legislature in enacting this chapter to provide that adult protective services agencies, local long-term care ombudsman programs, and local law enforcement agencies shall receive referrals or complaints from public or private agencies, from any mandated reporter submitting reports pursuant to Section 15630, or from any other source having reasonable cause to know that the welfare of an elder or dependent adult is endangered, and shall take any actions considered necessary to protect the elder or dependent adult and correct the situation and ensure the individual's safety.
(j) It is the further intent of the Legislature in adding Article 8.5 (commencing with Section 15657) to this chapter to enable interested persons to engage attorneys to take up the cause of abused elderly persons and dependent adults. (Amended by Stats. 1994, Ch. 594, Sec. 1. Effective January 1, 1995.)

15601.

The purposes of this act is to:
(a) Require health practitioners, care custodians, clergy members, and employees of county adult protective services agencies and local law enforcement agencies to report known or suspected cases of abuse of elders and dependent adults and to encourage community members in general to do so.
(b) Collect information on the numbers of abuse victims, circumstances surrounding the act of abuse, and other data which will aid the state in establishing adequate services to aid all victims of abuse in a timely, compassionate manner.
(c) Provide for protection under the law for all those persons who report suspected cases of abuse, provided that the report is not made with malicious intent.
(Amended by Stats. 2002, Ch. 54, Sec. 1. Effective January 1, 2003.)

15610.

The definitions contained in this article shall govern the construction of this chapter, unless the context requires otherwise. (Repealed and added by Stats. 1994, Ch. 594, Sec. 3. Effective January 1, 1995.)

15610.05.

"Abandonment" means the desertion or willful forsaking of an elder or a dependent adult by anyone having care or custody of that person under circumstances in which a reasonable person would continue to provide care and custody. (Added by Stats. 1994, Ch. 594, Sec. 3. Effective January 1, 1995.)

15610.06.

"Abduction" means the removal from this state and the restraint from returning to this state, or the restraint from returning to this state, of any elder or dependent adult who does not have the capacity to consent to the removal from this state and the restraint from returning to this state, or the restraint from returning to this state, as well as the removal from this state or the restraint from returning to this state, of any conservatee without the consent of the conservator or the court. (Added by Stats. 1997, Ch. 663, Sec. 2. Effective January 1, 1998.)

15610.07.

"Abuse of an elder or a dependent adult" means either of the following:
(a) Physical abuse, neglect, financial abuse, abandonment, isolation, abduction, or other treatment with resulting physical harm or pain or mental suffering.
(b) The deprivation by a care custodian of goods or services that are necessary to avoid physical harm or mental suffering.
(Amended by Stats. 1998, Ch. 946, Sec. 2. Effective January 1, 1999.)

15610.10.

"Adult protective services" means those preventive and remedial activities performed on behalf of elders and dependent adults who are unable to protect their own interests, harmed or threatened with harm, caused physical or mental injury due to the action or inaction of another person or their own action as a result of ignorance, illiteracy, incompetence, mental limitation, substance abuse, or poor health, lacking in adequate food, shelter, or clothing, exploited of their income and resources, or deprived of entitlement due them. (Amended by Stats. 1998, Ch. 946, Sec. 3. Effective January 1, 1999.)

15610.13.

"Adult protective services agency" means a county welfare department, except persons who do not work directly with elders or dependent adults as part of their official duties, including members of support staff and maintenance staff. (Added by Stats. 1994, Ch. 594, Sec. 3. Effective January 1, 1995.)

15610.15.

"Bureau" means the Bureau of Medi-Cal Fraud within the office of the Attorney General.(Added by Stats. 1994, Ch. 594, Sec. 3. Effective January 1, 1995.)

15610.17.

"Care custodian" means an administrator or an employee of any of the following public or private facilities or agencies, or persons providing care or services for elders or dependent adults, including members of the support staff and maintenance staff:
(a) Twenty-four-hour health facilities, as defined in Sections 1250, 1250.2, and 1250.3 of the Health and Safety Code.
(b) Clinics.
(c) Home health agencies.
(d) Agencies providing publicly funded in-home supportive services, nutrition services, or other home and community-based support services.
(e) Adult day health care centers and adult day care.
(f) Secondary schools that serve 18- to 22-year-old dependent adults and postsecondary educational institutions that serve dependent adults or elders.
(g) Independent living centers.
(h) Camps.
(i) Alzheimer's Disease day care resource centers.
(j) Community care facilities, as defined in Section 1502 of the Health and Safety Code, and residential care facilities for the elderly, as defined in Section 1569.2 of the Health and Safety Code.
(k) Respite care facilities.

(l) Foster homes.
(m) Vocational rehabilitation facilities and work activity centers.
(n) Designated area agencies on aging.
(o) Regional centers for persons with developmental disabilities.
(p) State Department of Social Services and State Department of Health Services licensing divisions.
(q) County welfare departments.
(r) Offices of patients' rights advocates and clients' rights advocates, including attorneys.
(s) The office of the long-term care ombudsman.
(t) Offices of public conservators, public guardians, and court investigators.
(u) Any protection or advocacy agency or entity that is designated by the Governor to fulfill the requirements and assurances of the following:
(1) The federal Developmental Disabilities Assistance and Bill of Rights Act of 2000, contained in Chapter 144 (commencing with Section 15001) of Title 42 of the United States Code, for protection and advocacy of the rights of persons with developmental disabilities.
(2) The Protection and Advocacy for the Mentally Ill Individuals Act of 1986, as amended, contained in Chapter 114 (commencing with Section 10801) of Title 42 of the United States Code, for the protection and advocacy of the rights of persons with mental illness.
(v) Humane societies and animal control agencies.
(w) Fire departments.
(x) Offices of environmental health and building code enforcement.
(y) Any other protective, public, sectarian, mental health, or private assistance or advocacy agency or person providing health services or social services to elders or dependent adults.
(Amended by Stats. 2002, Ch. 54, Sec. 2. Effective January 1, 2003.)

15610.19.

"Clergy member" means a priest, minister, rabbi, religious practitioner, or similar functionary of a church, synagogue, temple, mosque, or recognized religious denomination or organization. "Clergy member" does not include unpaid volunteers whose principal occupation or vocation does not involve active or ordained ministry in a church, synagogue, temple, mosque, or recognized religious denomination or organization, and who periodically visit elder or dependent adults on behalf of that church, synagogue, temple, mosque, or recognized religious denomination or organization.
(Added by Stats. 2002, Ch. 54, Sec. 3. Effective January 1, 2003.)

15610.20.

"Clients' rights advocate" means the individual or individuals assigned by a regional center or state hospital developmental center to be responsible for clients' rights assurance for persons with developmental disabilities. (Added by Stats. 1994, Ch. 594, Sec. 3. Effective January 1, 1995.)

15610.23.

(a) "Dependent adult" means any person between the ages of 18 and 64 years who resides in this state and who has physical or mental limitations that restrict his or her ability to carry out normal activities or to protect his or her rights, including, but not limited to, persons who have physical or developmental disabilities, or whose physical or mental abilities have diminished because of age.
(b) "Dependent adult" includes any person between the ages of 18 and 64 years who is admitted as an inpatient to a 24-hour health facility, as defined in Sections 1250, 1250.2, and 1250.3 of the Health and Safety Code. (Amended by Stats. 2002, Ch. 54, Sec. 4. Effective January 1, 2003.)

15610.25

"Developmentally disabled person" means a person with a developmental disability specified by or as described in subdivision (a) of Section 4512. (Added by Stats. 1994, Ch. 594, Sec. 3. Effective January 1, 1995.)

15610.27.

"Elder" means any person residing in this state, 65 years of age or older. (Added by Stats. 1994, Ch. 594, Sec. 3. Effective January 1, 1995.)

15610.30.

(a) "Financial abuse" of an elder or dependent adult occurs when a person or entity does any of the following:
(1) Takes, secretes, appropriates, obtains, or retains real or personal property of an elder or dependent adult for a wrongful use or with intent to defraud, or both.
(2) Assists in taking, secreting, appropriating, obtaining, or retaining real or personal property of an elder or dependent adult for a wrongful use or with intent to defraud, or both.
(3) Takes, secretes, appropriates, obtains, or retains, or assists in taking, secreting, appropriating, obtaining, or retaining, real or personal property of an elder or dependent adult by undue influence, as defined in Section **15610.70.**
(b) A person or entity shall be deemed to have taken, secreted, appropriated, obtained, or retained property for a wrongful use if, among other things, the person or entity takes, secretes, appropriates, obtains, or retains the property and the person or entity knew or should have known that this conduct is likely to be harmful to the elder or dependent adult.
(c) For purposes of this section, a person or entity takes, secretes, appropriates, obtains, or retains real or personal property

when an elder or dependent adult is deprived of any property right, including by means of an agreement, donative transfer, or testamentary bequest, regardless of whether the property is held directly or by a representative of an elder or dependent adult.
(d) For purposes of this section, "representative" means a person or entity that is either of the following:
(1) A conservator, trustee, or other representative of the estate of an elder or dependent adult.
(2) An attorney-in-fact of an elder or dependent adult who acts within the authority of the power of attorney. (Amended by Stats. 2013, Ch. 668, Sec. 2. Effective January 1, 2014.)

15610.35.

"Goods and services necessary to avoid physical harm or mental suffering" include, but are not limited to, all of the following:
(a) The provision of medical care for physical and mental health needs.
(b) Assistance in personal hygiene.
(c) Adequate clothing.
(d) Adequately heated and ventilated shelter.
(e) Protection from health and safety hazards.
(f) Protection from malnutrition, under those circumstances where the results include, but are not limited to, malnutrition and deprivation of necessities or physical punishment.
(g) Transportation and assistance necessary to secure any of the needs set forth in subdivisions (a) to (f), inclusive. (Added by Stats. 1994, Ch. 594, Sec. 3. Effective January 1, 1995.)

15610.37.

"Health practitioner" means a physician and surgeon, psychiatrist, psychologist, dentist, resident, intern, podiatrist, chiropractor, registered nurse, dental hygienist, licensed clinical social worker or associate clinical social worker, marriage and family therapist, licensed professional clinical counselor, or any other person who is currently licensed under Division 2 (commencing with Section 500) of the Business and Professions Code, any emergency medical technician I or II, paramedic, or person certified pursuant to Division 2.5 (commencing with Section 1797) of the Health and Safety Code, a psychological assistant registered pursuant to Section 2913 of the Business and Professions Code, a marriage and family therapist trainee, as defined in subdivision (c) of Section 4980.03 of the Business and Professions Code, an unlicensed marriage and family therapist intern registered under Section 4980.44 of the Business and Professions Code, a clinical counselor trainee, as defined in subdivision (g) of Section 4999.12 of the Business and Professions Code, a clinical counselor intern registered under Section 4999.42 of the Business and Professions Code, a state or county public health or social service employee who treats an elder or a dependent adult for any condition, or a coroner.
(Amended by Stats. 2011, Ch. 381, Sec. 49. Effective January 1, 2012.)

15610.39.

"Imminent danger" means a substantial probability that an elder or dependent adult is in imminent or immediate risk of death or serious physical harm, through either his or her own action or inaction, or as a result of the action or inaction of another person. (Added by Stats. 2002, Ch. 54, Sec. 6. Effective January 1, 2003.)

15610.40.

"Investigation" means that activity undertaken to determine the validity of a report of elder or dependent adult abuse. (Added by Stats. 1994, Ch. 594, Sec. 3. Effective January 1, 1995.)

15610.43.

(a) "Isolation" means any of the following:
(1) Acts intentionally committed for the purpose of preventing, and that do serve to prevent, an elder or dependent adult from receiving his or her mail or telephone calls.
(2) Telling a caller or prospective visitor that an elder or dependent adult is not present, or does not wish to talk with the caller, or does not wish to meet with the visitor where the statement is false, is contrary to the express wishes of the elder or the dependent adult, whether he or she is competent or not, and is made for the purpose of preventing the elder or dependent adult from having contact with family, friends, or concerned persons.
(3) False imprisonment, as defined in Section 236 of the Penal Code.
(4) Physical restraint of an elder or dependent adult, for the purpose of preventing the elder or dependent adult from meeting with visitors.
(b) The acts set forth in subdivision (a) shall be subject to a rebuttable presumption that they do not constitute isolation if they are performed pursuant to the instructions of a physician and surgeon licensed to practice medicine in the state, who is caring for the elder or dependent adult at the time the instructions are given, and who gives the instructions as part of his or her medical care.
(c) The acts set forth in subdivision (a) shall not constitute isolation if they are performed in response to a reasonably perceived threat of danger to property or physical safety. (Added by Stats. 1994, Ch. 594, Sec. 3. Effective January 1, 1995.)

15610.45.

"Local law enforcement agency" means a city police or county sheriff's department, or a county probation department, except persons who do not work directly with elders or dependent adults as part of their official duties, including members of support staff and maintenance staff. (Added by Stats. 1994, Ch. 594, Sec. 3. Effective January 1, 1995.)

15610.47.

"Long-term care facility" means any of the following:
(a) Any long-term health care facility, as defined in subdivision (a) of Section 1418 of the Health and Safety Code.
(b) Any community care facility, as defined in paragraphs (1) and (2) of subdivision (a) of Section 1502 of the Health and Safety Code, whether licensed or unlicensed.
(c) Any swing bed in an acute care facility, or any extended care facility.
(d) Any adult day health care facility as defined in subdivision (b) of Section 1570.7 of the Health and Safety Code.
(e) Any residential care facility for the elderly as defined in Section 1569.2 of the Health and Safety Code. (Added by Stats. 1994, Ch. 594, Sec. 3. Effective January 1, 1995.)

15610.50.

"Long-term care ombudsman" means the State Long-Term Care Ombudsman, local ombudsman coordinators, and other persons currently certified as ombudsmen by the Department of Aging as described in Chapter 11 (commencing with Section 9700) of Division 8.5. (Amended by Stats. 2002, Ch. 54, Sec. 7. Effective January 1, 2003.)

15610.53.

"Mental suffering" means fear, agitation, confusion, severe depression, or other forms of serious emotional distress that is brought about by forms of intimidating behavior, threats, harassment, or by deceptive acts performed or false or misleading statements made with malicious intent to agitate, confuse, frighten, or cause severe depression or serious emotional distress of the elder or dependent adult. (Amended by Stats. 2000, Ch. 559, Sec. 3. Effective January 1, 2001.)

15610.55.

(a) "Multidisciplinary personnel team" means any team of two or more persons who are trained in the prevention, identification, management, or treatment of abuse of elderly or dependent adults and who are qualified to provide a broad range of services related to abuse of elderly or dependent adults.
(b) A multidisciplinary personnel team may include, but need not be limited to, any of the following:
(1) Psychiatrists, psychologists, or other trained counseling personnel.
(2) Police officers or other law enforcement agents.
(3) Medical personnel with sufficient training to provide health services.
(4) Social workers with experience or training in prevention of abuse of elderly or dependent adults.
(5) Public guardians.
(6) The local long-term care ombudsman.
(7) Child welfare services personnel. (Amended by Stats. 2014, Ch. 62, Sec. 1. Effective January 1, 2015.)

15610.57.

(a) "Neglect" means either of the following:
(1) The negligent failure of any person having the care or custody of an elder or a dependent adult to exercise that degree of care that a reasonable person in a like position would exercise.
(2) The negligent failure of an elder or dependent adult to exercise that degree of self care that a reasonable person in a like position would exercise.
(b) Neglect includes, but is not limited to, all of the following:
(1) Failure to assist in personal hygiene, or in the provision of food, clothing, or shelter.
(2) Failure to provide medical care for physical and mental health needs. No person shall be deemed neglected or abused for the sole reason that he or she voluntarily relies on treatment by spiritual means through prayer alone in lieu of medical treatment.
(3) Failure to protect from health and safety hazards.
(4) Failure to prevent malnutrition or dehydration.
(5) Failure of an elder or dependent adult to satisfy the needs specified in paragraphs (1) to (4), inclusive, for himself or herself as a result of poor cognitive functioning, mental limitation, substance abuse, or chronic poor health. (Amended by Stats. 2002, Ch. 54, Sec. 8. Effective January 1, 2003.)

15610.60.

"Patients' rights advocate" means a person who has no direct or indirect clinical or administrative responsibility for the patient, and who is responsible for ensuring that laws, regulations, and policies on the rights of the patient are observed. (Added by Stats. 1994, Ch. 594, Sec. 3. Effective January 1, 1995.)

15610.63.

"Physical abuse" means any of the following:
(a) Assault, as defined in Section 240 of the Penal Code.
(b) Battery, as defined in Section 242 of the Penal Code.
(c) Assault with a deadly weapon or force likely to produce great bodily injury, as defined in Section 245 of the Penal Code.
(d) Unreasonable physical constraint, or prolonged or continual deprivation of food or water.
(e) Sexual assault, that means any of the following:
(1) Sexual battery, as defined in Section 243.4 of the Penal Code.
(2) Rape, as defined in Section 261 of the Penal Code.
(3) Rape in concert, as described in Section 264.1 of the Penal Code.
(4) Spousal rape, as defined in Section 262 of the Penal Code.

(5) Incest, as defined in Section 285 of the Penal Code.
(6) Sodomy, as defined in Section 286 of the Penal Code.
(7) Oral copulation, as defined in Section 288a of the Penal Code.
(8) Sexual penetration, as defined in Section 289 of the Penal Code.
(9) Lewd or lascivious acts as defined in paragraph (2) of subdivision (b) of Section 288 of the Penal Code.
(f) Use of a physical or chemical restraint or psychotropic medication under any of the following conditions:
(1) For punishment.
(2) For a period beyond that for which the medication was ordered pursuant to the instructions of a physician and surgeon licensed in the State of California, who is providing medical care to the elder or dependent adult at the time the instructions are given.
(3) For any purpose not authorized by the physician and surgeon. (Amended by Stats. 2004, Ch. 823, Sec. 18. Effective January 1, 2005.)

15610.65.

"Reasonable suspicion" means an objectively reasonable suspicion that a person would entertain, based upon facts that could cause a reasonable person in a like position, drawing when appropriate upon his or her training and experience, to suspect abuse.
(Added by Stats. 1994, Ch. 594, Sec. 3. Effective January 1, 1995.)

15610.67.

"Serious bodily injury" means an injury involving extreme physical pain, substantial risk of death, or protracted loss or impairment of function of a bodily member, organ, or of mental faculty, or requiring medical intervention, including, but not limited to, hospitalization, surgery, or physical rehabilitation. (Added by Stats. 2012, Ch. 659, Sec. 1. Effective January 1, 2013.)

15610.70.

(a) "Undue influence" means excessive persuasion that causes another person to act or refrain from acting by overcoming that person's free will and results in inequity. In determining whether a result was produced by undue influence, all of the following shall be considered:
(1) The vulnerability of the victim. Evidence of vulnerability may include, but is not limited to, incapacity, illness, disability, injury, age, education, impaired cognitive function, emotional distress, isolation, or dependency, and whether the influencer knew or should have known of the alleged victim's vulnerability.
(2) The influencer's apparent authority. Evidence of apparent authority may include, but is not limited to, status as a fiduciary, family member, care provider, health care professional, legal professional, spiritual adviser, expert, or other qualification.
(3) The actions or tactics used by the influencer. Evidence of actions or tactics used may include, but is not limited to, all of the following:
(A) Controlling necessaries of life, medication, the victim's interactions with others, access to information, or sleep.
(B) Use of affection, intimidation, or coercion.
(C) Initiation of changes in personal or property rights, use of haste or secrecy in effecting those changes, effecting changes at inappropriate times and places, and claims of expertise in effecting changes.
(4) The equity of the result. Evidence of the equity of the result may include, but is not limited to, the economic consequences to the victim, any divergence from the victim's prior intent or course of conduct or dealing, the relationship of the value conveyed to the value of any services or consideration received, or the appropriateness of the change in light of the length and nature of the relationship.
(b) Evidence of an inequitable result, without more, is not sufficient to prove undue influence.(Added by Stats. 2013, Ch. 668, Sec. 3. Effective January 1, 2014.)

15630.

(a) Any person who has assumed full or intermittent responsibility for the care or custody of an elder or dependent adult, whether or not he or she receives compensation, including administrators, supervisors, and any licensed staff of a public or private facility that provides care or services for elder or dependent adults, or any elder or dependent adult care custodian, health practitioner, clergy member, or employee of a county adult protective services agency or a local law enforcement agency, is a mandated reporter.
(b) (1) Any mandated reporter who, in his or her professional capacity, or within the scope of his or her employment, has observed or has knowledge of an incident that reasonably appears to be physical abuse, as defined in Section 15610.63, abandonment, abduction, isolation, financial abuse, or neglect, or is told by an elder or dependent adult that he or she has experienced behavior, including an act or omission, constituting physical abuse, as defined in Section 15610.63, abandonment, abduction, isolation, financial abuse, or neglect, or reasonably suspects that abuse, shall report the known or suspected instance of abuse by telephone or through a confidential Internet reporting tool, as authorized by Section 15658, immediately or as soon as practicably possible. If reported by telephone, a written report shall be sent, or an Internet report shall be made through the confidential Internet reporting tool established in Section 15658, within two working days.
(A) If the suspected or alleged abuse is physical abuse, as defined in Section 15610.63, and the abuse occurred in a long-term care facility, except a state mental health hospital or a state developmental center, the following shall occur:
(i) If the suspected abuse results in serious bodily injury, a telephone report shall be made to the local law enforcement agency immediately, but also no later than within two hours of the mandated reporter observing, obtaining knowledge of,

or suspecting the physical abuse, and a written report shall be made to the local ombudsman, the corresponding licensing agency, and the local law enforcement agency within two hours of the mandated reporter observing, obtaining knowledge of, or suspecting the physical abuse.
(ii) If the suspected abuse does not result in serious bodily injury, a telephone report shall be made to the local law enforcement agency within 24 hours of the mandated reporter observing, obtaining knowledge of, or suspecting the physical abuse, and a written report shall be made to the local ombudsman, the corresponding licensing agency, and the local law enforcement agency within 24 hours of the mandated reporter observing, obtaining knowledge of, or suspecting the physical abuse.
(iii) When the suspected abuse is allegedly caused by a resident with a physician's diagnosis of dementia, and there is no serious bodily injury, as reasonably determined by the mandated reporter, drawing upon his or her training or experience, the reporter shall report to the local ombudsman or law enforcement agency by telephone, immediately or as soon as practicably possible, and by written report, within 24 hours.
(iv) When applicable, reports made pursuant to clauses (i) and (ii) shall be deemed to satisfy the reporting requirements of the federal Elder Justice Act of 2009, as set out in Subtitle H of the federal Patient Protection and Affordable Care Act (Public Law 111-148), Section 1418.91 of the Health and Safety Code, and Section 72541 of Title 22 of California Code of Regulations. When a local law enforcement agency receives an initial report of suspected abuse in a long-term care facility pursuant to this subparagraph, the local law enforcement agency may coordinate efforts with the local ombudsman to provide the most immediate and appropriate response warranted to investigate the mandated report. The local ombudsman and local law enforcement agencies may collaborate to develop protocols to implement this subparagraph.
(B) Notwithstanding the rulemaking provisions of Chapter 3.5 (commencing with Section 11340) of Part 1 of Division 3 of Title 2 of the Government Code, or any other law, the department may implement subparagraph (A), in whole or in part, by means of all-county letters, provider bulletins, or other similar instructions without taking regulatory action.
(C) If the suspected or alleged abuse is abuse other than physical abuse, and the abuse occurred in a long-term care facility, except a state mental health hospital or a state developmental center, a telephone report and a written report shall be made to the local ombudsman or the local law enforcement agency.
(D) With regard to abuse reported pursuant to subparagraph (C), the local ombudsman and the local law enforcement agency shall, as soon as practicable, except in the case of an emergency or pursuant to a report required to be made pursuant to clause (v), in which case these actions shall be taken immediately, do all of the following:
(i) Report to the State Department of Public Health any case of known or suspected abuse occurring in a long-term health care facility, as defined in subdivision (a) of Section 1418 of the Health and Safety Code.
(ii) Report to the State Department of Social Services any case of known or suspected abuse occurring in a residential care facility for the elderly, as defined in Section 1569.2 of the Health and Safety Code, or in an adult day program, as defined in paragraph (2) of subdivision (a) of Section 1502 of the Health and Safety Code.
(iii) Report to the State Department of Public Health and the California Department of Aging any case of known or suspected abuse occurring in an adult day health care center, as defined in subdivision (b) of Section 1570.7 of the Health and Safety Code.
(iv) Report to the Bureau of Medi-Cal Fraud and Elder Abuse any case of known or suspected criminal activity.
(v) Report all cases of known or suspected physical abuse and financial abuse to the local district attorney's office in the county where the abuse occurred.
(E) (i) If the suspected or alleged abuse or neglect occurred in a state mental hospital or a state developmental center, and the suspected or alleged abuse or neglect resulted in any of the following incidents, a report shall be made immediately, but no later than within two hours of the mandated reporter observing, obtaining knowledge of, or suspecting abuse, to designated investigators of the State Department of State Hospitals or the State Department of Developmental Services, and also to the local law enforcement agency:
(I) A death.
(II) A sexual assault, as defined in Section 15610.63.
(III) An assault with a deadly weapon, as described in Section 245 of the Penal Code, by a nonresident of the state mental hospital or state developmental center.
(IV) An assault with force likely to produce great bodily injury, as described in Section 245 of the Penal Code.
(V) An injury to the genitals when the cause of the injury is undetermined.
(VI) A broken bone when the cause of the break is undetermined.
(ii) All other reports of suspected or alleged abuse or neglect that occurred in a state mental hospital or a state developmental center shall be made immediately, but no later than within two hours of the mandated reporter observing, obtaining knowledge of, or suspecting abuse, to designated investigators of the State Department of State Hospitals or the State Department of Developmental Services, or to the local law enforcement agency.
(iii) When a local law enforcement agency receives an initial report of suspected or alleged abuse or neglect in a state mental hospital or a state developmental center pursuant to clause (i), the local law enforcement agency shall coordinate efforts with the designated investigators of the State Department of State Hospitals or the State Department of Developmental Services to provide the most immediate and appropriate response warranted to investigate the mandated report. The designated investigators of the State Department of State Hospitals or the State Department of Developmental Services and local law

enforcement agencies may collaborate to develop protocols to implement this clause.
(iv) Except in an emergency, the local law enforcement agency shall, as soon as practicable, report any case of known or suspected criminal activity to the Bureau of Medi-Cal Fraud and Elder Abuse.
(v) Notwithstanding any other law, a mandated reporter who is required to report pursuant to Section 4427.5 shall not be required to report under clause (i).
(F) If the abuse has occurred in any place other than a long-term care facility, a state mental hospital, or a state developmental center, the report shall be made to the adult protective services agency or the local law enforcement agency.
(2) (A) A mandated reporter who is a clergy member who acquires knowledge or reasonable suspicion of elder or dependent adult abuse during a penitential communication is not subject to paragraph (1). For purposes of this subdivision, "penitential communication" means a communication that is intended to be in confidence, including, but not limited to, a sacramental confession made to a clergy member who, in the course of the discipline or practice of his or her church, denomination, or organization is authorized or accustomed to hear those communications and under the discipline tenets, customs, or practices of his or her church, denomination, or organization, has a duty to keep those communications secret.
(B) This subdivision shall not be construed to modify or limit a clergy member's duty to report known or suspected elder and dependent adult abuse if he or she is acting in the capacity of a care custodian, health practitioner, or employee of an adult protective services agency.
(C) Notwithstanding any other provision in this section, a clergy member who is not regularly employed on either a full-time or part-time basis in a long-term care facility or does not have care or custody of an elder or dependent adult shall not be responsible for reporting abuse or neglect that is not reasonably observable or discernible to a reasonably prudent person having no specialized training or experience in elder or dependent care.
(3) (A) A mandated reporter who is a physician and surgeon, a registered nurse, or a psychotherapist, as defined in Section 1010 of the Evidence Code, shall not be required to report, pursuant to paragraph (1), an incident if all of the following conditions exist:
(i) The mandated reporter has been told by an elder or dependent adult that he or she has experienced behavior constituting physical abuse, as defined in Section 15610.63, abandonment, abduction, isolation, financial abuse, or neglect.
(ii) The mandated reporter is not aware of any independent evidence that corroborates the statement that the abuse has occurred.
(iii) The elder or dependent adult has been diagnosed with a mental illness or dementia, or is the subject of a court-ordered conservatorship because of a mental illness or dementia.
(iv) In the exercise of clinical judgment, the physician and surgeon, the registered nurse, or the psychotherapist, as defined in Section 1010 of the Evidence Code, reasonably believes that the abuse did not occur.
(B) This paragraph shall not be construed to impose upon mandated reporters a duty to investigate a known or suspected incident of abuse and shall not be construed to lessen or restrict any existing duty of mandated reporters.
(4) (A) In a long-term care facility, a mandated reporter shall not be required to report as a suspected incident of abuse, as defined in Section 15610.07, an incident if all of the following conditions exist:
(i) The mandated reporter is aware that there is a proper plan of care.
(ii) The mandated reporter is aware that the plan of care was properly provided or executed.
(iii) A physical, mental, or medical injury occurred as a result of care provided pursuant to clause (i) or (ii).
(iv) The mandated reporter reasonably believes that the injury was not the result of abuse.
(B) This paragraph shall not be construed to require a mandated reporter to seek, nor to preclude a mandated reporter from seeking, information regarding a known or suspected incident of abuse prior to reporting. This paragraph shall apply only to those categories of mandated reporters that the State Department of Public Health determines, upon approval by the Bureau of Medi-Cal Fraud and Elder Abuse and the state long-term care ombudsman, have access to plans of care and have the training and experience necessary to determine whether the conditions specified in this section have been met.
(c) (1) Any mandated reporter who has knowledge, or reasonably suspects, that types of elder or dependent adult abuse for which reports are not mandated have been inflicted upon an elder or dependent adult, or that his or her emotional well-being is endangered in any other way, may report the known or suspected instance of abuse.
(2) If the suspected or alleged abuse occurred in a long-term care facility other than a state mental health hospital or a state developmental center, the report may be made to the long-term care ombudsman program. Except in an emergency, the local ombudsman shall report any case of known or suspected abuse to the State Department of Public Health and any case of known or suspected criminal activity to the Bureau of Medi-Cal Fraud and Elder Abuse, as soon as is practicable.
(3) If the suspected or alleged abuse occurred in a state mental health hospital or a state developmental center, the report may be made to the designated investigator of the State Department of State Hospitals or the State Department of Developmental Services or to a local law enforcement agency. Except in an emergency, the local law enforcement agency shall report any case of known or suspected criminal activity to the Bureau of Medi-Cal Fraud and Elder Abuse, as soon as is practicable.
(4) If the suspected or alleged abuse occurred in a place other than a place described in paragraph (2) or (3), the report may be made to the county adult protective services agency.
(5) If the conduct involves criminal activity not covered in subdivision (b), it may be immediately reported to the appropriate law enforcement agency.
(d) If two or more mandated reporters are present and jointly have knowledge or reasonably suspect that types of abuse of an

elder or a dependent adult for which a report is or is not mandated have occurred, and there is agreement among them, the telephone report or Internet report, as authorized by Section 15658, may be made by a member of the team selected by mutual agreement, and a single report may be made and signed by the selected member of the reporting team. Any member who has knowledge that the member designated to report has failed to do so shall thereafter make the report.
(e) A telephone report or Internet report, as authorized by Section 15658, of a known or suspected instance of elder or dependent adult abuse shall include, if known, the name of the person making the report, the name and age of the elder or dependent adult, the present location of the elder or dependent adult, the names and addresses of family members or any other adult responsible for the elder's or dependent adult's care, the nature and extent of the elder's or dependent adult's condition, the date of the incident, and any other information, including information that led that person to suspect elder or dependent adult abuse, as requested by the agency receiving the report.
(f) The reporting duties under this section are individual, and no supervisor or administrator shall impede or inhibit the reporting duties, and no person making the report shall be subject to any sanction for making the report. However, internal procedures to facilitate reporting, ensure confidentiality, and apprise supervisors and administrators of reports may be established, provided they are not inconsistent with this chapter.
(g) (1) Whenever this section requires a county adult protective services agency to report to a law enforcement agency, the law enforcement agency shall, immediately upon request, provide a copy of its investigative report concerning the reported matter to that county adult protective services agency.
(2) Whenever this section requires a law enforcement agency to report to a county adult protective services agency, the county adult protective services agency shall, immediately upon request, provide to that law enforcement agency a copy of its investigative report concerning the reported matter.
(3) The requirement to disclose investigative reports pursuant to this subdivision shall not include the disclosure of social services records or case files that are confidential, nor shall this subdivision be construed to allow disclosure of any reports or records if the disclosure would be prohibited by any other provision of state or federal law.
(h) Failure to report, or impeding or inhibiting a report of, physical abuse, as defined in Section 15610.63, abandonment, abduction, isolation, financial abuse, or neglect of an elder or dependent adult, in violation of this section, is a misdemeanor, punishable by not more than six months in the county jail, by a fine of not more than one thousand dollars ($1,000), or by both that fine and imprisonment. Any mandated reporter who willfully fails to report, or impedes or inhibits a report of, physical abuse, as defined in Section 15610.63, abandonment, abduction, isolation, financial abuse, or neglect of an elder or dependent adult, in violation of this section, if that abuse results in death or great bodily injury, shall be punished by not more than one year in a county jail, by a fine of not more than five thousand dollars ($5,000), or by both that fine and imprisonment. If a mandated reporter intentionally conceals his or her failure to report an incident known by the mandated reporter to be abuse or severe neglect under this section, the failure to report is a continuing offense until a law enforcement agency specified in paragraph (1) of subdivision (b) of Section 15630 discovers the offense.
(i) For purposes of this section, "dependent adult" shall have the same meaning as in Section 15610.23. (Amended by Stats. 2013, Ch. 673, Sec. 3. Effective January 1, 2014.)

15630.1.

(a) As used in this section, "mandated reporter of suspected financial abuse of an elder or dependent adult" means all officers and employees of financial institutions.
(b) As used in this section, the term "financial institution" means any of the following:
(1) A depository institution, as defined in Section 3(c) of the Federal Deposit Insurance Act (12 U.S.C. Sec. 1813(c)).
(2) An institution-affiliated party, as defined in Section 3(u) of the Federal Deposit Insurance Act (12 U.S.C. Sec. 1813(u)).
(3) A federal credit union or state credit union, as defined in Section 101 of the Federal Credit Union Act (12 U.S.C. Sec. 1752), including, but not limited to, an institution-affiliated party of a credit union, as defined in Section 206(r) of the Federal Credit Union Act (12 U.S.C. Sec. 1786(r)).
(c) As used in this section, "financial abuse" has the same meaning as in Section 15610.30.
(d) (1) Any mandated reporter of suspected financial abuse of an elder or dependent adult who has direct contact with the elder or dependent adult or who reviews or approves the elder or dependent adult's financial documents, records, or transactions, in connection with providing financial services with respect to an elder or dependent adult, and who, within the scope of his or her employment or professional practice, has observed or has knowledge of an incident, that is directly related to the transaction or matter that is within that scope of employment or professional practice, that reasonably appears to be financial abuse, or who reasonably suspects that abuse, based solely on the information before him or her at the time of reviewing or approving the document, record, or transaction in the case of mandated reporters who do not have direct contact with the elder or dependent adult, shall report the known or suspected instance of financial abuse by telephone or through a confidential Internet reporting tool, as authorized pursuant to Section 15658, immediately, or as soon as practicably possible. If reported by telephone, a written report shall be sent, or an Internet report shall be made through the confidential Internet reporting tool established in Section 15658, within two working days to the local adult protective services agency or the local law enforcement agency.
(2) When two or more mandated reporters jointly have knowledge or reasonably suspect that financial abuse of an elder or a dependent adult for which the report is mandated has occurred, and when there is an agreement among them, the telephone report or Internet report, as authorized by Section 15658, may be made by a member of the reporting team who is selected by

mutual agreement. A single report may be made and signed by the selected member of the reporting team. Any member of the team who has knowledge that the member designated to report has failed to do so shall thereafter make that report.
(3) If the mandated reporter knows that the elder or dependent adult resides in a long-term care facility, as defined in Section 15610.47, the report shall be made to the local ombudsman or local law enforcement agency.
(e) An allegation by the elder or dependent adult, or any other person, that financial abuse has occurred is not sufficient to trigger the reporting requirement under this section if both of the following conditions are met:
(1) The mandated reporter of suspected financial abuse of an elder or dependent adult is aware of no other corroborating or independent evidence of the alleged financial abuse of an elder or dependent adult. The mandated reporter of suspected financial abuse of an elder or dependent adult is not required to investigate any accusations.
(2) In the exercise of his or her professional judgment, the mandated reporter of suspected financial abuse of an elder or dependent adult reasonably believes that financial abuse of an elder or dependent adult did not occur.
(f) Failure to report financial abuse under this section shall be subject to a civil penalty not exceeding one thousand dollars ($1,000) or if the failure to report is willful, a civil penalty not exceeding five thousand dollars ($5,000), which shall be paid by the financial institution that is the employer of the mandated reporter to the party bringing the action. Subdivision (h) of Section 15630 shall not apply to violations of this section.
(g) (1) The civil penalty provided for in subdivision (f) shall be recovered only in a civil action brought against the financial institution by the Attorney General, district attorney, or county counsel. No action shall be brought under this section by any person other than the Attorney General, district attorney, or county counsel. Multiple actions for the civil penalty may not be brought for the same violation.
(2) Nothing in the Financial Elder Abuse Reporting Act of 2005 shall be construed to limit, expand, or otherwise modify any civil liability or remedy that may exist under this or any other law.
(h) As used in this section, "suspected financial abuse of an elder or dependent adult" occurs when a person who is required to report under subdivision (a) observes or has knowledge of behavior or unusual circumstances or transactions, or a pattern of behavior or unusual circumstances or transactions, that would lead an individual with like training or experience, based on the same facts, to form a reasonable belief that an elder or dependent adult is the victim of financial abuse as defined in Section 15610.30.
(i) Reports of suspected financial abuse of an elder or dependent adult made by an employee or officer of a financial institution pursuant to this section are covered under subdivision (b) of Section 47 of the Civil Code. (Amended by Stats. 2011, Ch. 373, Sec. 2.5. Effective January 1, 2012.)

15631.

(a) Any person who is not a mandated reporter under Section 15630, who knows, or reasonably suspects, that an elder or a dependent adult has been the victim of abuse may report that abuse to a long-term care ombudsman program or local law enforcement agency, or both the long-term care ombudsman program and local law enforcement agency when the abuse is alleged to have occurred in a long-term care facility.
(b) Any person who is not a mandated reporter under Section 15630, who knows, or reasonably suspects, that an elder or a dependent adult has been the victim of abuse in any place other than a long-term care facility may report the abuse to the county adult protective services agency or local law enforcement agency. Amended by Stats. 2012, Ch. 659, Sec. 3. Effective January 1, 2013.)

15632.

(a) In any court proceeding or administrative hearing, neither the physician-patient privilege nor the psychotherapist-patient privilege applies to the specific information reported pursuant to this chapter.
(b) Nothing in this chapter shall be interpreted as requiring an attorney to violate his or her oath and duties pursuant to Section 6067 or subdivision (e) of Section 6068 of the Business and Professions Code, and Article 3 (commencing with Section 950) of Chapter 4 of Division 8 of the Evidence Code. (Repealed and added by Stats. 1994, Ch. 594, Sec. 11. Effective January 1, 1995.)

15633.

(a) The reports made pursuant to Sections 15630, 15630.1, and 15631 shall be confidential and may be disclosed only as provided in subdivision (b). Any violation of the confidentiality required by this chapter is a misdemeanor punishable by not more than six months in the county jail, by a fine of five hundred dollars ($500), or by both that fine and imprisonment.
(b) Reports of suspected abuse of an elder or dependent adult and information contained therein may be disclosed only to the following:
(1) Persons or agencies to whom disclosure of information or the identity of the reporting party is permitted under Section 15633.5.
(2) (A) Persons who are trained and qualified to serve on multidisciplinary personnel teams may disclose to one another information and records that are relevant to the prevention, identification, or treatment of abuse of elderly or dependent persons.
(B) Except as provided in subparagraph (A), any personnel of the multidisciplinary team or agency that receives information pursuant to this chapter, shall be under the same obligations and subject to the same confidentiality penalties as the person disclosing or providing that information. The information obtained shall be maintained in a manner that ensures the maximum protection of privacy and confidentiality rights.

(c) This section shall not be construed to allow disclosure of any reports or records relevant to the reports of abuse of an elder or dependent adult if the disclosure would be prohibited by any other provisions of state or federal law applicable to the reports or records relevant to the reports of the abuse, nor shall it be construed to prohibit the disclosure by a financial institution of any reports or records relevant to the reports of abuse of an elder or dependent adult if the disclosure would be required of a financial institution by otherwise applicable state or federal law or court order. (Amended (as amended by Stats. 2005, Ch. 140, Sec. 5) by Stats. 2011, Ch. 372, Sec. 2. Effective January 1, 2012.)

15633.5.

(a) Information relevant to the incident of elder or dependent adult abuse may be given to an investigator from an adult protective services agency, a local law enforcement agency, the office of the district attorney, the office of the public guardian, the probate court, the bureau, or an investigator of the Department of Consumer Affairs, Division of Investigation who is investigating a known or suspected case of elder or dependent adult abuse.

(b) The identity of any person who reports under this chapter shall be confidential and disclosed only among the following agencies or persons representing an agency:

(1) An adult protective services agency.

(2 A long-term care ombudsperson program.

(3) A licensing agency.

(4) A local law enforcement agency.

(5) The office of the district attorney.

(6) The office of the public guardian.

(7) The probate court.

(8) The bureau.

(9) The Department of Consumer Affairs, Division of Investigation.

(10) Counsel representing an adult protective services agency.

(c) The identity of a person who reports under this chapter may also be disclosed under the following circumstances:

(1) To the district attorney in a criminal prosecution.

(2) When a person reporting waives confidentiality.

(3) By court order.

(d) Notwithstanding subdivisions (a), (b), and (c), any person reporting pursuant to Section 15631 shall not be required to include his or her name in the report. (Amended by Stats. 2002, Ch. 552, Sec. 2. Effective January 1, 2003.)

15634.

(a) No care custodian, clergy member, health practitioner, mandated reporter of suspected financial abuse of an elder or dependent adult, or employee of an adult protective services agency or a local law enforcement agency who reports a known or suspected instance of abuse of an elder or dependent adult shall be civilly or criminally liable for any report required or authorized by this article. Any other person reporting a known or suspected instance of abuse of an elder or dependent adult shall not incur civil or criminal liability as a result of any report authorized by this article, unless it can be proven that a false report was made and the person knew that the report was false. No person required to make a report pursuant to this article, or any person taking photographs at his or her discretion, shall incur any civil or criminal liability for taking photographs of a suspected victim of abuse of an elder or dependent adult or causing photographs to be taken of such a suspected victim or for disseminating the photographs with the reports required by this article. However, this section shall not be construed to grant immunity from this liability with respect to any other use of the photographs.

(b) No care custodian, clergy member, health practitioner, mandated reporter of suspected financial abuse of an elder or dependent adult, or employee of an adult protective services agency or a local law enforcement agency who, pursuant to a request from an adult protective services agency or a local law enforcement agency investigating a report of known or suspected abuse of an elder or dependent adult, provides the requesting agency with access to the victim of a known or suspected instance of abuse of an elder or dependent adult, shall incur civil or criminal liability as a result of providing that access.

(c) The Legislature finds that, even though it has provided immunity from liability to persons required to report abuse of an elder or dependent adult, immunity does not eliminate the possibility that actions may be brought against those persons based upon required reports of abuse. In order to further limit the financial hardship that those persons may incur as a result of fulfilling their legal responsibilities, it is necessary that they not be unfairly burdened by legal fees incurred in defending those actions. Therefore, a care custodian, clergy member, health practitioner, or an employee of an adult protective services agency or a local law enforcement agency may present to the California Victim Compensation and Government Claims Board a claim for reasonable attorneys' fees incurred in any action against that person on the basis of making a report required or authorized by this article if the court has dismissed the action upon a demurrer or motion for summary judgment made by that person, or if he or she prevails in the action. The California Victim Compensation and Government Claims Board shall allow that claim if the requirements of this subdivision are met, and the claim shall be paid from an appropriation to be made for that purpose. Attorneys' fees awarded pursuant to this section shall not exceed an hourly rate greater than the rate charged by the Attorney General at the time the award is made and shall not exceed an aggregate amount of fifty thousand dollars ($50,000). This subdivision shall not apply if a public entity has provided for the defense of the action pursuant to Section 995 of the Government Code. (Amended (as amended by Stats. 2005, Ch. 140, Sec. 7) by Stats. 2011, Ch. 372, Sec. 4. Effective January 1,

2012.)

15636.

(a) Any victim of elder or dependent adult abuse may refuse or withdraw consent at any time to an investigation or the provision of protective services by an adult protective services agency or long-term care ombudsman program. The adult protective services agency shall act only with the consent of the victim unless a violation of the Penal Code has been alleged. A local long-term care ombudsman shall act only with the consent of the victim and shall disclose confidential information only after consent to disclose is given by the victim or pursuant to court order.

(b) If the elder or dependent adult abuse victim is so incapacitated that he or she cannot legally give or deny consent to protective services, a petition for temporary conservatorship or guardianship may be initiated in accordance with Section 2250 of the Probate Code. (Added by Stats. 1994, Ch. 594, Sec. 18. Effective January 1, 1995.)

15637.

In any court proceeding or administrative hearing, neither the physician-patient privilege nor the psychotherapist-patient privilege applies to the specific information required to be reported pursuant to this chapter. Nothing in this chapter shall be interpreted as requiring an attorney to violate his or her oath and duties pursuant to Section 6067 or subdivision (e) of Section 6068 of the Business and Professions Code, and Article 3 (commencing with Section 950) of Chapter 4 of Division 8 of the Evidence Code. (Added by Stats. 1985, Ch. 1164, Sec. 13. Effective September 28, 1985.)

15640.

(a) (1) An adult protective services agency shall immediately, or as soon as practically possible, report by telephone to the law enforcement agency having jurisdiction over the case any known or suspected instance of criminal activity, and to any public agency given responsibility for investigation in that jurisdiction of cases of elder and dependent adult abuse, every known or suspected instance of abuse pursuant to Section 15630 or 15630.1 of an elder or dependent adult. A county adult protective services agency shall also send a written report thereof within two working days of receiving the information concerning the incident to each agency to which it is required to make a telephone report under this subdivision. Prior to making any cross-report of allegations of financial abuse to law enforcement agencies, an adult protective services agency shall first determine whether there is reasonable suspicion of any criminal activity.

(2) If an adult protective services agency receives a report of abuse alleged to have occurred in a long-term care facility, that adult protective services agency shall immediately inform the person making the report that he or she is required to make the report to the long-term care ombudsman program or to a local law enforcement agency. The adult protective services agency shall not accept the report by telephone but shall forward any written report received to the long-term care ombudsman.

(b) If an adult protective services agency or local law enforcement agency or ombudsman program receiving a report of known or suspected elder or dependent adult abuse determines, pursuant to its investigation, that the abuse is being committed by a health practitioner licensed under Division 2 (commencing with Section 500) of the Business and Professions Code, or any related initiative act, or by a person purporting to be a licensee, the adult protective services agency or local law enforcement agency or ombudsman program shall immediately, or as soon as practically possible, report this information to the appropriate licensing agency. The licensing agency shall investigate the report in light of the potential for physical harm. The transmittal of information to the appropriate licensing agency shall not relieve the adult protective services agency or local law enforcement agency or ombudsman program of the responsibility to continue its own investigation as required under applicable provisions of law. The information reported pursuant to this paragraph shall remain confidential and shall not be disclosed.

(c) A local law enforcement agency shall immediately, or as soon as practically possible, report by telephone to the long-term care ombudsman program when the abuse is alleged to have occurred in a long-term care facility or to the county adult protective services agency when it is alleged to have occurred anywhere else, and to the agency given responsibility for the investigation of cases of elder and dependent adult abuse every known or suspected instance of abuse of an elder or dependent adult. A local law enforcement agency shall also send a written report thereof within two working days of receiving the information concerning the incident to any agency to which it is required to make a telephone report under this subdivision.

(d) A long-term care ombudsman coordinator may report the instance of abuse to the county adult protective services agency or to the local law enforcement agency for assistance in the investigation of the abuse if the victim gives his or her consent. A long-term care ombudsman program and the Licensing and Certification Division of the State Department of Public Health shall immediately report by telephone and in writing within two working days to the bureau any instance of neglect occurring in a health care facility, that has seriously harmed any patient or reasonably appears to present a serious threat to the health or physical well-being of a patient in that facility. If a victim or potential victim of the neglect withholds consent to being identified in that report, the report shall contain circumstantial information about the neglect but shall not identify that victim or potential victim and the bureau and the reporting agency shall maintain the confidentiality of the report until the report becomes a matter of public record.

(e) When a county adult protective services agency, a long-term care ombudsman program, or a local law enforcement agency receives a report of abuse, neglect, or abandonment of an elder or dependent adult alleged to have occurred in a long-term care facility, that county adult protective services agency, long-term care ombudsman coordinator, or local law enforcement agency shall report the incident to the licensing agency by telephone as soon as possible.

(f) County adult protective services agencies, long-term care ombudsman programs, and local law enforcement agencies shall report the results of their investigations of referrals or reports of abuse to the respective referring or reporting agencies.

(Amended (as amended by Stats. 2005, Ch. 140, Sec. 9) by Stats. 2011, Ch. 372, Sec. 6. Effective January 1, 2012.)

15650.

(a) Investigation of reports of known or suspected instances of abuse in long-term care facilities shall be the responsibility of the bureau, the local law enforcement agency, and the long-term care ombudsman program.

(b) Investigations of known or suspected instances of abuse outside of long-term care facilities shall be the responsibility of the county adult protective services agency, unless another public agency is given responsibility for investigation in that jurisdiction, and the local law enforcement agency.

(c) The investigative responsibilities set forth in this section are in addition to, and not in derogation of or substitution for, the investigative and regulatory responsibilities of licensing agencies, such as the State Department of Social Services Community Care Licensing Division and the State Department of Public Health Licensing and Certification Division and their authorized representatives.

(d) Other public agencies involved in the investigation of abuse or advocacy of respective client populations, or both, include, but shall not be limited to, the State Department of State Hospitals and the State Department of Developmental Services. Other public agencies shall conduct or assist in, or both, the investigation of reports of abuse of elder and dependent adults within their jurisdiction in conjunction with county adult protective services, local ombudsman programs, and local law enforcement agencies.

(e) Each county adult protective services agency shall maintain an inventory of all public and private service agencies available to assist victims of abuse, as defined by Section 15610.07. This inventory shall be used to refer victims in the event that the county adult protective services agency cannot resolve the immediate needs of the victim, and to serve the victim on a long-term, followup basis. The intent of this section is to acknowledge that limited funds are available to resolve all suspected cases of abuse reported to a county adult protective services agency.

(f) Each local ombudsman program shall maintain an inventory of all public and private agencies available to assist long-term care residents who are victims of abuse, as defined by Section 15610.07. This inventory shall be used to refer cases of abuse in the event that another agency has jurisdiction over the resident, the abuse is verified and further investigation is needed by a law enforcement or licensing agency, or the program does not have sufficient resources to provide immediate assistance. The intent of this section is to acknowledge that ombudsman responsibility in abuse cases is to receive reports, determine the validity of reports, refer verified abuse cases to appropriate agencies for further action as necessary, and follow up to complete the required report information. Other ombudsman services shall be provided to the resident, as appropriate. (Amended by Stats. 2013, Ch. 76, Sec. 224. Effective January 1, 2014.)

15653.

(a) Minimum guidelines for use by county adult protective services agencies in determining when an investigation of abuse is warranted shall be maintained by the State Department of Social Services in cooperation with representatives of county government, and in consultation with the Department of Aging, the Department of Justice, and other concerned state departments for use by county adult protective services agencies.

(b) Uniform guidelines for local law enforcement assistance with investigations of allegations of abuse to elders and dependent adults as developed by the Department of Justice in consultation with the department, the Department of Aging, and other concerned state and local agencies pursuant to Section 15640, as amended by Chapter 769 of the Statutes of 1986, shall remain in effect until modified. Consistent with these guidelines, county adult protective services agencies may seek local law enforcement assistance with investigations of allegations of abuse to elder and dependent adults. (Added by Stats. 1994, Ch. 594, Sec. 22. Effective January 1, 1995.)

15653.5.

Training for determining when to refer for possible criminal prosecution a report of a known or suspected instance of abuse that occurred in a long-term care facility shall be included in the training provided by the Bureau of Medi-Cal Fraud and Elder Abuse pursuant to subdivision (h) of Section 12528 of the Government Code. (Amended (as added by Stats. 1998, Ch. 980) by Stats. 2002, Ch. 54, Sec. 12.3. Effective January 1, 2003.)

15654.

(a) As described in subdivision (h) of Section 12528 of the Government Code, the bureau shall offer training programs to local law enforcement and prosecutorial personnel in investigating and prosecuting crimes against elders and dependent adults, and to the State Department of Health Care Services, the State Department of Social Services, the county adult protective services agencies and to the long-term care ombudsman program in evaluating and documenting criminal abuse against elders and dependent adults.

(b) When producing new or updated training materials pursuant to this section, the bureau shall consult with the Commission on Peace Officer Standards and Training and other subject matter experts. Any new or updated training materials shall address all of the following:

(1) The jurisdiction and responsibility of law enforcement agencies pursuant to Section 368.5 of the Penal Code.

(2) The fact that the protected classes of "dependent person" as defined in Section 288 of the Penal Code and "dependent adult" as defined in Section 368 of the Penal Code include many persons with disabilities, regardless of the fact that most of those persons live independently.

(3) Other relevant information and laws.

(c) When the bureau offers or provides new or updated training materials pursuant to this section, the bureau also may inform

the agencies of other relevant training materials.
(Amended by Stats. 2010, Ch. 617, Sec. 14. Effective January 1, 2011.)

15655.

(a) (1) Each long-term health care facility, as defined in Section 1418 of the Health and Safety Code, community care facility, as defined in Section 1502 of the Health and Safety Code, or residential care facility for the elderly, as defined in Section 1569.2 of the Health and Safety Code, that provides care to adults shall provide training in recognizing and reporting elder and dependent adult abuse, as prescribed by the Department of Justice. The Department of Justice shall, in cooperation with the State Department of Health Services and the State Department of Social Services, develop a minimal core training program for use by these facilities. As part of that training, long-term care facilities, including nursing homes and out-of-home care facilities, shall provide to all staff being trained a written copy of the reporting requirements and a written notification of the staff's confidentiality rights as specified in Section 15633.
(2) Each long-term health care facility as defined in Section 1418 of the Health and Safety Code and each community care facility as defined in Section 1502 of the Health and Safety Code shall comply with paragraph (1) by January 1, 2001, or, if the facility began operation after July 31, 2000, within six months of the date of the beginning of the operation of the facility. Employees hired after June 1, 2001, shall be trained within 60 days of their first day of employment.
(3) Each residential care facility as defined in Section 1569.2 of the Health and Safety Code shall comply with paragraph (1) by July 1, 2002, or, if the facility began operation after July 1, 2002, within six months of the date of the beginning of the operation of the facility. Employees hired on or after July 1, 2002, shall be trained within 60 days of their first day of employment.
(b) Each long-term health care facility, as defined in Section 1418 of the Health and Safety Code, shall be subject to review by the State Department of Health Services Licensing and Certification Unit for compliance with the duties imposed in subdivision (a).
(c) Each community care facility, as defined in Section 1502 of the Health and Safety Code, and residential care facility for the elderly, as defined in Section 1569.2 of the Health and Safety Code, shall be subject to review by the State Department of Social Services Community Care Licensing Unit for compliance with the duties imposed in subdivision (a). (Amended by Stats. 2001, Ch. 196, Sec. 1. Effective January 1, 2002.)

15655.5.

A county adult protective services agency shall provide the organizations listed in paragraphs (v), (w), and (x) of Section 15610.17, and mandated reporters of suspected financial abuse of an elder or dependent adult pursuant to Section 15630.1, with instructional materials regarding abuse and neglect of an elder or dependent adult and their obligation to report under this chapter. At a minimum, the instructional materials shall include the following:
(a) An explanation of abuse and neglect of an elder or dependent adult, as defined in this chapter.
(b) Information on how to recognize potential abuse and neglect of an elder or dependent adult.
(c) Information on how the county adult protective services agency investigates reports of known or suspected abuse and neglect.
(d) Instructions on how to report known or suspected incidents of abuse and neglect, including the appropriate telephone numbers to call and what types of information would assist the county adult protective services agency with its investigation of the report. (Amended (as amended by Stats. 2005, Ch. 140, Sec. 11) by Stats. 2011, Ch. 372, Sec. 8. Effective January 1, 2012.)

15656.

(a) Any person who knows or reasonably should know that a person is an elder or dependent adult and who, under circumstances or conditions likely to produce great bodily harm or death, willfully causes or permits any elder or dependent adult to suffer, or inflicts unjustifiable physical pain or mental suffering upon him or her, or having the care or custody of any elder or dependent adult, willfully causes or permits the person or health of the elder or dependent adult to be injured, or willfully causes or permits the elder or dependent adult to be placed in a situation such that his or her person or health is endangered, is punishable by imprisonment in the county jail not exceeding one year, or in the state prison for two, three, or four years.
(b) Any person who knows or reasonably should know that a person is an elder or dependent adult and who, under circumstances or conditions other than those likely to produce great bodily harm or death, willfully causes or permits any elder or dependent adult to suffer, or inflicts unjustifiable physical pain or mental suffering on him or her, or having the care or custody of any elder or dependent adult, willfully causes or permits the person or health of the elder or dependent adult to be injured or willfully causes or permits the elder or dependent adult to be placed in a situation such that his or her person or health may be endangered, is guilty of a misdemeanor.
(c) Any caretaker of an elder or a dependent adult who violates any provision of law prescribing theft or embezzlement, with respect to the property of that elder or dependent adult, is punishable by imprisonment in the county jail not exceeding one year, or in the state prison for two, three, or four years when the money, labor, or real or personal property taken is of a value exceeding nine hundred fifty dollars ($950), and by a fine not exceeding one thousand dollars ($1,000), or by imprisonment in the county jail not exceeding one year, or by both that imprisonment and fine, when the money, labor, or real or personal property taken is of a value not exceeding nine hundred fifty dollars ($950).
(d) As used in this section, "caretaker" means any person who has the care, custody, or control of or who stands in a position of trust with, an elder or a dependent adult.
(e) Conduct covered in subdivision (b) of Section 15610.57 shall not be subject to this section.

(Amended by Stats. 2009, 3rd Ex. Sess., Ch. 28, Sec. 57. Effective January 25, 2010.)

15657.

Where it is proven by clear and convincing evidence that a defendant is liable for physical abuse as defined in Section 15610.63, or neglect as defined in Section 15610.57, and that the defendant has been guilty of recklessness, oppression, fraud, or malice in the commission of this abuse, the following shall apply, in addition to all other remedies otherwise provided by law:
(a) The court shall award to the plaintiff reasonable attorney's fees and costs. The term "costs" includes, but is not limited to, reasonable fees for the services of a conservator, if any, devoted to the litigation of a claim brought under this article.
(b) The limitations imposed by Section 377.34 of the Code of Civil Procedure on the damages recoverable shall not apply. However, the damages recovered shall not exceed the damages permitted to be recovered pursuant to subdivision (b) of Section 3333.2 of the Civil Code.
(c) The standards set forth in subdivision (b) of Section 3294 of the Civil Code regarding the imposition of punitive damages on an employer based upon the acts of an employee shall be satisfied before any damages or attorney's fees permitted under this section may be imposed against an employer. (Amended by Stats. 2004, Ch. 886, Sec. 3. Effective January 1, 2005.)

15657.01.

Notwithstanding Section 483.010 of the Code of Civil Procedure, an attachment may be issued in any action for damages pursuant to Section 15657.5 for financial abuse of an elder or dependent adult, as defined in Section 15610.30. The other provisions of the Code of Civil Procedure not inconsistent with this article shall govern the issuance of an attachment pursuant to this section. In an application for a writ of attachment, the claimant shall refer to this section. An attachment may be issued pursuant to this section whether or not other forms of relief are demanded.
(Added by Stats. 2007, Ch. 45, Sec. 1. Effective January 1, 2008.)

15657.03.

(a) (1) An elder or dependent adult who has suffered abuse as defined in Section 15610.07 may seek protective orders as provided in this section.
(2) A petition may be brought on behalf of an abused elder or dependent adult by a conservator or a trustee of the elder or dependent adult, an attorney-in-fact of an elder or dependent adult who acts within the authority of the power of attorney, a person appointed as a guardian ad litem for the elder or dependent adult, or other person legally authorized to seek such relief.
(b) For the purposes of this section:
(1) "Conservator" means the legally appointed conservator of the person or estate of the petitioner, or both.
(2) "Petitioner" means the elder or dependent adult to be protected by the protective orders and, if the court grants the petition, the protected person.
(3) "Protective order" means an order that includes any of the following restraining orders, whether issued ex parte, after notice and hearing, or in a judgment:
(A) An order enjoining a party from abusing, intimidating, molesting, attacking, striking, stalking, threatening, sexually assaulting, battering, harassing, telephoning, including, but not limited to, making annoying telephone calls as described in Section 653m of the Penal Code, destroying personal property, contacting, either directly or indirectly, by mail or otherwise, or coming within a specified distance of, or disturbing the peace of, the petitioner, and, in the discretion of the court, on a showing of good cause, of other named family or household members or a conservator, if any, of the petitioner.
(B) An order excluding a party from the petitioner's residence or dwelling, except that this order shall not be issued if legal or equitable title to, or lease of, the residence or dwelling is in the sole name of the party to be excluded, or is in the name of the party to be excluded and any other party besides the petitioner.
(C) An order enjoining a party from specified behavior that the court determines is necessary to effectuate orders described in subparagraph (A) or (B).
(4) "Respondent" means the person against whom the protective orders are sought and, if the petition is granted, the restrained person.
(c) An order may be issued under this section, with or without notice, to restrain any person for the purpose of preventing a recurrence of abuse, if a declaration shows, to the satisfaction of the court, reasonable proof of a past act or acts of abuse of the petitioning elder or dependent adult.
(d) Upon filing a petition for protective orders under this section, the petitioner may obtain a temporary restraining order in accordance with Section 527 of the Code of Civil Procedure, except to the extent this section provides a rule that is inconsistent. The temporary restraining order may include any of the protective orders described in paragraph (3) of subdivision (b). However, the court may issue an ex parte order excluding a party from the petitioner's residence or dwelling only on a showing of all of the following:
(1) Facts sufficient for the court to ascertain that the party who will stay in the dwelling has a right under color of law to possession of the premises.
(2) That the party to be excluded has assaulted or threatens to assault the petitioner, other named family or household member of the petitioner, or a conservator of the petitioner.
(3) That physical or emotional harm would otherwise result to the petitioner, other named family or household member of the petitioner, or a conservator of the petitioner.
(e) A request for the issuance of a temporary restraining order without notice under this section shall be granted or denied on

the same day that the petition is submitted to the court, unless the petition is filed too late in the day to permit effective review, in which case the order shall be granted or denied on the next day of judicial business in sufficient time for the order to be filed that day with the clerk of the court.
(f) Within 21 days, or, if good cause appears to the court, 25 days, from the date that a request for a temporary restraining order is granted or denied, a hearing shall be held on the petition. If no request for temporary orders is made, the hearing shall be held within 21 days, or, if good cause appears to the court, 25 days, from the date that the petition is filed.
(g) The respondent may file a response that explains or denies the alleged abuse.
(h) The court may issue, upon notice and a hearing, any of the orders set forth in paragraph (3) of subdivision (b). The court may issue, after notice and hearing, an order excluding a person from a residence or dwelling if the court finds that physical or emotional harm would otherwise result to the petitioner, other named family or household member of the petitioner, or conservator of the petitioner.
(i) (1) In the discretion of the court, an order issued after notice and a hearing under this section may have a duration of not more than five years, subject to termination or modification by further order of the court either on written stipulation filed with the court or on the motion of a party. These orders may be renewed upon the request of a party, either for five years or permanently, without a showing of any further abuse since the issuance of the original order, subject to termination or modification by further order of the court either on written stipulation filed with the court or on the motion of a party. The request for renewal may be brought at any time within the three months before the expiration of the order.
(2) The failure to state the expiration date on the face of the form creates an order with a duration of three years from the date of issuance.
(3) If an action is filed for the purpose of terminating or modifying a protective order prior to the expiration date specified in the order by a party other than the protected party, the party who is protected by the order shall be given notice, pursuant to subdivision (b) of Section 1005 of the Code of Civil Procedure, of the proceeding by personal service or, if the protected party has satisfied the requirements of Chapter 3.1 (commencing with Section 6205) of Division 7 of Title 1 of the Government Code, by service on the Secretary of State. If the party who is protected by the order cannot be notified prior to the hearing for modification or termination of the protective order, the court shall deny the motion to modify or terminate the order without prejudice or continue the hearing until the party who is protected can be properly noticed and may, upon a showing of good cause, specify another method for service of process that is reasonably designed to afford actual notice to the protected party. The protected party may waive his or her right to notice if he or she is physically present in court and does not challenge the sufficiency of the notice.
(j) In a proceeding under this section, a support person may accompany a party in court and, if the party is not represented by an attorney, may sit with the party at the table that is generally reserved for the party and the party's attorney. The support person is present to provide moral and emotional support for a person who alleges he or she is a victim of abuse. The support person is not present as a legal adviser and may not provide legal advice. The support person may assist the person who alleges he or she is a victim of abuse in feeling more confident that he or she will not be injured or threatened by the other party during the proceedings if the person who alleges he or she is a victim of abuse and the other party are required to be present in close proximity. This subdivision does not preclude the court from exercising its discretion to remove the support person from the courtroom if the court believes the support person is prompting, swaying, or influencing the party assisted by the support person.
(k) Upon the filing of a petition for protective orders under this section, the respondent shall be personally served with a copy of the petition, notice of the hearing or order to show cause, temporary restraining order, if any, and any declarations in support of the petition. Service shall be made at least five days before the hearing. The court may, on motion of the petitioner or on its own motion, shorten the time for service on the respondent.
(l) A notice of hearing under this section shall notify the respondent that if he or she does not attend the hearing, the court may make orders against him or her that could last up to five years.
(m) (1) The court may, upon the filing of a declaration by the petitioner that the respondent could not be served within the time required by statute, reissue an order previously issued and dissolved by the court for failure to serve the respondent. The reissued order shall remain in effect until the date set for the hearing.
(2) The reissued order shall state on its face the date of expiration of the order.
(n) (1) If a respondent, named in an order issued under this section after a hearing, has not been served personally with the order but has received actual notice of the existence and substance of the order through personal appearance in court to hear the terms of the order from the court, no additional proof of service is required for enforcement of the order.
(2) If the respondent named in a temporary restraining order is personally served with the order and notice of hearing with respect to a restraining order or protective order based on the temporary restraining order, but the respondent does not appear at the hearing, either personally or by an attorney, and the terms and conditions of the restraining order or protective order issued at the hearing are identical to the temporary restraining order, except for the duration of the order, then the restraining order or protective order issued at the hearing may be served on the respondent by first-class mail sent to the respondent at the most current address for the respondent that is available to the court.
(3) The Judicial Council form for temporary orders issued pursuant to this subdivision shall contain a statement in substantially the following form:
"If you have been personally served with a temporary restraining order and notice of hearing, but you do not appear at the

hearing either in person or by a lawyer, and a restraining order that is the same as this temporary restraining order except for the expiration date is issued at the hearing, a copy of the order will be served on you by mail at the following address: ____. If that address is not correct or you wish to verify that the temporary restraining order was converted to a restraining order at the hearing without substantive change and to find out the duration of that order, contact the clerk of the court."

(o) (1) Information on any protective order relating to elder or dependent adult abuse issued by a court pursuant to this section shall be transmitted to the Department of Justice in accordance with either paragraph (2) or (3).

(2) The court shall order the petitioner or the attorney for the petitioner to deliver a copy of an order issued under this section, or a reissuance, extension, modification, or termination of the order, and any subsequent proof of service, by the close of the business day on which the order, reissuance, extension, modification, or termination was made, to each law enforcement agency having jurisdiction over the residence of the petitioner, and to any additional law enforcement agencies within the court's discretion as are requested by the petitioner.

(3) Alternatively, the court or its designee shall transmit, within one business day, to law enforcement personnel all information required under subdivision (b) of Section 6380 of the Family Code regarding any order issued under this section, or a reissuance, extension, modification, or termination of the order, and any subsequent proof of service, by either one of the following methods:

(A) Transmitting a physical copy of the order or proof of service to a local law enforcement agency authorized by the Department of Justice to enter orders into the California Law Enforcement Telecommunications System (CLETS).

(B) With the approval of the Department of Justice, entering the order or proof of service into CLETS directly.

(4) Each appropriate law enforcement agency shall make available information as to the existence and current status of these orders to law enforcement officers responding to the scene of reported abuse.

(5) An order issued under this section shall, on request of the petitioner, be served on the respondent, whether or not the respondent has been taken into custody, by any law enforcement officer who is present at the scene of reported abuse involving the parties to the proceeding. The petitioner shall provide the officer with an endorsed copy of the order and a proof of service, which the officer shall complete and send to the issuing court.

(6) Upon receiving information at the scene of an incident of abuse that a protective order has been issued under this section, or that a person who has been taken into custody is the respondent to that order, if the protected person cannot produce an endorsed copy of the order, a law enforcement officer shall immediately attempt to verify the existence of the order.

(7) If the law enforcement officer determines that a protective order has been issued, but not served, the officer shall immediately notify the respondent of the terms of the order and where a written copy of the order can be obtained, and the officer shall at that time also enforce the order. The law enforcement officer's verbal notice of the terms of the order shall constitute service of the order and is sufficient notice for the purposes of this section and for the purposes of Section 273.6 of the Penal Code.

(p) Nothing in this section shall preclude either party from representation by private counsel or from appearing on the party's own behalf.

(q) There is no filing fee for a petition, response, or paper seeking the reissuance, modification, or enforcement of a protective order filed in a proceeding brought pursuant to this section.

(r) Pursuant to paragraph (4) of subdivision (b) of Section 6103.2 of the Government Code, a petitioner shall not be required to pay a fee for law enforcement to serve an order issued under this section.

(s) The prevailing party in any action brought under this section may be awarded court costs and attorney's fees, if any.

(t) (1) A person subject to a protective order under this section shall not own, possess, purchase, receive, or attempt to receive a firearm or ammunition while the protective order is in effect.

(2) The court shall order a person subject to a protective order issued under this section to relinquish any firearms he or she owns or possesses pursuant to Section 527.9 of the Code of Civil Procedure.

(3) Every person who owns, possesses, purchases, or receives, or attempts to purchase or receive a firearm or ammunition while subject to a protective order issued under this section is punishable pursuant to Section 29825 of the Penal Code.

(4) This subdivision shall not apply in a case in which the protective order issued under this section was made solely on the basis of financial abuse unaccompanied by force, threat, harassment, intimidation, or any other form of abuse.

(u) Any willful disobedience of any temporary restraining order or restraining order after hearing granted under this section is punishable pursuant to Section 273.6 of the Penal Code.

(v) This section does not apply to any action or proceeding governed by Title 1.6C (commencing with Section 1788) of Part 4 of Division 3 of the Civil Code, by Chapter 3 (commencing with Section 525) of Title 7 of Part 2 of the Code of Civil Procedure, or by Division 10 (commencing with Section 6200) of the Family Code. Nothing in this section shall preclude a petitioner's right to use other existing civil remedies.

(w) The Judicial Council shall develop forms, instructions, and rules relating to matters governed by this section. The petition and response forms shall be simple and concise, and their use by parties in actions brought pursuant to this section shall be mandatory.(Amended by Stats. 2012, Ch. 162, Sec. 227. Effective January 1, 2013.)

15657.04.

(a) The court shall order that any party enjoined pursuant to Section 15657.03 be prohibited from taking any action to obtain the address or location of any protected person, unless there is good cause not to make that order.

(b) The Judicial Council shall develop forms necessary to effectuate this section. (Amended by Stats. 2010, Ch. 572, Sec. 27.

Effective January 1, 2011. Operative January 1, 2012, by Sec. 28 of Ch. 572.)

15657.05.

Where it is proven by clear and convincing evidence that an individual is liable for abduction, as defined in Section 15610.06, in addition to all other remedies otherwise provided by law:
(a) (1) The court shall award to the plaintiff reasonable attorney's fees and costs. The term "costs" shall include, but is not limited to, costs of representing the abductee and his or her family in this state and any other state in any action related to the abduction and returning of the abductee to this state, as well as travel expenses for returning the abductee to this state and reasonable fees for the services of a conservator, if any, devoted to the litigation of a claim brought under this article.
(2) The award of attorney's fees shall be governed by the principles set forth in Section 15657.1.
(b) The limitations imposed by Section 377.34 of the Code of Civil Procedure on the damages recoverable shall not apply. However, the damages recovered shall not exceed the damages permitted to be recovered pursuant to subdivision (b) of Section 3333.2 of the Civil Code.
(c) The standards set forth in subdivision (b) of Section 3294 of the Civil Code regarding the imposition of punitive damages on an employer based upon the acts of an employee shall be satisfied before any damages or attorney's fees permitted under this section may be imposed against an employer. (Added by Stats. 1997, Ch. 663, Sec. 4. Effective January 1, 1998.)

15657.1.

The award of attorney's fees pursuant to subdivision (a) of Section 15657 shall be based on all factors relevant to the value of the services rendered, including, but not limited to, the factors set forth in Rule 4-200 of the Rules of Professional Conduct of the State Bar of California, and all of the following:
(a) The value of the abuse-related litigation in terms of the quality of life of the elder or dependent adult, and the results obtained.
(b) Whether the defendant took reasonable and timely steps to determine the likelihood and extent of liability.
(c) The reasonableness and timeliness of any written offer in compromise made by a party to the action. (Amended by Stats. 1994, Ch. 594, Sec. 23.5. Effective January 1, 1995.)

15657.2.

Notwithstanding this article, any cause of action for injury or damage against a health care provider, as defined in Section 340.5 of the Code of Civil Procedure, based on the health care provider's alleged professional negligence, shall be governed by those laws which specifically apply to those professional negligence causes of action. (Added by Stats. 1991, Ch. 774, Sec. 3.)

15657.3.

(a) The department of the superior court having jurisdiction over probate conservatorships shall also have concurrent jurisdiction over civil actions and proceedings involving a claim for relief arising out of the abduction, as defined in Section 15610.06, or the abuse of an elderly or dependent adult, if a conservator has been appointed for the plaintiff prior to the initiation of the action for abuse.
(b) The department of the superior court having jurisdiction over probate conservatorships shall not grant relief under this article if the court determines that the matter should be determined in a civil action, but shall instead transfer the matter to the general civil calendar of the superior court. The court need not abate a proceeding for relief pursuant to this article if the court determines that the civil action was filed for the purpose of delay.
(c) The death of the elder or dependent adult does not cause the court to lose jurisdiction of a claim for relief for abuse of that elder or dependent adult.
(d) (1) Subject to paragraph (2) and subdivision (e), after the death of the elder or dependent adult, the right to commence or maintain an action shall pass to the personal representative of the decedent. If there is no personal representative, the right to commence or maintain an action shall pass to any of the following, if the requirements of Section 377.32 of the Code of Civil Procedure are met:
(A) An intestate heir whose interest is affected by the action.
(B) The decedent's successor in interest, as defined in Section 377.11 of the Code of Civil Procedure.
(C) An interested person, as defined in Section 48 of the Probate Code, as limited in this subparagraph. As used in this subparagraph, "an interested person" does not include a creditor or a person who has a claim against the estate and who is not an heir or beneficiary of the decedent's estate.
(2) If the personal representative refuses to commence or maintain an action or if the personal representative's family or an affiliate, as those terms are defined in subdivision (c) of Section 1064 of the Probate Code, is alleged to have committed abuse of the elder or dependent adult, the persons described in subparagraphs (A), (B), and (C) of paragraph (1) shall have standing to commence or maintain an action for elder abuse. This paragraph does not require the court to resolve the merits of an elder abuse action for purposes of finding that a plaintiff who meets the qualifications of subparagraphs (A), (B), and (C) of paragraph (1) has standing to commence or maintain such an action.
(e) If two or more persons who are either described in subparagraph (A), (B), or (C) of paragraph (1) of subdivision (d) or a personal representative claim to have standing to commence or maintain an action for elder abuse, upon petition or motion, the court in which the action or proceeding is pending, may make any order concerning the parties that is appropriate to ensure the proper administration of justice in the case pursuant to Section 377.33 of the Code of Civil Procedure.
(f) This section does not affect the applicable statute of limitations for commencing an action for relief for abuse of an elderly

or dependent adult. (Amended by Stats. 2008, Ch. 179, Sec. 249. Effective January 1, 2009.)

15657.5.

(a) Where it is proven by a preponderance of the evidence that a defendant is liable for financial abuse, as defined in Section 15610.30, in addition to compensatory damages and all other remedies otherwise provided by law, the court shall award to the plaintiff reasonable attorney's fees and costs. The term "costs" includes, but is not limited to, reasonable fees for the services of a conservator, if any, devoted to the litigation of a claim brought under this article.

(b) Where it is proven by a preponderance of the evidence that a defendant is liable for financial abuse, as defined in Section 15610.30, and where it is proven by clear and convincing evidence that the defendant has been guilty of recklessness, oppression, fraud, or malice in the commission of the abuse, in addition to reasonable attorney's fees and costs set forth in subdivision (a), compensatory damages, and all other remedies otherwise provided by law, the limitations imposed by Section 377.34 of the Code of Civil Procedure on the damages recoverable shall not apply.

(c) The standards set forth in subdivision (b) of Section 3294 of the Civil Code regarding the imposition of punitive damages on an employer based upon the acts of an employee shall be satisfied before any punitive damages may be imposed against an employer found liable for financial abuse as defined in Section 15610.30. This subdivision shall not apply to the recovery of compensatory damages or attorney's fees and costs.

(d) Nothing in this section affects the award of punitive damages under Section 3294 of the Civil Code.

(e) Any money judgment in an action under this section shall include a statement that the damages are awarded based on a claim for financial abuse of an elder or dependent adult, as defined in Section 15610.30. If only part of the judgment is based on that claim, the judgment shall specify what amount was awarded on that basis. (Amended (as amended by Stats. 2010, Ch. 64, Sec. 5) by Stats. 2011, Ch. 296, Sec. 336. Effective January 1, 2012.)

15657.6.

A person or entity that takes, secretes, appropriates, obtains, or retains, or assists in taking, secreting, appropriating, obtaining, or retaining the real or personal property of an elder or dependent adult when the elder or dependent adult lacks capacity pursuant to Section 812 of the Probate Code, or is of unsound mind, but not entirely without understanding, pursuant to Section 39 of the Civil Code, shall, upon demand by the elder or dependent adult or a representative of the elder or dependent adult, as defined in subdivision (d) of Section 15610.30, return the property and if that person or entity fails to return the property, the elder or dependent adult shall be entitled to the remedies provided by Section 15657.5, including attorney's fees and costs. This section shall not apply to any agreement entered into by an elder or dependent adult when the elder or dependent adult had capacity. (Added by Stats. 2008, Ch. 475, Sec. 3. Effective January 1, 2009.)

15657.7.

An action for damages pursuant to Sections 15657.5 and 15657.6 for financial abuse of an elder or dependent adult, as defined in Section 15610.30, shall be commenced within four years after the plaintiff discovers or, through the exercise of reasonable diligence, should have discovered, the facts constituting the financial abuse. (Added by Stats. 2008, Ch. 475, Sec. 4. Effective January 1, 2009.)

15657.8.

(a) An agreement to settle a civil action for physical abuse, as defined in Section 15610.63, neglect, as defined in Section 15610.57, or financial abuse, as defined in Section 15610.30, of an elder or dependent adult shall not include any of the following provisions, whether the agreement is made before or after filing the action:

(1) A provision that prohibits any party to the dispute from contacting or cooperating with the county adult protective services agency, the local law enforcement agency, the long-term care ombudsman, the California Department of Aging, the Department of Justice, the Licensing and Certification Division of the State Department of Public Health, the State Department of Developmental Services, the State Department of State Hospitals, a licensing or regulatory agency that has jurisdiction over the license or certification of the defendant, any other governmental entity, a protection and advocacy agency, as defined in Section 4900, or the defendant's current employer if the defendant's job responsibilities include contact with elders, dependent adults, or children, provided that the party contacting or cooperating with one of these entities had a good faith belief that the information he or she provided is relevant to the concerns, duties, or obligations of that entity.

(2) A provision that prohibits any party to the dispute from filing a complaint with, or reporting any violation of law to, the county adult protective services agency, the local law enforcement agency, the long-term care ombudsman, the California Department of Aging, the Department of Justice, the Licensing and Certification Division of the State Department of Public Health, the State Department of Developmental Services, the State Department of State Hospitals, a licensing or regulatory agency that has jurisdiction over the license or certification of the defendant, any other governmental entity, a protection and advocacy agency, as defined in Section 4900, or the defendant's current employer if the defendant's job responsibilities include contact with elders, dependent adults, or children.

(3) A provision that requires any party to the dispute to withdraw a complaint he or she has filed with, or a violation he or she has reported to, the county adult protective services agency, the local law enforcement agency, the long-term care ombudsman, the California Department of Aging, the Department of Justice, the Licensing and Certification Division of the State Department of Public Health, the State Department of Developmental Services, the State Department of State Hospitals, a licensing or regulatory agency that has jurisdiction over the license or certification of the defendant, any other governmental entity, a protection and advocacy agency, as defined in Section 4900, or the defendant's current employer if the defendant's job responsibilities include contact with elders, dependent adults, or children.

(b) A provision described in subdivision (a) is void as against public policy.
(c) This section shall apply only to an agreement entered on or after January 1, 2013. (Amended by Stats. 2014, Ch. 442, Sec. 40. Effective September 18, 2014.

15658.

(a) A written abuse report required by this chapter, shall be submitted in one of the following ways:
(1) On a form adopted by the State Department of Social Services after consultation with representatives of the various law enforcement agencies, the California Department of Aging, the State Department of Developmental Services, the State Department of State Hospitals, the bureau, professional medical and nursing agencies, hospital associations, and county welfare departments. These reporting forms shall be distributed by the county adult protective services agencies and the long-term care ombudsman programs. This reporting form may also be used for documenting the telephone report of a known or suspected instance of abuse of an elder or dependent adult by the county adult protective services agency, local ombudsman program, and local law enforcement agencies.
(2) Through a confidential Internet reporting tool, if the county or long-term care ombudsman program chooses to implement such a system. This Internet reporting tool shall be developed and implemented in a manner that ensures the confidentiality and security of all information contained in the reports, pursuant to the confidentiality standards set forth in Sections 10850, 15633, and 15633.5.
(A) A county or long-term care ombudsman program that chooses to implement this system shall report to the Assembly Committee on Aging and Long-Term Care, the Assembly Committee on Human Services, the Senate Committee on Human Services, the Assembly Committee on Public Safety, and the Senate Committee on Public Safety one year after full implementation. The report shall include changes in the number of mandated reporters reporting through the confidential Internet reporting tool, changes in the number of abandoned calls, and any other quantitative or qualitative data that indicates the success, or lack thereof, in employing a confidential Internet reporting tool to better protect the safety and financial security of elder and dependent adults.
(B) Information sent and received through the confidential Internet reporting tool shall be used only for its intended purpose and shall be subject to the same confidentiality and privacy requirements that govern nonelectronic transmission of the same information, and that are set forth in Sections 10850, 15633, and 15633.5.
(b) The form required by this section and the confidential Internet reporting tool, if implemented, shall contain the following items:
(1) The name, address, telephone number, and occupation of the person reporting.
(2) The name and address of the victim.
(3) The date, time, and place of the incident.
(4) Other details, including the reporter's observations and beliefs concerning the incident.
(5) Any statement relating to the incident made by the victim.
(6) The name of any individuals believed to have knowledge of the incident.
(7) The name of the individuals believed to be responsible for the incident and their connection to the victim.
(c) (1) Each county adult protective services agency shall report to the State Department of Social Services monthly on the reports received pursuant to this chapter. The reports shall be made on forms adopted by the department. The information reported shall include, but shall not be limited to, the number of incidents of abuse, the number of persons abused, the type of abuse sustained, and the actions taken on the reports. For purposes of these reports, sexual abuse shall be reported separately from physical abuse.
(2) The county's report to the department shall not include reports it receives from the long-term care ombudsman program pursuant to subdivision (d).
(3) The department shall refer to the bureau monthly data summaries of the reports of elder and dependent adult abuse, neglect, abandonment, isolation, financial abuse, and other abuse it receives from county adult protective services agencies.
(d) Each long-term care ombudsman program shall report to the Office of the State Long-Term Care Ombudsman of the California Department of Aging monthly on the reports it receives pursuant to this chapter and shall send a copy to the county adult protective services agency. The Office of the State Long-Term Care Ombudsman shall submit a summarized quarterly report to the department based on the monthly reports submitted by local long-term care ombudsman programs. The reports shall be on forms adopted by the department and the Office of the State Long-Term Care Ombudsman. The information reported shall include, but shall not be limited to, the number of incidents of abuse, the numbers of persons abused, the type of abuse, and the actions taken on the reports. For purposes of these reports, sexual abuse shall be reported separately from physical abuse. (Amended by Stats. 2012, Ch. 440, Sec. 81. Effective September 22, 2012.)

15659.

(a) Any person who enters into employment on or after January 1, 1995, as a care custodian, clergy member, health practitioner, or with an adult protective services agency or a local law enforcement agency, prior to commencing his or her employment and as a prerequisite to that employment, shall sign a statement on a form that shall be provided by the prospective employer, to the effect that he or she has knowledge of Section 15630 and will comply with its provisions. The employer shall provide a copy of Section 15630 to the employee. The statement shall inform the employee that he or she is a mandated reporter and inform the employee of his or her reporting obligations under Section 15630. The signed statement shall be retained by the employer.

(b) Agencies or facilities that employ persons who were employed prior to January 1, 1995, and who are required to make reports pursuant to Section 15630, shall inform those persons of their responsibility to make reports by delivering to them a copy of the statement specified in subdivision (a).
(c) The cost of printing, distribution, and filing of these statements shall be borne by the employer.
(d) On and after January 1, 1995, when a person is issued a state license or certificate to engage in a profession or occupation the members of which are required to make a report pursuant to Section 15630, the state agency issuing the license or certificate shall send to the person a statement substantially similar to the one contained in subdivision (a) at the same time that it transmits to the person the document indicating licensure or certification.
(e) As an alternative to the procedure required by subdivision (d), a state agency may cause the required statement to be printed on all application forms for a license or certificate printed on or after January 1, 1995.
(f) The retention of statements required by subdivision (a), and the delivery of statements required by subdivision (b), shall be the full extent of the employer's duty pursuant to this section. The failure of any employee or other person associated with the employer to report abuse of elders or dependent adults pursuant to Section 15630 or otherwise meet the requirements of this chapter shall be the sole responsibility of that person. The employer or facility shall incur no civil or other liability for the failure of these persons to comply with the requirements of this chapter.(Amended by Stats. 2002, Ch. 54, Sec. 12.7. Effective January 1, 2003.)

15660.

(a) The Department of Justice shall secure any criminal record of a person to determine whether the person has ever been convicted of a violation or attempted violation of Section 243.4 of the Penal Code, a sex offense against a minor, or of any felony that requires registration pursuant to Section 290 of the Penal Code, or whether the person has been convicted or incarcerated within the last 10 years as the result of committing a violation or attempted violation of Section 273a or 273d, or subdivision (a) or (b) of Section 368, of the Penal Code, or as the result of committing a theft, robbery, burglary, or any felony, and shall provide a subsequent arrest notification pursuant to Section 11105.2 of the Penal Code, if both of the following conditions are met:
(1) An employer of the person requests the determination and submits fingerprints of the person to the Department of Justice. For purposes of this paragraph, "employer" includes, but is not limited to, an in-home supportive services recipient, as defined by Section 12302.2, an aged or disabled adult who is ineligible for benefits under Chapter 3 (commencing with Section 12000), who receives care by a person as described in paragraph (2), any recipient of personal care services under the Medi-Cal program pursuant to Sections 14132.95 to 14132.97, inclusive, and any public authority or nonprofit consortium, as described in subdivision (a) of Section 12301.6.
(2) The person is unlicensed and provides nonmedical domestic or personal care to an aged or disabled adult in the adult's own home.
(b) (1) If it is found that the person has ever been convicted of a violation or attempted violation of Section 243.4 of the Penal Code, a sex offense against a minor, or of any felony which requires registration pursuant to Section 290 of the Penal Code, or that the person has been convicted or incarcerated within the last 10 years as the result of committing a violation or attempted violation of Section 273a or 273d, or subdivision (a) or (b) of Section 368, of the Penal Code, or as the result of committing a theft, robbery, burglary, or any felony, the Department of Justice shall notify the employer of that fact. If no criminal record information has been recorded, the Department of Justice shall provide the employer with a statement of that fact.
(2) Any employer may deny employment to any person who is the subject of a report under paragraph (1) when the report indicates that the person has committed any of the crimes identified in paragraph (1).
(3) Nothing in this section shall be construed to require any employer to hire any person who is the subject of a report under paragraph (1) when the report indicates that the person has not committed any of the crimes indicated in paragraph (1).
(c) (1) Fingerprints shall be on a card provided by the Department of Justice for the purpose of obtaining a set of fingerprints. The employer shall submit the fingerprints to the Department of Justice. Within 30 calendar days of the receipt of the fingerprints, the Department of Justice shall notify the employer of the criminal record information, as provided in this subdivision. If no criminal record information has been recorded, the Department of Justice shall provide the employer with a statement of that fact as soon as possible, but not later than 30 calendar days from the date of receipt of the fingerprints. If new fingerprints are required for processing, the Department of Justice shall, as soon as possible, but not later than 30 calendar days from the date of receipt of the fingerprints, notify the employer that the fingerprints were illegible.
(2) Fingerprints may be taken by any local law enforcement officer or agency for purposes of paragraph (1).
(3) Counties shall notify any recipient of, or applicant for, in-home supportive services or personal care services under the Medi-Cal program, upon his or her application for in-home supportive services or personal care services or during his or her annual redetermination, or upon the recipient's changing providers, that a criminal record check is available, and that the check can be performed by the Department of Justice.
(d) (1) The Department of Justice shall charge a fee to the employer to cover the costs of administering this section.
(2) (A) If the employer is an in-home supportive services recipient, as defined in Section 123202.2, a recipient of personal care services under the Medi-Cal program pursuant to Sections 14132.95 to 14132.97, inclusive, or any public authority or nonprofit consortium as described in subdivision (a) of Section 12301.6, the fee shall be shared by the county and the state in the same ratio as described in Section 12306.
(B) (i) Notwithstanding any other provision of law, and except as provided in clause (ii), the department shall, no later than

January 1, 2009, implement subparagraph (A) through an all-county letter from the director.
(ii) No later than July 1, 2009, the department shall adopt regulations to implement the provisions listed in subparagraph (A).
(e) It is the intent of the Legislature that the Department of Justice charge a fee to cover its cost in providing services in accordance with this section to comply with the 30-calendar-day requirement for provision to the department of the criminal record information, as contained in subdivision (c). (Amended by Stats. 2009, Ch. 140, Sec. 217. Effective January 1, 2010.)

15670.

The Legislature finds and declares all of the following:
(a) Instances of elder and dependent adult abuse are on the rise, with the majority of the abuse occurring in the home of elderly or dependent person by noncertified caregivers.
(b) This state has a responsibility to protect these persons and to see that they are safeguarded from individuals who may pose a threat to their well-being.
(c) Criminal background checks of individuals who provide personal care services to elder and dependent adults, while not ending all occurrences of abuse, will serve as a factor in reducing some of these occurrences and giving senior citizens, dependent adults, and their families a sense of security that care is not being administered by individuals with dangerous criminal backgrounds.
(d) An effective background check program will be timely, affordable, and encompass caregivers in domestic and institutional settings.
(e) Individuals providing personal care services to elder and dependent adults should be well trained and appropriately compensated for their services to foster the creation of a long-term, professional work force.
(f) Therefore, it is the intent of the Legislature in enacting this article that certified nurse assistants and certified home health aides shall be subject to a criminal background check.
(g) It is the intent of the Legislature that the State Department of Social Services prepare a plan by January 1, 1996, to implement a program of criminal background checks for in-home care providers employed under the In-Home Supportive Services program (Article 7 (commencing with Section 12300) of Chapter 3 of Part 3). The plan shall be made available to the Legislature upon request. (Added by Stats. 1994, Ch. 1246, Sec. 16. Effective January 1, 1995.)

15671.

(a) All initial certified nurse assistant and certified home health aide applicants, shall as a requirement for certification, undergo a criminal background check pursuant to Section 1338.5 of the Health and Safety Code.
(b) Nurse assistants certified prior to July 1, 1998, shall, as a condition of renewal of their certificates, undergo a criminal background check pursuant to subdivision (a) of Section 1337.6 and Section 1338.5 of the Health and Safety Code. Commencing July 1, 1998, pursuant to Section 1338.5 of the Health and Safety Code, nurse assistant applicants whose applications were submitted on or after July 1, 1998, shall undergo a criminal background check. (Amended by Stats. 1997, Ch. 558, Sec. 8. Effective January 1, 1998.)

15673.

Home health aides certified prior to July 1, 1998, shall, as a condition of renewal of their certificates, undergo a criminal background check pursuant to Section 1736.6 of the Health and Safety Code. Commencing July 1, 1998, pursuant to Section 1736.6 of the Health and Safety Code, home health aide applicants whose applications are submitted on or after July 1, 1998, shall undergo a criminal background check. (Amended by Stats. 1997, Ch. 558, Sec. 9. Effective January 1, 1998.)

15675.

(a) Unless otherwise prohibited by law, the Department of Justice shall make available to the State Department of Health Services, at no cost, access to the California Law Enforcement Telecommunications System as established pursuant to Chapter 2.5 (commencing with Section 15150) of Part 6 of Division 3 of Title 2 of the Government Code.
(b) (1) As an alternative to the requirement of subdivision (a), the Department of Justice and the State Department of Health Services may negotiate and enter into a contract that specifies the method and terms upon which the cost of the Department of Justice to access the California Law Enforcement Telecommunications System for purposes of the State Department of Health Services are allocated between the respective departments.
(2) During the operation of this contract, subdivision (a) shall not apply. However, subdivision (a) shall apply upon the termination, for any reason, of the contract and the contract shall not contain provisions to the contrary.
(3) The contract shall not contain provisions inconsistent with any law that prescribes the extent to which an applicant for licensure, a permit, or certification, or employees, or volunteers shall or shall not pay for a criminal record background check. (Amended by Stats. 1997, Ch. 558, Sec. 10. Effective January 1, 1998.)

15700.

(a) The Legislature finds and declares all of the following:
(1) Elder and dependent adults may be subjected to abuse, neglect, or abandonment, and that this state has a responsibility to protect those persons.
(2) Most elder and dependent adults who are at greatest risk of abuse, neglect, or abandonment by their families or caretakers, suffer physical impairments and other poor health that place them in a dependent and vulnerable position.
(3) A significant number of these persons have developmental disabilities and that mental and verbal limitations often leave them vulnerable to abuse and incapable of asking for help and protection.
(4) In cases of severe elder and dependent adult abuse or neglect, endangered adults are often placed in situations that pose an

immediate risk of serious injury or death.
(5) In cases of severe elder and dependent adult abuse or neglect, endangered adults are frequently deprived of their personal autonomy and dignity by their abusers, thus preventing them from acting on their own needs or desires to free themselves from serious, and even life-threatening, abuse or neglect.
(6) Due to limited resources, court delays, and limitations of existing law, authorities are often unable to intervene in time to prevent victims of abuse and neglect from being seriously injured or killed.
(7) These limitations have left endangered adults, or elder and dependent adults subject to avoidable pain, suffering, and death, and has resulted in the expenditure of public funds of the treatment of major injuries and health conditions that could have been avoided with proper and timely intervention.
(b) It is the intent of the Legislature, in enacting this chapter, to enhance the protection of elderly persons and dependent adults by providing a mechanism for temporary emergency protective custody of elderly or dependent adults who are suspected victims of abuse or neglect, and who are found to be in a situation that poses an immediate risk of serious injury or death, and when no other means are available to mitigate the risk to the elderly or dependent adult. (Added by Stats. 1996, Ch. 913, Sec. 1. Effective January 1, 1997.)

15701.

The definitions contained in this article and Chapter 11 (commencing with Section 15600) shall govern the construction of this chapter. (Amended by Stats. 2002, Ch. 54, Sec. 13. Effective January 1, 2003.)

15701.05.

"Appropriate temporary residence" means any of the following:
(a) A home or dwelling belonging to a member of the endangered adult's family or next of kin, if it would not constitute a risk to the endangered or dependent adult.
(b) An adult residential care facility or residential care facility for the elderly designated by the county as an emergency shelter and that is licensed by the State of California to deal with the needs of elder or dependent adults.
(c) A 24-hour health facility, as designated by Sections 1250, 1250.2, and 1250.3 of the Health and Safety Code.
(d) This chapter shall not be used to circumvent or supplant the involuntary detention and evaluation process provided for pursuant to Chapter 2 (commencing with Section 5150) of Part 1 of Division 5. A person shall not be deemed an "endangered adult" for the sole reason that he or she voluntarily relies on treatment by spiritual means through prayer alone, in lieu of medical treatment.
(e) This chapter shall not be used to effectuate placement in jails or correctional treatment centers, as defined in paragraph (1) of subdivision (j) of Section 1250 of the Health and Safety Code. (Added by Stats. 1996, Ch. 913, Sec. 1. Effective January 1, 1997.)

15701.25.

"Endangered adult" means a dependent or elder adult who is at immediate risk of serious injury or death, due to suspected abuse or neglect and who demonstrates the inability to take action to protect himself or herself from the consequences of remaining in that situation or condition.
(Added by Stats. 1996, Ch. 913, Sec. 1. Effective January 1, 1997.)

15701.4.

"Appropriate temporary protective services" means those services provided to ensure that the endangered adult is protected from the immediate risk of serious injury or death due to suspected abuse or neglect, and that the effects of the abuse or neglect are remedied in accordance with the endangered adult's needs. These services may include, but not be limited to, any of the following:
(a) Social services case work and case management, including, but not limited to, evaluations of the endangered adult's functional capacity and community resources.
(b) The development of an appropriate individualized service plan.
(c) Appropriate referral and emergency response services.
(d) Counseling.
(e) Temporary shelter.
(f) Emergency services.
(g) Respite services.
(h) Alternative housing and housing assistance.
(i) In-home supportive services.
(j) Adaptive equipment.
(k) Transportation.
(l) Psychology services.
(m) Other health related services and referrals to legal services and advocate agencies. (Added by Stats. 1996, Ch. 913, Sec. 1. Effective January 1, 1997.)

15703.

(a) When, from personal observation, an authorized state or local law enforcement officer or designated employee of a county department of social services or mental health determines that an adult is an endangered adult, and no other option is available to mitigate the circumstances of that adult, the person may take the endangered adult into temporary emergency

protective custody, and initiate adult protective proceedings.
(b) When an authorized person takes an endangered adult into temporary emergency protective custody and initiates adult protective proceedings, the person shall cause the endangered adult to be transported to a hospital as soon as possible if medical evaluation and any necessary treatment is required.
(c) Upon taking an endangered adult into custody pursuant to this chapter, the law enforcement agency taking the endangered adult into custody shall notify:
(1) The superior court.
(2) The endangered person's next of kin, when appropriate.
(3) Adult protective services.
(d) This article shall not apply to state-licensed facilities.
(Added by Stats. 1996, Ch. 913, Sec. 1. Effective January 1, 1997.)
15703.05.
Whether or not medical treatment is required, a physician treating an adult may, if he or she determines that the person is an endangered adult, delay the release of the endangered adult until a local law enforcement agency takes custody of the endangered adult, it is determined by the responding agency the adult is not endangered, or the responding agency takes other appropriate action to ensure the safety of the endangered adult. (Added by Stats. 1996, Ch. 913, Sec. 1. Effective January 1, 1997.)
15703.1.
(a) Temporary emergency protective custody under this chapter shall not exceed a period commencing at the time the endangered adult has been taken into protective custody to the first court day commencing not more than 72 hours thereafter.
(b) Upon being taken into temporary emergency custody, the endangered adult shall be transferred to an appropriate temporary residence, pending the outcome of investigation and judicial hearing required by this chapter. (Added by Stats. 1996, Ch. 913, Sec. 1. Effective January 1, 1997.)
15705.
(a) A designated county agency shall initiate an investigation and file a petition for issuance of an emergency protective services order within 24 hours after the endangered adult has been taken into temporary emergency protective custody.
(b) (1) The court shall hold a preliminary hearing no later than the first court day commencing after a period of 48 hours after the endangered adult has been taken into temporary emergency custody to establish probable cause for grounds for protective custody.
(2) The court shall render its decision on the petition no later than the first court day following a period of 72 hours after the endangered adult has been taken into protective custody.
(Added by Stats. 1996, Ch. 913, Sec. 1. Effective January 1, 1997.)
15705.05.
If, as a result of the preliminary hearing, the court determines that probable cause does not exist to continue temporary emergency protective custody, the adult shall be released from temporary protective custody. (Added by Stats. 1996, Ch. 913, Sec. 1. Effective January 1, 1997.)
15705.1.
If, as a result of the preliminary hearing, the court determines that probable cause continues to exist for temporary emergency protective custody, the court may issue an order authorizing the provision of protective services on an emergency basis to an adult after finding on the record, based on clear and convincing evidence, that all of the following apply:
(a) The adult is an endangered adult.
(b) No other appropriate means are available to mitigate the situation that placed the endangered adult at risk of serious bodily harm or death. (Added by Stats. 1996, Ch. 913, Sec. 1. Effective January 1, 1997.)
15705.15.
In issuing an emergency order under this article, the court shall adhere to all of the following limitations:
(a) Only those protective services that are necessary to remove the conditions creating the emergency shall be ordered, and the court shall specifically designate the approved services in the emergency order.
(b) Protective services authorized by an emergency order shall not include hospitalization or a change of residence unless the court specifically finds that action is necessary and gives specific approval for that action in its order.
(c) Protective services may be provided through an emergency order for no more than 14 days, exclusive of Saturdays, Sundays, and legal holidays pending a hearing for long-term custody.
(d) (1) In its emergency order under this article, the court shall appoint the petitioner, next of kin, or other interested person, as appropriate, as a temporary conservator of the endangered adult.
(2) The court's appointee shall be responsible for the care of the endangered adult.
(3) The court's appointee may, until the expiration of the court's order, give consent for the provision of protective services for the endangered adult, in accordance with the emergency order.
(e) The issuance of an emergency order and the appointment of a temporary conservator of the endangered adult shall not deprive that endangered adult of any rights except to the extent provided in the order of appointment. (Added by Stats. 1996, Ch. 913, Sec. 1. Effective January 1, 1997.)
15705.2.

A petition for an emergency order under this article shall set forth all of the following information:
(a) The name, address, and interest of the petitioner.
(b) The name, age, and address of the person in need of protective service.
(c) The proposed protective services.
(d) The petitioner's reasonable belief, together with facts supportive thereof, of the existence of those circumstances that warrant the issuance of an emergency order.
(e) A statement of the petitioner's attempts to obtain the consent of the person for whom the protective services are proposed, and the outcome of those attempts. (Added by Stats. 1996, Ch. 913, Sec. 1. Effective January 1, 1997.)

15705.25.

(a) Notice of the filing of a petition for an emergency order shall be given, in language as understandable by the endangered adult as reasonably possible, at least 24 hours prior to the hearing on the petition for emergency intervention.
(b) The court may waive the 24-hour notice requirement on a showing that immediate and reasonably foreseeable physical harm to the person or other persons will result from the 24-hour delay, and reasonable attempts have been made to give notice. Notice of the final order of the court shall be given to each of the parties to the petition hearing. (Added by Stats. 1996, Ch. 913, Sec. 1. Effective January 1, 1997.)

15705.30.

The hearing on a petition for an emergency order under this article shall be held under all of the following conditions:
(a) The person with respect to whom an emergency order is sought shall be present unless that person knowingly and voluntarily waives the right to be present or due to the person's physical or psychological condition, he or she is unable to be present. Waiver or inability to be present shall not be presumed from that nonappearance of the endangered adult, but shall be determined on the basis of factual information supplied to the court by counsel or a representative appointed by the court.
(b) The endangered adult has the right to counsel, regardless of whether he or she is present at the hearing. If the person is indigent or lacks the capacity to waive counsel, the court shall appoint counsel. The attorney shall advise the endangered adult of his or her rights in relation to the proceeding and shall represent him or her before the court.
(c) The endangered adult or his or her representative may present evidence and cross-examine witnesses.
(d) The hearing shall be held no earlier than 24 hours after the notice of the hearing has been given, unless the notice has been waived by the court.
(e) The court shall issue, for the record, a statement of its findings in support of any order for emergency protective services. (Added by Stats. 1996, Ch. 913, Sec. 1. Effective January 1, 1997.)

15705.35.

Before any law enforcement agency may implement this article, including the taking of any person into protective custody pursuant to Section 15703, the law enforcement agency shall enter into a signed agreement with the county adult protective services agency that specifies the protocol that the county and the law enforcement agency shall follow in implementing this article. (Added by Stats. 1996, Ch. 913, Sec. 1. Effective January 1, 1997.)

15705.37.

This chapter shall be operative in a county only if the county board of supervisors has adopted a resolution to make this chapter operative in that county. (Added by Stats. 1996, Ch. 913, Sec. 1. Effective January 1, 1997.)

15705.40.

This article shall not be used to circumvent the involuntary commitment process provided for pursuant to Chapter 2 (commencing with Section 5150) of Part 1 of Division 5.
(Added by Stats. 1996, Ch. 913, Sec. 1. Effective January 1, 1997.)

15750.

The definitions contained in Chapter 11 (commencing with Section 15600) shall govern the construction of this chapter. (Added by Stats. 2002, Ch. 54, Sec. 19. Effective January 1, 2003.)

15751.

Each county welfare department shall establish and support a system of protective services to elderly and dependent adults who may be subjected to neglect, abuse, or exploitation, or who are unable to protect their own interest.
This system shall be known as the county adult protective services system. (Added by renumbering Section 15750 by Stats. 2002, Ch. 54, Sec. 18. Effective January 1, 2003.)

15752.

Each county shall establish and maintain a specialized entity within the county welfare department which shall have lead responsibility for the operation of the adult protective services program. (Added by renumbering Section 15751 by Stats. 2002, Ch. 54, Sec. 20. Effective January 1, 2003.)

15753.

The department shall, to the extent funding for this purpose remains with the department, establish one full-time position that reports to the director to assist counties with the following functions in their operation of the adult protective services system:
(a) Facilitating the review and update of state policies and procedures to promote best casework practices throughout the state, and providing technical assistance to local programs to promote consistent statewide adherence to these policies.
(b) Developing recommended program goals, performance measures, and outcomes for the adult protective services system,

and a strategic plan to accomplish these recommended goals, performance measures, and outcomes.
(c) Collaborating with other state departments and local communities that provide or oversee elder justice services to address the needs of elders and adults with disabilities and improve coordination and effectiveness of adult protective services.
(d) Exploring the development of a state data collection system that builds on existing statewide data and additionally tracks outcomes that will align with national data collection efforts.
(e) Participating in national, statewide, and regional discussions on adult protective services and elder justice issues and providing information on California's adult protective services programs.
(f) Participating in the development of federal and state policy that responds to new and emergent needs and develops suggested quality assurance measures to be implemented at the local level.
(g) Facilitating the development of a regionally based, ongoing, comprehensive and consistent statewide adult protective services training program that responds to new and emerging trends.
(h) In collaboration with experts in the field, developing guidelines for local adult protective services programs that will make recommendations for local practice in following areas:
(1) Caseload levels for adult protective services workers.
(2) Availability of tangible services for local programs.
(3) Educational and professional development of adult protective services workers.
(4) Structure for 24 hour adult protective services response.
(Added by Stats. 2015, Ch. 20, Sec. 29. Effective June 24, 2015.)
15754.
(a) Notwithstanding any provision of law governing the disclosure of information and records, persons who are trained and qualified to serve on multidisciplinary personnel teams may disclose to one another information and records which are relevant to the prevention, identification, or treatment of abuse of elderly or dependent persons.
(b) Except as provided in subdivision (a), any personnel of the multidisciplinary team that receives information pursuant to this chapter, shall be under the same obligations and subject to the same confidentiality penalties as the person disclosing or providing that information. The information obtained shall be maintained in a manner that ensures the maximum protection of privacy and confidentiality rights.
(Added by Stats. 1987, Ch. 1166, Sec. 7. Effective September 26, 1987.)

15755.
A law enforcement agency may seek a search warrant from a magistrate pursuant to the procedures set forth in Chapter 3 (commencing with Section 1523) of Title 12 of Part 2 of the Penal Code to enable a peace officer to have access to, and to inspect, premises if a county welfare worker has been denied access to the premises by the person or persons in possession of the premises and there is probable cause to believe an elder or dependent adult on those premises is subject to abuse. While executing the search warrant the peace officer may allow a county welfare worker, or any other appropriate person, to accompany him or her. (Added by Stats. 1994, Ch. 1246, Sec. 17. Effective January 1, 1995.)

15760.
Adult protective services shall include investigations, needs assessments, remedial and preventive social work activities; the necessary tangible resources such as food, transportation, emergency shelter, and in-home protective care; the use of multidisciplinary teams; and a system in which reporting of abuse can occur on a 24-hour basis.
(Amended by Stats. 2002, Ch. 54, Sec. 25. Effective January 1, 2003.)

15762.
When an allegation of abuse of an elder or dependent adult is reported to a county designated adult protective service agency and an agency social worker has reason to believe an elder or dependent adult has suffered or is at substantial risk of abuse pursuant to Section 15630, the social worker shall attempt to obtain consent to enter and meet privately with the elder or dependent adult about whom the report was made in the residence or dwelling in which the elder or dependent adult resides without the presence of the person's caretaker, attendant, or family or household member, unless the person requests the presence of the attendant, care giver, or family member, or refuses to meet with the social worker. (Added by Stats. 1998, Ch. 946, Sec. 13. Effective January 1, 1999. Section operative May 1, 1999, pursuant to Section 15765.)

15763.
(a) Each county shall establish an emergency response adult protective services program that shall provide in-

person response, 24 hours per day, seven days per week, to reports of abuse of an elder or a dependent adult, for the purpose of providing immediate intake or intervention, or both, to new reports involving immediate life threats and to crises in existing cases. The program shall include policies and procedures to accomplish all of the following:
(1) Provision of case management services that include investigation of the protection issues, assessment of the person's concerns, needs, strengths, problems, and limitations, stabilization and linking with community services, and development of a service plan to alleviate identified problems utilizing counseling, monitoring, followup, and reassessment.
(2) Provisions for emergency shelter or in-home protection to guarantee a safe place for the elder or dependent adult to stay until the dangers at home can be resolved.
(3) Establishment of multidisciplinary teams to develop interagency treatment strategies, to ensure maximum coordination with existing community resources, to ensure maximum access on behalf of elders and dependent adults, and to avoid duplication of efforts.
(b) (1) A county shall respond immediately to any report of imminent danger to an elder or dependent adult in other than a long-term care facility, as defined in Section 9701 of the Welfare and Institutions Code, or a residential facility, as defined in Section 1502 of the Health and Safety Code. For reports involving persons in a long-term care facility or a residential care facility, the county shall report to the local long-term care ombudsman program. Adult protective services staff shall consult, coordinate, and support efforts of the ombudsman program to protect vulnerable residents. Except as specified in paragraph (2), the county shall respond to all other reports of danger to an elder or dependent adult in other than a long-term care facility or residential care facility within 10 calendar days or as soon as practicably possible.
(2) An immediate or 10-day in-person response is not required when the county, based upon an evaluation of risk, determines and documents that the elder or dependent adult is not in imminent danger and that an immediate or 10-day in-person response is not necessary to protect the health or safety of the elder or dependent adult.
(3) The State Department of Social Services, in consultation with the County Welfare Directors Association, shall develop requirements for implementation of paragraph (2), including, but not limited to, guidelines for determining appropriate application of this section and any applicable documentation requirements.
(4) Notwithstanding Chapter 3.5 (commencing with Section 11340) of Part 1 of Division 3 of Title 2 of the Government Code, the department shall implement the requirements developed pursuant to paragraph (3) by means of all-county letters or similar instructions prior to adopting regulations for that purpose. Thereafter, the department shall adopt regulations in accordance with the requirements of Chapter 3.5 (commencing with Section 11340) of Part 1 of Division 3 of Title 2 of the Government Code.
(c) A county shall not be required to report or respond to a report pursuant to subdivision (b) that involves danger to an elder or dependent adult residing in any facility for the incarceration of prisoners that is operated by or under contract to the Federal Bureau of Prisons, the Department of Corrections and Rehabilitation, a county sheriff's department, a county probation department, a city police department, or any other law enforcement agency when the abuse reportedly has occurred in that facility.
(d) A county shall provide case management services to elders and dependent adults who are determined to be in need of adult protective services for the purpose of bringing about changes in the lives of victims and to provide a safety net to enable victims to protect themselves in the future. Case management services shall include the following, to the extent services are appropriate for the individual:
(1) Investigation of the protection issues, including, but not limited to, social, medical, environmental, physical, emotional, and developmental.
(2) Assessment of the person's concerns and needs on whom the report has been made and the concerns and needs of other members of the family and household.
(3) Analysis of problems and strengths.

(4) Establishment of a service plan for each person on whom the report has been made to alleviate the identified problems.
(5) Client input and acceptance of proposed service plans.
(6) Counseling for clients and significant others to alleviate the identified problems and to implement the service plan.
(7) Stabilizing and linking with community services.
(8) Monitoring and followup.

(9) Reassessments, as appropriate.
(e) To the extent resources are available, each county shall provide emergency shelter in the form of a safe haven or in-home protection for victims. Shelter and care appropriate to the needs of the victim shall be provided for frail and disabled victims who are in need of assistance with activities of daily living.
(f) Each county shall designate an adult protective services agency to establish and maintain multidisciplinary teams including, but not limited to, adult protective services, law enforcement, probation departments, home health care agencies, hospitals, adult protective services staff, the public guardian, private community service agencies, public health agencies, and mental health agencies for the purpose of providing interagency treatment strategies.
(g) Each county shall provide tangible support services, to the extent resources are available, which may include, but not be limited to, emergency food, clothing, repair or replacement of essential appliances, plumbing and electrical repair, blankets, linens, and other household goods, advocacy with utility companies, and emergency response units.(Amended by Stats. 2010, Ch. 617, Sec. 15. Effective January 1, 2011.)

15764.
Notwithstanding Section 10101.1, a county shall have no share of any nonfederal expenditures above the required expenditures for this program in the 1996–97 fiscal year, provided that the county has maintained the level of county matching funds it provided for this program in the 1996–97 fiscal year. (Added by Stats. 1998, Ch. 946, Sec. 13. Effective January 1, 1999. Section operative May 1, 1999, pursuant to Section 15765.)

15765.
This chapter shall become operative on May 1, 1999. Commencing with the 1999–2000 fiscal year, Sections 15760 to 15764, inclusive, shall be implemented only to the extent funds are provided in the annual Budget Act. (Amended by Stats. 2002, Ch. 54, Sec. 28. Effective January 1, 2003. Note: This section makes implementation of Sections 15760 to 15764 contingent upon Budget Act funding.)

15766.
The investigation of allegations of elder and dependent adult abuse pursuant to this chapter, and the case management of elder and dependent adult abuse cases shall be performed by county merit systems civil service employees. A county adult protective service agency may utilize a contracted private or nonprofit telephone answering service after normal working hours and on weekends and holidays. Such a contracted telephone service shall immediately forward to a county merit systems civil service employee any report of abuse or neglect of an elder or dependent adult, unless the caller is: (a) requesting routine information only; (b) reporting an incident of abuse which occurred prior to the date of the call, which does not at the time of the call put the victim at risk; or (c) requesting information not related to the adult protective service program, and the person answering the telephone meets the standards established by the department. (Added by Stats. 1999, Ch. 147, Sec. 36. Effective July 22, 1999.)

Chapter 15

Mental Health Records

Mental Health Records and Psychotherapy

The documentation of the clinical process serves two purposes: a) to provide a record of the client's assessment, diagnosis, and treatment if needed, and b) to protect MFTs should they face legal action. Though keeping mental health records is a legal requirement, it is far more important and beneficial to focus on how they serve to protect MFTs.

Appropriate mental health records provide MFTs with a clear reference point from which to begin the process of providing therapy. These records contain the structure that helps MFTs obtain and document all necessary client information. This information allows the clinician to establish an appropriate 5-Axis diagnosis supported with documented clinical symptoms and their duration. From the diagnosis, the clinician establishes a plan for treatment to resolve the presenting issues. This treatment plan also serves as an assessment tool to determine the effectiveness of the proposed treatment as it continues. As therapy progresses, the therapist can use the records to help keep progress in sight and to make new evaluations that may not have been apparent initially and now require attention.

Most clinicians would rather not think about the possibility of infirmity or their own demise. However, since no one has total control over these life events, the MFT has a responsibility to prepare his or her clients for outcomes of these possibilities. Mental health records thus become an important resource for providing continuity of treatment should a therapist no longer be able to treat her or his clients and avoid a possible malpractice action against him or her or his or her estate.

A client's mental health records can be subpoenaed for a variety of unpredictable reasons. These include auto accidents, personal injuries, divorce, custody evaluations, sexual harassment, malpractice and other legal actions that may take place many years after the completion of treatment. The client may require his or her records to defend a legal action or to sue the clinician for malpractice. In any one of these situations, the following law applies.

Civil Code 1016 addresses the lack of privilege as follows:

Evidence Code 1016: There is no privilege in any proceeding when the patient's emotional condition has been raised as an issue by the patient or the patient's representative.

Attorneys and mental health licensing boards rely on mental health records to evaluate alleged malpractice and claims of unprofessional conduct. Appropriate mental health records are the only legally acceptable documents that can illuminate what transpired in therapy. Keeping appropriate mental health records implies that the therapist applied standard of care in her or his practice in the area of keeping mental health records. These records can help protect clinicians by quashing an attorney's "fishing expedition" or formal investigation by providing appropriate documentation of the therapist's scope of practice, appropriate selection of client, assessment, diagnosis, treatment plan, consultations and treatment notes, and each component solidly supporting the best interests of the therapist and showing that he or she acted in a reasonable and prudent manner in the delivery of his or her services.

Mental Health Records: The Law and Ethical Standards

For California MFTs, keeping mental health records is a legal and ethical therapeutic duty. Legally, Business and Professions Code 4982(v) establishes that appropriate mental health records must be kept. Ethically, CAMFT Ethical Standard 2.4 complements the law. Thus, not keeping appropriate records can be considered both a legal and ethical violation of MFT practice.

Business and Professions Code 4982 (v): Failure to keep records consistent with sound clinical judgment, the standards of the profession, and the nature of the services being rendered Is considered Unprofessional conduct.

CAMFT Ethical Standard 2.4: Marriage and family therapists store, transfer, transmit, and/or dispose of patient records in ways that protect confidentiality.

Health and Safety Code 123130 — Foundation for the Content of Mental Health Records

Currently, California law does not specify the required content of mental health records. However, Health and Safety Code 123130 *indirectly* establishes what these records should contain. It does so by describing the content of the summary that MFTs may provide a client rather than their full records when the client requests these mental health records. (This decision to provide full records or a summary would occur after a client makes a written request of his or her records.) The law describes the minimum information that these records must contain. The following is the content of the summary:

a) Chief complaints, including pertinent history
b) Objective findings from the most recent physical examination
c) Findings from consultations and referrals to other health care workers
d) Pertinent reports of diagnostic procedures and tests
e) Diagnosis, when determined
f) Treatment plan
g) Progress of treatment
h) Prognosis, including significant continuing problems or conditions
i) Discharge summaries

For a discussion of the standard of care for mental health records, see chapters 16-18.

The Clinical Foundation for Content of Mental Health Records

Clinicians have the professional duty to assess, diagnose, and provide treatment to their clients regardless if they provide psychotherapy of social services. California law requires that MFTs maintain mental health records on their clients. There is however, a more compelling reason for doing so: protecting the clinician. Most clinical situations that require access to client records are unpredictable in nature. This means that the clinician is unable to determine when a clinical situation will aggravate to a serious level where the client presents danger to self and / or others. Once the critical point is reached, it's too late to return to a pre-morbid state and someone could experience a significant physical or emotional injury. To complicate matters, it is impossible to predict if or when the injured party will sue the clinician.

The clinician's best protection is to document the client's assessment, diagnosis, and treatment from the beginning. Regardless of whether this client initiates a legal action or not, the clinician's records will serve to document how he or she managed the presenting issues. More importantly, by documenting the decision-making process and actions taken to manage high-risk issues, the clinician can help ward off potentially devastating lawsuits in case of client injury.

Patient Access to His/Her Mental Health Records

Health and Safety Code 123130 addresses the right of patients to inspect and copy their records. It states that health practitioners must make these records available to clients who request these in writing. MFTs have 5 working days to provide a copy of the records. If the client requests copies of the records in writing, then MFTs can send a summary of the records within 15 working days. Should MFTs believe that releasing these records to a client would be injurious to his or her well-being, and then they can refuse to make these available to the client within 30 working days. The clinician must document why he or she refused to provide these records and must make them available to another mental health practitioner chosen by the client. The latter clinician must not release these records to the client; however, he or she can discuss the content with the client.

The guardian or legal custodian of a minor also has the same rights as an adult client when requesting his or her child's mental health records. There are three exceptions: a) when the minor has sought mental health treatment under the conditions established by law (minors over the age of 12, mature enough to participate in treatment, have been the alleged victim or incest or child abuse, or without treatment would present a danger to self or others), b) if the therapist believes that releasing these records to the adult would have a detrimental effect on the provider's professional relationship with the minor or the minor's physical safety or psychological well-being, and c) should the minor's well-being be jeopardized by releasing these records to a parent as established by *Daniel v. Daniel (1990)*. MFTs cannot deny non-custodial access to their child's mental health records. Clients cannot be denied access to their mental health record for lack of payment of therapeutic fees.

Computerized Records

Computerized records help clinicians improve accessibility, reduce storage space, enhance productivity, increase utilization, and maintain connectivity with insurance companies. Reasonable and prudent clinicians are required to maintain confidentiality when using a computerized format. To provide for the protection of confidentiality, the clinician must be aware of potential pitfalls with electronic storage. The clinician must avoid using a word-processing program to store these records. These programs allow for editing of text and thus do not allow the "fixing" of text. This is problematic for clinicians because should a legal action take place, the opposing attorney will attempt to prove that they created the records recently, and manipulated the data. If repair to the computer or hard containing the client data and the MFT uses a word processing program, confidential client data is easily accessible and retrieved. The only way to prove the actual creation date is to submit the hard drive to an expert who upon examination would determine when the exact date of creation of the data in question. This examination also exposes any data written about any other clients and thus, their confidentiality is violated by the clinician. The clinician must use appropriate software that allows text to be "fixed" upon pressing the "Accept" key. Should additional text be required, the program allows the clinician to append data with an accurate date stamp showing when the clinician entered the data into the program. Additionally, the software allows data to be stored in separate internal files. Should a third party require the client's records, a file containing that client's data can be exported singly and provided to the requesting party.

Clinicians must also address internal and external security of the computerized records. The computer must have a password and the software must have additional passwords: one master and additional user passwords allowing access to different parts of the program. Should the computer be disposed of, the clinician must use a "scrubber" program to safely delete the client data from the hard drive. Only then can the hard drive be disposed of.

Clinical Example # 1

Roger focuses his practice in treating mood disorders. Recently, one client has been challenging his clinical skills and Roger decided to consult a suicidologist regarding the client's emotional downturn into severe depressive symptoms. Being a busy clinician, Roger forgot to document the consultation and many of the risk assessments he performed on this client. While attending a weekend lecture in another city, the client attempted suicide and ended up in the intensive care unit. The client's father, a prominent attorney, asked his firm to subpoena the client's records for review by an expert witness who would report if the assessment, diagnosis, and treatment had conformed to the standard of care. If not, the firm would initiate a lawsuit against the therapist.

Questions for Clinical Example # 1

1. Roger receives the subpoena and realizes he did not document his assessment, diagnosis, and treatment in a manner that reflects the treatment he provided. What emotions do you believe he is experiencing at this moment?
2. Based on Roger's lack of discipline in writing his records, what do you imagine the expert witness will find when he or she reads the records?
3. Roger will most likely face a lawsuit for not conforming to the standard of care in this case. How could Roger have prevented this possibility? What documentation would have established that he conformed to the standard of care?
4. Had Roger documented his risk assessment for this client in a reasonable and prudent manner, he might not be facing a lawsuit. Now, he faces an additional complication to his professional life: a BBS investigation for unprofessional conduct. Does the BBS have ground to find that he violated California Business and Professions Code Section 4982? Why or why not?

Clinical Example # 2

Anthony prides himself in keeping excellent records. He details every interaction that takes place between himself and the client. Recently, he decides to keep his data on a computer after a friend told him how easy it was to print the records of a laser printer. Anthony decides to transfer all his records to a word-processing program and after he completed this task, he shredded his paper mental health records. Recently, a client made a written request for records, Anthony printed the client's records, and mailed these to the client who showed them to his attorney. The attorney questions the date of creation and issued a subpoena for Anthony's computer. Anthony attempted to have his attorney "quash" the request, however the judge ruled in favor of the client.

Questions for Clinical Example # 2

1. In retrospect, what should Anthony have done with the paper mental health records?
2. Has he kept these, would he be facing this difficulty? Why or why not?
3. Not only is Anthony violating all of his clients' confidentiality, he is now exposing himself to what type of accusation from the BBS?
4. What would you have advised Anthony had he asked you about how to keep computerized records?
5. If his intention was not to harm the client, will that make a difference with the Board of Behavioral Sciences if they investigate him for unprofessional conduct? Why or why not?

Chapter Questions

1. What specifically constitutes a legal and ethical therapeutic duty violation when records do not meet the standard of care?
2. What are the 8 minimum required components of mental health records?
3. What are the time elements therapists must follow when clients request their records from a therapist?
4. A therapist friend of yours calls you and asks your help with a case. She has been treating a suicidal patient for several weeks and is afraid the client has a plan, a weapon, and the client has not returned her calls. Your friend has not been keeping records on this case for the last six weeks. What would you advise her to do?
5. What is the importance of the treatment plan?
6. Consider the following scenario: An MFT treats a young woman with depressive symptoms for some time. During the course of the treatment, the young woman is involved in an automobile accident and she is injured. Her attorney initiates legal action against the other driver. A year later, the MFT receives a subpoena from the opposing attorney for the mental health records of this client. The MFT faces a quandary: she never documented the accident or the impact it had on the client. What recommendations would you have for this MFT?

Chapter 16

The Content of Mental Health Records

Appropriate Content of Mental Health Records

Mental health records serve to document the MFT's assessment, diagnosis, treatment, and legal challenges if present. These also provide clients with necessary information when required. The following components provide the necessary documentation of the elements discussed above. These include: intake form, informed consent form, mental status exam form, Beck Depression inventory form if needed, consultation form, written release of information form, diagnosis and treatment plan form, ledger form, progress notes, form, legal challenge documentation form, and discharge form.

Intake Form

This form provides the psychotherapist with important client information. For example, home or office address, telephone numbers, social security number, insurance information (if used by the therapist), family contact information (should an emergency arise), personal history, medical history, family history, referral source, history of previous therapy and/or hospitalizations, presenting issue, psychosocial issues, and other information the psychotherapist deems necessary. Having a thorough intake form establishes that the therapist took reasonable care to obtain all information necessary to make an accurate diagnosis, ensure safety and plan a course of treatment for the client.

Informed Consent Form

This form documents the creation of the therapeutic relationship and the genesis of therapeutic duty. This form also provides the patient with the necessary information concerning the proposed therapy allowing the client to determine if he or she wants to begin treatment. The information provided to the client includes the nature of the therapeutic approach used by the practitioner. It describes the benefits and risks of therapy, the estimated length of therapy, the cost of each session, the fee policy, a fee structure, the client rights, emergency policies, crisis management, insurance management, an explanation of unusual or experimental therapies, and a therapy termination policy. The psychotherapist and the client create a legal contract agreeing on therapeutic duty owed to the patient, the client's responsibilities owed to the therapist and to the therapeutic process, and a termination process should the client's lack of cooperation hinder the therapeutic process.

The client uses this form to consent to beginning of treatment, which includes all necessary assessments, appropriate psychometric testing, diagnosis, and the formulation of treatment. With this form, the patient acknowledges that he or she incurs a financial obligation for the treatment provided. This form also serves to hold both accountable should a legal issue arise between them.

Additional Informed Consent

There are times when MFTs must obtain a separate informed consent when the clinician utilizes experimental, difficult, unproven, risky, controversial, or challenging therapeutic techniques that are not yet considered acceptable standards of the profession. For example, in the past, experts recommended that MFTs obtain a separate informed consent when using Eye Movement Desensitization and Reprocessing. Since this modality has become part of the standard of care in treating trauma, it is no longer necessary required to obtain a separate informed consent. A reasonable and prudent clinician uses a separate informed consent form for such modalities as: Thought Field Therapy, Energy Therapy, Somatic Psychology, Perinatal Psychology or Past Life Regression Therapy prior to using these techniques. Therapeutic techniques that involve touch, such as Perinatal or Somatic Psychology, require a separate informed consent. The risks and benefits, scientific validation of the theoretical model, and the clinician's scope of competence with this approach are included in the informed consent. Using this document protects the client by providing necessary information to make an informed decision about beginning treatment. It protects clinicians by documenting that they provided this necessary information to clients.

Ledger Form

The Ledger form document the money paid to the therapist corresponding to the sessions and treatment provided and billed to the client. This form contains a financial history of the treatment history, including dates of services, service codes, fees charged, fees paid, adjustments, and current balance. This form also serves to null an accusation of fraud or other financial impropriety.

Psychometric Testing

Psychometric testing includes any psychometric test administered, ordered, or obtained by the psychotherapist. A recommended and important test to administer to all patients is the Mental Status Exam. It provides the psychotherapist with a baseline of cognitive, emotional, behavioral, physical, and other important mental processes about the patient. Using this test is an important step to establish that the therapist took a reasonable and prudent step to assess the patient initially. Continuously assessing the client's mental status provides MFTs with a comparative baseline should an opposing attorney question their assessment protocol. Patients presenting any depressive symptoms, MFTs must use the Beck's Depression Inventory and/or Hopelessness Scale. Sucidology experts indicate that these psychometric tests indicate and document the client's depressive process. Reasonable MFTs use these tests progressively to determine pattern of progress of the depression. Courts expect MFTs to document their client's depressive progress using the former tests.

Written Releases of Information

A written release of information serves to obtain or provide a client's confidential information to third parties. MFTs must follow a legal protocol to validate the exchange of information. MFTs who fail to follow this protocol are illegally breaching the client's confidentiality. (See Chapter 3 — Confidentiality).

DSM 5 Diagnosis, Treatment Plan and Prognosis

Standard of care dictates that MFTs complete a DSM 5 diagnosis according to the Diagnostic and Statistical Manual © published by the American Psychiatric Association. Since psychiatrists established this standard, it is likely that MFTs who fail to include it in their documentation will allow an opposing attorney to question their competence in diagnosis and documentation. This diagnosis includes the following:

- **Component 1 – Clinical Disorders**: Record of any mental disorders and/or V codes (MFTs document and support Axis I and Axis II diagnosis with corresponding clinical symptoms and their duration in the progress notes.)
- **Component 2 – Personality Disorders**: Record of mental retardation and personality disorders
- **Component 3 – Medical Information:** Record of medical conditions
- **Component 4 – Current Stressors:** Record of the factors impacting the presenting issues
- **Component 5– Psychosocial and Environmental Problems:** Compares the present Global Assessment of Functioning to the previous year.
- These components are written on a single line.

A treatment plan establishes the proposed pathway of treatment to resolve the presenting issue(s). The treatment plan also allows MFTs to determine the progress of treatment. Comparing progressive clinical results to the treatment plan allows MFTs to determine the progress and success of treatment provided. If the results are not succeeding, then the therapist can use the treatment plan to determine where treatment came to a halt. Next, MFTs develop a new and more effective treatment plan. Thus, this road map serves as a frame of reference against which to measure the success of goals, objectives, and interventions. The treatment plan must conform to the standard of care.

The prognosis creates a reasonable expectation regarding the outcome of treatment. This is neither a guarantee nor a prediction. Determining a prognosis depends on many factors, including the severity of the client's presenting issues, the ability and/or willingness of the client to cooperate, complicating factors (major depression, bipolar disorder, obsessive-compulsive disorder, etc.), and psychosocial factors. Clients have the right to receive information about the approximate prognosis of the proposed treatment.

Consultations and Medical Information

MFTs document all consultation with other practitioners in the client's mental health record. For example, when MFTs refer a patient to a psychiatrist or physician, they document the referral, the purpose, and the outcome of the referral. MFTs can ue a separate form labeled "Consultations" for this process. Additionally, MFTs use their progress notes to document how they will use the obtained information to modify the proposed treatment. Enclosed documents are also included in the mental health record.

MFTs obtain and document an important piece of information: their client's medical history. MFTs must rule out the possibility that the presenting psychological/emotional issues can have a physical etiology. Medical conditions that can cause psychological/emotional issues include hormonal imbalance, tumors of the pituitary, adrenal tumors, thyroid problems, brain tumor, or diabetes. In many states, case law has established that referral to a physician to rule out medical basis of emotional issues is a legal therapeutic duty. Treating a client with psychotherapy when a medical condition exists is a foundation for a malpractice action and for a licensing board action for incompetence.

Progress Notes

Progress notes constitute one of the most important components of mental health records. This component of the mental health records serves as a mechanism to document the client's overall progress in treatment. The documented narrative can be harmful and beneficial to MFTs, depending on how they write their notes. MFTs must be accurate in their progress notes. They must strike a balance between providing enough information to refresh their memory and avoiding excessive information that can jeopardize the client and clinician's needs. Excessive notes only help the opposing attorney when they initiate a malpractice action against MFTs.

When writing progress notes, MFTs assure that the dates of entries must correspond to the dates of treatment. They document information gathered at the initial assessment, correlation of diagnosis with behavioral symptoms and their duration, the results of consultations, the "progress" of treatment, the patient's affect, his or her behavior, and the response or reaction to clinical interventions. Importantly, to protect clinicians, they document crisis issues that require a legal/ethical action carefully and appropriately. Thus, MFTs use progress notes tell the progressive "story" and whether treatment progress has improved. A jury considers altering, erasing, or modifying progress notes after writing as tampering with a legal clinical record. Should tampering become apparent in a legal case, the court will most likely rule against the therapist. Therefore, it is important to avoid any change to progress notes after completing the documentation. However, it is permissible to append text in a progress note as long as MFTs identify it as such.

When MFTs use a word-processing program to store progress and treatment notes, they open the door to an accusation of violating their client's confidentiality. An opposing attorney explanation indicates that the information entered in file can be edited or deleted at a later date. Therefore, it is impossible to establish when MFTs entered the data initially. If a legal challenge occurs, the opposing attorney will request the judge to order the examination of the hard drive to determine the origin and date of the specific file in question. However, the data analysis engineer now has access to all other client files stored in the hard drive. The opposing attorney will request this information and use it for his or her benefit.

Discharge Summary

The discharge summary documents the official termination of therapy. It documents that the therapy was either successful or not successful depending on whether the client met the goals of therapy. Documenting the end of therapy establishes that the therapist acted professionally at this phase of treatment. For example, the discharge summary shows that MFTs did not abandon a client when he or she terminated therapy early. It also establishes that the client terminated therapy appropriately when he or she met the goals of therapy. Should a client injure him/herself and/or others after treatment ended, it serves to protect MFTs. It is possible that an opposing attorney will attempt to hold the MFT liable for the resulting injuries. This document establishes that the MFT no longer owes a therapeutic duty to the client.

Chapter Questions

1. How does the content of mental health records create clinical safety?
2. What is the purpose of the intake form?
3. What elements would be important for you to include in your informed consent Form?
4. A therapist friend of yours calls you and asks your help with a case. She has received a subpoena for treatment records, including all charges and payments. She doesn't have a patient ledger. What advice would you give your friend?
5. Not having treatment plans in the mental health records can be considered practicing below the standard of care. What are the reasons behind this possibility?
6. What is the importance of documenting consultations?
7. A therapist friend of yours asks you if she can erase her progress notes and make new ones up. What is your advice to her?
8. How does a discharge summary document create clinical safety?

Chapter 17

Sample Forms

SAMPLE INTAKE FORM

SAMPLE INFORMED CONSENT FORM

SAMPLE LEDGER FORM

SAMPLE MENTAL STATUS EXAM FORM

SAMPLE RELEASE OF INFORMATION FORM

SAMPLE DIAGNOSIS, TREATMENT PLAN, AND PROGNOSIS FORM

SAMPLE CONSULTATION FORM

SAMPLE PROGRESS NOTES FORM

Sample Intake Form

Personal History

Intake Date

Patient's Name______________ Birthdate_____________

Address____

Phone_____________________________ (OK to leave message?)_____________

Employer___________________________________ Occupation________________

Address ___________________________________ S.S. Number_______________

Family History

Single _______ Married______________ (how many times?)___

Spouse's Name____

Separated_________________ Date of Separation_________

Divorced_____ How many times?___ Date of Divorce(s)_________

Living with Significant Other/Roomate, if so, Name______________________________________

Children's Names/ Ages___________________ Phone #____________

Siblings' Names/ Ages____________________ Phone #____________

Parents' Names/ Ages____________________ Phone #____________

Religious Preference/Affiliation_________________________________

Medical History

Personal Physician_______________________ Phone # ___________

Address ____

Current Medications and Dosages_____________________________________

Date of last Medical Exam__________ Results__________________

Current Nonprescription Drug Use_________ Frequency of use_________________

Do (or did) your parents use drugs/alcohol? ____

Which parent?____________________ Which drugs?_____________

Have you been in psychotherapy before?__________ Dates_____________

With whom, where and why?____

What brings you to therapy now?____

What else would you like me to know?____

What would you like to achieve from therapy?__________________________________

Who referred you to me?____

Sample Informed Consent Form

TREATMENT CONTRACT

The Therapy Process • Participating in therapy can result in a number of benefits to you, including a better understanding of your personal goals and values, improved interpersonal relationships, and resolution of the specific concerns that led you to seek therapy. Working toward these benefits requires effort on your part and may result in your experiencing considerable discomfort. Change will sometimes be easy and swift, but more often it will be slow and frustrating. Remembering and resolving significant life events in therapy can bring on strong feelings of anger, depression, fear, etc. Attempting to resolve issues between marital partners, family members, and other individuals can also lead to discomfort and may result in changes that were not originally intended. As part of my therapeutic process, I use several techniques including hypnosis and Eye Movement Desensitization and Reprocessing. My theoretical perspective is a combination of Family Systems and Cognitive-Behavioral Approaches.

Client's Rights • You have the right to a confidential relationship with me. Within certain legal limits (see #3 below), information revealed by you during the course of therapy will be kept completely confidential and will not be revealed to any person without your written permission.

1. You have the right to know the content of your records at any time and I have the right to determine whether I will provide you with the complete records or a summary of their content.

2. If you ask me, I can release any part of your records on file to any person you specify. I will tell you whether or not I think releasing that information to that agency or person might be harmful to you.

3. Under certain legally defined situations, I have the duty to reveal information you tell me during the course of therapy to other persons without your written consent. I am not required to inform you of my actions if this occurs. These legally defined situations include:

a. If you reveal to me active child abuse, neglect, or abduction. An alleged perpetrator is in contact with minors and there is a reasonable suspicion that he or she may still be abusing minors. If active physical abuse of a dependent adult or an elder is taking place.

b. If you seriously threaten harm or death to another person, I am required to warn the intended victim and notify the appropriate law enforcement agencies.

c. If you are in therapy or are being tested by order of the court, the results of the treatment or tests ordered must be revealed to that court.

d. If a court of law issues a legitimate subpoena, I am required by law to provide the information specifically described in that subpoena.

e. If you are in a lawsuit claiming emotional harm, the opposing side may subpoena your therapy records.

4. You have the right to ask questions about any of the procedures used in the course of your therapy.

5. Should you choose not to enter therapy with me, I will provide you with names of other qualified professionals whose services you might prefer.

6. You have the right to terminate therapy with me at any time without any financial, legal, or moral obligations other than those you've already incurred. I have the right to terminate therapy with you under the following conditions:

   a. When I believe that therapy is no longer beneficial to you.

   b. When you fail to follow recommended treatment.

   c. When I believe that you will be better served by another professional.

   d. When you have not paid for the last two sessions, unless special arrangements have been made with me.

   e. When you have failed to show up for your last two therapy sessions without a 24-hour notice.

   f. If I determine during the first three sessions that I cannot help you, I will assist you in finding someone qualified. If I have written consent, I will provide that professional with information they request.

If any of these situations apply, I will send a certified letter to you at your address of record to inform you of my decision and I will give you the names of several therapists for your future counseling needs. As life can bring unexpected circumstance, should I be unable to continue your therapy, my trusted colleague, Jane Doe, Ph.D. will contact you to discuss what would be best for you at that time.

6Fees and Length of Therapy • I agree to enter therapy with James Doe, Ph.D., M.F.T., for fifty minute sessions during the next _______ weeks.

I agree to pay the fee of $____ for each completed fifty minute session. I will make payment in cash or by check at the time of the therapy appointment, unless we have made other arrangements. I understand that I can leave therapy at any time and that I have no financial, legal, or moral obligation to complete the maximum number of sessions listed in this contract. I am contracting only to pay for completed therapy sessions, or for any session I miss without providing 24-hour notice, and for telephone time as outlined in the Office Policies section.

Date ____________________ Client's Signature____________________________

Date ____________________ Therapist's Signature_________________________

Consent for Treatment • I ____________________________authorize and request that James Doe, Ph.D., L.C.S.W., carry out psychotherapeutic examinations, diagnostic procedures, and/or treatment which now or during the course of my care as a patient are advisable.

I understand that the purpose of any procedure will be explained to me and be subject to my agreement. I have read and fully understand this Consent for Treatment form.

Date _____________ Client's Signature______________________

Date _____________ Therapist's Signature____________________

OFFICE POLICIES

Payment for Service: You are expected to pay for services at the time they are rendered unless other arrangements have been made. Please notify me if any problem arises regarding your ability to make timely payment.

Insurance Reimbursement: Patients who carry insurance will bill their own insurance. I will provide you with the appropriate billing information, which you will send for reimbursement. I do not bill insurance companies nor do I accept payment from them.

Cancellation: Since an appointment reserves time specifically for you, a minimum of 24-hour notice is required for rescheduling or canceling of an appointment. Without such notification, The full fee will be charged for missed sessions without such notification. Most insurance companies do not reimburse for sessions missed.

Office Hours: My office hours are from 8:00 AM to 6:00 PM, Monday to Friday. If you need to contact me between sessions, please leave a message and I will return your call.

Telephone Time: After 5 minutes of telephone time, you will be charged at your regular fee.

Sessions Greater Than 50 Minutes: Sessions that go beyond the fifty minutes, will be prorated to the nearest quarter hour, unless you have made prior arrangements with me.

Emergency Procedure: An emergency is an unexpected event that requires immediate attention. If an emergency situation arises, please state this when you leave your message and I will return your call as soon as possible. After 5 minutes of telephone time, you will be charged on a prorated basis. If I have not called you back within 60 minutes and the emergency persists, and the emergency requires it, please call your physician or admit yourself to a hospital for observation.

I have read and understand these office policies.

Date ____________ Client's Signature ____________________________________

Date ____________ Therapist's Signature ________________________________

Sample Ledger Form

Name:____

Address:____

____

Telephone_________________________

Date	Code	Fee	Payment	Adjustment	Balance

Sample Mental Status Form

Initial Assessment

Name:______________________________ Date:________________

APPEARANCE: (How does patient present? Appropriately dressed, dishevelled, excessively neat and organized, immaculate and meticulous?)

Patient presents cleanly and appropriately dressed.

BEHAVIOR: (How does patient behave? Congruent or incongruent, contained or expansive, appropriate or inappropriate?)

Behavior is within normal limits.

SPEECH: (Describe patient's quality of talking.)

Speech is normal.

EMOTION/AFFECT: (Describe patient's emotional state and affect. Is emotion depressed, dysthymic, euthymic, manic, euthymic, hypomanic? Is affect expansive, labile, or flat, or other?)

Patient presents dysthymia, affect is slightly flat and restricted.

THOUGHT PROCESSES: (Is patient delusional, hallucinating, obsessive, or compulsive, or other? Is patient's thought process continuous and connected or disconnected and choppy?)

Within normal limits

ORIENTATION: (Is patient oriented to person/place/time?)

Oriented times 3

MEMORY: (Is patient's memory intact for recent/intermediate/remote?)

Short-term and long-term memory are intact.

GENERAL INTELLECTUAL ABILITIES: (Is patient's intellect within normal limits?)

Within normal limits.

JUDGMENT: (Is patient's judgement appropriate or inappropriate?)

Judgement appears appropriate.

INSIGHT: (Is patient's insight reasonable or unreasonable?)

Insight appears to be reasonable.

CLINICAL RECOMMENDATIONS:

Refer to physician for medical evaluation

Sample Release of Information Form

Your Name, MFT
5555 Anystreet Drive
Any City, CA 55555-5555

License #: MFC XXXXX
Tel 555-555-5555
Fax 555-555-5556

Authorization to Release Records

I, _____(Name of Patient)___________, hereby authorize ___(Other Communicant)_______ and (Your Name, MFT) to exchange my health records and information obtained during the course of treatment.

The disclosure of such records authorized herein is required for the following purpose(s):

____

____

Such disclosure shall be limited to the following use of information:

____

____

____

Such disclosure shall be limited to the following type of information:

____

____

____

This consent shall expire on:____

The patient can request a copy of this authorization. The patient has a right to refuse to sign this form. The patient understands that information that is used or disclosed according to this authorization may be subject to re-disclosure by the recipient. California law may provide additional protection regarding the possible re-disclosure. The provider will not make providing treatment a condition of signing this Authorization. The patient is entitled to receive a copy of this form. For revocation of this form, the Patient must provide a written request to the clinician named above.

Dated_____________ Signature of Client__________________________________

California Law Requires This Form To Be In Font Size 14 or Greater

In addition to complying with California legal requirements, this form is also HIPAA compliant. It is for illustration purposes only and not to be interpreted as a legal document. Always consult an attorney prior to using any of these published form to determine if they are appropriate for your practice.

Sample Diagnosis, Treatment Plan, and Prognosis Form

TREATMENT PLANNING & DIAGNOSIS

Name_______________________________________ Date__________________

DSM Diagnosis: Major depression, personality disorders not present, hypertension, loss of job and divorce, GAF last year 86 GAF this year 72

Treatment Plan

Crisis Issues

Goals:

Objectives:

Initial Phase

Goals:

Objectives:

Middle Phase

Goals:

Objectives:

Final Phase

Goals:

Objectives:

Prognosis: Excellent:_____Good:______Moderate:_______Poor:_____

Sample Consultation Form

CONSULTATIONS

Patient's Name: ____________________________

Date of Consultation_________________

Name of Consultant_________________

Reason for Consultation:____
____

Findings:____
____
____
____

Date of Consultation_________________

Name of Consultant_________________

Reason for Consultation:____
____

Findings:____
____
____
____

Date of Consultation_________________

Name of Consultant_________________

Reason for Consultation:____
____

Findings:____
____
____
____

Sample Progress Notes Form

Progress Notes

Name John Doe

Date

2-02-08	John began treatment because his depressive symptoms are interfering with his relationships. We agreed upon a fee of $100 per 50-minute hour. Obtained Informed Consent, discussed limits of confidentiality, discussed goals of treatment and length of therapy. Obtained family, medical, and personal history. Obtained a release of information to speak to previous therapist and his M.D.Completed Mental Status Exam and Beck Depression Inventory. Client presents with social isolation, flat affect, insomnia, not eating, and suicidal ideation during the last seven months. He denies having a weapon, a plan, or a desire to kill himself. I have asked him to bring his family at the next appointment. (TI)

Sample Discharge Summary

DISCHARGE SUMMARY

Date of Termination: 3-15-2003

Reason for Termination: Mr. Doe achieved completion of his goals in therapy and states that he no longer feels depressed or suicidal. He states that he has reconnected with his family, reconnected with his friends, is eating and sleeping well, and has found a joy in living. He states that he is no longer taking medication for depression and that he has maintained his stability for over one year. He states that his prospects for employment are very positive. We have addressed termination and he states he feels confident in being able to maintain a positive outlook on life without additional counseling. We have both agreed that he can return at any time to address future presenting issues should he require help. Case closed. *(Therapist's Signature)*

Chapter 18

Writing Case Notes

A Repeatable Format

Many psychotherapists have difficulty writing progress notes. Some fear that writing down any client information jeopardizes the client's confidentiality. Others are afraid that they will miss something important when they fail to include every bit of information given to them by clients. The answer lies somewhere in the middle. The following is a reasonable approach:

- Always follow the same format when writing mental health notes.
- Immediately establish your scope of practice in the first entry.
- Support your clinical diagnosis by describing the client's presenting clinical symptoms and their duration.
- Correlate the progress notes to each treatment session.
- Document "no-shows" and cancelled appointments.
- Use the progress notes to help you remember the course of treatment and not each interaction that took place).
- Use repeatable "key words" to help you remember the process of the session.
- Reflect the "core essence" of the session in the written entry.
- Avoid using extraneous details and information.
- When documenting legal/ethical decisions, describe in detail your decision-making process concerning which laws or ethical standards you applied, and identify the presenting issues dictating the need to apply legal standards.

Documenting Scope of Practice

After documenting the presenting "chief complaint," MFTs establish and document their scope of practice: the defined area of psychotherapy limited to MFTs. For example, if a client establishes a therapeutic relationship with a psychotherapist because depression is interfering with his or her life, a California MFTs write in their notes: "John Doe is seeking therapy because his depression is causing problems with his relationships" (the enhancement of relationships).

California LCSWs write: "John Doe is seeking therapy because his depression is interfering with his psycho-social adjustments" (the enhancement of psychosocial adjustments). A California psychologist would write: "John Doe came to therapy because his depression prevents joy in his life" (enhancing the resolution of any life issues). In case of legal action, this step establishes that the treating clinician provided services within of his or her scope of practice.

Documenting Diagnosis

After documenting "presenting complaint" and scope of practice, the next step is to document observable client behaviors and their duration that support a diagnosis. Should an opposing attorney challenge MFTs regarding their diagnostic protocol, this step documents that they followed an appropriate and reasonable protocol. Remember that clinicians are not expected to be perfect, only reasonable and prudent. For example, to support a diagnosis of Dysthymic Disorder, 300.4 the following documentation appears in the progress notes: "Within the last three years, Mr. Doe has experienced low energy and insomnia." The statement documents two behavioral elements (low energy and insomnia) and duration of the symptoms (more than two years). These are necessary to support this diagnosis. Not supporting a diagnosis with these two parameters helps the opposing attorney win a legal case against an MFT.

Consultations and Referrals

Documenting consultations in the "Consultations" page (see the previous chapter), allows the clinician to find this information immediately. Additionally, an opposing attorney would have a difficult time attempting to present an MFT as incompetent when the documentation shows that he or she acted as a reasonable and prudent psychotherapist. An additional observation is that the treating MFT defines him/herself as maintaining his or her clinical objectivity by obtaining appropriate consultations.

Writing Progress Notes

When documenting treatment with progress notes, MFTs remember that the purpose of these notes is to help the clinician recall the course of therapy or to help someone else take over where the clinician may have stopped in case he or she not be able to continue treatment. Therefore, the progress notes need only reflect the gist or essence of what transpired in therapy that day. I recommend the following steps:

Step 1:

Begin identifying each important segment of the therapy session and then separate each segment. See the example that follows:

During the course of a session, a client recalls how he and his wife end up fighting whenever they discuss finances. During their last fight at home, she accused him of being a "control freak" with the checkbook and he blamed her for spending too much money. The client is afraid that one day, during one of these fights, he may become violent and strike his wife. The therapist helps the client explore his emotional reactivity to regarding criticism and his fear of lashing back. During the exploration of these issues, the client remembers his father being hypercritical of his actions and links thinking he is a failure as a reaction to criticism.

Segment 1 includes the client's exploration of spousal conflict regarding finances with resulting criticism. Segment 2 involves his fear of expressing violence. Segment 3 includes the client's exploration of his emotional reactivity associated with parental criticism and belief of being a failure.

Step 2:

A clinician can create a list of repeatable words to help him or her remember the degree of affect expressed in session. I use the following words and each has a specific personal meaning: labile (broad range of expressed emotions), constricted (emotionally shut down), down (depressed), up (energized), sad, grieving, angry, etc. I also recommend using the following adverbs to qualify the degree of affect: mildly, moderately, and severely. A clinician can create his or her own repeatable language that can help him or her remember affect consistently. These terms can be integrated in the progress notes to help remember the affect of the session. To accentuate the description of affect, a clinician might close his or her eyes for a moment and recall the last clinical session he or she had yesterday. The clinician may attempt to connect with the "energy" of the session. He or she may see it, feel it, hear it, and even sense it in a more global manner. Now, the clinician can use a term or terms to describe this "energy." For example: "Client was flat and constricted." The personal meaning I give this sentence is that the client sat on the couch without showing much interest or emotion in his or her physical and verbal communications as he or she recounted the events of the week.

Step 3:

I recommend creating a sentence that condenses each segment of therapy. For example, "client addressed issues of abandonment and betrayal", or "client addressed conflict with spouse", or "client explored issues of child abuse". The clinician can use one sentence to identify each important segment of the therapy session. As practice continues, each clinician learns to develop the style that fits his or her needs. Perfection is not necessary: being reasonable and prudent is key.

Another consideration is to use the following words to relate to the process that took place in the session. "Explored" or "addressed" relates to the client having learned about the issues at hand. "Processed" related to the client having resolved the emotional blockage causing his or her emotional reactivity. "Integrated" relates to the client having incorporated successfully the "processed" issues into his or her schema.

Step 4:

Using the vignette in Step 1 as an example, a condensed sentence for segment 1 would read, "Client explored spousal conflict regarding finances with resulting mutual criticism." Segment 2 can be addressed in the following manner, "Client is fearful of expressing violence when criticized." Segment 3 can be written in this manner, "Client explored his emotional reactivity, parental criticism, and associated beliefs of being a failure." The complete entry would read as follows: "Client explored spousal conflict regarding finances with resulting mutual criticism. He's fearful of expressing violence when criticized. He explored his emotional reactivity, parental criticism, and associated belief system of being a failure. Client presented anger and sadness."

The following is an example of further condensation of the statement: Client is afraid of violence and criticism. He explored emotional reactivity, parent's criticism, and the belief being failure. His affect was angry and sad.

Both statements suffice to establish and document the process of therapy. The MFT's structural code chosen to write this entry serves as a reminder of what transpired in that session. The MFT can adapt the entry to fit his or her personal style. Remember that there is no "right" way of writing this entry. There is enough information in these two entries to help the therapist recapitulate the essence of what transpired in session. In case an opposing attorney queries the MFT about content, the MFT can read the entry, remember as much as possible, and provide the necessary information. During a deposition it is perfectly acceptable to reply: "I do not recall" to an attorney's question.

The benefits of writing such statements are:

- Extraneous data is avoided. Should the mental health records be subpoenaed, the MFT has avoided information that can cause harm to the client. Should an opposing attorney seek additional clinical information, the clinician determines how much information he or she will release when questioned. Using this protocol, the clinician is always in control of the client's information.
- The entry is concise yet complete. Using this method converts the task of writing mental records from being time-consuming to being time-effective.
- The process of therapy is documented. All the important elements of the session are present.
- The therapist can review the information and recall the essence of the session. By using personally meaningful language, the therapist can recall the nature of the session and what transpired.
- It is not necessary to be perfect: only reasonable and prudent. With time, the clinician will develop his or her personal style based on his or her degree of comfort.

Documenting Legal Issues and Challenges

When documenting legal actions based on either state law, or case law, it is imperative that clinicians establish their reasoning process from start to finish. Legal issues, by definition, require a greater degree of therapeutic duty, which is that responsibility placed upon the therapist to provide appropriate assessment, diagnosis, and treatment to their patients throughout the duration of treatment. Thus, these challenging situations, if not documented properly, can create problems for the clinician. For example, a client may kill him/herself and leave the MFT vulnerable to a malpractice action from his or her loved ones. When the MFT documents his or her appropriate management of the client's depression and suicidal ideation, he or she has a strong case to fend of an opposing attorney's consistent attack. Many clinical situations can initiate legal issues. Some of these include: breaching confidentiality to report mandated child abuse, breaching confidentiality to protect an identified victim, breaching confidentiality to report elder/dependent abuse, breaching confidentiality to protect a patient when he or she presents a danger to self or others, terminating the therapeutic relationship when treatment is incomplete due to lack of compliance, etc.

One complex example of a legal/ethical issue arising in psychotherapy or counseling is the management of a suicidal patient who indicates suicidal ideation yet tells the MFT that he or she will not harm him/herself. In this case, the standard of care dictates that MFTs must take reasonable steps to protect the life of the client yet the MFT may not have enough information to determine if the client presents a risk to him/herself. The MFT's bind lies in having enough information to suspect that a degree of risk of harm to self exists yet the client refuses to provide additional information about his or her degree of risk to harm him/herself. Rather than allow him/herself to be trapped in the bind, it serves this MFT to take reasonable steps to manage this client.

The suicidology literature is replete with clinical examples of what constitutes "reasonable steps." Bruce Bongar has written an excellent book (See the Reference Section) on this subject. For documentation purposes, the clinician begins documenting his or her assessment of the presenting crisis issue. This includes the clinician's observation of the client's behavior related to suicidality, results of psychometric testing (including use of Beck's Depression Inventory and Mental Status Exam), complete client history (including history of previous suicide attempts), family history (including history of suicides in the family), and history of previous treatment. MFTs note information in the progress notes. Next, the MFT supports his or her diagnosis with observable behaviors and their duration. Third, the clinician documents specific clinical interventions used to manage the possible suicidality (these may include referrals to psychiatrist and personal physician, increased telephone contact, "no-suicide" contract, voluntary hospitalization, etc.). If none of these interventions succeeds, the clinician faces a legal challenge, which is the possibility of breaching confidentiality to protect the life of the client. Should the therapist decide to do so or decides that the clinical information available does not warrant a breach of confidentiality, he or she begins the process of documenting his or her reasoning process for making one of the latter decisions and carrying it out.

The MFT begins the documentation process by noting the specific legal guidelines permitting the breach of confidentiality related to the issue at hand. Next, the clinician describes the clinical circumstances leading to this decision in detail. Third, the MFT establishes the specific action he or she followed including the names and roles of individuals involved, dates and times, and why they were involved. In any breach of confidentiality (as mandated or permitted by law), the clinician divulges only that clinical information about the client, and no more, that will permit the restoration of safety. MFTs note that process is carefully. It is important to remember that breaching confidentiality is a serious matter therefore the breach must be limited to the minimum information necessary to create clinical safety. Last, the clinician documents the outcome of the therapist's action. An example of clinical notes regarding a breach of confidentiality due to suicide follows:

> **11-29-95: Mr. Doe reported that his feelings of despair are becoming more intense and that he is afraid that he cannot handle them. He states that he does not have a way out of his problems except to end his life. He states he is ready to die to stop the feelings of hopelessness. He states he has a gun and will kill himself when he goes home. I reminded him of his "no-suicide" contract, his connection with his family and friends, and that once he kills himself there is no return. I asked him to have himself admitted to the hospital**

under his own volition and he refused. Under the present circumstances, my clinical impression is that his current mental state is such that he presents a danger to self and without intervention, he will commit suicide immediately (California Evidence Code 1024). Therefore, I have called his wife and disclosed to her Mr. Doe's present mental state. I have called the Psychiatric Assessment Team for an evaluation in my office for possible involuntary hospitalization (California Welfare and Institutions Code 5150). After the evaluation, the PAT Team decided that he was a danger to self and took him to the hospital for admission and observation for the next 72 hours. Since I have privileges at the hospital, I will consult with his psychiatrist to coordinate treatment after he is released. (Therapist's Signature).

Treatment Plans as Assessment and Documentation Tools

Expert witnesses would agree that one of the most important failings of clinicians accused of malpractice or wrongdoing is the inability to support their proposed, ongoing, or completed treatment. When deposing accused clinicians, opposing attorneys ask these therapists: "Were you ever aware during the time you treated my client that your proposed treatment was ineffective?" On the other hand, they may ask: "Can you show the jury where in your records did you document the treatment you proposed to my client?" Another question they may ask is: "What steps did you take to determine that my client no longer required or benefited from your treatment?" Unfortunately, these clinicians will provide answers that fail to support appropriate documentation. They also fail to recognize the importance treatment plans play in the overall documentation of the clinician's therapeutic duty. A woe for MFTs rests in not knowing when a client will become a threat of harm to self or others. This is an unpredictable aspect of clinical practice. Consider the following scenario:

A friend refers a client to a psychotherapist. The friend read in an article that this clinician treats anxiety issues with finger tapping. Being desperate to resolve his anxiety, the client makes an appointment. On the first appointment, the clinician takes a thorough history and discusses the proposed treatment, which strikes the client as being "weird" and "strange." The client tells the clinician he will think about it call later for an appointment. Instead, the client makes an appointment with a licensed clinical psychologist and discusses the proposed treatment. The psychologist tells client that this treatment falls below the standard of care and practiced by incompetent clinicians. After much consideration, the client submits a complaint to the clinician's state licensing board describing the statement made by the clinician and the licensed psychologist.

Later, a Board investigator visits the clinician and takes a statement from him. A week later, he receives a request for his records regarding this client. The board investigator turn over the records to the Board's expert witness and requests that the expert witness focus specifically on the documentation of the proposed treatment, the presence of informed consent discussing risks and benefits of this treatment and the clinician's scope of competence regarding the proposed treatment.

Upon receiving the records, the Board's expert witness searches for the following documents: a) informed consent addressing the risks and benefits of the treatment, b) a statement of the clinician's scope of competence regarding this treatment, and c) a reasonable treatment plan addressing the progressive phases of treatment including goals and objectives. If any of these components of treatment records are missing, then the Board's investigation regarding the clinician providing substandard care continue and the case will be turned over to the state's attorney general for prosecution. The clinician faces the danger of being unable to create a defense because he lacks the necessary documentation about the initial encounter with the client. In this meeting, he discussed the nature of the proposed unconventional treatment with the client, that he informed the client regarding the risks and benefits of this treatment, and that he informed the client regarding his scope of competence related to this treatment.

The Appropriate Use of the Treatment Plan

How can clinicians support their treatment if they face a challenge in a legal or board action? To answer this question, it is important to understand the nature of this documentation. Licensed clinicians must keep mental health records that meet the standards of the profession, including the therapeutic duty to treat appropriately. In addition to California Health and Safety Code 123130 requiring treatment plans as part of the set of records provided to clients when requested, the sole and best documentation tool to support proposed and ongoing treatment is a treatment plan as part of the mental health records. It serves two important functions: a) to document the proposed treatment and b) to assess the progress of treatment.

Aside for voluminous notes, the treatment plan is an effective and proven tool to support proposed treatment that is prudent and reasonable and conforms to the standard of care. In addition, a treatment plan serves to help the clinician assess for the effectiveness of the proposed treatment throughout the treatment process. MFTs modify the treatment plan as needed and they create a new one as presenting issues arise. Thus, the treatment plan serves to document that the proposed, ongoing, and completed treatments are reasonable and prudent. A reasonable and prudent clinician knows the following about treatment plans:

- They serve to document the proposed treatment.
- They separate treatment into four distinct stages: Crisis Phase, Beginning Phase, Middle Phase, and Ending Phase.
- The Crisis Phase addresses issues requiring immediate attention, like suicide, other harm to self or others.

- The Beginning Phase addresses the preparatory phase of treatment.
- The Middle Phase addresses the actual treatment that attempts to resolve the presenting issue or issues.
- The Ending Phase addresses closure, saying a healthy good-bye, and prepares the client for termination.
- Each phase contains goals and objectives. Goals are a broad-based direction that attempts to resolve the presenting issue. Objectives are the steps taken to meet the Goals.
- Treatment plans serve to assess if the proposed treatment is effective in resolving the presenting issue.
- Treatment plans serve to assess if the client met the goals of treatment and if he or she is ready to terminate.
- Treatment plans serve to document that the continuing treatment is in the best interests of the client.
- Treatment plans serve to document that the clinician is avoiding taking financial advantage of the client. This is extremely important when the clinician renders long-term, amorphous, and undefined treatment.
- Treatment plans serve to document and support that the clinician meets his or her therapeutic duty of assessing, diagnosing, and treating according to the standard of care.

Writing Discharge Summaries

MFTs write discharge summaries when the client completes the goals of therapy as defined by the treatment plan. This step documents that the clinician and the client have completed treatment regardless of success. For example, the client ends treatment without informing the clinician of his or her decision to terminate and discontinues treatment. Alternatively, the client completed the goals of treatment successfully. In another example, the client refuses to cooperate with treatment. Each example requires a specific discharge summary to indicate the nature of termination. Most importantly, the discharge summary emphasizes that the MFT's therapeutic duty owed to the client has terminated and that the clinician is no longer responsible for continuing patient care. By definition, this asserts that the MFT did not abandon the client. The summary needs to document that the possibility of future therapy has been discussed with the client and that he or she is welcome to return should the need arise. An example of a discharge summary follows:

> **Mr. Doe achieved completion of his goals in therapy and states that he no longer feels depressed or suicidal. He states that he has reconnected with his family, reconnected with his friends, is eating and sleeping well, and has found a joy in living. He states that he is no longer taking medication for depression and that he has maintained his stability for over one year. He states that his prospects for employment are very positive. We have addressed**

> **and processed termination and he states he feels confident he will able to maintain a positive outlook on life without additional counseling. We have both agreed that he can return at any time to address future presenting issues should he require help. Case closed. (Therapist's Signature)**

Another example follows:

> **Mr. Doe did not call for an appointment as promised. I left several messages were on his answering machine and he did not return them. According to the informed consent signed by the client, the client's lack of compliance is a reason to end treatment without patient abandonment. As of today, treatment has ended and the therapeutic duty owed to the client no longer exists. Case is closed. (Therapist's Signature).**

Clinical Charting for Hospital Consultations

MFTs receive hospital privileges throughout California as Allied Health Professionals. Some of the duties include providing treatment within the confines of a hospital setting and within their scope of practice. Some of their duties include treating their own hospitalized patients, providing family therapy to the families of hospitalized clients, and providing consultations to physicians when requested. This guideline will help MFTs provide legally prudent documentation when performing such consults.

<u>Reasons for Consultation:</u>
This section addresses the reason for the consultation. Usually, MFTs receive a request from a physician to evaluate a patient for a particular reason. Sometimes the MFT's own patient requests a consultation. This section needs to address scope of practice issues and relationship issues.

<u>Patient History:</u>
This section addresses the patient's complete medical history. As MFTs, we have a therapeutic duty to know the medical history of the patient and how it may be affecting mental health. In the hospital chart, a resident or the attending physician completes the patient's medical history. Thus, the MFT can review the history and state in the notes that he or she reviewed the patient history.

<u>Family History:</u>
This section addresses the patient's historical and present pertinent social and family history. The MFT notes significant relationships along with important social resources visiting the patient, including the frequency of visits.

<u>Mental Status Examination:</u>
This section addresses the evaluation of the patient's mental and physical state. This includes the following:

Appearance	Attention
Behavior	Orientation to
Speech	time, place, person

Emotion
Mood, affect, congruency
Thought processes
Stream of thought, continuity of thought
Content of thought, abstraction
Perception
Memory, immediate, recent, remote
Judgment
Intelligence and information
Insight

It is not necessary to include all these elements. Only the most important ones as the MFT deems necessary need to be included.

Observations:
This section addresses the patient's process that the MFT has observed in relation to the purpose of the evaluation. If the evaluation addresses the impact of depression on personal relationships, then the MFT must note how the depression is impacting the patient's inability to maintain contact with significant others while in the hospital, how the depression is manifested in the patient's behavior, those specific behaviors preventing contact with others, the severity of the depression, etc.

Recommendations:
In this section, the MFT notes what steps he or she believes are necessary to create a change in the patient's mental state. This may include educating the nursing staff, consulting with other mental health practitioners, educating family members, increasing the number of visits by significant others while the patient is in the hospital, etc.

After completing and documenting the evaluation, the nursing staff can benefit greatly from the MFT sharing the results with the individuals working directly with the patient.

Chapter 5

Subpoenas

Subpoenas

Subpoenas are a legal court order issued by attorneys informing clinicians that they are part of a lawsuit, requesting an item or items that the clinician holds and are pertinent to a malpractice action. They may request the presence of a clinician for testimony either at the courthouse or a designated office. The former is identified as a "Trial or Hearing." The latter is identified as a "Deposition."

Years ago, only judges could sign a court order or subpoena. However, judges were burdened by a large number of subpoenas required in legal transactions and the legislature gave attorneys the right to be officers of the court. This action allowed attorneys to issue subpoenas and their subpoenas have the same legal effect as those signed by a judge.

The Different Types of Subpoenas

There are several types of subpoenas that clinicians may encounter in their practice and each has a specific function which I will address later in the chapter. Being court orders, subpoenas must be complied with. A clinician who fails to comply may be responsible for the opposing attorney's costs to reissue a new one. The subpoenas pertinent to mental health clinicians are the following:

1. The Summons and Complaint Forms
2. A Civil Subpoena for Personal Appearance at Trial or Hearing
3. A Civil Subpoena for Personal Appearance and Production of Documents and Things at Trial or Hearing
4. Deposition Subpoena for Personal Appearance
5. Deposition Subpoena for Production of Business Records
6. Deposition Subpoena for Personal Appearance and Production of Documents and Things

A valid subpoena must be accompanied by the following documents:

1. A Notice to Consumer or Employee and Objection: This serves to establish that the person whose information is being sought has been informed of this process. The clinician uses the

Objection portion of this form to inform the opposing attorney why he or she is unable to comply. For example, the subpoena failed to include a Notice to Consumer and isn't legally binding.

2. Proof of Service: This document provides proof that the subpoena was served within the legal time limit.
3. Declaration of Records Released: This form is used when the subpoena only requests business records. The clinician records requested records that weren't sent and the reason. For example, the records were shredded, the records were damaged in a flood, etc.

The Purpose of Subpoenas

1. **The Summons and Complaint Forms**: This subpoena informs clinicians that they are being sued and the reason for a lawsuit. Clinicians should contact a defense attorney to respond to the subpoena.
2. **A Civil Subpoena for Personal Appearance at Trial or Hearing**: This subpoena requires the presence of the clinician at trial or a hearing.
3. **A Civil Subpoena for Personal Appearance and Production of Documents and Things at Trial or Hearing:** This subpoena requests the appearance of the clinician at trial or a hearing and the clinician must bring a copy of his or her extended records.
4. **Deposition Subpoena for Personal Appearance**: This subpoena requires that the clinician attend a deposition to answer questions from an attorney involved in a legal case where the clinician is a third party.
5. **Deposition Subpoena for Production of Business Records:** The clinician is required to provide client records, financial and clinical, to attorneys for a deposition.
6. **Deposition Subpoena for Personal Appearance and Production of Documents and Things:** This deposition requires the clinician's attendance at a deposition and requires he or she to provide a broad spectrum of client information, including client records, financial records, sign-in sheets, additional information pamphlets provided to the client, etc.

Managing Subpoenas Safely

All clinicians can experience a degree of anxiety after receiving a subpoena. It may be that the clinician wants to avoid making errors and causing problems for him or herself. A simple and efficient method to assure compliance follows:

1. A subpoena sent to a clinician being sued will arrive by mail. A subpoena sent to third parties must be hand delivered. Third parties are those clinician who provide treatment to a client involved in a lawsuit.
2. Upon receiving the subpoena, make sure it contains the required components which include the subpoena itself, the notice to consumer, the proof of service and the disposition of records.
3. Next, determine the type of subpoena you received. It could any of the following:
4. Summons and Complaint which informs the clinician that he or she is being sued and the reason for the lawsuit.
5. A Civil Subpoena for Personal Appearance at Trial or Hearing which informs the clinician that he or she is required to be present at a trial or hearing on a specific date, time and place.
6. A Civil Subpoena for Personal Appearance and Production of Documents and Things which requires the clinician to be present at a deposition and all items identified on the subpoena.
7. A Deposition Subpoena for Personal Appearance which requires the clinician to be present at a deposition on a specific date, time and location.
8. A Deposition Subpoena for Production of Business Records which requires the clinician to submit treatment records and other information related to the client's treatment. This request can include the client's financial records and treatment records.
9. Deposition Subpoena for Personal Appearance and Production of Documents and Things which requires the clinician to be present at a deposition at a specific time, place and date. The clinician is also required to bring all information regarding the involved client. This request is broader than the one requesting Business Records.
10. If the subpoena indicates that you are part of a legal action, consult with your attorney.
11. If the subpoena involves your client, inform him or her about the subpoena. If the client directs you to withhold the records, remind the client that you must comply with the court order. Document this interaction.
12. If your client directs you to communicate with his or her attorney, obtain a written release of information and provide the necessary information allowing the attorney to make an informed decision about managing the records. Document this interaction.
13. Remind the attorney that you must comply with the release of records within the time indicated in the subpoena. The attorney can request a hold on the subpoena from the court. If you haven't received notice from the attorney about issuing a hold, release the records and document your decision and action.
14. Ultimately, its important to assure that you understand what the subpoena requests, how you're going to manage it and to carry it out within the allotted time.

Actual Samples of Subpoenas

A full complement of the subpoenas discussed in this chapter can be found at the following California government website: http://courtinfo.ca.gov/cgi-bin/forms.cgi
After accessing the page, click on "No form group found" and choose "Subpoenas" then press "See Forms."

Document #1 Notice to Consumer

This is the "Notice to Consumer." It tells the recipient of the subpoena that the client has been informed that his or her mental health records are being requested. This form must accompany the subpoena to be valid.

Document #2 Proof of Service

This is the "Proof of Service." This document establishes that the subpoena was delivered legally. The recipient of the subpoena has 15 days from the date of service to produce the records, unless instructed differently by the client or the client's attorney.

Document # 3 Declaration of Records Released

This is the "Declaration of Records Released." This document is completed by the recipient of the subpoena. In this example, no records existed because they had been shredded. Therefore, it was returned to the person requesting records stating that "Records do not exist." If records did exist, then the statement would read: "All records enclosed."

Document # 1

NEY OR PARTY WITHOUT ATTORNEY *(Name and Address)*: TELEPHONE NO.: FOR COURT USE ONLY

[redacted] & Associates (805) [redacted]
:aig R. [redacted], Esq.,
[redacted] Santa Barbara St., 3rd Floor
:n Luis Obispo, CA 93401-0000

Ref. No. or File No.

NEY FOR *(Name)*: L.A. Hearne Co., et al.

ame of court, judicial district or branch court, if any:
ınta Barbara Superior Court
ok Division
.2-M East Cook Street
ınta Maria, CA 93454-5165

IFF/PETITIONER:
sus [redacted]

DANT/RESPONDENT:
A. [redacted] Co., et al.

NOTICE TO CONSUMER OR EMPLOYEE AND OBJECTION
(Code Civ. Proc.,§§ 1985.3, 1985.6)

CASE NUMBER:
SM[redacted]

NOTICE TO CONSUMER OR EMPLOYEE

TO *(name)*: Jesus Manuel [redacted]

PLEASE TAKE NOTICE THAT **REQUESTING PARTY** *(name)*: [redacted] & Associates
SEEKS YOUR RECORDS FOR EXAMINATION by the parties to this action on *(Specify Date)*: August 29, 2002
The records are described in the subpoena directed to **witness** *(specify name and address of person or entity from whom records are sought)*: Wilson [redacted], MD [redacted] N. La Cumbre Road, Ste. C, , Santa Barbara, CA 93110-0000

A copy of the subpoena is attached.

If you object to the production of these records, YOU MUST DO ONE OF THE FOLLOWING BEFORE THE DATE SPECIFIED IN ITEM a. OR b. BELOW:

a. If you are a party to the above-entitled action, you must file a motion pursuant to Code of Civil Procedure section 1987.1 to quash or modify the subpoena and give notice of that motion to the **witness** and the **deposition officer** named in the subpoena at least five days before the date set for the production of the records.

b. If you are not party to this action, you must serve on the **requesting party** and on the **witness,** before the date set for production of the records, a written objection that states the specific grounds on which production of such records should be prohibited. You may use the form below to object and state the grounds for your objection. You must complete the Proof of Service on the reverse side indicating whether you personally served or mailed the objection. The objection should **not** be filed with the court. **WARNING:** IF YOUR OBJECTION IS NOT RECEIVED BEFORE THE DATE SPECIFIED IN ITEM 1, YOUR RECORDS MAY BE PRODUCED AND MAY BE AVAILABLE TO ALL PARTIES.

YOU OR YOUR ATTORNEY MAY CONTACT THE UNDERSIGNED to determine whether an agreement can be reached in writing to cancel or limit the scope of the subpoena. If no such agreement is reached, and if you are not otherwise represented by an attorney in this action, YOU SHOULD CONSULT AN ATTORNEY TO ADVISE YOU OF YOUR RIGHTS OF PRIVACY.

Date: July 30, 2002

Craig R. [redacted] Esq. ▶ /S/
(TYPE OR PRINT NAME) (SIGNATURE OF ☐ REQUESTING PARTY ☒ ATTORNEY

OBJECTION BY NON-PARTY TO PRODUCTION OF RECORDS

☐ I object to the production of all of my records specified in the subpoena.
☐ I object only to the production of the following specified records:

The specific grounds for my objection are as follows:

Date:

▶
(TYPE OR PRINT NAME) (SIGNATURE)

(See reverse for proof of service)

Document # 2

PLAINTIFF/PETITIONER: James V. Doe	CASE NUMBER
DEFENDANT/RESPONDENT: Richard T. Client	XZ-123456

PROOF OF SERVICE OF DEPOSITION SUBPOENA FOR PRODUCTION OF BUSINESS RECORDS

1. I served this *Deposition Subpoena for Production of Business Records* by personally delivering a copy to the person served as follows:
   a. Person served *(name)*: Nancy K Therapist, MFT
   b. Address where served: 1234 Anystreet CA 95555
   c. Date of delivery: 12-12-02
   d. Time of delivery: 12:00 PM
   e. (1) ☐ Witness fees were paid.
      Amount: . . . . $ ______________
      (2) ☐ Copying fees were paid.
      Amount: . . . . $ ______________
   f. Fee for service: . . . . $ ______________
2. I received this subpoena for service on *(date)*: 12-12-02
3. Person serving:
   a. ☐ Not a registered California process server.
   b. ☒ California sheriff or marshal.
   c ☐ Registered California process server.
   d. ☐ Employee or independent contractor of a registered California process server.
   e. ☐ Exempt from registration under Business and Professions Code section 22350(b).
   f. ☐ Registered professional photocopier.
   g. ☐ Exempt from registration under Business and Professions Code section 22451.
   h. Name, address, telephone number, and, if applicable, county of registration and number:

I declare under penalty of perjury under the laws of the State of California that the foregoing is true and correct.

Date:

▶ ______________________________
(SIGNATURE)

(For California sheriff or marshal use only)
I certify that the foregoing is true and correct.

Date:

▶ [signature]
(SIGNATURE)

982(a)(15.2) [Rev. January 1, 2000]

PROOF OF SERVICE
DEPOSITION SUBPOENA FOR PRODUCTION

JURISEARCH
www.jurisearch.com

Page two

Document # 3

DECLARATION OF RECORDS RELEASED

TO: J. Smith, J.D.

RE: John Doe SSN: 123-45-6789

DOB: 1-1-50 Your File: XZ-12345

CERTIFICATION OF RECORDS RELEASED

I am duly authorized as a qualified witness with the authority to certify records for ***Santa Barbara Cottage Hospital***, Medical Records Department, Pueblo @ Bath St., Santa Barbara, CA 93102-0689.

The records were delivered to the agent for Deposition Officer or Requesting Party's representative for copying pursuant to subdivision (e) of section 1560 or section 1158 of the Evidence Code.

To the best of my knowledge, all such records were prepared or compiled by the personnel of the above named facility in the ordinary course of business, at or near the time of the acts, conditions, or events recorded.

All documents, records, or other things called for in the subpoena or authorization have been released for photocopy **with the following exceptions:**

[redacted] Records do Not exist

This certification is limited to the information supplied to me in the attached document: records may exist under another name, another spelling, or other identifying data.

I DECLARE under penalty of perjury the foregoing is true and correct.

Executed on May 15, 2001 at Santa Barbara, California

Signed ____________________

Clinical Example # 1

A young woman has been experiencing sexual harassment at work. A friend tells her of what a wonderful and supportive therapist Isobel was with her. She calls Isobel for an appointment and Isobel tells her she does not testify for clients and she will treat her only under this condition. The client agrees. Treatment ends successfully after one year. A few months later, Isobel receives two subpoenas: one for her records for this client and the other requiring her to testify on behalf of this client regarding a recent sexual harassment claim by this client. Isobel decides to ignore the subpoenas since she told the client she would not testify. Several months later, Isobel receives a letter from an attorney indicating that she is being sued for injuring this client by not testifying on her behalf. Additionally, Isobel receives a letter from the BBS indicating to her that an investigator will set up an appointment to talk to her about this case.

Questions for Clinical Example # 1

1. What, in your opinion, is the first error made by Isobel? What led her to make this error?
2. What should Isobel have known about subpoenas prior to initiating treatment with this client?
3. Since the client lost her case in the sexual harassment lawsuit, she is now suing Isobel for not responding to the subpoena. Do you believe that Isobel will win the lawsuit? Why or why not?
4. Had Isobel consulted with you, what would you have advised her when she received the subpoena a year ago?

Chapter Questions

1. A Marshall comes to your office and hands you a subpoena. He tells you he wants the records that moment and is willing to wait for you to copy them. You look at his badge and his appearance is imposing. You may feel threatened. What do you do?
2. Upon receiving a subpoena, you contact the client's attorney and are told to release the records. You find that it has been over seven years since you saw the client and the records have been shredded. What do you do?
3. You receive a subpoena for records. Upon contacting your client's attorney, she tells you not to release the records because they will hurt the client's case. You call the copying service and tell them what you have been instructed to do by your client's attorney. A few days later, you receive a call from the opposing attorney who is furious with you and tells you he will have you found in contempt of court (disobeying the Court) and have you thrown in jail. What do you do?
4. When facing an authority figure with a badge that threatens to take you to jail if you don't cooperate, what would be your greatest personal challenge as defined by you Internal Reality Perspective?

Chapter 20

Supervision of Trainees and Interns

Supervision Issues

The supervisor's role is important in the training of MFT interns and trainees. They serve as role models, mentors, and guides throughout the clinical learning process. The relationship between supervisor and supervisee begins in a power differential with the supervisor having greater knowledge, training, and experience than the supervisee. The supervisor evaluates the supervisee during their clinical experience progresses. Because of this increased responsibility, supervisors must know how to establish and respect appropriate clinical boundaries with their supervisees. Supervisors must know the appropriate application of California laws and CAMFT ethical standards as they relate to clinical practice and supervisory experience.

As part of their legal and ethical responsibilities, supervisors must continuously assess the supervisee's scope of competence (training, knowledge, and experience) before they assign cases to supervisees. This step helps avoid supervisees from treating clients that are beyond their clinical abilities. Supervisors must also know their own scope of competence regarding the management of cases with supervisees. Most importantly, supervisors are required to respect the trust that exists inherently in this important, yet fragile, relationship. They serve as positive role models in respecting this trust. Since their licenses are at stake during the course of supervision, it behooves supervisors to stay abreast of updates in California laws and CAMFT ethics. California law requires that supervisors receive 6 hours of continuing education in supervision issues every two years. These hours are included in the 36 hours MFTs complete every two years. Below are some important legal requirements for interns/trainees/supervisors:

- The supervisor must hold a valid license, which is not under suspension or probation.
- The supervisor must have been licensed for two years.
- The supervisor is responsible for the scope of competence of the intern/trainee.
- The supervisor must complete a 6-hour supervision training within the two year period preceding supervision and every two years thereafter.
- The supervisor is responsible for the application of California laws and CAMFT ethical standards by the intern/trainee.

- The supervisor must have practiced psychotherapy or directly supervised applicable interns or associates who perform psychotherapy as part of their clinical practice in two of the last five years immediately preceding the commencement of supervision.
- Whether a volunteer or a paid employee, the intern/trainee will be held accountable to the same standards. Interns/employees are not to be treated as independent contractors.
- Trainees shall receive an average of at least one hour of direct supervision for every five hours of client contact in which experience is gained.
- Interns shall receive an average of at least one hour of direct supervision contact for every 10 hours of client contact in each setting in which experience is gained (One hour of direct supervisor contact means one hour of face-to-face contact on an individual basis or two hours of face-to-face contact in a group of not more than eight persons).
- One third of the hours may include direct supervision contact and other professional enrichment activities (personal therapy, up to 100 hours which will be tripled in value).
- Trainees can only accrue experience in the following settings: a governmental entity, a school, college or university, a nonprofit and charitable corporation, a licensed health facility, as defined in Sections 1250, 1250.2, and 1250.3 of the Health and Safety Code, a social rehabilitation facility or a community treatment facility, as defined in subdivision (a) of Section 1502 of the Health and Safety Code, a pediatric day health and respite care facility, as defined in Section 1760.2 of the Health and Safety Code, or a licensed alcoholism or drug abuse recovery or treatment facility, as defined in Section 11834.02 of the Health and Safety Code, if the experience is gained by the trainee solely as part of the position for which he or she is employed.
- When an intern employed in private practice is supervised by someone other than the employer, the supervisor must be employed by and practice at the same site as the intern's employer.
- Interns and trainees are not allowed to gain any experience under the supervision of a spouse, relative, or domestic partner. Additionally, interns and trainees are not allowed to receive supervision from anyone who has ever been their therapist.
- Interns cannot begin private practice until they are registered with the Board. Interns are not allowed to pay for supervision in a private practice setting.
- Trainees and interns cannot be paid by the patient. They must be paid by the employer.
- Trainees and interns can only perform services at the place of employment or where the employer regularly conducts business (this can include other locations). They must be under direct control of their supervisor.
- Interns/trainees are not allowed to own part of their employer business.
- Interns/trainees may receive up to $500 in remuneration for expenses in a work setting and

they will still be considered employees. Any figure above that, they will be considered as being independent contractors. The Board has the authority to audit records from an applicant.

- Experience shall not be gained under the supervision of an individual who has provided therapeutic services to that applicant, nor has had a sexual relationship with that applicant, nor is married to that applicant.
- Individual supervision means one supervisor and one person being supervised.
- Group supervision means a group of no more than eight persons being supervised by one supervisor.
- Separate supervision is required for each work setting in which a supervisee is gaining hours of experience.
- A supervisor may supervise an unlimited number of interns and trainees in any appropriate work setting other than private practice, but is limited to supervising two interns when these interns are employed in private practice.
- A supervisor shall give at least one week's written notice to an intern or trainee of the supervisor's intent not to certify any further hours of experience for this person. A supervisor who has not provided such notice shall sign for hours of experience obtained in good faith where such supervisor actually provided the required supervision.
- Only three unlicensed interns my be supervised in private practice at any time.
- For information on corporations, see Business and Professions Code 44980.45.
- Interns and trainees are required to inform their clients, before beginning therapy, that they are unlicensed and working under the supervision of a licensed marriage and family therapist, licensed clinical social worker, licensed psychologist or licensed physician certified in psychiatry by the American Board of Psychiatry and Neurology.
- Licensees and registered interns are required to notify the BBS within thirty days of a change of address.

Dual Relationships With Interns/Trainees

Business and Professions Code 4982(r) explicitly states that any conduct in the supervision of any registered intern or registered trainee by any licensee that violates this chapter or any rules or regulations adopted by the board (will be considered as unprofessional conduct). If the supervisor becomes involved in a second relationship with the intern/trainee while in supervision, then the supervisor has created a dual relationship. Breaking this trust and dependency creates loss of objectivity or coercion. If the supervisor violates the supervisee's trust and dependency, then the supervisor has broken the law. He or she created a harmful dual relationship due to the presence of coercion or loss of objectivity. Examples of harmful dual relationships include: having the supervisee act as a secretary/housekeeper for the supervisor, having the supervisee run personal errands for the supervisor, having the supervisee baby-sit for the supervisor, and most importantly, having a sexual relationship with a supervisee.

Interns and Trainees as Employees

California law explicitly states that supervisees are employees and are not independent contractors. Only licensed MFTs are independent contractors. An independent contractor is an employment category described by the Internal Revenue Service where the "contractor" is responsible for paying his or her own taxes to the appropriate government agencies. The employer does not deduct any withholding taxes from the "draw" or payment received by the "contractor." The employer must file a form called "1099" with the I.R.S. every year stating the payment the "contractor" received during that year. As employees, supervisees must receive a "W-2" form every year, they must have payroll deductions taken from their income, and they must receive worker's compensation insurance. Without these conditions, the business relationship is illegal.

Supervisees cannot have ownership in the place of business that employs them. In addition, they do not pay for rental space, telephone lines, office equipment, etc. (Independent contractors can be charged for these items). Supervisees cannot set the fee with their clients; only the supervisor can. Should the BBS decide to audit the records of the supervisor/employer regarding the supervisee and if the employee status does not exist in this relationship, the supervisee will most likely lose the hours claimed in this traineeship/internship and the supervisor's license will be in jeopardy.

Additional Requirements for Interns/Trainees

Interns/trainees must identify their supervisory relationship with their clients at the beginning of therapy. It serves them to discuss with clients the role the supervisor will play in the supervisory relationship. Additionally, the supervisee identifies the supervisor by name, status (i.e., Ph.D., MFT, MD, or LCSW), how the supervisor will interact with the supervisee, and how they will manage the client's confidentiality. Supervisees must sign a form stating that they have read and understood their reporting requirements regarding child abuse and elder/dependent abuse. This form is kept in their employee file.

Advertising

Interns and trainees are allowed to advertise; however, they must follow specific guidelines. Ethical guidelines are discussed in Chapter 37. Legal guidelines are found in the Business and Professions Code. Also, see chapter 21 "Advertising."

Supervisor's Responsibilities

Supervisor's responsibilities are found in Business and Professions Code 1833.1.

- Any person supervising an intern or trainee (hereinafter "supervisor") within California shall comply with the requirements set forth below and shall, prior to the commencement of such supervision, sign under penalty of perjury the "Responsibility Statement for Supervisors of a Marriage, Family and Child Counselor Trainee or Intern" (Revised 1-00) requiring that:
- The supervisor possess and maintain a current valid California license as either a marriage, family and child counselor, licensed clinical social worker, licensed psychologist, or physician who is certified in psychiatry as specified in Section 4980.40 (a) of the Code; and
- Has been licensed in California as specified in Section 4980.40 (f) of the Code, and in any other state, for a total of at least two years prior to commencing supervision.
- If such supervisor is not licensed as a marriage, family, and child counselor, he or she shall have sufficient experience, training, and education in marriage, family, and child counseling to competently practice marriage, family, and child counseling in California.
- The supervisor keeps him/herself informed of developments in marriage, family, and child counseling and in California law governing the practice of marriage, family, and child counseling.
- The supervisor has a current license in good standing and will immediately inform the intern or trainee of any disciplinary actions, including revocation or suspension, even if stayed, probation terms, inactive license status, or lapse on licensing, that affects the supervisor's ability or right to supervise.
- The supervisor has practiced psychotherapy for at least two (2) years within the five (5) year period immediately preceding any supervision and has averaged at least five (5) patient/client contact hours per week.
- The supervisor has had sufficient experience, training, and education in the area of clinical supervision to competently supervise trainees and interns.
- Effective January 1, 2000, supervisors who are licensed by the board shall complete a minimum of six (6) hours of supervision training or coursework every two years. This training or coursework may apply towards the continuing education requirements set forth in Sections 4980.54 and 4996.22 of the Code.
- The supervisor knows and understands the laws and regulations pertaining to both the supervision of trainees and interns and the experience required for licensing as a marriage, family, and child counselor.

- The supervisor shall ensure that the extent, kind, and quality of counseling performed is consistent with the education, training, and experience of the intern or trainee.
- The supervisor shall monitor and evaluate the extent, kind, and quality of counseling performed by the intern or trainee by direct observation, review of audio or video tapes of therapy, review of progress and process notes and other treatment records, or by any other means deemed appropriate by the supervisor.
- The supervisor shall address with the intern the manner in which emergencies will be handled.
- The supervisor agrees not to provide supervision to a trainee unless the trainee is a volunteer or employed by one of the following settings permitted by law:
  a) government entity, b) school, college, or university, c) nonprofit or charitable corporation, d) a licensed health facility (Health and Code Sections 1250, 1250.2 and 1250.3), e) a social rehabilitation facility or a community treatment facility (Health Code Section 1252(a)) g) a pediatric day health and respite care facility (Health and Safety Code Section 1760.2).
- The supervisor agrees not to provide supervision to an intern unless the intern is a volunteer or employed in one of the following work settings permitted by law:
  a) a government entity, b) a school, college, or university, c) a nonprofit or charitable corporation, d) a licensed health facility (Health and Safety Code Sections 1250, 1250.2, and 1250.3), e) a social rehabilitation facility or a community treatment facility (Health Code Section 1252(a)), g) a pediatric day health and respite care facility (Health and Safety Code Section 1760.2), h) a licensed alcoholism or drug abuse recovery or treatment facility (Health and Safety Code Section 11834.02), and h) a private practice as specified in Section 4980.4 (f).
- Each supervisor shall provide the intern or trainee with the original signed "Responsibility Statement for Supervisors of a Marriage, Family, and Child Counselor Intern or Trainee" (Revised 1-00) prior to the commencement of any counseling or supervision. The intern shall provide the board with his or her signed "Responsibility Statement for Supervisors of a Marriage, Family, and Child Counselor Intern or Trainee" (Revised 1-00) from each supervisor upon application for licensure. The trainee shall provide the board with his or her signed "Responsibility Statement for Supervisors of a Marriage, Family, and Child Counselor Intern or Trainee" (Revised 1-00) from each supervisor upon application for internship.
- A supervisor shall give at least on (1) weeks written notice to an intern or trainee of the supervisor's intent not to certify any further hours of experience for such person. A supervisor who has not provided such notice shall sign for hours of experience obtained in good faith where such supervisor actually provided the required supervision.
- The supervisor shall obtain from any intern or trainee for which supervision will be provided, the name, address, and telephone number of the intern's or trainee's most recent supervisor and employer.

- In any setting that is not a private practice, a supervisor shall evaluate the sites where an intern or trainee will be gaining hours of experience toward licensing and shall determine that (1) the sites provide experience which is within the scope of marriage, family, and child counseling; and (2) the experience is in compliance set forth in this section.
- Upon written request of the board, the supervisor shall provide to the board any documentation which verifies the supervisor's compliance with the requirements set forth in this section.
- The supervisor's responsibility statement required by this section shall be used for supervisory relationship commencing on or after 1-1-98.
- The board shall not deny hours of experience gained towards licensing by any supervisee due to failure of his or her supervisor to complete the training or coursework requirements in subsection (a) (6).

The Supervisee's Dual Relationship With a Client Can Affect the Clinical Supervisor

The Board of Behavioral Sciences places upon clinical supervisors the responsibility to monitor the clinical development of their supervisees. Additionally, they must to assure that the supervisee avoids harming the client. Consider the following vignette:

> **Josh has been in clinical supervision as a marriage and family intern for two years. His clinical supervisor, Daniel, is a well-known and respected clinician in this community. Both meet regularly every week and Josh discusses his cases at length. Recently, one of Josh's clients made an appointment with an outside therapist to consult about her relationship with Josh. The client has been feeling more and more confused as time has passed. She asked the second therapist if it was appropriate for the therapist to hold the client in his arms during therapy. She also wanted to know if it was appropriate for the therapist to ask the client for massages during therapy. The client revealed a myriad of possible interactions that considered as a foundation of a harmful dual relationship. Not wanting to give a legal opinion, the second therapist referred the client to an attorney knowledgeable in malpractice actions for additional consultation.**

The consultation with the attorney reinforced the second clinician's suspicions, however of greater importance was the possible negligent behavior of the clinical supervisor. The client was confused because she never had had contact with the clinical supervisor. The attorney went on to explain that the clinical supervisor was directly responsible for the intern's clinical behavior and that there was a very strong possibility that she could sue both the intern and clinical supervisor for malpractice.

Some clinical supervisors may say: "This will never happen to me." I remind these clinicians that it is impossible to predict when something like this can happen. I advocate that each clinical supervisor take extra steps to make sure that his or her clinical supervisees maintain appropriate therapeutic relationships with clients, that the supervisee provides assessment, diagnosis, and treatment that meets the standard of care, and that the client isn't being harmed in any way. At minimum, the clinical supervisor can insist on reviewing recording of the supervisee's sessions. At maximum, the supervisor can observe the supervisee's clinical interactions and regularly review the mental health records. Failure to carry out these actions will open the door for a malpractice action against the clinical supervisor due to failure to supervise appropriately.

Contractual Agreements

One of the greatest areas of contention between supervisor and supervisee can occur after the supervisee leaves the supervisor's practice and starts his or her own practice. The supervisee takes his or her "clients" to the new practice. The supervisor contends that these clients are the property of the practice and the conflict ensues. CAMFT has created an ethical standard to prevent this conflict, however it may still develop. Importantly, California law attempts to prevent restriction of practice and at the same time protect the individual who has invested time and energy into developing a specific product: the supervisor's clinical practice.

CAMFT ethical standard 9.1 prohibits the clinical supervisor from charging a fee or accepting payment for referring clients to the supervisee for good reason. Doing so could lead to exploitation of the supervisee and the clinician's possible loss of objectivity. Both conditions would most likely harm the supervisor/supervisee relationship. However, clinical supervisors can take reasonable and prudent steps to manage this potentially precarious contractual situation. Stuart Zajic, an attorney in private practice focusing in contractual issues for small businesses proposes the premise that legally, clinicians can protect their practices and related interests by addressing "trade secrets" in the contractual agreement.

Mr. Zajic explains that this concept, based on California law, relates to that information clinicians uses in their mode of practicing, the list of clients served by the supervisor's practice, the names and addresses of these clients, and any other pertinent information about these clients obtained by the supervisor's practice. The importance of expanding this premise and developing a contractual agreement is to protect the client's welfare. The major complaint among supervisors is that supervisees obtain their license and "run away" with clients that belong the supervisor's practice. These supervisors tend to believe that supervisees do not appreciate the time and effort spent by supervisors in developing a stable and consistent clientele. Ultimately, supervisors can take the legal stance that when a supervisee takes clients away; the supervisor's "trade secrets" are being taken away from their practice. How would a reasonable and prudent supervisor manage this challenging issue? The reasonable and prudent clinician would consider incorporating these elements into his or her contract. It is important to obtain the counsel of a qualified attorney.

- Consult with an appropriate attorney to assure that the contract conforms to California law and CAMFT ethical standards.
- Assure that the supervisee understands the nature of the remuneration.
- Apply all confidentiality clauses that will be in effect even after the contractual relationship has ended.
- Define a remuneration package that conforms to ethical standards and is equitable for all parties involved.
- Define a process used in case that conflict ensues from the contractual relationship.

Ultimately, it is the responsibility of the clinician to avoid creating a situation that could lead to contractual conflict between supervisor and supervisee and which could affect the welfare of clients. Interested clinicians can obtain additional consultation from Mr. Zajic (805-963-4656).

Clinical Example # 1

A local agency advertises several internship positions. Jeannie, an MFT registered intern calls for information. She is told that as part of cost-saving measures, all supervisees rotate housekeeping duties once per week. That is a condition of supervision at this agency.

Questions for Clinical Example # 1

1. As a reasonable and prudent MFT, what would you tell Jeannie about this offer? Is it ethical? Why or why not?
2. What has this agency failed to recognize about their requirement to treat interns?
3. What is the potential ethical violation? What happens if the supervisor should lose objectivity or coerce the intern in the course of the type of relationship created in this situation?
4. Should Jeannie ignore your advice, what information could you provide her to help her obtain clarity?

Clinical Example # 2

Dominique and Rendi enter into a supervisory relationship. Three years later, Rendi obtains her MFT license and decides to open her office in another part of town. Meanwhile, she invites her current clients to her new location and many decide to follow her. Dominique is quite upset because she has expended a great deal of effort to develop a clientele and feels cheated by Rendi. She decides to sue Rendi for loss of income. Rendi counter sues for malicious intent to sue. Both end up having their respective attorneys send subpoenas to their clients.

Questions for Clinical Example # 2

1. What is the primary error both made regarding the welfare of their clients?
2. What is the secondary error both made regarding a contractual agreement?
3. It appears that both reacted from their anger and may have lost objectivity. What possible relationship did each create with the BBS? Why?
4. Had they begun their supervisory relationship with an appropriate contract, what could they have specified in the contract regarding ending the relationship in an appropriate manner?
5. If both were investigated by the BBS, what would be the accusation? If clients are involved in the lawsuit end up being injured, what could be the reasons for suing these therapists?

Chapter Questions

1. What is the primary responsibility of a supervisor to a supervisee?
2. An intern friend shares with you the unethical behavior of his or her supervisor. What would you counsel him or her to do?
3. What are the duties of a supervisee to a supervisor?

Chapter 21

Advertising

Advertising

The legal standard of care regarding advertising for MFTs is found under Business and Professions Code Section 651. It reads as follows:

> **Business and Professions Code Section 651(a) It is unlawful for any person licensed under this division or under any initiative act referred to in this division to disseminate or cause to be disseminated, any form of public communication containing a false, fraudulent, misleading, or deceptive statement, claim, or image for the purpose of or likely to induce, directly or indirectly, the rendering of professional services or furnishing of products in connection with the professional practice or business for which he or she is licensed. A "public communication" as used in this section includes, but is not limited to, communication by means of mail, television, radio, motion picture, newspaper, book, list or directory of healing arts practitioners, or other electronic communication.**

Business and Professions Code Section 651 establishes advertising requirements for MFTs. This law forbids "false, fraudulent, misleading, or deceptive" advertisement and extends it to a variety of advertising media. Therefore, when advertising, MFTs must use honesty and truthfulness. Business and Professions Code 4982 establishes that any deviation from truth is unprofessional conduct and thus, illegal behavior. The responsibility rests with MFTs to assure that their advertising venues do not violate this law. Violations can carry serious consequences. Business and Professions Code 4982 (p) establishes that the board may refuse to issue a license, or may suspend or revoke a license of any licensee if she or he is found guilty of improper advertising.

Additionally, there are some important details to incorporate into an advertisement to assure compliance with the legal requirements. First, the advertisement must include either the exact name of the license (marriage and family therapist) or the MFT's license number. Second, MFTs can use the term "psychotherapy" or "psychotherapist," however; the advertisement must establish that the practitioner is a licensed marriage and family therapist. Lack of disclosure of this information can define the ad as fraudulent: it can imply that the MFT is a licensed psychologist or psychiatrist. If the MFT is an unlicensed Ph.D., it is acceptable to include this degree after the clinician's name. The ad must clearly establish that the therapist holds a license of a marriage and family therapist. See Business and Professions Code 2902 (c).

Fictitious Names and Yellow Pages

A therapist can use a fictitious name as long as he or she avoids misleading the public. The use of a fictitious name requires that the MFT state whether the business is incorporated or not. If either the business is registered with the BBS as a corporation, or the true name is part of the business name (John Doe, MA, MFT, A Corporation), then these entities are exempt from disclosing their corporate status in advertising. MFTs must inform their clients at the beginning of therapy regarding the status of the "fictitious name" used in their business. This includes the name and license of the owner of the practice. To avoid misleading advertising in the "Yellow Pages", MFTs must be listed under the heading: marriage and family therapists rather than under psychologists.

Advertising And Interns/Trainees

It is not advisable for trainees to advertise since they are not permitted to enter into a private practice internship. If a trainee chooses to use a business card, the card must clearly state the trainee's licensing status as well as the name and license (including license number) of their supervisor.

Registered interns, on the other hand, may advertise as long as their ads are not misleading or false. The ad must clearly state that the intern is a registered intern under the supervision of a licensed therapist. The name, type of license and license number of the supervisor must be included. Any ad must clearly state that the intern has no ownership of the business he or she is working for and that the intern must follow the same guidelines established for licensed MFTs. It is the responsibility of the intern's supervisor to assure that advertising by the intern meets the standards of California Law.

Specialty Practice

MFT practice has changed considerably in the last few years as a result of external factors, such as new telecommunications developments, (faxing, telephone counseling services, etc.), legislative action expanding the role of MFT practice, and CAMFT's new ethical standards (effective 2008). CAMFT recognized that as MFT practice has evolved, new ethical standards were required to expand safety for clients and therapists. One such arena involves the advertising of a specialty practice. CAMFT Ethical Standard 10.8 addresses specialty practice as follows:

> **CAMFT Ethical Standard 10.8 — Marriage and family therapists may represent themselves either as specializing or having expertise within a limited area of marriage and family therapy, but only if they have the education, training, and experience which meet recognized professional standards to practice in that specialty.**

The following is an example of a violation of CAMFT Ethical Standard 10.8. An MFT advertises as a specialist in treating childhood trauma. One of the therapist's clients, whom he is treating for childhood trauma, sues the MFT for malpractice. At trial, while cross-examining the MFT, the opposing attorney focuses on this specialty. He questions the MFT about how he developed the advertised specialty and which professional organizations provided certification for this specialty. The MFT is unable to support a specialty status with any appropriate credentials. Although the initial action that began the malpractice lawsuit was marginal, the jury found for the plaintiff in its verdict. The jury perceived the MFT to be fraudulent because he advertised himself as a specialist when he had neither supporting credentials or certification by a recognized organization.

Advertising as specialists requires that practitioners obtain appropriate training and education from a recognized professional organization to establish a specialty practice. Some specialties include: a) hypnosis, b) EMDR, c) forensics, and d) sex therapy. Organizations such as the American Society of Clinical Hypnosis, the EMDR International Association, the American Board of Forensic Examiners, and the American Association of Sex Therapists support these areas of practice as specialties. The required training and education is determined by the executive boards of these organizations and can be found in their bylaws. Some organizations confer upon their members "diplomate" status; this status requires a minimum amount of experience in using the treatment modality and successfully completing a written and/or oral examination.

Practitioners who do not have any specialty certification can limit their practice to an area of psychotherapy within their scope of competence, for example: treating couples, children, adolescents, incest survivors, adult physical trauma, elderly, couples wanting to adopt children, and other such populations. However, the therapist cannot advertise as a specialist. Doing so would be a violation of this ethical standard.

Other Ethical Standards Addressing Advertising

CAMFT Ethical Standard 10 — Marriage and family therapists who advertise do so appropriately. Their advertising enables consumers to choose professional services based upon accurate information.

CAMFT Ethical Standard 10.1 — Marriage and family therapists accurately represent their competence, education, training, and experience relevant to their professional practice to patients and others.

CAMFT Ethical Standard 10.2 — Marriage and family therapists take reasonable steps to assure that advertisements and publications, whether in directories, announcement cards, newspapers, radio, television, Internet or any other media, are formulated to accurately convey information to the public.

CAMFT Ethical Standard 10.3 — Marriage and family therapists do not use a name which could mislead the public concerning the identity, responsibility, source, and status of those practicing under that name and do not hold themselves out as being partners or associates of a firm if they are not.

CAMFT Ethical Standard 10. 4 — Marriage and family therapists do not use any professional identification, including but not limited to, a business card, office sign, letterhead, or telephone or association directory listing, or any other electronic media, if it includes a statement or claim that is false, fraudulent, misleading, or deceptive. A statement is false, fraudulent, misleading, or deceptive if it a) contains a material misrepresentation of facts; b) fails to state any material fact necessary to make the statement, in light of all circumstances, not misleading; or c) is intended to or is likely to create an unjustified expectation.

CAMFT Ethical Standard 10.5 — Marriage and family therapists correct, wherever possible, false, misleading, or inaccurate information and representations made by others concerning the therapist's qualifications, services, or products.

CAMFT Ethical Standard 10.6 — Marriage and family therapists do not solicit testimonials from patients.

CAMFT Ethical Standard 10.7 — Marriage and family therapists make certain that the qualifications of persons in their employ are represented in a manner that is not false, misleading, or deceptive.

CAMFT Ethical Standard 10.8 — Marriage and family therapists may represent themselves as specializing within a limited area of marriage and family therapy, but only if they have the education, training, and experience, which meet recognized professional standards to practice in that specialty area.

CAMFT Ethical Standard 10.9 — CAMFT clinical, associate and prelicensed members may identify such membership in CAMFT in public information or advertising materials, but they must clearly and accurately represent whether they are clinical, associate, or prelicensed members.

CAMFT Ethical Standard 10.10 — Marriage and family therapists may not use the initials CAMFT following their name in the manner of an academic degree.

CAMFT Ethical Standard 10.11 — Marriage and family therapists may use the CAMFT logo only after receiving permission in writing from the Association. Permission will be granted by the Association to CAMFT members in good standing in accordance with Association policy on use of CAMFT logo. The Association (which is the sole owner of its name, logo, and the abbreviated initials CAMFT) may grant permission to CAMFT committees and chartered chapters in good standing, operating as such, to use the CAMFT logo. Such permission will be granted in accordance with Association policy on use of the CAMFT logo.

CAMFT Ethical Standard 10.12 — Marriage and family therapists, when publicizing their membership in CAMFT, do not do so in a manner that implies organizational endorsement of their activities.

Referral Services

Marriage and family therapists are permitted to join referral services. The function of these organizations is to promote the practice of its members and to refer clients to its members. However, it is unlawful for any MFT to use the services of any Referral Service that is not registered with the BBS.

In order to provide referral services, the MFT Referral Service must register with the Board of Behavioral Sciences. It must also submit the relationship between the MFT and the Referral Service to the BBS (Section 650.4 of the Business and Professions Code). Additionally, an example of the advertising employed by the Referral Service must be submitted to the BBS.

Clinical Example # 1

> Ross is very proud of his accomplishment, a PhD in clinical psychology. He is licensed as an MFT and his telephone greeting says: "Hello, this is Dr. Ross Smith, and I am not able to answer your call at this time. Please leave your name and number and I'll return your call as soon as possible."

Questions for Clinical Example # 1

1. If you were listening to this message, what would you consider Dr. Smith's to be licensed as?
2. Is this legal and ethical? Why or why not?
3. What steps are required by Ross to correct the misrepresentation?
4. If he doesn't correct it, what could he be accused of by the BBS in addition to the misrepresentation?
5. If he changed his telephone greeting, what two possibilities could allow him to say Dr. Ross Smith and comply with California Law and CAMFT ethical standards?

Chapter Questions

1. An MFT friend of yours opens her practice and shows you her new card. She has recently completed a Ph.D. in clinical psychology is very proud of being a Dr. Her new card reads: Dr. Jamie Dow, psychotherapist, specialist in relationships issues. What do you counsel her?
2. Another friend creates a business name which reads "Medical Psychotherapists" even though there are no physicians working under that name. What do you counsel him?
3. A therapist advertises his fees as affordable. Is this appropriate? Why or why not?

Chapter 22

Fees

Fees

In California, Business and Professions Code 4982 (n) and (o) regulate the issue of fees for MFTs. An MFT's unprofessional conduct regarding fees is defined below:

> **Business and Professions Code 4982 (n) Prior to the commencement of treatment, failing to disclose to the client or prospective client the fee to be charged for the professional services, or the basis upon which that fee will be computed.**
>
> **Business and Professions Code 4982 (o) Paying, accepting, or soliciting any consideration, compensation, or remuneration, whether monetary or otherwise, for the referral of professional clients. All consideration, compensation, or remuneration shall be in relation to professional counseling services actually provided by the licensee. Nothing in this subdivision shall prevent collaboration among two or more licensees in a case or cases. However, no fee shall be charged for that collaboration, except when disclosure of the fee has been made in compliance with subdivision (n).**

Under these laws, MFTs and their supervisees have the responsibility to inform clients, at the beginning of therapy, of the fee they will pay and how it will be computed. The supervisor is responsible for setting fees for his or her supervisees before client treatment begins.

Bartering

California law does not directly regulate bartering, however, CAMFT Ethical Standard 9.5 addresses it clearly:

> **CAMFT Ethical Standard 9.5 Marriage and family therapists ordinarily refrain from accepting goods, services, or other non-monetary remuneration from patients in return for professional services. Such arrangements often create conflicts and may lead to exploitation or distortion of the professional relationship.**

For MFTs, bartering is a practice fraught with many problems. For example, if the clinician applies value to the goods exchanged for service, he or she may find him/herself in a dual relationship because the he is acting simultaneously as a therapist and an appraiser. If the relationship sours and the conflict escalates, this dual relationship can become a harmful one because the clinician had the responsibility to avoid coercion or loss of objectivity. A harmful dual relationship becomes grounds for a malpractice action and a BBS investigation.

Disclosure of Fees

MFTs know that California law, Business and Professions Code, dictates disclosure of fees before the commencement of therapy. This disclosure is carried at before the first visit and usually at the time that the client calls to make an appointment. Waiting to state the fee at the end of the first appointment can cause difficulties for the therapist and the client. For example, once they have created a therapeutic relationship, the client may feel compelled to continue the relationship in spite of being financially unable to continue paying the fee. Additionally, the client may state that he or she cannot afford the reduced fee and refuses to begin treatment with another therapist, then the therapist is likely stuck seeing that client for a lower fee than the clinician would normally charge. Refusing to provide treatment under these conditions opens the door to an accusation of client abandonment with unpleasant potential outcome for the therapist.

The disclosure is best followed by a written statement, either in the form of a contract for services or a form letter agreeing on the fee, with the client's signature. Establishing the fee in writing creates greater safety for all involved.

Non-Affordability of Fees

Sometimes, clients cannot afford the fee quoted by the therapist. The therapist does not have a legal or ethical obligation to accept the client if the client cannot afford the fee. It is clear though, that the clinician informed the client in advance the fee. The therapist does have an ethical duty to refer the client to other therapists or low-cost clinics. If the client presents with a high-risk situation, then it is imperative that the therapist provide palliative treatment for a few sessions until the MFT manages the crisis. To prevent misunderstandings, the MFT obtains informed consent regarding the limited number of sessions at a lower fee and for specific goals. Abandoning the client in a high-risk situation will likely lead to an investigation of unprofessional conduct by the BBS and can also lead to a malpractice lawsuit. For additional discussion of this issue, see Chapter 36.

Collecting Unpaid Balances

Therapists are within their rights to take action to collect unpaid balances. They can use a collection service or small claims court, depending on the their preference. Should they choose of these services,

Evidence Code 1020 no longer protects the client's privilege. However, to avoid potential future problems with the client, it is important to remember that they must only provide specific information to the court. This information includes specific client attendance, the fee charged per session, the fee charged for additional services, any attempts to collect moneys owed and the therapeutic contract. If using a collection agency, MFTs must be judicious in the clinical information they provide. Providing extraneous clinical information can lead to retribution by an angry ex-client who will likely seek action against the MFT through the courts or the BBS.

Clinicians must be careful to prevent unpaid balances to grow uncollected. If the balance becomes a burden to the client, then an opposing attorney can accuse the MFT of causing injury to the client. The client's harm stems from having his or her debt become unmanageable yet having to continue treatment with this MFT. The MFT becomes responsible for causing the harm due to failure to recognize the stress and anxiety experienced by the client and for failing to take action to prevent the harm to the client. This again, opposing attorneys will consider this clinical behavior as unprofessional conduct, because MFTs have the responsibility to determine in advance the consequences of letting a balance accrue.

Maintaining Clinical Objectivity With Third Party Payers

MFTs often face a challenging clinical situation when a third party, such as a relative or a church fund offers to pay the client's clinical services. Though this may seem like an innocuous situation, MFTs have found it fraught with danger should they fail to manage it in a "reasonable and prudent" manner. Should the clinician fail to meet the payer's expectations, it is quite possible that the third party payer will sue the clinician for breach of contract based on the requirement to provide informed consent to the individual making the payment.

Some clinicians will ask "Am I required to provide informed consent per Rains v. Superior Court (1984) to those who are not my clients and pay for my client's treatment?" Opposing attorneys have stated that they would definitely take the stance in court that the clinician is required to provide appropriate information to the third party payer so they can make an informed decision when making payment for a client's clinical services. They also state that the clinician has the legal therapeutic duty to assure that he or she avoids the loss of objectivity when providing this limited informed consent to third party payers. The following clinical example illustrates these interacting duties.

Imagine the adult child of a wealthy individual seeking clinical treatment from a mental health clinician for a specific issue. The client tells the clinician he is unable to pay for the services, however he indicates that his parent will pay and have unlimited financial

> **resources to pay for treatment. The clinician informs the client that he requires an intensive treatment program and prolonged outpatient treatment, which will last several months. The clinician fails to inform that he is a part owner of the treatment facility. The father requests information regarding the clinician's scope of competence to address the presenting issue. The clinician assures him that he has the sufficient training, knowledge and experience to treat this issue. Based on the information provided, the parent agrees to pay for all services. Several months later, the client's condition has not improved and the parent has spent over $50,000 for inpatient and outpatient treatment. The parent consults with an attorney and decides to sue the clinician. The plaintiff's attorney informs the parent that the lawsuit will be for breach of contract: failure by the clinician's to provide the necessary and appropriate information regarding his scope of competence. The plaintiff's attorney includes the clinician's failure to maintain clinical objectivity when the client was referred to the inpatient program owned by the clinician.**

What could he have done differently? We can consider these steps as reasonable and prudent when facing a similar situation:

- Maintain an accurate and current curriculum vitae reflecting scope of competence. Update it monthly.
- Assure that clients and third party payers receive the necessary informed consent information in writing. Assure that all parties sign the necessary forms. The clinician can keep the signed original and provides a copy to the client and the third party payer.
- When providing information to third party payers, such as relatives, assure that accurate information regarding the clinician clearly notes his or her scope of competence.
- Should the clinician refer a client to a collateral facility where the clinician holds ownership, he or she must inform the client and/or third party payers of his or her ownership standing. Failure to do so can lead an opposing attorney to initiate an accusation for the loss of clinical objectivity. This attorney will highlight that the MFT made the referral for his or her own financial benefit.
- Always consult with an attorney trained in mental health law regarding the appropriate content of an informed consent document for third party payers.

Serious Challenges Faced By Clinicians When Third Parties Pay For Clinical Services

Another possible situation clinicians face when third parties pay for clinical services follows:

> **Jennie, an MFT who is a member of a church, receives a referral from the social outreach program of her church. The client, recently paroled for substance related violations, is under the supervision of her church. As a condition of her parole, she must attend counseling, which the church will pay for. The church made a special arrangement with Jennie who to provide short-term treatment and bill the church a lower fee than usual. Jennie and the client agree that the treatment will focus strictly on providing her with resources to help her integrate into her community. On the fifth and last session, the client begins to cry inconsolably and tells the Jennie that one of the guards in jail raped her. The client relates how she is having nightmares since the rape, having suicidal thoughts, and being unable to focus on daily tasks. She tells Jennie she is not sure she is going to make it.**

Compassionately, Jennie tells the client she understands her plight and needs to refer her to another therapist for treatment since their agreement was that Jennie would only provide 5 sessions. The client cannot understand why Jennie cannot continue treating her. "I don't want to see anyone else, I want to see you," she tells Jennie adamantly. Jennie picks up a package she had prepared in advance and gives it to her client. It contains the name of several low-cost agencies in the community and wishes her client good luck as she escorts her out the door.

Several months later, Jennie receives a subpoena from an attorney requesting this client's records. Jennie reads the subpoena and notices that in lieu of the client's name, she reads the daughter's name as legal representative for her mother, her former client. She complies with the subpoena. A few weeks later, she receives notice that the daughter is suing Jennie on behalf of her mother for several reasons. The two most prominent are patient abandonment and failure to protect her mother from suicide. Jennie is flabbergasted and scared. She calls her insurance carrier immediately to obtain the name of a malpractice attorney for a consultation.

Though the clinician's intentions were to help this client, she found herself in an untenable bind, much of it due to her making. Any expert witness assessing the forensic ramifications of this case would indicate that the following errors took place:

- Failure to treat the client with the required scope of competence.
- Failure to treat the client according to the standard of care.
- Failure to inform the client about the protocols of the therapeutic relationship.
- Failure to assess the client for risk of harm to self.
- Failure to protect the client for risk of harm to self.
- Failure to continue treatment in spite of client's evident risk of harm to self.
- Failure to use the informed consent to establish how the clinician would manage any additional treatment beyond the 5 sessions required by the client.
- Failure to provide referrals to the client in a manner that didn't foster abandonment.
- Failure to assess the client for possible danger to self during the referral process and managing this risk appropriately.
- Failure to apply clinical standard of care.

Ethical Guidelines Regarding Fees

CAMFT Ethical Standard 9 — Marriage and family therapists make financial arrangements with patients and supervisees that are understandable and conform to accepted professional practices and legal requirements.

CAMFT Ethical Standard 9.1 — Marriage and family therapists do not offer to accept payment for referrals, whether in the form of money or otherwise.

CAMFT Ethical Standard 9.2 — Marriage and family therapists do not financially exploit their patients.

CAMFT Ethical Standard 9.3 — Marriage and family therapists disclose, in advance, their fees and the basis upon which they are computed, including, but not limited to, charges for canceled or missed appointments and any interest to be charged on unpaid balances, at the beginning of treatment and give reasonable notice of changes in fees or other charges.
CAMFT Ethical Standard 9.4 — Marriage and family therapists give reasonable notice to patients with unpaid balances of their intent to sue, or to refer for collection. Whenever legal action is taken, therapists will avoid disclosure of clinical information. Whenever unpaid balances are referred to collection agencies, therapists will exercise care in selecting collection agencies and will avoid disclosure of clinical information.

CAMFT Ethical Standard 9.5 — Marriage and family therapists ordinarily refrain from accepting goods, services, or other non-monetary remuneration from patients in return for professional services. Such arrangements often create conflicts and may lead to exploitation or distortion of the professional relationship.

CAMFT Ethical Standard 9.6 — Marriage and family therapists represent facts regarding services rendered and payment for services fully and truthfully to third part;y payers and others.

See Chapter 36 "Financial Arrangements" for an in-depth discussion of fees.

Clinical Example # 1

Juan, a bilingual and bicultural therapist, has his practice in a rural and mainly agricultural part of California. He provides treatment to itinerant agricultural workers regarding substance abuse related issues. Many of his clients do not have much money and at times, bring produce they have picked in the fields where they work. At times, Juan finds himself in a dilemma. He remembers that he was taught in school that bartering was a bad idea and he finds that if he rejects these gifts, his clients feel disrespected. He does not want to hurt his clients' feelings yet he does not want to get into trouble with the BBS. Juan is sensitive of his clients' culture and he also wants to be a "good" therapist.

Questions for Clinical Example # 1

1. What is causing Juan's dilemma?
2. What is he failing to understand when facing such a dilemma?
3. Is it appropriate to accept these gifts to avoid disrespecting his clients? How can he create safety for himself and avoid a BBS investigation?
4. What steps would a reasonable and prudent clinician take in Juan's case?
5. What would you do?

Clinical Example # 2

Joanne has been developing a practice in Beverly Hills and serves mainly clients working in the movie industry. A recent strike in this profession caused her to lose 1/3 of her practice though she is well respected and is an excellent clinician. Her fee is now $300 for a 50-minute "hour" and most clients pay it. Recently, one of her clients, an up-and-coming movie star, became embroiled in a nasty divorce and his assets have been tied up for several months. He tells Joanne that he can't pay her current fee but would like to continue seeing her. She tells him: "For every client you refer, I'll give you three free sessions." He is afraid of losing the therapeutic relationship with her and says: "OK, I'll do it."

Questions for Clinical Example # 2

1. Is Joanne's proposal to her client coming from a clear and objective place? Why or why not?
2. If not, what do you believe clouded her clinical objectivity?
3. What causes her proposal to be illegal and unethical?
4. What options would a reasonable and prudent clinician have considered?
5 How can the client be hurt in this scenario?

Clinical Example # 3

Rodney opens his new practice as an MFT. His clinical supervisor told him that he could use a "sliding fee scale" to build his practice. He decides to start with a fee of $100 and provide flexibility to clients who can't afford his full fee. After 12 months, he realizes that the majority of his clients pay him an average of $45 per visit and he is dissatisfied with his income. He decides to charge more for future clients and changes his fee to $125. He receives a referral from a problematic client and the new potential client tells Rodney that he can't afford his new fee. Rodney asks him: "What fee can you afford?" The new client responds: "$45." Though Rodney is not happy with this arrangement, he accepts it with resentment. A few days later, he receives a phone call from the referring client. He complains to Rodney that his friend is only paying $45 while he has to pay $85. He tells Rodney that his friend can afford the full fee. He also wants Rodney to adjust his fee to $45. Rodney reacts angrily and tells this client that this is a fair fee and that he won't change it. The client reacts angrily and tells Rodney: "You're just going to blow me off? You'll be sorry!" Rodney replies: "Good riddance!"

Questions for Clinical Example # 3

1. Does Rodney's fee structure conform to acceptable standards of the profession? Why or why not?
2. If not, what are the problems that his current fee structure creates?
3. Describe Rodney's level of clinical objectivity regarding his fees. If you were consulting with him, what would you tell him about his state of clinical objectivity?
4. What feedback would you give Rodney regarding the manner in which he dealt with the question from his referring client regarding the issue of lowering his current fee?
5. What legal actions can this client take against Rodney? Would his accusations be reasonable?

Chapter Questions

1. What makes bartering a dangerous issue for therapists?
2. A therapist is in the habit of waiting until the interview is completed to establish his fee. He determines how much money the client is making before he arrives at the fee. What would you tell this therapist about his practice?
3. A supervisor tells an intern in private practice to charge what she wants to as long as it is not higher than the supervisor's fee? Is this approach unethical, illegal, or both? Why?
4. A therapist has allowed a client's unpaid balance accrue to 6,000 dollars. What ethical or legal

violations has this action caused? What makes this a challenge for psychotherapists? A client claims emotional injury because the clinician placed the client in an oppressive situation. The client worried extensively about the debt that he began to have nightmares and developed anxiety disorders. Would the court consider this a reasonable complaint?

Chapter 23

Insurance and Managed Care

Insurance and Confidentiality

When clients use insurance to pay for psychotherapy, it serves MFTs to inform clients of the benefits and risks of doing so (See CAMFT Ethical Standard 1.5). One of the major risks of using insurance is that the insurance company is entitled to receive the client's confidential information and can make it available to other insurance companies. When the insurance company enters into a contract with the client, the client agrees to provide the insurance company his or her medical information to process the insurance claim. When therapists sends a bill to the insurance company, bills through a website, or gives the client a self-bill form, they provide medical information to the insurance company. If the insurance company wants a pre-authorization completed before authorizing mental health care, again, the insurance company receives the client's confidential information. Once MFTs provide confidential information to the insurance company, neither the MFTs nor the client has any control over the utilization or storage of that information. Insurance companies tend to share medical information with each other companies through medical databases. Once other insurance companies and medical databases receive client information, it becomes "public" information.

Some would say that the client "should" know this process about insurance companies. MFTs must remember that they have a therapeutic duty to discuss with their clients how insurance companies will manage their confidential information. Clients may not want the insurance company or anyone else to know certain medical or personal information about them, yet they want to use their insurance. Therefore, to protect all involved, a reasonable and prudent therapist discusses how insurance confidentiality management can affect them. MFTs document this discussion in the client's mental health records. Not taking these steps places MFTs in a tenuous situation.

Insurance Fraud

Insurance fraud is any financial transaction with the insurance company, which is false or deceptive. When MFTs submit any information to insurance companies, they consider the submitted form a legal document. Once insurance companies become aware of a fraudulent insurance submittal, they use their resources to investigate and prosecute the perpetrator. After obtaining all available evidence against the MFT, they submit this evidence to the district attorney for criminal prosecution.

The following acts are considered fraudulent:

- MFTs enhance or worsen the client's diagnosis to benefit him or her and have the insurance pay benefits not otherwise provided.
- Billing insurance companies for "individual" therapy when in actuality the service were for couple's therapy.
- Billing for missed appointments as if they were attended sessions.
- Billing for sessions not rendered.
- MFTs increase the stated fee on the insurance billing to receive a larger payment from the insurance company.
- MFTs waive a client's insurance co-payment. Insurance companies view this action as a misstatement of the MFTs regular fee.
- Billing for services or sessions performed by someone else.
- Billing for non-covered services as office visits.
- Billing two insurance companies the same amount for couples' therapy, rather than billing each 1/2 the amount.
- Billing for services provided to one family member under the name of another family member to take advantage of unused sessions under the family's insurance plan.

Ultimately, it is important to remember that insurance fraud is not only illegal and unethical; it is also a criminal offense in certain jurisdictions. When in doubt, consult.

Ethical Standards Regarding Insurance Fraud

See CAMFT Ethical Standard 9.6 for a discussion on this topic.

Appealing Adverse Utilization Review Decisions in Managed Care

In 1986, *Wickline v. State of California*, a case law, issued the verdict that physicians had the duty to appeal adverse utilization review (UR) decisions by insurance companies and managed care companies. This is applicable to therapists too. When an insurance company's Utilization Review denies an "authorization for services," MFTs have the legal duty to challenge the denial. Otherwise, the client can pursue legal action against the therapist should the client be injured emotionally because the services were not rendered and the MFT failed to comply with this law. The law has placed the responsibility on the therapist, rather than on the insurance company for challenging these UR decisions.

Confidentiality and the Internet

The federal government introduced legislation in 1996 to address the management of confidentiality in the electronic media, and how it applies to the Internet. It is known as The Health Insurance Portability & Accountability Act of 1996 (HIPAA). Its purpose is to standardize electronic patient health, administrative and financial data. It establishes security standards protecting the confidentiality and integrity of "individually identifiable health information," past, present or future. It affects one-person offices, health plans, employers, public health authorities, life insurers, clearinghouses, billing agencies, information system vendors, service organizations, and universities.

"Electronic Health Transactions" as defined by HIPAA includes health claims, health plan eligibility, enrollment and disenrollment, payments for care and health plan premiums, claim status, first injury reports, coordination of benefits, and related transactions. Any communication through the Internet that involves the identity of a patient falls under the jurisdiction of this law. This includes E-mails directed to patients , such as newsletters, informational brochures, marketing approaches, electronic insurance claims, requests for information from insurance companies, and electronic transmission of patient information to insurance companies, etc. These transactions are covered under this federal law. Should these transactions be utilized by MFTs in their electronic transmittal of patient information, they must comply with this law. MFTs are required to know this law and apply it. For further clarification of this law see "HIPAA Made Easy: A Workbook For Mental Health Clinicians" ©, Grosso, 2003.

Reasonable And Prudent Action To Take Before The Client Runs Out of Insurance Benefits

John begins treatment with a licensed clinician hoping to use his insurance benefits. Although he has never used the benefits provided by this insurance company, he hopes he'll be able to address personal issues related to the impact on him and his family of a pending company relocation. He makes an appointment with Marcia, a licensed psychotherapist and finds out that his insurance company will only approve 10 sessions.

As John's treatment progresses, he finds out that his company's move has a severe impact on him and his family and realizes that 10 sessions may not be enough to process the upcoming upheaval and family disruption. His therapist, Marcia, attempts to obtain more sessions to continue his treatment and the insurance company denies her request twice. He asks her for a reduced fee, however Marcia informs him that she is unable to provide him a lower fee because he is already at a fee lower than her minimum threshold for low fee slots. Marcia informs him that she will refer him to someone else who can provide continuity of treatment. He does not want to change clinicians and attempts to change Marcia's mind. She is adamant in establishing firm boundaries regarding this issue and sends him a certified letter informing him that her ethical standards permit her to terminate treatment. She provides the names of three appropriate therapists in his community and tells him that she will make his records available to the therapist of his choice. Upon receiving the letter, feelings of

> **abandonment engulf him and he reacts angrily. He decides to pursue a malpractice action against her for inappropriate termination, abandonment, causing him emotional harm, failure to provide legally required informed consent, and practicing below the standard of care.**

Imagine how both MFT and client are in a bind. The MFT wants to refer him elsewhere and he does not want to terminate treatment with her. Clinicians will note that the bind need not happen. The MFT could have prevented this easily had she established an appropriate informed consent defining the specific conditions under which she could terminate treatment. This would have established a strong foundation to terminate treatment appropriately. Even if her client felt abandoned, that document would have served to protect her. Instead, she now finds herself trapped. The opposing attorney has reason to believe he will win the case against her and collect a large sum of money to benefit his injured client. To protect all involved, a reasonable and prudent clinician considers the following steps:

- Have a sound knowledge of legal and ethical requirements regarding the management of informed consent, therapeutic duty to assess, diagnose, and treat according to the standard of care throughout the duration of therapy, appropriate termination of treatment, and using appropriate referrals.
- Utilize an appropriate informed consent document addressing the issues discussed
- Discuss the risks and benefits of providing treatment when limited insurance benefits exist.
- Assure that the termination of treatment for the reason stated in previous paragraphs are clearly stated in the informed consent document.
- Make sure that the client signs the informed consent document without coercion.
- Establish the referral process in the informed consent document.

The above acts do not prevent malpractice actions against the clinician, however they can serve to strengthen the protection for all involved.

Clinical Example # 1

> Roger has been in practice since the mid-seventies and considers himself from the "old-school." Recently, a family in distress came to see him because they were facing financial problems and the father was in the process of losing his job. They wanted to use the company's mental health benefits, which provided 10 visits each and 5 conjoint visits. Roger considers himself to be a sensitive and caring therapist and when his clients ask him for favors, he complies as best he can. The father of this family opted to use only three of his visits and asked Roger to see his wife for her 10 allotted visits plus his 7. Wanting to help the family, Roger complied. Later, a misunderstanding arose regarding a broken appointment and the family stopped treatment. Six months later, Roger received a letter from the insurance company informing him he was being investigated for insurance fraud, that the information was being transferred to the BBS

and to the local District Attorney for criminal investigation. A week later, 2 white-collar crime detectives were at his door.

Questions for Clinical Example # 1

1. Can you imagine Roger's internal reality regarding wanting to be helpful? Describe it.
2. Imagine Roger taking himself into the future and having to face criminal investigation detectives versus wanting to help his clients. How do you believe he would respond differently?
3. What did Roger forget when he attempted to help this family and violated California laws and CAMFT ethical standards? If he had consulted with you, how would you have reminded him of his legal and ethical therapeutic duty without criticizing him?
4. How would a reasonable and prudent MFT process this issue, maintain appropriate boundaries, and be sensitive to the clients' needs?
5. Would personal therapy regarding "being helpful" to clients be of benefit to Roger? Why or why not?

Chapter Questions

1. A therapist is seeing a client for worker's compensation. During the course of treatment an MMPI is performed by a psychologist. The therapist receives a report from the psychologist and decides to bill the insurance company for the report. What would you recommend to this therapist regarding his or her actions?

Chapter 24

Forensics, Telephone and Online Counseling

Expert Witness

MFTs can provide expert testimony in a court of law as long as the testimony is within the scope of practice of a marriage and family therapist and within his or her field of expertise per his or her scope of competence. Being an expert witness requires specialized training in the specific field of interest. Being board certified adds to the clinician's credibility when testifying in court.

Child Custody Evaluations

MFTs can serve as child custody evaluators when appointed by the court or corresponding attorneys. It is important to note that serving in this capacity can open the door for malpractice lawsuits. Contentious and dissatisfied parents who are unhappy with the evaluator's recommendations tend to instigate these and seek retribution against the evaluator. Case law creates a degree of safety for evaluators by creating broad immunity for these activities. (See *Gootee v.. Lightner*). For Custody Evaluations Standards see rule 1257.3 of the California Rules of Court. To access California Laws on the Internet, see Chapter 35.

Personal Injury Evaluations

MFTs can serve as personal injury evaluators as long as they apply the scope of practice and scope of competence to this area of practice. Since MFTs can utilize any psychometric tool for assessment purposes (see the next section), they can assess clients injured in a diversity of situations and render a clinical opinion as to the nature and genesis of an emotional injury suffered. To do so effectively, the MFT must have the education, knowledge, and experience to assess pre and post morbidity function and status of emotional health. This requires the use of a clinical interview, use of assessment tools (i.e., the MMPI, MSE, etc.), collateral interviews, review of medical and mental health history, provision of appropriate treatment, the rendering of an opinion, and the writing of an appropriate report. The last requirement is the ability to testify to the facts in Court. As part of this testimony, the treating MFT will need to be prepared to quote the specific laws, legal opinions, and Business and Professions Code. Last, the MFT must have the ability to withstand cross-examination by an aggressive attorney intent on discrediting the client, the clinician's assessment and treatment, and the competence of the clinician. Ultimately, the best protection the clinician can develop for him/herself is having appropriate documentation of his or her therapeutic duty.

Psychometric Testing

MFTs can use psychological tests as long as the tests are used within the scope of practice and used as part of treatment. In 1984, the Attorney General published:

> **MFTs have statutory authority to construct, administer and interpret psychological tests but to do so only within the course of their practice, when within their field or fields of competence as established by education, training, and experience, and when such could be used and would be used to examine interpersonal relationships between spouses or members of families for the purpose of achieving more adequate, satisfying and productive marriage and family adjustments.**

Criminal Forensic Assessments

MFTs can render clinical opinions in this arena as long as the opinion is within the scope of practice for the MFT. MFTs cannot testify regarding the competency of a person since that assessment is outside their scope of practice. Psychiatrists and psychologists are the only clinicians permitted under California Law to perform competency assessments. However, an MFT can address how relationship issues, such as culture, family, belief systems, or religion, influenced a criminal act. It would be prudent for the MFT maintain their clinical focus on addressing their scope of practice.

CAMFT Ethical Standards Related to Forensic Activities

For a complete discussion on the clinical applications of these ethical guidelines, see Chapter 35.

Telephone and Online Counseling

Telephone counseling is an acceptable form of counseling when used for crisis intervention or when a therapeutic relationship is already established. Telephone counseling can be problematic when MFTs have not interviewed the client in person or have not been able to perform a mental status exam. MFTs tend to leave out much information when they conduct a clinical session via telephone. Experts indicate that the best method to interview the client is conducting a face-to-face meeting. Other problems might arise such as:

- The inability to obtain informed consent and releases of information within a reasonable period.
- In the event that the clinician conducts treatment outside of the client's state of residence, authorities may consider this action as a violation due to practicing outside of the licensing state.
- Internet counseling complicates the differentiation between the applications of crisis issues legal mandates.
- MFTs may have a difficult time determining if the client is a minor.

Legally, our society is reactionary and it creates laws after incidents take place; consider the Tarasoff Case Law. Telephone and online counseling will most likely be a testing ground for new laws as clients get hurt and initiate lawsuits. At this time, it is important for any California therapist to consult with an attorney knowledgeable in this arena before signing a contract with a telephone or Internet based psychotherapy provider.

Witness of Fact Versus an Expert Witness

Attorneys request and expect that clinicians will testify on behalf of their clients when they receive a subpoena. It is illegal for the clinician to deny this right to the client. The subpoena requires either a copy of the mental health records, the presence of the clinician in court, or both. The clinician's attendance may be postponed for a good reason, however he or she will ultimately appear in court as ordered by the subpoena. These clinicians are considered witnesses of fact; a witness that observed the client, his or her symptoms, performed an assessment, provided treatment, and noted the outcome of the treatment. These clinicians have a professional relationship with the client based on the therapeutic duty to assess, diagnose, and treat. These clinicians aren't permitted to render an opinion regarding the cause of the client's injuries. They can only testify as to the stressor related to the presenting symptoms. Should the client's attorney request that the treating therapist perform the role of the expert witness, the treating therapist or witness of fact must decline. Otherwise, he or she will enter in to dual relationship that could ultimately become harmful to the client. The claimed harm can stem from the clinician's inability to maintain clinical objectivity. The treating therapist maintains an empathic emotional connection with the client whereas the expert witness views the client objectively without any emotional attachment as he or she renders an opinion as to the cause of the client's injuries.

The expert witness is a clinician who is an expert in a specific arena of psychotherapy or social work. The expert witness will likely be board certified in his or her area of expertise. The opposing attorney retains the expert witness. He or she bills either the attorney or insurance company when a legal action begins. The expert's duty is to assess all individuals involved in the lawsuit, review all available documentation, interview all collateral witnesses, and render an opinion regarding the nature of the injures and what caused them. It's imperative that the forensic expert witness not have a previous professional relationship with any of those involved with the lawsuit, otherwise he or she would be accused of having a harmful dual relationship due to the inability to maintain clinical objectivity.

Business and Professions Code 2290.5

The following laws apply to Internet counseling:

Business and Professions Code Section 2290.5 - Telemedicine; informed consent procedures; written consent statement; compliance; application of section

(a) (1) For the purposes of this section, "telemedicine" means the practice of health care delivery, diagnosis, consultation, treatment, transfer of medical data, and education using interactive audio, video, or data communications. Neither a telephone conversation nor an electronic mail message between a health care practitioner and patient constitutes "telemedicine" for purposes of this section.
2) For purposes of this section, "interactive" means an audio, video, or data communication involving a real time (synchronous) or near real time (asynchronous) two-way transfer of medical data and information.
(b) For the purposes of this section, "health care practitioner" has the same meaning as "licentiate" as defined in paragraph (2) of subdivision (a) of Section 805.
(c) Prior to the delivery of health care via telemedicine, the health care practitioner who has ultimate authority over the care or primary diagnosis of the patient shall obtain verbal and written informed consent from the patient or the patient's legal representative. The informed consent procedure shall ensure that at least all of the following information is given to the patient or the patient's legal representative verbally and in writing:
(1) The patient or the patient's legal representative retains the option to withhold or withdraw consent at any time without affecting the right to future care or treatment nor risking the loss or withdrawal of any program benefits to which the patient or the patient's legal representative would otherwise be entitled.
(2) A description of the potential risks, consequences, and benefits of telemedicine.
(3) All existing confidentiality protections apply.
(4) All existing laws regarding patient access to medical information and copies of medical records apply.
(5) Dissemination of any patient identifiable images or information from the telemedicine interaction to researchers or other entities shall not occur without the consent of the patient.
(d) A patient or the patient's legal representative shall sign a written statement prior to the delivery of health care via telemedicine, indicating that the patient or the patient's legal representative understands the written information provided pursuant to subdivision (a), and that this information has been discussed with the health care practitioner, or his or her designee.
(e) The written consent statement signed by the patient or the patient's legal representative shall become part of the patient's medical record.
(f) The failure of a health care practitioner to comply with this section shall constitute unprofessional

conduct. Section 2314 shall not apply to this section.
(g) All existing laws regarding surrogate decision making shall apply. For purposes of this section, "surrogate decision making" means any decision made in the practice of medicine by a parent or legal representative for a minor or an incapacitated or incompetent individual.
(h) Except as provided in paragraph (3) of subdivision (c), this section shall not apply when the patient is not directly involved in the telemedicine interaction, for example when one health care practitioner consults with another health care practitioner.
(i) This section shall not apply in an emergency situation in which a patient is unable to give informed consent and the representative of that patient is not available in a timely manner.
(j) This section shall not apply to a patient under the jurisdiction of the Department of Corrections or any other correctional facility.
(k) This section shall not be construed to alter the scope of practice of any health care provider or authorize the delivery of health care services in a setting, or in a manner not otherwise authorized by law.

Clinical Example # 1

Judy prides herself in her clinical objectivity and ability to stay centered as a clinician. Her friends have told her she would make a wonderful forensic MFT. She begins training, taking courses, and reading. Though she's not certified as a forensic expert, she advertises as such and soon is sought by attorneys wanting to use her services. In a complex case where the father is accused of sexual child abuse, Judy agrees to testify against the him. She only reads the police interview and decides he is guilty and should be punished for his crime. She testifies on behalf of the District Attorney and attempts to portray the father as a pedophile. During cross-examination, the public defendant asks her how she reached her conclusion about the father's guilt. She answers that she relied on the police interview. She is asked if she conducted a personal interview with the accused and she states: "No." The public defender asks the judge to have her removed from the case, since she did not perform a complete assessment of the accused. The judge agrees and also tells her he is personally initiating a complaint against her with the BBS.

Questions for Clinical Example # 1

1. Judy wanted to do a god job and she got herself into trouble. What happened?
2. What mistake did Judy make? What information did she fail to understand and apply?
3. Had she complied with the CAMFT ethical standards addressing forensic activities, would she be in this difficulty? Why or why not?
4. What steps would you have advised her to carry out differently?

Clinical Example # 2

Andrew wants to expand his practice and signs up with an internet company that delivers mental health via online services. He recently took a law and ethics course and he heard something about the BBS requiring emergency contacts to be established where the clients reside. He knows from experience that emergencies seldom happen and decides that it's he doesn't have to comply. He eagerly begins providing Internet-based psychotherapy to clients outside the state. One client turns out to be challenging when he states: "I am have nothing to live for and my wife will find me dead tomorrow. That's what she gets for taking the kids away from me. Goodbye. Roger considers this pranks and does not address it. Several months later, he receives a notice of a lawsuit in federal court for violating a person's civil rights.

Questions for Clinical Example # 2

1. Andrew never believed this would be the outcome of expanding his practice. What did he overlook?
2. Would a consultation with an attorney prior to signing up with the internet company have been prudent and reasonable? Why or why not?
3. Had the attorney warned him that he could be sued in federal court should he face this issue, would Andrew have signed up with the internet company? Would you? Why or why not?
4. Had Andrew taken the suicide threat seriously and also had arranged for emergency coverage in the client's geographic area, would he have been sued? Why or why not?
5. What was Andrew's personal quality that prevented him from being prudent and reasonable in this situation?

Chapter Questions

1. What are the unresolved ethical and legal difficulties when performing therapy with a telephone service or Internet service?
2. A therapist decides to provide services with an internet-based company. After working with a client from another state, the client states that he is despondent and is planning to commit suicide. He states he has a weapon, plan, and he is serious. The therapist practices in California and doesn't know what laws to apply in the client's state? What would you counsel this therapist to do if he or she called you for guidance?

Chapter 25

Cultural Diversity

Cultural Diversity and Psychotherapy

As California's population becomes more culturally complex, MFTs have the added responsibility of understanding a wider range of human experiences. Meeting this responsibility enables MFT to provide effective and appropriate treatment to clients from different walks of life. CAMFT Ethical Code 1.1 addresses the MFT's responsibility to provide services to the diverse population.

> **CAMFT Ethical Code 1.1 — Marriage and family therapists do not condone, engage in discrimination, or refuse professional service to anyone on the basis of race, religion, national origin, age, sexual orientation, disability, socioeconomic or marital status. Marriage and family therapists make reasonable efforts to accommodate patients who have physical disabilities.**

CAMFT Ethical Standard 3.6 expands the MFT's responsibility to gain understanding of diverse populations.

> **CAMFT Ethical Standard 3.6 Marriage and family therapists strive to identify and understand the diverse cultural background of their clients by gaining knowledge, personal awareness, and developing sensitivity and skills pertinent to working with a diverse client population.**

When MFTs treat clients from a cultural background different from his or her own, they have the responsibility of enhancing their scope of competence to include cultural awareness of the population served . This may include consulting with a cultural expert, reading cultural anthropology books regarding the specific culture, attending lectures and seminars dealing with the treatment needs of diversity clients, and/or learning about the cultural undercurrents of each culture. The following segment can serve as a template to understand the therapeutic duty of treating culturally diverse clients.

Therapeutic Duty and Cultural Diversity: Example — The Mexican-American Client

California clinicians practice in an environment that creates numerous challenges regarding diversity issues. Mexican-Americans are one example. This population is rich in cultural and anthropological perspectives. For California psychotherapists and counselors, it is important to understand that when treating this population, culture and cultural values are valuable assets to consider. Attending to these values will assist the therapist in providing the therapeutic duty to assess, diagnose, and treat this population appropriately.

For example, when assessing a Mexican-American client it is important to determine the client's degree of acculturation. Many Mexican-Americans have been in the United States all of their lives while others have recently arrived. Although many immigrants from Mexico originate from an agricultural or "campesino" background with little or no formal education, others originate from urban centers and have a university education. Generally, the former will have a great deal of difficulty acculturating into American culture, whereas the latter will have an easier time due to their higher degree of education and better language skills. Additionally, immigrants from urban backgrounds tend to present different cultural perspectives, expectations and lifestyles than immigrants of agricultural communities.

One important undercurrent of Mexican-American culture is that of fatalism. Fatalism is the belief that everything in the universe is predetermined. This concept has its roots in Aztec religious belief, has transcended the Spanish conquest of Mexico and has embedded itself in modern Mexican culture. Many cultural anthropologists have noted that the impulsive, self-destructive behavior of Mexican-American males, such as killing a companion, a girlfriend, or someone else, in a moment of passion, is driven by fatalism and a narrowly defined sense of honor.

The second undercurrent is the Mexican-American concept of "honor". In this construct, the person believes that his or her personal dignity is damaged by or taken by another person. This disturbs the person's identity and they lose their sense of place and communal belonging. Additionally, the person believes that he regains his or her dignity and belonging by taking specific action. This belief has created a set of rules of behavior that predominately applies to males For example, a Mexican-American gang member kills someone and has no remorse. He believed he was "dissed," disrespected, by the other person. Since the gang member believes that his life has been predetermined, he has already been doomed to be a gang member and doomed to killing this person. The gang member believes that he can regain his "honor" by killing the person whom he believes has disrespected him.

It is important to remember that psychotherapeutic tools designed for one cultural group may be inappropriate for another cultural group. For example, in couple's therapy, the model of equality may not be applicable to understand the marital conflict in a Mexican-American couple. This couple may believe that if a man is to maintain his honor, he does not submit to a woman. Therefore, it is extremely important to understand the undercurrents of the client's cultural values when attempting to assess, diagnose, and treat appropriately. MFTs are required to understand the interaction of culture, educate themselves about the client's cultural values, and continue developing their scope of competence when treating cross-cultural clients. The following guidelines can help MFTs apply standard of care when treating diverse populations.

- Understand one's own cultural beliefs, values, roles and rules.
- Learn about the beliefs, values, roles and rules of the client's culture.
- Include the interplay of cultural values and the presenting issues when assessing and diagnosing and treating cross-cultural clients.
- Explore the client's individual cultural beliefs.
- Utilize appropriate consultation to facilitate treatment of cross-cultural clients.
- In the event that the therapist is unable to provide the standard of care for cross-cultural or diversity clients, he or she must refer to an appropriate resource.

CAMFT Ethical Standards are clear about the cross-cultural requirements placed on MFTs. As great diversity occurs in the population of California, those clinicians who stay abreast of this issue will succeed in meeting the needs of the changing population and will enrich their clinical practice.

Clinical Example # 1

Nguyen is proud of serving his community as a domestic violence prevention educator. He also has a small part-time practice treating mostly teenagers referred by the Probation Department. Though he is versatile in treating those within his culture, he has been struggling to treat a young Latino male recently referred to him. Nguyen doesn't understand why his customary interventions don't work with this boy. It's getting to the point that Nguyen dreads going to his office and treating him. Recently, he found himself yelling at him in frustration: "You're going to end up dead, just like your brother if you don't listen to me."

Questions for Clinical Example # 1

1. Is Nguyen's frustration causing his lack of clinical objectivity or could there be another reason? Why?
2. If his frustration is not the cause of his lack of clinical objectivity and only enhances it, what then could have caused him to lose objectivity in the first place?
3. What did Nguyen need to know before treating this adolescent?
4. Nguyen shares with you that he wants to prove to the Probation Department that he can handle all the cases they refer to him. What would you say to him in response?
5. You understand his driven desire to "prove" himself and yet he has a several therapeutic duties involving cross-cultural issues. What are these and how has he *not* addressed them or put them into action?
6. What steps would you recommend that he take to be a reasonable and prudent clinician in future similar situations?

Clinical Example # 2

Joseph is an ex-priest who became an MFT. He realized early in his career as a priest that he was gay and chose to leave. He now provides counseling for young men and women struggling with career choices. Recently, he received a call from a young man who was contemplating becoming a priest and wanted counseling. Joseph found himself ambivalent about helping this young man with his struggle. Several weeks into treatment and after careful consideration, Joseph said to the young man: "I am having a difficult time staying focused on this issue and have come to realize I may not be an appropriate therapist for you. To help you obtain help, it is best that I refer you to another colleague who can be more objective."

Questions for Clinical Example # 2

1. Did Joseph act reasonably and prudently when he made this statement to his client? Why or why not?
2. What do you believe prompted Joseph to make this decision? Was it made from clarity and clinical objectivity? Why or why not?
3. Was it fair to the young man to refer him after having begun treatment? Why or why not?
4. It took awhile for Joseph to become aware that he lacked cultural clinical objectivity in this case. Did he act inappropriately by taking on this client? Why or why not?
5. Would you have acted differently or the same as Joseph in the above case? Why or why not?

Chapter Questions

1.What is the prevailing therapeutic duty when treating diversity clients?
2. An MFT decides to treat a suicidal Mexican-American client. What steps would be necessary to take to assess this client correctly from a cultural perspective?

Chapter 26

Treatment of Minors,
Family Code (Marriage and Family Laws)

Treatment of Minors With Parental Consent

All clients under the age of 18 are considered minors in California and require parental consent for psychotherapy treatment. Treating a minor without parental consent is considered battery.

There are situations where the court becomes the "guardian" of the child and only the court can provide consent. This is usually done through a Court Order, via the Probation Department, or the Department of Corrections. It is important to establish who is authorized to provide consent in these situations, before beginning therapy. A reasonable and prudent clinician requests a copy of the court order.

Treatment of Minors Without Parental Consent

The law is specific regarding the treatment of minors without parental consent. Health and Safety Code 124260 describes these special circumstances.

> **Health and Safety Code Section 124260**: An MFT or MFT registered intern may treat a minor without parental consent if:
>
> 1) The minor is 12 years of age or older, *and*
> 2) The clinician determines that the minor is mature enough to participate intelligently in outpatient mental health treatment or counseling, *and*
> 3) The intent of this law is to include the parents in their child's treatment.
> 4) If, after consulting with the minor, the clinician determines that involving the parents is detrimental to the health of the minor, the parent shall be excluded.
> 5) The clinician must document: a) how the clinician determined that the minor was mature enough to receive counseling without parental consent, b) how the clinician determined that the parents could be included in the minor's treatment, c) how the clinician determined that the parents' participation was inappropriate, d) whether the clinician attempted to contact the parents and when , e) if the contact was successful or unsuccessful, and f) the reason it would be inappropriate to contact the parents.

When treating a minor under either of these conditions, the minor is financially responsible for the treatment. One of the goals of treatment in these situations is to incorporate the parents into treatment when appropriate. Once the parents are incorporated into treatment, they become financially responsible for treatment.

For clinicians who treat children, the changes in this law are significant. To avoid potential conflict with parents regarding the clinician's decision to treat the minor or the exclusion of the parents, its best to document carefully how they reasoned that the minor met the legal conditions for treatment and how they reasoned that the parents would be excluded from the minor's treatment ("the clinician deems the parental participation is inappropriate").

Treatment of Emancipated Minors

The court grants emancipated minors the right to make legal decisions without parental consent. They now have the same rights as an adult (expect as limited by law, for example: use of alcohol until the age of 21). Emancipated minors provide their own consent to treat and hold their own privilege. They are also responsible for payment of any treatment. To assure that the minor is indeed emancipated, consider obtaining the legal document granting the minor emancipation.

Treatment of Minors in Divorce Situations

When the parents of a minor client divorce, the parent awarded legal custody of the child by the Court is the only parent permitted to provide consent for treatment. If both parents have been given legal custody, it is in the best interest of the MFT to obtain consent from both parents prior to treatment. To clarify which of the parents have legal custody, consider obtaining a copy of the legal ruling that awarded legal custody.

Parents usually cooperate when the divorce has been amicable. When the divorce has been contentious, obtaining consent from both may be problematic. To manage this situation, first determine who has legal custody. If custody has been awarded to both parents and one of the legal custodians refuses to provide consent, it is best to ask the consenting parent to return to Court and ask the judge to order treatment. Treating without the second parent's consent can redirect unresolved anger that this parent holds against his or her spouse. This anger can be directed toward the therapist in the form of a malpractice or administrative board action.

Drug and Alcohol Counseling Treatment for Minors

Minors in California who are 12 years of age or older may consent to drug and alcoholism treatment on an outpatient basis under the following conditions:

- If appropriate, the treatment of the minor shall include the involvement of the minor's parents or guardian as determined by the psychotherapist.
- Attempts to contact the parents must be documented, including successful or unsuccessful attempts.
- If the therapist determines that contacting the parents would be detrimental to treatment of the minor: the MFT's reasoning must be documented.
- The parents are not liable for payment, unless they participate in the treatment.
- Under this law, minors are not allowed to receive replacement narcotic abuse treatment (methadone) without parental or guardian's consent.

The treatment rendered must be provided by a licensed clinician or organization identified by statute.

Holding Information Policy and Minors

Though minors are the holders of their privilege, by law they are not permitted to enter into legal contracts. Thus, they are not able to sign a written release of information document, nor can they provide informed consent to obtain psychotherapy services. Since parents provide informed consent for minors, it is logical that parents also must sign any written release of information form. Additionally, it is reasonable and prudent for a psychotherapist to discuss with the parent and the minor how he or she will hold sensitive information shared by the minor in an individual session. Most parents will likely want to know that their child is not at risk of harming him/herself. The MFT discusses his or her "Holding Information" policy with the minor and parent prior to seeing the minor alone. Should the minor share sensitive information with the MFT and demand that the therapist not share it with the parent, the MFT must respect the minor's confidentiality. A reasonable and prudent approach to take is to enroll the parent into allowing the therapist to hold sensitive information that may be shared by the minor. This allows trust to develop between the minor and therapist. The MFT can also have the minor allow the clinician to inform the parents should the MFT learn that the minor's behavior presents a danger to self and others.

Minors and Releasing Sensitive Clinical Information to Third Party Payers

A minor's confidentiality is as important as the adult. Third party payers require that MFTs provide a client's confidential information to third party payers if they are to pay for services. There are times when a minor's information though not confidential, is sensitive in nature. Such information includes any identifying information that can affect the minor seriously in the future. For example, a suicide attempt could prevent the minor from obtaining medical benefits on her own. Because parents and minors may lack the ability to consider the potential implication of releasing such information, this responsibility falls on MFTs. Thus, MFTs have the duty to inform the parents of the potential outcome of releasing this information. This action empowers the parents to decide for their children. There are times when the parent initiates the request that MFTs avoid sending such information. They must respect the parent's request as long as the demand does not place the minor in serious jeopardy. Failure to do so can cause the parent to initiate legal action against the MFT in question.

Family Code

The family code is the law that pertains to marriage, divorce, and custody issues in California. Since MFTs provide treatment in this arena, they are expected by law to be familiar with these laws.

300. Marriage is a personal relation arising out of a civil contract between a man and a woman, to which the consent of the parties capable of making that contract is necessary. Consent alone does not constitute marriage. Consent must be followed by the issuance of a license and solemnization as authorized by this division, except as provided by Section 425 and Part 4 (commencing with Section 500).

301. An unmarried male of the age of 18 years or older, and an unmarried female of the age of 18 years or older, and not otherwise disqualified, are capable of consenting to and consummating marriage.

302. An unmarried male or female under the age of 18 years is capable of consenting to and consummating marriage if each of the following documents is filed with the county clerk issuing the marriage license:

(a) The written consent of the parents of each underage person, or of one of the parents or the guardian of each underage person.
(b) A court order granting permission to the underage person to marry, obtained on the showing the court requires.

303. If it appears to the satisfaction of the court by application of a minor that the minor requires a written consent to marry and that the minor has no parent or has no parent capable of consenting, the court may make an order consenting to the issuance of a marriage license and granting permission to the minor to marry. The order shall be filed with the county clerk at the time the license is issued.

304. As part of the court order granting permission to marry under Section 302 or 303, the court shall require the parties to the prospective marriage of a minor to participate in premarital counseling concerning social, economic, and personal responsibilities incident to marriage, if the court considers the counseling to be necessary. The parties shall not be required, without their consent, to confer with counselors provided by religious organizations of any denomination. In determining whether to order the parties to participate in the premarital counseling, the court shall consider, among other factors, the ability of the parties to pay for the counseling. The court may impose a reasonable fee to cover the cost of any premarital counseling provided by the county. The fees shall be used exclusively to cover the cost of the counseling services authorized by this section.

305. Consent to and solemnization of marriage may be proved under the same general rules of evidence as facts are proved in other cases.

306. Except as provided in Section 307, a marriage shall be licensed, solemnized, and authenticated, and the certificate of registry of marriage shall be returned as provided in this part. Noncompliance with this part by a nonparty to the marriage does not invalidate the marriage.

307. This division, so far as it relates to the solemnizing of marriage, is not applicable to members of a particular religious society or denomination not having clergy for the purpose of solemnizing marriage or entering the marriage relation, if all of the following requirements are met:

(a) The parties to the marriage make, sign, and endorse on or attach to the license a statement, in the form prescribed by the State Department of Health Services, showing all of the following:

(1) The fact, time, and place of entering into the marriage.

(2) The signatures and places of residence of two witnesses to the ceremony.

(3) The religious society or denomination of the parties to the marriage, and that the marriage was entered into in accordance with the rules and customs of that religious society or denomination. The statement of the parties to the marriage that the marriage was entered into in accordance with the rules and customs of the religious society or denomination is conclusively presumed to be true.

(b) The License and Certificate of Declaration of Marriage, endorsed pursuant to subdivision (a), is returned to the county recorder of the county in which the license was issued within 30 days after the ceremony.

308. A marriage contracted outside this state that would be valid by the laws of the jurisdiction in which the marriage was contracted is valid in this state.

309. If either party to a marriage denies the marriage, or refuses to join in a declaration of the marriage, the other party may proceed, by action, to have the validity of the marriage determined and declared.

310. Marriage is dissolved only by one of the following:

(a) The death of one of the parties.

(b) A judgment of dissolution of marriage.

(c) A judgment of nullity of marriage.

350. Before entering a marriage, or declaring a marriage pursuant to Section 425, the parties shall first obtain a marriage license from a county clerk.

351. The marriage license shall show all of the following:

(a) The identity of the parties to the marriage.

(b) The parties' real and full names, and places of residence.

(c) The parties' ages.

352. No marriage license shall be granted if either of the applicants lacks the capacity to enter into a valid marriage or is, at the time of making the application for the license, under the influence of an intoxicating liquor or narcotic drug.

353. If an applicant for a marriage license is under the age of 18 years, the license may be granted only if both parties are capable of consenting to and consummating marriage as provided for in Section 302, and the consent or court order required by Section 303 are filed with the county clerk.

354. (a) Each applicant for a marriage license may be required to present authentic identification as to name.

(b) For the purpose of ascertaining the facts mentioned or required in this part, if the clerk deems it necessary, the clerk may examine the applicants for a marriage license on oath at the time of the application. The clerk shall reduce the examination to writing and the applicants shall sign it.

(c) If necessary, the clerk may request additional documentary proof as to the accuracy of the facts stated.

(d) Applicants for a marriage license shall not be required to state, for any purpose, their race or color.

355. (a) The forms for the application for a marriage license and the marriage license shall be prescribed by the State Department of Health Services, and shall be adapted to set forth the facts required in this part.

(b) The form for the application for a marriage license shall include an affidavit on the back, which the applicants shall sign, affirming that they have received the brochure provided for in Section 358.

(c) The affidavit required by subdivision (b) shall state:

AFFIDAVIT

I acknowledge that I have received the brochure titled ______________

Signature of Bride _______ Date _____________

Signature of Groom _______ Date_________________

356. A marriage license issued pursuant to this part expires 90 days after its issuance. The calendar date of expiration shall be clearly noted on the face of the license.

357. (a) The county clerk shall number each marriage license issued and shall transmit at periodic intervals to the county recorder a list or copies of the licenses issued.

(b) Not later than 60 days after the date of issuance, the county recorder shall notify license holders whose certificate of registry has not been returned of that fact and that the marriage license will automatically expire on the date shown on its face.

(c) The county recorder shall notify the license holders of the obligation of the person solemnizing their marriage to return the certificate of registry and endorsed license to the recorder's office within 30 days after the ceremony.

358. (a) The State Department of Health Services shall prepare and publish a brochure which shall contain the following:

(1) Information concerning the possibilities of genetic defects and diseases and contain a listing of centers available for the testing and treatment of genetic defects and diseases.

(2) Information concerning acquired immune deficiency syndrome (AIDS) and the availability of testing for antibodies to the probable causative agent of AIDS.

(b) The State Department of Health Services shall make the brochures available to county clerks who shall distribute a copy of the brochure to each applicant for a marriage license, including applicants for a confidential marriage license and notary publics receiving a confidential marriage license pursuant to Section 503.

(c) Each notary public authorizing a confidential marriage under Section 503 shall distribute a copy of the brochure to the applicants for a confidential marriage license.

(d) To the extent possible, the State Department of Health Services shall seek to combine in a single brochure all statutorily required information for marriage license applicants.

359. (a) Applicants for a marriage license shall obtain from the county clerk issuing the license, a certificate of registry of marriage.

(b) The contents of the certificate of registry are as provided in Division 9 (commencing with Section 10000) of the Health and Safety Code.

(c) The certificate of registry shall be filled out by the applicants, in the presence of the county clerk issuing the marriage license, and shall be presented to the person solemnizing the marriage.

(d) The person solemnizing the marriage shall complete the certificate of registry and shall cause to be entered on the certificate of registry the signature and address of one witness to the marriage ceremony.

(e) The certificate of registry shall be returned by the person solemnizing the marriage to the county recorder of the county in which the license was issued within 30 days after the ceremony.

(f) As used in this division, "returned" means presented to the appropriate person in person, or postmarked, before the expiration of the specified time period.

360. (a) If a certificate of registry of marriage is lost or destroyed after the marriage ceremony but before it is returned to the county recorder, the person solemnizing the marriage, in order to comply with Section 359, shall obtain a duplicate certificate of registry by filing an affidavit setting forth the facts with the county clerk of the county in which the license was issued.

(b) The duplicate certificate of registry may not be issued later than one year after issuance of the original license and shall be returned by the person solemnizing the marriage to the county recorder within 30 days after issuance.

(c) The fee for issuing the duplicate marriage license and certificate of registry is five dollars ($5).

400. Marriage may be solemnized by any of the following who is of the age of 18 years or older:
(a) A priest, minister, or rabbi of any religious denomination. (b) A judge or retired judge, commissioner of

civil marriages or retired commissioner of civil marriages, commissioner or retired commissioner, or assistant commissioner of a court of record or justice court in this state.

(c) A judge or magistrate who has resigned from office.

(d) Any of the following judges or magistrates of the United States:

(1) A justice or retired justice of the United States Supreme Court.

(2) A judge or retired judge of a court of appeals, a district court, or a court created by an act of Congress the judges of which are entitled to hold office during good behavior.

(3) A judge or retired judge of a bankruptcy court or a tax court.

(4) A United States magistrate or retired magistrate.

401.(a) For each county, the county clerk is designated as a commissioner of civil marriages.

(b) The commissioner of civil marriages may appoint deputy commissioners of civil marriages who may solemnize marriages under the direction of the commissioner of civil marriages and shall perform other duties directed by the commissioner.

402. In addition to the persons permitted to solemnize marriages under Section 400, a county may license officials of a nonprofit religious institution, whose articles of incorporation are registered with the Secretary of State, to solemnize the marriages of persons who are affiliated with or are members of the religious institution. The licensee shall possess the degree of doctor of philosophy and must perform religious services or rites for the institution on a regular basis. The marriages shall be performed without fee to the parties.

420. (a) No particular form for the ceremony of marriage is required for solemnization of the marriage, but the parties shall declare, in the presence of the person solemnizing the marriage and necessary witnesses, that they take each other as husband and wife.

(b) No contract of marriage, if otherwise duly made, shall be invalidated for want of conformity to the requirements of any religious sect.

421. Before solemnizing a marriage, the person solemnizing the marriage shall require the presentation of the marriage license. If the person solemnizing the marriage has reason to doubt the correctness of the statement of facts in the marriage license, the person must be satisfied as to the correctness of the statement of facts before solemnizing the marriage. For this purpose, the person may administer oaths and examine the parties and witnesses in the same manner as the county clerk does before issuing the license.

422. The person solemnizing a marriage shall make, sign, and endorse upon or attach to the marriage license a statement, in the form prescribed by the State Department of Health Services, showing all of the following:

(a) The fact, date (month, day, year), and place (city and county) of solemnization.

(b) The names and places of residence of one or more witnesses to the ceremony.

(c) The official position of the person solemnizing the marriage, or of the denomination of which that person is a priest, minister, rabbi, or member of the clergy.

(d) The person solemnizing the marriage shall also type or print the person's name and address.

423. The person solemnizing the marriage shall return the marriage license, endorsed as required in Section 422, to the county recorder of the county in which the license was issued within 30 days after the ceremony.

424. At the request of, and for, either party to a marriage, the person solemnizing the marriage shall issue a marriage certificate showing the facts specified in Section 422.

425. If no record of the solemnization of a marriage previously contracted is known to exist, the parties may purchase a License and Certificate of Declaration of Marriage from the county clerk in the parties' county of residence. The license and certificate shall be returned to the county recorder of the county in which the license was issued.

500. When an unmarried man and an unmarried woman, not minors, have been living together as husband and wife, they may be married pursuant to this chapter by a person authorized to solemnize a marriage under

Chapter 1 (commencing with Section 400) of Part 3, without the necessity of first obtaining health certificates.

501. Except as provided in Section 502, a confidential marriage license shall be issued by the county clerk upon the personal appearance of the parties to be married and their payment of the fees required by Sections 26840.1 and 26840.8 of the Government Code and any fee imposed pursuant to the authorization of Section 26840.3 of the Government Code.

502. If, for any reason, either or both of the parties to be married is physically unable to appear in person before the county clerk, a confidential marriage license shall be issued by the county clerk to the person solemnizing the marriage upon that person's presenting an affidavit to the county clerk, signed by the person and the parties to be married, explaining the reason for the inability to appear.

503. The county clerk shall issue a confidential marriage license upon the request of a notary public approved by the county clerk to authorize confidential marriages pursuant to Chapter 2 (commencing with Section 530) and upon payment by the notary public of the fees specified in Sections 26840.1 and 26840.8 of the Government Code. The parties shall reimburse a notary public who authorizes a confidential marriage for the amount of the fees.

504. A confidential marriage license is valid only for a period of 90 days after its issuance by the county clerk and may only be used in the county in which it was issued.

505. (a) The form of the confidential marriage license shall be prescribed by the State Registrar of Vital Statistics.

(b) The form shall be designed to require that the parties to be married declare or affirm that they meet all of the requirements of this chapter.

(c) The form shall include a certificate of marriage, which shall be filled out by the parties upon performance of the marriage and be authenticated by the person solemnizing the marriage.

(d) The form shall include an affidavit on the back, which the husband and wife shall sign, affirming that they have received the brochure provided for in Section 358.

(e) The affidavit required by subdivision (d) shall state:

AFFIDAVIT

I acknowledge that I have received the brochure titled __________

Signature of Wife __________________________ Date____

Signature of Husband _____________________ Date____

506. (a) The confidential marriage license shall be presented to the person solemnizing the marriage.

(b) Upon performance of the ceremony, the confidential marriage certificate shall be filled out by the parties to the marriage and authenticated by the person solemnizing the marriage.

(c) The certificate shall be returned by the person solemnizing the marriage to the office of the county clerk in the county in which the license was issued within 30 days after the ceremony.

507. Upon performance of the ceremony, the person solemnizing the marriage shall give a copy of the confidential marriage certificate to the parties who were married.

508. The person solemnizing the marriage shall provide the parties who were married with an application for a certified copy of the confidential marriage certificate which shall be filled out by the parties and sent by the person solemnizing the marriage to the county clerk.

509. (a) A party to a confidential marriage may obtain a certified copy of the confidential marriage certificate from the county clerk of the county in which the certificate is filed in any of the following ways:

(1) By submitting the application for a certified copy of the confidential marriage certificate provided to the

parties at the time of the marriage pursuant to Section 508.

(2) By personally appearing before a notary public or at the county clerk's office in the party's county of residence, producing proper identification, obtaining a certificate attesting to the party' s identity from the notary public or county clerk, and transmitting that certificate, together with a request for the certified copy of the confidential marriage certificate, to the county clerk of the county with which the certificate is filed.

(3) By personally appearing at the county clerk's office where the certificate is filed and producing proper identification.

(b) Copies of a confidential marriage certificate may be issued to the parties to the marriage upon the payment of a fee equivalent to that charged for copies of a certificate of marriage.

510. (a) If a confidential marriage certificate is lost, damaged, or destroyed after the performance of the marriage and before it is returned, the county clerk may issue a replacement upon the payment of a fee of five dollars ($5).

(b) The duplicate license may not be issued later than one year after issuance of the original license and shall be returned by the person solemnizing the marriage to the county clerk within 30 days after issuance.

511. (a) Except as provided in subdivision (b), the county clerk shall maintain confidential marriage certificates filed pursuant to Section 506 as permanent records which shall not be open to public inspection except upon order of the court issued upon a showing of good cause.

(b) The county clerk shall keep all original certificates of confidential marriages for one year from the date of filing. After one year, the clerk may microfilm the certificates and dispose of the original certificates or microfilm the certificates and send the original certificates to the Office of the State Registrar. The county clerk shall promptly seal and store at least one original negative of each microphotographic film made in a manner and place as reasonable to ensure its preservation indefinitely against loss, theft, defacement, or destruction. The microphotograph shall be made in a manner that complies with the minimum standards or guidelines, or both, recommended by the American National Standards Institute or the Association for Information and Image Management. Every reproduction shall be deemed and considered an original. A certified copy of any reproduction shall be deemed and considered a certified copy of the original.

(c) The county clerk may conduct a search for a confidential marriage certificate for the purpose of confirming the existence of a marriage, but the date of the marriage and any other information contained in the certificate shall not be disclosed except upon order of the court.

(d) The county clerk shall, not less than quarterly, transmit copies of all original confidential marriage certificates retained, or originals of microfilmed confidential marriage certificates filed after January 1, 1982, to the State Registrar of Vital Statistics. The registrar may destroy the copies so transmitted after they have been indexed. The registrar may respond to an inquiry as to the existence of a marriage performed pursuant to this chapter, but shall not disclose the date of the marriage.

720. Husband and wife contract toward each other obligations of mutual respect, fidelity, and support.

721. (a) Subject to subdivision (b), either husband or wife may enter into any transaction with the other, or with any other person, respecting property, which either might if unmarried.

(b) Except as provided in Sections 143, 144, 146, and 16040 of the Probate Code, in transactions between themselves, a husband and wife are subject to the general rules governing fiduciary relationships which control the actions of persons occupying confidential relations with each other. This confidential relationship imposes a duty of the highest good faith and fair dealing on each spouse, and neither shall take any unfair advantage of the other. This confidential relationship is a fiduciary relationship subject to the same rights and duties of nonmarital business partners, as provided in Sections 15019, 15020, 15021, and 15022 of the Corporations Code, including the following:

(1) Providing each spouse access at all times to any books kept regarding a transaction for the purposes of inspection and copying.

(2) Rendering upon request, true and full information of all things affecting any transaction which concerns the community property. Nothing in this section is intended to impose a duty for either spouse to keep detailed books and records of community property transactions.

(3) Accounting to the spouse, and holding as a trustee, any benefit or profit derived from any transaction by one spouse without the consent of the other spouse which concerns the community property.

750. A husband and wife may hold property as joint tenants or tenants in common, or as community property.

751. The respective interests of the husband and wife in community property during continuance of the marriage relation are present, existing, and equal interests.

752. Except as otherwise provided by statute, neither husband nor wife has any interest in the separate property of the other.

753. Notwithstanding Section 752 and except as provided in Article 2 (commencing with Section 2045), Article 3 (commencing with Section 2047), or Article 4 (commencing with Section 2049) of Chapter 4 of Part 1 of Division 6, neither spouse may be excluded from the other's dwelling.

754. If notice of the pendency of a proceeding for dissolution of the marriage, for nullity of the marriage, or for legal separation of the parties is recorded in any county in which the husband or wife resides on real property that is the separate property of the other, the real property shall not for a period of three months thereafter be transferred, encumbered, or otherwise disposed of voluntarily or involuntarily without the joinder of both spouses, unless the court otherwise orders.

755. (a) The terms "participant," "beneficiary," "employer," "employee organization," "named fiduciary," "fiduciary," and "administrator," as used in subdivision (b), have the same meaning as provided in Section 3 of the Employee Retirement Income Security Act of 1974 (P.L. 93-406) (ERISA), as amended (29 U.S.C.A. Sec. 1002). The term "employee benefit plan" has the same meaning as provided in Section 80 of this code. The term "trustee" shall include a "named fiduciary," as that term is employed in ERISA. The term "plan sponsor" shall include an "employer" or "employee organization," as those terms are used in ERISA (29 U.S.C.A. Sec. 1002).

(b) Notwithstanding Sections 751 and 1100, if payment or refund is made to a participant or the participant's, employee's, or former employee's beneficiary or estate pursuant to an employee benefit plan including a plan governed by the Employee Retirement Income Security Act of 1974 (P.L. 93-406), as amended, the payment or refund fully discharges the plan sponsor and the administrator, trustee, or insurance company making the payment or refund from all adverse claims thereto unless, before the payment or refund is made, the plan sponsor or the administrator of the plan has received written notice by or on behalf of some other person that the other person claims to be entitled to the payment or refund or some part thereof. Nothing in this section affects or releases the participant from claims which may exist against the participant by a person other than the plan sponsor, trustee, administrator, or other person making the benefit payment.

760. Except as otherwise provided by statute, all property, real or personal, wherever situated, acquired by a married person during the marriage while domiciled in this state is community property.

761. (a) Unless the trust instrument or the instrument of transfer expressly provides otherwise, community property that is transferred in trust remains community property during the marriage, regardless of the identity of the trustee, if the trust, originally or as amended before or after the transfer, provides that the trust is revocable as to that property during the marriage and the power, if any, to modify the trust as to the rights and interests in that property during the marriage may be exercised only with the joinder or consent of both spouses.

(b) Unless the trust instrument expressly provides otherwise, a power to revoke as to community property may be exercised by either spouse acting alone. Community property, including any income or appreciation, that is distributed or withdrawn from a trust by revocation, power of withdrawal, or otherwise, remains community property unless there is a valid transmutation of the property at the time of distribution or withdrawal.

(c) The trustee may convey and otherwise manage and control the trust property in accordance with the provisions of the trust without the joinder or consent of the husband or wife unless the trust expressly requires the joinder or consent of one or both spouses.

(d) This section applies to a transfer made before, on, or after July 1, 1987.

(e) Nothing in this section affects the community character of property that is transferred before, on, or after July 1, 1987, in any manner or to a trust other than described in this section.

770. (a) Separate property of a married person includes all of the following:
(1) All property owned by the person before marriage.
(2) All property acquired by the person after marriage by gift, bequest, devise, or descent.
(3) The rents, issues, and profits of the property described in this section.
(b) A married person may, without the consent of the person's spouse, convey the person's separate property.

771. The earnings and accumulations of a spouse and the minor children living with, or in the custody of, the spouse, while living separate and apart from the other spouse, are the separate property of the spouse.

772. After entry of a judgment of legal separation of the parties, the earnings or accumulations of each party are the separate property of the party acquiring the earnings or accumulations.

2010. In a proceeding for dissolution of marriage, for nullity of marriage, or for legal separation of the parties, the court has jurisdiction to inquire into and render any judgment and make orders that are appropriate concerning the following:
(a) The status of the marriage.
(b) The custody of minor children of the marriage.
(c) The support of children for whom support may be ordered, including children born after the filing of the initial petition or the final decree of dissolution.
(d) The support of either party.
(e) The settlement of the property rights of the parties.
(f) The award of attorney's fees and costs.

2011. When service of summons on a spouse is made pursuant to Section 415.50 of the Code of Civil Procedure, the court, without the aid of attachment or the appointment of a receiver, shall have and may exercise the same jurisdiction over:
(a) The community real property of the spouse so served situated in this state as it has or may exercise over the community real property of a spouse who is personally served with process within this state.
(b) The quasi-community real property of the spouse so served situated in this state as it has or may exercise over the quasi-community real property of a spouse who is personally served with process within this state.

2012. (a) During the time a motion pursuant to Section 418.10 of the Code of Civil Procedure is pending, the respondent may appear in opposition to an order made during the pendency of the proceeding and the appearance shall not be deemed a general appearance by the respondent.
(b) As used in this section, a motion pursuant to Section 418.10 of the Code of Civil Procedure is pending from the time notice of motion is served and filed until the time within which to petition for a writ of mandate has expired or, if a petition is made, until the time final judgment in the mandate proceeding is entered.

2040. (a) In addition to the contents required by Section 412.20 of the Code of Civil Procedure, the summons shall contain a temporary restraining order:
(1) Restraining both parties from removing the minor child or children of the parties, if any, from the state without the prior written consent of the other party or an order of the court.
(2) Restraining both parties from transferring, encumbering, hypothecating, concealing, or in any way disposing of any property, real or personal, whether community, quasi-community, or separate, without the written consent of the other party or an order of the court, except in the usual course of business or for the necessities of life and requiring each party to notify the other party of any proposed extraordinary expenditures at least five business days before incurring those expenditures and to account to the court for all extraordinary expenditures made after service of the summons on that party. However, nothing in the restraining order shall preclude the parties from using community property to pay reasonable attorney's fees in order to retain legal counsel in the proceeding.
(3) Restraining both parties from cashing, borrowing against, canceling, transferring, disposing of, or changing the beneficiaries of any insurance or other coverage, including life, health, automobile, and disability held for the benefit of the parties and their child or children for whom support may be ordered.
(b) In all actions filed on and after January 1, 1995, the summons shall contain the following notice:
"WARNING: California law provides that, for purposes of division of property upon dissolution of marriage

or legal separation, property acquired by the parties during marriage in joint form is presumed to be community property. If either party to this action should die before the jointly held community property is divided, the language of how title is held in the deed (i.e., joint tenancy, tenants in common, or community property) will be controlling and not the community property presumption. You should consult your attorney if you want the community property presumption to be written into the recorded title to the property."

2041. Nothing in Section 2040 adversely affects the rights, title, and interest of a purchaser for value, encumbrancer for value, or lessee for value who is without actual knowledge of the restraining order.

2200. Marriages between parents and children, ancestors and descendants of every degree, and between brothers and sisters of the half as well as the whole blood, and between uncles and nieces or aunts and nephews, are incestuous, and void from the beginning, whether the relationship is legitimate or illegitimate.

2201. (a) A subsequent marriage contracted by a person during the life of a former husband or wife of the person, with a person other than the former husband or wife, is illegal and void from the beginning, unless:
(1) The former marriage has been dissolved or adjudged a nullity before the date of the subsequent marriage.
(2) The former husband or wife (i) is absent, and not known to the person to be living for the period of five successive years immediately preceding the subsequent marriage, or (ii) is generally reputed or believed by the person to be dead at the time the subsequent marriage was contracted.

(b) In either of the cases described in paragraph (2) of subdivision (a), the subsequent marriage is valid until its nullity is adjudged pursuant to subdivision (b) of Section 2210.

2210. A marriage is voidable and may be adjudged a nullity if any of the following conditions existed at the time of the marriage:
(a) The party who commences the proceeding or on whose behalf the proceeding is commenced was without the capability of consenting to the marriage as provided in Section 301 or 302, unless, after attaining the age of consent, the party for any time freely cohabited with the other as husband and wife.
(b) The husband or wife of either party was living and the marriage with that husband or wife was then in force and that husband or wife (1) was absent and not known to the party commencing the proceeding to be living for a period of five successive years immediately preceding the subsequent marriage for which the judgment of nullity is sought or (2) was generally reputed or believed by the party commencing the proceeding to be dead at the time the subsequent marriage was contracted.
(c) Either party was of unsound mind, unless the party of unsound mind, after coming to reason, freely cohabited with the other as husband and wife.
(d) The consent of either party was obtained by fraud, unless the party whose consent was obtained by fraud afterwards, with full knowledge of the facts constituting the fraud, freely cohabited with the other as husband or wife.
(e) The consent of either party was obtained by force, unless the party whose consent was obtained by force afterwards freely cohabited with the other as husband or wife.
(f) Either party was, at the time of marriage, physically incapable of entering into the marriage state, and that incapacity continues, and appears to be incurable.

2211. A proceeding to obtain a judgment of nullity of marriage, for causes set forth in Section 2210, must be commenced within the periods and by the parties, as follows:
(a) For causes mentioned in subdivision (a) of Section 2210, by any of the following:

(1) The party to the marriage who was married under the age of legal consent, within four years after arriving at the age of consent.

(2) A parent, guardian, conservator, or other person having charge of the underaged male or female, at any time before the married minor has arrived at the age of legal consent.

(b) For causes mentioned in subdivision (b) of Section 2210, by either of the following:

(1) Either party during the life of the other.

(2) The former husband or wife.

(c) For causes mentioned in subdivision (c) of Section 2210, by the party injured, or by a relative or conservator of the party of unsound mind, at any time before the death of either party.

(d) For causes mentioned in subdivision (d) of Section 2210, by the party whose consent was obtained by fraud, within four years after the discovery of the facts constituting the fraud.
(e) For causes mentioned in subdivision (e) of Section 2210, by the party whose consent was obtained by force, within four years after the marriage.
(f) For causes mentioned in subdivision (f) of Section 2210, by the injured party, within four years after the marriage.

2212. (a) The effect of a judgment of nullity of marriage is to restore the parties to the status of unmarried persons.
(b) A judgment of nullity of marriage is conclusive only as to the parties to the proceeding and those claiming under them.

2250. (a) A proceeding based on void or voidable marriage is commenced by filing a petition entitled "In re the marriage of ____ and ____" which shall state that it is a petition for a judgment of nullity of the marriage.

(b) A copy of the petition together with a copy of a summons in form and content approved by the Judicial Council shall be served upon the other party to the marriage in the same manner as service of papers in civil actions generally.

2251. (a) If a determination is made that a marriage is void or voidable and the court finds that either party or both parties believed in good faith that the marriage was valid, the court shall:

(1) Declare the party or parties to have the status of a putative spouse.

(2) If the division of property is in issue, divide, in accordance with Division 7 (commencing with Section 2500), that property acquired during the union which would have been community property or quasi-community property if the union had not been void or voidable.

This property is known as "quasi-marital property".
(b) If the court expressly reserves jurisdiction, it may make the property division at a time after the judgment.

2252. The property divided pursuant to Section 2251 is liable for debts of the parties to the same extent as if the property had been community property or quasi-community property.

2253. In a proceeding under this part, custody of the children shall be determined according to Division 8 (commencing with Section 3000).

2254. The court may, during the pendency of a proceeding for nullity of marriage or upon judgment of nullity of marriage, order a party to pay for the support of the other party in the same manner as if the marriage had not been void or voidable if the party for whose benefit the order is made is found to be a putative spouse.

2255. The court may grant attorney's fees and costs in accordance with Chapter 3.5 (commencing with Section 2030) of Part 1 in proceedings to have the marriage adjudged void and in those proceedings based upon voidable marriage in which the party applying for attorney's fees and costs is found to be innocent of fraud or wrongdoing in inducing or entering into the marriage, and free from knowledge of the then existence of any prior marriage or other impediment to the contracting of the marriage for which a judgment of nullity is sought.

2310. Dissolution of the marriage or legal separation of the parties may be based on either of the following grounds, which shall be pleaded generally:

(a) Irreconcilable differences, which have caused the irremediable breakdown of the marriage.

(b) Incurable insanity.

2311. Irreconcilable differences are those grounds which are determined by the court to be substantial reasons for not continuing the marriage and which make it appear that the marriage should be dissolved.

2312. A marriage may be dissolved on the grounds of incurable insanity only upon proof, including competent medical or psychiatric testimony, that the insane spouse was at the time the petition was filed, and remains, incurably insane.

2313. No dissolution of marriage granted on the ground of incurable insanity relieves a spouse from any obligation imposed by law as a result of the marriage for the support of the spouse who is incurably insane, and the court may make such order for support, or require a bond therefor, as the circumstances require.

2320. A judgment of dissolution of marriage may not be entered unless one of the parties to the marriage has been a resident of this state for six months and of the county in which the proceeding is filed for three months next preceding the filing of the petition.

2321. (a) In a proceeding for legal separation of the parties in which neither party, at the time the proceeding was commenced, has complied with the residence requirements of Section 2320, either party may, upon complying with the residence requirements, amend the party's petition or responsive pleading in the proceeding to request that a judgment of dissolution of the marriage be entered. The date of the filing of the amended petition or pleading shall be deemed to be the date of commencement of the proceeding for the dissolution of the marriage for the purposes only of the residence requirements of Section 2320.

(b) If the other party has appeared in the proceeding, notice of the amendment shall be given to the other party in the manner provided by rules adopted by the Judicial Council. If no appearance has been made by the other party in the proceeding, notice of the amendment may be given to the other party by mail to the last known address of the other party, or by personal service, if the intent of the party to so amend upon satisfaction of the residence requirements of Section 2320 is set forth in the initial petition or pleading in the manner provided by rules adopted by the Judicial Council.

2322. For the purpose of a proceeding for dissolution of marriage, the husband and wife each may have a separate domicile or residence depending upon proof of the fact and not upon legal presumptions.

2330. (a) A proceeding for dissolution of marriage or for legal separation of the parties is commenced by filing a petition entitled "In re the marriage of ____ and ____" which shall state whether it is a petition for dissolution of the marriage or for legal separation of the parties.

(b) In a proceeding for dissolution of marriage or for legal separation of the parties, the petition shall set forth among other matters, as nearly as can be ascertained, the following facts:

(1) The state or country in which the parties were married.

(2) The date of marriage.

(3) The date of separation.

(4) The number of years from marriage to separation.

(5) The number of children of the marriage, if any, and if none a statement of that fact.

(6) The age and birth date of each minor child of the marriage.

(7) The social security numbers of the husband and wife, if available, and if not available, a statement to that effect.

2330.1. In any proceeding for dissolution of marriage, for legal separation of the parties, or for the support of children, a supplemental complaint may be filed, pursuant to Section 464 of the Code of Civil Procedure either before or after a final judgment, seeking a judgment or order of paternity or support for a child of the mother and father of the child whose paternity and support are already in issue before the court. A supplemental complaint for paternity or support of children may be filed without leave of court either before or after final judgment in the underlying action. Service of the supplemental summons and complaint shall be made in the manner provided for the initial service of a summons by this code.

2330.5. Notwithstanding any other provision of law, if no demand for money, property, costs, or attorney's fees is contained in the petition and the judgment of dissolution of marriage is entered by default, the filing of income and expense declarations and property declarations in connection therewith shall not be required.

2331. A copy of the petition, together with a copy of a summons, in form and content approved by the Judicial Council shall be served upon the other party to the marriage in the same manner as service of papers in civil actions generally.

2332. (a) If the petition for dissolution of the marriage is based on the ground of incurable insanity and the insane spouse has a guardian or conservator, other than the spouse filing the petition, the petition and summons shall be served upon the insane spouse and the guardian or conservator. The guardian or conservator shall defend and protect the interests of the insane spouse.

(b) If the insane spouse has no guardian or conservator, or if the spouse filing the petition is the guardian or conservator of the insane spouse, the court shall appoint a guardian ad litem, who may be the district attorney or the county counsel, if any, to defend and protect the interests of the insane spouse. If a district attorney or county counsel is appointed guardian ad litem pursuant to this subdivision, the successor in the office of district attorney or county counsel, as the case may be, succeeds as guardian ad litem, without further action by the court or parties.

(c) "Guardian or conservator" as used in this section means:

(1) With respect to the issue of the dissolution of the marriage relationship, the guardian or conservator of the person.

(2) With respect to support and property division issues, the guardian or conservator of the estate.

2333. Subject to Section 2334, if from the evidence at the hearing the court finds that there are irreconcilable differences which have caused the irremediable breakdown of the marriage, the court shall order the dissolution of the marriage or a legal separation of the parties.

2334. (a) If it appears that there is a reasonable possibility of reconciliation, the court shall continue the proceeding for the dissolution of the marriage or for a legal separation of the parties for a period not to exceed 30 days.

(b) During the period of the continuance, the court may make orders for the support and maintenance of the parties, the custody of the minor children of the marriage, the support of children for whom support may be ordered, attorney's fees, and for the preservation of the property of the parties.

(c) At any time after the termination of the period of the continuance, either party may move for the dissolution of the marriage or a legal separation of the parties, and the court may enter a judgment of dissolution of the marriage or legal separation of the parties.

2335. Except as otherwise provided by statute, in a pleading or proceeding for dissolution of marriage or legal separation of the parties, including depositions and discovery proceedings, evidence of specific acts of misconduct is improper and inadmissible.

2336. (a) No judgment of dissolution or of legal separation of the parties may be granted upon the default of one of the parties or upon a statement or finding of fact made by a referee; but the court shall, in addition to the statement or finding of the referee, require proof of the grounds alleged, and the proof, if not taken before the court, shall be by affidavit.

(b) If the proof is by affidavit, the personal appearance of the affiant is required only when it appears to the court that any of the following circumstances exist:

(1) Reconciliation of the parties is reasonably possible.

(2) A proposed child custody order is not in the best interest of the child.

(3) A proposed child support order is less than a noncustodial parent is capable of paying.

(4) A personal appearance of a party or interested person would be in the best interests of justice.

(c) An affidavit submitted pursuant to this section shall contain a stipulation by the affiant that the affiant understands that proof will be by affidavit and that the affiant will not appear before the court unless so ordered by the court.

2337. (a) In a proceeding for dissolution of marriage, the court, upon noticed motion, may sever and grant an early and separate trial on the issue of the dissolution of the status of the marriage apart from other issues.

(b) The court may impose upon a party any of the following conditions on granting a severance of the issue of the dissolution of the status of the marriage, and in case of that party's death, an order of any of the following conditions continues to be binding upon that party's estate:

(1) The party shall indemnify and hold the other party harmless from any taxes, reassessments, interest, and penalties payable by the other party if the dissolution of the marriage before the division of the parties' community estate results in a taxable event to either of the parties by reason of the ultimate division of their

community estate, which taxes would not have been payable if the parties were still married at the time the division was made.

(2) Until judgment has been entered on all remaining issues and has become final, the party shall maintain all existing health and medical insurance coverage for the other party and the minor children as named dependents, so long as the party is legally able to do so. At the time the party is no longer legally eligible to maintain the other party as a named dependent under the existing health and medical policies, the party or the party's estate shall, at the party's sole expense, purchase and maintain health and medical insurance coverage that is comparable to the existing health and medical insurance coverage. If comparable insurance coverage is not obtained, the party or the party's estate is responsible for the health and medical expenses incurred by the other party which would have been covered by the insurance coverage, and shall indemnify and hold the other party harmless from any adverse consequences resulting from the lack of insurance.

(3) Until judgment has been entered on all remaining issues and has become final, the party shall indemnify and hold the other party harmless from any adverse consequences resulting to the other party if the bifurcation results in a termination of the other party's right to a probate homestead in the residence in which the other party resides at the time the severance is granted.

(4) Until judgment has been entered on all remaining issues and has become final, the party shall indemnify and hold the other party harmless from any adverse consequences resulting to the other party if the bifurcation results in the loss of the rights of the other party to a probate family allowance as the surviving spouse of the party.

(5) Until judgment has been entered on all remaining issues and has become final, the party shall indemnify and hold the other party harmless from any adverse consequences resulting to the other party if the bifurcation results in the loss of the other party's rights to pension benefits, elections, or survivors' benefits under the party's pension or retirement plan to the extent that the other party would have been entitled to those benefits or elections as the surviving spouse of the party.

(6) Prior to entry of judgment terminating status, both of the following shall occur:

(A) The party's retirement or pension plan shall be joined as a party to the proceeding for dissolution.

(B) If applicable, an order pursuant to Section 2611 shall be entered with reference to the defined benefit or similar plan pending the ultimate resolution of the distribution of benefits under the employee benefit plan.

(7) The party shall indemnify and hold the other party harmless from any adverse consequences if the bifurcation results in the loss of rights to social security benefits or elections to the extent the other party would have been entitled to those benefits or elections as the surviving spouse of the party.

(8) Any other condition the court determines is just and equitable.

(c) A judgment granting a dissolution of the status of the marriage shall expressly reserve jurisdiction for later determination of all other pending issues.

2338. (a) In a proceeding for dissolution of the marriage or legal separation of the parties, the court shall file its decision and any statement of decision as in other cases.

(b) If the court determines that no dissolution should be granted, a judgment to that effect only shall be entered.

(c) If the court determines that a dissolution should be granted, a judgment of dissolution of marriage shall be entered. After the entry of the judgment and before it becomes final, neither party has the right to dismiss the proceeding without the consent of the other.

2339. (a) Subject to subdivision (b) and to Sections 2340 to 2344, inclusive, no judgment of dissolution is final for the purpose of terminating the marriage relationship of the parties until six months have expired from the date of service of a copy of summons and petition or the date of appearance of the respondent, whichever occurs first.

(b) The court may extend the six-month period described in subdivision (a) for good cause shown.

2340. A judgment of dissolution of marriage shall specify the date on which the judgment becomes finally effective for the purpose of terminating the marriage relationship of the parties.

2341. (a) Notwithstanding Section 2340, if an appeal is taken from the judgment or a motion for a new trial is made, the dissolution of marriage does not become final until the motion or appeal has been finally disposed of, nor then, if the motion has been granted or judgment reversed.

(b) Notwithstanding any other provision of law, the filing of an appeal or of a motion for a new trial does not stay the effect of a judgment insofar as it relates to the dissolution of the marriage status and restoring the parties to the status of unmarried persons, unless the appealing or moving party specifies in the notice of appeal or motion for new trial an objection to the termination of the marriage status. No party may make such an objection to the termination of the marriage status unless such an objection was also made at the time of trial.

2342. Where a joint petition under Chapter 5 (commencing with Section 2400) is thereafter revoked and either party commences a proceeding pursuant to Section 2330 within 90 days from the date of the filing of the revocation, the date the judgment becomes a final judgment under Section 2339 shall be calculated by deducting the period of time which has elapsed from the date of filing the joint petition to the date of filing the revocation.

2343. The court may, upon notice and for good cause shown, or on stipulation of the parties, retain jurisdiction over the date of termination of the marital status, or may order that the marital status be terminated at a future specified date. On the date of termination of the marital status, the parties are restored to the status of unmarried persons.

2344. (a) The death of either party after entry of the judgment does not prevent the judgment from becoming a final judgment under Sections 2339 to 2343, inclusive.

(b) Subdivision (a) does not validate a marriage by either party before the judgment becomes final, nor does it constitute a defense in a criminal prosecution against either party.

2345. The court may not render a judgment of the legal separation of the parties without the consent of both parties unless one party has not made a general appearance and the petition is one for legal separation.

2346. (a) If the court determines that a judgment of dissolution of the marriage should be granted, but by mistake, negligence, or inadvertence, the judgment has not been signed, filed, and entered, the court may cause the judgment to be signed, dated, filed, and entered in the proceeding as of the date when the judgment could have been signed, dated, filed, and entered originally, if it appears to the satisfaction of the court that no appeal is to be taken in the proceeding or motion made for a new trial, to annul or set aside the judgment, or for relief under Chapter 8 (commencing with Section 469) of Title 6 of Part 2 of the Code of Civil Procedure.

(b) The court may act under subdivision (a) on its own motion or upon the motion of either party to the proceeding. In contested cases, the motion of a party shall be with notice to the other party.

(c) The court may cause the judgment to be entered nunc pro tunc as provided in this section, even though the judgment may have been previously entered, where through mistake, negligence, or inadvertence the judgment was not entered as soon as it could have been entered under the law if applied for.

(d) The court shall not cause a judgment to be entered nunc pro tunc as provided in this section as of a date before trial in the matter, before the date of an uncontested judgment hearing in the matter, or before the date of submission to the court of an application for judgment on affidavit pursuant to Section 2336. Upon the entry of the judgment, the parties have the same rights with regard to the dissolution of marriage becoming final on the date that it would have become final had the judgment been entered upon the date when it could have been originally entered.

2347. A judgment of legal separation of the parties does not bar a subsequent judgment of dissolution of the marriage granted pursuant to a petition for dissolution filed by either party.

2400. (a) A marriage may be dissolved by the summary dissolution procedure provided in this chapter if all of the following conditions exist at the time the proceeding is commenced:

(1) Either party has met the jurisdictional requirements of Chapter 3 (commencing with Section 2320) with regard to dissolution of marriage.

(2) Irreconcilable differences have caused the irremediable breakdown of the marriage and the marriage should be dissolved.

(3) There are no children of the relationship of the parties born before or during the marriage or adopted by the parties during the marriage, and the wife, to her knowledge, is not pregnant.

(4) The marriage is not more than five years in duration at the time the petition is filed.

(5) Neither party has any interest in real property wherever situated, with the exception of the lease of a residence occupied by either party which satisfies the following requirements:

(A) The lease does not include an option to purchase.

(B) The lease terminates within one year from the date of the filing of the petition.

(6) There are no unpaid obligations in excess of four thousand dollars ($4,000) incurred by either or both of the parties after the date of their marriage, excluding the amount of any unpaid obligation with respect to an automobile.

(7) The total fair market value of community property assets, excluding all encumbrances and automobiles, including any deferred compensation or retirement plan, is less than twenty-five thousand dollars ($25,000), and neither party has separate property assets, excluding all encumbrances and automobiles, in excess of twenty-five thousand dollars ($25,000).

(8) The parties have executed an agreement setting forth the division of assets and the assumption of liabilities of the community, and have executed any documents, title certificates, bills of sale, or other evidence of transfer necessary to effectuate the agreement.

(9) The parties waive any rights to spousal support.

(10) The parties, upon entry of the judgment of dissolution of marriage pursuant to Section 2403, irrevocably waive their respective rights to appeal and their rights to move for a new trial.

(11) The parties have read and understand the summary dissolution brochure provided for in Section 2406.

(12) The parties desire that the court dissolve the marriage.

(b) On January 1, 1985, and on January 1 of each odd-numbered year thereafter, the amounts in paragraph (6) of subdivision (a) shall be adjusted to reflect any change in the value of the dollar. On January 1, 1993, and on January 1 of each odd-numbered year thereafter, the amounts in paragraph (7) of subdivision (a) shall be adjusted to reflect any change in the value of the dollar. The adjustments shall be made by multiplying the base amounts by the percentage change in the California Consumer Price Index as compiled by the Department of Industrial Relations, with the result rounded to the nearest thousand dollars. The Judicial Council shall compute and publish the amounts.

2401. (a) A proceeding for summary dissolution of the marriage shall be commenced by filing a joint petition in the form prescribed by the Judicial Council.

(b) The petition shall be signed under oath by both the husband and the wife, and shall include all of the following:

(1) A statement that as of the date of the filing of the joint petition all of the conditions set forth in Section 2400 have been met.

(2) The mailing address of both the husband and the wife.

(3) A statement whether or not the wife elects to have her maiden or former name restored, and, if so, the name to be restored.

2402. (a) At any time before the filing of application for judgment pursuant to Section

2403, either party to the marriage may revoke the joint petition and thereby terminate the summary dissolution proceeding filed pursuant to this chapter.

(b) The revocation shall be effected by filing with the clerk of the court where the proceeding was commenced a notice of revocation in such form and content as shall be prescribed by the Judicial Council.

(c) The revoking party shall send a copy of the notice of revocation to the other party by first-class mail, postage prepaid, at the other party's last known address.

2403. When six months have expired from the date of the filing of the joint petition for summary dissolution, the court may, upon application of either party, enter the judgment dissolving the marriage. The judgment restores to the parties the status of single persons, and either party may marry after the entry of the judgment. The clerk shall send a notice of entry of judgment to each of the parties at the party's last known address.

2404. Entry of the judgment pursuant to Section 2403 constitutes: (a) A final adjudication of the rights and obligations of the parties with respect to the status of the marriage and property rights.

(b) A waiver of their respective rights to spousal support, rights to appeal, and rights to move for a new trial.

2405. (a) Entry of the judgment pursuant to Section 2403 does not prejudice nor bar the rights of either of the parties to institute an action to set aside the judgment for fraud, duress, accident, mistake, or other grounds recognized at law or in equity or to make a motion pursuant to Section 473 of the Code of Civil Procedure.

(b) The court shall set aside a judgment entered pursuant to Section 2403 regarding all matters except the status of the marriage, upon proof that the parties did not meet the requirements of Section 2400 at the time the petition was filed.

2406. (a) Each superior court shall make available a brochure, the contents and form of which shall be prescribed by the Judicial Council, describing the requirements, nature, and effect of proceedings under this chapter. The brochure shall be printed and distributed by the Judicial Council in both English and Spanish.

(b) The brochure shall state, in nontechnical language, all the following:

(1) It is in the best interests of the parties to consult an attorney regarding the dissolution of their marriage. The services of an attorney may be obtained through lawyer referral services, group or prepaid legal services, or legal aid organizations.

(2) The parties should not rely exclusively on this brochure which is not intended as a guide for self-representation in proceedings under this chapter.

(3) A concise summary of the provisions and procedures of this chapter and Sections 2320 and 2322 and Sections 2339 to 2344, inclusive.

(4) The nature of services of the conciliation court, where available.

(5) Neither party to the marriage can in the future obtain spousal support from the other.

(6) A statement in boldface type to the effect that upon entry of the judgment, the rights and obligations of the parties to the marriage with respect to the marriage, including property and spousal support rights, will be permanently adjudicated without right of appeal, except that neither party will be barred from instituting an action to set aside the judgment for fraud, duress, accident, mistake, or other grounds at law or in equity, or to make a motion pursuant to Section 473 of the Code of Civil Procedure.

(7) The parties to the marriage retain the status of married persons and cannot remarry until the judgment dissolving the marriage is entered.

(8) Other matters as the Judicial Council considers appropriate.

6920. Subject to the limitations provided in this chapter, notwithstanding any other provision of law, a minor may consent to the matters provided in this chapter, and the consent of the minor's parent or guardian is not necessary.

6921. A consent given by a minor under this chapter is not subject to disaffirmance because of minority.

6922. (a) A minor may consent to the minor's medical care or dental care if all of the following conditions are satisfied:

(1) The minor is 15 years of age or older.

(2) The minor is living separate and apart from the minor's parents or guardian, whether with or without the consent of a parent or guardian and regardless of the duration of the separate residence.

(3) The minor is managing the minor's own financial affairs, regardless of the source of the minor's income.

(b) The parents or guardian are not liable for medical care or dental care provided pursuant to this section.

(c) A physician and surgeon or dentist may, with or without the consent of the minor patient, advise the minor's parent or guardian of the treatment given or needed if the physician and surgeon or dentist has reason to know, on the basis of the information given by the minor, the whereabouts of the parent or guardian.

6924. (a) As used in this section:

(1) "Mental health treatment or counseling services" means the provision of mental health treatment or counseling on an outpatient basis by any of the following:

(A) A governmental agency.

(B) A person or agency having a contract with a governmental agency to provide the services.

(C) An agency that receives funding from community united funds. (D) A runaway house or crisis resolution center.

(E) A professional person, as defined in paragraph (2).

(2) "Professional person" means any of the following:

(A) A person designated as a mental health professional in Sections 622 to 626, inclusive, of Article 8 of Subchapter 3 of Chapter 1 of Title 9 of the California Code of Regulations.
(B) A marriage, family, and child counselor as defined in Chapter 13 (commencing with Section 4980) of Division 2 of the Business and Professions Code.

(C) A licensed educational psychologist as defined in Article 5 (commencing with Section 4986) of Chapter 13 of Division 2 of the Business and Professions Code.

(D) A credentialed school psychologist as described in Section 49424 of the Education Code.

(E) A clinical psychologist as defined in Section 1316.5 of the Health and Safety Code.

(F) The chief administrator of an agency referred to in paragraph (1) or (3).
(3) "Residential shelter services" means any of the following: (A) The provision of residential and other support services to minors on a temporary or emergency basis in a facility that services only minors by a governmental agency, a person or agency having a contract with a governmental agency to provide these services, an agency that receives funding from community funds, or a licensed community care facility or crisis resolution center.

(B) The provision of other support services on a temporary or emergency basis by any professional person as defined in paragraph (2).

(b) A minor who is 12 years of age or older may consent to mental health treatment or counseling on an outpatient basis, or to residential shelter services, if both of the following requirements are satisfied:

(1) The minor, in the opinion of the attending professional person, is mature enough to participate intelligently in the outpatient services or residential shelter services.

(2) The minor (A) would present a danger of serious physical or mental harm to self or to others without the mental health treatment or counseling or residential shelter services, or (B) is the alleged victim of incest or child abuse.

(c) A professional person offering residential shelter services, whether as an individual or as a representative of an entity specified in paragraph (3) of subdivision (a), shall make his or her best efforts to notify the parent or guardian of the provision of services.

(d) The mental health treatment or counseling of a minor authorized by this section shall include involvement of the minor's parent or guardian unless, in the opinion of the professional person who is treating or counseling the minor, the involvement would be inappropriate. The professional person who is treating or counseling the minor shall state in the client record whether and when the person attempted to contact the minor's parent or guardian, and whether the attempt to contact was successful or unsuccessful, or the reason why, in the professional person's opinion, it would be inappropriate to contact the minor's parent or guardian.

(e) The minor's parents or guardian are not liable for payment for mental health treatment or counseling services provided pursuant to this section unless the parent or guardian participates in the mental health treatment or counseling, and then only for services rendered with the participation of the parent or guardian. The minor's parents or guardian are not liable for payment for any residential shelter services provided pursuant to this section unless the parent or guardian consented to the provision of those services.

(f) This section does not authorize a minor to receive convulsive therapy or psychosurgery as defined in subdivisions (f) and (g) of Section 5325 of the Welfare and Institutions Code, or psychotropic drugs without the consent of the minor's parent or guardian.

6925. (a) A minor may consent to medical care related to the prevention or treatment of pregnancy.

(b) This section does not authorize a minor:

(1) To be sterilized without the consent of the minor's parent or guardian.

(2) To receive an abortion without the consent of a parent or guardian other than as provided in Section 25958 of the Health and Safety Code.

6926. (a) A minor who is 12 years of age or older and who may have come into contact with an infectious, contagious, or communicable disease may consent to medical care related to the diagnosis or treatment of the disease, if the disease or condition is one that is required by law or regulation adopted pursuant to law to be reported to the local health officer, or is a related sexually transmitted disease, as may be determined by the State Director of Health Services.

(b) The minor's parents or guardian are not liable for payment for medical care provided pursuant to this section.

6927. A minor who is 12 years of age or older and who is alleged to have been raped may consent to medical care related to the diagnosis or treatment of the condition and the collection of medical evidence with regard to the alleged rape.

6928. (a) "Sexually assaulted" as used in this section includes, but is not limited to, conduct coming within Section 261, 286, or 288a of the Penal Code.

(b) A minor who is alleged to have been sexually assaulted may consent to medical care related to the diagnosis and treatment of the condition, and the collection of medical evidence with regard to the alleged sexual assault.

(c) The professional person providing medical treatment shall attempt to contact the minor's parent or guardian and shall note in the minor's treatment record the date and time the professional person attempted to contact the parent or guardian and whether the attempt was successful or unsuccessful. This subdivision does not apply if the professional person reasonably believes that the minor's parent or guardian committed the sexual assault on the minor.

6929. (a) As used in this section:

(1) "Counseling" means the provision of counseling services by a provider under a contract with the state or a county to provide alcohol or drug abuse counseling services pursuant to Part 2 (commencing with Section 5600) of Division 5 of the Welfare and Institutions Code or pursuant to Division 10.5 (commencing with Section 11750) of the Health and Safety Code.

(2) "Drug or alcohol" includes, but is not limited to, any substance listed in any of the following:

(A) Section 380 or 381 of the Penal Code.

(B) Division 10 (commencing with Section 11000) of the Health and Safety Code.

(C) Subdivision (f) of Section 647 of the Penal Code.

(3) "LAAM" means levoalphacetylmethadol as specified in paragraph (10) of subdivision (c) of Section 11055 of the Health and Safety Code.

(4) "Professional person" means a physician and surgeon, registered nurse, psychologist, clinical social worker, or marriage, family, and child counselor.

(b) A minor who is 12 years of age or older may consent to medical care and counseling relating to the diagnosis and treatment of a drug or alcohol related problem.

(c) The treatment plan of a minor authorized by this section shall include the involvement of the minor's parent or guardian, if appropriate, as determined by the professional person or treatment facility treating the minor. The professional person providing medical care or counseling to a minor shall state in the minor's treatment record whether and when the professional person attempted to contact the minor's parent or guardian, and whether the attempt to contact the parent or guardian was successful or unsuccessful, or the reason why, in the opinion of the professional person, it would not be appropriate to contact the minor's parent or guardian.

(d) The minor's parents or guardian are not liable for payment for any care provided to a minor pursuant to this section, except that if the minor's parent or guardian participates in a counseling program pursuant to this section, the parent or guardian is liable for the cost of the services provided to the minor and the parent or guardian.

(e) This section does not authorize a minor to receive replacement narcotic abuse treatment, in a program licensed pursuant to Article 3 (commencing with Section 11875) of Chapter 1 of Part 3 of Division 10.5 of the Health and Safety Code, without the consent of the minor's parent or guardian.

7000. This part may be cited as the Emancipation of Minors Law.

7001. It is the purpose of this part to provide a clear statement defining emancipation and its consequences and to permit an emancipated minor to obtain a court declaration of the minor's status. This part is not intended to affect the status of minors who may become emancipated under the decisional case law that was in effect before the enactment of Chapter 1059 of the Statutes of 1978.

7002. A person under the age of 18 years is an emancipated minor if any of the following conditions is satisfied:

(a) The person has entered into a valid marriage, whether or not the marriage has been dissolved.

(b) The person is on active duty with the armed forces of the United States.

(c) The person has received a declaration of emancipation pursuant to Section 7122.

7050. An emancipated minor shall be considered as being an adult for the following purposes:

(a) The minor's right to support by the minor's parents.

(b) The right of the minor's parents to the minor's earnings and to control the minor.

(c) The application of Sections 300 and 601 of the Welfare and Institutions Code.

(d) Ending all vicarious or imputed liability of the minor's parents or guardian for the minor's torts. Nothing in this section affects any liability of a parent, guardian, spouse, or employer imposed by the Vehicle Code, or any vicarious liability that arises from an agency relationship.

(e) The minor's capacity to do any of the following:

(1) Consent to medical, dental, or psychiatric care, without parental consent, knowledge, or liability.

(2) Enter into a binding contract or give a delegation of power. (3) Buy, sell, lease, encumber, exchange, or transfer an interest in real or personal property, including, but not limited to, shares of stock in a domestic or foreign corporation or a membership in a nonprofit corporation.

(4) Sue or be sued in the minor's own name.

(5) Compromise, settle, arbitrate, or otherwise adjust a claim, action, or proceeding by or against the minor.

(6) Make or revoke a will.

(7) Make a gift, outright or in trust.

(8) Convey or release contingent or expectant interests in property, including marital property rights and any right of survivorship incident to joint tenancy, and consent to a transfer, encumbrance, or gift of marital property.

(9) Exercise or release the minor's powers as donee of a power of appointment unless the creating instrument otherwise provides. (10) Create for the minor's own benefit or for the benefit of others a revocable or irrevocable trust.

(11) Revoke a revocable trust.

(12) Elect to take under or against a will.

(13) Renounce or disclaim any interest acquired by testate or intestate succession or by inter vivos transfer, including exercise of the right to surrender the right to revoke a revocable trust.

(14) Make an election referred to in Section 13502 of, or an election and agreement referred to in Section 13503 of, the Probate Code.

(15) Establish the minor's own residence.

(16) Apply for a work permit pursuant to Section 49110 of the Education Code without the request of the minor's parents.

(17) Enroll in a school or college.

Clinical Example # 1

Marianne receives a phone call from the 14-year-old son of one of her current clients. She tells Marianne that he needs her help because recently, she found out that she is pregnant and does not want her mother to know. She refuses to say who the father is and if pressured, she'll run away. Marianne feels stuck. She wants to help both mother and daughter and is afraid that if the mother finds out she is seeing her daughter, she will leave treatment. Marianne tells the daughter she can't see her without parental consent.

Questions for Clinical Example # 1

1. What do you believe is causing Marianne's "stuckness?"
2. Is she able to be objective from that place of "stuckness? Why or why not?
3. What options has Marianne ignored when providing treatment alternatives to the 14 year-old?
4. On the one hand, Marianne seems to be attempting to prevent a conflict of interests between the needs of the mother and the needs of the daughter? How could she have managed this issue in a reasonable and prudent manner?
5. How would you manage this situation in a reasonable and prudent manner?

Clinical Example # 2

Rodney's parents are struggled through a contentious divorce. Each accused the other of infidelity and lack of interest in their son. Both have legal custody of Rodney and tend to undermine each other's legal decisions. Rodney is referred to an MFT for counseling by his father's therapist due to depressive symptoms and dad makes an appointment ASAP. Mother finds out that Rodney has been seeing this clinician and she was not consulted for consent. Feeling betrayed again by her husband, she decides to take action against the MFT and retains an attorney.

Questions for Clinical Example # 2

1. What possible legal actions could the MFT face?
2. As a consultant to the MFT, what steps would you have told her to take prior to seeing Rodney?
3. The MFT's intention was to help Rodney, however she now is facing possible legal action. What could be her best defense? Will it hold in court? Why or why not?
4. Could the MFT have made an appointment with Rodney without parental consent? Why or why not? Would this have been an effective clinical action? Why or why not?
5. What steps would you take to avoid this dilemma?

Chapter Questions

1. Under what conditions can a therapist treat a minor without parental consent?
2. A 16 year-old calls a therapist because he wants to quit smoking cigarettes. What does the law say about MFTs treating minors for this issue?
3. What makes the age of 12 years so important in distinguishing the need for parental consent?

4. What are the requirements for marriage in California?
5. What elements are required for consent for marriage?
6. What is required to dissolve a marriage?
7. What are the requirements for two underage persons to marry?
8. Who is legally able to carry out a marriage ceremony?
9. What is required to obtain a confidential marriage license?
10. What do the following terms mean: community property, tenants in common, and joint tenants?
11. What is separate property in a marriage?
12. What areas of marriage can the court examine when dissolution of marriage takes place?
13. What are the elements for claiming dissolution of marriage?
14. What is the definition of a court-appointed guardian?
15. What is a summary dissolution of marriage and what are the conditions for granting it?
16. How can a minor become emancipated?

Chapter 27

Clinical Challenges With Legal Implications

Clinical Objectivity: The Foundation of Making Clinical Decisions

Experts would tell us that making clinical decisions is not an "all-or-nothing" process. Clinical objectivity is an integral part of making decisions and in some circumstances clinicians maintain clarity and balance while in other circumstances, clinicians delve into the loss of clinical objectivity. The process of transitioning from clarity to loss of objectivity is subtle and progresses sequentially to an overt state. Even seasoned clinicians may be unaware of this process and they act out instinctively without attending to the client's well-being.

This observation is significant because it explains the clinicians' inability to extricate themselves from this process once it begins. It appears that the initial stage of the loss of objectivity begins with the clinician's inability to separate his or her feelings from the client. Through this emotional enmeshment, the clinician fails to discern empathy from sympathy for the client and becomes one with the client's emotions. Thus, the client's anger integrates with the clinician's anger and the clinician's unresolved family of origin issues increases by an amount related to the severity of the pain or trauma of the unresolved "family of origin" issues.

Emotional enmeshment arising from positive feelings can also trigger the loss of clinical objectivity. This process is the same as the one discussed above, except that we substitute positive for negative ones. For example, the clinician identifies a client's positive qualities to those of a loved one in childhood. This identification causes positive feelings within the clinician and he or she wants to replicate them as an adult. At this point, the clinician begins a subtle loss of clinical objectivity and this progresses as the clinician increases the enmeshment. The latter increases in intensity and at some point, the childhood feelings become real adult feelings existing in the present and the clinician sinks into a deeper level of loss of clinical objectivity. Though the clinician may have crossed minimal professional boundaries, the time comes when the clinician is unable to help him/herself and his or her loss of objectivity causes him or her to cross a significant professional boundary that will cause harm to the client.

Likely, some clinicians will eschew the "psychic stunt double" theory while telling themselves that this is all fine and good, however they know better. True and for clinicians, the danger lies in the subtle and insidious expression of this dynamic. The subtle engagement can be difficult to identify as it engulfs and obfuscates the psychotherapist's clinical and decision making processes. Without a mechanism providing awareness and recognition of these traps, the clinician will figuratively gravitate slowly in a downward spiral into a state of progressive loss of clinical objectivity until he or she makes a clinical decision that injures the client.

The Risks and Benefits of Keeping Minimal vs. Voluminous Records

When clinicians discuss this topic, they create three camps: those who keep no records, those who keep minimal records, and those who keep voluminous records. Regardless of which camp clinicians find themselves in, they will not learn the efficacy of their method until they face a malpractice action. Experts agree that regardless of the method used for documentation, the best protective method assures that the following components are included in both methods.

1. I use a separate intake form to obtain client information, emergency contacts, medical information, and history of past treatment providers.

2. The consent form discusses the legally required elements according to Rains v. Superior Court (1984). It includes a discussion on the limits of confidentiality, disposition of records, management of subpoenas, signed consent to treat, financial policies, office policies, termination policy, emergency management.

3. The release of information form complies with California law and HIPAA.

4. Use the Mental Status Exam to document the client's mental state. If a client presents minimal depressive symptoms, use the Beck Depression Inventory.

5. Assure that the 5-Axis diagnosis is accurate and based on observable clinical symptoms and their duration. State a treatment prognosis.

6. The 4-Phase treatment plan addresses the presenting issue. Modify it as needed and use it as an assessment tool to determine the progress of treatment.

7. The progress notes indicate how treatment is progressing. Never use process notes because they open a "can of worms" in case of a lawsuit.

8. In case of a legal clinical challenge, such as a mandated breach of confidentiality, document your rationale and actions carefully.

9. Always use a discharge summary to make sure those involved know that treatment has ended for appropriate reasons or that the client has been referred appropriately.

Clinicians would that it serves them to use a minimal system of keeping records. However, the therapist who faced a lawsuit would help other therapists understand the risks and benefits of keeping minimal of records. Each clinician will decide for him/herself as to how much to write and which format is best. However, they would agree that the recommended content serves and protects them.

Clinicians Ignore Risk Factors At Their Own Risk

When clinicians experience a client's suicide or suicide attempt, the client's family seeks someone to blame for their loved one's death or near death. They immediately turn to the psychotherapist an attempt to hold him or her accountable for the client's act of harm to self. The opposing attorney determines the clinician's culpability as determined by how he or she assessed and applied risk factors to the risk treatment plan. The opposing attorney's expert witness indicates which risk factors, if any the clinician documented in his or her treatment records. This attorney knows that clinician's cannot predict harm, thus they fail to prepare for when a high-risk client acts out. Clinicians ignore some of the following important risk factors:

- The literature states that mental health clinicians have the duty to recognize risk factors. MFTs must know that depending on the severity of these risk factors, clinicians must know that in conjunction, these represent a danger to self or others.

- It is well documented that clinician miss the first set of risk factors and fail to obtain additional clinical information when the client presents a mild form of mood related behaviors: a history of mild depression, lack of psychotropic medication, and failure to obtain relevant suicidal ideation information from previous clinicians.

- When the client's symptoms worsen, they tend to miss the next set of risk factors: the client statements about not wanting to live any more, a history of making these types of statements to other therapists, deviating the conversation into a different subject to avoid discussing explicitly about harm to self.

- Finally, the client indicates a verbal desire to kill himself and may act out immediately while leaving the therapist unprepared to manage the pending act of harm to self. Unfortunately, the client places the clinician in a legal bind that requires addressing according to Bellah v. Greenson, the clinician fails in his duty to protect the client.

Recommendations:

- Know your legal responsibilities regarding managing high-risk clients.

- Know, recognize, and act upon risk factors indicating harm to self or others.

- Make sure your clinical records are integrative and complementary to protect you.

- Should someone sue you for malpractice, make sure your attorney is competent in mental health cases and that you have an expert witness who can help your attorney prepare any contingency to afford you the best protection possible.

The Out of Compliance and Uncooperative Client

One of the most challenging clients in clinical practice is that client who is uncooperative and out of compliance with the clinician's clinical boundaries. Imagine the following client:

> **The client interviews six clinicians until she finds the "perfect" one. She tells the last one that she does not want to end treatment prematurely, she wanted the "best" one in the community, and she wanted "in-depth" psychotherapy. After a few weeks of weekly treatment, the therapist has minor reservations about this client: she has not signed all the required forms for informed consent.**
>
> **Months later, the clinician realizes that her forms are not signed. She has hears a "million" excuses from her client and finally decides to hold her client accountable. Upon recounting the numerous promises her client made, the client delivers a tirade about how she had to put up with substandard therapy. The therapist invites the client to find someone else and the client's retort is: "You'll have to fire me and you can't because I did not sign your informed consent. And if you keep pushing me, you'll drive me to suicide."**

The clinician's challenge is severe: she lacks the appropriate foundation to terminate the therapeutic relationship using a legally and ethically sound approach. Instead, she created a bind for herself. Her only avenue open for termination is to declare that she does not have the competence to treat this client and provides her with appropriate referral. The client can accuse her of abandonment and sue her for malpractice. The therapist will have to determine if that path is acceptable to her. Ultimately, it is important to recognize that having the client sign the appropriate forms is the best protection to terminate a therapeutic relationship with an uncooperative client who is out of compliance.

The Impaired Clinician and His or Her Immediate Colleagues

Drinking or the use of drugs does not necessarily cause impairment. Illness or psychosocial stressors also cause it. The common denominator is the clinician's inability to function as a psychotherapist due to impaired judgment, inability to focus, loss of clinical objectivity, and the inability to track cognitive processes. Regardless of the reason, the impaired clinician is a threat to the client's well-being and must dissociate him/herself until he or she is healthy enough to return to practice. It may be that the clinician may never return due to a fulminating illness or destructive neurological illness.

When an impaired clinician practices in the proximity of other clinicians, the others may be at risk. If the impaired clinician should cause a severe injury to a client, the opposing attorney will seek out anyone and everyone who had contact with the impaired clinician and will sue them to obtain the maximum financial reward possible. Unfortunately, they will face several years of extremely uncomfortable malpractice experience. These clinicians can take the following steps to protect themselves and their well-being:

- Clinicians have an ethical duty to recognize and address a colleague's impairment with the appropriate regulatory bodies.
- An impaired clinician who injures a client becomes primarily responsible for the injury. His co-workers become secondarily responsible for failing to stop the impaired clinician and thus permitting the impaired clinician to injure the client.
- Thus, clinical co-workers must define their professional role to other clinicians. Though having a "group" practice may sound impressive, it may have untold negative consequences. Obviously consulting with a qualified attorney regarding this issue is imperative.
- Practicing clinicians must educate themselves to recognize the subtle and clear symptoms of impairment. They must teach other members of their group to practice appropriate interventions and the management of ethical responsibilities to be compliant with professional and licensing agencies.
- Once clinical co-workers become aware of an impaired clinician who is a member of their group, they must take appropriate action and document it thoroughly.
- If necessary, legal consultation regarding the management of this issue should be obtained to avoid a lawsuit by the impaired clinician.

The "It'll Never Happen to Me" Syndrome

There are two types of clinicians: those of prepare and those who gamble. The former will be ready regardless of the challenge they face. The latter hope that they never face a negative situation in practice. When it does, they are always unprepared and ask for immediate help at the last minute. It is unproductive to ask why, instead it is far more productive to ask: "What can I do to become the former?"

This clinician might ask: "What knowledge must I know aside from the fact that I'm required to keep mental health records? I kept an intake sheet and some notes. Isn't that enough for simple cases?" Sadly, this clinician fails to appreciate the degree of protection afforded him or her by using appropriate records, especially a treatment plan. When used appropriately, the complementary components of treatment plans connect and build upon each other to strengthen the clinician's documentation of how he or she managed the client's clinical treatment process.

During the initial part of treatment, the clinician applies this knowledge sequentially and begins obtaining personal information, pertinent family history, medical consultations, past treatment history, observed clinical symptoms, and other pertinent information. Next, the clinician performs all necessary psychometric assessments including the Mental Status Exam and Beck Depression Inventory if needed. Now, the clinician integrates this clinical information to arrive at a working 5-Axis diagnosis. The clinician utilizes the 5-Axis diagnosis, the client's presenting symptoms, and defined clinical needs to develop a progressive treatment plan. These assessments help the clinician develop the necessary treatment to stabilize a crisis issue or proceed with non-crisis related treatment.

The treatment plan, which is the foundation of strength and protection for the clinician, creates a radial and interconnected protection for the clinician. For example, the Crisis Phase of treatment establishes that the clinician assessed and managed all immediate high-risk issues that could place the client and/or others in danger. Additionally, this first phase of the treatment plan establishes that the client and/or others are no longer in danger of harm. The clinician can now proceed to the next phase of treatment.

The next phase of the treatment plan establishes that the clinician obtained all necessary clinical information. He or she may have used psychometric assessment tools, referrals, family consultation, obtained medical and psychiatric information, and any other information necessary to complete the this phase of treatment. The completion of this phase indicates that the clinician assessed the client as necessary to obtain an appropriate diagnosis. Without completing this phase and the multi-axis diagnosis, the clinician is unable to proceed to the next phase of treatment.

The middle phase defines the treatment necessary to resolve the client's presenting clinical issues and symptoms. The clinician integrates the presenting clinical symptoms, other pertinent information, and the multi-axial diagnosis to arrive at a working treatment plan. Additionally, the treatment plan will change as the client's clinical needs change. For example, a bipolar client in the depressive phase of the illness may suddenly move into the manic phase. The treatment for depression would immediately change to address the mania within the context of bipolar disorder.

Some clinicians may say: "The concept presented above is ludicrous. Treatment plans are not necessary and they are burdensome. They take away precious time from treating the client." For those clinicians who refuse to protect themselves from any type of legal action, this may be true. However, for those clinicians who want the maximum protection from lawsuits, using treatment plans appropriately is another important component of the overall protective mechanism.

It is a known fact among expert witnesses who help attorneys in cases involving licensed clinicians that astute attorneys will use the clinicians' weaknesses to undermine their credibility and present them and their clinical actions in the worst manner possible to the court. When these attorneys know that mental health records and especially treatment plans do not exist, they will continue to ask for proof of documentation repeatedly. Imagine how unnerving a clinician may feel after having to answer that he or she failed to document his or her assessment, diagnosis, and treatment.

Working and Collaborating With Unlicensed Mental Health Clinicians

MFT collaborate with substance abuse or dependence counselors in a variety of settings. Often, drug and alcohol counselors provide this treatment in outpatient or inpatient settings. Collaborating with these clinicians usually leads to a legal challenge when attempting to protect the client's confidentiality. The challenge stems in the differing legal protection awarded to licensed versus non--licensed mental health clinicians. California law grants legal protection to MFTs regarding the holding of a client's confidentiality including mandated or permitted breaches to protect clients from harm to self and/or others. Drug and alcohol counselors do not have this legal protection or a mandate or permit to breach confidentiality when managing the safety of the client and/or others.

When MFTs share a client's confidential information, only the MFT is required to protect it. Drug and alcohol counselors cannot promise holding confidential and if they promise so to clients, they expose themselves to a malpractice action for breaching a therapeutic contract. Should MFTs share confidential information with these clinicians, they must be aware that the shared information lacks legal protection and a third party can easily access it. Yet, MFTs must cooperate with and provide confidential information to these clinicians. When challenged in these situations, MFTs can consider the following steps to protect themselves:

- Determine the license status of the mental health clinicians he or she will cooperate or consult with. Assess if this clinician is required legally to protect client confidentiality.
- If the clinician lacks the legal mandate to protect confidential information, inform and discuss with this counselor the clinical implications of treating the client due to this bind.
- Add information to the release of information informing the client that providing clinical information to this counselor is not protected legally and a third party can access it.
- Make sure your written release of information conforms to legal requirements.
- Continuously confer with and discuss the status of the clinician information you have provided to this clinician.

Closing an Office and Avoiding Harm to Clients

There will be a time when an MFT retires from practice. Though this transition can be bittersweet, it is also fraught with danger if not managed properly because client injury may arise from the office closure. To avoid injuring clients, MFTs take protective steps. The first step is to assess the clinical status of clients and determine if any of them are in a potential crisis modem regardless of how minimal is the emotional disturbance. Next, make sure that they document each client's evaluation. Use the evaluation to formulate each client's individual needs and document these with a thorough 5-Axis diagnosis and treatment plan. Establish a reasonable transition structure, which assures that each referral matches the scope of competence of the new clinician and that the new clinician has access to a copy of the client's record. Finally, any client in a crisis status receives continued until he or she is stable. Only then does the MFT refer this client to the appropriate clinician. MFTs make themselves available with the new clinicians and they set protective storage facilities to keep client records for at least 6 years.

The Clinician's Malpractice Experience

Clinicians who have experienced a malpractice lawsuit or BBS administrative action have the same feedback: "It is hellish." Attorneys sue MFTs because they have determined that their client suffered an injury caused by an MFT and they believe they have an excellent chance of receiving a positive verdict awarding them a large sum of money to address the client's injury. The attorney is due a large percentage of the financial award. To prepare their case for success, opposing attorneys follow these steps:

- They obtain all written, verbal, and printed records from the MFT.
- They provide all gathered information to an expert witness for review and analysis.
- They question the MFT at length attempting to establish that he or she withheld important information and thus the opposing attorney questions his or her veracity during trial.
- The trial usually lasts between one and one-half to two years after the lawsuit begins. However, the case may have settled or dismissed prior to the starting the trial. The trial will take place in front of a jury and its task is to determine if the client was injured and if the MFT's negligence caused the injury. If they rule against the MFT, they will award a financial verdict to the client. The more egregious the injury, the larger the award. If the award exceeds $9,999.99, it is reported to a national database, which will provide this information to the BBS.

Chapter 28

CAMFT Ethical Standard 1

Responsibility to Patients

In developing ethical standards for MFTs (marriage and family therapists), the California Association of Marriage and Family Therapists established the norms for professional responsibility and created the means of creating safety for therapists and their clients when involved in the therapeutic process. This responsibility rests on the underlying concept that if growth, change, and/or development are to take place within the therapeutic environment, the client and the therapist must experience a degree of safety. Ethics are one part of the complete structure that creates this safety. Without ethics, the other components are limited in scope. These ethical guidelines create an additional therapeutic duty upon the therapist; he or she is expected to create a safe therapeutic relationship with the client. The clinician relies on other elements of the therapeutic structure such as clinical, scientific, and legal standards of care and the therapist's personal values or internal reality to generate safety.

1. RESPONSIBILITY TO PATIENTS:

Marriage and family therapists advance the welfare of families and individuals, respect the rights of those persons seeking their assistance, and make reasonable efforts to ensure that their services are used appropriately.

When providing treatment, MFTs have one primordial consideration: the welfare of families and individuals. This consideration assumes the nature of this welfare is emotional, behavioral, or the condition of the mental state of families and individuals. The clinician's focus is to help the client(s) learn how to resolve the impasses that prevent their well-being. This CAMFT ethical standard identifies the goal of psychotherapy: addressing the welfare of clients. The clinician is expected to know that California law places an additional responsibility upon MFTs; legal responsibility or legal therapeutic duty to assess, diagnose, and to treat according to the standard of care throughout the duration of treatment. This means that a reasonable and prudent clinician follows the standards that are scientifically, clinically, and legally in MFT psychotherapy even if the outcome is less than ideal.

A reasonable and prudent clinician recognizes that to enhance the client(s) welfare, he or she must use recognized and professionally acceptable psychometric tools and sound theoretical constructs.

These tools help therapists create a n assessment baseline to consider the client's progress throughout the duration of treatment. Should improvement fail to take place, it is the responsibility of the MFT to reassess the direction and format of treatment. Should change continue to fail even after reassessment and redirection of treatment, a referral to another therapist would be appropriate ethical clinical behavior.

A reasonable and prudent clinician makes his/her diagnosis throughout the duration of treatment according to the prevailing standard of care. This means that the MFT obtains all necessary information to make a DSM 5 diagnosis supported by the presenting clinical symptoms and their duration and adjusts his or her diagnosis as needed throughout the duration of treatment. Treating the client according to the standard of care means that the MFT follows accepted theoretical modalities and utilizes psychotherapeutic techniques that present proof of scientific validity in obtaining results. If an MFT uses questionable, experimental, or challenging modalities to provide treatment, the MFT has the therapeutic duty to obtain a separate and appropriate informed consent regarding these alternate treatment modalities.

Since this standard requires MFTs to advance the welfare of client, they must also be aware of when clients' welfare may be in jeopardy. A prudent MFTs would have an assessment protocol in place to determine if the presented treatment is adequate to advance the clients' welfare and to assure that the MFT's clinical objectivity will be such as to assure that clients won't suffer harm due to the application of the proposed treatment. Not doing so could lead to an accusation of acting unethically.

When working with families, couples, or groups, the therapist has an even higher degree of professional responsibility, because in addition to the well-being of each individual member of the treatment unit, the MFT takes into consideration the compounded well-being of the treatment unit. Imagine the potential harm caused to a family unit when a therapist recommends to a family of an adult drug abusing son or daughter that the family must disengage completely from the son until he "reaches bottom." Not all family members are in agreement and the fabric of the family unit begins to fray. As this family breaks apart, each family member will tend to react emotionally. Those family members, who experience this separation unjust, will react the strongest. In time the injured family will most likely blame the therapist for the family rift and may not rest until he or she faces legal action.

Should this case come to be resolved by the legal system, the Court may find that the therapist's inappropriate action caused injury to this family by imposing his or her personal judgement and depriving family members of the opportunity to to make a decision that suited the family. The injury would be more aggravated if the therapist had little knowledge of applicable legal and ethical therapeutic duties in this situation. From a perspective of creating safety, the therapist must consider the impact of this clinical intervention on the whole family and not just individual ones. Additionally, he or she must consult with objective peers to determine how this clinical action compares to the standard of care. The latter is that care that a prudent and reasonable therapist in the community would provide his or her clients.

There will be times when the proposed treatment may cause harm to the client. This can occur when an MFT is asked to perform a custody evaluation where one of the parents will result with less custodial privileges than the other. In addition, during treatment a client experiences emotional trauma when clinician tells him or her that divorce appears to be the only path to achieve emotional well-being. Harm can occur when the clinician reports child abuse, the authorities interrogate the minor and later drop the investigation for lack of evidence. Imagine the accused adult seeking retribution. These are examples of clinical and ethical actions that can cause harm to clients. In these cases, a reasonable and prudent clinician would document his or her reasoning process used to reach a specific conclusion, the steps taken to address the issue at hand, and the outcome. The clinician can remember that he or she is not required to be perfect in his or her assessment, diagnosis, and treatment. Rather, he or she can rely on being a reasonable and prudent clinician to consider the possible alternatives that best meet the needs of the client.

In review, this standard places additional responsibilities on MFTs to assure that their services are used appropriately. A reasonable and prudent clinician determines if the proposed services meet the presenting needs of the client. In addition, the clinician establishes that the provided services are not being used to manipulate, abuse, or take advantage of a situation, a condition, or a person. Consider a client using psychotherapy to obtain additional disability funds even though he or she is not disabled any longer. Ultimately, in a malpractice action opposing attorneys will utilize this standard as the primary obligation placed upon MFTs to consider and manage the clients' well-being.

<u>1.1 NON-DISCRIMINATION:</u>

Marriage and family therapists do not condone or engage in discrimination, or refuse professional service to anyone on the basis of race, religion, national origin, age, sexual orientation, disability, socioeconomic or marital status. Marriage and family therapists make reasonable efforts to accommodate patients who have physical disabilities.

This standard establishes that MFTs must be aware of their personal biases and must take special measures to prevent these from interfering with their clinical work. Note that this standard does not state that MFTs must provide services to every client who comes to their practice because not all MFTs have that degree of scope of competence in all aspects of psychotherapy and in working with a wide array of client populations. It is appropriate to refer clients when the MFT does not meet the required scope of competence to treat the presenting issue(s) and specific clients.

For example, if a bilingual and monocultural Hispanic client seeks a therapist's services, the therapist could not deny treatment based on this client's cultural heritage. However, if the therapist did not have an understanding of Hispanic family dynamics, the therapist would do well to refer the client to another therapist with the appropriate level of experience with this culture. For example, a particular therapist may not agree with the gay and lesbian lifestyle, or any other form of personal sexual preference expression. This does not justify a refusal to treat to this segment of the population. Doing so could mean that this therapist is being prejudicial and is violating this ethical code. Again, lacking the scope of competence to treat the issues of this population requires a referral to an appropriate clinician. The clinician refusing to provide services to a client after the client initiated a HIPAA complaint against the clinician with the Department of Human and Health Services evidences another example of discrimination.

The code was expanded to include the duty of MFTs to make reasonable accommodations to provide treatment to clients with disabilities. This does not mean that the therapist will install an elevator if the building they practice in does not have one. However, it does mean that the therapist must make reasonable modifications in scheduling, provide flexibility of session time, and in some cases, request that the landlord construct a ramp to allow wheel-chair-bound clients access to the office. Ultimately, what is reasonable conduct also depends on the context of the situation.

1.2 DUAL RELATIONSHIPS-DEFINITION:

Marriage and family therapists are aware of their influential position with respect to patients, and they avoid exploiting the trust and dependency of such persons. Marriage and family therapists, therefore, avoid dual relationships with patients that are reasonably likely to impair professional judgment or lead to exploitation. A dual relationship occurs when a therapist and his/her patient engage in a separate and distinct relationship either simultaneously with the therapeutic relationship, or during a reasonable period of time following the termination of the therapeutic relationship. Not all dual relationships are unethical, and some dual relationships cannot be avoided. When a concurrent or subsequent dual relationship occurs, marriage and family therapists take appropriate professional precautions to insure that judgment is not impaired and that no exploitation occurs.

This standard acknowledges that in a therapeutic relationship, a power differential exists by default. Clients usually enter into this relationship seeking help or guidance from the therapist and present themselves in a vulnerable state. Until clients are able to access their own power and establish appropriate boundaries, they rely upon the MFT to provide guidance in making appropriate decisions. To help clients make appropriate decisions, a reasonable and prudent ethical MFT must maintain personal and clinical objectivity and avoid taking advantage of the client's vulnerability. Clinical and personal objectivity can be lost when the therapist extends him/herself beyond the clinical role by entering into a second non-clinical and harmful dual relationship with he client. The latter is one in where exploitation or loss of objectivity takes place. Under these circumstances, it is virtually impossible for the client to maintain a relationship of equality with the therapist. The resulting imbalance between the two distinct and unequal relationships tends to confuse clients and create greater dependency on the therapist. By definition therapists who do not maintain objectivity and/or exploit their clients, fail to advance the welfare of families and individuals" and they are harming their clients.

For example, a client who is confused and hurt because his or her spouse is having an affair seeks the help of an MFT. Initially in this relationship, the MFT holds greater power than the client does. Should the MFT take advantage of the client's confusion regarding the status of the marriage and make a sexual advance toward the client, the MFT has lost clinical objectivity and if sued, the opposing attorney will show that this therapist exploited the client's vulnerability. Making sexual advances to a client is a harmful dual relationship because the therapist has crossed over the therapeutic boundary and has become a potential sexual partner who knows the client's emotional vulnerabilities.

Other examples of harmful dual relationships include: borrowing money from clients; lending money to clients; setting up a business venture with clients; socializing with clients; providing psychotherapy to a close friend and continuing the friendship; providing massage and coaching at the same time to clients; being both an expert witness and a treating therapist for a client in a legal situation; asking clients for favors; asking clients to employ family members and relatives; and/or arranging dates between clients. These are harmful because the MFT has not addressed or discussed his relation to the client's emotonal vulnerability in advance. Its unavoidable for exploitation and injury of the client to occur. Usually in these situations, the therapist has most likely lost objectivity within this power differential. It is the MFT's therapeutic duty to avoid either loss of objectivity or coercion of the client.

This standard accepts the fact that in some locations or in some circumstances, dual relationships cannot be avoided. The latter includes residing in a small town, a close knit community, sharing specific language and culture with a community. In these situations, a therapist may take additional professional precautions to assess the impact of the dual relationship on the therapeutic relationship and thus act as a reasonable and prudent MFT. By consulting with experts in the legal/ethical arena and documenting the results of the consultation, MFTs support their intent to remain objective. Therapists living in a small town or who are members of a close-knit ethnic community sometimes face the following challenges. An MFT must use the services of the only bank in the community where the bank manager is a client. The clinician seeks medical services for her children from the only local physician who is also a client. The MFT is invited to culturally significant events at clients' homes. After being injured in a car accident, the MFT obtains medically necessary physical therapy from a client who is the only physical therapist in the community. In these circumstances, it is impossible to avoid dual relationships with clients. However, the nature of the relationship must be evaluated contextually and managed safely by the therapist to avoid coercion of the client or loss of objectivity by the clinician. For services that require a greater depth of relationship, which could result in loss of objectivity or exploitation of the client, evaluating each situation carefully, obtaining objective consultation, and documenting this process may provide the best possible solution.

1.2.1 UNETHICAL DUAL RELATIONSHIPS:

Other acts which would result in unethical dual relationships include, but are not limited to, borrowing money from a patient, hiring a patient, engaging in a business venture with a patient, or engaging in a close personal relationship with a patient. Such acts with a patient's spouse, partner or family member may also be considered unethical dual relationship.

This standard helps MFTs identify other possibilities of unethical dual relationships. These examples include, having meals regularly with clients, meeting the client for coffee, caring for a client's house or pets while the client is on vacation, asking the client for personal favors, or taking a client home to protect them from a spousal abuse situation. As society continues to evolve and new opportunities for social interaction develop, therapists face the possibility of entering into a potential dual relationship with a client. A reasonable and prudent clinician assures that he or she avoids loss of clinical objectivity, that the clinician avoids coercing the client in any manner, and more importantly that the MFT avoids injuring the client in any form.

1.2.2 SEXUAL CONTACT:

Sexual intercourse, sexual contact or sexual intimacy with a patient, or a patient's immediate family member, during the therapeutic relationship, or during the two years following the termination of the therapeutic relationship, is unethical.

Should a marriage and family therapist engage in sexual intimacy with a former patient or patient's spouse or partner, or a patient's immediate family member, following the two years after termination or last professional contact, the therapist shall consider the potential harm to or exploitation of the former patient or to the patient's family.

This standard clearly states that any violation of the therapeutic boundary through sexual contact with a current client, the client's spouse or partner, or a client's immediate family member, is unequivocally unethical behavior. The term sexual intimacy extends the sanction to the spoken word and includes verbal sexual harassment. Of all possible harmful dual relationships, a sexual relationship with a client can be the most confusing and destructive to the client. The California Legislature has wisely identified the destructiveness of this form of client involvement and has made it a punishable offense in both criminal and civil court. A sexual relationship of any kind with a client, or client's spouse or partner, or intimate family member within two years after termination is considered unethical behavior. Additionally, terminating the therapeutic relationship for the sole purpose of having a sexual relationship with a client is also unethical. As such, this clinical action does not advance the welfare of the client.

Similar violations can take place in other clinical situations where MFTs are not actually performing as a licensed marriage and family therapist. The MFT who violates the therapeutic relationship boundary, regardless of licensing activity, will still be held accountable to this CAMFT Ethical Standard. For example, an MFT works as a drug and alcohol counselor in a university environment. The employment regulations do not require an MFT license to perform this job. The MFT begins dating and becomes sexually intimate with a client. Even though the MFT claims that he or she was not functioning in the scope of practice as an MFT, the Board will still hold him or her accountable to the MFT scope of practice and ethical standards. Board of Behavioral Sciences administrative action or malpractice action have found clinicians accountable for harm suffered by clients due to the above violation of the therapeutic boundary.

<u>1.2.3 PRIOR SEXUAL RELATIONSHIP:</u>

A marriage and family therapist does not enter into a therapeutic relationship with a person with whom he/she has had a sexual relationship or enter into a therapeutic relationship with a partner or the immediate family member of a person with whom he or she has had a sexual relationship.

It is a breach of the ethical therapeutic duty for a therapist to provide treatment to individuals with whom sexual relationships have been established. This standard classifies this form of professional relationship as a harmful dual relationship. It is difficult, if not impossible, for a therapist to maintain professional objectivity or avoid coercion of clients when a history of sexual relationship exists between them or the client's loved ones. Intimate romantic relationships may generate unresolved power differentials which can be aggravated should a professional relationship, such as that created in psychotherapy, be established.

Consider the following scenario. A therapist receives a phone call from a previous lover. The ex-lover describes being in a difficult emotional situation in a new relationship and requests that this therapist become the provider of psychotherapy to the ex-lover and the new significant other. The ex-lover makes the case that the therapist's awareness of the issues involved would expedite the process of therapy. "Besides," the ex-lover states, "I don't know if I can trust anyone else as much as I trust you." As appealing as this request may be, the reasonable and prudent MFT refers these potential clients to an objective therapist and ultimately creates therapeutic safety for all involved. In another situation, the clinician provides couple's therapy and in time, begins a romantic relationship with the spouse. A reasonable and prudent clinician would ask: "How can the clinician maintain clinical objectivity during treatment?" A second question that follows is: "How can the clinician avoid a power differential with the spouse in the romantic relationship even after therapy is terminated?" The MFT has the duty to ask these questions of him/herself before he or she begins such a relationship. Ultimately, the clinician must ask how he or will harm the client and or his family.

1.3 TREATMENT DISRUPTION:

Marriage and family therapists are aware of their professional and clinical responsibilities to provide consistent care to patients, and maintain practices and procedures that assure undisrupted care. Such practices and procedures may include, but are not limited to providing contact information and specified procedures in case of emergency, or therapist absence, conducting appropriate terminations, and providing for a professional will.

This standard dictates that MFTs must be aware of the process to end the therapeutic relationship or treatment in a manner that avoids harm to the client. Inversely, the MFT is also required to know how treatment can be disrupted and how to avoid disruptions that can lead to client abandonment. A reasonable and prudent clinician initially establishes clinical expectations and procedures through informed consent. This document informs the client in advance how the clinician will manage potential disruptions that range from the mundane to the catastrophic.

The informed consent document section specifies the precise conditions to manage clinical disruptions. Some of these include the client's inability to pay for sessions at the agreed upon fee, the clinician must contact a significant family member due to a clinical emergency, the clinician takes a leave of absence, the clinician increases his or her fees, the client must contact the clinician in an emergency, the clinician relocates to another city, the clinician discontinues practice, or the clinician died or suffered a debilitating injury and cannot continue to practice.

This standard requires that MFTs create the structure and process, which allows the client the ability to maintain continuity of care. I believe that each clinician can best benefit by developing his or her specific answers to how he or she practices. Doing so establishes that the MFT acted as an ethical, reasonable, and prudent clinician.

> **1.3.1 TERMINATION:**
> **Marriage and family therapists use sound clinical judgement when terminating therapeutic relationships and do so in an appropriate manner. Reasons for termination may include, but are not limited to, the patient is not benefiting from treatment, continuing treatment is not clinically appropriate, the therapist is unable to provide treatment due to the therapist's incapacity or extended absence, in order to avoid an ethical conflict or problem.**

This standard establishes the ethical therapeutic duty upon MFTs to know how to recognize the clinical elements required for termination and how to terminate treatment appropriately. This awareness and knowledge has implications affecting treatment and the therapeutic relationship. This awareness requires that the clinician ask the following questions before termination takes place: "Has the client completed all phases of the treatment plan? Has the client failed to cooperate with treatment? Has the client terminated treatment prematurely? Has the client terminated treatment for reasons other than these?" Answering these questions helps the clinician how to proceed reasonably and prudently.

There are times when the MFT makes clinical recommendations, such as having the client seek a medical or psychiatric evaluation and the client refuses. When this happens, it would be important to document the client's decision and explore with the client the refusal to obtain appropriate information that would enhance treatment. Should the client continue to refuse, it serves the MFT to consider referring the client to another therapist. Appropriate management of termination of the therapeutic relationship is via the discharge summary after the MFT gives the client various referrals.

In some extreme cases, clients have sued therapists for abandonment when they have died or have contracted a debilitating illness and have not established a reasonable mechanism to transfer the client to another clinician. Since a precedent exists making this action standard of care, reasonable and prudent MFTs create a therapeutic will. This will is documented in the informed consent document and informs clients who will contact them should the therapist not be able to continue treatment due to death or debilitating infirmity. Additionally, providing for continuity of care during clinical absences makes professional sense. This standard establishes this therapeutic duty. There have been cases where clients have committed suicide when they could not contact the treating therapist in an emergency. A reasonable and prudent clinician informs the client in his/her informed consent document how to reach the therapist should an emergency arise. Not doing so opens the door for an accusation of malpractice and administrative action to contributing to the "wrongful death" of the client.

The ethical MFT knows that appropriate termination recognizes that the client's needs were met and the final phase of treatment was completed appropriately. This requires that the clinician assess the client's readiness to terminate. This assessment involves utilizing a Mental Status Exam to determine the client's mental or emotional stability, discussing the client's benefits from treatment, and in some cases practicing a prevention program. Conversely, the clinician refers the client elsewhere if he or she determines that the client has not benefited from treatment. It may be that the clinician lacks the scope of competence to address developing clinical issues. Regardless of the reason for termination, it is in the clinician's best interest to document the reasons for termination, the rationale for terminating treatment, and the clinical outcome of termination. These clinical actions are expected of a reasonable, prudent, and ethical MFT.

> 1.3.2 ABANDONMENT:
> **Marriage and family therapists do not abandon or neglect patients in treatment. If a therapist is unable or unwilling to continue to provide professional services, the therapist will assist the patient in making clinically appropriate arrangements for continuation of treatment.**

A reasonable and prudent clinician is required to help the client continue obtaining therapeutic services in the even that he or she is unable to continue providing these services for appropriate reasons. There are times when the clinician lacks the scope of competence to treat the client's developing issues. It may be that the client is unable to pay the clinician's fees and the clinician is unable to provide a low fee slot. Regardless of the reason, it is the MFT's duty to assure that the client transitions into new treatment without disruption that could harm the client. The reasonable and prudent transition mechanism requires that the MFT provides the names of appropriate referrals to the client and obtains the authorization to provide the necessary clinical information to the new clinician. These referrals could include low-cost clinics, or other therapists who have the scope of competence to provide the necessary treatment. Should the client present imminent danger to self or others and the crisis is not managed, it would be unethical to refer the client elsewhere until the crisis issue is managed. In this situation, the treating therapist is required to provide pro bono treatment until he or she has managed the crisis and the client is stable. Of course, it is in the best interest of the clinician to assure that he or she documents the factors that led to transferring the client elsewhere, how that decision was made, and the rationale behind the decision.

1.3.3 FINANCIAL GAIN:

Marriage and family therapists do not maintain therapeutic relationships solely for financial gain.

When establishing a therapeutic relationship, reasonable and prudent MFTs attend to the financial well-being of the client and don't focus on benefiting from the client's financial status. Rather, they attend to the client's financial welfare and respect it throughout the therapeutic relationship. MFTs assess how the client manages the financial transactions and how these affect the client's ability to focus on the therapy rather than on financial transactions. CAMFT and the BBS will view any violation that causes MFTs to gain from the professional relationship as unprofessional conduct and will likely lead to administrative action.

1.3.4 NON-PAYMENT OF FEES:

Marriage and family therapists do not terminate patient relationship for non-payment of fees except when the termination is handled in a clinically appropriate manner.

In this standard, CAMFT recognizes that when the client is unable to pay the agreed-upon-fee, the therapist has the choice to lower the fee or to terminate the treatment relationship in an appropriate manner as discussed in previous sections. Terminating treatment for this reason is not considered unethical behavior. A reasonable and prudent clinician documents the client's inability to pay and refers to the informed consent document, which defines the termination process that will be followed should this condition arise. The clinician's informed consent document clearly establishes how treatment will be ended to avoid harm to the client and the client is provided with names of therapists that can provide service at a lower fee. Ending treatment for non-payment of fees and not following the described procedure could lead to an accusation of abandonment.

1.4 PATIENT AUTONOMY:

Marriage and family therapists respect the right of patients to make decisions and help them to understand the consequences of their decisions. When clinically appropriate, marriage and family therapists advise their patients that decisions on the status of their personal relationships, including dissolution, are the responsibilities of the patient(s).

This standard establishes that MFTs must be aware of the power differential that exists in therapy and must assure that they do not abuse it. Creating a dialogue with the client regarding the process of making decisions and that these are the responsibility of the client, identifies clinicians as appropriate teachers and healthy role models. Decisions made by clients will have negative and positive consequences and should the MFT make decisions for the client, it is likely that emotional dependency or reactivity will result. Instead, the clinician can bring the decision making process to the clients' awareness and utilize this process to help them obtain greater objectivity and thus in time learns how to make appropriate and healthy personal decisions.

As clients integrate this decision-making process into their scheme of life, they can begin to take personal responsibility for their behaviors, rather than blame others or life circumstances for their problems. As they make choices about relationships, they can explore the benefits and liabilities inherent to these relationships. Imagine a client struggling as to whether to stay in a marriage versus seeking divorce indicates two possible choices faced by many clients. Should the client ask the clinician: "What should I do?" A reasonable and prudent clinician avoids making the decision for the client. Next, the clinician focuses the therapy towards helping the client develop awareness of the ramifications of the choices at hand and help the client make the decision for him/herself. This process enhances the client's well-being.

The power differential tends to be corrected in this growth process. It would be unethical for the therapist to abuse his or her privileged position by telling the client "Get out of the marriage, you don't belong there," or " It's your duty to stay married to this person." These statements would negate the client's ability to learn to make personal decisions and would foster dependency on the therapist. Sometimes clients ask the therapist for solutions to their life dilemmas. It may be easy for the therapist to provide an answer and move on to the next one. However, giving an answer can be disempowering the client and foster the client dependency on the therapist for solving future challenges. The therapist has the responsibility to be aware of his or her conscious and unconscious processes that serves to undermine the client's independence. Fostering this form of dependence can easily lead to an accusation of unprofessional conduct.

1.4.1 ELECTRONIC THERAPY:

When patients are not physically present (e.g., therapy by telephone or Internet) during the provision of therapy, marriage and family therapists take extra precautions to meet their responsibilities to patients. Prior to utilizing electronic therapy, marriage and family therapists consider the appropriatness and suitability of this therapeutic modality to the patient's needs. When therapy occurs by electronic means, marriage and family therapists inform patients of the potential risks, conseqences, and benefits, including but not limited to, issues of confidentiality, clinical limitations, transmission difficulties, and ability to respond to emergencies. Marriage and family therapists ensure that such therapy complies with the informed consent requirements of the California Telemedicine Act.

Electronic technologies have transitioned into effective treatment modalities for MFTs. These include the use of teleconferencing, video and voice communication via the Internet, and telephony utilization through the Internet. This standard dictates to MFTs to be aware of the inherent and progressive risks and benefits of the electronic modality. Once aware, the clinician can make appropriate and healthy decisions to enhance the welfare of the client.

First, the clinician must address the primordial issue of confidentiality. The MFT must ask, what are the confidentiality risks for my client and for me? First, the MFT cannot guarantee confidentiality. Electronic communication begins at the MFT's computer, travels to the sender's internet provider's server (large computer), from there to the recipient's internet provider's server (another large computer), and finally to the client's computer. At each computer, we find data indicating the content of the conversation. Though at first approximation it appears that the communication is protected, in reality it is not. A technician who specializes in data recovery can access this stored information. One may ask, who would be interested and why would they access the computer? Imagine an auto collision involving the client and resulting in a severe physical injury or fatality. The opposing attorney will attempt to obtain all information available, written or electronic, to strengthen his or her case. Since the hard drives, personal and servers are accessed, all contained information is now available to an expert who will provide it to the opposing attorney. This is an important risk of this type of therapy.

Another danger for MFTs is inability to determine the patient's age of consent and thus cannot determine if the client is a minor. MFTs know that treating a minor without parental consent is illegal. Next, MFTs must determine the state where the client is conducting electronic media treatment. Since MFTs are licensed in a specific state, the mandate to report laws do not apply in another state. In an emergency, MFTs cannot legally contact another state's authorities to prevent a client from harming him/herself or others. Doing so is a breach of confidentiality. A reasonable and prudent MFT prearranges emergency contacts in the client's vicinity to manage any emergency that arises.

MFT providing these services would take prudent action by establishing a pre-arranged emergency protocol should the client face an emergency that requires management. This protocol would include having a local emergency contact where the client resides. Of present concern is the yet undefined standard of care in the electronic psychotherapy arena. Expert witnesses would have a difficult time defending an MFT who faces a legal challenge because of undefined practice standards. Should an MFT decide to practice in this arena, he/she has the ethical therapeutic duty to do so safely as established by this standard. To establish reasonable and prudent clinical actions in this arena of psychotherapy, the MFT uses informed consent thoroughly and effectively. The California Telemedicine Act clearly addresses the required consent.

1.5 THERAPIST DISCLOSURES:

Marriage and family therapists provide adequate information to patients in clear and understandable language so that patients can make meaningful decisions about their therapy.

When providing informed consent, MFTs must provide it in clear and understandable language. This requirement addresses the elimination of obfuscation and confusion, which result when lack of clarity exists in any communication. MFTs must address the standard of care in this facet of informed consent. The standard of care requires that the MFT perform four functions: a) The MFT assesses the competency of the client, b) The MFT assures that the disclosure provides enough material allowing the client to make an appropriate and educated decision, c) The MFT makes sure that the client understands the material presented in the informed consent, and d) the client's consent must be voluntary. From this moment forward, the MFT establishes the foundation of clear and understandable communication. The ensuing communication dynamic continues to evolve through clarity and understanding allowing the therapeutic relationship to strengthen. The clear communication enhances trust and accountability, which enhance clarity and understanding. Thus, the MFT applies standard of care and addresses the client's well-being simultaneously.

1.5.1 RISKS AND BENEFITS:

Marriage and family therapists inform patients of the potential risks and benefits of therapy when utilizing novel or experimental techniques or when there is a risk of physical harm that could result from the utilization of any technique.

This ethical standard is a complement to the legal mandate established by Rains v. Superior Court (1984), which mandates that MFTs provide informed consent to clients before the initiation of treatment. Standard of care requires clinicians to provide clients with adequate information, which includes the risks and benefits of treatment to make informed decisions. This empowers the client and creates a greater degree of equality in the therapeutic relationship.

This standard requires MFTs to recognize those treatment modalities, theoretical constructs that due to their lack of proven validity and reliability can cause harm to the client. It is common for clinicians to attend courses and educational seminars introducing innovative techniques. In their eagerness to utilize these, MFTs may fail to recognize that a result of using these is injury to the client. Thus, MFTs must ask themselves if the innovative approach, they are using causes physical or emotional harm. Next, they must determine if using this approach warrants the possibility of harming the client. Third, MFTs must inform the client as to the nature of this new, untested, or potentially injurious approach. Last, MTFs must assure that their informed consent conforms to standard of care, conforms to Rains v. Superior Court, and to specific elements identified in the professional literature.

1.5.2 EMERGENCIES/CONTACT BETWEEN SESSIONS:

Marriage and family therapists inform patients of the extent of their availability for emergencies and for other contacts between sessions. When a marriage and family therapist is not located in the same geographic area as the patient, he/she shall provide the patient with appropriate resources in the patient's locale for contact in case of emergency.

This standard places the responsibility on MFTs to provide clients with a protocol to reach the clinician should an emergency arise after hours. A reasonable and prudent clinician informs clients in the informed consent document the definition of a clinical emergency, the contact process the client must follow, and the approach to take after hours when the clinician is not available for phone contact. It is insufficient to provide this information to clients via a telephone message system. It must be in writing in the informed consent document in case a legal challenge occurs and the client challenges the clinician's credibility. At times, an interactive telemedicine relationship may encounter a true clinical emergency. If the client resides in a geographical location separate from the MFT, it is impossible for the MFT to utilize familiar emergency protocols. This standard requires MFTs who perform telemedicine to set up emergency contacts before engaging in a professional relationship with the client. Next, the clinician informs the client about the presence and utilization of these emergency resources in the clients locality should it be necessary. Without these emergency resources and plan of action in case a situation arises that requires these, the MFT can face a malpractice action, an administrative board investigation, and a challenge of unethical conduct.

1.5.3 CONSENT FOR RECORDING OBSERVATION:

Marriage and family therapists obtain written informed consent from clients before videotaping, audio recording, or permitting third party observation.

MFTs are required to consider how videotaping, audio recording, or allowing a third party observation, influences treatment. Before initiating any of these venues, MFTs discuss the implications with clients. Next, documenting the client's decision via the informed consent document satisfies this ethical therapeutic duty. A reasonable and prudent clinician considers the potential ramifications these recording or observations could have in the client's future. Consider the following example. A client agrees to videotape treatment sessions that will be used for educational purposes. Later, the videotapes end up in a commercial product unbeknownst to the client. Even though the client gave consent, if such a possibility was not discussed in advance, then the clinician could be sued for "breach of contract." This standard attempts to protect client by placing an ethical duty on MFTs to clarify in advance the possibilities of how confidentiality may be affected and to establish that the clients understand the possible impact of giving their authorization. The clinician informs the client as to the purpose and use of the taping or observation, and what population would have access to it. A written consent ultimately protects all involved.

1.5.4 LIMITS OF CONFIDENTIALITY:

Marriage and family therapists are encouraged to use clear and understandable language to inform patients as to as to the exceptions to confidentiality, including but not limited to, child abuse reporting, elder and dependent adult abuse reporting, and patients dangerous to themselves or others.

MFTs are required to consider an important element of informed consent: how to manage confidentiality safely. Since maintaining confidentiality helps establish trust within the professional relationship, managing appropriately is fundamental in addressing the client's welfare. A reasonable and prudent clinician informs clients at the beginning of treatment about the legal requirements regarding confidentiality. The client is informed that the clinician will protect confidentiality except as mandated or permitted by law. When mandated, the clinician addresses a reasonable suspicion of child, elder/dependent adult abuse, or a serious threat to harm. It may be that the MFT chooses to breach confidentiality when the client presents harm to self or others. Regardless, having this discussion strengthens the therapeutic relationship and protects those involved in therapy: they know in advance that their confidentiality could be breached. Ultimately, the MFT addresses these limits in a sensitive and caring maner to reduce fear or anxiety in clients. Importantly, should the clinician face a reporting issue, documenting the discussion with the client regarding this issue can serve to displace a potential malpractice action.

1.5.5 THERAPIST BACKGROUND:

Marriage and family therapists are encouraged to inform patients at an appropriate time and within the context of the psychotherapeutic relationship of any information that affects the nature of the services to be provided or the policies to be implemented. This information includes, but is not limited to the therapist's experience, education, specialties, theoretical and professional orientation.

This standard relates to the ethical therapeutic duty of obtaining informed consent, which provides the client the necessary information to make an informed choice. Providing clients with this information gives them the choice to continue or end the relationship before investing time, money, and energy in establishing this important relationship. This specific information of the MFT's training, knowledge, experience, and treatment modalities, helps strengthen the therapeutic relationship and facilitate the client's acceptance of the therapist's ability to treat their presenting issue(s). This form of empowerment also helps to balance the power differential inherent in the therapeutic relationship and enhances the client's growth process. Should a clinician fail to provide this information, he or she can be held legally and ethically accountable for failure to provide appropriate informed consent, and in some situations of misleading the client for financial gain.

1.6 EXPLOITATION:

Marriage and family therapists do not use their professional relationships with patients to further their own interests.

MFTs recognize the inherent power differential between therapist and client and continuously respect it in their actions. As clients learn from their therapists, they establish the process of making healthy decisions for themselves. This process also involves recognizing and establishing appropriate boundaries. The MFT's task is to teach the client how to recognize these, apply them in their interpersonal relationships, and help the client make appropriate decisions without taking advantage of the client's vulnerability. The therapist remembers that he or she is responsible for his or her personal issues that may cloud clinical objectivity, cause personal blind spots to develop, and lead to behaviors that injure the therapeutic relationship and the client.

Abusing the power imbalance inherent in therapy is one of the most injurious acts that a clinician can inflict on a client. Therefore, a reasonable and prudent therapist safeguards against impairment of clinical objectivity and prevents hurtful clinical behaviors by being aware of his or her internal reality. The safest and healthiest path an MFT can take to address this issue is to understand his or her motivation of personal actions. Consulting with objective peers when personally challenged, and exploring necessary issues in their own therapy as needed helps safeguard the loss of clinical objectivity.

Consider the following examples and imagine how the therapeutic relationship and the client are affected. A therapist opts not to refer a socially influential client for additional counseling with a second therapist who has greater expertise because referring this client would mean loss of income or recognition. Another therapist extends treatment in spite of the client's readiness to terminate. The clinician is afraid to lose her current level of income and her emotional need to maintain and unconscious dependency in their relationship. A famous television host who is the client invites the clinician to appear on his television program to promote the clinician's practice and he accepts. Another therapist asks a client to provide employment for unemployed relatives at the client's company while concurrently providing psychotherapeutic services. The therapist reminds the owner that they must continue "working" on addressing the tragedy that took place at his factory and several workers were injured. He feels guilty and agrees with her. In considering the impact of the clinicians' action on their clients, imagine how they consciously or unconsciously furthered their personal interests in the therapeutic relationship. An investigation of unprofessional conduct easily opens the door to a malpractice action.

> 1.7 PATIENT BENEFIT:
> **Marriage and family therapists continually monitor their effectiveness and take steps to improve when necessary. Marriage and family therapists continue therapeutic relationships only as long as it is reasonably clear that patients are benefiting from the relationship.**

Ethically, this standard requires MFT to assess continuously how they affect the client's growth and development during treatment. To do so, the MFT must be able to recognize what progress means to the client. A clinician attempting to define progress of treatment without consulting the client is essentially ignoring the welfare of the client. This action is oppressive and unethical. The MFT must be aware of the different factors that redirect the progress of treatment. In addition, the MFT must also be aware of the different methods available to assess the client's progress.

Clinicians are aware that a multitude of factors driving the direction of treatment. These include psychosocial, financial, personal, interpersonal, spiritual, employment, parenting, and cultural. Knowledgeable clinicians accept that these factors are an important component of diagnosis and prognosis. As the clinician begins developing a treatment plan, he or she assesses these issues individually and in group. This information is invaluable to the clinician since it provides an understanding of factors that can enhance or interfere with treatment. In awareness, the clinician prevents these factors from derailing treatment.

The clinician also has an excellent assessment tool to determine if treatment is progressing. This tool is the treatment plan. Treatment plans serve as a pathway to achieve success in treatment. It also serves to assess if the client has stopped progressing towards his or her goals. To be effective in this task, the clinician must have a relevant treatment plan in place and must know how to view goals and objectives as assessment tools. The treatment plan, when used correctly, serves to indicate where the client's progress has come to a halt. Being progressive, the goals and objectives indicate the specific point of stoppage. An observant and knowledgeable clinician observes that point and determines how the treatment plan must be modified to initiate momentum. If this change is ineffective, the clinician's task is to determine the cause for the lack of progress. In making this determination, the MFT considers several factors. These include inappropriate treatment, lack of understanding by the client, overwhelming treatment, unconscious lack of the client's motivation and cooperation, and possibly the therapist's ineffectual management of the therapeutic modalities. Regardless of the reason, it is the clinician's responsibility to assess for the lack of progress and create an effective treatment approach. Once the clinician determines this finding, he or she develops a program of expanding his or her scope of competence. This improvement includes attending classes, obtaining consultation with more experienced colleagues, reading, viewing films, joining a discussion group, and other similar activities.

Should the clinician realize that he or she is the reason for the lack of progress in treatment and is unable to enhance his or her competence, the clinician must take appropriate action. It is unethical for the clinician to continue treatment when he or she is ineffective in the treatment delivery. What reasonable options are open to the MFT at this point? The first step is to converse with the client and present finding indicating that the clinician is no longer effective in providing treatment. Next, the concept of the client's well-being is addressed. This means that the clinician's interventions always focus on the welfare of the client. The clinician follows with the consideration that referring the client to another therapist with greater experience and knowledge is in the best interest of the client. Acting below that standard could only cause harm to the client. Once the referral contact is established, the MFT assures that the referral process is in the best interest of the client. This means that the client is not referred when in crisis and only when stable.

1.8 EMPLOYMENT AND CONTRACTUAL TERMINATIONS:

When terminating employment or contractual relationships, marriage and family therapists primarily consider the best interests of the patient when resolving issues of continued responsibility for patient care.

This standard directs MFTs who are employers, employees, or independent contractors to be aware of the possible conflict that arises in contractual arrangements due to inappropriate expectations and misunderstandings. When the employment relationship ends, there may be times when a conflict ensues between the employer and employee regarding the "ownership" of the client. Any conflict resulting from the employment relationship can jeopardize the patient's welfare. A reasonable and prudent clinician, as employer or employee, educates him/herself regarding employment law and statutes, Case Law, and employment regulations affecting contractual agreements. The clinician assures that all such agreements conform to state law. Not doing so can jeopardize the clinician's status with the state department of labor, lead to an accusation of unprofessional conduct, face a civil action for breach of contract, and even face a BBS investigation for unprofessional conduct in case the contractual agreement involves the client's participation for resolution of the conflict.

It is the responsibility of MFTs in these situations to resolve such conflict and avoid placing the client in the middle of their struggle. That is, it is in the clients' best interest if the employer-employee difference is addressed in the form of an appropriate contract between the employer and the employee before providing clinical services to clients.

1.9 FAMILY UNIT/CONFLICTS:

When treating a family unit(s), marriage and family therapists carefully consider the potential conflict that may arise between the family unit(s) and each individual. Marriage and family therapists clarify at the commencement of treatment, which person or persons are clients and the nature of the relationship(s) the therapist will have with each person involved in the treatment.

This standard states that when the treatment unit is comprised of more than one person, a concurrent relationship exists among those being treated. Then the therapist takes reasonable and prudent steps to insure that these clients understand to whom the therapist owes the therapeutic duty. It may be that the MFT does not owe this duty to some of the unit members. The clinician informs all the treatment unit members at the same time who are the actual clients, what role they play in the treatment, what steps the therapist will take to insure that each person forming part of this relational group is protected throughout the therapeutic process, and how that protection will take place.

For example, a couple seeks therapy to determine if they will stay together. Through written informed consent, the therapist clarifies that the couple is the client and that he or she will keep individual records for their individual protection in case they divorce. The therapist also clarifies that he or she owes the therapeutic duty to the couple until they divorce. Should they divorce, the therapeutic duty reverts to each one of them individually. As a dictum for insuring safety for clients, the reasonable and prudent therapist obtains written informed consent, which delineates these important concepts. Should the MFT be called to testify as a witness on behalf of one or the other client, this consent clearly clarifies the therapist's role. The therapist's "Holding Information Policy" is stated at the beginning of therapy, adding further safety to this complicated situation.

In another example, an adult client brings a sibling to therapy to provide the therapist with additional information. The MFT establishes that the sibling is not part of the therapeutic relationship and serves only as an informational resource or consultant to the therapist. It serves the MFT to establish in writing with this sibling that therapeutic duty does not exist between them and that the nature of the relationship is only for informational purposes. This clarity of this action creates safety should the sibling believe that the MFT owes him or her a confidential therapeutic relationship.

1.10 WITHHOLDING RECORDS/NON PAYMENT:

Marriage and family therapists do not withhold patient records or information solely because the therapist has not been paid for prior professional services.

Though mental health records are the property of the MFT, the information contained in these records is the property of the client and the therapist holds it in a confidential manner. When this information is required for a client's continuity of treatment or to address legal matters, the MFT behaves unethically if he or she withholds records due to non-payment of therapeutic services. This decision and action can injure the client and the client can initiate legal, administrative, and professional action when injured.

Several conditions exist where clients would require access to their mental health records. These include changing therapists, obtaining emergency care, experiencing the death of a therapist, obtaining supplemental services, involvement with forensic situations, geographic relocations an auto collision resulting in a physical injury, or displeasure with the present therapist. In addition, the client can decide to avoid paying for services. This action can result from a misunderstanding to an outright conflict between client and therapist. Regardless of the reason for non-payment of services, the MFT must act ethically and avoid withholding mental health records or information because the client failed to pay for services.

1.11 CONSULTATION:

When appropriate, marriage and family therapist consult, associate, collaborate with, and refer to physicians, other health care professionals, and community resources in order to improve and protect the health and welfare of the patient.

In some clinical situations, the MFT's therapeutic duty to provide appropriate treatment to clients includes obtaining consultation with more experienced colleagues, association with other treatment providers, and/or collaboration with other professionals. When complying with this ethical standard, MFTs refer clients to an M.D. or to a psychiatrist to determine if psychotropic medication is appropriate. Examples of other referrals include a psychologist to treat a issue outside of an MFT's scope of practice, referring to other mental health clinicians, referring to support groups, referring to educational activities, referring to group psychotherapy.

These referrals broaden the treatment perspective and strengthen the treatment delivery unit, especially if a crisis issues develops. Such issues, which include active suicidality, a serious threat to harm, child abuse, substance abuse with danger to self or others, anorexia nervosa, elder/dependent abuse, are potentially dangerous situations. These situations warrant an extended treatment approach, which includes a multidisciplinary approach to protect the client and clinicians.

In the middle and ending phase of treatment, MFTs can enlist additional resources to help manage presenting clinical issues. Examples of this are support groups, 12-step programs, educational programs, group therapy, and specialized treatment programs. It is prudent to make these referrals part of the MFT's treatment considerations. MFTs are expected to consult with colleagues to expand treatment considerations when the client is not achieving the treatment goals, when the treatment is not successful, or when it is necessary to enhance treatment considerations. Reasonable and prudent MFTs use appropriate referrals to augment treatment.

1.12 ADVOCATE WITH THIRD-PARTY PAYERS:

When appropriate, marriage and family therapists advocate for mental health care they believe will benefit their patients. In appropriate circumstances, they challenge denials of care, or denials of payment for care, by managed care organizations, or other payers.

This standard identifies the importance of the legal therapeutic duty established by the Wickline case (1986) and expands this duty onto an ethical therapeutic duty as well. The Wickline case establishes that all health professionals, including psychotherapists, have the responsibility to appeal a negation of medical services made by a managed health care or insurance company. MFTs who treat clients under managed care or insurance programs must pay close attention to this standard. When receiving an insurance company's refusal to pay for client services, MFTs must resubmit the request for services. If necessary, MFTs assess the client's progress to determine if treatment has been completed as defined by the treatment plan goals. If new information requires inclusion in the resubmitted request, MFTs have the ethical therapeutic duty to provide the insurance company with this additional medically necessary information. MFTs base their second request on objective clinical findings, the presence of a mental disorder, and/or psychosocial impairments.

For example, in the case of managed care, an MFT receives an insurance authorization for 7 sessions. Treatment begins addressing depressive symptomatology, which interferes with the client's relationships. After the client completes first 7 sessions, the MFT submits a treatment plan and a pre-authorization form to request 36 additional sessions to manage the client's depressive as well as psychosocial impairments. The managed care company informs the MFT stating that they deny the requested services because the pre-authorization form does not support the diagnosis of a "medically-necessary" impairment. According to this standard, the MFT must challenge the managed care company's denial of services. An appropriate challenge involves resubmitting the request with any additional explanation of the requested services and their medical necessity. Should this MFT accept the first negation of services without a challenge, the MFT's conduct is unethical. If the insurance company denies the services a second time, the clinician has met his ethical therapeutic duty. Ultimately, it is the MFT's responsibility to assess the client accurately, document the client's "medically-necessary" services and advocate for the client by challenging the negated services or payments.

1.13 TREATMENT ALTERNATIVES:

Marriage and family therapists discuss appropriate treatment alternatives with patients. Marriage and family therapists do not limit their discussions of treatment alternatives to what is covered by third party payers.

Informed consent is a legally established concept, which requires that MFTs provide clients with adequate information allowing them to make an informed decision before beginning treatment. When clinicians provide clients with reasonable variety treatment alternatives, they offer clients empowerment regarding this decision-making process. As clients consider and evaluate treatment alternatives, some of which MFTs may not provide, they can decide for themselves the approach that best suits their emotional and/or financial needs. This standard establishes the ethical therapeutic duty that reasonable and prudent MFTs must present clients with reasonable treatment alternatives even though managed care providers or third party insurers do not cover some or all of these services.

Clients who present for counseling under managed care programs, insurance, or other third party program, may not be fully informed of their complete benefits package. While this standard does not require the MFT to educate the insured on their specific insurance benefits, it does recognize that due to the complexities of insurance programs, clients may be uninformed or even misinformed as to the covered treatment modalities. In some cases, a degree of misinformation may preclude appropriate benefit utilization by unaware clients. Thus, MFTs are required to address potential misinformation that may exist and help clients understand how they treat a presenting issue even though insurance benefits may not cover these. Should MFTs present treatment modalities that do not provide a working solution for the client, they have the duty to refer the client to other clinicians who provide alternatives that can meet the needs of clients. Failure to do so invites an opposing attorney to initiate a malpractice in case the client suffers injury. The attorney's accusation would include: failure to treat appropriately, failure to refer, and failure to recognize personal limitations to treat.

<u>1.14 POTENTIAL CONFLICTS:</u>

Maariage and family therapists carefully consider the potential conflicts when providing concurrent or sequential individual, couple, family, and group treatment, and will take reasonable care to avoid or minimize such conflicts.

When a group of individuals, regardless of the nature of the relationship, engages in relational therapy, MFTs must be aware of interpersonal conflicts that can exist in human interactions. Additionally, this standard requires that MFTs place these potential conflicts within the appropriate context when providing therapy. Reasonable and prudent MFTs know that invariably, conflicts will arise between members of such a treatment unit regardless of the size. Ethically, MFTs must conceptualize how these conflicts can affect each individual client and the interpersonal relationship(s) between and among members. This preparedness provides MFTs the opportunity to diminish the potential conflict destructiveness and injury and manage these appropriately. MFTs can teach clients that they do not have to fear conflict. Instead, they can welcome it as an opportunity to strengthen their relationships. Thus, MFTs can avoid clinical imbalance and disruption when such conflict arises and simultaneously model for clients how they can turn a liability into an asset.

<u>1.15 DOCUMENTING TREATMENT DECISION:</u>

Marriage and family therapists are encouraged to carefully document the decision-making process when significant clinical judgment has been exercised, e.g., determining reasonable suspicion of child, elder, or dependent adult abuse, determining when a patient is a danger to self or others when making major changes to the treatment plan, or when changing the unit being treated.

Reasonable and prudent MFTs know that challenging clinical situations require careful monitoring and management when they occur. These legal challenges are adversarial and as such, a high degree of tension exists. In these charged clinical situations, opposing parties may want to intentionally place MFTs in tenuous situations to benefit from clinical decisions made by MFTs. One such situation is the confidentiality bind when facing a legal mandate to report child abuse. MFTs must decide if a reasonable suspicion of abuse exists. From that point, they either report or not report. Opposing parties will attempt to attempt to blame the clinician for inappropriate conduct for reporting or not reporting.

Experts in documentation protocols and the content of mental health records state that in challenging clinical situations, reasonable and prudent MFTs consider the nature of the challenge, regardless of it's presentation, as a fluid process with a beginning and an end. Their experience leads them to recognize that only a comprehensive and progressive documentation protocol is helpful to clinicians when having to support their clinical decision. Such a protocol begins with a description of the nature of the issue, the clinical challenge the clinician faces, the clinical information they obtained, the supporting information leading to their decision, identification of legal standards applicable to the present situation, rationale for the action taken, outcome of the decision, and the outcome. This documentation serves to protect the client and the clinician when facing a legal challenge in the future.

1.16 NON-THERAPIST ROLES:

Marriage and family therapists that engage in professional roles other than treatment or supervision (including, but not limited to, managed care utilization review, consultation, coaching, adoption service provider, or behavior analyst), act solely within that role and clarify, when necessary, to avoid confusion with consumers and employers, how that role is distinguished from the practice of marriage and family therapy.

This standard differentiates MFTs as service providers and psychotherapy providers. Ethically, both roles differ in that the latter utilizes psychotherapeutic methodologies. Each role provides different benefits to clients and has separate requirements of MFTs. They must inform clients when they serve in roles other than marriage and family therapists. For example, they inform clients the nature and function of the separate service role, the services the client can expect, and that psychotherapy is not a part of the service provided. However, MFTs must remember that licensed clinicians providing secondary services must abide by all California law, especially the mandated reporting laws.

1.17 THIRD PARTY PAYER DISCLOSURES:
Marriage and family therapists advise patients of the information that will likely be disclosed when submitting claims to managed care companies, insurers, or other third party payers, such as, dates of treatment, diagnosis, prognosis, progress, and treatment plan.

When using client insurance, MFTs must provide a variety of client clinical client information to authorize payment for services. Though a necessity for some, other clients may object to the MFT providing such records to third party payers. Some of these records can have a negative impact on the insurability of the client. MFTs must remember that released information is not retrievable. This standard requires that those MFTs providing treatment and billing third party payers on behalf of clients provide them with informed consent regarding the third party payer disclosure requirement and the nature of the disclosed information. The client makes the decision to disclose or not to disclose.

Clinical Example # 1

Jeanette and Tyrone, an interracial couple, are having difficulties in their marriage and seek counseling with an MFT. At the first appointment, both sense a degree of discomfort in the therapist. However, soon they begin to argue and the MFT raises her voice and orders them to leave her office immediately. She says: "I don't have to put up with this abuse from anyone."

Questions for Clinical Example # 1

1. After reading the vignette, did it appear that Jeanette and Tyrone were being abusive towards the therapist? Why or why not?
2. Was the MFT's sudden termination of the session in the best interest of the treatment unit? Why or why not?
3. If the MFT's Internal Reality was such that she was biased against interracial couples, was her behavior reasonable and prudent? Why or why not?
4. If the MFT had been aware of her bias, what steps could she have taken to prevent the sudden and inappropriate termination of treatment?
5. Which CAMFT ethical standards were violated and why?

Clinical Example # 2

Tim is a physician in diversion treatment for alcohol abuse. The medical board received several complaints about him being drunk at work and to avoid losing his medical license, he opted for treatment with Pamela, an MFT. Pamela is a single mother and her daughter has been ill with pneumonia. She forgot to pick up medication for her daughter at noon and it will take her several hours to have her physician call in the prescription to the pharmacy. Instead, she opts to ask Tim for a prescription. She reasons that he won't mind after all she's done for him. Upon hearing the request, Tim's initial reaction is to comply, however, he begins to consider that since he has not examined the child, he might be liable if she has a reaction with the medicine. Also, if he doesn't give Pamela the prescription, she might not help him avoid the loss of his medical license. He agrees only because he feels trapped.

Questions for Clinical Example # 2

1. What makes the interaction between Pamela and Tim a dual relationship? Is it a harmful dual relationship? Why or why not?
2. Pamela did not intend to coerce Tim, yet he felt coerced by her. Does this matter if he were to be harmed by the resulting harmful dual relationship?
3. Some clinicians might say: "No one will know so it's OK to ask." Do you agree? Why or why not?
4. What questions would a reasonable and prudent clinician have asked of himself/herself prior to asking Tim for a prescription?
5. If a reasonable and prudent clinician considers the impact of his/her clinical actions on treatment or the therapeutic relationship, what would be the first question that Pamela needed to ask of herself?
6. Which CAMFT ethical standards were violated and why?

Clinical Example # 3

Judy receives a call from a potential client referred by one of Judy's ex-clients. Judy tells him her fee and he states he can't afford that. She tells him she will gladly provide him with names of clinicians with a lower fee. He becomes angry and tells her she is unethical and will lodge a complaint against her.

Questions for Clinical Example # 3

1. Did Judy violate any CAMFT ethical standards? Why or why not?
2. Is she ethically required to treat clients at a lower fee? Why or why not?

Clinical Example # 4

Roberta is a staff MFT at a battered women's shelter. One of her clients recently returned with severe injuries to her upper body and face. Upon seeing the client's injuries, Roberta couldn't help herself and reacted by saying: "You've got to divorce the S.O.B. or he will kill you."

Questions for Clinical Example # 4

1. Was Roberta justified in reacting emotionally? Why or why not?
2. Did she maintain clinical objectivity? Why or why not?
3. Though it is understandable to be angry when facing her client's injuries, what is Roberta's ethical therapeutic duty regarding telling clients what to do?
4. Which CAMFT ethical standards did she violate?

Clinical Example # 5

Josephine has not taken a vacation since she opened her practice. Her focus has been on creating a successful practice and save enough money to buy a small condominium. After putting a d down payment on one, she gave herself the luxury of accepting a sudden invitation from her sister to go away for the weekend. She took her cell phone, however, service was not available in the remote area they visited. During the weekend, a particular vulnerable client faced an emergency and could not reach Josephine. Ultimately, she ended in the emergency room after an overdose of prescription pills and alcohol.

Questions for Clinical Example # 5

1. Josephine probably thought: "Nothing will happen to my clients during the weekend." Is this reasonable and prudent reasoning? Why or why not?
2. Had Josephine informed her client how to safely manage a crisis in her absence, would the client have ended in the emergency room? Why or why not?
3. What is Josephine's ethical therapeutic duty according to CAMFT ethical standard 1.4.2?
4. Did Josephine comply with this duty? Why or why not?

Chapter Questions

1. In CAMFT Ethical Standard 1, what does "advancing the welfare of individuals and families" mean?
2. In the same Ethical Standard, what does "make reasonable efforts to ensure that their services are used appropriately" mean?
3. In Ethical Standard 1.2, the term "influential position" appears. What is its significance in therapy?
4. What is the difference between a dual relationship and a harmful dual relationship?
5. What makes having sex with a client an egregious violation?
6. CAMFT Ethical Standard 1.3 prohibits providing therapy to persons with whom the therapist has had a sexual relationship. Were the therapist to do so, how will this affect his/her objectivity?
7. An MFT tells a client that he needs therapy for at least five years after the client discloses that he received a very large inheritance and can pay full fee. What would you tell this MFT about this action?
8. An MFT tells a couple that they must divorce because their conflict is extremely caustic and hurting the children. Which Ethical Standard has been violated and why?
9. A client considers suicide and calls her MFT. A recorded message answers stating that a message can be left and the MFT will return the call later. What is the ethical violation and why?
10. A therapist receives a lucrative job offer in another city and the job begins in two days. The therapist leaves a message onthe answering machine of each of his clients telling them of her move. She tells them they need to seek another therapist. What is the ethical violation and why?
11. An MFT begins treating a couple. She then has a few sessions with each individually. The husband tells the MFT that he has been in an affair for the last two years and wants to bring his lover to therapy. Which ethical standard could be violated if the MFT proceeds and why?
12. A client presents with codependent issues. The client asks if Alanon would be of help. The therapist responds: "I don't believe in their approach and I can treat you by myself." What is the ethical violation and why?
13. A deeply troubled teenager is not benefiting from a religion-based therapeutic approach and their insurance has stopped paying for treatment. He is told by the therapist that the only way to heal is to pray fervently. What is/are the ethical violation(s) and why?

Chapter 29

CAMFT Ethical Standard 2

Confidentiality

Therapeutic safety is the foundation of effective psychotherapy and counseling. A critical aspect of safety is the appropriate management of confidentiality within the therapeutic relationship. This means respecting the client's privacy and promoting the secure continuation of the therapeutic process. Enacted state law in the mental health field creates a legal framework that continues to evolve in the direction of protecting the client's privacy. Professional ethics too, contribute to the maintenance of a client's privacy and their appropriate use by MFTs extends the foundation of safety for their clients and themselves as well.

> 2. CONFIDENTIALITY
> **Marriage and family therapists have unique confidentiality problems because the "patient" in a therapeutic relationship may be more than one person. The overriding principle is that marriage and family therapists respect the confidences of their patient(s).**

This section addresses the unique challenge MFTs face when treating more than one client within the context of the therapeutic relationship. This standard requires that MFTs assess and respect their clients' confidentiality when the "treatment unit" is comprised of more than one person. The clients can be individual members of a family, a couple, or any other group of people, including clients in group therapy, who seek the services of an MFT for help in improving their relationships. In this situation, the clinician can face a difficult challenge regarding confidentiality. The challenge being that should one or more members of the "treatment unit" share sensitive information at an individual session with the therapist and want not to have that information shared with the rest of the unit, the clinician must hold that information. Holding this information prevents the clinician from utilizing this held information to address issues that may be preventing the advance of the welfare of the unit. In other words, the clinician is stuck: he or she must hold this information and cannot use to help "treatment unit."

MFTs manage confidentiality in a reasonable and prudent manner for this "treatment unit" by initially addressing and applying a "Holding Information" policy. Standard of care requires that MFTs manage this "Holding Information" policy in the following manner, First, they inform the "treatment unit" of how treatment and the treatment unit can be impacted by holding versus not holding sensitive information. Next, MFTs inform their clients that holding sensitive information can create individual safety and possibly slow down the treatment process while not holding this information can create increased tension between the members of the treatment unit. Possibly, feelings of betrayal may arise in one of the clients should the held information be revealed by the therapist. In addition, it may be that treatment may accelerate when MFTs disclose the sensitive information. Ultimately, MFTs have the choice to hold all information, no information, or some information while giving the holder of the privilege the opportunity to bring up the held information in session should this held information interfere with treatment. Any of these approaches are acceptable forms of standard of care. The important point is to inform the clients up front about which approach MFTs use after obtaining agreement from their client. If not, then MFTs negotiate an approach that is satisfactory to their clients. It is important for MFTs to make sure everyone understands the implications of the chosen "Holding Information" policy.

When treating minors with parental consent, reasonable and prudent MFTs create safety by having the parents and child agree on the parameters of the sensitive information held versus not held. MFTs inform parents that they will share this information should the minor present a danger to self or others. This allows MFTs to create trust with the minor by not revealing information to the parents that could breach the trust in the therapeutic relationship. Alternatively, MFTs establish trust by applying appropriate boundaries in this delicate negotiation.

2.1 DISCLOSURE OF CONFIDENTIAL INFORMATION:

Marriage and family therapists do not disclose patient confidences, including the names or identities of their patients, to anyone except a) as mandated by law, b) as permitted by law, c) when the marriage and family therapist is a defendant in a civil, criminal or disciplinary action arising from the therapy (in which case patient confidences may only be disclosed in the course of that action), or d) if there is an authorization previously obtained in writing, and then such information may only be revealed in accordance with the terms of the authorization.

This standard establishes the ethical duty to maintain confidentiality with all client communications. To maintain this privacy, MFTs create a safe therapeutic environment in which the client explores issues with little or no fear of injury caused by disclosures of confidential information. However, in some specific clinical situations, the law mandates that third party safety supersedes the individual client's interests: confidentiality releases are mandated or permitted to protect the client or others. For MFTs, mandated situations include child abuse reporting requirements (Penal Code 11166-11174), elder abuse reporting requirements (Welfare and Institutions Code 15610-15650), dependent adult abuse reporting requirements (Welfare and Institutions Code 15610-15650), and a serious threat to harm (Tarasoff v. Regents of the University of California and Civil Code 43.92). Permitted disclosures include a threat of harm to self or others (Evidence Code 1024), when the therapist is defending himself or herself in a legal action that arises from therapy (Evidence Code 1020), and when MFTs receive a valid written release of information (Civil Code Section 56 through 56.37).

Reasonable and prudent MFTs evaluate all clinical situations carefully and assess for imminent danger. To manage danger, they seek consultation from an objective and experienced peer when necessary, substantiate and document decisions affecting the issue at hand, and only release that information pertinent and necessary to address the issue at hand. Consider a client telling a therapist that he or she is considering suicide because there is little reason to live. The client talks about a lack of employment and increased social isolation making his life worse. The therapist assesses for suicidality, hopelessness and perturbation and the client continues to assert the possibility of attempting suicide, though no actual attempts have ever been made. After assessing that the client's mental or emotional state poses a danger to self or others, the MFT considers breaking confidentiality as a clinical intervention. However, doing so may be considered unethical behavior unless the therapist first obtains a consultation from experienced peers, clearly establishes suicidality risk factors, continues objective assessment for hopelessness, perturbation, and potential imminent danger to self, and determines that breaching confidentiality is the only possible clinical intervention to save the life of the client.

The question of whether to breach confidentiality in this case is considered only when all reasonable steps to protect the life of the client, per Bellah v. Greenson (1978), have been exhausted. The reasonable and prudent MFT document all reasonable steps taken to protect the life of the client in the progress notes including the rationale for making this decision. MFTs breach confidentiality as minimally as possible per Evidence Code 1024. First, MFTs notify significant others or the appropriate authorities and later, the authorities can invoke Welfare and Institutions Code 5150, a 72-hour involuntary hold intended to protect the client.

2.2 SIGNED AUTHORIZATIONS — RELEASE OF INFORMATION:

When there is a request for information related to any aspect of psychotherapy or tratment, each member of the unit receiving such therapeutic treatment must sign an authorization before a marriage and family therapist will disclose information received from any member of the treatment unit.

This standard states that to release any information to anyone outside of the treatment unit (this unit includes all interconnected persons who are seeking therapy with the same MFT at the same time) the MFT protects the clients by obtaining the appropriate written consent to release such information (Civil Code Sections 56 through 56.37). In addition, therapists inform their clients at the onset of therapy that they will obtain the client's consent to release any requested information. Therapists will further clarify that if any person within the unit refuses to give consent, the therapist will owe an ethical and legal therapeutic duty to this unit and will withhold the requested information. For example, a conflicted family seeks the services of an MFT to improve interpersonal relationships. In time, the parents decide to divorce and the father wants to introduce the information discussed in therapy to obtain legal custody of the children. If the mother refuses to provide a written release of information to the therapist, the MFT must protect the confidentiality of the whole family unless directed by a judge to do otherwise.

2.3 ELECTRONIC MEDIA:

Marriage and family therapists are aware of the possible adverse effects of technological changes with respect to the dissemination of patient information, and take care when disclosing such information. Marriage and family therapists are also aware of the limitations regarding confidential transmission by Internet or electronic media and take care when transmitting or receiving such information via these mediums.

Communication technology continues to evolve rapidly, especially as it affects the practice of psychotherapy. Facsimile machines, E-mail, voice mail, telephone answering machines, wireless networking, cellular phones, cordless phones, satellite communications, hard drive storage, Bluetooth adapters, electronic web based communications, and similar instruments have expanded communication technology to the benefit and detriment of MFT practice. This expansion affords therapists the ability to accelerate communication and transmit large volumes of information instantaneously. However, these communication facilitators also present a challenge to MFTs. Thanks to this rapidly evolving technology, client confidentiality may be jeopardized, and in some situations MFTs may unknowingly allow unauthorized access.

Some examples are: facsimile machines may be programmed incorrectly and sensitive information about a client may be forwarded to unintended recipients, telephone answering machines may be accessed by anyone within reach or by someone knowing the security access code, E-mail can be accessed by computer hackers or others who know how to access Internet Service Provider database computers, computers with password protection can also be accessed by persons with appropriate skills including repair technicians, those servicing the communication company servers can also access cellular phone communications. Currently, the only secure communication is a "hard-wired" line between two direct telephones using a direct wire transmission or by using expensive electronic signal scramblers or computer encryption programs.

This standard requires that reasonable and prudent MFTs must be aware of how confidentiality can be jeopardized by the utilization of these communication technologies. Additionally, when using these instruments, MFTs must take reasonable steps to protect client confidentiality. For example, when using facsimile machines, MFTs use a disclosure statement warning the recipient that in case an unintended party receives the message, notifies the sender of the error and appropriate steps are taken to correct it. It is quite possible that an unintended recipient could read the facsimile, and taking these steps would be a prudent and reasonable approach to act ethically. I recommend that MFTs send a test fax in advance. A cover page requests that the recipient contact the sender when he or she receives the test fax. When the recipient returns the phone call to the sender, the recipient verifies his or her identity. It is in MFTs' best interest that uses a facsimile machine to double check the recipient's telephone number for accuracy before sending confidential information.

When using cellular or cordless phones, MFTs take reasonable steps to ensure that an immediate eavesdropper does not listen to confidential information. This may mean not using these telephones for communicating confidential information. Alternatively, MFTs only use first names. Information that identifies the client is avoided.

The user of E-mail transmissions and computer technology also safeguards confidentiality. Again, reasonable steps are taken to safeguard any confidential information stored or transmitted via computers or the Internet. One of these steps is to use encryption programs in the computer hard drive. These protect computer disk files from being read by someone without the proper computer program and security password. Additionally, encryption allows files to be erased completely from the computer and even a file recovery program cannot retrieve the encrypted erased file thus providing true confidentiality protection when using computers. When transmitting E-mail and client records through the Internet, again encryption of data would protect these files from random access by computer hackers. Those therapists sending patient information via the Internet should apprise themselves of the federal HIPAA requirements regarding this subject. MFTs protect hard drives or laptop computers from theft to avoid disclosure of confidential information.

For those therapists using computer programs to store mental health records, it is prudent to avoid word-processing computer programs to store client information and treatment records. Should a legal challenge occur, the opposing attorney will likely subpoena the word processing program and the complete hard-drive because these programs cannot "fix" the entered data. That is, the writer can edit this information at any time. Therefore, the possibility exists that MFTs using such programs have altered the client's mental health records. When a third party subpoenas the complete hard drive, client confidentiality is breached. The individual checking for data alteration will access other client data contained within the hard drive to determine the date of creation. If MFTs are considering using a computer program for data storage, the program used must a "fix" feature to lock the entered information with the appropriate date. Additionally, the program must have the capability to "import-export" an individual patient file, which means that a single client's information is retrieved as a single file and given to the party legally requesting this information. Password protection must also be part of the mental health computer program. Should a client's mental health record be subpoenaed, the exported file is provided along with a copy of the program allowing the third party to read only the information in that file. Thus, MFTs protect the confidentiality of all their clients.

2.4 MAINTENANCE OF PATIENT RECORDS —CONFIDENTIALITY:

Marriage and family therapists store, transfer, transmit, and/or dispose of clinical records in ways that protect confidentiality.

While the clinical records themselves are the property of the MFT, the information contained within these records belongs to the client. The client is the holder of the privilege and the therapist upholds this privilege for the client by protecting the information contained in the records. It is the responsibility of MFTs to manage clinical records to protect client confidentiality.

Storing clinical records appropriately requires that MFTs always kept them under lock and key. Transferring records from one location to another also requires the protection of the client's confidentiality. It would be best to place them in a locked box in the trunk of an automobile, rather than leaving them in the front or rear seat. The first option would needlessly leave the records vulnerable to stealing or other possible loss. Consider this example: an MFT enters a car wash and leaves mental health records in the back seat. One of the attendants picks up the charts out of curiosity and recognizes the name of a local celebrity. As the attendant begins to read the record, he finds that the celebrity had been involved in a damaging affair. Soon, the information becomes public to the chagrin of the celebrity. He knows that only the MFT knows of the affair and decides to pursue legal and administrative action. MFTs store clinical records appropriately to prevent legal action. Others might expand this scenario. They would ask: "If someone stole her car, would she still be liable?" An expert witness answers this by stating that she needs to show that her actions were reasonable and prudent for the circumstances. Ultimately, the question becomes: "Were her actions reasonable and prudent?"

Disposing of the clinical records in an appropriate manner requires that the appropriate amount of time pass before mental health records be disposed. Second, MFTs shred mental health records to protect confidentiality. Placing mental health records in the trash whole, or left relatively intact is considered unethical and illegal behavior.

This standard extends the ethical therapeutic duty upon MFTs to consider the storage of clinical files in computers. The question to ask is: "Will my hard-drive be subpoenaed due to inappropriate use of computer programs?" Computer programs that do not fix the entered text to avoid deleting and/or altering of text are potentially dangerous to use. Also, computer programs that do not allow for the separation of each client record as a separate file open the possibility that the complete hard-drive could be subpoenaed. Should any of these conditions exist, an expert witness would reasonably suggest to the attorney that the MFT's hard drive be subpoenaed to rule out the possibility that the files were altered in any way. Text alteration is considered unethical and unprofessional conduct. Should the complete hard-drive be subpoenaed by the opposing attorney, then client confidentiality would most likely be jeopardized. When deleting any computer files from a computer, the reasonable and prudent clinician uses a "scrubber" application to remove traces of these files in the hard drive. In addition, reasonable and prudent MFTs consider placing the hard drive containing client information in a locked cabinet.

Overall, this standard establishes that MFTs must be aware of possible breaches of confidentiality during storage, transfer, and disposal of mental health records including interfacing with computers. Taking this responsibility seriously assures that confidentiality be maintained and protected. For computer applications, see the previous standard.

<u>2.5 EMPLOYEES — CONFIDENTIALITY:</u>

Marriage and family therapists take appropriate steps to ensure, insofar as possible, that the confidentiality of patients is maintained by their employees, supervisees, assistants, and volunteers.

Maintaining confidentiality is both a legal and ethical therapeutic duty that MFTs owe to clients. MFTs with employees, supervised interns, assistants or volunteers under their clinical direction, have the ethical duty to assure, within reason, that these individuals will hold client confidentiality. When the treatment provider unit extends to include other professionals who are members of the practice, this duty also applies to them. This also applies to agencies where the confidentiality "umbrella" extends to all parties working for the organization.

MFTs as employers or supervisors cannot truly control the behavior of other members of the treatment component. However, they can take reasonable and prudent steps to manage confidentiality in these circumstances. For example, they can establish the use of a confidentiality contract with all employees and volunteers. This contract requires these individuals to hold confidentiality for the rest of their lives. Though pre-licensed supervisees are already required to maintain confidentiality, they must be also included in the contract because should they stop the licensing track, the law does not require them to hold client confidentiality.

Reasonable and prudent MFTs discuss with employees, volunteers, assistants, and supervisees all applicable clinical, legal/ethical, and professional implications of breaching and maintaining confidentiality. For example, it may be that employees and supervisees may not have the legal and ethical foundation to understand totally the clinical ramifications of breaching this important component of treatment. Alternatively, each of the participating members of the team may have a different understanding of the requirements of maintaining confidentiality. Inviting experts in the application of law and ethics in supervision helps educate the participants on confidentiality requirements for MFT interns, trainees, and employees. This approach serves to address the responsibilities established by this standard upon supervisors. Employees can be forewarned that client names not be shouted or spoken publicly, that telephone messages be given to clinical staff in writing rather than verbally in front of other clients, that mental health records be stored under lock and key, that no mental health records should be left on desks unguarded, and employees refrain from revealing to their own family members the identify of clients.

> <u>2.6 USE OF CLINICAL MATERIALS — CONFIDENTIALITY:</u>
> **Marriage and family therapists use clinical materials in teaching, writing, and public presentations only if a written authorization has been previously obtained in accordance with 2.1 d), or when appropriate steps have been taken to protect patient identity.**

This standard dictates that reasonable and prudent therapists have an ethical therapeutic duty to protect their clients' confidentiality when clinical material is used in a public manner such as publications, lectures, or teaching. This standard provides two alternatives for the safe use this clinical material. MFTs obtain the client's written consent or they alter the name and other client identifying information to protect client identity. All materials to be presented publicly are reviewed for possible identifiable information that could reveal a client's identity and modified as needed. Ultimately, the risk of breaching a client's confidentiality under these circumstances takes precedence over the benefits of developing new clinical or experimental approaches. When managing the confidentiality of clients under these circumstances, these approaches maintain safety for the client and the therapist and protect both of them.

2.7 GROUPS — CONFIDENTIALITY

Marriage and family therapists, when working with a group, educate the group regarding the importance of maintaining confidentiality, and are encouraged to obtain written agreement from group participants to respect the confidentiality of other members of the group.

Group therapy provides clients an opportunity to explore themselves in an interpersonal setting under the leadership and direction of a professionally trained therapist. Due to the number of participants, the potential of breaching confidentiality increases. MFTs are not expected to monitor each client's management of the group's confidential information. Reasonable and prudent MFTs discuss with their group clients the need to maintain confidentiality, thus allowing them to feel safe in their exploration of interpersonal dynamics. Lack of safety undermines the group's process. Standard of care dictates that a safe approach for MFTs is to establish a contractual agreement to hold confidentiality between members. Should any member breach another member's confidentiality in the group, the aggrieved party can seek legal action against the party that caused the injury.

Clinical Example # 1

Angelina provides substance related treatment at a county jail facility. Her skills as a bilingual MFT are required to treat the large Hispanic population within the jail. Due to funding limitations, her program involves group therapy. She believes she doesn't have to deal with confidentiality issues with the inmates because she will hold their confidentiality. One of the inmates revealed in group therapy that he had robbed a liquor store several months ago. A few days later, he was taken out of the program, charged with the crime, and transferred to another facility for dangerous criminals. A few months later, Angelina received notification that her program at the jail was being terminated due to a major lawsuit by this inmate. The County, the county jail, the jail administrators, and the substance abuse counselors were being sued for violation of confidentiality and for violation of the inmate's civil rights.

Questions for Clinical Example # 1

1. Angelina ignored an important issue regarding addressing confidentiality management within group therapy. What did she ignore?
2. What specific CAMFT ethical standard did she violate?
3. What could she have done differently?

Clinical Example # 2

> John and Mary have decided to terminate couples treatment with Joanne because they decided to divorce. Both blame each other for the pending divorce and each wants control of the children. A custody evaluator contacts Joanne and tells her he has written authorization from both clients to obtain their records. Without question, Joanne talks to the evaluator without first obtaining a copy of the authorization. Later, one of the clients initiates a lawsuit against Joanne for breach of confidentiality. It appears that only one client provided written authorization for release of his records. Because Joanne released too much information, the wife lost custody of the children.

Questions for Clinical Example # 2

1. Joanne wanted to be helpful to the custody evaluator yet she forgot an important ethical requirement. What did she forget?
2. Which CAMFT ethical standards did she violate? How?
3. What prudent and reasonable steps could she have taken upon receiving the phone call from the custody evaluator requesting client information?

Clinical Example # 3

> Maryanne works in an agency notorious for it's lack of structure. Many interns who have trained there have commented, "It's an accident waiting for a place to happen." One evening while seeing clients until late, she forgot to put her mental health records away thinking that she would put them away in the morning. The next day, she is unable to find them and no one knows where they are. A week later they get a call from the recycling center; an employee found these records in a recycling bin, he recognized his friend's name and shared the content of the records with other employees. A few weeks later, Maryanne and the agency are sued for causing emotional harm to the client whose records were "recycled" inadvertently.

Questions for Clinical Example # 3

1. Maryanne never imagined this could ever happen to her. How did she lose clinical objectivity and stop acting in a reasonable and prudent manner?
2. At what point was the client's confidentiality violated?
3. Who is responsible for the breach of confidentiality: Maryanne, the agency, or both? Why?
4. In court, Maryanne tries to blame the breach on the housekeeping staff. Will this hold up in Court? Why or why not?
5. What reasonable and prudent steps needed to have been taken to prevent this breach of confidentiality?
6. Which CAMFT ethical standards were violated and why?

Chapter Questions

1. A "Holding Information" policy prevents a therapeutic bind if it isn't established at the beginning of treatment. What is the bind? How could this ethical violation impact the therapeutic relationship and/or treatment?

2. CAMFT Ethical Standard 2.2 discusses the need for a written release of information. How does this standard compare with Civil Code 56-56.37?
3. What are the ethical challenges when using electronic devices for wireless communication?
4. List 5 ways that violate ethical standard 2.4 when storing, transferring, and disposing of mental health records?
5. A local well-known politician begins treatment with an MFT. The MFT uses a billing company to complete her insurance billing. One of the employees of this company tells a friend about the politician seeking therapy and the friend contacts the local TV station. What is the ethical violation and why?
6. An MFT faxes a request for services to an insurance company. The fax, including the patient's complete mental history and identity is faxed to the local sandwich shop. How could this ethical violation have prevented?
7. A delicate and painful issue is brought up in group therapy about one of the members. Another group member goes home and shares this with his wife. She, in turn, shares it with a friend who happens to be the first man's employer. The first man is fired from his job and is told why. He decides to sue the therapist. How could this ethical violation have been prevented?
8. A couple buys the latest book on important clinical cases and bipolar treatment. Upon reading it, they recognize another prominent couple discussed in the book. They call their friends and the response is a state of shock. They decide to complain to the BBS and initiate legal action. Which ethical violations are involved?

Chapter 30

CAMFT Ethical Standard 3

Professional Competence and Integrity

Professional ethics and the law complement each other to create therapeutic safety. MFTs address competence, integrity, and therapeutic safety by establishing that they will have the training, knowledge, and experience required to manage the issues clients present in therapy. These standards also dictate the process MFTs use in a variety of clinical situations and circumstances requiring clinical and professional competence.

> 3. PROFESSIONAL COMPETENCE AND INTEGRITY
> **Marriage and family therapists maintain high standards of professional competence and integrity.**

This section establishes the ethical therapeutic duty to address the level of training, experience, and education required of MFTs in the areas of practice, teaching, and research. Before providing services in any of these three areas within the profession of marriage and family therapy, MFTs must develop appropriate levels of competence. The professional literature defines competence as the training, knowledge and experience a "prudent and reasonable" therapist in the community will use when providing care to clients. Additionally, honesty, fairness, objectivity, and respect of self, and other qualities as implied by law and ethics, are expected of therapists as members of this profession.

This section implies that MFTs without appropriate levels of competence in specific professional arenas, such as treating borderline clients, can harm a client severely if MFTs provide professional services without an appropriate knowledge base and clinical safeguards. These safeguards include seeking clinical consultation, guidance, or education from an experienced peer. In addition, ethical standard 3.0 places the onus of responsibility on MFTs to determine their own level of competence for all therapeutic issues they treat. All therapists continue to assess their clinical skills in relation to what the profession considers as a "reasonable and prudent" level of competence. This self–assessment may range from reading the current clinical and scientific literature to staying abreast of latest changes in treatment approaches.

3.1 CONVICTION OF A CRIME:

Marriage and family therapists are in violation of this Code and subject to termination of membership, or other appropriate action, if they: a) are convicted of a crime substantially related to their professional qualifications or functions; b) are expelled from or disciplined by other professional organizations; c) have licenses or certificates that are lapsed, suspended or revoked or are otherwise disciplined by regulatory bodies; d) continue to practice when they are no longer competent to practice because they are impaired due to physical or mental causes or the abuse of alcohol or other substances; or e) fail to cooperate with the Association or the Ethics Committee at any point from the inception of an ethical complaint through the completion of all proceedings regarding that complaint.

This standard establishes the importance of maintaining appropriate levels of integrity in professional practice. Integrity includes honesty, fairness, and respectfulness toward self and others, as implied by California law and CAMFT ethics. When MFTs violate their responsibility of professional integrity, CAMFT can discipline them. Resulting discipline can include termination of membership, which can also have disciplinary ramifications with the Board of Behavioral Sciences (BBS). Such actions include: committing insurance fraud, misrepresenting the clinical license though inappropriate advertising, falsifying information in the license renewal application, practicing under the influence of drugs or alcohol, embezzling funds from a non-profit agency where the therapist is employed, practicing under the influence of addictive substances, practicing while mentally or physically disabled, or being convicted of driving under the influence, any other action where the safety of clients is being jeopardized, or refusing to cooperate with an investigation by CAMFT's Ethics Committee. This section states that therapists have the ethical therapeutic duty of maintaining appropriate clinical safety by managing their own integrity within the confines of therapeutic practice, research, or teaching.

3.2 FINANCIAL INCENTIVES:

Marriage and family therapists avoid contractual arrangements which provide financial incentives to withhold or limit medically / psychologically necessary care.

With managed care and the use of insurance becoming the norm in the field of marriage and family therapy, competitiveness and financial pressures may determine how insurance programs will be managed. If the sole purpose of an insurance program is to curtail medical or psychological services to patients for financial gain, then according to this standard, MFTs who become members of these programs are not acting in the best interest of the client. Instead, the insurance company's financial interests supersede the client's. It is important to remember that MFTs have an ethical therapeutic duty to advance the welfare of the client. An insurance program that restricts medical/psychological services to patients for whatever reason is not advancing the welfare of clients. Joining these programs can constitute unethical behavior in the part of MFTs.

3.3 CLINICAL RECORDS:

Marriage and family therapists create and maintain patient treatment records, whether written, taped, computerized, or stored in any medium, consistent with sound clinical practice.

This standard places an ethical responsibility upon MFTs to follow established definitions of "sound clinical practice." Experts have written that section 123130 of the Heath and Safety Code indirectly establishes the minimum content of mental health records in general. These experts state that Health and Safety Code 123130 clearly defines the minimum content of the mental health records that MFTs provide to a client when that client makes a request in writing for these records. Other experts have established that mental health records serve to document the clinician's therapeutic duty owed to the client. MFTs meet this duty by documenting assessment, diagnosis, treatment, and management of crisis issues in a reasonable and prudent manner. When releasing these records to the client, MFTs must provide the legislated content, or when not releasing the records, provide a written explanation regarding the refusal to release these records. The legislated contents are: chief complaints and pertinent history, treatment plan, diagnosis, prognosis, medical findings and consultations, progress notes, and discharge summary. It would be prudent to consider that these components reflect the minimal requirements of records according a "sound clinical practice."

Keeping mental health records is a legal and ethical therapeutic duty. Reasonable and prudent MFTs consider the following as appropriate content: personal client history, family history, medical history, previous treatment history, consultations, referrals, psychometric testing including a Mental Status Exam and Beck's Depression Inventory when appropriate, informed consent document, additional informed consent documents when using "challenging" therapies, written releases of information when appropriate, a complete financial history, a 5-Axis diagnosis, prognosis, treatment plan, progress notes, and discharge summary. Specific clinical needs dictate additional content. MFTs lacking this level of content in their notes are practicing below the standard of care.

When storing mental health records, maintaining confidentiality is paramount. This means that records are locked in a cabinet. Experts recommend keeping records a minimum of seven years after the therapeutic relationship has ended. For clients under 18 years of age, they recommend keeping the records for one year after the 18th birthday and for no less than seven years. To dispose of mental health records appropriately and to maintain confidentiality, records are shredded. Avoid throwing the records in the recycling bin in a plastic bag believing that a recycling engineer will shred them. Imagine a curious worker at the recycling center opening the bag and perusing the records.

This standard also applies when using computerized records. An appropriate software program allows saving text entries and making these entries "non-editable" once, the "Accept" button is pressed. The software program also allows for each patient record in its entirety to be "imported-exported" as a separate file. This allows only the release of one record to be given to the requesting party should records be subpoenaed. Otherwise, the whole program and database, which includes all patient data is handed over to the party who subpoenas the records. This action breaches the confidentiality of other clients. This program must also have a multi-level password utility allowing security at different levels to prevent unauthorized parties from making changes and editing or deleting important information. The software program must also be HIPAA compliant. Not using these safeguards can lead to practicing below the standard of care. Ultimately, MFTs have the duty to practice reasonably and prudently in this arena.

3.4 PROFESSIONAL ASSISTANCE:

Marriage and family therapists seek appropriate professional assistance for their professional problems or conflicts that impair work performance or clinical judgment.

This standard dictates that MFTs monitor their personal life for signs of difficulties that could impair their professional performance or clinical objectivity. These problems can include marital or family discord, employment or financial problems, endogenous or exogenous depression, substance abuse or dependence, sexual addiction, major illnesses, or any other life crisis that interferes with work. Upon recognizing such impairments, reasonable and prudent MFTs act appropriately to ensure the safety of their clients. These measures include consultation with objective peers, personal therapy, obtaining assistance for substance-impaired professionals, medical help, and if necessary, taking a leave of absence. Consider an MFT who practices with an unmanageable bipolar disorder, enters into the manic phase of the disorder, severely abuses therapeutic boundaries, and causes severe harm to a client. This and similar actions are considered unethical behaviors. However, taking appropriate medication and managing the bipolar disorder can allow the MFT to continue practicing in a safe manner.

Ultimately, reasonable and prudent MFTs ensure the safety their clients' safety by temporarily or permanently limiting, suspending, or terminating professional activities when a personal problem influences the ability to practice therapy in a safe manner. Should MFTs decide to terminate professional activities, they provide their clients with continuation of professional services through referrals to other qualified therapists and avoid abandoning clients.

3.5 STAYING CURRENT:

Marriage and family therapists remain abreast of developments in their field through educational activities and clinical experiences. Marriage and family therapists, when acting as teachers, supervisors, and researchers, stay abreast of changes in the field, maintain relevant standards of scholarship and present accurate information.

This standard places a responsibility on MFTs who provide psychotherapy, teach, supervise, and conduct research to stay current with scientific and professional information as it develops. MFTs are responsible for maintaining a "reasonable and prudent" level of competence in each professional skill area. MFT maintain their level of clinical, educational, or supervisory competence by seeking peer consultation from more experienced professionals, using peer study groups, attending continuing education courses, reading appropriate materials (including referred journals and texts,) presenting or attending workshops, and/or teaching at a recognized university. MFTs, who begin to supervise interns without receiving any education and/or training in supervisory skills, are practicing unethically since CAMFT has established the educational requirements for this activity. Additionally, MFTs are responsible to be conversant with the extensive scientific literature addressing supervision issues and even consider becoming certified voluntarily under CAMFT's supervisory protocol. Any information presented in clinical practice, teaching, research, and supervision must be scientifically accurate and based on professionally and scientifically founded knowledge obtained from appropriate sources.

3.6 CULTURAL SENSITIVITY:

Marriage and family therapists actively strive to identify and understand the diverse cultural backgrounds of their clients by gaining knowledge, personal awareness, and developing sensitivity and skills pertinent to working with a diverse client population.

Psychotherapy practice in California exposes MFTs to clients with a variety of cultural backgrounds. Reasonable and prudent MFTs assure that they have the necessary cultural understanding to provide services to these diverse cultural groups. MFTs also consider the specific needs of each cultural or diversity group. Elements that must be considered when providing psychotherapy to culturally different clients include the following: the degree of acculturation of the individual into the prevalent society, the belief system and social values of each culture, how morality is expressed within the culture, the role of the psychotherapist as an authority figure or as a peer, how a power differential is expressed in the culture, whether counseling is valued as an educational or psychodynamic process, and an awareness of the therapist's own internal reality and value system. MFTs also consider these elements when diversity issues arise, such as sexual orientation, gender differences, religion, etc. MFTs can develop additional skills and obtain education through continuing education courses, workshops, consultation, and staying abreast of the scientific literature in this area of psychotherapy.

3.7 THERAPIST CULTURAL VALUES:

Marriage and family therapists make continuous efforts to be aware of how their cultural/racial/ethnic identity, values and beliefs affect the process of therapy.

Providing psychotherapy requires that MFTs understand their clients' process but also their own. Reasonable and prudent MFTs are aware of their personal values and understand how these values regarding cultural differences affect the psychotherapeutic process. The California legislature gave MFT educators who teach students California law and CAMFT ethics to integrate into their teaching how the students' own sense of self and human values will affect their professional judgment and actions. This ethical standard dovetails with the legal provision as defined by legislation (Business and Professions Code 4980.41-5) that requires the above-mentioned exploration of self and human values. It addresses the personal and professional competence of MFTs to become aware of what values they identify with regarding cultural, ethnic, or racial differences.

3.8 HARASSMENT OR EXPLOITATION:

Marriage and family therapists do not engage in sexual or other harassment or exploitation of patients, students, supervisees, employees, or colleagues.

Ethically, this section addresses the power imbalance found in therapeutic relationships including relationships with clients, students, interns, trainees, supervisees, employees, or colleagues. Sexual harassment, exploitation, and other forms of harassment seriously violate the power differential. Sexual or other harassment appears in the form of flirting, playfulness, teasing, requesting favors or privileges, or using sexual innuendoes. Due to the nature of the therapeutic relationship, MFTs are on the upper echelons of the power differential. As such, MFTs model appropriate boundaries and provide a healthy role model for those in a professional relationship with them, especially students, trainees, interns, employees, and patients. Consider an MFT who is a teacher. He invites a student for a cup of coffee after class and both begin talking about their personal lives. Should loss of objectivity develop or coercion take place as a result of this intimacy, the MFT, as clinical supervisor, would be acting below the standard of care and behaving in an unethical manner. Ultimately, MFTs are responsible to avoid harmful dual relationships by assessing how they can lose objectivity or exploit those under their care.

3.9 SCOPE OF COMPETENCE:

Marriage and family therapists do not assess, test, diagnose, treat, or advise on problems beyond the level of their competence as determined by their education, training, and experience. While developing new areas of practice, marriage and family therapists take steps to ensure the competence of their work through education, training, consultation, and/or supervision.

This section establishes the ethical therapeutic duty to assess, diagnose, and treat according to the standard of care. In psychotherapy's rapidly evolving and challenging arenas, MFTs are not relieved of the duty to protect their clients from lack of competence when providing professional services. All MFTs have the duty to establish a personal standard of competence for the issues and problems they treat professionally. This competence must meet the standards of the profession, also known as the standard of care.

When MFTs assess appropriately, they obtain all necessary information to arrive at a diagnosis. This includes the client's personal information, family history, medical history, previous treatment history, present symptomatology, cross-cultural issues, and assessment of current mental status via a Mental Status Exam. MFTs diagnose appropriately when they have obtained all necessary information and establish the most reasonable diagnosis, which includes a 5-Axis diagnosis. It is important to support the diagnosis via observable clinical symptoms and duration of the symptoms. This information leads to developing an appropriate treatment plan. Treating appropriately means that MFTs apply his or her standard of competence (i.e. knowledge, experience, and training) to address the presenting symptoms in a way that meets the client needs. The client receives reasonable alternatives to treatment, hears about the risks and benefits of these, and makes a decision whether to proceed with the presented treatment. A treatment plan would document the proposed treatment via goals, objectives, and serves as an assessment tool to determine if the clinical work is effective. Should it prove ineffective, MFTs modify the treatment plan. Not having an appropriate treatment plan is practicing below the standard of care due to lack of documentation

3.10 PATIENT SEEING TWO THERAPISTS:

Marriage and family therapists do not generally provide professional services to a person receiving treatment or therapy from another psychotherapist, except by agreement with such other psychotherapist or after termination of the patients's relationship to the other psychotherapist.

MFTs are required to clarify who is the primary therapist when clients are simultaneously obtaining services from more than one therapist. The primary therapist owes the legal and ethical therapeutic duty to the client and is responsible to provide an appropriate treatment plan of action to the client. This plan can include appropriate referrals to expand the treatment container and, ultimately, the primary therapist is responsible for the overall management of the client's treatment. When a second therapist becomes involved in the client's treatment unbeknownst to the primary therapist, the treatment could be undermined and therapeutic safety could also be jeopardized. If the client is dissatisfied with the primary therapist, it is the client's responsibility to address that dissatisfaction and resolve any multiple therapeutic relationships. Should the second therapist become aware of this dissatisfaction, it is in the best interest of the client to refer the client to the primary therapist for clinical resolution of the "dissatisfaction." Once this has been resolved and if the client has terminated the relationship with the first therapist, the second therapist may become the primary treatment provider.

In some cases, the primary therapist may be unaware that the client is seeking additional services from a second therapist. In these cases, it is impossible to address this issue. Should the primary treating therapist's assessment lead him or her to believe that the client is seeing a second therapist, it is reasonable and prudent to ask the client directly. If the answer is "yes," then this therapist has the duty to clarify the situation with the client and if necessary, obtain a written Release of Information to contact the other clinician and make his or her aware of the potential conflict. Ultimately, one of the therapeutic relationships must terminate before the second therapist becomes the primary therapist as defined in legal and ethical standards.

3.11 ELECTRONIC SERVICES:

Marriage and family therapists provide services by Internet or other electronic media to patients located only in jurisdictions where the therapist may lawfully provide such services.

With the advent of Internet and electronic media therapies, an increasing number of MFTs are providing treatment via these mediums. CAMFT recognizes that it may be an appropriate medium when certain conditions exist. It requires that MFTs be available in the immediate geographic area where the clinician is licensed. This standard attempts to assure that the laws of California are applicable in the provision of treatment. CAMFT would consider MFTs who provide services outside of their geographic area of practice as unethical. The BBS would consider this practice as unprofessional.

It is reasonable for MFTs to limit their practice to the location where their license allows them to practice. The concept of client confidentiality, including mandated and permitted reporting based on California law applies only to California. Practicing outside of the state via the Internet could prove problematic to MFTs and to their clients. Not only is it difficult to establish emergency resources for client, MFTs are unable to protect clients when high-risk issues arise in Internet practice. Additionally, providing services via this medium prevents clinicians from performing a personal interview of the client, which is one of the essential requirements to practice according to the standard of care. Thus, when performing psychotherapy over the Internet or other electronic medium, it is best to assure that the services provided are limited to the location where MFTs' license allows them to practice safely and protect their clients' well-being.

3.12 RESEARCH FINDINGS:

Marriage and family therapists take reasonable steps to prevent the distortion or misuse of their clinical and research findings.

This section directs that MFTs who publish their clinical and/or research results and find that their results have been misinterpreted or distorted through any public media must take reasonable steps to correct such errors. This media includes such as publications, lectures, online continuing education, E-books, or workshops. Consider an MFT who publishes a book regarding treatment for anxiety disorders in children. A media review favorably misinterprets the therapist's findings. As a result, the MFT is overwhelmed with new clients and decides not to correct the misquoting and possibly inhibit the flow of new clients to her practice. This action represents an example of unethical conduct under this standard.

Though it may be difficult, or even impossible, to address every single error, MFTs must take reasonable steps to make appropriate corrections when found. These reasonable steps may include writing letters, making telephone calls, having private communications with the appropriate individuals, and if necessary, taking legal action to stop the continued publication of the misquoted material.

3.13 PUBLIC STATEMENTS:

Marriage and family therapists, because of their ability to influence and alter the lives of others, exercise care when making public their professional recommendations and opinions through testimony or other public statements.

This section draws attention to the inherent power differential that exists between MFTs and the public. This power differential may be explicit or implicit, and, ultimately, reasonable and prudent MFTs have the responsibility to manage this differential in a safe manner. Making public statements to support a political, social, religious, or financial organization can have both positive and negative repercussions. Some may benefit and some may be harmed. MFTs weigh both outcomes carefully before making such public statements. Before MFTs make any public endorsements or public statements about any organization, it serves them to obtain consultation with appropriate individuals and consider the possible ramifications of these actions. Consider an MFT who publicly supports a political candidate and makes a statement such as: "Based on my professional experience as a therapist, I know that this person is an excellent community leader and would serve our community with integrity. I recommend your approving vote." Some of her clients may ask: "Why doesn't she support my cause?" These individual may feel hurt and cast aside by her actions. When making supportive statements, the need for caution and consultation must be considered when determining if it is ethical conduct to make this type of statement.

3.14 LIMITS OF PROFESSIONAL OPINIONS:

Marriage and family therapists do not express professional opinions about an individual's mental or emotional condition unless they have treated or conducted an examination of the individual, or unless they reveal the limits of the information upon which their professional opinions are based, with appropriate cautions as to the effects of such limited information upon their opinions.

This standard clearly establishes that it is unethical conduct when MFTs provide a professional opinion about a client whom they have never assessed, examined, or treated. The ramifications of this action can be detrimental to the well-being of the recipient of this opinion. Once they make these statements, it is impossible to retract them. When MFTs release this information, the public interprets it as if the individual is a client presenting a mental disorder or emotional challenge and has been or is currently being treated by this MFT. This recipient can suffer great harm should this happen to him or her.

Imagine a couple seeking marital counseling to avoid divorce. After several months of treatment, they have an acrimonious divorce. Later, the ex-wife seeks individual therapy. During the course of treatment, she discusses her ex-husband's comportment and foibles. In time, her therapist begins to discuss his mental disorders and personality disorders as if she had examined him personally. Eventually, the ex-wife is convinced that her ex-husband is quite ill and that he took advantage of her financially during the divorce procedures. She returns to Court and requests a new hearing based on this new evidence about his illness affecting his ability to make financial decisions. Ultimately, both parties will end up injured or worse. This standard requires MFTs to be cognizant of their impact on individuals whom they have never treated yet diagnose without a sound clinical foundation.

Clinical Example # 1

Jason complained to his supervisor that he needed more clients in his private practice internship. To comply, his supervisor began referring more difficult cases. The last one involved a severely depressed young man, Robert, who lost his wife in a horrible car accident. Jason had learned about mood disorders in school, however, he knew very little about suicidality or how to assess for risk. Jason tried using reflection and empty chair work with Robert to no avail. Robert now began talking about suicide and Jason kept using his usual techniques.

Questions for Clinical Example # 1

1. What specifically have Jason and his clinical supervisor not paid attention to?
2. Which CAMFT ethical standards were violated and why?
3. The boundary between depression and suicide is very thin and actually the former can merge into the latter very quickly. What is the danger that Jason faces as he avoids assessing Robert for risk of suicide?
4. What is the danger the clinical supervisor faces by having Jason treat beyond his *Scope of Competence?*
5. Should Robert commit suicide, which clinician would be held responsible for not taking steps to protect his life: Jason, his supervisor, or both? Why?
6. It is obvious Jason has no training regarding the treatment of suicide clients or how to assess for risk of suicide. Who has the primary responsibility to assure that he is trained prior to treating clients with this issue: Jason, his clinical supervisor, or both? Why?

Clinical Example # 2

Armelle, a licensed MFT, recently found out she had breast cancer. She finds herself crying uncontrollably in session with clients. She recognizes it is a problem yet she needs to make money to support herself since she doesn't have disability insurance. She can't afford to see a therapist: her medical insurance doesn't cover therapy.

Questions for Clinical Example # 2

1. If Armelle continues treating clients under these conditions, what could possibly happen?
2. If she were unable to maintain clinical objectivity and make a decision that ends up hurting a client, would she be held responsible for this action even though she is in "shock" herself? Why or why not?
3. You are her colleague and recently one of your clients told you that her friend, one of Armelle's clients, began complaining about the quality of her services. What would you do to help Armelle? How would you do it to avoid breaching your client's confidentiality?
4. Which CAMFT ethical standards were violated and why?
5. What steps would a reasonable and prudent clinician have taken in this situation?

Clinical Example # 3

Majawi began her internship at an inner-city program for homeless children. She feels fortunate to be paid for her hours of training and enjoys working with children. Her clinical supervisor invites his interns to his home for gatherings and parties. In one occasion, he approached her and told her: "You are a beautiful woman and it's hard to stay focused when I am around you." Then he leaned over to smell her fragrance. She didn't know what to do and smiled out of nervousness and anxiety. He informed her by way of innuendos that he can have her fired. She's afraid of not being able to support herself and his is becoming more aggressive in his pursuit.

Questions for Clinical Example # 3

1. Is Majawi's clinical supervisor coercing her? Why or why not?
2. Would you consider his behavior to be sexual in nature? Why or why not?
3. Would you consider his behavior to be predatory? Why or why not?
4. Majawi finds herself in a difficult bind. If she reports him, she could lose her job. If she doesn't, in time he will probably demand sex from her. If she were consulting with you, what advice would you give her?
5. What CAMFT ethical standards have been violated?
6. Majawi decides to pursue a sexual harassment accusation against her supervisor and a BBS accusation. Do you agree with this approach? Why or why not?

Chapter Questions

1. How are "standards of competence" in treating different psychotherapeutic issues established?
2. An MFT with dual licenses in California and Idaho receives a letter from the State Board in Idaho telling her that she is being found in violation of fraud and her license is revoked. CAMFT finds out about this violation and expels the therapist from membership. Soon thereafter, the BBS initiates an investigation against this therapist. Describe the ethical violation that initiated the California action by the BBS.
3. A substance-abusing troubled teenager learns that her therapist is "scoring" speed from a local source. When confronted by the teenager, the therapist replies "I need it for weight control." The teenager notices the trembling of the therapist's hands. What are the ethical violations and why?
4. A current client is injured in an auto accident. Her attorney needs the mental health records to show that her pre-morbid (before the accident) state did not show severe anxiety about driving and fear of being rear-ended. The therapist notifies her attorney that she keeps minimal records and did not document her pre-morbid condition. The client cannot prove association of her symptoms to the accident and loses her legal case. She sues the therapist. What caused this to happen?
5. An insurance company is seeking new treating therapists. Their acceptance into the program requires that they control all treatment to six sessions or more; otherwise they will not receive future referrals. What is the ethical violation for an MFT who joins this program and why?
6. A therapist keeps his mental health records in a new computer program. One night, his office is robbed and the computer is stolen. A few weeks later, the police notify him that the hard drive is found in a "swap meet." The police find that the hard drive is fully operational and the program is accessible. What are the ethical violations and why?
7. An Employment Assistance Program refers a client who practices Hinduism to an MFT to treat his depression. The therapist considers herself to be deeply religious in her own faith and views other religions as an affront to her religious beliefs. She tells the client that his depression is due to his lack of acceptance of the "True God" and that his depression will lift when he initiates exploration of her religion. She is adamant that prayer is the best way to heal depression. He becomes despondent and his family has him hospitalized. They consult with an attorney who initiates legal action against the company and the therapist. What are the ethical violations?
8. A supervisor tells an intern that she can have the choice cases at the agency if the intern baby-sits her 2-year old on a regular basis. The supervisor has not taken a legal and ethical course in many years. What are the ethical violations?

Chapter 31

CAMFT Ethical Standard 4

Responsibility to Students and Supervisees

MFTs as teachers and supervisors play an important role in modeling appropriate behavior to their students and supervisees. MFTs have the responsibility to create safety within the relationships they develop with students and/or supervisees. Since students and supervisees will use their relationship with supervisors as the foundation for future therapeutic relationships they will develop with their clients, reasonable and prudent MFTs assures that they maintain clear and appropriate boundaries in their relationships with students or supervisees.

4. SUPERVISOR, STUDENT AND SUPERVISEE RESPONSIBILITIES:

Marriage and family therapists do not exploit the trust and dependency of students and supervisees.

Section 4 establishes the ethical therapeutic duty upon MFTs who supervise to recognize and protect the special relationship that exists between them and their students/supervisees. This relationship is based on a unique power differential based on the teacher or supervisor's greater knowledge and experience and the student/supervisee's lack of professional experience, knowledge and training. Gender differences, social status, professional standing, or economic status may enhance this power imbalance. Reasonable and prudent MFTs have the responsibility to appreciate the fragility of this power differential, respect it, model appropriate behavior and soundly manage the trust and dependency that exists between student/supervisee and the teacher/supervisor. Exploiting this trust and/or dependency is a violation of CAMFT's ethical standards.

4.1 DUAL RELATIONSHIPS:

Marriage and family therapists are aware of their influential position with respect to students and supervisees, and they avoid exploiting the trust and dependency of such persons. Marriage and family therapists therefore avoid dual relationships that are reasonably likely to impair professional judgment or lead to exploitation. Provision of therapy to students or supervisees is unethical. Provision of marriage and family therapy supervision to clients is unethical. Sexual intercourse, sexual contact, or

sexual intimacy and/or harassment of any kind with students or supervisees is unethical. Other acts which would result in unethical dual relationships include, but are not limited to, borrowing money from a supervisee, engaging in a business venture with a supervisee, or engaging in a close personal relationship with a supervisee. Such acts with a supervisee's spouse, partner or family member may also be considered unethical dual relationship.

This standard establishes that MFTs who supervise and/or teach hold a greater power than their students and/or supervisees. The students/supervisees expect that their teachers/supervisors will protect them whereas the inverse is not true. Reasonable and prudent MFTs are expected to understand, respect this power differential, model appropriate behavior, and restrain themselves from injuring this fragile relationship. The relationship between student/supervisee and teacher/supervisor holds the same potential for abuse as a therapeutic relationship. Violating the trust and dependency of this relationship can cause the same harm as violating the therapist-client relationship due to an inappropriate dual relationship where loss of objectivity or exploitation takes place.

This section explicitly prohibits the creation of harmful dual relationships such as having a sexual relationship, performing therapy with students and/or their families, or harassing students or supervisees in any manner. This standard also expands the meaning of the supervisor/supervisee/student relationship in that it includes intimate family members. Supervisors and teachers are prohibited from developing abusive, coercive, or harmful relationships with these individuals. If teachers/supervisors believe they may be vulnerable to developing such a relationship with their student/supervisee, it would be appropriate to obtain necessary consultation and, if necessary, the therapist's own therapy to prevent an injurious situation from developing. Doing so would model appropriate behavior for future therapists.

4.2 COMPETENCE OF SUPERVISEES:

Marriage and family therapists do not permit students, employees, or supervisees to perform or to hold themselves out as competent to perform professional services beyond their training, level of experience, and competence, prelicensed or unlicensed status.

This standard requires that MFTs take appropriate steps to prevent those under their supervision from providing treatment beyond their clinical capacity. The first aspect of this responsibility is to comprehend the scope of competence as defined by law and ethics; the second, to evaluate their supervisee's education, training and experience in therapeutic areas they will be addressing as a supervisee; and the third, to ensure that the supervisee does not exceed this level without adequate support and monitoring from the supervisor.

Evaluating a supervisee's level of competence, is a continuous process that the supervisor addresses in supervision and documents in attendance records for courses and workshops and lists of books and journals read. Ensuring that their supervisees/employees do not extend beyond their level of competence requires that the supervisor continually evaluate their supervisees' training, experience, and knowledge and match clinical challenges accordingly. The latter may involve clinical interaction with the supervisee to monitor his or her competence. If a case provides excessive clinical challenges, ultimately it is the responsibility of the supervisor to manage this issue safely for all involved, especially for the client. The supervisor can accomplish this by asking the supervisee to take additional courses, seek additional supervision, obtain appropriate consultation from a more experienced professional, and, if necessary, refer the client to a more knowledgeable clinician.

4.3 MAINTAINING SKILLS OF SUPERVISORS:

Marriage and family therapists who act as supervisors are responsible for maintaining the quality of their supervision skills and obtain consultation or supervision for their work as supervisors whenever appropriate.

MFTs who supervise trainees and interns have the responsibility to evaluate their personal competence to provide this service. The BBS clearly states the requirements for MFTs providing supervision: they must complete six CEUs every two years regarding supervision issues. With this standard, CAMFT expands the supervisory accreditation via an educational process. If MFTs agree to supervise interns and trainees using a modality that as supervisor he or she lacks appropriate training then the MFT is in violation of this ethical standard. MFTs who allow supervisees to practice below the legal and ethical standard of care are practicing unethically in their supervisory duties. Ultimately, this ethical standard places upon MFTs who provide supervision, the responsibility of creating safety for those supervisees who are dependent on their supervisor for the development of their clinical skills.

4.4 KNOWLEDGE OF SUPERVISORS:

Supervisors and educators are knowledgeable about supervision, relevant laws and regulations, and the practice of marriage and family therapy. Supervisors and educators are knowledgeable about and abide by the laws and regulations governing the conduct of supervisors and supervisees.

MFTs who supervise trainees and interns have the responsibility to assure that their education and knowledge in important facets of marriage and family psychotherapy practice meet the prevalent standard of care. These areas include California laws and ethical standards related to marriage and family therapy, and the standard of care related to the practice of marriage and family therapy. Additionally, supervisors know California law regarding supervision, apply it appropriately in their supervisory functions, and assure that they supervise according to the standard of care.

4.5 CHANGES IN LAWS AND ETHICS:

Supervisors and supervisees are aware of and stay abreast of changes in professional and ethical standards and legal requirements and supervisors ensure that their supervisees are aware of professional and ethical standards and legal responsibilities.

California law regarding marriage and family therapy continues to evolve. As supervisors, MFTs are required to know about changes in the law and ethical standards and their appropriate clinical application in supervisory practice. As supervisors, MFTs assess the knowledge of law and ethics of their supervisees. If deficient in this arena, the supervisor takes reasonable and prudent steps to assure that supervisees rise to the level of accepted knowledge of California law and its application.

4.6 CULTURAL DIVERSITY:

Supervisors and educators are aware of and will address the role that culture and diversity issues play in the supervisory relationship, including but not limited to evaluating, terminating, disciplining, or making decisions regarding supervisees or students.

CAMFT recognizes that MFTs represent a varied cultural diversity as supervisors and supervisees. At times, MFTs and supervisees can misinterpret each other's comments, behaviors, clinical recommendations, and even termination of the supervisory relationship. CAMFT requires both supervisor and supervisee to be aware of how diversity can affect the supervisory relationship, to consider its impact on the supervisory relationship, and to manage it appropriately within the supervisory relationship.

4.7 POLICIES AND PROCEDURES:

Supervisors and educators create policies and procedures that are clear and that are disclosed to supervisees and students at the commencement of supervision or education.

This standard requires that educators and supervisors clarify the structure and boundaries of the professional relationship. The structure and boundaries serve to clarify the nature of the interactions, expectations, method of communication, and process of termination. By performing this process at the beginning of the professional relationship, MFTs provide safety, structure, and stability for all involved.

4.8 PERFORMANCE APPRAISALS:

Supervisors and educators provide supervisees with periodic performance appraisals and evaluating feedback throughout the supervisory relationship and identify and address the limitations of supervisees and students that might impede their performances.

MFTs have the responsibility to assess their supervisees periodically and communicate their assessments in a timely fashion and in a manner that benefits the supervisee. Without such feedback, the supervisee fails to determine his or her progress in the path towards becoming a licensed MFT. This assessment and feedback allows both supervisor and supervisee to "course correct" should the supervisee require additional knowledge, training, or experience to enhance or modify his or her scope of competence. Supervisors also benefit from this symbiotic interaction: they learn to sharpen their assessment skills and to continuously improve their communication skills with their supervisees.

4.9 BUSINESS PRACTICES:

Supervisors follow lawful business practices and employer policies when employing and/or supervising interns, trainees, applicants, and associates.

MFTs, as supervisors, educate themselves regarding the appropriate financial requirements when interacting with supervisees. California law is clear about the nature of the only remuneration method available permissible in this professional relationship and supervisors must know it and apply it. Violating

California law means that MFTs are acting both illegally and unethically. Another related aspect of this standard requires that supervisors must refrain from taking financial advantage of their supervisees. For example, supervisors can take advantage of the professional relationship as indicated by the following: failure to remunerate the supervisee fairly, asking the supervisee to perform personal tasks for the supervisor as part of the financial remuneration, and provide an appropriate fanatical termination structure.

4.10 PERFORMANCE ASSISTANCE:

Supervisors and educators guide supervisees and students in securing assistance when needed for the supervisee to maintain or improve performance, such as personal psychotherapy, additional education, training, or consultation.

MFTs as educators and supervisees have the ethical responsibility to guide their students or supervisees to obtain appropriate help when needed. At times, students or supervisees may face a personal or interpersonal challenge that prevents them from continuing in their professional endeavors. At other times, their charges may lack the necessary educational base to transition into the next phase. Others may find themselves lacking clinical or personal objectivity and the only solution available is to obtain consultation from an outside and objective party. Ultimately, supervisors and educators must recognize the impasses experienced by their students and supervisees and take appropriate action to help them seek a satisfactory solution.

4.11 DISMISSAL:

Supervisors shall document their decisions to dismiss supervisees.

Termination of supervisees is a difficult time for all involved especially when conflict arises between supervisor and supervisee. Though supervisors may have an appropriate reason to terminate the professional relationship between themselves and their supervisees, ultimately they must protect the client from harm from the ensuing conflict. Documenting their reasons for terminating their supervisees serves to establish a reasonable foundation and supports this difficult and challenging decision. Should conflict between supervisor and supervisee ensue, the documentation serves to establish the supervisor's reasonable and prudent clinical actions. Thus, supervisors address this ethical requirement and at the same time address the standard of care when addressing this issue.

4.12 <u>REVIEW OF TRAINEE AGREEMENTS:</u>
Supervisors are aware of and review any trainee agreement with qualified educational institutions.

MFTs as supervisors have the professional responsibility to assess for the existence of an agreement between their supervisee who is an intern due to their special status. Since their academic programs for clinical training refer these supervisees, supervisors review the documentation allowing this individual to begin a supervisory relationship. Should the agreement be incomplete, lack important information, contain inadequate language, supervisors have the duty to contact the referring academic institution and request any necessary changes to make this agreement valid.

4.13 <u>PATIENTS ARE PATIENTS OF EMPLOYER:</u>
Supervisees understand that the patients seen by them are the patients of their employers.

When supervisees begin a "private practice" internship under the guidance of their supervisors, they understand and accept that their clients belong to the practice. This means that should the supervisee become licensed, want to move to another locality, and take those clients they have been treating with them, this action is unethical. This is an important standard because it attempts to prevent potential conflict from ensuing between supervisor and supervisee when their relationship ends and the supervisee wants to transfer his or her clients to a practice located in a different location. This type of conflict is one of the most onerous in clinical practice. The person most harmed is the client. Thus, this standard requires supervisees to be aware that they have an ethical obligation to prevent harm to the client in these circumstances by recognizing their role within the supervisory relationship and their relationship with clients.

4.14 KNOWLEDGE OF LAWS AND REGULATIONS:

Supervisees and students have a responsibility to become knowledgeable about relevant laws and regulations pertaining to the license and practice of marriage and family therapy.

Those clinicians under the supervision of licensed MFTs have the responsibility to educate themselves regarding the laws and regulations pertinent to the practice of marriage and family therapist. Throughout their clinical practice as interns or trainees, supervisees will find that California laws continue to change and evolve. These laws affect the client, the supervisee, and the supervisor. CAMFT expects supervisees to stay abreast of all California laws involving the practice of marriage and family therapy.

4.15 MAINTAINING REGISTRATIONS:

Supervisees maintain registrations when required by law and/or regulation and function within this limited role as permitted by the licensing laws and/or regulations.

When practicing as a supervisee, whether as an intern or trainee, the individual must obtain and maintain the proper registrations as required by their state board. Failing to do is considered as practicing in an unethical manner.

CAMFT Ethical Standard 4 — Responsibility to Students and Supervisees

Clinical Example # 1

A local agency is looking for new interns to replace those who have passed their license as MFTs. An ad in placed in the local newsletter with a contact name and phone number. Maria wants this internship because the clinical supervisor has an excellent reputation. The agency's director, also an MFT, interviews Maria and tells her that all interns must take turns to clean the only bathroom. She says: "It's the best way for interns to learn personal humility."

Questions for Clinical Example # 1

1. Does having interns perform this type of housekeeping duty an appropriate method for interns to learn humility? Why or why not? Would you do it? Why or why not?
2. What possible dual roles are interns expected to perform as part of their internship?
3. Would you consider this to be a harmful dual relationship? Why or why not?
4. Which CAMFT ethical standards have been violated?
5. Would the clinical supervisor be held accountable for supporting this harmful dual relationship even though the clinical director originated it? Why or why not?
6. If you were consulting with this agency, what steps would you recommend that they follow to comply with CAMFT ethical standards?

Chapter Questions

1. How are "trust and dependency" related to a power differential in a supervisor/supervisee or student/teacher relationship?

2. Ethical Standard 4.1 is quite broad in its scope. It attempts to create safety for interns/trainees/students in a relationship where they have less power than the other professional. You hear from your best friend that he is being supervised by an MFT with a large referral base; however, you also hear that his supervision also includes personal therapy. Another friend tells you "I am so lucky to be supervised by my therapist. Another friend tells you that her supervisor always begins individual supervision with lengthy hugs, which she tells you feel "dirty." What do you tell each one of these friends?

3. A fellow trainee tells you that she saw her first client a few weeks ago. She also tells you that she feels overwhelmed in session because there are so many complicating issues present with her client that she doesn't know where to start. Your suggestion is to approach her supervisor and discuss her discomfort. She tells you that she did and that the supervisor told her she needed to learn through exposure with the hard cases. What do you tell her about her ethical challenge?

Chapter 32

CAMFT Ethical Standard 5

Responsibility to Colleagues

MFTs play an important role in creating safety in their interaction with colleagues by being honest, respectful, considerate, and sensitive. Their primary consideration in these interactions is the welfare of the client.

5.0 RESPONSIBILITY TO COLLEAGUES:
Marriage and family therapists treat and communicate with and about colleagues in a respectful manner and with courtesy, fairness, and good faith, and cooperate with colleagues in order to promote the welfare and best interest of the patient.

Interpersonal professional relationships parallel the therapeutic relationship. When cooperating with other mental health professionals, MFTs behave in a professional manner. These interactions are based in good faith, cooperation, respect, courtesy and fairness, must safeguard the welfare of the client at all times. Should acrimonious interpersonal conflict result between two cooperating mental health professionals, their conflict can deflect attention away from the client and causing the client injury. CAMFT considers such behavior between MFTs as unethical.

5.1 RESPECT CONFIDENCE OF COLLEAGUES:
Marriage and family therapists respect the confidences of colleagues that are shared in the course of their professional relationships.

In a cooperative professional relationship, MFTs may share personal and sensitive information in confidence with the other clinician. Such disclosures occur in consultation settings, supervision, or other professional interactions. Though the shared information is not considered as technically confidential under California law, it is shared in confidence with the expectation that this information will be respected and not shared with others. CAMFT requires that MFTs holding such information abstain from divulging it and keep it private.

Consider a treating MFT seeking the services of another MFT to obtain substance abuse treatment for a client. During the consultation, the first MFT shares his own struggle with substance abuse. Though he asks the second MFT to hold this information private, the second MFT shares it with a close friend. She asks her friend to keep it confidential. Unfortunately, the information continues the sharing process until it comes back to the first MFT. CAMFT's ethical standard considers the breach of personal information as a violation of this standard.

5.2 IMPAIRED COLLEAGUES:

Marriage and family therapists are encouraged to assist colleagues who are impaired due to substance abuse, emotional problems, or mental illness.

This standard clearly states that it encourages MFTs to help colleagues who practice while impaired. MFTs are not required to take unilateral action to stop impaired colleagues, however they are encouraged to be alert for signs and symptoms of early impairment due to substance abuse, emotional problems or mental illness. These symptoms include short and reactive temper outbursts, unmanageable family conflict, apparent mood disorders, unexplained behavior, changes in eating or sleeping habits, evidence of subtle or overt substance abuse or dependence, or in some extreme cases, the potential of suicide. MFTs will first note changes in behavior or personality before the impaired person decides to become aware of personal changes. This standard reminds MFTs that an early intervention with impaired colleagues can help prevent future emotional and/or physical pain for them and their families.

5.3 FRIVOLOUS COMPLAINTS:

Marriage and family therapists do not file or encourage the filing of ethics or other complaints that they know, or reasonably should know, are frivolous.

As a professional organization, CAMFT upholds its professional ethics through a process of investigating ethical violations. CAMFT takes these ethical violations seriously and investigates each one carefully to protect the rights of individual members and prevent the besmirching of someone's professional reputation. MFTs in the processes of investigation can suffer emotionally when they are accused unjustly via an unmeritorious complaint. This standard establishes the responsibility upon MFTs to refrain from filing or encouraging others to file ethical complaints, which are known to have lack of merit or validity. If an MFT who files or encourages others to file an unmeritorious complaint, CAMFT considers this behavior as unethical. CAMFT considers the filing of any frivolous ethical complaint as unprofessional conduct.

5.4 SOLICITING OTHER THERAPIST'S PATIENTS:

Marriage and family therapists do not agree to see or solicit the clients of other therapists or encourage clients to leave other therapists, except as addressed in Section 3.10.

MFTs must respect the therapeutic relationship established by other MFTs with their clients. Attempting to undermine this relationship can harm the sense of trust established between these two parties. CAMFT also considers the solicitation of other MFTs' clients or encouraging these clients to terminate their established therapeutic relationship for the sake of personal or emotional gain as unprofessional conduct.

Clinical Example # 1

Roxanne is one of a few mental health professionals in a small community. Recently, she was interviewed on television to promote the development of a school-based psychotherapy program for troubled youth. Her positive presentation was a success and as a result, her practice has grown considerably. One of the other clinicians, whose practice has shrunk, decides to get even by complaining to CAMFT about Roxanne's unethical conduct in the interview.

Questions for Clinical Example # 1

1. How has Roxanne's colleague lost objectivity?
2. If Roxanne can prove that the complaint was frivolous, what recourse does she have in regards to the clinician who submitted the complaint against her?
3. Would you pursue action against the clinician? Why or why not?
4. Which CAMFT ethical standards were violated?

Chapter Questions

1. Two therapists find themselves competing for the same client pool at their local university. One of the therapists is invited to the Chancellor's house for a party. The second is not and feels slighted. She blames the first therapist for not being invited and decides to punish her peer by not returning phone calls, cooperating with client treatment, and making false statements about the first therapist's sobriety. What are the ethical dangers for the second therapist? If you were consulting with the second therapist, what recommendations would you make?

2. The second therapist submits a complaint to the CAMFT Ethics Committee accusing the first therapist of abusing her position at the university. If you were an Ethics Committee member, how would you address these complaints?

3. As an Ethics Committee member, you receive a second complaint regarding the first therapist. This complaint alleges that the first therapist did not provide assistance to a fellow therapist who was incapacitated due to a mental problem. How would you respond?

Chapter 33

CAMFT Ethical Standard 6

Responsibility to Research Participants

MFTs as researchers play an important role in protecting their research participants. MFTs are responsible to create as safe of an environment as possible within this relationship. This relationship extends into several areas including, but not limited to, the scope of competence of the researcher, obtaining informed consent, respecting confidentiality, and avoiding harmful dual relationships while conducting research. Ultimately, MFTs attend to the well-being of the research participants.

6. RESPONSIBILITY TO RESEARCH PARTICIPANTS:

Researchers respect the dignity and protect the welfare of participants in research and are aware of federal and state laws and regulations and professional standards governing the conduct of research.

Conducting research competently requires that MFTs respect the dignity and welfare of research participants. This involves, but is not limited to: evaluating the research protocol and assuring that participants can give informed consent. Participants are debriefed after completing the project. All appropriate elements of confidentiality are protected. Participants are assured that the research is conducted ethically by the researchers and/or the assistants. All psychometric tests are scored properly. All applicable laws are followed. Cultural differences of the research participants are respected. Institutional approval is granted. Participants are not exposed to harm, and appropriate consultation is obtained when required. MFTs follow these steps to assure that they protect research participants from harm.

6.1 SAFEGUARDS:

Researchers are responsible for making careful examination of ethical acceptability in planning studies. To the extent that services to research participants may be compromised by participation in research, researchers seek the ethical advice of qualified professionals not directly involved in the research and observe safeguards to protect the rights of research participants.

This standard establishes the importance of determining if the research project follows ethical guidelines. Researchers have the ethical responsibility to obtain appropriate consultation from a more experienced researcher who can evaluate the project objectively. Of paramount importance is the researchers' level of competence in conducting specific research. If researchers do not have the required level of competence for this project and fail to obtain it through consultation, experience, and training, these MFTs may be in violation of this ethical standard. An example that may apply here is the following: MFTs create an effective intervention for couples where a spouse is diagnosed with cancer. In their zeal to pursue an investigation of the validity and reliability of this intervention, the researchers omit taking a thorough medical history of the research participants, and accept candidates who are inappropriate for this study. If these MFTs continue with the project without obtaining consultation on this issue, they may be in violation of this standard.

6.2 DIMINISHED CONSENT WHEN RECEIVING SERVICES:
Researchers requesting participants' involvement in research inform them of all aspects of the research that might reasonably be expected to influence willingness to participate. Researchers are especially sensitive to the possibility of diminished consent when participants are also receiving clinical services, have impairments which limit understanding and/or communication, or even when participants are children.

This standard states that MFTs have the responsibility to obtain appropriate informed consent from the research participant. MFTs use an appropriate disclosure of the research project, which must be in language that is easy to understand. The disclosure addresses all reasonable uncomfortable possibilities that may be encountered in the project, informs the participants that they have the option to decline to participate or withdraw from the project at any time, informs the participants of the implications on the professional relationship between researcher and participant, determines if a previous therapeutic relationship affects the participant's decision to continue or withdraw from the project, discusses the management of confidentiality, sets a protocol for debriefing after completion of the project, and answers all questions, within reason, about the project.

MFTs conducting research are expected to determine if the individual has the competence to understand the content and meaning of informed consent. If not, then these MFTs take steps to protect participants by not including them in the study. If the participants are children, MFTs inform parents of the previously listed factors and the MFTs provide the parents with informed consent before their children can participate. MFTs must also take reasonable steps to assure that the children understand what they can expect to experience during the research by using age-appropriate language.

6.3 DUAL RELATIONSHIPS WITH RESEARCH PARTICIPANTS:
Researchers respect participants' freedom to decline participation in or to withdraw from a research study at any time. This obligation requires special thought and consideration when researchers or other members of the research team are in positions of authority or influence over participants. Marriage and family therapists, therefore, make every effort to avoid dual relationships with research participants that could impair professional judgment or increase the risk of exploitation.

This standard dictates that MFTs conduct research must protect participants when they decline participation in or withdraw from the project at any time. MFTs assure participants that the researcher and/or research assistants will not abuse a present or previous professional power differential. When clients, students, or supervisees are involved as potential candidates for the research project, they may be vulnerable to abuse. Creating this level of safety requires that MFTs conducting research avoid harmful dual relationships with research participants.

Consider an MFT who has established a friendship with current students or supervisees and invites this person to participate in her research project. Since she is using her previous relationship based on trust and a power differential, she may be conducting herself unethically under this standard. The reason is that since she abused the trust of the research participant, they may have felt compelled to participate to avoid a conflict with her. The fact that a friendship exists already may cloud the researcher's objectivity with her friends. These students may feel pressured to participate in the research project because failure to do so could affect their friendship with the researcher and could affect their grades negatively. This MFT would best not invite her students with whom she has already established a dual relationship to participate in her study.

6.4 CONFIDENTIALITY:
Information obtained about a research participant during the course of a research project is confidential unless there is an authorization previously obtained in writing. When the possibility exists that others, including family members, may obtain access to such information, this possibility together with the plan for protecting confidentiality, is explained.

This standard creates a responsibility for MFTs conducting research to follow established procedure to maintain confidentiality. This includes releasing information only when the research participant obtains an appropriate written Release of Information. MFTs know that it is impossible to maintain confidentiality in certain circumstances. MFTs must inform potential participants that their confidentiality may not be protected and under specific circumstances where this could take place. Following these steps, the researcher provides appropriate information to the potential participants and thus is providing informed consent. Consider an example when a research participant's identity could be deduced by family members who know that their daughter was involved in a specific research project because their daughter's emotional descriptive characteristics were provided as part of the discussion of the research participants. Allowing this disclosure to take place without informing the participant of the potential breach of confidentiality would be unethical.

In summary, when conducting research, MFTs must follow ethical standards as discussed in this chapter. These steps include obtaining informed consent, addressing scope of competence, preventing harm or injury of the research participants, creating a process allowing participants to terminate involvement with the project, and providing participants with information and debriefing after completion of the project.

Clinical Example # 1

> Charles, a clinical MFT, has been given a part-time faculty appointment at a local university. One of his duties is to conduct and supervise clinical research with students. Though he is not familiar with the research protocol, he tells himself: "Fake it until you make it." Recently, a student pointed out a conflict of interest in one of the research projects. Charles decided to ignore it since it would impact their funding and he did not want to "rock the boat."

Questions for Clinical Example # 1

1. How has Charles lost objectivity?
2. If the conflict of interest emerges at a later date and the research has to be rejected, will Charles be held responsible for this decision? Why or why not?
3. Do you believe the university has a valid reason to submit a complaint to CAMFT for unethical behavior? Why or why not?
4. Which CAMFT ethical standards would the university identify as having been violated by Charles?

Chapter Questions

1. An MFT who is a professor at a local university conducts field research on the outcome divorce on children and their school grades. He approaches many of the local schools to enroll them in the program. Since she is also a clinical supervisor for many of these schools, he tells the parents that it is a school-based project. Had she based the project at his university, the school authorities would have most likely denied the project. The parents believe that the project is part of the evaluation their children receive each year. If you were consulting with the MFT, what ethical guidance would you give him? Would you support a complaint regarding an ethical violation? Why or why not?

2. An MFT wants to study the outcome of her treatment on her patient population. She tells her clients that they must consent to the study as part of their treatment. Is this ethical? Why or why not?

Chapter 34

CAMFT Ethical Standard 7

Responsibility to the Profession

In this section, the CAMFT Ethical Guidelines consider MFTs' social responsibility that extends into professional and social communities. MFTs serve as role models of appropriate behavior in arenas where a personal or professional interaction takes place. As such, they have the ethical duty to exemplify appropriate social and professional relationships whenever possible.

7. RESPONSIBILITY TO THE PROFESSION:

Marriage and family therapists respect the rights and responsibilities of professional colleagues and participate in activities that advance the goals of the profession.

This section recognizes the differences among MFTs that may include, but are not limited to, cultural, political, social, economic, religious, and sexual orientation issues. It establishes that MFTs will respect other professionals' rights to hold varying personal values and apply them in a healthy way to their own profession. Additionally, this section recognizes that MFTs also hold inherent responsibilities to their clients and to the profession, and that they will carry out these responsibilities in a respectful and professional manner. For example, colleagues who do not want a specific type of political activity in their community shall not prevent an MFT who chooses to advocate politically for HIV-infected clients from doing so. However, this section does not say that unacceptable professional behavior, such as practicing under the influence of drugs or alcohol, shall be tolerated by other professionals in the community.

This section supports those activities by MFTs that expand public awareness regarding the practice of marriage and family therapy. These activities include public speaking, television and radio interviews, education, career fairs, publications, and similar activities that enhance public awareness about the profession.

7.1 ACCOUNTABLE TO THE STANDARDS OF THE PROFESSION:

Marriage and family therapists remain accountable to the standards of the profession when acting as members or employees of organizations.

This standard establishes that MFTs are responsible for professional accountability when representing him/herself as a member of an organization such as a service club or school board, or when acting as an employee of an organization such as a local non-profit agency or a for-profit organization. This means that confidentiality of clients and clients' issues are respected, harmful dual relationships are avoided, credentials are not misrepresented, state and federal laws applying to the MFT practice are adhered to, and all applicable CAMFT Ethical Standards are respected. All members of the profession are held to the same degree of ethical accountability regardless of employment situation.

7.2 PUBICATION CREDIT:

Marriage and family therapists assign publication credit to those who have contributed to a publication in proportion to their contribution and in accordance with customary publication practices.

This standard states that MFTs who publish their work have a responsibility to recognize all contributors to the publication regardless of their relative professional status and degree of contribution. However, this does not mean that all individuals who participated in the development of a publication receive authorship credit. Rather, individuals can be acknowledged in the footnotes, introduction section, acknowledgment section, and any other pertinent section of the book. An MFT practices unethically when he or she describes him/herself as an author of a book when in reality he or she wrote it cooperatively with others.

7.3 AUTHORS – CITING OTHERS:

Marriage and family therapists who are authors of books or other materials that are published or distributed appropriately cite persons to whom credit for original ideas is due.

This standard dictates that MFTs have an ethical responsibility to protect the original ideas of other professionals who either have published or are yet to publish. Ethical MFTs do not plagiarize another's ideas as their own and give due and appropriate credit to others' work. MFTs give credit to others by quoting the exact material and referring to the page number and citing the publication, or by acknowledging them as the source for the ideas when appropriate.

7.4 AUTHORS – ADVERTISING BY OTHERS:

Marriage and family therapists who are the authors of books or other materials published or distributed by an organization take reasonable precautions to ensure that the organization promotes and advertises the materials accurately.

This standard creates a responsibility for MFTs who publish to prevent the inaccurate promotion and advertisement of published materials by marketing department of a publishing or marketing organization. MFTs consult with the publishing or marketing departments and assure that errors in the promotional messages will not take place. MFTs also take appropriate steps to clarify the intended marketing message that accurately states the content of the publication. Should an advertisement or promotion be inaccurate, MFT have the responsibility to contact the individual responsible for the inaccuracy and formally request a correction of the error.

7.5 PRO BONO SERVICES:

Marriage and family therapists are encouraged to participate in activities that contribute to a better community and society, including devoting a portion of their professional activity to services for which there is little or no financial return.

Ethically, MFTs have a social responsibility to provide some form of professional services to their community pro bono or for small financial remuneration. The intention here is not to give away services; rather its intent is to provide services to those members of the community who are unable to obtain counseling or other services due to their economic or social position. MFTs can provide these services in different ways. Having some low fee slots, serving as an officer in the local or state CAMFT organization, volunteering as a therapist to a local non-profit counseling organization, providing consultation at no charge to local counseling agencies that utilize interns or trainees, or serving as a volunteer supervisor or consultant to non-profit counseling agencies would satisfy this ethical standard.

7.6 DEVELOPING A PUBLIC POLICY:

Marriage and family therapists are concerned with developing laws and regulations pertaining to marriage and family therapy that serve the public interest, and with altering such laws and regulations that are not in the public interest.

From an ethical perspective, California MFTs have an obligation to advocate for legislation that advances marriage and family therapy as an art, a science, and a mental health profession. Monitoring the legislative process of proponents or detractors of such laws, writing letters to individual legislators, becoming involved at the local chapter level, and voting to support or defeat appropriate legislation, are reasonable steps that an MFT can follow as a member of the profession.

<u>7.7 FAILURE TO COOPERATE WITH COMMITTEE:</u>

Marriage and family therapists cooperate with the Ethics Committee and truthfully represent facts to the Ethics Committee and truthfully represent facts to the Ethics Committee. Failure to cooperate with the Ethics Committee is itself a violation of these standards .

The CAMFT Ethics Committee addresses situations arising from complaints made against members of this organization. The committee follows due process as explained in the Ethical Standards for Marriage and Family Therapists Part II. The Ethics Committee expects each member to cooperate fully with an investigation. To protect all parties involved, the committee respects everyone's confidentiality as well as obtains legal releases of information. The committee expects that MFTs participating in an investigatory process will represent all facts truthfully to the Ethics Committee.

Should the Ethics Committee attempt to settle the dispute or make a formal recommendation to the Board of Directors, participating members are mandated to cooperate fully. Non-compliance of this section is a serious violation of the CAMFT Ethics Standards and the committee "may appropriately impose more stringent sanctions upon members previously found to have violated the CAMFT Ethical Standards for Marriage and Family Therapists."

Clinical Example # 1

Barbara, a licensed MFT, has recently published a book where she is identified as a licensed clinical psychologist. Though she did not make this mistake, she decided to ignore it and leave it as is. She thought: "It might improve my income by giving me greater professional credibility and no one will know the difference."

Questions for Clinical Example # 1

1. Do you agree with Barbara's reasoning? Why or why not?
2. What questions would a reasonable and prudent clinician in the same situation ask of him/herself?
3. Though Barbara did not create this error of commission, does her lack of action violate CAMFT ethical standards? Why or why not?
4. Which CAMFT ethical standards were violated?
5. What do you believe led Barbara to lose objectivity and avoid taking reasonable and prudent steps to correct this error?

Chapter Questions

1. An MFT decides to send out a patient newsletter. She contacts a professional organization that sells her a commercial newsletter with her name as the author. What is the ethical violation?
2. An MFT travels extensively in South America. There, he finds a book that, he believes, would sell well in the United States. He translates the book and publishes it under his name. What is the ethical violation?
3. An MFT receives a letter from the CAMFT Ethics Committee asking her to provide information about her friend's practice. She decides to ignore the letter since her friend could get into trouble. What would you say to this MFT?

Chapter 35

CAMFT Ethical Standard 8

Responsibility to the Legal System

As MFTs have increased their interactions with the legal system, CAMFT recognizes that the advocacy and conflictive nature of our judicial system require appropriate guidelines for MFTs to create greater safety for clients and for themselves. Forensic activities differ from therapy services provided to clients and insofar as specific rules of conduct exist, these must be followed carefully to prevent harm to those involved. Unlike therapy, forensic activities require clinical and emotional detachment by the therapist to provide objectivity during forensic evaluations. Without these guidelines, MFTs could make costly and injurious mistakes.

8. RESPONSIBILITY TO THE LEGAL SYSTEM:
Marriage and family therapists recognize their role in the legal system and their duty to remain objective and truthful.

MFTs perform different roles within the legal system. For example, they can be appointed as child custody evaluators, perform personal injury assessments, consult with attorneys on different matters of mental health, serve as expert witnesses in specific areas of marriage and family therapy, assess worker's compensation injuries and personal injuries, perform forensic sexual or physical child abuse assessments, be involved in criminal law when the scope of practice applies, and be "witnesses of fact" when they provide psychotherapy to emotionally injured clients involved in litigation and testify on behalf of their clients. Additionally, MFTs may be asked to comply with a mental health records subpoena, which requires sequentially appropriate responses as indicated by legal experts.

In some situations, MFTs providing clinical services to clients may be asked to serve as expert witnesses. Doing so could create a conflictive situation for these therapists. It can be difficult for a therapist to maintain forensic objectivity when a treating therapist has established a strong therapeutic relationship. When these roles overlap, it is important to remember that ethical MFTs clarify their roles with clients in advance of any legal action. Regardless of the MFTs' role in the legal system, this standard places an ethical therapeutic duty upon them to understand the full implications of his or her role as forensic expert. In addition, MFTs must maintain objectivity and be truthful when providing services in the legal arena. MFTs must set aside their personal biases and prejudices when performing clinical or forensic services in court-related cases or when testifying. In addition, MFTs must provide factual and accurate information to the court. MFTs who provide testimony in a challenging legal case involving sexual abuse of a child may want to withhold important evidence that could exonerate the accused parent because an MFT believes that parent is guilty. The act of withholding information in this case is unethical. It is important to remember that only the judge or the jury can determine guilt or innocence.

8.1 TESTIMONY:
Marriage and family therapists who give testimony in legal proceedings testify truthfully and avoid making misleading statements.

Testimonial MFTs must be honest and truthful to the best of their ability. Due to the legal process, at times it is difficult for MFTs to provide all the information they wish in these proceedings. In spite of these limitations, MFTs must strive to maintain their objectivity and honesty rather than allow biases or prejudices to cloud their testimony. MFTs can reply in a misleading manner when their answers are unclear, confusing, partly true, or they fail to clarify an answer. Regardless of the intent, answering questions in this fashion is unethically. Therapists can take appropriate steps to clarify their answers by telling the questioning attorney who asks a "yes or no" question that this question cannot be answered with a simple yes or no. Another appropriate step would be to assure that testimony presented is based on scientifically based accurate data and clinical findings. If MFTs modify scientific data inaccurately to strengthen their client's case, this behavior is another example of unethical conduct.

8.2 EXPERT WITNESSES:
Marriage and family therapists who act as expert witnesses base their opinions and conclusions on appropriate data, and are careful to acknowledge the limits of their data or conclusions in order to avoid providing misleading testimony or reports.

Serving as an expert witness places additional responsibilities upon MFTs, which are beyond the ones MFTs uphold when providing therapy. These responsibilities include affecting the emotional, personal and financial life of clients in a significant manner. Consider an MFT involved as an expert witness in a personal injury case who does not know the scientific literature regarding the emotional impact of experienced pain on relationships. His or her testimony in Court will likely be replete with incomplete and inconsistent information, which could negatively affect the client's case. In another situation, an MFT testifies as an expert witness in a child custody case without having interviewed all pertinent parties. The MFT makes statements in court regarding which parent would be the best legal and physical custodian of the child. This inappropriate forensic activity is considered as unethical conduct and the MFT will likely find a malpractice action filed against him or her for misrepresenting his or her scope of competence.

This standard also requires MFTs in the legal arena to know the scientific literature in their field of expertise, the validity and reliability of this literature, state and case law, applicable ethical standards, the limitations of their findings, the cultural and cross-cultural implications of the population involved, and the nature of the problems involved in a forensic assessment. Ultimately, MFTs in this position are being required to avoid harm to the parties involved that can result from providing misleading statements due to incomplete or incompetent work and/or reports.

8.3 CONFLICTING ROLES:

Whenever possible, marriage and family therapists avoid performing conflicting roles in legal proceedings and disclose any potential conflicts. At the onset of the service to be provided and as changes occur, marriage and family therapists clarify role expectations and the extent of confidentiality to prospective clients, to the courts, or to others as appropriate.

This standard addresses the development of harmful dual relationships when providing forensic services. In some situations, clients enter therapy with MFTs because they experience physical injuries, are having emotional difficulties adapting to the injury and struggling with their relationships. As an MFT develops a strong therapeutic relationship with the client, the latter develops greater trust in the MFT and in the therapeutic process. Before the anniversary of the injury, the client must file a civil lawsuit against the plaintiff (the person who caused the injury) to comply with the statute of limitations. Due to the trust established in the therapeutic relationship, the client asks the MFT to testify as an expert and witness of fact. As a witness of fact, the MFT provides information about the client's process in therapy. The expert witness' experience and training in forensics permits him or her to testify about the causation of the injury and the impact of the injury upon the client's physical and emotional well-being. In these situations, MFTs always consider the well-being of the client and avoid entering into any type of harmful dual relationship (it is impossible for a therapist to serve as both expert witness and therapist for the client). Both roles are distinct and separate in their function; require different approaches, and different clinicians. In a forensic situation, the MFT considers all possibilities that could take place. Whereas in therapy, only the material presented by the client is considered important.

When determining what is in the best interest of the client, the therapist who faces a potentially negative dual relationship in the legal system must address the consequences of choosing either approach. If the therapist declines the invitation to carry out both roles, then the client may feel rebuffed and betrayed. If the therapist accepts the invitation, then potentially the MFT's objectivity may be compromised as an expert witness and this could affect the client's legal case negatively. It behooves the MFT to discuss these therapeutic issues with clients, thus empowering them. Initiating this discussion with the client opens the opportunity to strengthen the therapeutic relationship by managing difficult emotional material.

Though it would be in the best interest of the MFT to avoid this potentially harmful relationship, the therapist will most likely appear in court as a fact witness. The MFT must clarify this role with the client and his or her attorney to avoid creating unreasonable expectations. Doing so will allow the MFT to maintain clear boundaries on his or her role as a fact witness. If the MFT continues to be confused about this decision, a reasonable approach would be to consult with a legal expert in this arena. The MFT must remember to do no harm to the client and to establish appropriate boundaries with the client.

> 8.4 DUAL ROLES:
> **Marriage and family therapists avoid providing both treatment and court-ordered evaluations for the same clients or treatment units in legal proceedings such as child custody, visitations, dependency, or guardianship proceedings, unless otherwise required by law or initially appointed pursuant to court order.**

MFTs must refrain from entering into dual relationships with clients in situations that involve custody issues, family or individual treatment, or issues about guardianship. Providing concurrent services and serving in two capacities at the same time is considered conflictual and can harm those involved. Thus, should MFTs be invited to serve as providers of these mutually exclusive roles, they refuse one or other. MFTs clarify with attorneys, parents, judges, and others involved that they can only provide one service unless directed by the court to do othewise. Should MFTs be in doubt of their duty, it is best that they consult with an appropriate attorney for guidance.

> 8.5 IMPARTIALITY:
> **Marriage and family therapists, regardless of their role in a legal proceeding, remain impartial and do not compromise their professional judgment or integrity.**

Maintaining objectivity in the legal arena requires that MFTs understand the full implications of their role and the expectations placed upon them by clients, attorneys, and the court system. Once MFTs identify a specific role within the court system, they can clarify for themselves the ramifications of their actions. Additionally, MFTs must address and manage personal biases and prejudices toward clients, attorneys, and the confrontational court system. If MFTs allow these biases to cloud their objectivity, then errors in judgment or relevant opinions may cause undue harm to those involved in litigation.

MFTs can also compromise their professional judgment by allowing attorneys to unduly influence their testimony when preparing for a deposition or a court appearance. Some attorneys, in advocating for their clients, may subtly guide testifying MFTs to make statements, which may not be completely true or may be misleading. Should MFTs not take steps to clarify these statements, the resulting behavior can be unethical. This standard requires MFTs to be objective and maintain a high degree of professional integrity and judgment.

8.6 MINORS AND PRIVILEGE:

Marriage and family therapists confirm who is the holder of the psychotherapist-patient privilege on behalf of minor clients prior to releasing information or testifying.

When MFTs interact with the legal system and are involved with children, they have the duty to determine who is the holder of the privilege. Though California law grants each client the right to hold his or her privilege, including minors, there are times when other entities, such as the court system or the probation department, may be the actual holders of the minor's privilege. Thus, to avoid violating the rights of the minor, it is imperative that MFTs take the extra step of clarifying with the appropriate authorities that are the actual holder of the privilege for their minor client.

8.7 OPINIONS ABOUT PERSONS NOT EVALUATED:

Marriage and family therapists shall only express professional opinions about clients they have treated or examined. Marriage and family therapists, when expressing professional opinions, specify the limits of the information upon which their professional opinions are based. Such professional opinions include, but are limited to, mental or emotional conditions of parenting abilities.

There are circumstances when the court requires that MFT provide professional opinions when MFTs have not assessed the client directly. For example, if a therapist is asked to render an opinion on a hypothetical situation, then it would be appropriate for MFTs to do so as long as it they state to the court how they reached their conclusion and what material they examined to reach such a conclusion. At other times, the court requests MFTs to examine test data; case notes, professional reports, pertinent history, and other appropriate information and render a general opinion based on these findings. Again, MFTs are permitted to do so as long as they discuss the limitations of their findings and they clearly present these as part of the findings. However, MFTs are not permitted to render a clinical or professional opinion about an individual they have never evaluated personally. Doing so is considered practicing below the standard of care and this clinical action is unethical.

8.8 CUSTODY EVALUATORS:

Marriage and family therapists who are custody evluators (private or court-based) or special masters provide such services only if they meet the requirements established by pertinent laws, regulations, and rules of court.

MFTs must have the required competence to practice in all aspects of marriage of family therapy and that includes providing services as a custody evaluator or special master. Competence means that MFTs working professionally in this arena obtain the necessary training, appropriate training, and continuing education to meet state, local, board certification if required, and standard of care. Should MFTs practice in this capacity without the required competence, they can face sanctions from the court, malpractice actions, and investigations by CAMFT.

8.9 CONSEQUENCES OF CHANGES IN THERAPIST ROLES:

Marriage and family therapists inform the patient or the treatment unit of any potential consequences of therapy-client role changes. Such role changes include, but are not limited to, child's therapist, family's theapist, couple's therapist, individual's therapist, mediator, evaluator, and special master.

MFTs may face instances where the clinician may be asked to transition from one professional role to a different one with the same clients. For exampe, the MFT provides child custory evaluation services to a couple and will report to the court and soon thereafter, he or she is asked to perform family counseling since he or she if "familiar" with the family conflict. In another situation, an MFT serving as an advisor to a mediator who provides services to a conflictual couple. A few months later, the treating clinician becomes ill and the advising MFT is asked to serve as the new treating clinician. Though the latter clinician is permitted to transition into the new clinical circumstance, he or she must be aware of the new situation may be fraught with danger.

Its important to remember that when the MFT transitions into the new professional relationship, he or she brings a previously established power differential from the previous relationship. Therein lies the danger. A power differential is an imbalance of knowledge, experience and training held by the clinician. Should the clinician fail to consider the effect of this power diffential upon the new relationship, it may be possible that he or she may cause emotional injury to the client. To avoid doing so, the clinician would need to maintain an ongoing consultative relationship with another clinician to monitor his or her clinical objectivity and assure that all clinical decisions and actions avoid harm to the client.

8.10 FAMILIARITY WITH JUDICIAL AND ADMINISTRATIVE RULES:
Marriage and family therapists, when assuming forensic roles, are or become familiar with the judicial and administrative rules governing their roles.

MFTs in general practice must know the application of legal standards upon marriage and family practice. This standard expands that requirement to include administrative, judicial, and California law that apply the forensic practice. Since forensic MFTs have a serious impact on the lives of clients involved in the legal system, they have the responsibility to know and practice the appropriate clinical and forensic application. MFTs who fail to comply with this standard and cause injury to a client can expect to be held accountable for failing to protect the welfare of the client.

Clinical Example # 1

Kathie has been treating a young woman involved in an auto collision for panic attacks and insomnia. Kathie completed a full assessment and supports the client's complaint that the collision caused her to suffer emotionally. The client's attorney tells Kathie that he will use her as an expert witness since she knows the client's issues due to her excellent treatment. Kathie is honored and agrees to his request. At the deposition, the opposing attorney begins to ask Kathie about her role: "Are you a treating MFT or a forensic expert? Both, she replies." Later, Kathie finds out that the case was dismissed due to her dual relationship. The client sues Kathie for economic loss and for practicing forensically below the standard of care. She also receives a letter of complaint filed with the BBS for unprofessional conduct.

Questions for Clinical Example # 1

1. What information did Kathie fail to take into consideration?
2. Do you believe she lost objectivity after the attorney complemented her? Why or why not?
3. Kathie could either perform treatment with this client or serve as an expert witness. Based on her initial therapeutic relationship, which role would have been the most appropriate for her? What do you base your answer on?
4. Could Kathie have been the treating therapist, later ended the therapeutic relationship with this client, and began as a forensic expert for this client? Why or why not?
5. Which CAMFT ethical standards were violated?
6. Could Kathie have prevented her current legal problems? Why or why not?

Chapter Questions

1. An MFT, who was involved in an acrimonious custody battle with her husband and lost custody of her children, decides to engage in custody evaluations. She knows that is the time for "pay-back" against those "sleazy" dads. What advice would you give this MFT?
2. After serving many years as an expert witness, an MFT decides to work only for the defense since insurance companies pay her full fee. What are the ethical ramifications of this behavior?
3. During a heated trial, an MFT serving as an expert witness, after reviewing the clinical data, testifies that he had a previous relationship with the plaintiff (the person suing) many years ago. He also states that in his opinion, the defendant (the person being sued) has a severe mental disorder, even though he superficially reviewed the test data since he does not perform the MMPI himself. Where does this person stand ethically?

Chapter 36

CAMFT Ethical Standard 9

Financial Arrangements

The issue of fees within the therapeutic context can sometimes challenge MFTs. Addressing the fee issue immediately and clearly at the onset of therapy helps MFTs create therapeutic safety for all involved. Appropriate use of the ethical guidelines by MFTs minimize these dangers in the financial aspect of marriage and family therapy practice and create a foundation of safety for the welfare of their clients and for themselves.

> 9. FINANCIAL ARRANGEMENTS:
> **Marriage and family therapists make financial arrangements with patients and supervisees that are understandable and conform to accepted professional practices and legal requirements.**

This section addresses the importance of managing and clarifying with clients the fee structure in marriage and family therapy practice. The presented fee structure becomes a contractual arrangement that requires that the client have the competence to give informed consent. MFTs have the responsibility to provide all and not withhold any information to clients. MFTs are free to set their own fees, use a sliding fee scale based on financial ability to pay, provide low-fee slots, or even provide free services. However, MFTs must inform clients those services for which they will be charged.

Regardless of the fees and financial structures that MFTs choose in their practice, they must conform to acceptable professional practices and standardize their forms and language allowing clients to easily understand the provided material. Examples of unacceptable financial practices with clients are bartering where exploitation or loss of objectivity takes place, insurance fraud, avoiding collecting insurance co-payments, or allowing clients to accrue large unpaid balances that may create an undue financial burden. Examples of unacceptable professional practices with supervisees are: bartering in lieu of providing a salary, charging a fee for providing supervision in a private practice environment, coercing a supervisee to accept an unusually low salary in exchange for having the opportunity to accrue hours toward licensing, or providing private practice interns a 1099 IRS form in lieu of a W-2 to avoid reporting appropriate payroll taxes.

Experts consider that bartering is not specifically considered as an unethical clinical action. However, it is fraught with danger should MFTs lose objectivity or exploit their clients. The following example clarifies this possibility. A client gives the therapist a piece of jewelry appropriately appraised by a reputable third party, in exchange for services. Both agree on the exchange. The client feels dissatisfied with the outcome of therapy and he accuses the MFT of taking advantage of his emotional vulnerability when the MFT took a "family heirloom." He also accused the MFT of knowing how much this memento from his grandmother meant to him and the MFT took advantage of the client's momentary weakness and vulnerability. In this case, it would be difficult for the MFT to defend the decision to accept the "heirloom" since it is expected that this therapist would have taken appropriate steps, such as obtaining consultation, to prevent the unethical behavior of developing a harmful dual relationship. Also, consider the following example. An MFT trades services with a painting contractor. The contractor finishes ahead of the MFT and soon afterwards, the paint begins to peel off the wall. The MFT accuses the painter of performing shoddy work and should the therapist seek legal action against the painter, he or she lacks a solid foundation to pursue the case. Actually, other therapists in similar situations have found themselves sued for malpractice.

<u>9.1 PAYMENT FOR REFERRALS:</u>

Marriage and family therapists do not offer to accept payment for referrals, whether in the form of money or otherwise.

This standard identifies the potential abuse that can take place when MFTs accept payment in money or in trade for client referrals. MFTs who accept such remuneration for referring clients are not considering the welfare of the client. Instead, they are only considering the interest of the person making the payment for referrals and their own interest. When MFTs experience a financial gain, the client's welfare is jeopardized. An example of unethical conduct is an MFT giving a percentage of the collected fee to anyone who refers clients to them. This standard also requires MFTs acting as employers/supervisors to avoid contractual agreements with employees/supervisees that remunerate the supervisor on a fee structure based on charging a fee for every client referred to the supervisee. This behavior constitutes unethical behavior by both supervisor and supervisee.

<u>9.2 FINANCIAL EXPLOITATION:</u>

Marriage and family therapists do not financially exploit their patients.

This standard requires that MFTs recognize the inherent power differential in the therapeutic relationship as it pertains to finances. When the client begins therapy, he or she is dependent on the therapist to guide him or her through the therapy process. Should MFTs fail to consider the client's vulnerability in their client's trust, MFTs could act in a manner that causes harm to the client. For example, MFTs could exploit clients financially by setting an inflated fee when the clients' emotional or physical state is such that they are unable to contract for therapeutic services in an informed manner. Another form of exploitation occurs when MFTs continue to treat clients for financial reasons without any further benefit to the clients. Increasing fees upward because the client is wealthy would also constitute a violation of this standard. Failing to address termination of therapy for financial gain when the client is to terminate would be considered be a breach of this ethical standard. Ultimately, reasonable and prudent MFTs have the ethical duty to assure that they will give clients an opportunity to obtain informed consent and make a competent decision about the fee charged and the reasonable duration of therapy for which they will pay this fee.

9.3 DISCLOSURE OF FEES:

Marriage and family therapists disclose, in advance, their fees and the basis upon which they are computed, including, but not limited to, charges for canceled or missed appointments and any interest to be charged on unpaid balances, at the beginning of treatment and give reasonable notice of changes in fees or other charges.

This standard dictates that therapists have an ethical responsibility to protect their client's ability to give informed consent when contracting for therapeutic services. Reasonable and prudent MFTs utilize a fee structure consistent with state law. These MFTs introduce their fee prior to the first session and an agreement is made before the client is seen. There may be reasonable situations where the fee cannot be agreed upon immediately, either because the client is too emotionally distraught to focus on financial matters, or is extremely agitated (when the client faces a crisis issue) to reasonably discuss fees. This would require documentation in the mental health records. Clinically, MFTs would be required to document their judgment, discuss and come to an agreement regarding the fee with the client as soon as possible or when the client's mental or emotional state is appropriately clear.

It is ethically acceptable to increase fees during the course of therapy as long as clients are given a reasonable notice as to when the fee increase will take effect and by how much. This expands the requirement that clients must continue giving informed consent for contractual changes. A "reasonable" length of time is that time that clients would need to determine if they can or cannot pay the new fee. For some clients it may be a few days, for others it may be a few weeks. There is no set time standard. The therapist must clarify this time requirement with clients prior to changing the previously set fee. If clients inform the MFT that they cannot pay the new fee, the MFT must either continue treatment at the old fee or take reasonable and prudent steps to assure that the client will continue their therapy with another therapist. If an MFT raises his fees indiscriminately because "the client can now afford it.,:" or when MFTs only consider their financial well-being, by default their actions aare injurious to the client.

9.4 COLLECTING UNPAID BALANCES:

Marriage and family therapists give reasonable notice to patients with unpaid balances of their intent to sue, or to refer for collection. Whenever legal action is taken, therapists will avoid disclosure of clinical information. Whenever unpaid balances are referred to collection agencies, therapists will exercise care in selecting collection agencies and will avoid disclosure of clinical information.

This standard does not preclude MFTs from collecting unpaid balances through legal or collection services. However, reasonable and prudent MFTs have the responsibility to inform clients (after providing an adequate amount of time) that they will use collection services to collect the unpaid balance. An example of unethical behavior involves an MFT who automatically turns late accounts for collections after three months of unpaid status without notifying clients of this decision. The unethical behavior stems from failing to notify clients of the impending action and for failing to provide clients with an adequate time to remedy the unpaid status of their bill.

MFTs must be judicious when taking legal or collection action as mentioned above. Reasonable and prudent MFTs only release that information that is pertinent to the legal action, such as dates of services, fees owed, the therapeutic contract that addresses how MFTs collect unpaid bills, and any written communication informing the client that legal action used to collect the unpaid balance. Therapists are required to be careful in selecting only those collection agencies that are professional in their practice and not breach a client's confidentiality to others. An example of such a breach would be an MFT choosing a collection agency that attempts to collect moneys owed by leaving messages at the client's place of employment and stating in the message that this client owes money to a particular therapist. At this point, the collection agency breached the client's confidentiality. Since the MFT contracted with this agency, ultimately he or she becomes responsible for the breach of confidentiality.

9.5 BARTER:

Marriage and family therapists ordinarily refrain from accepting goods, services, or other non-monetary remuneration from patients in return for professional services. Such arrangements often create conflicts and may lead to exploitation or distortion of the professional relationship.

This standard does not prohibit bartering between MFTs and clients. However, CAMFT discourages it due to the potential problems inherent with this practice. In some circumstances, bartering may be the only method of payment by a client in dire need of services from MFTs. Should this condition arise, MFTs would be advised to obtain appropriate consultation, assess for any possible loss of objectivity or coercion, discuss the risks and benefits with the client, obtained written informed consent, and even then proceed with caution.

CAMFT advises against bartering based on its experience when evaluating ethical complaints against members. Though the intention of bartering seems innocuous at first glance, eventually, any disagreements between therapist and client end up exacerbated by the lack of agreed upon value of the goods bartered. The resulting conflict can severely injure the therapeutic relationship to the point where an aggrieved client may seek legal redress against the therapist. For example, an MFT accepts a client who is a local farmer and both agree to exchange his produce for therapy. After several weeks, the therapist begins to complaint about the quality of the farm goods. He tells her he saves his best produce for the market to make enough money to provide for his family. Both end up angry at each other and blame one another. Eventually, the MFT "fires" the client who lodges a formal complaint of unethical behavior against the therapist for abandonment and for taking advantage of him.

9.6 THIRD PARTY PAYERS:

Marriage and family therapists represent facts regarding services rendered and payment for services fully and truthfully to thrid party payers and others.

This standard requires reasonable and prudent MFTs to provide accurate information regarding how they will correlate fees to therapeutic services. MFTs must inform clients if they will charge for telephone time and at what fee. In addition, MFTs must discuss how they will charge for written reports and for home visits. If they provide extraordinary services, they must also disclose these fees. If the client uses insurance, MFTs must know what constitutes insurance fraud. For example, providing an inappropriate DSM 5 code to obtain insurance approval, billing the same amount to different insurance companies, billing for missed appointments and identifying these visits as treatment, billing higher fees to insurance companies, and using one family member's benefits to provide services to another member of the family are all examples of insurance fraud. Not only is this unethical conduct, it is also a criminal act.

When supervisees provide clinical care under the supervision of MFTs, the supervisors have the added responsibility of assuring that the supervisees follow this ethical guideline in the same manner that "reasonable and prudent" MFTs follow. Ultimately, it is the MFTs' responsibility to fully inform their clients how they will charge for services provide. This includes their fee, how they will bill the insurance company in a manner that is consistent with the law, and for any additional service rendered. One common example of fraud follows. Three family members have five insurance visits each. The wife and daughter have used them all up. The husband approaches the MFT and requests that he provide treatment for his wife under his five visits. The MFT agrees. Later, the couple divorce and sue the MFT for inappropriate treatment and they submit a complaint to the insurance company. Under this standard, MFTs must avoid this form of unprofessional and criminal behavior.

Clinical Example # 1

Harold is a student at a local university and an heir to a large fortune. All his expenses are paid by a trust established by his parents prior to their untimely death when their small plane crashed. Recently, he's been questioning his sexual preference and is unsure if he prefers men or women. Deeply troubled, he sets up an appointment with Dean. Dean prefers not to scare clients away by discussing his fee at the first visit. Upon meeting with Harold and finding out that payment will be made by a trust, he doubles his usual fee. Ignorant of the Dean's customary fee, he consents.

Questions for Clinical Example # 1

1. Do you agree with Dean's premise of not scaring clients away by discussing the fee in advance? Why or why not?
2. Initially, Dean feels slightly remorseful, however, he rationalizes his action by telling himself: "Now I'll be able to provide more sliding fee slots to deserving clients." Do you agree with this premise? Why or why not?
3. Has Dean lost clinical objectivity? Why or why not?
4. What do believe led him to lose it?
5. Which CAMFT ethical standards were violated?

Clinical Example # 2

Victoria wants desperately to enter into a private practice internship with Julie, a well-known MFT in the community. Julie is known to provide many clients to interns, however she wants to be paid $100 up front and "under the table" for every client she refers to her interns. Victoria shares her process with you and you can sense her distress as she asks you to lend her $400 to get started. She does not have this amount of money and is afraid she will lose this opportunity. She tells you "everyone" know about Julie's fee and won't turn her in because she's a great teacher and she'll pay you later after Julie gives her the first check.

Questions for Clinical Example # 2

1. Do you agree with Victoria's impression that Julie is a great teacher? Why or why not?
2. Would you lend her money to help alleviate her distress? Why or why not?
3. Would you call CAMFT and report Julie's irregular fee structure with her interns? Why or why not?
4. Which CAMFT ethical standards did Julie and Victoria violate?
5. Are Julie's license and Victoria's registered intern status in jeopardy with the BBS? Why or why not?

Clinical Example # 3

Tammy has provided services to clients in the past and they have not paid her and she decides to set strong boundaries regarding payment. A wealthy couple asks her to treat their housekeeper from Guatemala for Post Traumatic Stress Disorder. Juana saw her family killed by guerrillas and has not fully recovered since then. They offer to pay and want Tammy to bill them monthly. They want to submit the bill to their self-insurance program and request that a diagnosis be included. Tammy complies since Juana has difficulty understanding how the bill will be paid, though she speaks English.

Questions for Clinical Example # 3

1. Did Tammy manage the financial arrangements in a reasonable and prudent manner? Why or why not?
2. Did she violate confidentiality when she submitted Juana's information directly to her employers? Why or why not?
3. What caused Tammy to lose objectivity in this case?
4. Which CAMFT ethical standards did she violate and how?
5. What reasonable and prudent steps could she have taken at the onset?

Chapter Questions

1. An MFT regularly waits until the third session to determine her fee. She finds that by the third week she has enough information to set her fee based on how difficult the case is. She tells her clients that this is her standard practice. She also tells her clients that if for every referral they make to her, she will give them a 5% discount on their fee. Ethically, what would you say about these actions?
2. After several years of receiving treatment at a reduced rate, a client is told by her MFT that he must now pay double her original standard fee since he has received an inheritance and can make up the difference, otherwise he'll have to start all over with someone else. What are your ethical observations about this behavior?
3. An intern receives an offer to start a private-practice internship with a well-respected MFT. She is told that because she is a close friend of the MFT, the percent of the fee split will be 5% higher than usual, however, the intern will still have to pay an extra $300 for office expenses in addition to the fee split. What would you advice the intern and supervisors?
4. A despondent client has been in therapy for several years. She has been recently told that her company will be sold and that she will lose her job. Her insurance has run out and she doesn't want to stop her therapy. She decides to exchange with her therapist her grandmother's ring, which her therapist admired on a previous session. The MFT agrees and decides to give the client 20 sessions in exchange for the ring. What are the possible future dangers for the MFT and how has she acted unethically?
5. After not receiving payment for an insurance co-payment of $300 owed to her by a patient, an MFT sends the bill to a collection agency. She warns the agency not to call the client after 5:00 PM because she is a "rage-a-holic" and blows up immediately. What is the ethical violation?
6. An MFT, whose fee is $150, bills a couple's insurance each for $150. What is the ethical violation?

Chapter 37

CAMFT Ethical Standard 10

Advertising

Professional advertising within the therapeutic context can challenge MFTs ability act according to legal and ethical standards. When used appropriately, advertising can serve to educate, promote, enhance, and market the MFTs' practices in the community. Conversely, advertising can also be "false, fraudulent, misleading and deceptive" when it is inaccurate, unclear, or a misrepresentation of facts. The latter is problematic for MFTs as they continue to strive toward distinctiveness within their local communities. Appropriate use of the advertising ethical guidelines by MFTs provides a foundational basis to advertise, promote, and market their practices in a legally and ethically safe manner.

> 10. ADVERTISING:
> **Marriage and family therapists engage in appropriate advertising, including advertising that enables consumers to choose professional services based upon accurate information.**

This section addresses the importance of using accurate information when MFTs communicate their professional identity to their communities. This form of communication may appear as education, advertising, marketing, promotion, and statements made by others. MFTs may use business cards, brochures, newspaper, radio and television advertisement, yellow pages, Internet home pages, etc., as long as the information contained is accurate, clear, and honest.

Inappropriate advertisement activities involve paying a finder's fees to advertisers for each new client obtained as a result of the advertising, leaving out the completely written license name "licensed marriage and family therapist" or leaving out the license number in an ad, or soliciting testimonials from clients to market the therapist. Reasonable and prudent MFTs avoid fraudulent, deceptive, misleading, or false communications that may misinform potential and current clients. Another example of unethical behavior is MFTs who advertise as Dr. when in actuality they are not licensed psychologists. This can be deceptive behavior a reasonable person can believe that the clinician is a licensed psychologist or psychiatrist.

10.1 ACCURACY Re: QUALIFICATIONS:

Marriage and family therapists accurately represent their competence, education, training, and experience relevant to their professional practice to patients and others.

This section enhances the importance of providing potential clients and the community at large an accurate presentation of skills, education, training, knowledge, and abilities, otherwise known as professional competence. When MFTs provide clients with appropriate informed consent informing them about the MFTs' education, training, and experience, they can make appropriate choices to begin treatment. MFTs rely on the informed consent document to inform clients regarding the extent of their education, the depth of their knowledge in the specific arena of practice, and the length of practice. An example of a violation would be MFTs without a degree in clinical psychology representing themselves as psychologists. Another ethical violation would be MFTs describing themselves as specialists without the educational, experiential, and certification basis to make such a claim.

10.2 ASSURING ACCURACY:

Marriage and family therapists assure that advertisements and publications, whether in directories, announcement cards, newspapers, or on radio or television, Internet or any other electronic media, are formulated to accurately convey information to the public.

This section addresses the importance of providing true, accurate, and honest communications when using the media to disseminate information describing MFTs' professional identity. MFTs may use business cards, brochures, newspaper ads, publications, radio and television advertisement, yellow pages, internet web pages, etc., as long as the information contained is accurate, clear, and honest. If an advertisement, brochure, radio spot, television ad, or any other form of advertisement is incorrect, it is the responsibility of MFTs to address and correct the error. If dissemination of the promotional material took place, MFTs have the responsibility to stop the distribution of misleading material and to discard it in such manner that prevents future utilization. MFTs must provide honest, clear, and accurate information to clients and the community at large regarding their qualifications, training, and experience, thus allowing clients to choose their professional services from an informed stance.

10.3 FICTITIOUS/OTHER NAMES:

Marriage and family therapists do not use a name which could mislead the public concerning the identity, responsibility, source, and status of those practicing under

that name and do not hold themselves out as being partners or associates of a firm if they are not.

This standard dictates that MFTs must be clear, honest, and accurate in the representation of the ownership of their practice that provides services to their clients. They must have the ability to determine who is providing clinical services and who is responsible for the quality of the care. Should a question arise regarding these services, the client must know whom to contact to seek redress. If the owner of this treatment facility gives it a fictitious name, this standard requires that clients must be informed at the onset of therapy which person is the owner of the registered practice.

This standard also addresses the need for clarity when describing the affiliations and ownership of a practice or place of business. It is unethical for MFTs to describe themselves as partners or associates in a business when in reality they may be employees. MFTs are in violation of this standard when stating to the client that he or she is a partner of the "Psychological Offices of Dr. Smith," when in reality the therapist only rents space. Additionally, using the name "psychological offices" may be misleading since implies that the place of business is a psychologist's office and the MFT does not have such a license. Clarity in this issue can prevent misunderstandings and potential problems for MFTs.

10.4 FALSE, MISLEADING, OR DECEPTIVE:
Marriage and family therapists do not use any professional identification, including but not limited to, a business card, office sign, letterhead, or telephone or association directory listing, Internet or any other media, if it includes a statement or claim that is false, fraudulent, misleading, or deceptive. A statement is false, fraudulent, misleading, or deceptive if it a) contains a material misrepresentation of facts; b) fails to state any material fact necessary to make the statement, in light of all circumstances, not misleading; or c) is intended to or is likely to create an unjustified expectation.

This standard addresses the nature of a false, fraudulent, misleading, or deceptive professional identification statement. A statement can be false, fraudulent, misleading, or deceptive by both omission and commission. Adding or detracting from a statement can change its intended message. If a statement modifies the facts enough to make it false, omits facts, which would make the statement true, or creates an expectation in the client, which cannot be fulfilled, then the statement is considered false, misleading, fraudulent, or deceptive.

Examples of unethical behavior follow: instances in which MFTs list publications in their office promotional material that they did not write, adding their names to commercially available articles and publishing them in newspapers as their own, adding a degree to their name that they do not possess, describing themselves as specialists when they have not indeed had specialized training or professionally recognized certification, using the CAMFT logo on business cards without being members of CAMFT and without written authorization from CAMFT's board of directors. Omitting the MFT license number or failing to add, "licensed marriage and family therapist" to the advertisement are also examples of unethical conduct. Since MFTs can only practice when licensed by the state, then it is necessary to identify one's licensed status in promotional and educational material. Ultimately, MFTs are responsible to prevent such errors of omission or commission by scrutinizing all materials, printed or electronic, used to disseminate information about their practitioner.

> 10.5 CORRECTIONS:
> Marriage and family therapists correct, wherever possible, false, misleading, or inaccurate information and representations made by others concerning the therapist's qualifications, services, or products.

This standard addresses the nature of a false, fraudulent, misleading, or deceptive professional identification statement. A statement can be false, fraudulent, misleading, or deceptive by both omission and commission. Adding or detracting from a statement can change its intended message. If a statement modifies the facts enough to make it false, omits facts, which would make the statement true, or creates an expectation in the client, which cannot be fulfilled, then the statement is considered false, misleading, fraudulent, or deceptive.

Examples of unethical behavior follow: instances in which MFTs list publications in their office of promotional material that they did not write, they add their names to commercially available articles and publishing them in newspapers as their own, they add a professional degree to their name that they do not possess, they describe themselves as specialists when they have not had specialized training or professionally recognized certification, they use the CAMFT logo on business cards without being members of CAMFT and without written authorization from CAMFT's board of directors. Therapists who omit the MFT license number or fail to add, "licensed marriage and family therapist" to the advertisement provide examples of unethical conduct. Since MFTs can only practice when licensed by the state, then it is necessary to identify one's licensed status in promotional and educational material. Ultimately, MFTs are responsible to prevent such errors of omission or commission by scrutinizing all materials, printed or electronic, used to disseminate information about their practitioner.

10.6 SOLICITATION OF TESTIMONIALS:

Marriage and family therapists do not solicit testimonials from patients.

Reasonable and prudent MFTs refrain from seeking testimonials from current and past patients. Doing so takes advantage of the inherent power differential between therapist and client and can damage the client's welfare. Asking a client to provide a testimonial places the client in an awkward position: if the client refuses, the therapist's feelings may be hurt and the client may feel responsible for causing these feelings. On the other hand, the client, fearing the therapist's rejection may comply with the request to avoid this feeling. In one example, an MFT was engaged to assess a custodial issue in an acrimonious divorce. The MFT found in favor of the father, who was a prominent actor and could be an excellent referral source. The MFT solicited a written testimonial from the father who felt pressured by this request. The father felt he was in a bind: if he rejected the request, he was fearful of losing the support of the MFT in court; however, agreeing to the request felt extremely uncomfortable to him. In requesting a testimonial from this father, the therapist acted unethically because the client was vulnerable to undue influence.

10.7 EMPLOYEE – ACCURACY:

Marriage and family therapists make certain that the qualifications of persons in their employ are represented in a manner that is not false, misleading, or deceptive.

MFTs employing interns or other licensed MFTs take the precaution of verifying their licensing or registration status. Additionally, all written and spoken information indicating the license status and competence of their employees must be accurate, honest, and clear. An example of an ethical violation follows. An MFT who is an employer introduces a registered intern as a newly licensed MFT. Additionally, the employer sates that the registered intern has the competence and training to provide treatment in special situations even though the intern has not had such training or experience. In another situation, an MFT also exaggerates the experience of an employee who is a licensed MFT to make this clinician "look good" to clients. MFTs as employers are ultimately responsible for preventing misleading, false, or deceptive representation of the qualifications and competence of their employees.

10.8 SPECIALIZATIONS:

Marriage and family therapists may represent themselves either as specializing or having expertise within a limited area of marriage and family therapy, but only if they have the education, training, and experience which meet recognized professional standards to practice in that specialty area.

Ethically, MFTs who identify themselves as "specialists" must follow guidelines set for specialty status by recognized boards. These organizations require a specific number of years of clinical experience, knowledge of the literature knowledge base for the specialty area, completion of a set number of hours of continuing education in this arena, and passing a comprehensive examination before the clinician becomes certified as specialists. Simply because MFTs state that they have specific areas of interest in their practice and treat these areas does not make them "specialists." Doing so can invite both a Board investigation and CAMFT investigation for false advertising.

There are areas of MFT practice that do not have recognized specialties. Ethical MFTs seek a comparable specialty board in psychology and follow a parallel course of study, training, and experience before calling themselves specialists. It is the responsibility of all MFTs to have the knowledge base, training, and experience in the treatment issue or area of practice before they can call themselves specialists.

> <u>10.9 ADVERTISING OF CAMFT MEMBERSHIP:</u>
> **CAMFT clinical, associate and prelicensed members may identify such membership in CAMFT in public information or advertising materials, but they must clearly and accurately represent whether they are clinical, associate, or prelicensed members.**

The California Association of Marriage and Family Therapists allows members to identify themselves as belonging to the professional organization as long as they correctly identify their membership status. Currently, CAMFT recognizes three separate categories: a) clinical members, which includes all members who have been licensed by the Board of Behavioral Sciences in California as MFTs, b) associate members, which includes all individuals who wish to join CAMFT and are not licensed MFTs, and c) pre-licensed members, which includes all members who are registered interns or trainees.

> <u>10.10 USE OF "CAMFT":</u>
> **Marriage and family therapists may not use the initials CAMFT following their name in the manner of an academic degree.**

It is unethical for members of CAMFT to add the initials "CAMFT" to their name as if these represented an academic degree. Doing so would be misleading since any reasonable person could assume that these initials represented a formal degree.

> <u>10.11 USE OF CAMFT LOGO:</u>
> **Marriage and family therapists may use the CAMFT logo only after receiving**

permission in writing from the Association. Permission will be granted by the Association to CAMFT members in good standing in accordance with Association policy on use of CAMFT logo. The Association (which is the sole owner of its name, logo, and the abbreviated initials CAMFT) may grant permission to CAMFT committees and chartered chapters in good standing, operating as such, to use the CAMFT logo. Such permission will be granted in accordance with Association policy on use of the CAMFT logo.

Members of CAMFT who are in good standing may include the CAMFT logo in their professional presentations. This includes the use of business cards, letterhead or advertising in a directory. Requesting the use of this logo requires the following: a) the request is made in writing to the Association, b) defining a statement that the user will include the words "California Association of Marriage and Family Therapists" with the logo including the category of membership, c) the statement describes where the logo will be used (letterhead, advertising, etc.), d) the request is accompanied by a copy or copies of the final products, and e) the recipient has obtained written authorization from the Association prior to use of the logo. An MFT who does not follow the policy on use of the logo as defined by CAMFT is in violation of this ethical standard.

CAMFT chapters may use the logo for official chapter business when the Association has given appropriate permission. Uses include using it on Chapter letterhead, advertising, leaflets, and brochures. The chapter officers would follow CAMFT's policy on use of the logo before official use. It would be unethical for a chapter to use the CAMFT's logo in conjunction with any other logo from any other organization. Such use would imply official sanction of CAMFT for the second organization. This action would be a misrepresentation of fact.

10.12 CAMFT MEMBERSHIP:

Marriage and family therapists, when publicizing their membership in CAMFT, do not do so in a manner that implies organizational endorsement of their activities.

It is unethical for any members of CAMFT to utilize their membership in CAMFT in any arena outside of clinical and professional activities. An example of unethical conduct involves MFTs who are running for office for a local school board state in their ad campaign literature that they are members in good standing of CAMFT. This would imply that CAMFT has given this MFT official sanction for his or her personal activities. This action would be a misrepresentation of fact.

CAMFT Ethical Standard 10 establishes the nature of clear, honest, correct, and proper advertising and public communications. Any deviation from this can lead to false, fraudulent, misleading, or deceptive professional communications that can adversely affect the therapeutic relationship and process. Additionally, this section creates further boundaries of safety for the therapeutic environment.

Clinical Example # 1

> Mary, a licensed clinical psychologist, is watching television. She recognizes a local prominent MFT being interviewed by a newscaster regarding a recent child abuse case. The newscaster states: "Dr. Smith, tell us about your qualifications." She replies: "I am a licensed psychologist" and practice marriage and family therapy in town." Mary remembers that this clinician has a Ph.D. in sociology and is licensed as an MFT. Mary is extremely upset, picks up the phone and calls the BBS.

Questions for Clinical Example # 1

1. What do you believe caused this MFT to misstate her qualifications?
2. Could she have retracted her statement and avoided a BBS investigation? Why or why not?
3. Which CAMFT ethical standards did she violate?
4. How could she have maintained objectivity and have acted in a reasonable and prudent manner?

Chapter Questions

1. You decide to advertise in the Yellow Pages and you find an ad in the marriage and family therapists section, which states that John Doe, MFT, CAMFT, is a leading expert in the area of business consultation. What would you advice this therapists?
2. An MFT tells a supervisee that he should place his own ad in the Yellow Pages to promote his practice. His ad reads John Doe, MFT including his address and telephone number. What is wrong ethically?
3. An MFT asks you to share expenses with her regarding a promotional campaign on the radio. The two of you will be presented as specialists in family therapy. What would you say to this therapist and why?
4. The MFT in question #2 receives a letter from CAMFT informing his that he is in violation of a CAMFT Ethical Standard. If he does nothing about the ad, what other ethical standard will he violate?
5. A local newspaper approaches you with a radio campaign. They want to test a new market and are willing to discount their fee to you. In exchange, they want you to discount your fee to those clients who respond to the ad. You agree and when you hear the ad, the following is said about your fees: "The most reasonable fees in town." Where do you stand with the Ethics Committee?

Chapter 38

A Structure to Process Legal and Ethical Decisions

Managing Legal and Ethical Challenges Safely

MFTs are facing a greater number of challenges in the profession. Managed care, increasing number of therapists competing for the same market, providing "coaching" instead of psychotherapy, increased vigilance and control by the licensing board, Internet psychotherapy, increasing malpractice actions, and a mounting number of complaints filed with the BBS's and CAMFT's Ethics Committees, all make clinical practice an ongoing challenge. Some therapists have decided to change professions. Others practice from a position of fear, worrying continuously about attorneys, malpractice lawsuits, and the BBS. Sadly, these approaches are based on fear of the worst-case scenarios and may lead to a lack of enjoyment of clinical practice. The following approaches come from a perspective of *Creating Safety,* which includes the therapist and client in the safe therapeutic environment:

A. ***Transform fear of the legal and ethical issues into an environment of safety.*** I have proposed a different perspective to clinical practice: one based on creating clinical safety rather than fear. This approach relates to ethical guidelines and the law as boundaries, which create a foundation of safety for clinical practice. In this perspective state law, case law and CAMFT's ethical guidelines serve as the container of a safe and effective therapeutic practice much as do sidelines in tennis. This approach helps the therapist become free of fear-based injunctions and helps open up opportunities to relate differently and freely to ethics and the law. There is greater personal freedom in asking "How can I create safety for my client and myself?" Rather than asking, "What do I need to do to keep from getting sued?"

B. ***Know all applicable state and federal laws.*** Since the Tarasoff case law became effective, there have been an increasing number of state and federal regulations impacting the practice of marriage and family counseling. With new clinical challenges come new laws. Sometimes it is difficult to keep track of every new regulation. CAMFT's legal articles in ***The California Therapist*** are an excellent resource to track new developments in the legislative arena or read "The Legal and Ethical Corner," a monthly newsletter appearing at http://www.fgrosso.com. An important development impacting this perspective is that as of 2004, MFTs will be expected to present 6 accrued continuing education credits on California law and CAMFT ethics required toward licensing every two years. Ignorance of the law is not an excuse for unprofessional conduct.

C. ***Know, explore and discuss ethical standards with knowledgeable peers.*** Expanding the safety container means that the "reasonable and prudent" MFT will also know CAMFT's Ethical Standards and apply them appropriately. Expert witnesses and attorneys focus on ethical violations by therapists to show how the clinician presented a pattern of unethical conduct and of practiced below the standard of care. Exploring and discussing these standards with informed peers helps generate familiarity with the ethical standards should a challenging ethical issue arise. "Be prepared!" This is the Scout motto and it is also applicable in the practice of marriage and family therapy.

D. ***Recognize personal countertransference issues, which could lead to potential ethical challenges.*** Ethically, MFTs are expected to be aware of personal biases, preconceptions, weaknesses, belief systems, and limitations, which could create a lack of objectivity when faced with some professional treatment issue or situation. This insight helps create additional safety within the therapeutic container: the more MFTs know themselves, the greater freedom they have to avoid difficult and challenging ethical situations which could lead to potential unethical conduct. For additional information, I invite the reader to explore my article titled "Avoiding the Transference-Countertransference Confrontation Trap," (see Appendix A).

E. ***Create a personal structure to prevent potential ethical conflicts.*** Some relevant questions that "prudent and reasonable" MFTs may ask themselves follow: (1) is this case addressing ***interpersonal*** relationship issues? (scope of practice), (2) Do I have the training, experience, and education to address the treatment issues in this case? (scope of competence), (3) Am I maintaining confidentiality except for the breaches permitted or mandated by law, addressing my "Holding Information Policy" and using appropriate written releases of information? (Confidentiality/Privilege), (4) Am I addressing crisis issues as permitted or mandated by law? (Evidence Code 1024, Welfare and Institutions Code 5150, Welfare and Institutions Code 15630, Penal Code 11165-11174, Tarasoff case law and Civil Code 43.92, *Bellah v. Greenson*, etc.), (5) Am I addressing management practice issues appropriately? (Fees, insurance, managed care, Health Code 123130, termination, referrals, etc.), (6) Am I avoiding and preventing dual relationships where I will lose objectivity or exploit my clients? (Business and Professions Code 4982), and am I keeping mental health records according to the standard of care? (See" Mental Health Records Made Easy: A Workbook for Mental Health Professionals" in Appendix A).

F. ***Practice within the legal/ethical, clinical, and scientific standards of care.*** Know the scientific literature to understand the advantages and disadvantages, strengths and weaknesses of applied clinical modalities and interventions, utilized psychotherapeutic theories, information given to clients regarding treatment, and what the experts say about specific clinical treatment approaches.

G. ***Consult with peers and experts who know the application of the law and ethical standards.*** CAMFT attorneys are an excellent professional resource for members of CAMFT. For those who are not members of CAMFT, attorneys specializing in this area are available for consultation. Ultimately, it is the responsibility of each MFT to seek appropriate consultation when faced with an ethical challenge, which could cause potential harm to a client.

As a friend of mine has reminded me on several occasions, "measure twice, cut once!" After the decision has been made and action taken, it is very difficult to change the course of events that ensue, especially if the client is harmed as a result of the action taken. If MFTs do not deliberately create and maintain an environment of safety for their clients, ultimately the licensing board will take appropriate and restrictive steps to create safety for the consumers of the state. It is the responsibility of each therapist to create safety in the practice of marriage and family counseling. By diligently creating this container of safety, all MFTs have the opportunity to enjoy their practice.

Chapter 39

Accessing the Internet for California Codes

Accessing the California Code Through the Internet

Any person with an Internet Service Provider account can obtain the California Code through the Internet via the Official California Legislative Information Server (http://www.leginfo.ca.gov/). As an exercise, access this server and go to the home page, which should be titled "Official California Legislative Information" and display the seal of the State of California. Proceed to the bottom of the page and access "California Law." Press the button and go to the next page, which is titled "California Law." The law consists of 29 statutes, and each one has a box to the left of its name.

Continue by checking the box to the left of "Business and Professions Code." Proceed to the bottom of the page and find the search engine. Type in "Marriage, Family, and Child Counselor" and press "Search."

When the next page appears, proceed to the first listed legislation and access it. Congratulations! You have learned how to access California legislation applicable to MFTs.

Return to the previous page and uncheck "Business and Professions Code." Check "Code of Civil Procedure" and leave "Marriage, Family, and Child counselor"

Continue this process until you have explored all California code categories for "MFCC or MFT" content. Please print the image of the search engine page for the California Legislative Information server and hand it in.

Appendix

Answer Key

Chapter 1

Your Internal Reality

1. Internal reality means a compilation of life experiences, belief systems, morality, religious and social values, biases, prejudices, fears, myths, and socioeconomic values. It is everything that makes up how you feel and think about your world and how you relate to it. Your internal reality affects how you do therapy and how you make legal and ethical decisions.2. This question can be answered only by you.

3. Blind spots are those areas in our lives where we lack objectivity for whatever reason. Identify yours.

4. Therapeutic safety means creating a therapeutic environment in which the client and the therapist can generate trust in the process and in each other. This creation of trust allows the client to safely explore his or her issues.

5. Primarily, by knowing and applying the laws and ethics of MFT practice. Next by obtaining appropriate consultation with a knowledgeable peer. Third, by establishing a healthy therapeutic relationship with the client.

Chapter 2

Informed Consent

1. Informed consent is providing clients with necessary information about the psychotherapeutic process to make an informed decision.

2. Providing clients with informed consent creates a balance in the power differential inherent to psychotherapy.

3. Informed consent must address (a) the competency of the client, (b) the disclosure of material information, (c) the client's understanding of the presented material, and (d) the voluntary consent of the client.

4. Informed consent creates safety by addressing expectations both therapists and clients may have of each other at the beginning of therapy and what they can expect from each other. In some situations, clients can feel overwhelmed by the information provided.

5. Create a document and check with your instructor.
6. Create a document and check with your instructor. It will probably expand.

Chapter 3

Confidentiality

1. When an MFT treats more than one person as part of the treatment unit, each person's unique confidentiality needs must be taken into consideration. The therapist must provide his or her clients with

possible ways of managing the confidentiality needs.

2. A legal release of information must contain the following items: see page 21.

3. I would create a group contract and have the members sign it. Ethically, I have a mandate to create safety for the group.

4. A "holding information" policy addresses how this multiple confidentiality issue will be maintained to protect everyone's interests.

5. There are three possibilities of secrets policies. A not-holding-information policy is best used when clients have a high degree of differentiation and good ego strength. The implications are that the couple must be able to manage whatever tension arises by themselves. A limited-holding-information policy can be used when the clients are not in total accord with the goals of therapy and a difference in ego strength between the parties exists. The implications are that the clients rely on the therapist for guidance during the course of therapy. An all-holding-information policy is best used when the couple has a low degree of differentiation and poor ego strength. The implications are that all responsibilities lie on the therapist regarding managing tension between the couple.

6. I would assess each one carefully and determine their ability to share "secrets." If either one could not share secrets initially, I would language an intervention that would allow for the couple to create a holding information policy that works for both of them (the weakest denominator would dictate how sensitive information would be managed). I believe I would work with them because it would be a clinical challenge to bring them to the same level of ego strength.

7. This question addresses my internal reality and my knowledge of ethics and the law. Essentially, I have to take his confidentiality needs into consideration and those of his parents. Though his parents hold the privilege, I also need to acknowledge the parent's confidentiality needs. If these two are in conflict, I need to create safety for all of them by addressing my holding information policy previously established with the family (the parents gave consent for treatment and want to be informed should the son be in danger). I would need to address Evidence Code 1024 should he be in danger to self or others. And I believe it would be important for him to know he is loved by his parents who are concerned about his well being. I would use a clinical intervention that would establish this and invite him to tell his parents himself. This action would be the most enhancing for the progress of treatment.

8. Electronic devices are not conducive to maintaining confidentiality, therefore, I would use them with care and selectively. Being aware of the limitations of these products.

Chapter 4

Privilege

1. Privilege deals with the legal system. Confidentiality deals with the clinical environment.
2. Privilege and confidentiality both manage the information given to the therapist in treatment.
3. Privilege can be broken when mandated by law.
4. The client is the holder of the privilege. The guardian or conservator if the client has one of these. Or the executor if the client is deceased.
5. The therapist asserts or claims privilege for the client when the therapist receives a subpoena for records and refuses to hand these to the requesting person at the time the subpoena is received.
6. I would tell the Marshall that I claim privilege for my client and that he is welcome to call my client's attorney.
7. That she is violating Business and Professions Code 4982 (v).
8. When client's claim emotional injuries in a legal case, mental health records can be subpoenaed by the opposing attorney.

Chapter 5

Important legal Concepts in MFT Practice

1. Scope of Practice for MFTs is defined as enhancing relationships. An intrapersonal issue would be becoming a better reader by learning to overcome an emotional trauma (this does not enhance relationships). An interpersonal issue would be addressing depression because it interferes with relationships.
2. By taking courses, consulting with more experienced peers, reading books on the subject, and taking on clients under an experienced supervisor.
3. Answer this on your own.
4. Personal question.
5. Consult with a more experienced peer or legal/ethical consultant.
6. Therapeutic duty is the responsibility placed upon therapist by law and ethics to create safety for the client. I see it as a conduit between myself and the client that becomes stronger as we manage challenging issues in therapy.
7. Informed consent is providing information at the beginning of therapy which allows the client to be informed about the process of therapy.
8. Therapeutic duty is based on contract law.
9. Therapeutic safety requires objectivity by the therapist. Therapeutic duty is created by law and ethics. As these two concepts intertwine, the therapist becomes more knowledgeable of law and ethics and allows him/herself to become more objective through his or her own therapy.
10. To seek consultation on this issue and to follow through with my own therapy.
11. Standard of care is the best care a therapist can give a client and is based on what experts have defined care to be in the field of psychotherapy. It creates a model of what is expected of each and every therapist to provide his or her clients.
12. Scientific standard of care relates to research findings as they apply to therapy.
13. Clinical standard of care relates to clinical interventions, theories of psychotherapy, and other clinical elements that apply to therapy.
14. Legal/ethical standard of care relates to the laws and ethics as they apply to psychotherapy.
15. It can enhance it, diminish it, or terminate it, depending on how the client perceives he or she is receiving mental health care from the therapist.
16. Case law creates a Therapeutic duty on the therapist to apply appropriate legal standards.
17. Read the official publication of CAMFT "The California Therapist" to stay abreast of case law in California.
18. Personal answer.

Chapter 6

Business and Professions Code as it Applies to Marriage and Family Therapists

1. For MFT's, the focus of practice is on enhancing relationships.

2. A marriage and family therapist receives remuneration for services.

3. Each MFT is encouraged to provide his or her client informed consent.

4. Unprofessional conduct is any activity that violates the regulations of marriage and family counseling.

5. Confidentiality must be maintained except as permitted or mandated by law.

6. Fees must be disclosed at the beginning of therapy.

7. Sexual contact with any client is prohibited and the therapist can lose the license if he or she engages in such conduct.

8. First, if doing business under a fictitious name, the name of the owners of the business must be disclosed to the clients. Second, the fee to be charged must be disclosed to the client before counseling begins.

Chapter 7

Malpractice and Unprofessional Conduct

1. It means that an MFT will be expected to know the laws and ethics of this profession thoroughly.

2. By losing clinical objectivity.

3. He failed to inform the client that this was a new approach to therapy. He failed to take the client's emotional state into consideration.

4. He failed to consider that the new therapy he was using did not meet the Standard of Care in psychotherapy.

5. Creating safety invites the client to participate and creates partnership. Protecting oneself does not take into consideration the needs of the client and only considers the welfare of the therapist.

Chapter 8

The Therapeutic Relationship

1. The therapeutic relationship is the vehicle by which all change takes place in therapy.

2. It can be enhanced when the therapist role models appropriate behavior, such as taking responsibility for errors in judgment.

3. The therapist's frustration could be easily "felt" by the client. The client could be emotionally reacting to the therapist and the therapeutic relationship could be weakened.

4. If the therapist abuses the therapeutic relationship, the client may want to seek redress through a malpractice action.

5. A BBS investigation is an administrative action against the license of the therapist. A malpractice action is a civil legal action against the therapist. I would advice this therapist to contact his or her malpractice carrier as soon as possible.

Chapter 9

Dual Relationships

1. Personal answer. Personal answer.

2. It is illegal. A therapist can be sued through civil court and criminal court. Also, he or she can lose his or her license. Personal answer.

3. Civil court means that a malpractice action has taken place and monetary damages can be assessed against the therapist. Criminally, the therapist can go to jail and be fined.

4. Some therapists take advantage of the therapeutic relationship and the power differential that takes place in therapy. These therapists use the sexual relationship to take advantage of the client's weaknesses.

Chapter 10

Managing High-Risk Clients and Creating Therapeutic Safety

1. Clinical issues become crisis issues when danger to self or others is imminent.

2. Crisis issues have one thing in common: a breach of confidentiality is mandated or permitted by law.

3. Sometimes they parallel each other and sometimes they complement each other.

4. This is a personal answer.

5. This is a personal answer.

6. This is a personal answer.

Chapter 11

The Suicidal Client, Evidence Code 1024

1. At all times take reasonable steps to protect the life of the client.

2. First, establish a firm therapeutic relationship. Next, follow a sound theoretical approach that works well with suicidal clients, such as a cognitive-behavioral approach. Use clinical interventions that are part of the standard of care.

3. Assess the client's mental or emotional state via a mental status exam. Next determine if the client presents a danger to self or others. If so, breach confidentiality only if absolutely needed. Document this decision thoroughly.

4. If no other intervention worked to contain the suicidality of my client, I would breach confidentiality to create safety.

5. Personal answer. I would stay in contact with my own therapist to process my thoughts and feelings and maintain objectivity. Next, I would consult with an expert in suicide. I would make sure I was abreast of all legal and ethical requirements regarding suicide. I would document all my legal and ethical decisions carefully.

6. I would remind the therapist that *Bellah v. Greenson* places the therapeutic duty on therapists to take reasonable steps to protect the client's life. I would also recommend to the therapist that he or she see their own therapist to maintain objectivity.

Chapter 12

Serious Threat to Harm (Tarasoff Case Law) and Civil Code 43.92

1. The lack of predictability of dangerousness makes this a challenging issue. Not being able to foresee a dangerous action by the client makes this difficult to manage.

2. Assess the client carefully and thoroughly. Refer as necessary. Consult with more experienced peers.

Document my decisions. Breach confidentiality as mandated by law.

3. Personal answer.

4. Tarasoff is a legally mandated breach of confidentiality when an identifiable victim has been threatened by a client and the therapist hears the serious threat to harm. It places a duty to protect this identifiable victim upon the therapist. Civil Code 43.92 establishes how the therapist will protect the identifiable victim: a) by calling the police, and b) by taking reasonable steps to warn the identifiable victim.

5. Calling the police and taking reasonable steps to warn the identifiable victim.

6. After assessing the situation carefully, would warn those around me and call the police.

7. No, because she heard the threat and is not technically an identifiable victim. She can take steps to protect herself. Had she not known that the serious threat to harm was made against her, then it would be a Tarasoff situation.

Chapter 13

Mandated Child Abuse Reporting

1. Reasonable suspicion means that the context of the statement made to the therapist is evaluated carefully to determine whether this is a reasonable statement.

2. Immediately by phone and within 36 hours by written report to CWS.

3. Both of them equally.

4. Personal answer.

5. Assess the situation carefully. Consult with more experienced peers. Check my emotional reactivity with my own therapist. Know the laws and ethics regarding this issue.

6. Personal answers.

7. Assess the case carefully. Consult and seek my own therapy to check my emotional reactivity. In this case, I would need to work with the mother to reiterate that her children need to be protected by law. Ask her how can we work together and still stay within the law to achieve this. If she refuses to call CWS, I will call, knowing that she may terminate therapy.

8. The treatment could slow down or end. The therapeutic relationship can have a positive effect on treatment. The stronger my relationship with the client, the greater the chance that we can work through this challenging issue together for the benefit of the family.

9. I would direct her to consult with an expert in this field.

Chapter 14

Elder and Dependent Abuse Reporting

1. First, I would document the bruising I noticed in previous sessions. I would continue to ask her about the bruising. I would refer her to a physician for evaluation. I would consult with Adult Protective Services without revealing my client's name. I would invite my client to call APS herself. If she refuses, I would call and give them all the pertinent information, including her fears of being abandoned by her daughter.

2. I would call APS immediately and report the possible financial abuse.

Chapter 15

Mental Health Records

1. Business and Professions Code 4982 (v) and CAMFT Ethical Standard 2.4 require that MFTs keep appropriate mental health records.

2. The following components must be kept: a) chief complaints, including pertinent history, b) findings from consultations and referrals to other health care workers, c) diagnosis, when determined, d) treatment plan. e) progress of treatment, f) prognosis, including significant continuing problems or conditions, g) pertinent reports of diagnostic procedures and tests and all discharge summaries, h) objective findings from the most recent physical examination

3. If a client wishes to examine his or her mental health records, the therapist must allow this within 5 working days. If the client wishes a copy of his or her records, then the therapist must provide a copy within 15 working days. If the therapist wishes to provide a summary, then the summary must be completed and mailed within 15 working days.

4. I would have her call CAMFT immediately and consult with their staff attorney. I would also recommend that she contact her own attorney and consult.

5. Treatment plans are a required component of mental health records. They serve to provide a path directing treatment.

Chapter 16

The Content of Mental Health Records

1. The content of mental health records is dictated by law. Not having the minimum legal requirement could be considered as practicing below the Standard of care.

2. It provides identifying information about the client, including medical information, previous therapy, family history, and emergency contact information.

3. It would be important to include the following: limits of confidentiality, office procedures, emergency procedures, procedure for termination of therapy, and consent to assess, diagnose, and treat.

4. I would have her call CAMFT immediately and consult with their staff attorney. I would also recommend that she contact her own attorney and consult.

5. Treatment plans are a required component of mental health records.

6. Documenting consultations and referrals serves to show that the therapist has acted within Standard of Care in obtaining additional help when necessary.

7. If this therapist were to change her treatment notes, she would be altering a legal document and this is an illegal action.

8. The Discharge summary creates a legal documentation of the termination of therapeutic duty when therapy ends.

Chapter 19

Subpoenas

1. 1. You "claim privilege" for your client and tell the Marshall you will contact him or her after you have spoken to your client's attorney.

2. You sign the "Affidavit" stating that these records no longer exist and send that to the copying service.

3. You are legally bound to release the records by the date stated on the subpoena.

4. Personal answer.

Chapter 20

Supervision

1. The primary responsibility is to serve as a guide and role model appropriate conduct when performing therapy. This includes respecting the relationship between supervisor/supervisee which resembles the therapeutic relationship.

2. Call CAMFT and ask to speak with the staff attorney.

3. Follow the guidelines established by the supervisor. Know the laws and ethics of MFT practice. Follow Standard of Care. Consult with the supervisor continuously.

Chapter 21

Advertising

1. First, her card is illegal because it states false or misleading information. She needs to include either her license number or the name licensed marriage and family therapist. Also, there is no recognized specialty in relationship issues and therefore she is acting unprofessionally. She can say she limits her practice to relationship issues. That would be acceptable and legal.

2. Again, this would be misleading and false since he is not a physician nor a psychiatrist. He needs to change the name.

3. It is not appropriate because he is not being specific and is using a relative value which can be misinterpreted by a potential client.

Chapter 22

Fees

1. Bartering can lead to creating a harmful dual relationship. To barter, the therapist must create a value for the items involved. That is the job of an appraiser and this creates a dual relationship. There can be loss of objectivity in pricing below the market value the items exchanged.

2. He is practicing illegally and unethically. He needs to establish one fee and provide that fee at the beginning of treatment. Doing it his way creates personal gain and he is taking advantage of the clients.

3. It is the duty of the supervisor to establish the fee, not the intern. This is both an illegal and unethical practice which can lead to the loss of both the intern's future license and the license of the supervisor.

4. This is a loss of objectivity of the therapist. Allowing a large balance to accrue creates an undue burden on the client and the therapist lost his or her objectivity in the treatment of this client. The client can sue the therapist for malpractice.

Chapter 23

Insurance and Managed Care

1. This action is illegal and unethical. The therapist cannot bill insurance companies for work performed by others.

Chapter 24

Forensics, Telephone and Online Counseling

1. There are many. Some are that the laws have not yet been defined for this type of practice. This includes which state's laws will be applied, the one where the therapist practices or the one where the client resides? If there is a difference in addresses, is the therapist practicing illegally in another state? Many others.

2. Call CAMFT's staff attorney immediately and seek their counsel. Consult with his or her own attorney immediately.

Chapter 25

Cultural Diversity

1. The prevailing Therapeutic duty is to assess, diagnose, and treat correctly. The MFT must take into consideration cultural issues that could impact the treatment and are relevant to the client. In assessing correctly, the MFT must maintain personal clinical objectivity and have the Scope of Competence when treating diversity clients.

2. A Mexican-American client may have a belief system that revolves around "fatalism," which means that he or she cannot help the outcome of the future and that he or she is "doomed" to suffer and die. In assessing this perspective, the MFT would obtain appropriate consultation to determine how best to treat this fear of living a "doomed" life.

Chapter 26

Treatment of Minors, Family Law

1. When they are 12 years or older and are capable of benefiting from therapy, and without treatment they would be a danger to self or others, or when they have been the alleged victim of a crime or incest.

2. She must obtain parental consent.

3. Age 12 appears to be the age of reason in California law.

4. Both parties must be 18 years of age and capable of consenting to and consummating a marriage. If underage, parental consent or court consent must be granted for the underage person.

5. As part of consent, the court requires, for minors, that both parties participate in premarital counseling.

6. The willingness to proceed with a divorce, irreconcilable differences, insanity, and a six-month waiting period.

7. Both parties must have parental consent or the consent of the court.

8. Anyone who is recognized by the state.

9. Both parties must have lived together for over one year.

10. Community property means property belonging to both parties of the marriage. Tenants in common

means both parties hold equal ownership with or without marriage. Joint tenants means both parties share ownership without it being equal.
11. Separate property is property brought into the marriage before the marriage took place.
12. The status of the marriage; custody of minor children of the marriage; support of children for whom support may be ordered, including children born after the filing of the initial petition or final decree of dissolution;, support of either party; the settlement of the property rights of the parties; and award of attorney's fees and costs.
13. Insanity and irreconcilable differences.
14. An individual with court-appointed authority to manage the affairs of the marriage.
15. A dissolution is granted without a protracted legal process. It takes place when one of the parties does not contest the divorce.
16. The minor must have the ability to understand what treatment is about.

Chapter 27

New Trends in Legal and Ethical Aspects of Psychotherapy

1. Coaching involves guiding the client through an educational experience and helping him or her become proficient in a specific area including the changing of behaviors. Coaching does not provide a legal basis for holding confidentiality. Psychotherapy involves the addressing of conscious and unconscious motivation of behavior. This process focuses on the management of emotions utilizing acceptable psychotherapeutic techniques. Licensed psychotherapy provide a legal basis for holding confidentiality.
2. MFTs acting as coaches may promise holding confidentiality to coaching clients. As coaches, they cannot provide the holding of confidentiality. Should they promise confidentiality and breach it, they could face malpractice actions for "breach of contract". Also, MFTs are versed in the use of psychotherapeutic techniques. It may be that the MFT may be unable to prevent him/herself from using these techniques when a coaching client faces a difficult emotional moment. Doing so, would be considered as psychotherapy without a license, crossing over onto a separate clinical relationship, and possibly causing harm to the client.

Chapter 28

1. It means that the therapist has the duty to assure that the proposed treatment is in the vest interest of the client and to take steps to avoid harming clients.
2. The clinician must take appropriate steps, such as assessment, diagnosis, and treatment, to avoid harming the client.
3. Without appropriate consideration of a power differential, the client could influence the clients decision even if they aren't in the best interest of the client.
4. A dual relationship involves a concurrent relationship with the client where harm isn't present. In the harmful dual relationship, the clinician has either lost clinical objectivity or coerced the client with resulting client harm.
5. This type of violation is the most severe violation that can take place in a therapeutic relationship, besides the possibility of murder.
6. A sexual relationship usually involves an emotional attachment between the parties involved. To provide appropriate therapy, objectivity must be clear. A sexual relationship most likely creates a loss of objectivity in the therapist.

7. That the possibility exists that the therapist is providing therapy for his or her own benefit in violation of CAMFT ethical standard 1.5.
8. CAMFT ethical standard 1.7 has been violated. Therapist never tell their clients what to do. Rather, they help clients understand the consequences of their own decisions and respect the right of patients to make their own decisions.
9. It appears that CAMFT ethical standard 1.8 was violated. It states that therapists must inform patients on their availability for emergencies.
10. CAMFT ethical standards 1.10, 1.11, and possibly 1.12 were violated. The first one requires that therapist assure that clients have continuity of care when they can't provide treatment. The next one, requires that therapists not abandon their patients, and if for some reason the therapist cannot continue treatment, then the therapist must arrange for the continuity of treatment with another therapist. The third one would be violated if the therapist worked for someone else and did not take into consideration the best interest of the patient when terminating employment.
11. CAMFT ethical standard 1.12 requires that, when treating a family unit, therapists consider the potential conflict that may arise between the family unit and each family member. In this case, there could be a conflict of interest if the therapist treats the couple and the lover at the same time.
12. CAMFT ethical standard 1.15 requires that therapists utilize community resources when necessary to improve and protect the health and welfare of the patient. Not referring the client to ALANON for additional support for codependency would be a violation of this standard.
13. CAMFT ethical standard 1.16 requires that therapists challenge denials of treatment by insurance companies, when appropriate. 1.17 requires that alternatives to treatment be discussed with patients when there is no coverage by an insurance company. This therapist appears to have violated both standards.

Chapter 29

1. If the therapist does not establish a holding information or secret's policy at the beginning of therapy, then a client, when seen alone, could share information with the therapist and request that the therapist not divulge it to their partner or family member. If the information stops the therapy, then the therapist is in a bind because he or she cannot breach the client's confidentiality

2. Civil Code 56-56.37 also requires a written release of information before information will be released to a third party. The exception is that the latter establishes the exact requirements for the release to be legal.

3. Electronic devices do not protect confidentiality.

4. When storing records, a therapist neglects to store them in a locked cabinet and the cleaning service people peruse the records. When transferring the records, the therapist leaves them in the car and the records are stolen from the car. When disposing of records, the therapist leaves them in the trash and someone reads them. The therapist stores the records in a computer program without a password protection system. Anyone can open the computer and access the records. When working in an agency, a therapist leaves her records by the front desk and the entering clients can read the names on the charts.

5. Per CAMFT ethical standard 2.5, this therapist did not take appropriate steps to ensure that the confidentiality of patients is maintained by his or her employees.

6. Per CAMFT ethical standard 2.3, therapists must be aware of possible adverse effects of technological

changes with respect to the dissemination of patient information. This therapist could have sent a test fax to assure that the appropriate party received the fax and prevent a breach of confidentiality.

7. The therapist, per CAMFT ethical standard 2.7 are encouraged to obtain agreement from group participants to respect the confidentiality of other members of the group. This could be done through a contract holding each member legally responsible for respecting the group's confidentiality.

8. This therapist violated CAMFT ethical standard 2.6 by not obtaining a written authorization from clients to use clinical material that could violate a client's identity.

Chapter 30

1. Scope of Competence is established by experts in the field who publish their expertise in the scientific literature.

2. CAMFT ethical standard 3.1 states that therapists are in violation of CAMFT ethical standards if they are convicted of a crime substantially related to their professional qualifications or functions.

3. This therapist is in violation of CAMFT ethical standard 3.1 for practicing when impaired due to physical or mental causes or the abuse of alcohol or other substances.

4. CAMFT ethical standard 3.3 requires that MFTs maintain patient treatment records consistent with sound clinical practices. Standard of Care dictates that the client assess, diagnose and treat appropriately. This therapist did not keep appropriate records.

5. This therapist is violating CAMFT ethical standard 3.2 which states that therapists avoid contractual arrangements which provide financial incentives to withhold or limit medically/psychologically necessary care.

6. This therapist, per CAMFT ethical standard 3.3, failed to consider protecting access to the computer by utilizing a password system.

7. This therapist appears to have violated CAMFT ethical standards 3.6 and 3.7 which address striving to understand a client's cultural perspective and a therapist's understanding of his or her own cultural values affect therapy.

8. Per CAMFT ethical standard 3.8, therapists stay abreast of developments in their field through education and 3.9 which prevents the exploitation of supervisees, this therapist appears to have violated both standards.

Chapter 31

1. Trust and dependency are related to the inherent power differential that exists in the described relationships.

2. In all these instances, a harmful dual relationship exists where loss of objectivity or coercion exists. I would tell each one of these supervisees to seek consultation regarding the supervisory relationship.

3. I would tell her that the supervisor could be in violation of CAMFT ethical standard 4.2, which requires that supervisors assess the competence level of their supervisees and do not allow them to treat patients beyond their level of competence.

Chapter 32

1. The second therapist appears to be in violation of CAMFT ethical standard 5.0, which requires therapists to treat colleagues with respect, courtesy, fairness, and good faith, and cooperate with colleagues in order to promote the welfare and best interest of the patient. By violating this standard, this therapist may also be violating CAMFT ethical standard 3.1. I would recommend to this therapist that she pursue her own therapy and explore her behavior, and stop her destructive behavior to prevent an ethical violation.

2. After investigating the accusation by the second therapist, I would remind her of CAMFT ethical standard 5.3 which states that therapists do not file frivolous ethical complaints.

3. I would remind this therapist that according to CAMFT ethical standard 5.2 he is only encouraged to assist colleagues who are impaired and it is not a requirement to do so.

Chapter 33

1. This therapists appears to have violated all the CAMFT ethical standards from 6.0 to 6.4. The violation is severe and I would support a complaint with the CAMFT Ethics Committee.

2. It is not ethical because it appears to violate CAMFT ethical standard 6.3 which requires that research participants have the freedom to decline or withdraw from a research project at any time.

Chapter 34

1. This therapist appears to be in violation of CAMFT ethical standard 7.2 which requires that therapists assign publication credit to those who have authored a publication. By placing her name as author of this newsletter, this therapist is in violation of this standard.

2. By not giving credit to the original author, this therapist appears to have violated CAMFT ethical standard 7.3.

3. I would remind this therapist that she has a responsibility to cooperate with CAMFT's Ethics Committee per CAMFT ethical standard 7.7.

Chapter 35

1. I would remind this therapist that she could be in violation of CAMFT ethical standard 8.0 which requires that she maintain her objectivity when serving as a custody evaluator in the legal system.

2. Per CAMFT ethical standard 8.4, this therapist is required not to compromise her professional judgment or integrity. By basing her decision to serve as an expert witness solely due to financial gain, this therapist may be violating this standard.

3. Per CAMFT ethical standard 8.3, this therapist could be in violation of this ethical standard. He is required to prevent conflicting roles when serving as an expert witness. Having had a previous relationship with the plaintiff, his objectivity is compromised. Additionally, it appears that he is in violation of CAMFT ethical standard 8.5 since he did not conduct an examination of the defendant.

Chapter 36

1. Per CAMFT ethical standards 9.0, 9.1, 9.2, 9.3, this therapist may be in violation of all these standards. I would tell her that by establishing her fee due based on how difficult the case is, not disclosing her fee at the beginning of therapy, and offering a fee discount for every referred patient, she appears to be on shaky ethical ground.

2. This behavior appears to be violating several CAMFT ethical standards. These include 9.0, 9.2, and 9.3. The ethical violations appear to be changing the fee without having informed the patient at the beginning of therapy how it would be changed. It appears that the therapist is also exploiting the patient financially.

3. There appear to be various CAMFT ethical violations. First, therapists do not exploit the trust and dependency of supervisees (4.0). Next, supervisors do not exploit their supervisees financially (4.1), and finally, supervisors make financial arrangements with supervisees that conform to accepted professional standards.

4. Per CAMFT ethical standard 9.2, therapists do not exploit their patients financially which appears to be happening when the therapist takes advantage of the client's financial plight and accepts the ring in lieu of payment. Per CAMFT ethical standard 9.5, avoid accepting goods in lieu of payment when doing so can lead to loss of objectivity or exploitation of the therapeutic relationship. Again, accepting this ring at this time appears to be a loss of objectivity and even coercion by the therapist.

5. Per CAMFT ethical standard 9.4, this therapist seems to have violated this ethical standard by divulging clinical information.

6. Per CAMFT ethical standard 9.6, the therapist appears to have committed fraud by "double-billing" for the session. Each member's insurance should have been billed $75, which would reflect an accurate description of the fee charged. By billing each insurance $150, this therapist is stating that the fee was $300.

Chapter 37

1. Per CAMFT ethical standard 10.10, therapists are not permitted to use "CAMFT" as a degree or title after one's name. CAMFT ethical standard 10.4 prohibits therapists from advertising in a false or misleading manner.
2. Per CAMFT ethical standard 10.9, therapists must state their clinical status. By advertising in this manner, this intern appears to be a licensed therapist practicing on his own which is also a false and misleading statement (10.4).

3. Per CAMFT ethical standard 10.8, the term "specialist" is limited for those therapists who have completed training in an area of therapy that has recognized professional standards. There is no official organization that certifies therapists in the area of family therapy.

4. Per CAMFT ethical standard 10.5, false and misleading advertising must be corrected by the therapist when they occur. Not doing so is a violation of this standard.
5. Per CAMFT ethical standard 10.4, this advertisement could be described as misleading and deceptive since this therapist cannot prove that his or her fees are indeed "reasonable." This is a relative term and using it creates a misleading and fraudulent statement.

References

Appelbaum, P. S., & Gutheil, T. G. (1991). *Clinical Handbook of Psychiatry and the Law.* Baltimore, MD: Williams & Wilkins.

Babitsky, S., Mangraviti, J.J., Todd, C., (2000). *The Comprehensive Forensic Services Manual: The Essential Resources for All Experts.* Falmouth, MA: S.E.A.K, Inc.

Benke, S. H., Preis, J. J., & Todd Bates, R. (1998). *California Mental Health Law.* New York, NY: W.W Norton & Company.

Bersoff, D. N. (1995). *Ethical Conflicts in Psychology.* Washington, DC: American Psychological Association.

Boland, W. E. (1997). *SecComm Solutions.* Elbert, CO: Personal Communication.

Bongar, B., (1991). *The Suicidal Patient: Clinical and Legal Standards of Care.* Washington, DC: American Psychological Association.

California Association of Marriage and Family Therapists. (1997). *Ethical Standards for Marriage and Family Therapist, Part I.* San Diego, CA: Author.

California Association of Marriage and Family Therapists. (1997). *Ethical Standards for Marriage and Family Therapist, Part II.* San Diego, CA: Author.

California Association of Marriage and Family Therapists. (1987). *The Association's Policy on Use of Logo.* San Diego, CA: Author.

Canter, M. C., et al. (1995). *Ethics for Psychologists: A Commentary on the APA Ethics Code.* Washington, DC: American Psychological Association.

Caudill, O. B., & Pope, K. S. (1995). *Law and Mental Health Professionals: California.* Washington, DC: American Psychological Association.

Corey, G., et al. (1993). *Issues and Ethics in the Helping Professions.* Pacific Grove, CA: Brooks/Cole Publishing Company.

Dickson, D. T. (1995). *Law in the Health and Human Services: Guide for Social Workers, Psychologists, Psychiatrists, and Related Professionals.* New York, NY: The Free Press.

DSM IV, (1994), Diagnostic and Statistical Manual of Mental Disorders, Washington, DC, The American Psychiatric Association.

DSM 5, (2013), Diagnostic and Statistical Manual of Mental Disorders, Washington, DC, The American Psychiatric Association.

Grosso, F. C. (1995, February). *Standard of Care Versus Standard Care*. Newsletter of the Santa Barbara Chapter of the California Association of Marriage and Family Therapists.

Grosso, F. C. (1995, March). *Therapeutic Duty*. Newsletter of the Santa Barbara Chapter of the California Association of Marriage and Family Therapists.

Grosso, F. C. (1995, May). *Informed Consent: What Is It?* L. A. Therapist Update, Newsletter of the LosAngeles Chapter of the California Association of Marriage and Family Therapists.

Grosso, F. C. (1995, May). *Standard of Care Versus Standard Care*. Santa Barbara Chapter of CAMFT Newsletter.

Grosso, F. C. (1995, June). *The Suicidal Patient: Clinical, Legal, and Scientific Standard of Care.* L. A. Therapist Update, Newsletter of the Los Angeles Chapter of the California Association of Marriage and Family Therapists.

Grosso, F. C. (1995, October). *Professional Competence.* L. A. Therapist Update, Newsletter of the Los Angeles Chapter of the California Association of Marriage and Family Therapists.

Grosso, F. C. (1995, August). *Mental Health Records and Notetaking: Creating Safety.* L. A. Therapist Update, Newsletter of the Los Angeles Chapter of the California Association of Marriage and Family Therapists.

Grosso, F. C. (1995, September). *The 21st Century: Being a Good Therapist Won't Be Enough to Avoid Malpractice.* L. A. Therapist Update, Newsletter of the Los Angeles Chapter of the California Association of Marriage and Family Therapists.

Grosso, F. C. (1996, January / February). *Mental Health Records and Notetaking.* L. A. Therapist Update, Newsletter of the Los Angeles Chapter of the California Association of Marriage and Family Therapists.

Grosso, F. C. (1997, June). *Termination in Therapy: The Clinical, Legal/Ethical, and Scientific Standard of Care* L. A. Therapist Update, Newsletter of the Los Angeles Chapter of the California Association of Marriage and Family Therapists.

Grosso, F. C. (1997, July / August). Avoiding the "Transference–Countertransference Confrontation Trap." *The California Therapist,* pp. 46–47.

Grosso, F. C. (1997). Ethics for Marriage, Family, and Child Counselors: *A Commentary on the Association of Marriage and Family Therapists Ethical Standards.* Santa Barbara, CA: Federico C. Grosso, DDS, PhD, MFT.

Grosso, F. C. (2001). Treatment Planning Made Easy: *A Workbook for Mental Health Professionals.* Santa Barbara, CA: Federico C. Grosso, DDS, PhD, MFT.

Grosso, F. C. (2001). Mental Health Records Made Easy: *A Workbook for Mental Health Professionals.* Santa Barbara, CA: Federico C. Grosso, DDS, PhD, MFT.

Grosso, F. C. (2001). Advanced Applications of Law and Ethics: *A Workbook for California Clinical Social Workers.* Santa Barbara, CA: Federico C. Grosso, DDS, PhD, MFT.

Grosso, F. C. (1997). Advanced Applications of Law and Ethics: *A Workbook for California Marriage and Family Therapists.* Santa Barbara, CA: Federico C. Grosso, DDS, PhD, MFT.

Grosso, F. C. (2013). Complete Applications of Law and Ethics for California Marriage and Family Therapists. Santa Barbara, CA: Federico C. Grosso, DDS, PhD, MFT.

Grosso, F. C. (2013). Advanced Applications of Law and Ethics for California Licensed Professional Clinical Counselors. Santa Barbara, CA: Federico C. Grosso, DDS, PhD, MFT.

Grosso, F. C. (2000). Treatment Planning Made Easy: *A Workbook for Mental Health Professionals.* Santa Barbara, CA: Federico C. Grosso, DDS, PhD, MFT.

Grosso, F. C. (2001). Mental Health Records Made Easy: *A Workbook for Mental Health Professionals.* Santa Barbara, CA: Federico C. Grosso, DDS, PhD, MFT.

Haas, L. J., & Malouf, J. L. (1995). *Keeping Up the Good Work: A Practitioner's Guide to Mental Health Ethics.* Sarasota, FL: Professional Resource Exchange, Inc.

Koocher, G. P., & Keith-Spiegel, P. C. (1990). *Children, Ethics, and the Law.* Lincoln, Nebraska: University of Nebraska Press.

Leslie, R. S. (1983, January / February). Nutritional Advice. *The California Therapist.*

Leslie, R. S. (1989, July / August). Confidentiality. *The California Therapist,* pp. 35–36.

Leslie, R. S. (1989, January / February). Authorization to Release Information. *The California Therapist,* pp. 45–46.

Leslie, R. S. (1989, September / October). Dual Relationships: The Legal View. *The California Therapist,* pp. 9–11.

Leslie, R. S. (1989, September / October). Patient Access to Records. *The California Therapist,* pp. 25–26.

Leslie, R. S. (1990, May / June). Advertising: A Legal and Ethical Perspective. *The California Therapist,* pp. 7–16.

Leslie, R. S. (1990, November / December). Recent Court Decisions Establish Immunity: Custody Evaluations, Mediation Affected. *The California Therapist,* pp. 37–39.

Leslie, R. S. (1991). Recent Rulings Shed Light on "Tarasoff Warnings." *The California Therapist*, 13(6), 25–27.

Leslie, R. S. (1992). Information / Disclosure Statements: Informed Consent. *The California Therapist*, pp. 7–8.

Leslie, R. S. (1993). Ethical Standards. *The California Therapist*, 5(13), 24–25.

Leslie, R. S. (1993). The Relationship Sours. *The California Therapist*, 5(4), 29–31.

Leslie, R. S. (1993). Telephone Counseling Services. *The California Therapist*, 5(6), 40–42.

Leslie, R. S. (1994). Retaining Clinical Records: Problems and Considerations. *The California Therapist*, 6(2), 11–15.

Leslie, R. S. (1994). Managed Care: Ethical and Legal Considerations in Appealing Adverse UR Decisions. *The California Therapist*, 6(2), 24–29.

Leslie, R. S. (1994). Child and Sexual Abuse Repressed Memories—Real or Imagined?: Staying Clear of Unethical Behavior. *The California Therapist*, 6(1), 22–25.

Leslie, R. S. (2000). Personal Communication.

Myers, J. E. (1992). *Legal Issues in Child Abuse and Neglect.* Newbury Park, CA: Sage Publications.

Nurcome, B., & Partlett, D. F. (1994). *Child Mental Health and the Law.* New York, NY: The Free Press.

Pelchat, Z. (2002, January / February). Minor's Privilege: Florida Follows California. *The California Therapist*, 25-27.

Rave, E. J. & Larsen, C. C. (1995). *Ethical Decision Making in Therapy: Feminist Perspectives.* New York, NY: The Guilford Press.

Riemersma, M. (1989, January / February). Intern / Trainees: Not Independent Contractors. *The California Therapist*, pp. 16–17.

Riemersma, M. (1990, November / December). What is Insurance Fraud?. *The California Therapist*, pp. 21–24.

Riemersma, M. (1992) The Dos and Don'ts of Interviewing Interns and Trainees. *The California Therapist*, 4(3), 13–15.

Woody, R. H. (1988). *Fifty Ways to Avoid Malpractice: A Guidebook for Mental Health Professionals.* Sarasota, FL: Professional Resource Exchange, Inc.

Van de Creek, L., & Knapp, S. (1993) Tarasoff and Beyond: Legal and Clinical Considerations in the Treatment of Life-Endangering Patients. Sarasota, FL: Professional Resource Press.

Zajic, S. J. (2004). Personal Communication.

Index

Index

E

Index

F

G

H

I

N

O

P

Q

R